SECRET FLOTILLAS

Volume II: Clandestine Sea Operations in the Mediterranean, North Africa and the Adriatic 1940–1944

WHITEHALL HISTORIES: GOVERNMENT OFFICIAL HISTORY SERIES

ISSN: 1474–8398

The Government Official History series began in 1919 with wartime histories, and the peacetime series was inaugurated in 1966 by Harold Wilson. The aim of the series is to produce major histories in their own right, compiled by historians eminent in the field, who are afforded free access to all relevant material in the official archives. The Histories also provide a trusted secondary source for other historians and researchers while the official records are still closed under the 30-year rule laid down in the Public Records Act (PRA). The main criteria for selection of topics are that the histories should record important episodes or themes of British history while the official records can still be supplemented by the recollections of key players; and that they should be of general interest, and, preferably, involve the records of more than one government department.

The United Kingdom and the European Community:
Vol. I: The Rise and Fall of a National Strategy, 1945–1963
Alan S.Milward

Secret Flotillas
Vol. I: Clandestine Sea Operations to Brittany, 1940–1944
Vol. II: *Clandestine Sea Operations in the Mediterranean, North Africa and the Adriatic, 1940–1944*
Brooks Richards

SOE in France
M.R.D.Foot

The Official History of the Falklands Campaign:
Vol. I: The Origins of the Falklands Conflict
Vol. II: The 1982 Falklands War and Its Aftermath
Sir Lawrence Freedman

SECRET FLOTILLAS

Volume II:

Clandestine Sea Operations in the Mediterranean, North Africa and the Adriatic 1940–1944

BROOKS RICHARDS

FOREWORD BY M.R.D.FOOT

WHITEHALL HISTORY PUBLISHING
in association with
FRANK CASS
LONDON • PORTLAND, OR

First published in 2004 in Great Britain by
FRANK CASS PUBLISHERS
reprinted by the Taylor & Francis e-Library, 2005

This edition printed in 2013 by
PEN AND SWORD Books Ltd
An imprint of
Pen & Sword Books Ltd
47 Church Street
Barnsley,
South Yorkshire
S70 2AS

ISBN 978 1 78159 303 5

A CIP catalogue record for this book
is available from the British Library

Printed and bound in England
by CPI Group (UK) Ltd, Croydon, CR0 4YY

Pen & Sword Books Ltd incorporates the Imprints of Pen & Sword Aviation,
Pen & Sword Family History, Pen & Sword Maritime, Pen & Sword Military,
Pen & Sword Discovery, Pen & Sword Politics, Pen & Sword Archaeology,
Pen & Sword Atlas, Wharncliffe Local History, Wharncliffe True Crime,
Wharncliffe Transport, Pen & Sword Select, Pen & Sword Military Classics,
Leo Cooper, The Praetorian Press, Claymore Press, Remember When,
Seaforth Publishing and Frontline Publishing

For a complete list of Pen & Sword titles please contact
PEN & SWORD BOOKS LIMITED
47 Church Street, Barnsley, South Yorkshire, S70 2AS, England
E-mail: enquiries@pen-and-sword.co.uk
Website: www.pen-and-sword.co.

The author of this work, as of the official histories of the Second World War, has been given free access to official documents. He alone is responsible for the statements made and the views expressed; also for the accuracy of any information *not* obtained from official British documents.

Contents

List of Illustrations

Between pages 172 and 173

30. *Sea Giant.*
31. MGB 179 (2 prints).
32. MGB 191, Ancona, 1945.

List of Maps

Preface to the Second Edition

This second edition of *Secret Flotillas* differs from its predecessor in two respects:

1. Whereas the 1996 book covered only the clandestine sea lines to France and what was in 1940–44 French North Africa, the present one includes operations to and from Italy in 1943–45.
2. Though written in two parts covering missions from United Kingdom ports and those from Gibraltar and other bases in the Western Mediterranean respectively, these were published as a single volume. This has now been divided into two.

The reasons for these changes are that the ships and crews operating to the south of France in 1943 and 1944 from Corsica were working at the same time to the west coast of Italy and the adjacent islands and that the same flotillas operated in the Adriatic and the Tyrrhanean.

To have included all this in a single volume would have made an already large and expensive book unmanageable and unsaleable. The division will also provide visitors to the coasts of the West Country and Brittany with a conveniently-sized account of the part of this epic likely to be of the most interest to them.

A further consideration which weighed heavily with the author in deciding to include Italy in this edition is that more than half of the 390 operations in Italian and adjacent waters were carried out by Italian vessels with Italian crews. It was a contribution to the Allied war effort which, like the shelter and the succour of the *contadini* to Allied ex-prisoners after the Armistice of 1943, ought not to be forgotten.

Foreword

Sir Brooks Richards wrote most of this book in the early 1990s—that is, half a century or so after the events described in it took place; but he had the enormous advantage of having been present in person at many of the crucial occasions he discussed. In an age when not many military historians have had a chance to hear shots fired in anger, it is an extra delight to find a participant who thinks so clearly and writes so well.

He took part in running agents to and fro across the Channel between Cornwall and Brittany, and earned the first of his two DSCs for gallantry under fire while doing so. The second of them was awarded for operations behind the German right flank in the Tunisian campaign. He could still, when he wrote this book, recall precisely the difficulties that in the pre-satellite age attended on navigation close to shore, when Breton rocks and tidal streams, or Moroccan surf and indistinguishable dunes, not to speak of enemy land, sea and air patrols, presented incessant dangers. Every sortie had to be most precisely timed, to fit in with the known perils; for the unexpected, one could do nothing but improvise and hope.

He moved on in 1943 from his seaborne career to land-based work for SOE, running agents into southern France from Algiers, and next year began a long and distinguished diplomatic career, which culminated in his own embassy in Athens from 1974 to 1978. Retirement from the diplomatic service, on reaching the age of sixty, did not mean for him retiring from public life: he had held several responsible posts in Whitehall already, and became the Crown's adviser on security in Northern Ireland.

Sir Brooks Richards never forgot those who had served with him in the war. He was long one of the pillars of the Special Forces Club. In this book, he recaptures with wonderful vividness the minute details of secret sea operations; and in this second edition, which alas he did not live to see in print, he expands it beyond the Tunisian campaign to cover small boat work on to the coasts of Italy, both before and after the Italian change of sides. Some of this was conducted by his friend Andrew Croft, from bases in Corsica, with exceptional daring. Over and over again, he uses his knowledge of the personalities involved to illuminate what went on.

This is one of the books that brings out the horror, the exultation and the chanciness of war, by one who knew what he wrote about from inside, and used the most secret surviving archives, sealed off from me forty years ago. This is not a piece of history that will need writing again: it is conclusive.

M.R.D.Foot

Acknowledgements to the First Edition

This book grew out of a chance encounter with Professor Guy Vourc'h in Paris in 1979. It was a name that awoke echoes: we had met soon after the Liberation. I knew that he and his three younger brothers had escaped in turn from Brittany to England during the Occupation and that he had been one of the first Frenchmen to fight their way ashore on D-Day. I told him that I had been involved in contacts with Brittany in 1941 and 1942: he knew more of the Breton side of my first operation than I did. And he sent me Roger Huguen's *Par les Nuits les plus Longues*.

The book was a professionally researched account of wartime escapes from Brittany, which I found fascinating. It covered a number of British-organised evacuations by sea and he had had help from various British sources. But most naval and paranaval operations to Brittany did not concern evacuation of escapers and evaders and fell outside the scope of M.Huguen's researches. I knew too that Brittany was not the only part of France to which sea lines had operated. I found myself regretting the lack of a comprehensive record of clandestine sea transport into and out of French territory during the war years. This lacuna seemed anomalous since Hugh Verity, who commanded the Lysander and Hudson Flight of 161 Special Duties Squadron in 1943 when it was at the peak of its activity, had long since published a history of the corresponding air operations. This had been translated and published also in France, where it evoked much interest. Unless a maritime counterpart were produced promptly, it would be too late to draw on the testimony of surviving participants to amplify any surviving official records. Since no-one seemed better placed to tackle the job, I decided to set about it myself.

My especial thanks are due to Gervase Cowell, SOE Adviser to the Foreign and Commonwealth Office, for his help in enabling me to gain access to the essential records on the terms applied to Official Historians. He later helped me to surmount pitfalls on the way to publication. I am grateful to Professor M.R.D.Foot and John Debenham Taylor for helpful advice and briefing.

The records provided an indispensable armature of fact and chronology, but they contained important gaps and were too lacking in detail to yield a satisfactory narrative on their own. I have had help from many quarters in redressing these deficiencies.

Operations to the west coast of Brittany had to be carried out by fishing boats or a combination of submarines and fishing boats as the distances involved were beyond the reach of high-speed vessels such as motor gunboats. In dealing with the sea lines to this area I have received invaluable help from Daniel Lomenech, Steven Mackenzie, Patrick Whinney, Richard Townsend, Jean Le Roux, Roger Huguen, René Pichavent and Capitaine de Vaisseau Jean Pillet. Daniel Lomenech's assistance extended beyond his own remarkable involvement to that of Hubert Moreau, his precursor, the first man to return to France on an intelligence mission. He found copies of an incomplete series of articles by Moreau published in the 1950s. Lt-Col. Moreau, Hubert's son, who was approached on my behalf by Claude Huan, produced a most interesting unpublished article in which his father carries forward his account of the three missions he undertook in July, August and September 1940.

I am most grateful to Steven Mackenzie for allowing me to reprint his scintillating account of the MARIE-LOUISE operations, which appeared in *Blackwood's Magazine* not long after the end of the war.

Operations on the north coast of Brittany by motor gunboats from Dartmouth or Falmouth enjoyed spectacular success from October 1943 onwards. In this field, papers in the possession of the late David Birkin, longest-serving of the specialist navigating officers attached to the 15th MGB Flotilla, are by far the most important supplementary source. Not only did he keep copies of 33 official reports of operations in which he was involved, but he and his widow, Judy, have allowed me to make use of two unpublished articles by David, track charts, diagrams and photographs from his collection. I am much indebted to them for their help.

I am also most grateful to Peter Williams, Charles Martin, Lloyd Bott, Tom Long, Michel Guillot and Derek Carter for help with this section of the book.

When I arrived in Gibraltar at the end of October 1942, a brilliantly successful run of operations by Polish-manned feluccas was just coming to an end. Little has appeared in print about them, but, on the advice of Professor M.R.D. Foot, I approached Dr Josef Garliński, who remembered seeing records of the Polish Naval Mission at Gibraltar in the Sikorski Institute. I am most grateful for that tip; the Institute possessed an almost complete set of operational reports and related correspondence in Polish, which I was able to sample thanks to the kindness of Dr Andrjez Suchcitz, who is in charge of the collection and who most helpfully summarised their contents. Full translations of all the key documents were needed, so I enlisted the help of Dr Keith Sword of the School of Slavonic and Eastern European Languages. I am most grateful for his translations, researches and background advice. I hope that we have between us rescued a small-scale epic from oblivion. Captain Marian Kadulski has added valuable personal details to the narrative represented by reports and correspondence that he wrote, under very great pressure, at the time. I am most grateful to the Sikorski Institute for permission to publish material of which they hold the copyright.

In relation to operations to and from Corsica, I am much indebted to Pat Whinney and Andrew Croft and Michael Lumby.

Throughout my researches, I received much help and advice from Capitaine de Vasseau Claude Huan, the well-known French naval historian. His knowledge of the French naval archives and his energy and skill in extracting information from them and other documentary and human sources only accessible in Paris helped my project forward very greatly. I am particularly grateful to him for compiling a list of the special operations undertaken by French submarines from Algiers in 1943 and 1944 for the French clandestine services and for obtaining from Capitaine Paul Paillole the names of more than 100 of the 150 passengers who travelled to or from France by this route.

The subject of operations by British submarines for SOE and SIS also required basic research. I am grateful to David Brown, Head of the Naval Historical Branch at the Ministry of Defence; to Commodore Bob Garson; to Commander Compton-Hall and Commander Jeff Tall, successively Directors of the RN Submarine Museum; to Gus Britten; and to Charles Beatty for their help in this connection. It was the last-named who kindly lent me Jean L'Herminier's book.

I am much indebted to Roger Huguen for generous advice and help and allowing me to make use of maps prepared for his book; to Daniel Lomenech, Richard Townsend, Derek Carter, Pat Whinney, Judy Birkin, Andrew Croft, Charles Martin, Lloyd Bott, Mary Holdsworth, Hilary Rust, the Musée de la Marine and the Etablissement Cinématographique et Photographique des Armées (ECPA) in Paris for help over photographs. My thanks are due to Mrs E.A.G.Davis for permission to use a painting of MGB 318 on the dust jacket; and to my brother Robin for resolving various problems of chart-work and nomenclature. It is to him and to Mrs Honer that I owe the drawing of *Seawolf* by the late Eric Honer. My brother and his wife, Kate, kindly photographed and transcribed the panels in the museum on the Ile-de-Sein recording escapes by Breton vessels during the Occupation.

While the project was still trying to make its way, the Imperial War Museum gave it unconditional backing, whether publication ensued or not. On the strength of this the Leverhulme Foundation gave it an invaluable two-year grant. Without their generous help it could never have come to maturity.

At a critical stage, the interest of Admiral Sir Julian Oswald, the First Sea Lord, and of Kenneth Carlisle MP, Parliamentary Under-Secretary at the Ministry of Defence, were a great encouragement, as was that of Amiral Emile Chaline, historian of the Free French naval forces.

I owe an immense debt to Patricia Andrews, Head of the Historical and Records Section of the Cabinet Office; without her support the book would never have been published. I am most grateful to Margaret Russell, who undertook the task of putting the text on to word processor and seeing it through many revisions of detail.

I am much obliged to Ingrid Cranfield for her careful editing of the text; to Steven Carruthers and HMSO for further editing and proof-reading; and to my wife for critical advice and much practical help.

HMSO wishes to acknowledge with grateful thanks the following for their kind permission to reproduce photographs: Beken of Cowes, marine photographers for the photograph of S502; Mrs. Mary Collins, for the photographs of RAF 360 and *Sunbeam II;* Conway Maritime Press for the photograph of *Minna,* taken from *Model Shipwright* (Vol. II, No. 3, Spring 1974); M. le Capitaine de Vaisseau Jannot, director of the Service d'Information et de Relations Publiques des Armées/Établissement Cinématographique et Photographique des Armées (SIRPA/ECPA) of the French Ministry of Defence for the photographs of Capitaine de Frégate Jean L'Herminier and Admiral Darlan; the Musée de la Marine in Paris for the photographs of Capitaine de Frégate Jean L'Herminier one taken in the wardroom of *Casabianca* and the other of Capitaine de Frégate Jean L'Herminier and Admiral Darlan; the Musée de la Marine in Paris for the photograph of Capitaine de Frégate Jean L'Herminier standing by *Casabianca*'s periscope and the photograph of *Casabianca* at Algiers; Universal Pictorial Press & Agency Ltd. for the photograph of Commander F.A.Slocum at his CMG investiture in 1953; Tom Maxted for the photograph of the Felucca *Seawolf;* M. Sebastien Briec for his painting used on the frontispiece. Extracts from *Michelin Green Guide to Brittany,* 1991 edition, are reproduced by permission of Michelin, authorisation no. 95–027.

The author and publisher have attempted to trace Gordon Ellis, the artist whose painting *Mayflower* has been used on the dust jacket for this publication. If the copyright holders of this (or other material not acknowledged above) wish to contact HMSO, we shall ensure that the correct acknowledgement appears in any future edition of this book.

Brooks Richards, 1996

Acknowledgements to the Second Edition

Sadly my father died shortly after completing the text of the second edition of *Secret Flotillas,* but I know that he would have wished to acknowledge again all those whom he thanked for helping him produce the first version and the extensive acknowledgements to the first edition are reproduced here unamended.

I am sure that he would also wish me to extend warm thanks to those who were in any way involved in helping him to get this updated and extended version prepared for publication. In particular he would have wished me to thank: Capitaine de Vaisseau Pierrick Roullet, the translator of the French edition of *Secret Flotillas;* Tessa Stirling, Richard Ponman and Sally Falk of the Histories and Records Unit of the Cabinet Office, without whose help and support the revised editions of *Secret Flotillas* would never have been published; Christopher Woods, who provided him with his research on SOE in Italy; Duncan Stuart and Mark Seaman, who gave valued help and support; and Geoffrey Hudson, who provided some of the photographs and diagrams for the new sections of the book.

An attempt has been made to trace the source of the photographs and diagrams which are reproduced in this edition, but not in every case successfully. I know my father would have wished to have thanked and acknowledged those who supplied the material. If the copyright holders of any of the material reproduced in this edition wish to contact the Cabinet Office, we shall ensure that the correct acknowledgement appears in any future edition of this book. And to anybody else—there must be a number—whose help deserved a personal acknowledgement but ignorance has prevented me from giving it, I can only express my gratitude and my apologies.

Francis Richards
March 2003

I
The Polish Predicament

Under the terms of the armistice concluded in June 1940 between the Axis powers and the French government formed by Pétain at Bordeaux, the Germans completed their occupation of France's Atlantic seaboard, but left the Mediterranean coast in French hands.

Vichy was hampered by severely restricted numbers of armed forces and shortages of fuel. The controls it exercised over this residual coastline and that of the unoccupied French North African territories were therefore less effective than the defences that the Germans proceeded to develop from the Hook of Holland to Hendaye. Gibraltar, the nearest base in British hands, was 1,100km (700 miles) or more from the beaches of Languedoc and the *calanques*—the long deep creeks on the coast of Provence. It was thus some time before the British clandestine services sought to exploit what was for them a rather roundabout route to and from occupied France.

For the Poles, who faced genocide at the hands of the Nazis, and, on a lesser scale, the Czechs, the problem of organising escape routes from unoccupied France was more urgent.[1] In the eight months between Hitler's conquest of their homeland and the fall of France, the Poles had set up a government-in-exile in Paris and proceeded to regroup and re-form Polish forces on Allied territory. A number of their naval vessels and the bulk of their merchant fleet had found refuge and a new operational base in Great Britain. It was in Britain, too, and with the support of the RAF, that senior Polish air force officers would have preferred to concentrate the effort to rebuild an air force. But General Sikorski, who was both Prime Minister and Commander-in-Chief, believed profoundly in France as he remembered it from 1918 and wished this to be done in France. Under the terms of a compromise reached at the end of October 1939, Polish air force personnel who had made their way to the West were divided equally between the two countries. The new Polish army was wholly raised and equipped in France, however, though one brigade had been reconstituted in Syria, then French mandated territory.

To extricate Polish troops from the neutral countries where they had taken refuge and been interned at the end of the campaign in Poland was no easy task. They had first to escape from internment and then find civilian clothes, identity documents and transport. There were about 40,000, including most of an armoured brigade, in Hungary and 30,000 troops and 20,000 civilian refugees in Romania: many of the latter had had military training and were of an age to be called up. Some 13,800 had sought refuge in Lithuania. By June 1940, 22,000 had been extricated from Romania and 21,000 from Hungary. From these two countries the escape line to France ran through Yugoslavia and Italy, which, despite Mussolini's alliance with Hitler, showed sympathy with the Poles and respected their Embassy. The French authorities also allowed Sikorski to mobilise suitable age groups from the Polish community in France, which was almost half a million strong, many still Polish citizens. Though this process of reforming and training the new Polish armed forces was still far from complete at the time of the German breakthrough north of the Maginot Line, those under arms in France or serving with the Podhalańska Brigade at Narvik numbered about 82,000.

It had been agreed between Sikorski and Gamelin, the French Commander-in-Chief, that Polish units, when ready for action, would form their own corps and operate as a single unit, but this had still not been done when the battle of France began and such Polish units as were ready for action were widely dispersed. The 1st Grenadier Division formed part of the French 20th Corps and was deployed south-west of Nancy in defence of the Maginot Line. The 2nd Infantry Fusiliers was in the Belfort area, not far from the Swiss border, and became part of the French 15th Corps. The 10th Armoured Cavalry Brigade was partly available and there were eight Polish infantry companies and two anti-tank batteries serving in French regimental formations. The still untrained 3rd Division and two equally untrained battalions at Coëtquidan in Brittany were drawn into the battle eventually, but none of these units, whose strength totalled approximately 40,000, was in action before 14 June, the day Paris was occupied. They were all determined to fight, and the 1st and 2nd Divisions both did so with distinction, but the battle was already lost and organised French military resistance crumbled around them in growing confusion.

The Polish government had by this time moved to Angers, but General Sikorski, wishing to be as near as possible to the two Polish divisions then in action, went forward to his field headquarters near Nancy but then only added to the confusion by moving from place to place and becoming difficult to find. His faith in France was such that he had never considered the possibility of its defeat or made any plans for the withdrawal of Polish forces-which their dispersion and integration in French formations made impracticable in the prevailing chaos.

By 17 June, the Polish government and President had retreated to Libourne and their French counterparts to Bordeaux, where Pétain succeeded Reynaud as Prime Minister and asked the Spanish government to ascertain Hitler's terms for an armistice. Sikorski met Pétain next day and subsequently issued a declaration of Polish determination to fight on at the side of Great Britain. He flew to London in an aircraft provided by Churchill, who, at a conference on 19 June, confirmed that Great Britain would continue the war, receive the Polish President and government and do what was possible to evacuate Polish troops from France. In a radio bulletin broadcast that same day by the BBC, General Sikorski ordered his men to break through to ports in southern France or cross into Switzerland.

The evacuation of Polish troops began forthwith from ports on the west coast of France. Some 3,000 left Brest before it fell into German hands on 19 June. Others embarked at Saint-Malo and La-Rochelle. Two days later the process continued from Bordeaux, Bayonne and Saint-Jean-de-Luz, where the Polish liners *Batory* and *Sobieski* took off 4, 000 troops and 500 civilians. The evacuation continued until 25 June from south-western French ports while British naval vessels kept the Luftwaffe at bay. Polish airmen embarked meanwhile at Port-Vendres and Sète in the Mediterranean. Estimates of the numbers rescued vary between 16,000 and 23,000: the official figure quoted in London at a meeting of the Polish National Council some weeks later was 19,457.

As Garliński, historian of Poland in the Second World War, has pointed out, this was not a bad result given the chaos of the time, the lack of transport and the dispersion of Polish units. Moreover, a significant number of men mobilised in France were *émigrés* living there who would have preferred to stay. There remained however many thousands who had no roots in France and who were extremely bitter at finding themselves abandoned by their senior officers and civilian authorities in a foreign country, without money, papers or advice.

One of those who had failed to get away from Saint-Jean-de-Luz was a professional Polish intelligence officer named M.Z. Slowikowski, who had been serving at Kiev under consular cover when war broke out and had then, with his wife and 13-year-old son, quickly made his way to France via Finland, Sweden, Norway, Great Britain, Holland and Belgium.[2] Slowikowski, who held the rank of major and was already 53 years old, was given the job of second in command of one of the new Polish divisions being formed in France. Four months later, in February 1940, with the Russians in occupation of eastern Poland and the Russo-Finnish War in full swing, he was brought back to Paris to serve in the intelligence section of the Polish General Staff, where his knowledge of the Soviet Union could be put to use.

Early on, Slowikowski foresaw the outcome of the battle in France and sent his wife and son for safety to Salies-du-Salat, a small town south of Toulouse. On the day before the Germans entered Paris he was put in charge of a group of officers from the General Staff and told to evacuate them by train to Saintes in the Charente-Maritime, not far north of Bordeaux, which he did with considerable difficulty. Together with another professional intelligence officer named Captain Jankowski, who had served in Germany before the war, he found lodgings and took stock of the situation, in which everyone seemed panic-stricken and obsessed with a desire to get out of France as quickly as possible.

Slowikowski and Jankowski found it hard to decide whether to attempt to join in the evacuation or to stay on in France, where they felt there would be great opportunities for successful intelligence collection while the Germans digested the spoils. In any case, they drove to Toulouse next morning, having obtained permission to collect their families from their refuge. The Polish Consulate at Toulouse was packed up, expecting to be evacuated to Spain, but they persuaded the Consul to issue them passports, collected their families and somehow all reached Saint-Jean-de-Luz. There, the question whether to leave or stay was taken out of their hands because the Polish general acting as port commandant had decided to embark soldiers and airmen in priority and to relegate officers of their age with families to the back of the queue. The weather was most unpleasant, with heavy showers and strong winds, and they had to sleep in the open.

While awaiting embarkation, Slowikowski and Jankowski went down to Hendaye to have a look at the Spanish frontier. There they ran into a French Deuxième Bureau officer whom they knew. He told them that, under the terms of the armistice, the Germans would occupy the whole of the French Atlantic coast, but that there would be a 'free zone' under French government control and he advised them to make their way into it if they had to remain in France. Realising that the possibility of their being evacuated from Saint-Jean-de-Luz had vanished, the two families returned to Salies-du-Salat, where they found their previous accommodation still available. Moreover, the town and nearby Toulouse lay, in what was to be the unoccupied zone.

Slowikowski was soon in contact with another Polish secret-service officer named Zarembski, who had also worked in the Soviet Union under consular cover and had subsequently been briefly in charge of the Polish counter-intelligence post in Paris, this time with commercial diplomatic cover. They went together to Toulouse, which they found packed with refugees: Polish could be heard spoken everywhere and Polish uniforms were much in evidence. The Consulate was overwhelmed by soldiers seeking documents and advice: the other ranks were bitterly hostile to officers, particularly those of senior rank. Slowikowski, who had been born near Warsaw in what was then part of Czarist Russia, was unpleasantly reminded of the behaviour of Russian troops during the 1917 Revolution. Fortunately, the appointment of a diplomat named Bitner to take charge of the Consulate defused this explosive situation: his concern for the troops' welfare was unmistakable.

Bitner accepted in principle Slowikowski's suggestion that he and Zarembski should organise the evacuation to Great Britain of as many of the stranded Polish servicemen as possible, but he was less happy to cooperate in practice when he learned of Slowikowski's and Zarembski's secret-service backgrounds. The arrival of Colonel Kobylecki, pushing a bicycle that had borne him south from the Breton battlefield, resolved the question. Kobylecki had been Slowikowski's chief on the latter's arrival in France and he had gone on to command the Podhalańska Brigade at Narvik. After the evacuation of the Allied Expeditionary Force from Norway, the Brigade had been disembarked at Brest and thrust immediately into the battle, notwithstanding the loss of all its heavy equipment. The active support of so senior an officer settled Bitner's qualms and the procedure began. Zarembski assumed responsibility for security vetting of candidates for evacuation.

During the first two months—as Szumlakowski, the Polish Ambassador at Madrid, subsequently told General Sikorski—anybody, irrespective of age, could and did travel through Spain—even those who bore arms and wore uniforms.[3] The Spanish authorities allowed Poles in without the Portuguese visas for which would-be evacuees later had to wait for weeks on end. The Ambassador considered that, because the evacuation from France had been inadequately organised, this period was not used to full advantage. After this there were two possible ways to get the evacuees across Spain to Portugal, whence passages to the United Kingdom were available. The evacuee could be equipped with a Polish passport and granted a visa to some exotic country such as China. This gave him the right to a Portuguese transit visa and a Spanish conditional visa. To obtain the Portuguese visa, he needed to produce a receipt from the Cook's travel agency showing that he had paid part of the cost of the passage by sea to China. Provided the Polish passport proved the bearer to be less than 20 or more than 45 years of age, he could then travel to Perpignan and obtain, through the Polish Consulate there, a French exit permit from the local Prefecture. Anyone who had surmounted this series of bureaucratic obstacles could then travel to Lisbon legally.

The alternative was to introduce the evacuees illegally into Spain and hope to get them through to Portugal without their being arrested by the Spanish police. This became increasingly difficult. Szumlakowski had argued strongly against methods such as the use of false documents and visas, which he considered compromised his mission and damaged Polish interests in Spain. Police controls had been much tightened up following a change of Spanish Foreign Minister and of pressure from the Gestapo. He complained that, in spite of this, Poles were still being sent over the border from France without adequate preparation and that of every 16 crossing the 'green frontier', not more than four succeeded in reaching Madrid.

There was, indeed, a great deal of mutual recrimination amongst the Polish authorities involved in the evacuation scheme. One of the officers concerned, Major Adam Szydlowski, who had been imprisoned in Spain, wrote subsequently to his former commanding officer that, thanks to the complete incompetence of the authorities in France responsible for organising the evacuation and to the lack of coordination between the Polish authorities in France and in Spain, many wasted months passed; moreover, there was no prospect that the situation would improve in future.[4]

A more comprehensive appraisal, and one markedly more appreciative of Slowikowski's and Bitner's efforts at Toulouse, is contained in a report by a former staff officer of the Polish 2nd Infantry Division who managed to leave France at the end of July. His name appears at the head of the report as Lt Cdr Czeslaw Chieconski but he signed it

Chiconski. In the report, written in London two months later, he recorded his own experiences and made his own recommendations to General Sikorski's Chief of Staff on ways of evacuating Polish troops left behind in southern France.[5]

Those who had not managed to leave France in June were, he reported, grouped in a few centres, which should be regarded as reservoirs of potential military manpower. The most important centres were Toulouse and Marseilles but there were smaller concentrations at Lyons, Nice and a camp near Port-Vendres. He estimated the number of Poles at Toulouse in July at 5,000: after dispersal of the soldiers who were inhabitants of France, there might possibly be 3–4,000 still left there.

The attitudes and quality of the men at Toulouse varied. They had been subjected to Gestapo and Soviet propaganda, to which some of the weaker characters—both officers and other ranks—had succumbed. Some were prepared to return to Poland; others shrank from active service and preferred to await the outcome of the war. Still others, however, of more robust outlook, were constantly looking for opportunities to leave for England to continue the fight against the Germans. The soldiers at Toulouse were very short of money and, if left there long, might be lost to the cause.

Chiconski predicted that relations between the French authorities and the Poles, which in most cases were at present quite good, would probably deteriorate. Quartering and food were bad. The Polish Consulate at Toulouse was working efficiently and with tremendous dedication, but under very difficult circumstances.

At Marseilles the military element was prepared to take any risks to find ways of getting to England. Morale here was very high. The total number of officers and men in the Marseilles area was estimated at 600–700. The material circumstances of the officers were good because they had received their pay for June and some for July as well. For the other ranks, by contrast, living conditions were abysmal: they had been left to find their own quarters, as best they could, in hospices and places of refuge. Food was unsatisfactory and the French authorities were passive and unfriendly. The Polish Consulate at Marseilles was performing poorly and unproductively by comparison with the one at Toulouse.

Lyons was no more than a staging post for men on the way to Toulouse, Marseilles or other centres where Poles had congregated.

Nice was an assembly point for officers hoping to leave for Italy and thence travel to Poland. Some hoped to pursue their journey from Italy to Yugoslavia, Greece and Turkey with a view to joining the Polish forces in Palestine, but this was a very unrealistic plan. Chiconski did not know how many soldiers were in the camp at Port-Vendres. Quarters and food there were not bad and the soldiers there were prepared to continue the fight against the Germans.

After describing the formalities for evacuation through Spain by the legal route, Chiconski set out in detail how to avoid trouble with the authorities while on Spanish soil. These ranged from tips about the currency regulations at the Spanish and Portuguese frontier posts to advice to the evacuee not to carry weapons or any part of his uniform, not to carry any documents about his real reason for travelling through Spain, not to stay in Spain even for the most plausible reasons, to avoid restaurants, coffee-houses and brothels; and to avoid any form of conflict with members of the public and particularly with the authorities. Any breach of Spanish law or currency regulations would lead to immediate arrest and incarceration. On arrival in Barcelona, the British Consulate would issue a third-class ticket to Madrid and the Polish Consulate would provide a small allowance and all necessary information. Evacuees should not overstay in Madrid without a valid reason. The Polish Consulate there would issue third-class tickets to the Portuguese border, but their advice that travel was allowed without payment in Portugal was incorrect: permission for free travel had to be obtained from the Polish Consulate in Lisbon. The Consulate in Madrid did not work well and tended to dismiss enquiries in a perfunctory and slapdash manner. Cooperation between the Consulates in the two capitals was very unsatisfactory, but the Consulate at Lisbon was very active and all matters concerning the evacuation of Polish military personnel were handled by Col. Mally, the Military Attaché, or by Dubicza, the Minister, who was the most approachable official Chiconski had ever encountered.

Holders of Chinese, Portuguese and Spanish visas who lacked French exit permits might cross the French frontier illegally near Andorra or near a small town named Saint-Laurent, where the French authorities were usually cooperative. Soldiers crossing in such circumstances should report to the Spanish Customs. The Spanish authorities would respect all visas even when the French exit visa was missing.

In Chiconski's opinion, group travel with the permission of the French authorities would not be practicable because of pressures exerted by the Gestapo, but it might be feasible, with the cooperation of the British Navy, to evacuate large groups of Poles assembled on the Mediterranean coastline, as already at the camp near Port-Vendres.

How far this report influenced official thinking at General Sikorski's headquarters in London is unclear: probably not very much, since an annotation in longhand, dated 1 October 1940, at the bottom of the document records the Chief of Staff's s opinion that the above person was not trustworthy and was the subject of a pending criminal case.

The Polish government-in-exile managed to establish, rather precariously, an Embassy at Vichy when the Pétain government moved there from Bordeaux. Within it, General Kleeberg, the Military Attaché, assumed overall control of evacuation arrangements in July. But, by the autumn of 1940, under increasing German pressure, the French authorities had virtually ceased to cooperate over the issue of exit permits. At the beginning of October, moreover, Kleeberg had to order the route through Spain to be closed, owing to the complete lack of co-operation by the Polish agencies on the Spanish side of the border. As he subsequently reported to General Sikorski, anyone who attempted to escape by that route and whom luck did not favour generally found his way into Spanish internment camps or, if not, might be thrown back to the French side of the border, sometimes from as far away as Madrid or even the Portuguese frontier.[6]

Internment in Spanish camps such as that at Miranda-del-Ebro was a serious matter for Poles. The British Embassy was able to secure the release of British evaders and escapers within a few weeks, since the Spanish government badly needed British cooperation over the contraband control of essential commodities such as flour and petrol. The Poles had no such leverage, however, and many of the 700 or so Polish escapers from France who were interned in Miranda languished there for two years or more.

Little wonder, then, that those concerned began seriously to consider the alternative of evacuation by sea from southern France. Even before the end of July 1940, Kleeberg had elaborated a scheme for removing several hundreds of soldiers by sea in one fell swoop. Having bought a cargo ship lying in Marseilles, he asked Slowikowski to transfer 250 men from the Toulouse area, for which he was responsible, to Marseilles for embarkation.[7] The men duly travelled by train in groups of ten, under the noses of the French gendarmerie, and once in Marseilles, were escorted to the English Seamen's Hospital to await embarkation. Kleeberg had, however, based his plan on the mistaken assumption that it would receive official approval by the Vichy authorities. Instead of granting Kleeberg permission, General Dentz, who, after surrendering Paris to the Germans, had become the general officer commanding the south-east military region, threatened to arrest him and anyone else using the ship for such a purpose. This turn of events, which ought to have been foreseen but was not, left the organisers with the acute administrative problem of dealing with the men assembled in the English Hospital, which also served as a reception centre for Polish troops arriving to be demobilised.

After this disaster, Kleeberg offered Slowikowski command of Polish evacuation from the whole of France—an offer which the latter felt unable to refuse. Having taken stock of the situation, Slowikowski, who adopted the alias 'Dr Skowronski', decided that Marseilles was the obvious centre for organising departures by sea. When he got there he found that nearly 300,000 Francs had been spent locally on 'research' but that not one man had as yet actually been evacuated. One officer was planning to ferry evacuees out to Gibraltar by motor boat. Slowikowski wanted him first to report to him on the cost and likely results but this advice was disregarded and a small party of officers set off anyhow, though Slowikowski noted that the organiser himself preferred to travel by the land line into Spain. Before leaving Marseilles he claimed to have been robbed at gunpoint by the Frenchmen who had helped him purchase the boat; for obvious reasons, he had been unable to report the matter to the police. Reproaching Slowikowski for forbidding evacuation by sea, the officer also maintained that by dispatching the boat to Gibraltar, he had proved this method to be possible. Slowikowski subsequently discovered that the boat had in fact been intercepted by the French maritime gendarmerie and its passengers sent to a special penal camp in the Pyrenees.

This was not the only unsuccessful attempt by Poles to escape by sea in small vessels. A fishing boat named *Marie-Thérèse,* of a type known locally as a *bateau boeuf* (because two worked together towing a single trawl, like yoked oxen with a plough) lay at the

Quai-Aspirant-Herbert at Sète in November 1940.[8] Some 200 Polish soldiers were to be involved in this operation, which was headed by a Polish sapper Captain. He was assisted by a lieutenant and a naval sub-lieutenant, who had left hospital clandestinely with the help of two Bretons who hoped to use this Polish venture to leave the country themselves. They were denounced by local fishermen and the two Bretons were arrested on board the *Marie-Thérèse* by two police inspectors from the crime squad, who had come all the way from Vichy. René Poujade and Raymond Cauvel, the Bretons, admitted that they planned to escape to Gibraltar but they said nothing about the Poles involved in the enterprise, all of whom got away to Nîmes in a hurry.

The cargo ship bought by General Kleeberg for the abortive mass evacuation still lay in Marseilles port and, in due course, Slowikowski decided that, since the French police seemed to have lost interest in her, it was worth trying again to use her for an escape operation, this time without informing the French authorities.[9] Her holds were filled with bunks, which were supposed to be racks for oranges. The plan was that the ship would sail from Marseilles in ballast and would embark the evacuees by night from a nearby point on the coast. After dropping them at Gibraltar, she would put into a Spanish port and pick up a genuine cargo of crates of oranges before returning to land these at Marseilles. A French crew and captain were signed on and preparations were far advanced when news leaked out to the port authorities, who sealed the ship and denied access to her by anyone other than the crew. Since there was no longer any hope of reviving the project, the ship was sold, which realised a small profit.

On 1 October 1940, the Germans compelled Vichy to close down the Polish Embassy and all the Polish Consulates. With the Ambassador's departure, General Kleeberg lost his diplomatic status and was able to stay on in France as unofficial head of the Polish forces only by invoking his friendships with a number of high-ranking French officers. He moved to Marseilles and from then on all plans and arrangements for evacuation had to be pursued on a wholly clandestine basis.

The Germans tried several times to infiltrate agents into the Polish evacuation network; the network at least twice foiled the attempt by executing the individuals concerned. Fortunately Slowikowski had links with a pro-Allied French inspector of police at Marseilles who was prepared to lend them support and protection. Soon afterwards, warned by the Poles that his name was on a blacklist at Vichy, this officer was able to get himself transferred to Morocco, where he eventually became one of Slowikowski's most valuable contacts in organising an intelligence network.

Direct evacuation by sea to Gibraltar proved extremely difficult. Permission to buy a boat had to be obtained from the port police and no ship could sail from a French port without the approval of the German Armistice Commission. There was, moreover, an acute shortage of fuel even on the black market. Nevertheless, Slowikowski felt that it was well worth evacuating men to French North Africa, from which escape might well prove easier. As early as October 1940, he had predicted that there would be an Allied landing in North Africa because of its strategic value. Poles who could get there would thus find themselves among friends sooner than would be the case if they remained in metropolitan France. Kleeberg agreed that in French North Africa they would be safer from the risk of falling into German hands. Lieutenant Kiersnowski, commander of the Polish naval outpost at Marseilles, was therefore ordered to establish friendly contacts with French merchant seamen on the Marseilles-North Africa run and to find out whether they would help stowaways. Kiersnowski knew his way around the waterfront bars of the Vieux-Port and spoke their argot; he soon gained their confidence and reported that evacuation by this route and method would be possible at a price of between 100 and 300 Francs per transportee, depending on the number to be carried.

The next step was to organise a network of evacuation outposts in French North Africa to receive men on arrival and direct them to safe houses pending their transfer to Casablanca, which Slowikowski judged would prove the best and safest port of refuge. Given the distances involved and the administrative division of French North Africa into three separate territories, each with guarded borders and the requirement for a permit to travel between them, there were substantial problems to be overcome. Five officers were selected to set up these outposts at Tunis, Algiers and Casablanca. They left for North Africa in November 1940 to make the necessary contacts and reported that conditions were rather better, and the officials more helpful, than in metropolitan France. Kleeberg therefore authorised Kiersnowski to begin shipments.

Batches of up to 40 evacuees would be assembled at the English Hospital reception centre when a suitable ship was due to sail and the necessary payments had been made. Late at night, they were collected and moved to waiting boats, which, with all due precautions, rowed them round to the side of the ship remote from the quay. They climbed on board via a rope ladder hanging down the ship's side and were immediately ushered to their hide-outs in parts of the ship rarely visited by officers, such as the shaft tunnel and coal-bunkers. Conditions were often extremely uncomfortable and made great demands on the physical stamina of the stowaways, who needed to remain hidden for several days before being disembarked at a North African port with similar speed and secrecy. Any man who broke bounds and ventured forth from his cramped quarters to stretch his legs or snatch a breath of fresh air might ruin the whole venture. This is doubtless what happened in December 1940 when an early RAF evader, the future Air Chief Marshal Sir Lewis Hodges, whose Hampden bomber had made a forced landing in Brittany, arranged to be smuggled on board the *Ville-de-Verdun*, to Casablanca.[10] On their first day at sea, the ship's captain was alerted to the presence of other stowaways. The subsequent search brought to light altogether 40 illicit travellers. He turned the ship round and handed them all over to the Vichy police at Marseilles, who interned them, with the result that Hodges ended up with other British officers in what had been the French Foreign Legion transit depot in the Fort-Saint-Jean, instead of in Casablanca as he had hoped.

The Czechs had also had troops in France, though far fewer than the Poles, and these were equally subject to internment at the hands of the Vichy authorities. Among the places used for this purpose were camps on the coast between Sète and Perpignan, which had been built to accommodate interned Spanish Republican refugees. Gradually, groups of both Czech and Polish demobilised internees were transferred under armed guard into the Alps and Massif Central to do forestry work.

When the Polish Embassy had to be closed in November 1940, Kleeberg sought an audience with General Huntzinger, Pétain's Secretary of State for War, to discuss with him the status and future of the Polish soldiers in France. On 16 January 1941, when Huntziger refused to see him, Kleeberg wrote to him instead.[11]

The situation imposed on the Poles, he wrote, seemed incompatible with the real feelings of the French population for his compatriots and with the mutual engagements, both moral and material, contracted between Poland and France. Polish soldiers had been called up, trained and engaged in combat in accordance with agreements concluded between the two Governments. On the orders of the French High Command, Polish units had been thrust into battle: the First and Second Infantry Divisions and even the Third, which was in process of being formed, the Northern Brigade, and the scarcely trained and formed Maczec Motorised Group. These units had all, without exception, done their duty. On the Polish side, all engagements had been fulfilled. Despite this, these soldiers, who had contributed unflinchingly to the vital task of holding back the enemy and saving honour, were now considered superfluous foreigners and treated on the same basis as the Spanish Republicans (law of 27 September 1940). Not surprisingly therefore, Polish officers and soldiers, rejected by their erstwhile brothers in arms, sought to leave France.

Senior officers and soldiers with long service stripes, who had committed no other crime than to wish to fight on and to fulfil their duty as soldiers, found themselves in chains and treated as common criminals. Although the tribunal at Aix-en-Provence had recently set them free, the police were now about to send them to the camp at Le-Vernet with Communists, thieves and crooks. One of them, a senior officer of the greatest merit, had gone out of his mind. These soldiers asked for no favours. They wished only to be treated as ex-servicemen, with dignity.

Lastly, Kleeberg argued, it ought to be possible to avoid exposing these men to the risk of falling into enemy hands once more. It was clear, from reports of officers and other ranks who had escaped, that Polish soldiers captured in France by the Germans were particularly ill treated. He concluded:

> I know that I am only doing my duty, General, in begging you to take the necessary steps to ensure that Polish soldiers, who have merely carried out the orders of their commanding officers, are not once more surprised by the enemy, as were, among others, the troops of the Narvik Brigade in Brittany.

> I ask you to facilitate their transfer to North Africa where they will know how to make themselves useful, whatever the circumstances.
>
> I beg you to believe, General, that I am not acting in a spirit of recrimination but from a sense of my responsibility as a chief, from a love of my soldiers and from my attachment to France, which long residence entitles me to consider my second homeland. We are at a moment of history where our actions are of more than passing consequence, for they will determine the future.

This plea seems to have elicited no response.

Slowikowski reckoned that almost 3,000 more Poles had been evacuated from France to the United Kingdom by one means or another before the beginning of May 1941. Several hundreds more had been smuggled to French North Africa. By Christmas 1940, Kleeberg thought he should send a more senior officer there to take charge and recommended Major Wysoczanski. Slowkowski did not know Wysoczanski, but he briefed him, explained his duties and told him he was expected to report on the local situation and on progress in carrying out his mission. He gave him funds and a list of the officers already actively engaged on the problem, but made it clear that Wysoczanski was free to make such changes as he thought necessary.[12]

Wysoczanski arrived at his post in North Africa at the end of 1940 with a team of his own associates and proceeded to replace most of the existing outpost commanders. Flouting orders, he sent no reports either to Slowikowski or to Kleeberg but instead sent telegrams demanding money. Slowikowski noted dourly that he and Kleeberg both thought it would be unwise to send money for unknown purposes.

Evacuation from the south of France to North Africa continued with reasonable success until mid-March 1941. It had been Slowikowski's policy to regroup the evacuees in North Africa according to their service of origin; the airmen had been concentrated in Tunisia, where good accommodation was available and Admiral Esteva, the French Resident-General, was particularly well disposed.

Unfortunately, the Polish commandant of this camp overreached himself by staging military parades on festive occasions. Alerted to this, the Italo-German armistice commission took the matter up officially with Esteva and a full-scale enquiry was launched, which brought to light not only the illegal camps in Tunisia but the clandestine sea traffic from France that had led to this concentration of Polish airmen in the Protectorate. A number of French officials who had been helpful to the Poles lost their jobs, while the airmen were transferred back to France and interned under penal conditions. The French sailors who had been involved in smuggling Poles into North Africa on merchant ships were arrested. Slowikowski had no choice but to suspend evacuation by this method.

Shortly afterwards, Slowikowski was himself appointed to North Africa to organise an intelligence network to cover the whole range of French territories from the Tripolitanian border to Dakar. He handed over the evacuation work in metropolitan France to his deputy, Major Mizgier-Chojnacki.

II
Mass Evacuations from the Marseilles Area and the *Fidelity* Tragedy

A quite separate scheme for a large-scale evacuation by sea of Polish ex-servicemen immobilised in southern France had been under discussion in London since December 1940 between the Polish General Staff and the British Admiralty.[1]

Sikorski's staff reckoned that there were still at least 3,000 officers and other ranks to be brought out. The original plan aimed to evacuate in a single operation all the internees in two main camps in the Marseilles area by means of a cargo steamer, the *Czardasz*. Slocum was in close touch with the Directorate of Naval Intelligence and it seems inherently likely that he was involved in these discussions as he was at the same time fitting out another small cargo steamer for an expedition to the south coast of France on behalf of the British clandestine services. He was quite prepared to meet Polish and Czech operational needs in the course of this projected voyage as well.

As a result of the *Czardasz* scheme, a Polish naval lieutenant named Marian Kadulski was sent out to Gibraltar in March 1941. Kadulski, who is one of the real heroes of this book, was born in December 1909 in Nowy Sacz, south of Krakow, in the foothills of the Tatras. His father soon thereafter obtained a job in the Austro-Hungarian Imperial dockyard at Pola (now Pula) on the Adriatic coast of what subsequently became Yugoslavia. At the end of the First World War, in the resurrected Poland, Kadulski Senior joined the army, pieced together from ex-Austrian-German—and Russian—trained personnel. For the three Kadulski children, of whom Marian was the eldest, their father's changing assignments meant changing schools, which had also quite recently begun to merge satisfactorily. His mother often recalled in later years how surprisingly Marian caught up each time in the new surroundings and was always top of the class or very near it. When he was 13, his secondary schooling at Lwów (now L'viv in the Ukraine) was on the lines of a German *Realgymnasium,* with a curriculum which stressed mathematics, physics and natural history. Again he was at the top. Languages came to him easily. He matriculated at 18, second out of about 30. He could well have been first, but he had a handicap, which also plagued him at naval college: he looked much younger than his age and, while not short of stature, did not look 100 per cent 'The Good Soldier Schweik'.

At the naval college (in Torun), where the three-year course was interspersed with summer cruises in warships, Kadulski was top in English and French, with quite good German as well. Having read Jules Verne's *The Fifteen-Year-Old Ship's Captain,* he longed to learn astronomical navigation. Indeed, thanks to the manuals available at the school, he mastered the subject before the first lectures on it began, taking observations of Jupiter and Saturn in the morning watch on the training ship in order to identify them by the reversed mathematical process. It was a skill that, as will become apparent, stood him in good stead during his Gibraltar appointment in 1941 and 1942.

At the time of his arrival on the Rock, Kadulski was 31 years old and had been in the Polish navy since 1928. He had done an extra year's training on the French navy's *Jeanne d'Arc,* where the cadets were required to take observations at noon each day and work out a fix, served in submarines and received some training in intelligence work during the summer of 1939. After postings to the Polish Naval Missions in Copenhagen and Amsterdam during the early months of the war, possibly on intelligence duties, he had become temporary first lieutenant of the destroyer *Blyskawica,* a post in which he was subsequently confirmed. He remained in this ship until November 1940 and saw active service in the Norwegian campaign. His appointment to Gibraltar on 3 March 1941 was nominally as head of a new Polish Naval Mission there, but this was no more than cover: he had in fact been detached from the navy to the branch of the Polish clandestine services dealing with evacuation operations. In this new capacity he was responsible to Colonel Frederyk Mally, whose cover post was Military Attaché in Lisbon, rather than to the Polish naval authorities. He adopted the name Krajewski for this new job and will be so described hereafter.[2]

Within a very few weeks of Krajewski's arrival at Gibraltar, it became evident that the Czardasz plan was no longer practicable: mass escapes from the camps would be impossible in view of the enhanced French security measures adopted after Slowikowski's escape line to French North Africa was exposed. However, Commander Slocum's planned operation went ahead and it included a small-scale attempt to pick up Polish or Czech escapers from the coast of Languedoc. It also landed Bitner, previously Polish Consul at Toulouse, who was being sent back to investigate, in conjunction with SOE (Special Operations Executive), whether the large Polish population in the Nord and Pas-de-Calais Departments could be drawn into active resistance.

The vessel to be used for this, Slocum's first operation in the Mediterranean, was an unusual ship which has passed into history as HMS *Fidelity.* For better security, *Fidelity* was to be sailed on this voyage direct from the United Kingdom, where she had been fitted out and commissioned, rather than from Gibraltar. She was built in 1920 at Hartlepool as a cargo vessel with an overall length of 270 feet, a beam of 41 feet and a gross registered tonnage of 2,450. Her triple-expansion Mackie and Baxter engine, yielding 1,100h.p. from two boilers, had originally given her a top speed of 9.5 knots; 21 years later, in wartime service with poor coal, this was reduced to nearer 6 knots. Fitted to carry 20 passengers in seven cabins, she was put into service as *Le-Rhin* by the French firm of Devéry et Chaumet, who in 1923 sold her to the Compagnie Paquet of Marseilles. She was then used to transport vegetable oils from Senegal and general cargo to Morocco, the eastern Mediterranean and Black Sea ports.[3]

In June 1940, as organised French military resistance to the German onslaught was collapsing, *Le-Rhin* lay at Marseilles unloading a cargo from North Africa, when a French naval officer of Corsican origin, Claude André Péri, engaged on special service for the French Admiralty and the Cinquième Bureau, arrived there armed with an *ordre de mission* and looking for a ship to take him to Gibraltar to join the British.

Péri had a previous connection with *Le-Rhin:* indeed, he had used her only six weeks earlier as a mobile base from which to mount an attack on a German merchant ship, the SS *Corrientes,* lying in Las Palmas harbour in the Canaries. This operation was carried out on 10 May, the day on which Hitler launched his western offensive into the Low Countries. Péri used limpet mines and plastic explosive, a novelty of Czech origin, in this attack. As *Le-Rhin* sailed from the neutral Spanish port, Péri had slipped back in her launch and placed the mines. He then rejoined the ship and was well offshore before they detonated. How much damage was caused is not clear: some accounts say Péri sank her, but an SIS report casts doubt on this.

Finding that almost all the evacuees had already gone, Péri took charge of the *Le-Rhin,* although he was a mere sub-lieutenant, while her regular captain held the rank of Corvette Captain in the naval reserve. Helped by a handful of junior officers, he reloaded *Le-Rhin* with whatever lay to hand on the quay and joined a belated convoy sailing to Morocco. As the convoy was passing through the Straits of Gibraltar, Péri altered *Le-Rhin*'s course and brought her into Gibraltar harbour, complete with her cargo of silks, wines, bicycles, blankets and refrigerators. There she was kept idle for some months. Meanwhile, Péri was joined by a Belgian army doctor named Albert Guérisse, who shared his determination to fight on. The ship was finally sailed to Barry Docks to be refitted. In Britain Péri, who had scorned an attempt by the French Consul at Gibraltar to enlist him to carry out a sabotage attack on HMS *Hood,* opted to join the Royal Navy, rather than the Gaullist forces; so did his officers and they were, accordingly, granted RN (Royal Navy) ranks equivalent to their French ones. The ship had been visited by Admiral Muselier while she lay at Gibraltar, however, and the decision to allow Péri and his crew to join the Royal Navy caused great resentment at de Gaulle's Carlton Gardens headquarters—so much so that SOE decided not to take over the ship. They reckoned they already had enough trouble on their hands in the form of opposition from Passy and de Gaulle to their Independent French Section, which, however, they were determined to maintain because they could not be certain that their view of the need for paramilitary action in France would always coincide with de Gaulle's.

For reasons of security, Péri and his crew joined the Royal Navy under assumed names. Péri became Lt Cdr Jack Langlais, RN, and remained in command, with Guérisse as first lieutenant under the name Lt Cdr Patrick O'Leary, RN.

Slocum had fewer inhibitions than SOE and was ready to take over responsibility for *Le-Rhin,* which Langlais had proposed should be refitted as what would have been called in the First World War a Q-ship—a disguised armed merchant cruiser. Slocum's idea from the outset was to use her for clandestine sea-transport operations in the western Mediterranean. The refit at Barry was carried out under the direction of Langlais and with the help of one of Slocum's staff officers, Lt Patrick Whinney, RNVR. Whinney, like his colleague Steven Mackenzie, had been a member of the British Naval Mission at Admiral Darlan's headquarters at the Château de Maintenon before the fall of France. When they reached London and reported for duty at the Admiralty, they were sent by Ian Fleming, special assistant to the Director of Naval Intelligence, to join Slocum's Section of SIS (Special Intelligence Service).

At the end of her refit, *Le-Rhin* was renamed *Fidelity* and, with her French crew, commissioned under the white ensign, de Gaulle's objections notwithstanding. The programme for her first operational voyage in April 1941 involved landing two parties of agents and embarking three groups of evaders and escapers on the south coast of France. She needed to put into Gibraltar briefly to refuel and disembark some officers of SOE's Spanish Section, but it was decided to do this under cover of darkness, since ship movements in and out of the port could be observed from adjacent Spanish territory and it had to be assumed that the daily influx of 4,000 Spanish workers included a quota of Axis spies. Thereafter, she proceeded through the Straits before dawn and up the Spanish coast.

Fidelity had been equipped with several disguises of Spanish and Portuguese character and her crew had been trained in altering the ship's appearance overnight. She passed inspection by German aircraft more than once and arrived on 25 April at her first pinpoint, the Etang-du-Cannet, close to the eastern end of the Pyrenees, where Bitner and an elderly Maltese civil engineer named Rizzo were landed by night. Rizzo had worked in Paris as a science teacher: he hated the Germans and was being infiltrated for Leslie Humphreys's Section of SOE, to establish a two-way link across the Pyrenees in conjunction with the professional Spanish smugglers working in the area. These were, for the most part, Republican exiles who made a living by carrying contraband tobacco into Spain. Rizzo accomplished his mission with great success and his trans-Pyrenean Spanish 'passers' formed an essential part of the land lines run by Humphreys into and out of France.

The next day *Fidelity* arrived off the small French port of Cerbère, which lies close to the Spanish frontier. She was due to collect a party of Polish evaders. The arrangement was that a boat would put into the harbour in daylight, embark passengers from the jetty in quick time and leave again before too many questions were asked. A small fishing boat of local type was carried for this purpose in the *Fidelity*.

On 26 April 1941, this boat entered Cerbère under command of 'Pat O'Leary' (an alias of Albert Guérisse). A Polish agent met them and went off to collect his party, which was waiting nearby. But while he was doing this, two French gendarmes arrived and asked awkward questions, which forced O'Leary to leave hurriedly. His boat was pursued by a French *chasseur* and captured. O'Leary and his crew, with the exception of one man who got away by swimming into Spanish territorial waters, were taken prisoner by the Vichy authorities—but not for long. Guérisse and a fellow-member of *Fidelity*'s crew named Lalande were interned in Fort Saint-Hypolite-du-Gard, but their potential value as native French speakers was soon spotted by a Scottish officer named Ian Garrow, who had himself escaped from internment and was building an organisation to repatriate members of the British forces left behind after Dunkirk and airmen who had been shot down and evaded capture. Garrow decided to arrange for the escape of Guérisse and Lalande to work with him if London agreed. Having secured MI9's approval, Garrow got them out and incorporated them into his escape organisation. In the spring of 1942, he sent them to Gibraltar via Spain for consultations with MI9's representatives. They returned by sea (see page xxx). Lalande was supposed to work as the escape line's radio operator, but the arrangement was not a success and he was eventually sent home. In July 1942, Garrow was arrested—having been betrayed by a British sergeant named Cole, who had become a double agent. Guérisse took over Garrow's escape line and became one of MI9's most successful agents, though he repeated Garrow's mistake of trusting Cole. He became Belgium's greatest hero of the Second World War. Not long before Guérisse's death in 1989, the King of Belgium broke with precedent and conferred on him the title of Count, in recognition of his outstanding services to the Resistance.

Fidelity's first voyage is not well documented. She had been due to pick up a group of British evaders and escapers from a pinpoint in the Gulf of Lyons but was prevented from doing so by the appearance of a French seaplane. Slocum's 1946 report on his Section's wartime activities says of *Fidelity*'s voyage only than that 'she completed her programmes satisfactorily and returned to the United Kingdom with a long list of defects and complaints.' The fact that he did not list any of the five operations that had been planned does not suggest that they were notably successful, apart from the landing of Bitner and Rizzo.

A major refit proved necessary and there were constant political squabbles over the crew, owing to continued Free French objections to the employment of Frenchmen in the Royal Navy. In September 1941, *Fidelity* was again ready for sea and this time her programme included operations on the Algerian coast. Again she sailed direct from the United Kingdom. The SOE records show that she once more made a stop, presumably nocturnal, at Gibraltar.

She had lost time on the outward passage owing to bad weather and poor coal. The first pinpoint in the Gulf of Lyons was reached 24 hours late on 14 September and the British evaders and escapers who should have been there could not be found. She then sailed for the Algerian coast, where she was due to embark a second party of escaped British prisoners of war and evaders for MI9 on 16 September, but she again found no one at the pinpoint. However, two other operations were, according to Slocum's 1946 report, carried out before *Fidelity* returned to the first pinpoint for a further attempt to embark the British evaders and escapers. She tried twice—on 20 and 21 September—but again failed.

The SOE files provide confirmation that four of their agents were successfully landed in the course of this voyage. This seems to have taken place at Barcaire, near Perpignan, on 19 September: the agents were F.Basin ('Olive'), R.Leroy ('Louis'), R.B.Roche and A.J.R. Dubourdin—all of whom were destined to join the de Vomécourt brothers' AUTOGYRO circuit, the first such group that SOE's independent F Section had got going. They appear to have been landed as a single party. No details of a second disembarkation, as suggested by Slocum, have emerged.

Fidelity's September sortie to the western Mediterranean was thus not entirely fruitless, but Slocum apparently decided at this point that enough was enough and that she could not be further employed for his purposes. Apart from her slowness, she was too large and conspicuous for repeated clandestine ventures in the confined waters of the western Mediterranean. She was refitted once more towards the end of 1941, this time by Messrs Harland and Wolff at Southampton under the guidance of the Admiralty's Plans Division for work in the Far East, the 'spirit and personality' of her commanding officer having attracted the attention of the new C-in-C (Commander-in-Chief) Eastern Fleet, Admiral Somerville.[4] Langlais, now promoted Acting Commander, knew the area well, having worked there before the war for the French Colonial Intelligence Service. The plan was that *Fidelity* should operate in this theatre as a proper Q-ship, carrying, for offensive purposes, Royal Marine Commando personnel, two small amphibious aircraft and a 45-foot motor torpedo boat of a type based on a First World War Coastal Motor Boat (CMB) design, capable of giving a top speed of 52 knots when fully loaded or 58 knots without armament, under the impulsion of a Rolls-Royce Merlin main engine of the type used in Spitfire and Lancaster aircraft. This thorough refit was followed by intensive working-up with the Royal Marine Unit, which had been training at Chale on the south coast of the Isle of Wight.

In December 1942, *Fidelity* sailed for Panama as part of convoy ONS 154 on what proved to be her last voyage. Despite her apparent offensive capability, she was not considered a member of the escort. In fact, an Admiralty directive of November 1941 had said that, even if she were refitted (as she now had been), she was considered 'a most unsuitable ship to work on regular convoy escort as long as she is manned as she is at present'. Eight days later the two groups of German U-boats that had been shadowing

ONS 154 since it emerged from St George's Channel pressed in and the biggest wolf-pack attack yet experienced began: it was to reduce the convoy of 45 ships to 30.

At the most critical moment of this running battle, at dusk on 29 December, Langlais was asked by the senior officer of the escort, Lt Cdr Windeyer, RCN, in HMCS *St-Laurent,* to fly off one of his two Kingfisher seaplanes to cover an alteration of course against submarine attack. Langlais, only too delighted to take part in the fight, complied and *Fidelity* hove to while the aircraft was hoisted out over the starboard quarter and deposited in the water. The pilot, Lt Cdr (A) Ben Schröder, RNVR—a distinguished Paris dentist in peacetime—and his observer/gunner, Sub-Lt J.-J.Allen, RN, clambered into the tandem cockpits. Schröder realised that his chance of making a safe take-off in the prevailing conditions was poor. He shouted to Langlais to request the cooperation of the *St-Laurent.* The destroyer duly obliged and set off to steam at full speed into the wind, thus creating by her wake a broad strip of smooth water to provide a runway for the seaplane, but to no avail, the sea was altogether too rough and the Kingfisher became unstable. One wing-tip float dug into the water and broke off. The aircraft slewed round almost 90° and came to a standstill pointing back towards *Fidelity.* Very quickly, the seaplane settled into the water. Schröder and Allen extricated themselves from their harness and clung on as long as they could to the waterlogged fuselage. Allen's attempt to inflate the dinghy was unsuccessful and he was swept away, sustained only by his Mae West. It was two hours before first Schröder and then he were picked up by the *St-Laurent.*

The Kingfisher had been equipped with six aircraft-type depth charges, three slung beneath each wing. They were set to go off at 50-foot depth and, as the aircraft sank, there was a series of explosions, which were felt with great force in *Fidelity*'s engine-room. The condenser was extensively damaged and the engines had to be shut down in some haste, leaving the ship disabled and dead in the water. The convoy pressed on with a Canadian corvette, HMCS *Shediac,* detached to stand by *Fidelity,* though she was forced to leave in the early hours of 29 December as she was short of fuel.

The U-boat pack had followed the main convoy, which continued to lose merchant ships. *Fidelity,* in improving weather, launched her MTB at about noon on 29 December and an hour later the second Kingfisher seaplane was able to take off for a brief reconnaissance, which revealed an apparently disabled U-boat on the surface some 16 miles to the south-west and two heavily laden lifeboats in the same area. The aircraft was hoisted back aboard and the MTB was sent to investigate the sightings, though only her auxiliary engine was working. Langlais subsequently ordered her to resume her anti-submarine patrolling and sent the two landing craft carried by *Fidelity* to search for the lifeboats.

In mid-afternoon, the fractured condenser pipes had been temporarily patched up and *Fidelity* got underway again at a speed that eventually rose to 5 knots. In due course, the landing craft returned with some 40 survivors including the commander of the convoy.

That same evening *Fidelity* was twice attacked. U 225 fired one torpedo, which missed. Langlais dropped a pattern of depth charges. The MTB sighted the U-boat on the surface and tried to close in on her, but at 7½ knots this proved impossible. The U-boat dived and broke off the action. Less than an hour later, U 615, which was making a sweep behind the convoy, sighted *Fidelity* and fired three more torpedoes, to no apparent effect. Once again Langlais dropped depth charges and the submarine withdrew. However, *Fidelity*'s engines broke down and, when she was able to get underway again, it was at no more than 2 knots. The MTB was in equally great mechanical trouble by this stage and lost sight of her mother ship during the night. With failing batteries, she lost R/T contact as well. Langlais had failed to make his position clear to the Admiralty when he left the convoy route, heading for the Azores; and in the forenoon of 30 December the Admiralty lost radio contact with *Fidelity,* which fell victim to two of three torpedoes fired by U 435 that afternoon. Langlais, belligerent to the last, fired two last depth charges as the ship sank.

Strelow, the U-boat commander, came up to periscope depth to view the destruction he had wrought. He estimated, with some accuracy, that there were between 300 and 400 survivors in the sea or on rafts in the gathering gloom, although he did not specify a figure in the signal he sent three hours later to his base at Saint-Nazaire, reporting the sinking. The reply told him in rather chilling tones to report if survivors were on board or whether 'their destruction in the weather prevailing can be counted on'.

Not one of the 406 souls on board *Fidelity* when she sank lived to tell the tale. Among those who died were Lt Cdr J.W.F.Milner-Gibson, her first lieutenant, who had played an important part in clandestine sea transport as one of only two navigators used by Slocum on all cross-Channel operations of this type before September 1941. One of the ten members of the ship's company who survived because they were either on board the first Kingfisher aircraft or on MTB 105 was Schröder's observer, 'J.-J.Allen', later known as J.-J.Tremayne, real name Gilbert. Eight months later he assumed command of MFV 2023, Slocum's high-speed version of a French west-coast sardine *pinasse,* when Daniel Lomenech brought his three-year career as a clandestine operator to an end and transferred to submarines.

Fidelity and her commanding officer hold a unique, if controversial, place in the annals of the Royal Navy. Even three years after her demise, Slocum was predicting that many a supply officer would blench, many a civil servant tear his hair for years to come at the mere mention of her name. Seldom, he continued, could a single ship have caused such diverse opinions in high circles. The Flag Officer Commanding North Atlantic in Gibraltar referred to her as HMS *Futility,* but the ship and Langlais were highly thought of by the Commanders-in-Chief of Western Approaches and of the Far Eastern Fleet. Reviled by many and loved by few, she was the first British warship to sail in wartime with a female officer (First Officer Madeleine Barclay, WRNS, was her cipher officer). Under the name Bayard, this woman is said to have worked as an agent for Péri in the Far East and to have followed him home. At one time she had certainly been his mistress.

Péri was the only Frenchman in modern times to become an Acting Commander, RN. His methods of maintaining discipline included kicking a defaulter down the ladder leading to the ship's bridge. Slocum, who knew him well, described him as having the appearance and mentality of an eighteenth-century buccaneer, but he considered Péri a great man and his death a real loss to Britain. Peter Kingswell, in his carefully-researched monograph *Fidelity Will Haunt Me till I Die,* written for the Royal Marine Historical Society, took a less charitable view: he deemed Péri a supreme opportunist who, in pursuit of his dream of personal glory and his insatiable lust for contest, caused vast sums of money to be squandered on converting an entirely unsuitable vessel into an armed merchant cruiser. He considered *Fidelity*'s very presence on convoy ONS 154 futile and her enormous armament pointless. For the loss of 406 lives and the waste of the invaluable assault troops in T Company of 40 Royal Marine Commando, Péri's megalomania and ability to bend people of influence and authority to his will qualify him, in Kingswell's view, for a heavy share of the blame.

III
Operations from Gibraltar to Morocco: July–October 1941

On 29 April 1941, after the plan to use the cargo steamer *Czardasz* to evacuate Poles from the Marseilles area was abandoned (see previous chapter), Krajewski, who had been sent to Gibraltar to organise that operation, received from Colonel Mally, his chief in Lisbon, details of a quite different plan, which the Polish General Staff had put to the Admiralty in London.[1]

The Poles suggested the British naval authorities should help them acquire a motor vessel that could be used to collect Polish internees from the Casablanca area. If a suitable craft could not be made available for their exclusive use from the existing stock of vessels at Gibraltar, a ship should be bought in Portugal or possibly Spain and sailed to Gibraltar. It would obviously attract undesirable attention if the Poles were seen to be the buyers. They would need help, too, in finding a crew for the vessel and a suitable place for it to be berthed at Gibraltar.

Once these conditions were fulfilled and they had been able to locate a suitable embarkation point at the Casablanca end, Mally would send a courier to Wysoczanski, their representative in Morocco, to discuss with him in secrecy how to put the plan into effect. The courier would take a letter from General Bohusz for Wysoczanski to give to Colonel Molle, Chief of Staff to General Béthouart, who commanded the French division at Casablanca, asking Molle to give them all possible help. On the courier's return to Lisbon, Mally would inform the British authorities of the proposed arrangements so that they could issue the operation orders.

The evacuees would not be told how they were to be evacuated: they would, indeed, be given the misleading impression that it would be organised via Gambia or Tangiers. They would be required, as a condition of embarkation, to sign an undertaking to join the Polish army in England. No families or other dependants would be taken off. Evacuation would be carried out in secret and at night. All immigration and security-vetting procedures would be applied on arrival in the United Kingdom and evacuees would be held incommunicado while in transit through Gibraltar. The Poles asked that the costs of fitting out and maintaining the vessel, cost of fuel, pay for the crew and subsistence for the evacuees should be met locally from British sources and recovered from the Polish treasury in London.

The Admiralty was prepared to back the venture and written confirmation of this would be forthcoming. They suggested that Krajewski liaise in Gibraltar with Flag Officer Commanding North Atlantic (FOCNA) who would probably be able to provide a suitable craft from local resources but, if not, would be able to help Krajewski buy one in Spain or Portugal.

The Admiralty thought it would be better for the crew to be Polish, in case the boat were stopped by French patrols, when the presence of British sailors might endanger the whole operation. The British Ministry of Shipping would, if necessary, send a crew of Poles out from the United Kingdom, but it might be possible instead to recruit crew from the Polish motor ship *Oksywia,* which had been seized by the French authorities in Morocco but whose crew were expected to be released. Krajewski could choose volunteers and one officer to take command of the vessel. This crew should be retained in Gibraltar even if the required vessel had not been handed over when they arrived there.

FOCNA would give Krajewski advice and instructions about the operational aspects of the scheme—choice of a suitable time to approach the French Moroccan coast, embarkation point and possible support by British naval forces.

The Polish proposals presented the Admiralty with a means not only of rescuing their troops interned in the Casablanca area but also of meeting longer-term needs. A vessel based at Gibraltar and its Polish crew might be used to mount similar operations to other points on the French coast.

Mally was instructed by General Sikorski's Chief of Staff to put the plan into effect, in close cooperation with the British authorities and with Krajewski. Mally cabled Krajewski and followed this up with a letter telling him to begin the search for a vessel and asking whether it would be possible to draw from the crew of the *Oksywia.* Krajewski was to establish and maintain contact with FOCNA.

This was not the first clandestine sea contact with Morocco. In September 1940, a British destroyer from Gibraltar had landed three Gaullist emissaries between Mogador and Agadir, but their mission had been short-lived: all had been arrested soon after their arrival.[2]

As well as the Poles, a number of Allied ships and their crews were detained by the Vichy French authorities in Morocco. The Belgians had made one abortive attempt, through their Consulate in Lisbon, to smuggle out a group of about 40 people from Port Lyautey on a 200-ton Portuguese merchant ship, but the executants fell into the hands of a double agent working for the Vichy administration. The Portuguese captain, who was not privy to the plan, was arrested and sent to France.[3] Local initiatives by the interned ship's crews had been rather more successful. Six Danes and a Belgian had escaped from

Port Lyautey in January 1941 in a ship's lifeboat, followed on 11 March by four more Danes and a Norwegian, by ten Danes a week later, and by three Norwegians at the beginning of April.[4] On the other hand, two Norwegians, who left Casablanca on 15 January in a ship's boat, were cast ashore near Fedhala, and five Danes, who had stolen a yacht to get away from Safi, were arrested off Mazagan by a French naval vessel. The project that emerged from the Poles' discussions with the Admiralty, however, was different in kind from any of these previous enterprises, and more ambitious, in that it envisaged an ongoing series of clandestine sea-transport operations from the Gibraltar base.

Krajewski reported on 9 May that he had found a boat that he could use without charge.[5] It was a seagoing motor fishing vessel, which could be used without arousing suspicion. She would require a maximum of four crew—possibly fewer—apart from the captain, a role he would take on himself. He would like to have a W/T operator who could double as a deck-hand, so as to maintain communications with Gibraltar when at sea.

The crew of the *Oksywia* were not at Gibraltar, nor could he find any trace of their having been there in transit. Foreigners arriving at Gibraltar were sent on to the United Kingdom as quickly as possible. There were no communications between Gibraltar and French Morocco. Since crew might therefore have to be chosen in Lisbon, Krajewski spelt out for Mally the qualities he was looking for. An ability to keep one's mouth shut was the first prerequisite. He stressed the need for stability of character because of prevailing conditions in the fortress of Gibraltar, where a lengthy stay must be anticipated, for his operations would take place over some months. On the positive side, a pay supplement would be available.

There was no regular means of smuggling letters to Morocco, Krajewski reported, but he had promises of help and hoped to know more within a few days. He assumed Mally would send detailed information and instructions by letter to Wysoczanski and asked permission to append details of his seagoing technical needs. Obviously, rapid communications apart from these letters would be needed, W/T communications in particular, and these would need to be direct to avoid loss of time in decoding and recoding in Lisbon. But he confessed he was ignorant about conditions in Casablanca, and how much freedom their people enjoyed.

Krajewski knew that the British in Gibraltar had tried to evacuate a group of their own people by sending some form of naval vessel. The French authorities were terrified that, if they helped the Poles, the news would get back to Germany. While making these preparations for operations to Morocco, Krajewski had not lost sight of the far more important problem of evacuation from France. In a letter to Mally dated 17 May 1941, forwarding a report on communications to Morocco, he suggested that for urgent operational matters it would be better to use coded cable. Were there, he went on, direct communications between Lisbon and Marseilles? Was it General Kleeberg himself or his deputy who would be involved at the other end? He asked also if there had been any important change of status regarding the camps and what Kleeberg had replied to his earlier question about the delivery of people to certain places.

Mally replied on 21 May to both these letters.[6] He sent Krajewski Wysoczanski's address in Casablanca and an alternative means of contacting him through a bar. He had renewed a request to London headquarters for a code for use in direct communications between Mally and Casablanca which was indispensable for evacuation work. The Czechs, Mally continued, had recently been planning an evacuation of about 30 people from just north of Rabat, using a fishing boat. If this operation succeeded, they would be able to make use of the experience gained through it. Mally knew that there were at least 80 Poles to be evacuated from the Casablanca area, but this figure was some months out of date and he was convinced the total would turn out to be about 100. They were grouped in camps 150–200 km (95–125 miles) from the coast and their freedom of movement was restricted. There was considerable difficulty about getting hold of passes to Casablanca; and it would not be easy to get these people down to the coast.

Wysoczanski had reported to Mally the names of the officers in charge of the camps in French North Africa. He was pessimistic about the chances of organising even the smallest evacuation without French complicity and thought that any attempt to take people out would cause a worsening of conditions in the camps. Mally said he was insisting that Wysoczanski should persist, as this was the only hope of getting these valuable people out of Africa. Wysoczanski had made proposals for evacuation by legal means, all of which, however, would require interminable efforts to get visas.

On 2 June, Mally wrote to say that the French military and civilian authorities in Morocco were, for the time being, well disposed to the evacuation of the Poles from Africa.[7] This opportunity must be seized, for it was conceivable that the French would be obliged by the Armistice Commission to send the Poles who had reached Algeria and Morocco back to German-occupied France. Mally instructed Krajewski to get the British naval authorities to agree that, in that event, the ship carrying them would be intercepted and the Polish internees rescued: what had happened in Tunisia might equally well occur in Algeria and Morocco.

In a postscript, Mally wrote that a cable from London, just arrived, informed him that the British Admiralty had now issued the instruction for his own operations to France to begin. GHQ wanted Krajewski to report on progress. It was fairly typical that Mally's letter took three-and-a-half weeks to reach Krajewski from Lisbon.

On 14 June, Mally wrote again to Krajewski to say that he was still awaiting formal British Admiralty approval for operations to begin.[8] Wysoczanski meanwhile was urging the soonest possible evacuation because of the conditions prevailing in French North Africa. Mally repeated that they must abandon the idea of using crew from the *Oksywia,* as the French were refusing to release them; Krajewski must find an alternative crew in Gibraltar.

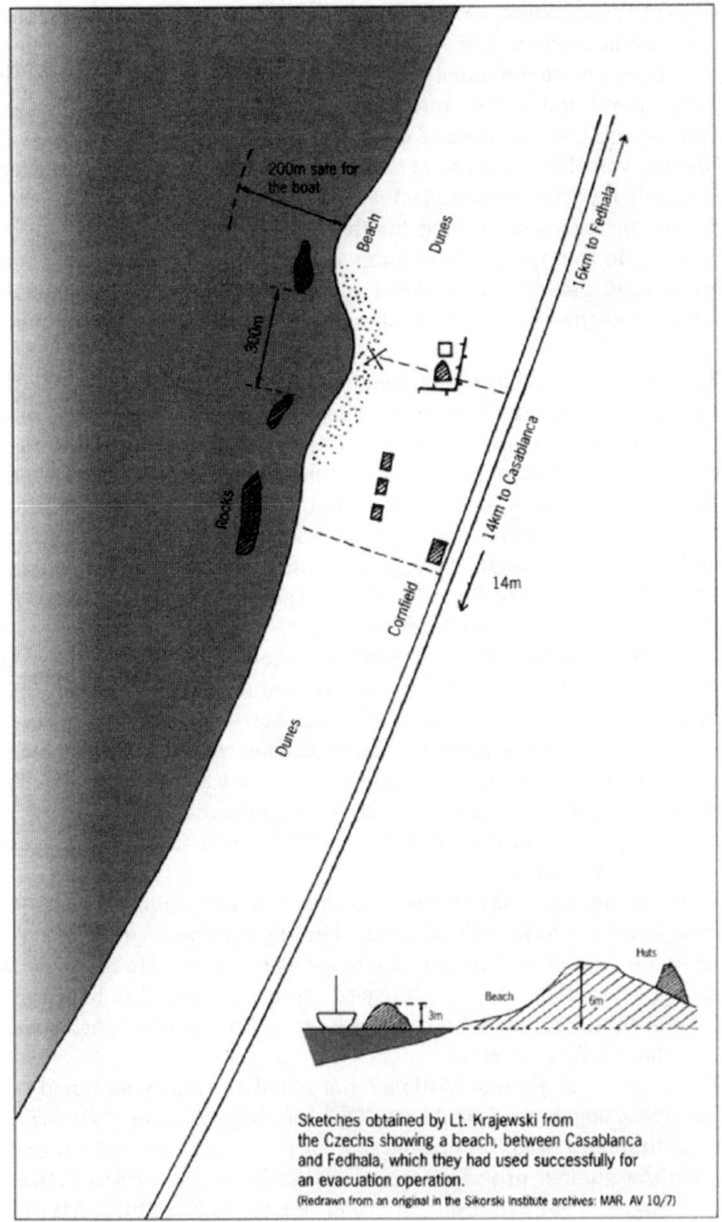

Sketches obtained by Lt. Krajewski from the Czechs showing a beach, between Casablanca and Fedhala, which they had used successfully for an evacuation operation.

(Redrawn from an original in the Sikorski Institute archives: MAR. AV 10/7)

Mally had sent Wysoczanski technical details, such as recognition signals, and he told Krajewski he must be ready to carry out an operation to Algeria at seven days' notice and to Morocco at five. This letter must have crossed with one that Krajewski wrote on 15 June to Mally about the radio and courier problems he was experiencing in his communications with both Lisbon and Casablanca.[9] Friendly British Officers had just told him that a fishing vessel had arrived at Gibraltar from Morocco with Czechs on board. He attached a separate report on this subject, and sent another ten days later.

Particular circumstances accounted for the high cost of the Czech operation—10,000 Francs per person. In fact, the price—a lump sum of 115,000 Francs—was to have covered the evacuation of 30 persons (i.e. 4,000 Francs per capita). This cost per head rose *de facto* when the police prevented 21 members of the expedition from making their way to the boat.

Krajewski's informants had been detained by the police with the other 21 Czechs. There was, however, no evidence against them, since they were not carrying any bundles of possessions. (Evacuees, against organisers' orders, sometimes carried packages of belongings or suitcases with papers in them; one man had too many layers of clothing on.) The informants simply told the police that they had 'come to the beach' and were released with orders to return to camp before 10 o'clock.

Krajewski thought these events of obvious significance for the Poles; Wysoczanski must be informed of them. The Czechs, with their experience of evacuations, had proved a useful source of information. They advised that the best time of day for concentration at the evacuation point was the afternoon; evacuees should be divided into groups of two to four and should travel to the beach by various means. The police were in the habit of checking the papers of everyone who got off a bus. Nevertheless, the Czechs believed that escape was easy so long as it was well organised. They gave Krajewski excellent sketches of the area. A person who knew the place well was a Czech Lieutenant named Riedel, who had organised matters competently at the Casablanca end. Krajewski suggested it might be worth using him in cooperation with their own local representative. He gave Riedel's address in Casablanca.

Krajewski wrote that he could evacuate as many as 110 people if he used a passenger vessel that was available to him in Gibraltar. For any number over 50, he could ask for a British naval escort. If it proved impossible to get as many as 50 to the embarkation point, he would use an unescorted felucca. As regards crew, he wanted to have three, or at least two, Poles, rather than foreigners he could not trust. An engineer was indispensable, but he could do without a W/T operator.

Krajewski replied on 26 June to Mally's letter dated 14 June, which had taken ten days to reach him. They ought possibly to use Quennell's (SOE) bag.[10] He still had to find, requisition and fit out a vessel. He needed to hear from Casablanca about the place for the evacuation and the number of people, so as to decide on the most suitable type of boat. Then he would have to get Admiralty approval for the expenditure. All this would take time. He had suggested to Wysoczanski one possible pinpoint 14 km south of Casablanca, but this was subject to Wysoczanski's report back on any buildings or guard posts in the area. An alternative, which he preferred, was 14km from Casablanca towards Fedhala. The Czechs had used it and been able to find a hide-out on the coast while waiting for evacuation. The spot was so isolated that they did not even consider a silenced engine in the boat necessary.

Krajewski pointed out that Casablanca was 190 nautical miles from Gibraltar. He estimated (not entirely accurately) that, allowing 12 hours in hand for contingencies, the round trip would take 70 hours at 7 knots or 52 hours at 10 knots. Oran was 250 nautical miles and a round trip would require 85 hours at 7 knots or 62 hours at 10 knots. Algiers was 450 nautical miles and a round trip would take 132 hours at 7 knots or 85 hours at 10 knots. He would need two months' notice and a no-moon period would be necessary.

Krajewski asked whether it would be possible to recruit a couple of Poles in Lisbon as crew. If not, he would attempt to find Spaniards, with discreet help from the British. Anticipating this, he had been learning Spanish for some time. He had proposed to Wysoczanski that priority be given to evacuating the crew of the Oksywia, including an engineer, but only if they agreed to serve in evacuation operations. In that case, the Spaniards would be needed for the first mission only.

On 13 June, Hugh Quennell, SOE's senior representative at Gibraltar, had informed Krajewski, to whom he was helpful in a number of ways, of a plan he had elaborated, which would involve leaving Polish military personnel in French North Africa for eventual use in special operations rather than evacuating them.[11] He told Krajewski he had been in Lisbon a week previously and had discussed this idea with Mally: he showed Krajewski a document in English, which purported to summarise Mally's reaction. The Polish military personnel left *in situ* would be organised in case the Germans invaded French North Africa or France entered into the Axis camp. The Poles would then disperse and place themselves at the head of Arab groups to create diversions. He undertook to provide money in sufficient quantity and would that week be sending 100,000 Francs to a named contact in Casablanca. Quennell claimed that Mally had more or less accepted his plan. Asked his own position, Krajewski replied that he could not adopt any policy but that of his own headquarters in London, which, to date, had given him instructions to evacuate. He was not prepared to hazard a personal view, not being familiar with the terrain in French North Africa. He suggested that Quennell might wire SOE Baker Street to discuss the matter with Polish headquarters in London.

Quennell set out his requirements in a memorandum to Krajewski dated 2 July 1941.[12] If Polish headquarters were to give permission for Polish military personnel other than air and armoured troops to be used for fifth-column activities, he would need answers to the following questions:

(a) How many Poles would be at SOE's disposal?

(b) In what districts could they become active?
(c) What were the numbers in particular districts?
(d) Who might become leaders of the proposed bands?
(e) Could the bands organise themselves as an effective fifth column for tasks such as cutting communications, sinking ships, distributing propaganda leaflets and other acts of sabotage?
(f) How much money would be necessary for such a scheme?
(g) What kind of material would need to be supplied?
(h) Could targets for sabotage be suggested?

In exchange, SOE could offer the following:

(a) To convey to French North Africa the radio station that was indispensable.
(b) Signals from the radio station could be transmitted to Gibraltar.
(c) Letters could be sent from Tangiers to the French North African territories.
(d) Money could also be forwarded by the same route.

Quennell asked if these questions and proposals could also be conveyed to the Czechs in French North Africa.

Mally replied on 8 July, enclosing a record of a meeting he had had with Quennell and Jack Beevor, SOE's representative in Lisbon, on 12 June.[13] This, he said, would prove to Krajewski that Quennell had mislead him. Agreement had been reached with Mr Quennell to stop evacuation of Polish military personnel from French North Africa and to leave them there for special operations, but only in the circumstances of a German invasion of French North Africa or of an attempt by the French to transfer Polish troops back to the French mainland. He asked Krajewski to remind Quennell of the basic assumptions on which their collaboration had been agreed.

The minutes of the meeting of 12 June recorded that Wysoczanski had a certain freedom of movement and was able to travel all over French North Africa to visit the Polish camps. Mally had described the distribution of the camps and the numbers involved: Casablanca and Oran served as transit points. He had enumerated a range of possible means of arranging evacuation:

(a) United States visas, as had been obtained for individual British detainees.
(b) Evacuation by means of motor vessels under the command of Krajewski, working from Gibraltar. This project was in process of being firmed up in discussions between Polish GHQ and the British Admiralty.
(c) Evacuation with the help of British warships patrolling along the African coast. This would require that notice be given by Krajewski to Wysoczanski and would be possible only for small parties.

(d) Visas for neutral states via Lisbon: the British authorities had promised to evacuate most of the Poles from Portugal and, when this had been done, the Portuguese would be more likely to grant transit visas.
(e) The chartering of a Portuguese ship in Casablanca. In this case Portuguese visas would not be necessary: the ship would officially be sailing for Tangiers but would in fact go to Gibraltar.
(f) The remaining question was what should be done with their people should the Germans move into North Africa before evacuation was complete. Col Mally thought it would not be possible to disperse the Polish internees without the support of the Arab population because of the latter's pro-German sympathies. In the light of Mr Quennell's statement that there were Caids, tribal chieftains, of friendly disposition, matters presented themselves rather differently: dispersal would thus be an excellent solution if there were a German invasion or an order by the French authorities for the Poles to be returned to France.

Proper preparations for their welfare and money for their subsistence would be necessary and should be arranged as for those held in the British camp at Carnot.

Mally had described the siting of the camps in French Morocco and the provenance of those held there; the Polish evacuation outposts at Algiers and Oran, whose personnel had a certain freedom of movement and access to the ports; and the 'Polooffices', which were the former Consulates at Algiers and Casablanca. Some further form of representation was contemplated in Tangiers.

The British wanted sabotage groups of six in Tangiers and Casablanca, and cooperation with preparations for an uprising of the local population. The Polish side was uncertain whether it would be possible to establish Poles secretly in Tangiers, but could find people in French Morocco, including the crew of the Oksywia at Safi, where they were in contact with the interned Norwegians. With financial help they could achieve quite a lot. Lt Goguel, second mate of the *Oksywia,* would be a suitable leader. In Safi there were a number of large Norwegian ships whose crews were dreaming of escape. It would be worth helping them.

Mally noted that the possibility of an insurrection would depend on contact with the Arab chiefs and on the availability of money for them. It would be necessary to assign a liaison officer to the Caids. He had asked for 100,000 Moroccan Francs to be sent to an address he had given. Further financial needs would depend on progress with evacuation. Mally had said that French control of the port at Casablanca was stringent, but at Safi it was comparatively mild.

The Poles had excellent opportunities for monitoring movements of troops and merchant shipping at Oran and Safi and possibly also at Casablanca. This intelligence could be relayed to Krajewski in Gibraltar.

Code words had been agreed for the British emissary to Wysoczanski. He should bring greetings from Mally, who had worked with him in the registration office in Paris. Wysoczanski could be found via someone named Komar or the Poloffice.

Before receiving this information from Mally, Krajewski had reported (on 22 June) the arrival at Gibraltar of three boats carrying 15 Norwegians and Danes from Morocco: two were from Port Lyautey, one from Rabat.[14] The boats had simply been stolen during the night. The most important of their preparations was to provide a few boxes of biscuits and some fresh water. In the case of Port Lyautey, as the port lies some way up a river, they took advantage of the current and the ebb tide. The determination of the escapers could be judged from the fact that the boat from Rabat did not even have a compass. The voyage to Gibraltar had been accomplished in three to four days without incident. There were almost no controls on the coast and, if there were any look-out posts, they must have been asleep.

Krajewski felt that, if only the Poles had set about the task with energy, they would already have evacuated some dozens of their people. On 3 July Krajewski wrote to Wysoczanski and copied the letter to Mally. He reported that Major Brzozowski had arrived from Africa.[15] To avoid further delay, he had begun preparations. The boat he had acquired had a diesel engine and auxiliary sails: it could carry up to 30 passengers and was said to be very reliable. Work on this vessel would take up to 12 July. The first evacuation operation would begin on 19 July at 0300. He was frustrated by the delay in their communications and had decided to take the initiative. He would use the embarkation point between Casablanca and Fedhala recommended by the Czechs and he attached to his letter a copy of their sketch of it. This stretch of coast was featureless and monotonous. He proposed to signal to the shore unless there was some other vessel in the vicinity. His crew on this first mission would consist of foreigners but he asked Wysoczanski to include some Polish sailors among the evacuees: he needed two reliable mechanics, only one of whom need be fully qualified, and one deck-hand. It would be desirable to get some undertaking from them of their readiness to serve. The second officer of the *Oksywia* (Goguel) would be useful. Each group of evacuees should include at least one person familiar with Morse code.

Krajewski said he was planning a second contact on Sunday 27 July and a third on Sunday 3 August, both at 0300. He repeated the Czech advice that the evacuees should avoid carrying bundles of their possessions and should be split into groups of not more than two to four persons, taking different routes to the pinpoint. He asked about the possibility of organising evacuation from the Oran area.

On 5 July, Krajewski reported to Mally that he had taken on a Norwegian crew at a wage of £18, the rate paid on British ships.[16] They would also receive £20 by way of 'hard-lying' or danger money. He had not told them the whole story. The conversion was progressing well: the additional fuel and freshwater tanks were being fitted by RN specialists, rather than by the civilian shipyard, in the interests of security. He expected to receive a second boat.

As regards communications, Quennell was being helpful at present, but in return he was asking Krajewski to help him over 'diversionary' activities. He had received a reply from [Polish] GHQ to his telegram. After the evacuation of air force and armoured warfare personnel, they said that others could be used for 'diversionary activities'. Krajewski had queried this: he wondered whether this ruling was not out of date in view of the decisive change in the political situation since the Germans had engaged themselves in the east. Perhaps a certain Father Misieuda might be landed at Casablanca for special operations of the type Quennell wanted.

In discussion with Krajewski, Admiral Collins [FOCNA] agreed that, if advised in time, and other commitments permitting, Royal Navy vessels might be used to intercept any French ship carrying Polish ex-service personnel back to metropolitan France.

Replying to earlier letters from Krajewski, Wysoczanski reported that on 7 July there had been a major change in the situation regarding the camps.[17] An order had been issued to transfer all the internees to the eastern frontier of Morocco, near the Algerian border, whence their chances of getting to the Atlantic coast would be impossible and to the Mediterranean coast nearly so. This forced Wysoczanski to make use of the fisherman Krajewski had recommended. The transfer was to begin on 11/12 July. A first group consisting of one officer and 16 other ranks must be ready for collection by this fisherman at midnight on 10 July and a second group, one officer and 24 other ranks, at midnight on 13 July. Mally would need to provide the funds.

Wysoczanski said he had reconnoitred the stretch of coast proposed by Krajewski and did not consider it suitable: the German Armistice Commission had an outpost at a village not many kilometres away and the whole district was closely patrolled. He had chosen an alternative approximately 7 km south-west of Fedhala lighthouse and 14 km north of the Roches-Noires lighthouse. The place would be easily recognisable. He had given it the code name HADDA. There were, he said, more than 200 Polish internees in Algeria. As he could not bring them into Morocco, their evacuation from the Mediterranean coast should be considered. He had carried out a preliminary investigation and forwarded a report and map covering the area he thought of using for embarkation, code-named ZORRA.

Since Wysoczanski had started writing the letter, the first embarkation had had to be postponed for 24 hours as the fisherman had not turned up. Making use of a series of fishermen was an expensive and unsuitable method of evacuating large numbers. Events had shown that the fishermen were unreliable, which had meant that the intended evacuees were left in hiding near the beach.

The Czechs would be due to repay their share in the evacuation: The first combined Czech-Polish group had gone up from 1+16 to 1+24 and the bill would be 100,000 Francs in all: 20,000 of which should be reclaimed from the Czechs in respect of their eight passengers.

After an abortive sortie on 19 July in the felucca he had been fitting out, Krajewski got back to Gibraltar on 25 July. On 3 August, just before he set off again on a further attempt, he wrote again to Mally.[18]

Communications with Casablanca continued to be unsatisfactory. Wysoczanski had not received via Quennell either the money or the radio. Quennell said he had a receipt from Tangiers signed by Komar, so they must face the possibility that someone in the line was either stealing or betraying. He would check with Wysoczanski as soon as possible to see whether he had after all now received the parcels.

If Krajewski's letter of 3 July had fallen into the wrong hands, it would be highly compromising, since it contained complete instructions for the evacuation operation and, what was worse, some intelligence and sabotage instructions sent by Major Brzozowski. The consequences would be catastrophic, so he asked Mally to try to find out through his own channels what had happened. Krajewski, for his part, had drawn the necessary conclusions and was using other means of contact with Casablanca.

Since Wysoczanski had not received his instructions by 20 July, Krajewski continued, it was entirely understandable that the first voyage should have been such a fiasco and that they had not found a single soul at the intended point of embarkation. Krajewski said he had tried to postpone the operation by telegram in code, but in the absence of the explanatory letter this would have meant nothing to Wysoczanski.

The boat's engine needed a thorough overhaul. There was no alternative vessel available at Gibraltar and looking for one in Spanish ports posed considerable security problems. Krajewski was reticent about what was wrong with the engine but, three months later, when he had achieved a run of successes, he noted that the dockyard engineer had stopped reminding him of his felucca's 'spoiled engine'. This rather suggests that his improvised initial crew of two Norwegian seamen—survivors from a torpedoed ship—neither of whom was a mechanic, had been guilty of some sin of omission, such as failing to top up the oil in the crank-case, so that it had run dry and the big-end bearings had melted. Krajewski left no report of this abortive sortie and conferred the title of 'first evacuation mission' on what was actually his second voyage to Morocco, though he somewhat inconsistently called the immediately following operation his 'third' and numbered the series consecutively thereafter.

The salient features of his first surviving report to Mally can be rendered thus in translation:

> *REPORT OF THE FIRST EVACUATION MISSION*
> (follows my cable of 8 viii '41)[19]
>
> 1) *AN UNEXPECTED OPPORTUNITY.* As I reported on 3 August, despite having a crew and being aware that people might still be waiting for me, my felucca was still undergoing basic repairs. In these circumstances... I received your telegram containing the information that dispersed all our doubts about possibly letting Major

Wysoczanski down. The situation on that day made it glaringly obvious to us how exhausted our people must have been both physically and mentally, waiting since 10 July, and, in the majority of cases at least, sleeping on the beach.

When I informed Mr Quennell about my frustration he said, completely unexpectedly, 'Why don't you take my boat.' It turned out that he was prepared to give us his 'special operations' vessel for this task—an offer which, considering the situation here, I have to take as an expression of the utmost confidence.

I managed to prepare the ship for the voyage within 24 hours of being informed that we could use it (Sunday afternoon). On Monday 4 August I weighed anchor. I should add that I did not have my own crew (which would have been too small for this ship) but the ship's normal complement of personnel, together with its captain. Happily the latter was well disposed towards the operation, and also accepted certain suggestions from me regarding camouflage and the conduct of the ship, the route, etc. On board, apart from myself and the normal crew, there was Major Brzozowski, who was to be put ashore should we not find the people at the rendezvous, in order to make contact with them... There was in addition a young English officer, whom I took along at the request of Mr Quennell ostensibly to 'keep his hand in', although in reality perhaps as an apprentice for similar operations or as a discreet observer of our proceedings on behalf of the local representatives of British security intelligence. As it happened, it also served my purpose when we returned after a successful mission: his enthusiastic accounts of the operation helped our cause greatly and strengthened both the 'propaganda' success and its practical consequences at local level—the scale of support.

As for the first voyage, neutral identification signs were painted on the ship's side during the night. The journey to Casa was without incident. The number of ships and fishing vessels was even less than during my first trip. On 6 August at 0200 hrs we began to approach the coast, an operation of which I had already some considerable experience from my previous foray. Generally speaking, everything favoured an operation of our kind, since visibility had been reduced by a sea mist down to around 4,000 metres and the moon, which had been very bright (it was two days before the full moon) just before our arrival, became shrouded by a light layer of cloud. Having purposely arrived at our destination with time in hand...we began to patrol along the shore at a distance of 800 metres, giving our previously agreed identification signals as we went... The shoreline was generally rocky with some beaches and the hinterland was uninhabited for a distance of some kilometres. After half an hour of agitated suspense, when we had sighted what was beyond doubt the rock described by the Czechs and by Major Wysoczanski—and we had almost lost hope of receiving a reply from the shore—we made out the agreed signal. We approached the shoreline as far as the depth would allow, given the fairly large draft of our ship...and we dropped anchor. A small dinghy was launched and, having taken a volunteer in the shape of the English observer, I rowed the two of us towards the beach, towing behind me a light line, in accordance with the plan which I had drawn up to enable us to cross the breakers.

At a distance of 100 metres from the shore—as I soon realised—began the place where the waves broke into surf. Although we exercised the greatest care, we could not cross that line without a wetting, as we were thrown from the boat, which rapidly became filled with water. Since we had to swim across this none-too pleasant stretch of water, we experienced this phenomenon for some 15 minutes.

Meanwhile, when thrown out of the boat, I had luckily managed to grab the line from it and, after I had swum to the shore, our people there helped me pull it out. Captain Roehr, the head of the local evacuation operation, was waiting for me on the beach together with 27 people, three of whom were Czechs. After an initial 'conference' with Captain R., which, because it was held in such difficult conditions, did not explore in full all the matters we had to discuss, I took a first group of nine people who knew how to swim. Since we were uncertain whether we could pass through the line of breakers with our wet clothes weighing down the boat, I ordered them to be left on the beach, allowing the men to take only their money, documents and items of value. I disposed the people around the boat, ordering them also to keep hold of the line. At an arranged signal the crew of the ship began to draw the line in, and we helped by walking alongside it until we were out of our depth. That line proved to be invaluable: the evacuees did not exhaust themselves, since their only efforts were expended in keeping afloat. The boat unfortunately filled with water once again, so that its contents were soaked. Apart from two people who at a certain point betrayed signs of panic and clawed their way on to the boat already filled with water, the whole group swam out most efficiently to the ship, where, with the help of the crew, they clambered up on to the deck. Each received a blanket and the crew made over its living quarters to them until the end of the voyage.

I returned to the shore; once again it proved impossible to cross the line of breakers without being tipped from the 'saddle'... After a final conversation with Captain Roehr, who made a favourable impression on me, and having received from him a letter for you [Mally] and me, I got together the second and final group. After the first attempt, I decided to risk the crossing with the whole remaining party at once (16 people). The procedure would be just the same—that is, we would cross the breakers to reach the ship. However, I must say that the second group conducted itself even more calmly than the first, even though its members did not know how to swim. The Englishman also returned from the shore with this second group. He—as it later turned out—was impressed by the courage and determination of our people in making their way from Africa to join the Polish army.

So, at 0530, after 2½ hours, we completed the embarkation, after the disagreeable experience of touching the bottom a few times. The night was unsuitable for the operation insofar as the tides were concerned; high water being at 0200 hours, so we were compelled to work on a falling tide...

The only anxious moment of the voyage was the passage of a French aircraft some 1,000 metres away from us. Luckily it was a transport aircraft destined—to judge by its course—for Dakar. Also, as we approached the Straits of Gibraltar, where...we had a gale blowing against us, on the edge of Spanish territorial waters we met a Spanish patrol boat, which...suddenly, having passed us, turned about and followed us for a few minutes.

2) *ECHOES OF A SUCCESSFUL EXPEDITION.* Our mission acquired a relatively large, although discreet, fame amongst the senior people here. This is possibly because the attempts mounted so far, if my information is correct, have in general produced results such as the seizure of trawlers by the French or the failure of the evacuees to materialise, etc. The Governor himself [Lord Gort] took an interest in the mission and I have been informed that he will be summoning me within the next few days. Congratulations are coming in from all sides and, something that is most important in this situation, help for my people in the form of uniforms, equipment, and many lesser items...

3) *NEWS FROM CAPTAIN ROEHR.* During the period when they were awaiting our arrival, 13 people were caught in a series of searches. One of them managed to escape for a second time. After the first escape on 25 July, Major Wysoczanski was called to the French military command and told that they did not believe that the escape had taken place without his knowledge, and that he had 'lost their confidence'. At present, as Captain R. says, they will await the reaction of the authorities for around two weeks, after which they were even going to inform the French that these people were 'already in Tangiers'.

They are not going to use the radio, although it is ready, as they are still exercising extreme care since the arrests. They have not given up the idea of using it, though, as long as it does not worsen the situation.

Apparently the French are going to clear the Casablanca region of foreigners, and house searches are being forecast (in the newspapers) under the pretext of requisitioning accommodation.

When the observation period has elapsed they will give us dates for further expeditions.

Wysoczanski will attempt to gain permission to travel to Algeria, where he will organise evacuations.

The Birgemayer affair, so strikingly coinciding with the Czechs' account, demands an immediate reaction. I am trying to establish the date on which the courier handed Mr Quennell the letter (there are difficulties and delays). If it is proved that the letter was deliberately delayed—this amounts to nothing other than treason. If they had received the letter on 19 July, I would have brought out 12 more people and there would have been less bad feeling from the French brought down on Wysoczanski's head, since the people would have disappeared without trace...'

(signed) M.Krajewski

The letter from Wysoczanski to Krajewski bears a note written by the latter to the effect that Roehr handed it over on the beach at Fedhala at 0400 on 6 August. It was written from Casablanca on 5 August and has survived time as well as immersion.[20] Wysoczanski wrote that he was assuming that the boat would come that night. He would need another operation to Morocco and, if he could obtain a permit, he would then go to Algeria. He would arrange for telegrams to be sent in code from Casablanca, Oran or Algiers about the next operation in the series. A telegram from Casablanca would mean that the boat should go to the HADDA pinpoint; sent from Oran or Algiers, to the ZORRA pinpoint. A reference in the telegram to 'transit visas' would indicate the number of evacuees, while one to 'resident's visas' would indicate the date on which the operation should take place. ZORRA was the beach from Les-Andalouses village to Cap-Falcon; because of its length, he had divided it into three sections: a reference in the telegram to 'IMMEDIATE' meant that the westernmost section, marked '1' on the plan (which he enclosed), would be the embarkation point; 'TRÈS URGENT would denote the middle part of the beach; 'URGENT' the easternmost.

Wysoczanski said he would try to send the telegram about a week before the embarkation. If he had to cancel, he would telegraph at least 48 hours before the date on which the boat would need to sail from Gibraltar. He also indicated how Krajewski could warn him if the operation had to be cancelled from his side.

In a postscript, Wysoczanski said he had received Krajewski's letter dated 3 July only at 1800 hours that day: the courier had not distinguished himself and some other arrangement would be necessary in future. The arrest of his people on 25 July had led, as he saw it, to a vote of no confidence in him personally from the French authorities. The lack of premises made the installation of his W/T set more difficult. Household searches seemed likely and would affect foreigners first of all. The radio specialist mentioned by Krajewski did not reach Casablanca until the end of June and, owing to carelessness on the part of Marseilles, was picked up immediately after landing in Africa. The two sailors asked for by Krajewski should have been in the operation on 10 July but were arrested on 25 July. Arrangements for getting the crew of the *Oksywia* out were proving difficult, but he would include them in the next batch. Wysoczanski said he was in touch with Captain Nierojewski of the *Oksywia,* but, apart from a few officers and men of her crew, they had no-one who spoke English.

Mally too had written to Krajewski on 5 August, forwarding details of the number of people awaiting evacuation in Morocco and of the camps where they were held.[21] The arrests had been only partial: about 10 had been taken into custody, but approximately 30 were still awaiting Krajewski's arrival, in very difficult and arduous circumstances.

Mally asked Krajewski to pass on an order from himself as soon as effective contact with Wysoczanski was established: Wysoczanski's letters, cards and cables, all on the same subject, had attracted the attention of the censorship at Madrid; this kind of nonsense must cease forthwith.

Krajewski set sail once more for Morocco on 17 August and, when he returned eight days later, he reported as follows:

REPORT OF THE THIRD EVACUATION MISSION
(follows my cable of 26 August)[22]

1) As I reported in my evacuation report of 10 August, following the first evacuation, Major Wysoczanski intended to wait for some two weeks, in order to ascertain how the French authorities would react; after this waiting period, as long as their attitude did not worsen, he was to indicate by telegram his readiness to continue with further missions.

The first news from Wysoczanski in this regard was the cable you yourself received on 12th inst. with the information that Casablanca 'was asking why no-one has arrived to pick up the next group'.

As I reported by cable, replying to the above-mentioned enquiry, I had prepared a third evacuation mission irrespective of whether or not we received a signal from Casablanca. This was because I was aware of the unsatisfactory state of communications with Africa, especially regarding the speedy transmission of information *from Wysoczanski to me,* since the only route at the moment is via Lisbon.

2) My own evacuation vessel was still not ready (the workshops have promised to have it ready a week from now) so that, once again, certain technical difficulties arise. A trawler was not suitable on this mission, since I intended to wait close to the shore for up to a few days under the new plan I had devised for the mission.

Finally, I obtained, or rather borrowed, thanks to Mr Quennell's help, a fishing smack with room for cargo/passengers, although small. It had a 30 h.p. engine and sails. The motor, though, was 30 years old, and the condition of the sails left much to be desired. I include these details in order to convey to you some idea of the limited technical facilities here—despite the full-hearted support of the Gibraltar authorities and private help from a whole range of the officers here.

3) *PLAN OF THE MISSION.* This, by contrast with the evacuation of 4–8 August, was based on changing the evacuation point

a) because I regard the HADDA location as too severely compromised following the month-long vigil of some 40 of our people on this stretch of the coast;
b) because of the recruiting of a certain number of Arabs and one Frenchman into the organisation by our people (feeding them during the period of their vigil?); we had to count on the fact then that our activities might be revealed by idle chatter;
c) because the gendarmes seized 13 of our people on this precise stretch of coastline; this apart, during the night of 5/6 August, when the evacuation was underway, the gendarmerie was alerted by an Arab informer; they attempted to arrest one of our people, but were put to flight by superior numbers;

d) because, given the particular circumstances surrounding our embarkation and departure, our people had also left behind on the beach a number of items (clothing), and we had to assume that it might have come to the notice of the authorities (through markings left in the sand) even though Roehr had promised to send a friendly Frenchman to pick them up; we left though at a fairly late hour (0550 hrs).

After considering the above points, and sounding out the opinions of people who had been evacuated from that spot, I decided to change the point of evacuation. By a coincidence it seemed that one place definitely identified as suitable for evacuations already existed. A certain Officer Cadet Staggart, a Czech staying at Gibraltar, who himself wanted to use it for such purposes, knew the Moroccan terrain perfectly, having served for ten years in the Foreign Legion. He speaks Arabic, has fluent French, and he has to his credit a rather important achievement: he managed successfully to evacuate Czechs from Fedhala on 8–10 June *without any outside help.*

Staggart suggested a spot 3 km to the north of the wall of the town of Sali (near Rabat). He claimed to have reconnoitred this place as an embarkation point during the spring, in connection with a certain evacuation plan devised with the aid of the Czech Consul in Lisbon (the plan though was never put into operation since the Consul was apparently transferred).

Nevertheless, Staggart undertook to accompany us, which ruled out any worries that by myself I might not recognise the correct location, etc. Staggart moreover was putting himself in some danger, since, if he were caught, he risked being put in front of a court martial and shot as a deserter from the Legion. This argued in his favour, but in any case, you only needed to look at him to have confidence in him. (The British authorities trusted him completely until…our return.)

My mission plan was based on putting Staggart ashore. He would then make contact with Major Wysoczanski and his own compatriots (only three of them were intending to leave), and he was to bring them to the agreed embarkation point within 24 hours. If this could not be accomplished in time, then within 2 days, during which I was to wait offshore (so as to conserve fuel).

An important advantage of the cooperation with Staggart was that he had a very good Czech friend in Rabat, the director of some business, who, as he said, would be sure to help by hiding our people for a few days.

4) We weighed anchor on 17 August after a week of the customary problems with technical preparations (by some dreadful quirk, circumstances forced me to prepare *three* different ships for these three missions…). The crew consisted of: Siembieda, in the role of engine-man; two Norwegians; and Staggart. At about 0300 hrs on the 19th we were already close to the port of Rabat, from where I began the passage along the coast to try to locate the agreed spot. However, in spite of the Czech's assurances that the spot could be discerned even at night 'thanks to the *marabout*' [Moslem shrine], we had to wait until dawn; then it became clear that, at the agreed

point, *there was no beach* (!), simply a rock wall. (Staggart's comment: 'It looked different from above...') Because of this I moved further along the shore in a northerly direction, looking for some other suitable site. Only when I had travelled to a point almost halfway between Sali and Mehedia (Port Lyautey) did I come to a beach which was very long and suited our purpose completely–provided, of course, that the hinterland beyond the hills did not hide any surprises. Apart from numerous Arabs, there were no special patrols visible on the shore, nor a dense network of observation posts. The only thing, as it turned out later, was the spotter aircraft constantly flying along the coastline at a height of some 100 metres: they paid no attention to us at all because of our obvious 'fishing' appearance, complete with nets hung out to dry. Since I could not begin by putting Staggart ashore by day under the eyes of the Arabs, I dropped anchor some 500 metres from the shore to await dusk.

After sunset I advised the Czech to get into the water with a container tied to a line, inside which were his clothes, money, etc. I changed our anchorage specially in order to shorten the distance to the shore (to some 50 m). The plan had of course been agreed with Staggart completely. I did not give him the rubber dinghy on purpose, since he said he was a good swimmer and it made the manoeuvre considerably easier. The line was to serve both for safety and to draw the container back to the ship (it was supposed to serve as a means of loading items without getting them wet—a need based on experience of the first trip). Twenty minutes after his descent into the water, as a result of calls from the water, we drew the line back in. It seemed that Staggart had not reached the shore; he explained that the line got in his way, etc. Since I still had complete confidence in him, I believed him, assuming that after all he probably lost his sense of direction in the dark.

We spent the night anchored further from the beach, since there is a powerful surf near the shore, and the presence of even a fishing boat would be suspect. On the morning of 20 August I once again approached to within 50 m, risking the loss of my anchor and the destruction of the felucca on the shore owing to the dangerous oceanic surf (for people swimming, or on a dinghy or life-raft, it presents a danger, as we learned during the embarkation on 6 August, when the state of the sea was the same. A clear beach without rocks is essential since the force of such waves falling on to rocks can kill...). I did in fact lose one anchor as the line broke, unable to withstand the tension. We were saved by the second anchor which was being held ready, the engine, which was also standing by, and—perhaps most important—the specially placed sailor, whose task was to observe the soundings taken to discover immediately the slightest dragging of the anchor.

Now, in such a perilous position, Staggart, having been called on deck, said that he was absolutely exhausted and in no state even to attempt making for the shore. After having tried vainly to persuade and entreat him, I again drew out from land to some 500 m, hoping that an additional day-long rest would restore his morale. At midday he was himself once more and, seeing that it was such a beautiful day and that the beach was completely safe (fine sand), he promised to set off the following night. At dusk on 20 August, I anchored once again, this time even closer (calmer spot) and—I must emphasise—I offered him a rubber boat with oars (from a German ship), together with a sailor to help him. In addition, he would be on the safety line. (I had already tried to send him by this inflatable boat in the morning.)

Staggart refused in spite of the fact that the whole crew volunteered to travel with him in the boat. (The conduct of the crew, including the Norwegians, deserves the highest praise. They displayed unflagging enthusiasm and energy as well as discipline. In spite of unbelievably difficult conditions and the fact that the voyage was eventually extended to eight days, two of them taken up by a fierce storm, there was not a word of complaint about the conditions, which were imaginable only by someone who has himself experienced life on a small fishing vessel.)

My further efforts to appeal to his sense of pride and to remind him that, because of him, some 40 people were going to have to wait, threatened by danger of arrest, etc., were in vain.

Given the situation, I began to weigh up the possibility of perhaps entering the port of Rabat or Mehedia at dawn, and dropping him off in the dock area, counting on the fact that the port police would not pay any attention since they would assume that it was one of their own boats returning with a catch. Staggart again promised that he would land, but when, at dawn on the 21st, I approached the entrance to Mehedia, he again began to display his symptomatic 'doubts'.

Since the risk of entering the port was too great to allow the Czech to proffer one more refusal—as usual at the last moment—I decided to return.

5) The return journey was not without adventure. Just before we entered the Straits of Gibraltar on the morning of 22 August (Friday), a strong gale blew up. With my weak engine I had no chance of making progress against the storm (which was from the east). After a few hours the storm blew itself out and I had to set a course for the north. In this way I tacked between Cadiz and Spanish Morocco for two days, driven by the ocean. After a lull on Sunday 24th, a wind from the south-west enabled me to return to Gibraltar at 2230 on the 25th.

6) As I discovered on reaching port, after a period of searching and waiting, the people here had almost given up hope of my return, which, in spite of the negative outcome, was a pleasant surprise...all the more so since they had been aware of the weather conditions at sea. Those who had been searching for us had not recognised us.

As regards Staggart, certain conclusions were drawn from the episode and he was sent to England.

7) Thinking over the case, I am now convinced that during his first attempt to swim, having arrived at the line of breakers, he was terrified by the waves, turned back and—not being able to find the boat in the darkness—experienced an overwhelming moment of fear, which broke him psychologically, so that even

mentally he could not believe he could cross the breakers—a feat which 27 of our people had achieved previously.

8) Since people are waiting for me somewhere near Rabat, my intention is to repeat the mission, despite the risk, using HADDA, which after a few weeks will surely be a little safer. I intend to put to sea on Saturday 30 August and carry out the operation on the night of 31 August/1 September. As a precaution I am taking along Midshipman Kleybor, who has distinguished himself already by his courage and is a good swimmer. The object is to establish communication, if no telegrams have arrived by then.

(signed) M.Krajewski

Krajewski followed up this report on 28 August with a long letter to Mally.[23] Simbieda, who had been used for the first time on the 17–25 August operation, had been a disappointment. The weather had been bad and he had felt seasick. The magneto had got wet and had had to be stripped down in particularly trying conditions. Simbieda, had tried to do the job but had proved such a poor mechanic that Krajewski, though he had no particular mechanical aptitude, had had to spend a great deal of time working on the engine himself. This episode made it easier to understand why the *Sobieski* had been prepared to relinquish Simbieda to the army at a time when there was such an acute shortage of specialists. The man had positive qualities—he was a hard worker—but Krajewski was now looking to exchange him against someone better qualified from the crew of the *Oksywia*.

Krajewski was left with the two packets of Moroccan Francs and could not say how he would forward them. Also, he had not been able to land the new W/T set. He thought Casablanca were perhaps being unduly cautious in not using the set they already had.

He observed that all transients in Gibraltar, not just the Poles but also, for example, French and Belgians from Miranda, were accommodated in difficult conditions in the Spanish Pavilion, which was a kind of barracks. In spite of being disinfected every few weeks, even days, Polish soldiers still complained about fleas. They also had to sleep on the floor with a couple of blankets. A considerable part of the British garrison was similarly affected: London had met a request for beds with the rejoinder that there was a war on! It was really not possible for him to combine the functions of seagoing operations officer and liaison officer although he had achieved some progress in matters of this kind. It was only through his efforts that those arriving would be issued with tropical uniforms rather than battledress. Their soldiers were completely satisfied with the supply of equipment. The officers were separately quartered in hotels—admittedly cheap ones.

Father Misieuda had done his best on his first mission: he had even gone ashore in the rubber boat. Reporting was a problem, as there was so little time between missions, and he had to deal with quartering of the evacuees and with their medical needs (malaria was on the increase). He could not delay missions to attend to the welfare of those already evacuated. After each operation, he had to report in detail to the Admiral, his Chief of Staff, to naval intelligence, army intelligence, the Governor's Chief of Staff, the head of counter-intelligence, to the dockyard concerning technical matters and to a number of lesser figures. His courtesy visits elicited great interest and friendly offers of help. From him, for example, the Governor learned of the fleas and as a result the barracks were disinfected the next day. He also had to take care of his own crew. He cited the many tasks assigned to him not by way of complaint but because he had now been reproached a second time for being behind with his reports.

In the light of increased Polish business, the British authorities had suggested he ought to have an assistant, and Krajewski now concurred. The French, Belgians and Czechs all had or were forming missions. The other missions also had responsibility for evacuating their nationals from French North African territory, though only the French had actually got to the executive stage: he knew they had had boats arrested in the Casablanca area. The name of Kasimir Badeni, an officer cadet who spoke good English, was put forward as assistant to Krajewski, who suggested he be given the rank of second lieutenant.

Father Misieuda was taking the Belgian ship *René-Paul* to Lisbon. Quennell told him that Birgemayer had been arrested at Casablanca: the news had reached him via Madrid. It was not clear whether this was linked with their evacuation operations or not, but his arrest might affect future missions, as he might reveal too much under interrogation.

From: Marian KRAJEWSKI, Gibraltar, 8 September 1941.
To: Colonel Fryderyk MALLY (Lisbon)

REPORT OF THE FOURTH EVACUATION MISSION TO FRENCH AFRICA (follows my cable of 6 September '41) *24*

l) Following the unsuccessful mission of 17–25 August I weighed anchor again, after the indispensable minimum period of time needed to

a) inform Major Wysoczanski by telegram, giving him at the same time a few days to prepare things at his end;
b) repair the felucca's engine, which had taken in water;
c) add to our reserves, etc.

2) I informed Major Wysoczanski that, as he had concentrated his people in the vicinity of Rabat in line with my previous plan, I would not ask him to transfer them 70 km to the south. I told him that he alone should establish contact with me at the HADDA point, and show me the place at which he wanted them to embark (near Rabat).

3) We weighed anchor on 30 August, or just under five days from the time of our return from the third mission. On the felucca, apart from the crew, 2 Norwegians and Siembieda, were: Kleybor, taken in case the telegram had not reached Wysoczanski, and Lt Killick, an officer of the British army, whom I took along as a volunteer, in

return for the great deal of help he had given me with technical preparations of the boat, which is formally under his care. This officer showed himself to be very brave and efficient, completely dedicated to the undertaking. He travelled with me already on the second mission (27 people brought back), when his official role was that of an observer.

For the first time, too, I carried some weapons, in case of a meeting with a motor patrol boat or, on land while we were embarking, an armed patrol: these consisted of a machine-pistol (tommy-gun), a carbine and two pistols.

4) The voyage to Casablanca passed without incident. I arrived at the spot several hours ahead of schedule (1750 hrs on 31 August). Until 2200 hrs I lay hove-to at a distance of 6 km offshore. Then I began to make an approach to the correct location. Conditions at first were foul (v. thick fog) but luckily they improved at the last moment and we proceeded along the shore from the Fedhala lighthouse in order to find the rocks with which I was familiar. The moon was almost full, but a slight fog reduced visibility to around 5,000 metres. At 0030 hrs on 1 September I found myself near the rock. Immediately after giving the signal, we received the agreed response. I approached the shore as near as possible, to just a little more than the vessel's draft, as it seemed, and to the edge of the breakers (around 250 m.), which are dangerous on open oceanic beaches. Having dropped two anchors and taken soundings to establish whether the heavy swell might not cast the felucca on to the breakers, I launched the rubber boat which was already prepared and secured to a line, which was later paid out from the felucca. A second coil of rope was in the boat: this was later paid out from the beach, when the felucca drew the boat back in.

At a distance of around 20 m from the rubber boat a watertight tin can was fastened to the line, in which I conveyed to the shore post for Casablanca, pistols for the look-outs covering the landing, and money. Additionally it had to serve to bring on board the documents, money, watches, etc. of those being evacuated. A distance of 20 m was maintained so as not to injure those swimming in the surf.

5) I made my way to the beach with Kleybor. During the first trip to the shore in the rubber boat we had of course to row: on the next the 'ferry' system began to function, with the line being drawn in by turns from the boat and from the shore. We were dressed only in our swimming gear and lifebelts.

On the beach Major Wysoczanski was waiting with Capt Roehr and Lt Jozefkiewicz. After putting the embarkation procedure in motion, I left Midshipman Kleybor by the rubber boat in charge of the technical side of the operation, while I had a conference with the leaders of the evacuation.

As it turned out, the number of people brought together was 48, of whom four were Belgians.

The boarding operation passed off without incident: one Arab was chased away by a look-out.

6) At 0300 hrs I had already made my way back to the ship and, having weighed anchor, started on the return journey: first parallel with the shore and then direct to the Straits of Gibraltar.

As might have been foreseen, the conditions under which such a large group of people were accommodated on a small fishing boat were unspeakably difficult (it is 9 tons; my own felucca, which is bigger, will be ready in a few days). This was especially the case during the first night when these people were wet through (they received a ration of rum to warm them and a blanket each) and during the later nights of the voyage—of which more below. Half of the evacuees had to sleep on the deck, and the nights even in these regions are damp and cold at sea. Mind you, the crew had to put up with identical conditions.

In spite of these difficulties, the general mood was very good and one could see that these people were happy to have got out of Morocco. The meals were varied and, during the first days, until we were seriously delayed, of sufficient quantity.

Among the evacuees was the entire crew of the *Oksywia* with its Captain (Lipkowski).

7) After a day's sailing, we were at the entrance to the Straits (morning of 2 September), having travelled 140 nautical miles. But it was here that our difficulties began. A strong easterly wind began to blow, coming from the very direction in which I wanted to enter the Straits. After a few hours' unsuccessful attempts to make my way against the current and the storm-force wind, in conditions of dangerously heavy swell, and relentless soaking of half the evacuees and the crew, I turned back and sought shelter behind Cape Spartel, the northernmost promontory of Africa (in the Straits of Gibraltar). There I prepared to ride out the storm, or at least wait for it to blow in a more favourable direction in relation to my course.

In these conditions we waited out the 2nd and 3rd of September. The wind neither weakened nor turned. The conditions under which we slept at night were worse than uncomfortable, and the food supplies were almost exhausted: the crew of Oksywia and the presence of other sailors among the evacuees—in other words, the absence of people suffering from seasickness—meant that food reserves ran low, they being limited because of the lack of space. So when, on the morning of 4 September, the wind seemed to abate, I made an attempt to break through to Gibraltar. I managed only to get to the Spanish coast and came under the lee of Tarifa, the southernmost promontory of Spain. The wind developed almost into a hurricane. I dropped anchor initially in the vicinity of Tarifa, off a beach where there happened to be a fort. Either in order to have a practice shoot or else to frighten away the intruding 'unknown fishermen', a Spanish army platoon came directly level with us (distance 500 m) and began firing along the beach towards their target. Owing to the fact that bullets were falling in the water at a distance half-way between me and the shore—and not finding any pleasure in conjecturing whether it was being done accidentally or on purpose—I weighed anchor after a stay of two hours and, having made one further abortive attempt to make my way against the current, I put into the small fishing port of Tarifa. (Tarifa is called, because of its fortifications, the 'Spanish Gibraltar'). According to the laws and customs of the sea, I always had the right to do this because of bad weather, and, in the event of questions from the Spanish authorities about the crowding on my felucca, I had a cover story prepared. For a few hours, nobody even turned up. Only when I requested supplies from a few 'fellow fishermen', who paid me a neighbourly visit and wanted to help me—did they go off to the authorities, in order to obtain not only fruit, which I had asked for, but also items distributed only on ration cards. They recounted to the authorities the story they had heard from me about having picked up the survivors from a torpedoed ship.

8) Eventually a Sub Lieutenant in the Spanish navy turned up (a sort of commissary-paymaster, or expert in maritime law) together with a couple of customs officials. After looking at the one document from Gibraltar that I had, on which it was noted that I had gone to sea to catch fish, and after listening to my story—that I was a fisherman from Gibraltar who at the beginning of my voyage had come across a group of survivors from the SS *Kirken*—he invited me along to his office. There, in my presence, he telephoned through to the naval authorities in Algeciras, repeating my story faithfully, and asking whether he could give me supplies for the survivors. While awaiting the reply (2½ hours, since it was quite a late hour), I met the commander of the fortress, a Lt Colonel, who informed me very kindly that, given the difficult situation created by the presence of these survivors, they would certainly 'not let us starve to death'. They added that, once they had received a positive reply from Algeciras, for as long as I judged the weather too severe to put to sea, they would provide me with food on a daily basis. That night, despite the lateness of the hour, after 10 o'clock, the above-mentioned naval officer came with me around the shops and supply offices, in order to help me with provisions.

9) I had an unexpected visit after returning to the ship. Another naval officer appeared, a Lieutenant Commander, who spoke unexpectedly good English, although not well enough to realise that I am not English myself—which I had stated at the outset. After giving us tea and sugar (for the 'survivors'), he began some discreet questioning: which ship had it been (he asked for the exact name), where was it torpedoed, had it been travelling alone or in a convoy before being torpedoed, had any of the crew died? For most of the details of the ship, I called upon the officers of the *Oksywia,* as the crew of the *Kirken*. Having listened to the story and asked searching questions, the Spanish officer left, promising to inform the British authorities.

We had a curious visit next day when the same officer approached again. He asked if he could see 'the Captain of the torpedoed ship'. Luckily, Captain Lipkowski *(Oksywia)* had been briefed on my fairy-tale, so there were no inconsistencies. To the question, 'Has the name of your ship been changed, since there seems to be no trace of it on Lloyd's List?', Captain Lipkowski answered that it had, but he had only sailed in her under the new name and did not know the old one.

But this time too he was left with no doubts for even if there had been any inconsistencies, it would hardly have been surprising, since in wartime losses, names and other details are concealed. The only weak point in my story, which happily no-one pressed, was the professional aspect of my 'fishing knowledge'. But it was the regular navy with whom we were dealing, so they were not familiar with such things either.

10) Around 1500 hrs on 5 September two British naval motor launches [110-foot 'B'-Class Fairmile MLs] from Gibraltar arrived at the port of Tarifa. After being welcomed by the Spanish officer (mentioned above) they began preparations for loading the passengers. Since the wind was still at storm level and so too strong for my engine, I took a tow-line from them. During the towing, though, I helped by using my own engine, thanks to which we managed to reach Gibraltar at the 'exceptional' speed of 10 knots. I entered the port of Gibraltar and approached the pier under my own power (the weather, ironically, had improved markedly—after four days of storm —half-way to Gibraltar).

11) In Gibraltar quite a number of officers were awaiting my arrival—both in an official and in a private capacity. Also waiting was Major Brzozowski, whom the authorities had still not found a means of sending to England. Our return had something of a triumphal entry about it. In spite of my unusual dress (fisherman's) and the need to maintain a low profile, the congratulations began. People were immediately taken to cars and driven off to quarters prepared for them. In the meantime a number of things were put right: for example, each soldier received a mattress; they were divided among the regiments, because of overcrowding, which gave certain benefits, since the regiments, of their own initiative, are giving them many 'perks', and show a great deal of friendship and warmth towards them.

It turned out that the information from the Spanish authorities [about their arrival at Tarifa] was understood correctly [by the authorities in Gibraltar], in spite of lack of details, and only the number of 'survivors' was considered to be impossible for that sort and size of boat.

After settling in the new arrivals and the crew, there began the usual round of reporting on the mission: to the Admiral commanding the base, the naval Chief of Staff and other functionaries of the navy and army. In addition, Admiral Somerville, Commander of the Mediterranean Squadron, famous for the battle with the Italians, asked the base commander if he could put me up for a British decoration. They all expressed their sincere admiration for the morale and attitude of the Polish army, that, in the most difficult conditions, despite all adversities, the men manage to rejoin their forces. As for the undertaking itself, they themselves underlined the poverty of the resources with which such results were achieved.

12) As I anticipated, after two successes, the second larger than the first, thus ruling out any suspicion that it was all due to luck, all the officials here are asking in what way they can give more help. I am of course making the most of the situation with a view to evacuating the next region.

I should add that, up until, and including, the last evacuation, I was still forced to use a boat that was not my own, but borrowed, since mine is in the last stages of refitting.

13) *NEWS FROM WYSOCZANSKI. 'With this last mission the evacuation from Morocco is completed'*—Wysoczanski told me on the beach. The remaining element consists of people not suitable for evacuation (mainly from the Foreign Legion). He himself, together with his two helpers, will now attempt to secure an official transfer to Algeria: if the French authorities refuse this request, he will wire me via Lisbon, to come and pick them up, and put them ashore in Oran. There, being familiar already with the technique of evacuation and having now experience of the kind of embarkation point needed for such an operation (what was very important were places to hide large groups of people, in case of a delay in the date of departure and other obstacles), they will examine embarkation points suggested by me and also a plan of their own.

Birgemayer was arrested as a result of his own carelessness. When one hears assessments of his character from all sides, it is quite difficult to believe that he could be used for special duties. He talked too much and boasted of his 'special' missions: they found a radio code in his apartment.

As regards my letter of 3 July, which arrived in Major Wysoczanski's hands on 4 August, Wysoczanski discovered that Birgemayer received it on 21 July. In other words he allowed an unpardonable delay of two weeks to pass before handing it on—and this was in spite of the fact that the letter was opened and B. knew that the dates of my arrival mentioned therein would in the meantime have passed. Thus the fiasco of my first voyage.

As for Komar, the matter is not serious: he was arrested because a Morse key was found in his apartment, of the type that radio-telegraph operators use for training. They think that he will soon be released.

As for the money, I gave them only 75,000 *French* Francs, since these were the only kind in the package I received, despite the reference in the letter to 'Moroccan Francs'. I tore open the package en route, in order to load the contents into watertight containers. Major Wysoczanski was astonished by the French currency. He took the amount allocated, however, and asked for the rest to be sent on to him via the United States Consulate, which I will do. In case he leaves, 'Poloffice' will send it after him.

Incidentally I repeated to Major Wysoczanski the recommendation that correspondence using plain-language code should be kept to a minimum.

As for the radio, the matter is completely dead and buried, according to Major Wysoczanski, following the arrest of the radio-telegraphist. They must be very careful. Files, for example, have been burned for the same reason.

14) As regards our successful mission, I consider it my duty to tell you that the expedition succeeded thanks to the good organisational work involved in concentrating the people on shore; credit for this must go to Major Wysoczanski and

> his helpers, Capt. Roehr and Lt Jozefkiewicz, who ran considerable risks in making direct contacts.
>
> After talking to a number of the people evacuated, I was able to appreciate the excellent organisation of the evacuation on the spot. After receiving a telegram from me, Major Wysoczanski managed, through skilful planning, to gather together people from such places as Berguent (500 km), a whole crew from Safi who had come on a pass to Casablanca in order to have a 'medical examination'; and people from hospital; he managed to maintain the morale of people who had arrived too late for the first evacuation and who had to wait in the undergrowth or in a small hut for several weeks.
>
> In addition I would like to inform you that the following distinguished themselves during this mission: Midshipman Kleybor, who ventured ashore with me, and Midshipman Pelipeyko. Kleybor was in fact a member of the crew and, in the course of the return journey lasting several days, his help in cooking and feeding the numerous passengers went unappreciated. He nevertheless carried out his normal watches day and night. Pelipeyko also kept watch (I know him from the navy) and when we were leaving Tarifa and other evacuees found themselves in more comfortable conditions on the MLs, he applied to make up the numbers of my small crew which—as might have been expected—meant a complete soaking for several hours and very hard work.
>
> (signed) M.Krajewski

Although Wysoczanski had told Krajewski on 1 September at Fedhala that, with this last mission, evacuation from Morocco was complete, he did in fact require one more operation. On 27 September, Mally wrote to Gibraltar asking what had happened with preparations for this further expedition: as he had already informed Krajewski by cable, Wysoczanski was pressing for news about the next date for embarking his people.[25] The letter reached Krajewski only on 6 October, the day before he sailed once more in *Dogfish,* the ship lent to him by Quennell.

Mally asked for a repetition of a cable regarding a man named Sumliez, of which they had only been able to decode the beginning. He had orders from London that this man should on no account be admitted to England, even if they had to throw him back over the Portuguese border. He had been delivered to Mally by the Portuguese under armed guard straight from prison. The Madrid Embassy believed he was working for the Gestapo. London were furious that he had been embarked on a British warship without a British visa and Krajewski was enjoined to find some way of stopping him. It was not the first case in which Madrid had sent on someone working for foreign intelligence: not long before they had helped Ejsymont, who was working for the Germans and had given away all their evacuation arrangements. The evacuation organisation was still suffering from the effects. The file copy is annotated, 'Too late, he left on 2/x'.

Krajewski was asked to find out from the British whether they would be prepared to provide 700 blankets and how these could be forwarded to the Miranda-del-Ebro camp. He was also to investigate the possibility of sending food and reading matter via the British to the inmates of the camp. Gibraltar was also to send Lisbon a list of names of the soldiers they had collected from Casablanca, together with particulars of their experience in the military field. Krajewski was to report such information automatically in future.

Mally wrote that they had prepared in Lisbon a motor vessel, which could carry up to 20 people. They hoped this would spare them the task of keeping transients illegally in Portugal and avoid mass arrests such as had taken place a month previously.

Krajewski by this time had acquired an assistant and was probably glad to be able to leave him to wrestle with these problems and himself escape to sea, but it was to be a trying experience, as his report shows:

From: Marian KRAJEWSKI, Gibraltar, 13 October 1941
To: Colonel Fryderyk MALLY (Lisbon)
REPORT OF THE FIFTH EVACUATION MISSION
(Follows my cable 1938/10/10)[26]

1) Having learned from you that Major Wysoczanski was awaiting my news concerning the date of the evacuation, I once again found myself in a difficult situation because...the evacuation boat was still not ready. It is two months now and the workshops here have still not completed the refit of a 50h.p. engine. (It appears that this is a fairly common occurrence in these parts: all the workers in the dockyard are Spanish and they work at a slow pace.)

However, relying on the solemn promise of the engineer, and above all being myself aware that the engine had already been *assembled* and required only a few workshop tests, then to be fitted and tested on the boat itself, I sent a cable to Wysoczanski naming Sunday 5 October for the evacuation. Meanwhile the workshop, in spite of the intervention of the Chief of Staff, whom I kept *au courant* with the date of my departure, did not manage to have the engine working even by the time of the next deadline I gave to Major Wysoczanski, that is, Wednesday 8 October.

Not wanting to postpone the evacuation date yet again, I once more borrowed the *Dogfish,* familiar from my two previous missions. I had tried to avoid this since it is a coastal vessel rather than an ocean-going one and in any case is too small. Luckily the weather in general improved, exceptionally for the time of year, and as a result I was ready to weigh anchor on the morning of 7 October.

2) Composition of the crew, apart from myself, as captain: Siembieda, first mechanic; Filipkowski (for the first time) as second mechanic; and Jensen and Eggum (Norwegians) as deck-hands, the first in addition serving as cook.

I made efforts to take with me the radio-telegraphist, Lt Riedel (a Czech), in case of an accident, or the need to give our position to a ship sent to rendezvous with us, but I was not provided in time with suitable radio equipment for the difficult operating conditions on a small fishing boat.

An important improvement in the present plan was the promise that a British naval trawler would be sent to meet me, and an aircraft to relay my position. Because of this, the whole mission took on the character of a regular operation, in which the prerequisites for success were: my finding the people on the beach; my picking them up at any price, in spite even of adverse conditions which were always a possibility; and finally—something which caused a number of people to have doubts about the feasibility of the operation—to pick up the people *on time* and then *navigate precisely* after leaving the shore immediately after the pick-up, so that the rendezvous could take place. They knew that on the felucca there was no log and the compass was wildly inaccurate, so that the course of the operation was followed by the staff here with a certain interest, giving us an even greater incentive to succeed.

3) On 7 October at 0950 hrs we weighed anchor. The passage through the Straits and almost all the 190-mile journey down was without incident. The weather was in our favour and at this point I was even expecting that the breakers—that most important factor on which both the timing and the success of the landing depends—would be less, since the swell was relatively small. Only at the end of the trip, after the whole of the second day of the journey out of sight of land, as I approached the shore of French Morocco near Fedhala to make a landfall, a thick fog descended, so I took a course parallel with the shore. (A foretaste of what would have awaited us had we travelled further came during a momentary thinning of the fog, when for a minute we saw huge surf breaking on to rocks at a distance of 2–3 thousand metres.) The fog continued, so that at around 1230 hrs on 8 October—having estimated our position to be in the vicinity of Fedhala (the lighthouse from which I start my usual 'march' along the shoreline to the rocks)—I stopped the engine so as not to 'overrun' the spot. In any case, ten minutes later the fog lifted and we saw Fedhala on course at a distance of 4,000 metres. Since I was too close to the shore, I pushed out to a distance of a few nautical miles to sit out the rest of the day until dusk, hove-to.

4) At 2115 hrs I started up the engine and moved to the pinpoint. The night was bright—a full moon—and visibility, depending upon the direction, was from 6,000 metres towards the moon to 4,000 away from it. At 2315 hrs we were already near the 'rock' and we began to send out the agreed signals. The answer came back after some 15 minutes—'Everything in order'.

However the surf was unusually unfavourable. It turned out that there was a considerable swell, imperceptible from the open sea and, for the first time since I had started my evacuation missions, the breakers *began almost twice as far from the shore as usual,* at a distance of some 400–500 m. In the light of this I made an attempt to reach the shore in the rubber boat once again from outside the surf, not wanting to risk lying at anchor, given the exceptional size of the swell and, what was worse, the breakers, whose 'manes' represented a considerable danger because of the ease with which they can overturn small boats or break their anchor cables. At 2340 hrs I got into the dinghy, together with Filipkowski. As usual, one line was taken ashore in a coil and the other paid out from the boat. As early as the first minute on the line of the breaking surf, we were both thrown from the rubber boat by waves of huge size and it turned over. This story was repeated several times before we reached the neutral zone between two stretches of breakers (450 and 200 metres). There, however, in spite of strenuous rowing, we made no progress: the weight of the line's slack—in spite of being supported by several containers and a package of inflated lifebelts (for the 'passengers')—turned out to be too great. We gave the signal for them to draw us back in. Filipkowski, after this half-hour spent in the water, had a feverish attack, so for the next two attempts I had to take the Norwegian, Eggum, with me in the rubber dinghy. Because of the difficult conditions, I decided to cross the line where the breakers began and anchor inside the surf line in the 'calm' zone. We crossed the critical line safely, in spite of a few dangerous moments, by proceeding in reverse. To reduce the distance to a minimum I dropped anchor for the second time just by the edge of the second line of breakers. After waiting to be sure that the anchor was holding, I entered the water for the second time. We had hardly struck away from the ship's side when the crew began signalling to draw us back again. Owing to the pitching of the boat on the anchor chain, and because of the quite extraordinary difference of level caused by the ocean swell, the boat had struck the bottom, once or twice, in spite of the fact that our soundings had shown there to be 4. 5 metres' clearance. (The boat's draught was about 1.2m.) Once again we were compelled to raise the anchor (especially difficult because of the surf) and move out a further 50 metres. Our distance from the shore at that point must have been about 300m.

After half an hour's rowing—with, of course, inevitable falls from the rubber boat in spite of shouting a warning to each other before each major wave and then lying flat—we reached the shore and drew the boat up on to the beach. Only then did we appreciate how much heat we had lost through a soaking lasting by then a number of hours.

5) On the beach I found 13 Poles, three Belgians and Mr Wysocki, known to me already as the owner of one of the hide-outs. One of the Belgians told me what had happened. The day before my arrival Major Wysoczanski had been sent by the French authorities to Algeria. This was of course in accordance with his intentions, but he had wanted to see me before his departure in order to discuss embarkation sites and other details of evacuation from Oran. Wysoczanski, Roehr, Jozefkiewicz and Komar, released from prison, also left. In addition I was informed that the whole Kasbah Tadla camp had been sent to Algiers some considerable time ago (that is, those who still remained after the last evacuation of 1 September). The Belgian, Durieux, known commonly as 'Maurice', was sent by Major Wysoczanski to the embarkation site, to show the others the way and also to receive the mail from me. Luckily, having anticipated the absence of Major Wysoczanski or his helper, I had ready a letter, or rather a note, with my observations and the latest information about

possible landing sites in Algeria. This apart, I handed over all the letters received from Lisbon for Wysoczanski and other addressees in Casablanca.

In addition, because of guarantees given by Mr Wysocki about the trustworthiness of the Belgian Officer, I handed him 100,000 French Francs for Major Wysoczanski.

The whole of the mail was to have reached its intended recipients, according to Durieux, 'the day after tomorrow'. He himself already had a visa and reckoned he would be at Gibraltar, via Lisbon, in two weeks.

Because of the trying cold, I kept the conversation down to the minimum and, having instructed the group how to use the life belts and tied two bags of clothes to the rubber dinghy, I gave the signal for those on the boat to draw in the line. Pushing the dinghy in front of us we moved out to the spot where the ground began to disappear beneath our feet, and then began to swim holding on to the line round the rubber dinghy.

Only then did we realise, as never before in any of the previous four expeditions, how horribly dangerous a strong surf can be. The extreme force of the waves—which on the way *to* the shore had acted to push us—was now opposing the efforts of the three-man crew, as they pulled the 15 of us hanging on the dinghy—a number which hitherto had been feasible. After some 20 minutes we felt that the pulling almost stopped, at precisely the moment when we were at the critical line where the surf broke. Even when the people involved are exceptionally brave, such a situation, when so protracted, can lead to panic. I had reason also to be very worried about the strength of the line, subjected to abnormal stress when the waves broke underneath the dinghy, which shot upwards at the impact of the wave. At last however we crossed the critical line and after another half an hour we reached the boat, where we found that the crew were at the limits of their endurance and had injured their hands.

It was 0300 hrs, 3½ hrs since we had first put the boat into the water and we had brought only one group. During the fourth mission four trips took around 2½ hours.

All those who came out of the water received a tot of rum and two blankets, after which we accommodated them, because they were so few in number, in the fo'c's'le. Our return through the outer line of breakers took place without difficulty. After two hours following the coast, we made a course straight for Cape Spartel, which was also the course for our rendezvous.

7) In the morning most of our passengers were 'as normal', that is, those who were suffering from seasickness felt worse, but morale was high, for the weather too was calm and generally sunny. It was then that I discovered to my astonishment that among the passengers I had *three Spaniards*—a very unpleasant surprise for reasons I detail below.

As I had calculated from a noon sight, I was as far north as Mehedia (Port Lyautey) at a distance of around 22 miles from the shore; in other words, in the area where our meeting was to take place. Indeed, at 1220 hrs an aircraft appeared (a Swordfish, as I later discovered) directly in front of us, flying very low. After the first 'look out, hide yourselves'—since I had encountered French aircraft too in the course of my missions—I ordered the passengers to come on deck and wave their hands to let the pilot know that the landing operations had succeeded, and so that he could send a message to that effect.

In the afternoon fog descended again and it had already begun to seem that the rendezvous with the trawler would not take place. When the fog lifted however, at 1430 hrs, I saw the outline of a ship. After changing course it became evident that it was the trawler, which also immediately picked up speed and moved in our direction. After we had recognised its colours and exchanged signals by means of the Aldis lamp, he came alongside and, without difficulty, since the sea was fairly calm, I transferred my passengers to him. Afterwards he got under way for Gibraltar. According to his calculations I was less than 5 miles off course.

In the end the trawler arrived at Gibraltar at 0330 hrs on 10 October; however the *Dogfish,* to the astonishment of all and sundry, came in exceptionally early, at 1215 that day; but, more important than the time saved, our passengers were spared an uncomfortable night and morning fighting against the usual east wind near Cape Spartel and in the Straits of Gibraltar.

Thanks to the presence, during my mission, of my new assistant in Gibraltar, the matter of organising the newcomers' stay, i.e. making lists, kitting them out, making payments on account, etc, does not have to wait for me but swings into operation immediately. Upon my return, as events have shown, I am still involved for a certain time with the maintenance and equipping of the ship since, because of my boat's lying in the [naval] dockyard, I have nowhere to keep stock for her. All these administrative and housekeeping matters now are dealt with quite smoothly, since we are working in tandem; and of course the paymaster now has a precedent, so there is no need to waste time in the tussle over some trivial items, as was the case at the beginning. In any case, by contrast with the first two groups, this group of Poles is due to leave very shortly, around Wednesday 15 October.

9) Unfortunately, as I had feared from the beginning, bringing the three Spaniards to Gibraltar without the agreement of the British was nothing other than a 'blunder'; the British authorities were shocked since

a) the evacuation operation had been assumed to be for Allies only;
b) the Spanish are not trusted here;
c) the British were afraid that General Franco's people might demand they be handed over, if they heard of their arrival in Gibraltar (a similar case occurred a month ago when a runaway Spaniard attempted to swim across from La Linea but left his clothes on the beach).

I was given to understand quite clearly that such 'mistakes' were not desirable in the future.

I cannot explain why Wysoczanski added not only two Belgians but these Spaniards to the group as well. He should have understood that if we took Czechs or Belgians it was because they are Allies.

I hope, however, that this sorry incident will shortly be cleared up and forgotten, since the head of the Free French mission is due tomorrow, and it seems he is to recruit them to the Foreign Legion…

10) I must add in this report of the mission that during the boarding operation, one of the containers holding a pistol broke away. Also, at the time the raft with evacuees was crossing the line of breakers, both bundles broke away, despite the fact that they had been secured with rope. This was an event that even perhaps tilted the scale to our advantage, owing to the considerably reduced area on which the waves broke…

11) Among those evacuated is—apart from the Polish soldiers without specialist qualifications—Mr Tadeusz Wysocki, born on 26 June 1899 in Dabrów, district of Nowy Sacz, a representative of the Bank of Poland. Although I cannot attempt to assess his professional banking qualifications, he creates a very favourable impression. He is however a special case, as a 42-year-old civilian who has never served in the army.

The decision to evacuate Wysocki should, in my opinion, be beyond discussion; Major Brzozowski agrees with this; Wysocki, as the official owner or subtenant of the hide-out, put himself in considerable danger helping the evacuations and without this safe house it is possible we would not have so many Poles evacuated from Morocco already…

(signed) M.Krajewski

On 10 October 1941, Mally wrote to Krajewski forwarding, with his heartiest congratulations, the following commendation bestowed on him by General Sikorski on 13 September:[27] 'On behalf of the Service I commend him for having evacuated from hostile territory in difficult circumstances, without any concern for his personal safety and in spite of two unsuccessful missions, 68 of our soldiers, as well as 3 Czechs and 4 Belgians.'

A covering letter addressed to Mally by General Klimecki, Sikorski's Chief of Staff, asked him for a list of the crew members of the boat, adding that he trusted that the Commander-in-Chief's commendation would not be the last that Major *(sic)* Kadulski (Krajewski) and the crew of his boat would receive, and that he would again have the opportunity to convey to him messages of similar content or, indeed, other means of bestowing distinctions in respect of Captain *(sic)* Kadulski and his crew.

By the time these accolades reached Gibraltar, the score of those evacuated by Krajewski had risen by a further ten Poles, two Belgians and, of course, three controversial Spaniards.

Sketch maps of two beaches in Algeria used by Lt Krajewski in Polish evacuation operations during winter 1941–42.

(Redrawn from originals in the Sikorski Institute archives)

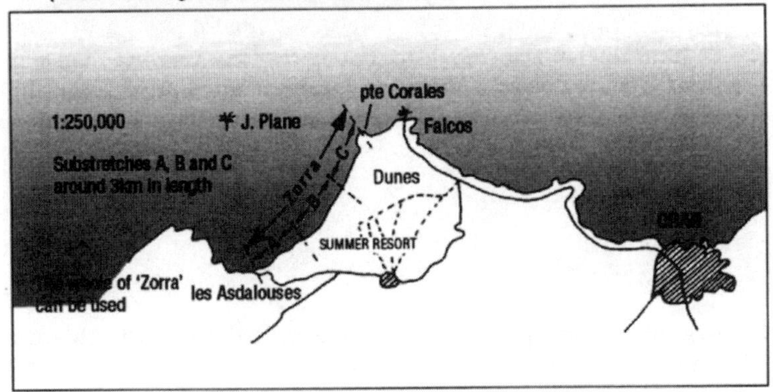

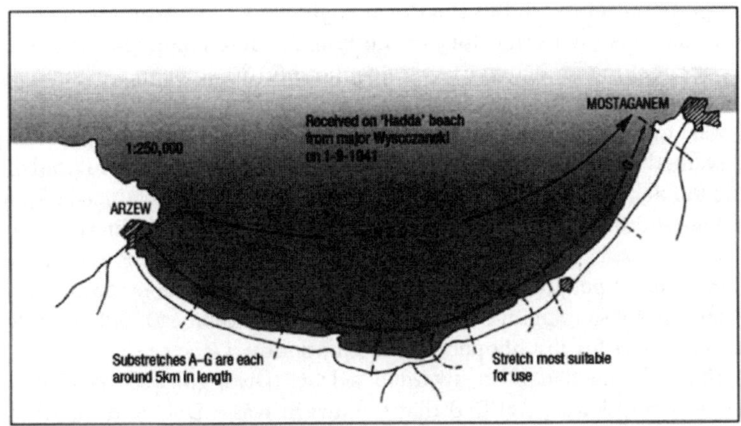

IV
Krajewski's Operations to Western Algeria: October 1941–January 1942

'Not until hair grows on the palms of my hands will the Poles in this camp join the Allies.'[1] This had been the habitual boast of the French camp commandant in Morocco, where Krajewski's first Polish evacuees had been interned.

By the time he had completed his five missions to Morocco, Krajewski had begun to make his mark not only at Polish GHQ in London but also at senior levels on the Rock (Gibraltar). When HRH the Duke of Gloucester paid a visit, Krajewski was not only invited to a garden party but presented to His Royal Highness by the Admiral. Krajewski elicited a laugh from the Duke with the story of the French camp commandant's boast and with his observation that the Frenchman must now be sporting some unwelcome hair. The fact that he had been singled out for presentation and had amused the royal visitor seemed to help Krajewski quite significantly. People who had previously belittled the importance of things he wanted done and had put difficulties in his way now invited him to their messes; and the dockyard engineer stopped reminding him of his felucca's spoiled engine. At a time when nothing much was happening in the western Mediterranean, his Scarlet Pimpernel role, enhanced by the hush-hush character of the business and the success of his embarkations, caught people's imaginations in the small official community on the Rock. He could not otherwise explain how he came to be awarded a DSO before he had begun his even more successful run of operations to the south of France.

He was first told he had been awarded a DSC (Distinguished Service Cross). Soon afterwards he was officially notified that the award was a DSO and heard that the King had had to sign the relevant documents twice, probably because the Admiral and the Governor had put up separate, and uncoordinated, recommendations. He clearly thought the whole matter rather a joke, though he did claim credit for having swum ashore in the course of each successful operation in order to gain first-hand knowledge of the conditions and to establish effective liaison on shore in person.

The escapes by foreigners from the Protectorate came to the attention of the German Armistice Commission, which lodged protests both at Vichy and in Morocco.[2] On 18 October, Admiral Darlan, Secretary of State for the French Navy, called for a report from Admiral d'Harcourt, whose head of Deuxième Bureau replied on 23 October saying that no British fishing vessel had ever been reported off the coast of French Morocco nor did he think that clandestine escapers could have reached Gibraltar in that way.[3] He forwarded a list of 14 known escapes since 1 January 1941, which involved 77 foreign seamen from Danish, Norwegian and Greek ships interned in French Moroccan ports, but all these escapes had been made at night in ships' lifeboats or other small boats from the ships in question or had been stolen locally. If these people had succeeded in reaching Gibraltar he thought they must have done so in the boats on which they had left, unless they had been picked up by Spanish feluccas, which fished in great numbers off the coast. The list also gave particulars of five further attempted escapes that had failed or been foiled. The 13 members of the crew from the Oksywia, who had been under enforced residence at Safi, had left there for Casablanca by bus on 31 August after obtaining the proper authorisation, but they had disappeared in the course of the journey and police enquiries had thus far failed to trace them.

D'Harcourt's staff had made a similar statement direct to Herr Laube, the armistice commission's local representative, giving figures of approximately 50 known escapes since 1 January and 10 since 1 August. He had appeared satisfied with this reply.

The number of escapes had, in fact, been twice as great as d'Harcourt reported. Apart from the 13 missing members of the *Oksywia*'s crew, Krajewski had successfully evacuated 65 other Poles, six Belgians and three Czechs. A French submarine-chaser was temporarily based at Port Lyautey to carry out patrols in an area extending 32 km offshore, with the object of intercepting and seizing any possible British fishing vessels, but the horse had already bolted: Krajewski's objective was now Oran.

The first two operations to Algeria took place from 23 to 29 October and from 1 to 6 November in such quick succession that Krajewski had time to report to Mally between them only by telegraph. It was not until 8 and 9 November that his full accounts were completed and dispatched.

REPORT OF THE SIXTH EVACUATION MISSION
(follows my cables of 23 and 31 October)[4]

1) After the last evacuations from Morocco (my report of 13 October), I was waiting for the first signal from Major Wysoczanski following his transfer to Algeria, so that I could set out to pick up people from this—for me—new evacuation region.

The first word I received was Major Wysoczanski's cable of 10 October, sent on by letter…which I did not receive until 17 October. Major Wysoczanski's wire required me to arrive as early as 19 October, but since the message was conveyed to me by letter rather than by telegraph, clearly I was not informed in time to make the necessary preparations, which I could only do once I had definite knowledge of the *date* of evacuation. Indeed, the journey itself to the agreed spot (280 nautical miles to the Bay of Mostaganem) would take three days, given the speed of which the felucca is capable.

2) Faced with this situation, I sent you cable no. 1840/17/10 in which I drew attention to two possible evacuation sites: DORULA and BRZOZA; also I requested that the necessary cable be sent 'en clair' to Oran. Not having received a reply before my departure, I sent cable no. 1620/23/10 on the day we weighed anchor, repeating the mission plan (place of embarkation).

3) We weighed anchor on 23 October at 0930 hrs. Once again, my own evacuation felucca had still not been finished by the workshops and once again I had to set out in the 'borrowed' *Dogfish,* a small ship, not constructed for use on the open sea, but in fact perfectly suitable for our purposes. The crew was made up, apart from myself, of Siembieda and Filipkowski as mechanics, and Eggum (Norwegian) as a deck-hand and cook in place of Jensen (Norwegian) who had been dismissed for drunkenness. In addition, in the light of experience—'just in case'—I took along Second Lt Lisek as a possible messenger who might be able to establish contact in the event of a 'jam', etc.

4) Our course led past the Tres-Forcas (Melilla) peninsula in order to fix our position and then from the Habibas Islands (about 25 nautical miles west of Oran) along the Algerian coast to the Bay of Mostaganem. The journey was very arduous, both because of the weather, which turned bad on the second day, and the fact that we were towing a sailing boat, which I was taking along for the first time in order to save people being drenched in sea-water, which by now was quite cold. It reached the stage that every few hours we had to let a sailor down into the small boat with a scoop to bail out the water. Worse was the fact that the extreme tension that built up in the tow-line tore away, one after the other, the cleats around which the line was fastened. Eventually, when the weather deteriorated even further, we were forced to attempt to haul the boat on to the felucca. This proved almost impossible, since we had to stop the engine and the boat itself was already full of water, but we succeeded, thanks to the efforts of the whole crew. This, I should underline, was one of many characteristic incidents that illustrated the exemplary attitude of the present crew.

5) On 25 October the stormy weather still continued, while the strong wind had turned about through 180°—a characteristic occurrence for these regions—and taken the worst possible direction for us: from dead ahead. Under these conditions it took me six hours to travel 16 miles from the Habibas Islands to the Cap-Falcon lighthouse, while tons of water poured down on to the deck. My calculations showed that, travelling at such 'terrific' speed (around 3 knots), I would not reach the rendezvous point on time, nor, more important, would we be in a position to carry out embarkation in a bay open to a wind from the north-east. I therefore decided on a complete change of plan. I changed to a diametrically opposite course, towards the embarkation point code-named DORULA, some 50 km to the west of Oran. After

turning about, we made a speed of 10 knots. Since the pilot-book warns that this bay 'is suitable only for small ships with knowledge of local conditions' and since our chart was too small-scale to show details of such a small bay—it did not give a precise idea of the location of the submerged rocks at the entrance—I ordered the crew to put on their life-jackets and gave instructions 'in case we founder'. The entry, though, passed off successfully. The little bay gave ideal shelter against storms from almost any direction, and it was situated in an almost unpopulated region, if you do not count Arabs tending their cattle, or one family group living in widely dispersed huts.

6) After sunset I put into action the second stage of the plan—sending a messenger to Oran with the information that I was at another point and giving directions for reaching it. Second Lt Lisek was put ashore in the rubber dinghy, reckoning that he would be in Oran by the second day. All the following day I waited in the little bay, the one drawback of which was that it was visible from the high Habibas Islands, on which there is a lighthouse (distance about 10,000 metres). We waited through the whole of the next night for the agreed signal, enduring unusually cold temperatures.

On the morning of 27 October, when I had already started to fear that some accident had occurred, an individual appeared on the shore undressed and swam across to our boat, causing a near sensation among the Arabs. It turned out to be Second Lt Polanski, liaison officer to the division in Oran, who, having been shown the way by Second Lt Lisek, had at the last moment gone on ahead, fearing that we would weigh anchor and move off. A moment later Lisek also appeared and we fetched him in the rubber dinghy. After a few words of explanation, we weighed anchor and left the bay, just in time to make out a French patrol boat emerging from behind the headland and travelling slowly at a distance of some 4,000 metres from the shore. In order not to arouse suspicion, I continued on the same course, in other words towards him, and only at a distance of 2,000 metres did I change course towards Oran, which in the circumstances must have seemed normal behaviour. Fortunately it passed off without any questioning…

7) *A NEW SITUATION.* When sending Second Lt Lisek ashore I had asked him to recommend those in charge to organise a mass evacuation, that is, in groups of more than 25 people, like the one that Wysoczanski had arranged for me in Morocco. I even said that I was prepared to supply tinned food and fresh water to help keep people alive in empty desert regions. If we carried out the evacuation in small groups, we might alert the French authorities, who would probably step up their level of vigilance. Indeed, it emerged from Second Lt Lisek's account that, since their telegram to Lisbon on 10 October, the leaders of the Oran group were thinking along the same lines and had worked out a plan for total evacuation. As a result, on the night in question there were not 25 people at the embarkation point but only Major Wysoczanski and Capt Roehr. I was to take these two off because the French authorities in Algeria had issued an order for their arrest on the charge of arranging

evacuations from Morocco. They had received prior warning in confidence and gone into hiding.

The DORULA site, the little bay in which I had sheltered for a day and a half, was unfortunately ruled out because of its distance from Oran (50 km), as well as the necessity of travelling through desert regions and small settlements where the sight of any strange and white face immediately drew attention. The only possibility, they thought, was BRZOZA; it was easy to reach (road and railway passed a few hundred metres away) without having to travel through Oran, and there was a hinterland covered in brush and bushes in which people could conceal themselves while awaiting the felucca.

On the way there I familiarised Second Lt Polanski with our sailing problems and at the same time I familiarised myself with the peculiarities of the new embarkation site and the plan for total evacuation.

8) *TOTAL EVACUATION FROM THE ORAN REGION.* The plan was based on the premise that for the two days of the forthcoming holiday—All Saints and Sunday—there would be no attempt to carry out a roll-call in the camps. So, starting on Friday evening, small groups of our people were to make their way in a trickle by bus, train and even by car (arrangements were being made) to the agreed spot, led by those who had been let into the secret—basically only a handful of officers. It was a great risk but had considerable chance of success, and its success would have dramatically resolved the question of evacuation from all Africa.

My main difficulty was that I had very little time for technical preparations, because of the very large number of people involved. However, because of the high stakes I could not hesitate with my reply.

9) That evening (27 October), after passing the well-known Mers el-Khebir [naval base] at a distance of about 8 miles, we entered Mostaganem Bay. I was struck at first—and this was confirmed by my later observations as well as by those of others—by the lack of shipping movement of any kind, even of fishing boats, which are normally a very common sight on the coast of Morocco.

At 2140 hrs we altered course to travel parallel with the coast at a distance of 250 metres, in order to reconnoitre the shoreline. Second Lt Polanski helped me with my reconnaissance of the shore, he having been one of the first to check out this site. At 2200 hrs we received the agreed signal, which was followed by the usual preparations and the lowering of the raft. One fundamental difference struck me about this new location: the complete absence of breakers. Here it was connected with the fine weather and the direction of the wind (off shore). But on the Moroccan coast there are breakers *even in the finest weather.*

Major Wysoczanski, Capt Roehr, Lt Wyganowski and Lt Jozefkiewicz, were already waiting on the beach and Polanski came ashore with me. While we were discussing the plan, it emerged that, after Polanski's departure, still further disturbing changes had taken place: an order was being prepared for the arrest of Polanski and Capt Szewalski, who played important roles in the local cell. Contacts had informed them of this confidentially. My proposal to off-load supplies was willingly accepted, as it would ease the logistical demands of maintaining a large group of people, for whom there was no question of purchasing food during the waiting period. In total I unloaded two boxes of biscuits, four boxes of tinned meat, 130 litres of fresh water and 400 litres of petrol for vehicles.

Those present accepted the plan for total evacuation and I promised to turn up at all costs on the night of Sunday/Monday 2/3 November. I warned that, in the event of an accident, very bad weather or other unexpected obstacles, I might turn up late—but *I would be coming.*

10) At 0145 hrs on 28 October we finished unloading the supplies and took on board Major Wysoczanski and Capt Roehr, after which we weighed anchor. The journey from Oran to Gibraltar took place in excellent weather (an exception for these missions of ours…) and in phenomenal visibility: one could see the coastlines of Spain and of Spanish Morocco simultaneously from a distance of 50 nautical miles. This time I set a course to the small island of Alboran—the shortest route—so as to get used to the currents on this route (during the evacuations from Morocco, experience gained on frequent journeys allowed me to make use of currents, an important factor considering my speed of 6 knots).

That day at 2005 hrs we had a breakdown of the circulation pump (a pin had broken away), which happily the duty mechanic, Filipkowski, detected by ear immediately. He thus saved the engine: if it had continued working for a few minutes without being cooled, it would have been irreparably damaged and the return to Gibraltar would have had to be carried out under sail.

On 29 October at 2115 hrs I moored in Gibraltar, not without emotion, having been shot at by the trawler on guard off the port. The staff officer had not issued a warning in time and the trawler, seeing a 'mysterious' fishing boat approaching the entrance, fired a warning shot across our bow (as happened last with the Chief of Staff's launch).

11) During this trip Second Lt Lisek and the motor mechanic, Filipkowski, distinguished themselves.

Second Lt Lisek not only volunteered unhesitatingly for the dangerous mission of messenger but showed great strength of character and physical endurance. He travelled 50 km, partly at night, through hilly (400 m above sea-level) terrain, the first section of it trackless. After only a few hours' rest, and having accomplished his mission entirely, he set out again on the return journey. In total he covered 100 km and was on the move for 38 hrs with only a few hours' break. (How much more commendably this *one-armed* officer performed than the Czech Staggart during the third evacuation mission.)

Also deserving of commendation is Second Lt Polanski, for his brave and decisive action, demanding great physical effort, in informing the evacuation vessel of the change in situation, despite the fact that in doing so he jeopardised his very good official relations with the French authorities in Oran.

From: Marian KRAJEWSKI, Gibraltar, 9 November 1941.
To: Colonel Frederyk MALLY (Lisbon)
REPORT OF THE SEVENTH EVACUATION MISSION
(follows my cables of 31.x and 7.xi)[5]

1) After returning from the 6th evacuation mission, I had a little less than three days to prepare for the next mission. In the prevailing conditions, of which I will say more below, this was so little time that it was reminiscent, in the feverishness of the preparations and frequent disappointments, of the worst days of July, before the first expedition.

My plan was to use, for the first time, our own evacuation felucca; workshop tests were complete on the engine and it had only to be installed. The felucca could hold, not officially, but squeezed in together, 60 people, at a pinch. If it were merely to ferry them to another, larger ship, I estimated that I could take as many as 120 people —equivalent to the maximum the leaders of the local evacuation expected on the night of 2/3 November. On Monday 3 November a second group of some 30 people were to filter in, whom I planned to collect in a repeat performance on that night. A trawler-like vessel of around 70 tons, familiar to us from the second mission, would be standing by to take off any excess passengers. Using her presented a complication since in the first instance there was no engineer officer, no cook and no stoker. I made up the numbers from the crew of the *Oksywia,* not without trouble from one particular mechanic who at first allowed his anxiety not to miss the convoy to England to overshadow his patriotism. *Seawolf,* the evacuation felucca, might also have been ready, since the workshop had anticipated completing the job two days after our departure: following the intervention of the Chief of Staff at the base, they worked day and night, and it looked at long last as though she would be used for the first time.

2) On the day of our departure, Saturday, 1 November, we fitted the engine, which had supposedly been overhauled in the workshop, but it turned out that this was not the case and that once again the 'specialists' could not deliver the goods. I was forced to change the whole plan at the last moment and turn to a motor boat, the *Seagull,* of around 50 tons, which I had used in July. Luckily, thanks to the Chief of Staff, I was able to take charge of it immediately, although the owner (Customs and Excise) warned comfortingly that, ever since it had returned from the workshop, the engine was so undependable that they would be afraid to travel 20 miles with it. The mechanic and I looked over the engine and decided to take the motor boat and demonstrate that it was not the engine but Spanish mechanics who are undependable.

It was characteristic of that morning that, almost simultaneously with the Seawolf fiasco, I was told that the *Quarto,* the civilian trawler that was to travel with me to carry back evacuees, had while raising steam burst some pipes in the boiler; as it turned out these pipes had corroded through repeated use of salt-water in the boiler.

Happily the *Seagull* had enough room on board for all the people who might turn up.

Our departure was delayed, however, owing to various small difficulties such as requisitioning the motor boat, loading her up with an ample supply of stores (170 blankets, tinned food, biscuits and fresh water—enough for 150 people for four days). Thus we lost the extra reserve of time we had allowed in case of bad weather and unforeseen occurrences.

3) I cast off at 1525 hrs on 1 November. The crew was composed of: Siembieda and Filipkowski (mechanics), Eggum (deck-hand), and Skulimowski (cook and deck-hand taken on in place of Jensen...). In addition Capt Roehr, who knew local conditions, went with us, in order to contact the people on shore should any complications arise during the operation.

The outward passage took place without any incident worth mentioning, though a temporary breakdown of the engine occurred nine hours after our departure. It turned out that the cause was a blocked oil filter, which the Spanish mechanic had failed to clean. Once again our motor mechanic, Filipkowski, distinguished himself: he at once discovered the fault and sorted it out in 45 minutes. By Monday night (3/4 November) I had reached the latitude of Oran. Although the currents had been favourable to me on the first part of the journey, I had calculated that I would reach the agreed spot at 0400 hrs, the last possible moment to begin embarkation. However, at the last moment the weather and opposing currents dashed my hopes, so that it was not until 0300 hrs (after detour to avoid the Mers el-Kebir naval base that I reached the vicinity of Cap-Aiguille, in other words scarcely beyond Oran. I would not therefore arrive at the pinpoint until 0600 hrs. Accordingly, I had to make use of the remaining hours of darkness (very relative, as the night was bright and the moon full) to move away out of sight of the high shoreline (600m).

We spent the whole of the next day—in stormy weather particularly unsuitable for this motor boat, which was built for use in sheltered waters and was not sufficiently stable—riding out the storm some 35 miles north-east of Oran. In spite of our unfortunate outline and colours (typical of a motor torpedo boat), no-one paid any attention to us, as there was almost no traffic to speak of and all we saw was something like a trawler passing at a distance of around 10,000 m. Immediately the sun went down, I started the approach to Mostaganem Bay, in which I found the agreed embarkation point, familiar from the previous successful operation when we took aboard Major Wysoczanski and Capt Roehr.

4) The night fortunately was not as light as the previous one, since the full moon was obscured for most of the time by a layer of cloud. At 0015 hrs on 4 November we were already near Brzoza, or rather the stretch of shore where this pinpoint is situated, and we started on a course parallel to the shore. However, in spite of giving the agreed signals that had been used successfully several times before, no reply came back. After about half an hour of travelling along the coast, which at this point was a steep rock wall about 10m high, with a few small beaches below it (like *Brzoza*), we

noticed, to our amazement, several figures moving stealthily along the shoreline, trying with some difficulty to keep up with the boat, forcing their way through the bushes and the rocky terrain. We were able to see them because of our proximity to the shore (some 250m) and also because their silhouettes stood out against the background of the lighter sky. A few of them moved so incautiously that they were even more clearly discernible.

All of this was incomprehensible to us, so, in order to make absolutely sure that they were our people,... I changed course 180 degrees and gave out the agreed signals with a signalling lamp, although I knew that, if they were Frenchmen, our signals would be compromised. Figures on the shore began to run back in the other direction. These were certainly the same figures, since towards the end of the second tour a signal was given from the shore—an answer to my blue flashes—with a *white* light. The correct answer should have been a *blue* light, moreover not one flash but a series of short flashes. Whoever was faking the signals was confused by the fact that my signals were long, as had been agreed. Equally, it was obvious that they were not using an electric lamp but some improvised light. The man in charge of the interception group, for such I took them to be, was caught by surprise by the blue lamp and improvised an answer—but it is not easy to improvise a blue lamp.)

Capt Roehr, who was on board with us, confirmed that our people invariably have a blue lamp at their disposal, since they carry several. I therefore set course for the open sea. Visibility was so good that we could see both sides of the bay and, if the trap had been better organised and they had called in the navy to cooperate, it would have been comparatively easy to have caught us. When the sun rose we could still see the shore.

5) On 4 November I set a course not directly to Gibraltar, but to the Spanish cape Cabo del Gata, so as to avoid any possible pursuit. In order to fix my position between the lighthouse and Mesa de Roldan, I took a course to the Isle of Alboran, which, because of a continuing heavy swell coming then from the east, slowed our progress tiresomely. The waves were at times dangerous for our shallow-draft motor boat, with no keel or ballast. We reached the level of Alboran at 1035 hrs on 5 November. On the same day at 1800 hrs a British Fulmar flew over and, as agreed before my departure, signalled in Morse, 'Please indicate number of passengers'. On this occasion I had to answer, 'No passengers'. On the next morning at 0800 hrs we were already moored at Gibraltar, where news of the trap set for us aroused a great deal of understandable interest and the comment, 'You were lucky'...

Krajewski went on to set out at some length the possible reasons for this failure. Perhaps when the first checks had been carried out in the camps at 10 a.m. on 3 November and most of the internees found to have disappeared (only 50 had not been included in the plan), the French authorities had immediately sounded the alarm and begun searching the coast, specifically, by deduction, the stretch of coast where the Brzoza pinpoint lay.

Deploying an extended line of soldiers or police would have enabled them to capture, as in Morocco, if not all at least most of the escapers. The weak point in this hypothesis was that it assumed a very un-French organisational efficiency, since no more than 14 hours could have elapsed from the alarm to the time the vessel appeared off the coast.

A further possibility was that the escape had been accidentally discovered, perhaps though some indiscretion on the part of their people, a chance meeting with strangers in the forest or perhaps an encounter with some suspicious policeman who wanted to check their papers. But the most likely explanation, in Krajewski's opinion, was that the plan had been given away by informers among the internees, whose existence had been suspected by their leaders in the camps for some time. It was too soon to lay the blame at anyone's door: they had known from the outset that any mass evacuation would be a risky venture. Still, if they had attempted to bring people out in small groups, the disappearance of the first 25 or so would have led to the present state of alert. The French authorities were undoubtedly very vexed by the successful 100 per cent evacuation from Morocco, as had been evident from their orders to arrest Wysoczanski, Roehr, Polanski and Szewalski, and were determined to apply preventive measures in Algeria. News from Algeria would soon show the real reason for the fiasco. Krajewski asked Mally to make sure that he was cabled any information arriving either from there or from Morocco, since it was quite possible that a certain number of the escapers might still be hiding near the coast or that the French might, even now, be unable to prevent the escape of smaller groups.

Krajewski then turned his attention to sea evacuation from France, which remained his main objective, since the number of Polish troops immobilised there was far larger than in Algeria. Mally had written on 18 October instructing him to consult the British naval authorities about the possibility of carrying out two different types of evacuation operations from France and to report whether he would be able to put them into effect.[6]

The first of these plans, both of which emanated from General Kleeberg in France, would involve sending 100 evacuees to sea from Marseilles in a ship which would follow a predetermined course for a distance of 140 nautical miles from the French coast. There the ship would be met and her passengers taken off, and she would be given a return cargo of 10 tons of SOE stores. To Mally, the plan seemed wholly impracticable, though Kleeberg had had the benefit of naval advice in working it out. Sailors with whom Mally was in touch maintained that such transfers at sea would be impossible in the prevailing stormy season, but that they might be carried out later in the winter when seas would be calmer.

In Kleeberg's second plan, a British warship would take delivery at sea of groups of 50 evacuees travelling on foreign ships to Oran, Algiers or Tunis. He wanted to know if this would be possible, provided the Admiralty were informed a week before a ship's departure of her name and anticipated course. Krajewski thought both proposals naive and said so in a letter to Mally.[7] He put forward his own ideas on tackling the problem in a paper for Mally, copies of which he sent to General Sikorski's Chief of Staff and to the Polish Naval Attaché in London.

Krajewski proposed that internees should be picked up from the coast of metropolitan France at night, using a small fishing vessel, which could transport them directly to Gibraltar. The distance from the Rock to Marseilles was 700 nautical miles—a passage of five days at 6 knots and a round trip of 12 days, allowing 48 hours for contingencies. At 10 knots, the round trip would take 8 days, with the same spare time in hand. At 12 knots, only 2½ days would be needed on passage to and from the pick-up area. From the technical and security points of view, groups of 50–100 could be managed. Operations would be easier than in North Africa, but a larger vessel would be needed. A minimum speed of 10–12 knots was desirable and the vessel's range must be sufficient for the double voyage of 700 miles, plus two additional days' steaming. The engine must be economical in its fuel consumption, simple to service and reliable: a diesel would probably best match these requirements.

The vessel should be able to carry 100, apart from the crew. She must be seaworthy and look like a fishing boat. She should not be too large—70 gross registered tons would probably be about right. There should be no need to build a vessel for the job, since boats of that size were common on the coasts of Spain and Portugal. The British were looking for something similar. Krajewski envisaged packing the evacuees into every corner of the ship, even if they had to sleep on deck. In wartime such conditions were acceptable. He had views, too, about what would be needed at the Marseilles end. The English Hospital could accommodate only about 40 and there was the perennial problem of chatter in bars; he proposed to send Roehr to take charge.

Four days later, Krajewski wrote to Mally again.[8] He described their current communications problems, including the radio link they were trying to establish, and went on to say a new 50h.p. engine was needed for the felucca *(Seawolf)* under repair. Four months had been wasted, during which he had had to struggle with various *Dogfishes*. A new engine was indispensable: a Kelvin A4 from Bergius of Glasgow could be made available in four weeks if the Admiralty backed the order and the factory were told.

In this winter period it was impossible to think of carrying out operations in the smaller vessel. The problem of a new engine was quite separate from his recommendation that a larger vessel be obtained for evacuations from France, advice based on six months' experience and a year's observation. Although his hitherto unavowed ambition had been to return to the fleet, he was putting forward this proposal because he saw the need to help their colleagues in France. Without capable and skilled assistance from outside, they were forced to take desperate steps, such as attempting to escape on yachts powered with car engines or, more frequently, to make their way over the 'green frontier', across the whole breadth of Spain and then over the Portuguese border. Unfortunately, most ended up in Miranda camp, from which there was no release until the end of the war. At the time of writing, there were 400 people in that notorious detention centre, compared with only 160 as recently as 26 June.

Krajewski plan was a counter to the proposals of Kleeberg, who lacked the necessary technical expertise. The serious drawbacks in Kleeberg's plan had become very evident when he had in vain asked the Admiralty to send a ship to intercept a French ship on which evacuees had been sent out. He knew that several dozen Poles were currently trying to escape from Sète on a motor fishing vessel. The projected cooperation with the Belgians was not necessary. Objections to the smallness of the ship were ridiculous: small was best. They would manage without the Belgian ship and security and organisation would be better without their help. As regards communications with Marseilles, Krajewski also found London HQ's objections to a direct link ridiculous.

Krajewski put to sea again on 18 November, still with no news of what had happened in the Orannais. His report to Mally on this mission was as follows:

From: Marian KRAJEWSKI, Gibraltar, 4 January 1942[9]
To: Col. Fryderyk MALLY (Lisbon)
REPORT OF THE EIGHTH EVACUATION MISSION
(follows my wire of 27.xi.41)

1) The aim of the mission was chiefly to re-establish communications after the unsuccessful 7th mission. Major Wysoczanski had forecast that, even if the mission had failed through betrayal, communication would still be possible through certain intermediaries; in spite of this, we did not receive a single telegram, nor any other form of news. We considered beforehand that some of the officers and soldiers might possibly still be in hiding and that we would be able to direct them to the boarding-point.

This time we chose a different embarkation place, not *Brzoza,* which had been revealed to the Vichy authorities after the previous mission, but Zorra to the west of Oran, near the Falcon lighthouse. Our felucca was the *Dogfish* (*circa* 10 tons)—the veteran of our missions.

2) Our departure from Gibraltar took place at 1100 hrs on 18 November. The first day of the voyage and almost the whole of the second passed in very difficult weather conditions; there was a strong wind (Force 4) and a heavy swell, and, to make things worse, the wind was from the east, which meant that in our small felucca we were continually taking water on deck, and everything became wet through, both on the deck and unfortunately in the living quarters. This gave us a foretaste of what to expect during the winter period, when even the local fishermen do not generally venture out to fish. Luckily, by the evening of the second day, the sea became almost completely calm, which gave us some hope that conditions would permit putting a runner ashore.

3) At 2110 hrs on 19 November we could already make out the lighthouse on the Habibas Islands; this came as a surprise since we had skirted Alboran Island (half-

way to Oran) at such a distance that it had been out of sight; I had estimated that we would have lost far more time as a result of the earlier bad weather. At 0230 hrs I passed around Plane Island, which is at the entrance to the bay—our destination. From this island we set a course to the landing point, which was a new one, but of which we would gain experience during this operation (from the land side it was to be reconnoitred by Capt Roehr).

At 0330 hrs I dropped anchor opposite a small beach; I was some 250 metres from it in water about 3–4m deep. Midshipman Buslowicz (the messenger) and Skulimowski (to help with the rowing) were put into the rubber dinghy and then we began the usual procedure of letting out the line to which the dinghy was attached, as those in it rowed their way towards the shore. Midshipman Buslowicz's effects were wrapped up in waterproof clothing, in case they fell into the water. The conditions here, by comparison with the Atlantic coast, were more favourable also in that the rowers got their legs wet to knee height only (and it was quite cold). At 0400 hours we weighed anchor, having of course pulled in Skulimowski once he had given the signal with his torch. Next, we set a course to the north, with the aim of distancing ourselves from the coast. At 1000 hrs we were hove-to some 25 miles from the coast, which was nevertheless still visible because of some high mountains.

We used this period of waiting until the evening to carry out some minor repairs such as changing the gaskets, changing the oil in the crank-case and trying out the sea anchor, which had been given us only recently. We also sighted an aircraft in the direction of the land, but it did not spot us. At 1700 hrs we set course again for the landing point.

4) The plan in putting the messenger ashore was as follows: the messenger had received from Major Wysoczanski a few addresses of people working with us; in the first place that of a Mr E., a Spaniard. He in turn was to find out what had happened to the Polish soldiers after the failed mission to La Macta; where and how they were being held; if they had freedom of movement, were able to communicate with us—and most important of all, he had to establish contact with Capt Szewalski and Lt Polanski (local leaders of the evacuation) if indeed they had not been arrested.

The messenger had received instructions to return in *24 hours;* if he did not appear, I was to return for him in 48 hours. However, if that too produced no answer to our signals as we moved along the coast, I would assume that the first had been arrested and would put a second messenger ashore. Since it was difficult to obtain an electric torch in Oran, I gave him a ship's flashlight so as to ensure that he had something with which to signal.

5) On reaching the narrow entrance to the bay, with Plane Island in the centre and both shorelines plainly visible, we slipped in successfully, at the last moment going 'at full speed' (as fast as 7½ knots) and moving out of the path of a patrol boat, which was slowly following a course to the west, a mile from the shore. In the bay we were comparatively safe. At 0015 hrs we were level with the point on the shore where, proceeding slowly, we sent out the agreed signal. There was, however, no answer. I

therefore withdrew further out into the middle of the bay, and, after an hour had passed, I repeated the operation, again without success. It seemed to us at one stage that we saw a light but there was no answer to our repeated signalling. When, after a further two hours (at 0200 hrs) we had had no further success and the most probable period for our messenger to arrive was drawing to a close, I set a course that would take us out of the bay.

6) Meanwhile, out at sea, there was an unusual amount of traffic for the time of year. The patrol boat that we had avoided with difficulty three hours earlier was now returning from the Habibas Islands. In addition, not very far from us, a small ship with bright lights was moving from Oran to Plane Island, and, having quite obviously noticed us (without lights), changed course 90º and began to travel along with us. After a time he did turn off his lights completely but at the same time he ceased to tread on our heels. I took a course to the west in order to shelter in Mersa Ben Nuar Bay, since the sea was becoming heavier, and waiting all day in a small felucca in the open sea is not one of life's more pleasurable experiences.

This course however lay between a large ship, which, as we guessed from the navigation lights, lay hove-to, but with its engine still turning over (another unusual phenomenon in this spot and at this hour) and the patrol boat mentioned earlier. The patrol boat in the end passed us quite close by without seeing us, perhaps because of our lowish profile.

7) At 0600 hrs, after passing the Habibas Islands, we approached the shore with the intention of locating the small bay of Mersa Ali, familiar to us from previous missions, and, of putting Lt Lisek and Lt Polanski ashore there in broad daylight, in spite of the presence of the Arabs. Even at a distance of 2,000m it was difficult to recognize the entrance to this crack in the steep, high, rocky shoreline, since the night seemed somehow to have become even darker. Eventually we managed to slip in past the underwater rock at the entrance and at 0630 hrs we were already anchored and preparing to hang out the fishing nets in order to give ourselves an innocent look. The whole day passed quietly, except that we watched an Arab family group on the shore with some suspicion, worried that they might despatch a messenger to the nearest guard-post with the information that the people 'who once took on board a group of people on a raft' had come back. One Arab did pay us a visit, but he only asked about the fishing, to which we answered that the catch was poor.

This period of waiting was very much to our advantage, since we had been frozen and wet through during the night because of the swell and the cold. In addition, the crew had not had much sleep because of our night-time manoeuvres along the coast.

8) At 2130 hrs we weighed anchor. The weather had improved a great deal. At 0130 hrs we were again close to the shoreline, and we recognised the spot where the first messenger had been put ashore; it turned out too that the spot was at the edge of a village (Les Andalouses) of which we had not known beforehand (the stretch on

which the landing had to be made was relatively short, only a few kilometres long, and was bounded at one end by underwater rocks and at the other by this village).

However on this occasion, too, there was no answer to our signals. So I at once withdrew from the vicinity and anchored, using two anchors (one anchor further from the shore, in order that we could haul ourselves off from the shallows if we touched bottom while our stern was close to the minimum depth; the position achieved by this method is parallel to the line of the coast and it permits lying closer to the shore, because the anchor further out provides added security).

According to the agreed plan, I put a second messenger ashore (Skulimowski), who had already spent some time in this area, so that at 0320 hrs we were able to weigh anchor. At 0430 hrs we had a breakdown of the cooling-pump, which was potentially very unpleasant, since we might have to remain after sunrise at a distance of less than 5,000 m. from the shore. Luckily at 0700 hrs we managed to repair the breakdown and precisely at that moment the familiar lights of the approaching patrol boat from the previous night appeared shining on the horizon.

9) At 1100 hrs we were waiting hove-to in the open sea in fine weather. The mechanics used this wait to improve the working of the pump, in which they displayed some ingenuity: they cut off two large brass pins and drilled holes and threaded them, then used them to bring together the broken bolts of the pump. This incident boosted the morale of the crew, who were also cheered by the appearance of a shark right alongside the ship, together with the pilot fish, although we tried in vain to catch the shark to turn it into fishmeat.

10) At 2045 hrs on 23 November we started up the engine in order to move along the shore for the third time, now perhaps just a little concerned about the fate of the colleagues we had put ashore. At 0200 hrs, having approached the shore and given our 'call signal' for the first time, WE RECEIVED A REPLY. After anchoring at the nearest point we could (depth 2½m.), we sent the raft to the shore. By 0245 hrs we had on board both messengers (Midshipman Buslowicz, Skulimowski), Second Lt Gromnicki and Branco Nekic (officer of the Yugoslav merchant navy). We had hardly made away from the beach, however, and were merely 1,000 metres from the shore when our engine broke down again. This time our situation was even more critical, since the spot was only a few kilometres distant from the Cap-Falcon lighthouse, which we knew to be also a look-out point. This time the problem was only damp in the magneto and at 0430 hrs the engine was working again.

11) Now everything seemed to turn against us as we were hurrying to return to base. The weather became stormy and, just when we could have done with an easterly wind such as there had been for several days, the storm came from the WEST. At 0830 hrs, when we were still at the latitude of the Habibas Islands and the wind had grown to Force 4–5, we began to worry about the stability of this shallow-draught boat during a journey of at least a day, and that against both waves and wind; so I decided to seek shelter, albeit perhaps not complete, in the Ali Bay again.

At 0930 hrs we entered the bay only to discover that it did not give real shelter and that the waves, because of the shallow depth, were transformed into SURF—the most dangerous kind of wave. We tried to shelter in one of the corners of the bay, behind a ridge, but the anchor we dropped would not hold and the felucca started to drag to the beach some 100m away. In these critical conditions I decided to seek alternative shelter where normally I would never have gone: the Habibas Islands, with their lighthouse-keeper's accommodation and—most probably—a telephone.

12) An hour later we entered the tiny bay of the main island of Habibas, where however, to our astonishment, we found a whole armada of our 'fellow fishermen' beckoning to us with friendly gestures to approach as near to them as possible, where it was best to shelter from the wind. We did not of course show any enthusiasm for this idea, fearing their professional eye. Eventually I dropped anchor at the entrance to the bay, at a discreet distance from our 'colleagues', but not without great difficulty since the anchor—dropped several times—dragged along the rocky bottom.

The local fishermen looked on curiously and again, for a time, tried to encourage us to change our position; the lighthouse-keeper too came down from his lighthouse high aloft to satisfy his curiosity. Next, two fishermen made their way out in a small boat to meet us and they too encouraged us to move. Although they were very friendly, their conversation was sprinkled with intriguing remarks such as, 'We are all only fishermen'... 'There was once a ship of Spanish smugglers here'... 'There are no soldiers here, nor any navy; there is no telephone either'. It all pointed to the conclusion that they had recognised something unusual about the newcomers and this was confirmed when one of them said, 'We here read the newspapers from both sides'... I was not sure how far these two fishermen had gone in their speculation. They made good-natured but pointed complaints about the lack of food and lack of petrol for their engines (5 litres a month, which is nothing for a fisherman, enough for only half an hour under power...).

Eventually I established more intimate contact with them while we waited until the next morning. They were Algerians of Spanish origin, and did not harbour any particularly friendly sentiments towards the current French regime. A few litres of fuel, tinned meat or biscuits did a lot, of course, to loosen up our conversations. They answered in kind by supplying us with fresh bread. I gained a great deal of valuable information from them about the appearance of the motor patrol boat and the location of look-out posts, and was much reassured by their offers to 'help with anything at all'. After this I took their addresses, in case we needed to organise additional safe-houses (I checked these addresses to confirm that the men were trustworthy, and that this was not merely a ploy, or a double cross).

13) On 24 November I weighed anchor, since the weather had improved, and arrived at Gibraltar without further incident during the night of 25 November. The epilogue to this journey took place the following day when I moved the *Dogfish* to another mooring-place: the clutch broke. If this had happened at sea a day earlier, it

would certainly have meant a return journey...under sail. This breakdown was of course a warning that the 30-year-old engine was already 'tired' and not completely reliable.

14) The following is a summary of the news brought by Lt Gromnicki from Algeria:

In the course of a few days, from Friday 30 October to Sunday 2 November, very nearly 200 people gathered on the coast at the secret concentration point called BRZOZA, near La Macta. This was possible mainly because of forged passes, breaking the number up into small groups and favourable conditions over the holiday period. This luck turned out to be only partial since, by real misfortune, the Prefect of Oran arranged a charity hunt (and, as though Fate intended to make fun of us, the proceeds were intended for the benefit of French POWs in German captivity) in exactly the same area of La Macta on Sunday 2 November. The result, completely unforeseen by the organisers of the escape, was that, during the hunt (with dogs) the hunting guests found under almost every bush of this fairly small forest not game but Poles. So THE ESCAPE WAS DISCOVERED A DAY EARLIER THAN HAD BEEN ANTICIPATED. In fact there was no immediate reaction on the spot.

However that same night the police and army were mobilised (a whole division of troops, since it was feared that a British landing was in the offing) and the navy was alerted too. The search was limited to one small area, with shooting in the air and calls to 'Give yourselves up!'; the results were, for the time being, poor (around 30–40 were caught). Next morning, however, several companies of soldiers and the police, walking abreast through the forest in daylight, caught almost all the rest; all those who were not caught then gave themselves up during the next few nights. At sea meanwhile warships and aircraft patrolled.

The French authorities were apparently aghast at this mass flight of two whole camps; for our troops and officers, however, it was to have regrettable results, since the other ranks were transferred immediately from Saida deep into the Sahara (Béchar) and the officers for the time being are held under guard with fixed bayonets. In due course they too are to be moved much further inland; their situation will be very unpleasant. The one person who remained at liberty was Capt Szewalski, saved by unusual quick-wittedness: he told the French that he had opposed the whole plan. They put him under guard nevertheless. And it was only with some difficulty that he managed to see my messenger and convey the above information to him.

15) The conclusions I draw from this information are as follows: A mass evacuation had a chance of succeeding and we would have managed to take off at least half the people if

1) we had possessed on the day in question our own LARGE evacuation felucca, and not the *Dogfish*, which is good for around 40 people only, and that in awful conditions;

2) there had been an earlier decision from the organisers of the operation from the land side about the plan for the mass evacuation, and this had been communicated sufficiently early to the organisers of the seagoing part of the operation. Evacuation of 200 people required different preparations from those for groups of 40 people. The organisers of the naval side were not informed until the morning of Wednesday 29 October so that, after returning to Gibraltar on Wednesday night, we would have had to be ready on Saturday morning equipped with two new feluccas or ships, whereas only one was ready. This was why, at the organisational briefing on the beach at La Macta on the morning of 29 October, I had guaranteed only Monday 3 November as a deadline. The discovery of our people by the hunt took place on the Sunday;
3) the people on shore had been dispersed to several embarkation points, with the aim of not placing all our eggs in one basket, in case the operation were uncovered. At the very least, instructions should have been issued to the evacuees that, if one site were compromised, they should make their own way to another. Some of them would always have managed to get through.

Regarding the possession of a felucca—I reported on this earlier. The only one lying at Gibraltar was being prepared for our use, but, in spite of the intervention of HQ at my request and the assurances that there would be a positive and early conclusion to the refit, the dockyard spent four months repairing the engine in the workshop and then fitted it into the felucca (still expressing optimism), only to declare that...this engine was not suitable for the vessel in question.

16) The ship's complement during the voyage apart from myself consisted of: Siembieda and Filipkowski (mechanics), Skulimowski (cook and deck-hand), Eggum (Norwegian, deck-hand) and Midshipman Buslowicz as courier, to carry out the mission in Oran.

(signed) M.Krajewski

Further details of the failed mass evacuation from La Macta (Brzoza) reached Krajewski in a letter from Casablanca dated 20 November. [10] It confirmed that on 2 and 3 November French patrols had arrested 148 Polish soldiers and officers assembled at the agreed embarkation point near Oran. Evacuation from the camps at Saida and Mascara had gone off unusually well. After the departure from Saida of all those earmarked for embarkation, only 39 of the normal complement of 206 remained: at Mascara, only six of the previous total of 67 were left. Apart from the 148 arrested on the beach, the balance were rounded up on their way to the pinpoint. All of those arrested were transferred to Saida, where the other ranks were placed behind barbed wire and carefully guarded. Officers were confined to a barracks at Mascara. Those officers who had not left Mascara at all were not allowed to leave the hotel where they were accommodated: they were cut off from communication with the outside world. An inquiry was taking place.

According to information from Algeria, it was forestry guards and members of a shooting party who had on Sunday 2 November appeared in the district near the shore and chanced upon the tracks of groups of people in abnormal numbers. They alerted the gendarmes immediately and French naval patrols were carried out in the forest.

Szewalski was immediately directed by the French authorities to Mascara: there were hopes that he would be able to return to Oran. Lt Polanski had been arrested and imprisoned at Oran.

Though he did not send his full written report on it to Mally until 29 January 1942, Krajewski went back to Algeria in the *Dogfish* between 12 and 19 December. His account was as follows:

REPORT OF THE NINTH EVACUATION MISSION
(follows my wire of 30 Dec. 1941) [11]

1) As I have already reported, Capt Szewalski most insistently asked Midshipman Buslowicz, who was put ashore in Algeria between 22 and 25 Nov., to arrange for a felucca to be sent around 15 December in order to take off those people whom he had managed to collect and hide, and—he stressed the need most forcefully—that a sum of at least 500,000 Fr. Francs be sent to him by the same route.

However, prospects of finding available sea-going resources were gloomy then, and still are. I reported on this in my wire no. 1748 of 29 November, sent via the British Naval Attaché. Namely,

a) The *Seawolf,* our own felucca, was to have received a new engine after four months' overhaul of the old engine by this incompetent dockyard; discussions about this were beginning at the time we left for the 9th mission;
b) The *Dogfish,* a very small felucca with a very antique engine, was being repaired after a serious breakdown of the clutch mechanism. The breakdown indicated that many unpleasant surprises are hidden behind the general wear and tear on this 30-year-old engine;
c) There was no other felucca or smaller vessel at our disposal, and I knew only that the local agencies were looking on the Lisbon market for a 'special purposes' ship with the characteristics needed for our evacuations.

2) In these circumstances, and in view of the urgency of Capt Szewalski's requests and the dire situation of our people in Africa after the discovery of the escape at La Macta, I decided to embark on one more voyage with the *Dogfish,* the engine of which had had only its most basic faults repaired (the clutch—and that only partly). The weather posed anther risk. According to the pilot-book and accounts of fishermen, the period of continuous bad weather should already have begun. I counted on another couple of days' delay.

As events showed, we succeeded almost completely, but we had to pay for our boldness during the next mission.

3) We weighed anchor at 1405 hrs on 13 December and, as if it wanted to indicate that to demand another 500 nautical miles from it was too much, the *Dogfish*'s engine took half an hour to start, seized up at the exit from the port—which was guarded very closely following the most recent sinkings and sabotages—and would not start again until an hour later.

Apart from myself, the crew was composed of: Siembieda and Filipkowski (mechanics), Skulimowski (cook), Eggum (deck-hand) and Second Lt Gromnicki, brought back recently from Oran, as a courier to put ashore.

4) The voyage to Oran lasted almost two days and passed off without incident. At 2130 hrs on 14 December we sighted the now very familiar lighthouse on the Habibas Islands. The weather for almost all of the outward journey was tolerable and only at the end did the wind betray signs of growing to almost storm strength. At 0330 hrs I dropped anchor at a depth of 2½m off the shore, at a point equidistant from the Falcon lighthouse and the village of Les Andalouses (about 1½km from each), the ZORRA pinpoint. After we had put Second Lt Gromnicki ashore with the money, I weighed anchor at 0400 hrs. Then, because of the increasingly heavy swell, happily then coming from ENE, which left Zorra sheltered, I withdrew about 15 miles to the west to the little bay of Ali Ben Nuar, which we had already used a couple of times, and which my crew had christened 'Rio de Janeiro'. It is a small bay surrounded by mountains and has underwater rocks at the bar but, as we were familiar with this stretch of coastline, we had no trouble in locating it. We entered the bay at 0710 hrs 15 December.

5) Just before noon that day, a young Arab with only one arm paid us a visit. He came from a very poor family, who had recently settled in this desolate little bay... He did appear greatly suspicious. In the end we bought two chickens from him to vary our monotonous menu.

At 1430 hrs we had a far less welcome visit, which may yet have serious repercussions. A man in a boat borrowed from an Arab family approached our felucca. His dress contrasted strongly with the rags of the ordinary Arabs, although he may have had the same Semitic roots. He treated us to some very good cigarettes, certainly not an Arab custom. He asked some searching questions: 'Where have you come from?' 'Do you have any fish?' 'Do you know the Falcon family at Nemours?' (from which we had supposedly come). He also put some silly questions, such as, 'What do you catch using a net with such large holes?' (here he pointed to the net that we habitually hung out to improve our 'fishing appearance', although closer examination would reveal that it could be used in trawling for particular types of fish only). To which we answered, 'Anything we can'. After a time he gave up and returned to the shore, then walked rapidly uphill.

The identity of this person was of course clear to me: he was an agent of the secret police, or simply a police informer, of which, in the French colonies—where a police regime prevails—there are a great many. So I ordered the anchor to be weighed, although we did not need to hurry especially, since the agent had to travel 25 km to the nearest guard-post and the sun would set in three hours.

Whether we wanted to or not, we had to set out against a strong swell and wind and spend the night on the sea anchor. That night the man on watch at 0230 hrs saw lamp lights in the region of our bay, which of course did not come as a surprise to us.

6) Since I had arranged with Second Lt Gromnicki that I would pick him up two days later, in order to give him more time to sort things out, we continued to wait at sea the whole of the next day at a distance of about 30 nautical miles to the north-west of Oran—until 1900 hrs. At 0140 I entered the Andalouses Bay and, an hour later, having received the agreed signal from the shore, I anchored and sent the life-raft to the shore.

I took Second Lt Gromnicki on board again, along with five officers whom he had brought to the spot…

7) The return journey was initially propitious: there was almost no swell during the first day. However it grew heavier during the afternoon of 17 December, so that my speed dropped to 4 knots.

Worse came when the engine seized up that night about 20 miles from Gibraltar, almost in the Straits, in regularly patrolled waters. However, from that distance I was able to send an agreed recognition signal with the Aldis lamp to the look-out post at Gibraltar. As we had not returned to port at the expected time, they sent out a motor launch to help. We were towed for 10 minutes, after which the engine recovered and we were able to return to Gibraltar under our own steam at 0230 hrs on 18 December.

8) The news brought to me by Second Lt Gromnicki and the evacuated officers was communicated to you earlier. In short, the situation has not changed. Apparently there was a chance that former camp conditions might be restored (as at Saida and Mascara), but because of the treachery of two of our officers (Second Lt Schonfeld and Capt Jakubowski, according to Capt Szewalski), the French authorities moved the officers and the camps deeper inland…

9) This voyage showed once again that the *Dogfish* is not at all suitable for this time of the year. Its inadequate accommodation places excessive demands on the crew, who therefore have to spend the whole journey on deck, as do any passengers. This is to say nothing of its faults associated with age—leaks and the ancient engine.

(signed) M.Krajewski.

On 20 December, the day after Krajewski returned from his ninth mission, Mally wrote to him agreeing that Roehr should leave for France to prepare evacuations by sea from there on the lines proposed by Krajewski.[12] He then raised the entirely new idea that some of those evacuated from France to Spain might possibly be directed into the Malaga area, where they would be hidden by priests. If so, the question would arise of exfiltrating these people by sea from somewhere in that vicinity. He asked Krajewski to look into this possibility on the basis of existing resources.

Mally had acquired a fishing vessel in Portugal, but its delivery to Krajewski in Gibraltar had been delayed because the Belgian who was to act as skipper took fright when the Portuguese 'official' owner of the boat started to explain the navigational difficulties and the danger from submarines, and at the last minute refused to make the voyage. Mally was pressing the shipping office and would send her on as soon as a crew was available.

Meanwhile, he had been authorised by his London headquarters to buy a larger fishing vessel with the characteristics specified by Krajewski for operations to the south coast of France. His source of advice on seafaring matters in Lisbon thought, however, that it would be difficult to find a vessel which reconciled the required fuel capacity and range with the desired speed, carrying capacity and overall need to look like a fishing vessel. Furthermore, London imagined the cost of a suitable ship would be of the order of £2, 000. Mally doubted whether this price would buy anything suitable in Portugal. He asked Krajewski to confirm whether a new ship was still needed now that a new engine had been promised for the existing felucca. To put Krajewski in the picture, Mally advised that the felucca they would be sending to Gibraltar for him would be able to carry 15 people in addition to the crew.

Krajewski was instructed to retain a radio operator who was in Gibraltar, rather than send him on to the United Kingdom. He was also to ask Captain Kaminski, who had been evacuated by the British from Madrid, whether Chojnacki would be suitable as organiser of the landward side of the planned sea evacuations from metropolitan France.

On 24 December, Mally followed this letter up with a two-page plan for evacuations by sea from Spain, on very similar lines to those previously arranged from Africa, although he acknowledged that this scheme would not be necessary if direct evacuation from France proved possible. The landward side of any such operations would be organised by Madrid, the maritime side by Gibraltar. The object would be to extract groups of up to 50 people at a time on innocent-looking vessels.

On a day indicated by Gibraltar, the boat would turn up at the appointed place. Agreed identification signals would be needed. Embarkation might have to be carried out in rubber dinghies because of the surf. Mail might be handed over and there might be an opportunity for land and sea operational personnel to confer. The embarkation point might be between 100 and 200 km from Gibraltar. He proposed Malaga as a suitable collecting point for evacuees. Naval charts indicated that the shore 10–18km outside the town might be suitable: there were beaches and no off-lying rocks. Embarkation points should be hidden and suitable for people to be picked up at night (2400–0200 hrs) without the need to wait for particularly dark conditions. Areas where there were underwater rocks should be avoided, to allow the ship to approach as near as possible and anchor in

4–5m of water. A little bay that would provide shelter from any breakers would be ideal, but an open beach might do.

There would have to be a recognisable navigational landmark on which the vessel could make its landfall: the boat would then follow the coast at distance of 500m. Suitable landmarks might be a rock, a building or patches of undergrowth. At least three pinpoints should be chosen and, in order to facilitate recognition, each should be given a code name for telegraphic purposes, e.g. DORA. The paper ended with notes about recognition signals and laid down coding arrangements to be used between Madrid and Gibraltar.

Krajewski's hopes of avoiding any further mid-winter operations in the nine-ton felucca Dogfish had been further raised by a visit paid to Gibraltar by Commander Slocum in December 1941. Slocum still held no Admiralty appointment: he was at that time no more than the SIS officer responsible for meeting that organisation's requirements for physical communications with occupied western Europe. He was, however, well on the way to establishing control of all Allied clandestine sea transport to the north and west coasts of France and his visit to Gibraltar proved a first step towards his acquiring at least theoretical control in the western Mediterranean as well.

In the event, his presence did not spare Krajewski from one further, unusually trying, sortie in *Dogfish*. This was the report submitted on it to Mally:

> *REPORT OF THE TENTH EVACUATION MISSION*[13]
>
> 1) In the course of a meeting between Second Lt Gromnicki and Captain Szewalski during the 9th mission (13–19.xiii.1941), Captain Szewalski asked for a felucca to be sent on 10 January, by which date he expected to have gathered around 15 people in a newly organized safe house.
>
> During that 9th mission, we expected to receive a new felucca more suited to the task, by the beginning of January. After Commander Slocum's visit, the matter of vessels for use in special operations moved forward much more energetically. It was possible we might be able to use either *Seawolf,* after the arrival of a new engine ordered by cable from London on 13.xi; or the *Ville-De-Fedala,* a very good fishing vessel freshly acquired by the authorities here. We did not take the *Dogfish* into consideration, because of her complete unsuitability for that kind of mission during bad weather. Moreover according to Commander Slocum, two special ships for this kind of operation were due to arrive at Gibraltar from England.
>
> By the time the operation was due to start, however, the feluccas I then had at my disposal were in just the same state as on so many previous occasions. Consequently, I was compelled to fall back on the 10-ton *Dogfish* with its old engine. This meant taking considerable risks, if only navigational, since she would be required to undertake a journey of some 600 miles, lasting at least six days, during the winter period. Having no other choice, I could only hope that, as on the last two

missions we would have the good fortune to encounter a period of mild weather and avoid any serious breakdown of the engine.

The sometimes turbulent 16-day voyage did not bear out our initial hopes…

2) We put to sea on the morning of 8 January. The crew, apart from myself, was composed of Siembieda and Filipkowski (mechanics), Skulimowski (cook), Eggum (deck-hand, Norwegian), Second Lt Gromnicki (liaison courier to be put ashore) and for the first time an English sergeant, Guilder. This man was seconded to me almost at the last moment in order to test some special radio apparatus for the authorities here. I was more than ready to do this favour for our hosts (and the owners of the *Dogfish*) since it provided a chance to use radio communications in the event of difficulties during the voyage. I do not use my own apparatus on the *Dogfish* because of the likelihood of damage from the damp, etc.

For the first two days of the voyage the wind was from the west—i.e. to our advantage—even though its strength (4–5) was rather dangerous for our little felucca. Far from easing, it strengthened, so that on the evening of 9 January, as we approached the Cap-Falcon lighthouse, near our usual landing and pick-up point, I had to decide whether to put Second Lt Gromnicki ashore on the *eastern* side of the peninsula, since the western shores were completely exposed to the north-west swell. Around 2200 hrs on the 9th we were only a few miles from the lighthouse and being driven in the direction of that rocky shoreline by the storm-force wind from aft. Passing us at a distance of a few thousand metres was a convoy of three French merchant vessels which, advancing slowly along the coast, exchanged recognition signals with the lighthouse. No-one could have noticed us in the complete darkness though.

3) At this point we suffered a mechanical breakdown. The clutch mechanism gave out a characteristic rattle and the propeller ceased to rotate, which was a sure indication of serious damage to the cog-wheels, something that just could not be repaired on a felucca. This was a very critical moment for a breakdown: we were drifting on to a rocky shore, now only a few thousand metres distant, in a very large swell. We raised the sails almost immediately, from the outset strongly reefed. After entering the Bay of Oran I realised that, unfortunately, I had not found the expected shelter from the north-westerly storm; the swell was even more dangerous for us in the shallower waters, since it broke into surf. We had a foretaste of what awaited us as we approached the shore near the Falcon lighthouse, when the swell nearly covered us completely. I ordered the crew to put on their lifebelts. Taking shelter in the port of Oran or in Mers el-Kebir was out of the question, even if we did look like a fishing boat, because of the possibility that the entrance was closed by a boom.

In the light of this, I set a course as close to the wind as possible, about N 30° E, counting on being able to shelter in the little port of Arzew, east of Oran, and there dismantle the clutch.

4) In the midst of this severe storm, which demanded the full concentration of the crew in exceptionally difficult conditions, we were driven by the wind all night. In

the end I was unable to manoeuvre in such a way as to enter the Bay of Arzew, which, with hindsight—after the experience of the shooting on 13 January—would have presumably ended in imprisonment, since our 'fishing appearance' had already been compromised. The storm remained at full force throughout 10 January and the following night. The only safe course I could hold was that of 30°, so that by the morning of the 11th, when it had calmed somewhat, we found ourselves drifting almost 100 miles from the Falcon light.

The dismantled clutch was immediately revealed to be seriously damaged and looked quite beyond repair. However, in view of the gravity of our situation (some 350 miles from Gibraltar, the proximity of the shore, the stormy season of the year), Siembieda undertook to attempt to repair the clutch, so that we could at least use the engine to go ahead. The experiment was entirely successful and, after two days of strenuous work, on the evening of 12 January, we were ready to set off in the direction of Oran. Siembieda again demonstrated the talent and experience of a fine specialist technician, since the repair required such things as drilling some 20 holes in iron or steel, threading them, cutting the bolts, etc, and all this while subjected to a continuous rolling motion, in conditions as remote from an engine repair-shop as could be imagined.

5) Nevertheless we had no guarantee that we could rely on the clutch, and we still lacked a reverse gear. With these considerations in mind, I decided to set a return course for Gibraltar. In spite of everything, though, I thought we could hazard careful use of the engine in order to approach the shore and put our runner ashore. The weather that night was considerably improved and, having travelled 300 miles, I did not want to return without having picked up the people who were no doubt waiting impatiently in hiding. And lest that be thought something of a risk, then I must state that I considered any voyage in the *Dogfish* was one continuous risk.

On the morning of the 13th we were in the vicinity of Oran again, intending to wait 24 hours in order to carry out our assignment. Once more—although not for the last time on this trip—the weather forced us to change our plans. The wind rose again and became very strong, forcing us to search for a suitable sheltered anchorage. I moved off therefore in the direction of the Habibas Islands, which I knew from the 8th mission. The waves mounted and the wind grew ever stronger (Force 5), however, so that, after a day-long attempt to cross that scarcely 25-mile stretch, I was forced to seek shelter at all costs. The larger waves threatened to overturn the felucca, which has no keel or inside ballast.

The only place I could reach and seek shelter, given the direction of the wind, was in Oran Bay, specifically near Cap Falcon; this had the advantage of not being a port with the various customary authorities...also, it was the point indicated by the pilot-books. In other words, it was a natural place for a fisherman to seek shelter from the storm.

6) At around 1700 hrs, shortly before sunset, we dropped anchor. We intended to move closer to the shore during the night, hoping still to be able to put a courier

ashore in the same place. Soon afterwards we noticed more than a dozen Arab soldiers, who appeared to be drawing in a net on the narrow beach. They must have seen us drop anchor (we were the only ship visible). A few of the soldiers then gathered opposite our anchorage (at some 250–300m from the shore) and called to us. Since we could not understand what they wanted, and there was not a great deal of choice of possible anchorages, we did not pay a great deal of attention to their shouting; sunset was near, and we hoped they would quickly tire of it. When, however, the watch informed me that an officer had joined them and was carefully studying us through a telescope, before evidently giving the order to launch their small boat, I understood that the game was starting to become more serious. Before they had travelled very far, I managed to turn the felucca around and set a course for the open sea, cutting the anchor cable without recovering the anchor to save time. We thus began a race. We were extremely lucky in all this since the engine started up at once: even a few minutes' delay would have delivered us into the hands of the French.

Not only did they give chase but they had hardly seen the movement on our deck indicating that we were getting under way before they began firing with rifles—both from the boat and from the shore. Their shooting was reasonably accurate: no-one was hit but we found four bullet holes in the hull and on the mast. Two were on the stern, very close to me and to the fuel tank. Obviously they judged me, as helmsman, a more worthwhile target than the others… Needless to add, we took cover, insofar as cutting the anchor cable and steering permitted. So once again we were on the open sea, in a storm that rated at least point 6 on the Beaufort scale.

7) This was decidedly the worst night we spent at sea during the evacuation missions, perhaps even during our whole careers at sea. We struggled continuously with the endless waves that poured over us. The trick was to avoid all the largest breakers, which represented not just danger but possible disaster for our felucca. Worse, in spite of clothing that was generally excellent and waterproof, we were soaked through and suffered from the cold.

This lasted until the morning of 14 January. On that day as the sun rose, we made out the Spanish coast, viz. Mesa de Roldan. The Gata peninsula, known for its navigational features, was not much further. We had travelled all night under sail and with our engine running so as to get as far as possible out of range of the French air force, which might have been searching for us.

The weather gradually improved during the day, which was fortunate since the clutch was again refusing to respond to the controls. The pins that had been drilled into the cog-wheel and the propeller shaft to fasten them together had held for barely a single stormy night, although this was quite an achievement in itself. Luckily, this time the repair was easier. During the night, more pins were put in and we were able to move again.

8) There was only one direction we could choose: Gibraltar. Our supplies of fuel were exhausted and also the alarm had been raised among the French authorities on the coast after the last bout of shooting.

Our return journey seemed at first to be progressing well: the wind at Capo de Gata was in our favour and 15 January passed calmly. Indeed, we had enough fuel for the return only if the weather remained reasonably calm, but not if the winds against us were strong, reducing our speed from between 6 and 4 knots to 3 or even less—moreover, at the cost of severely straining the felucca's hull.

On the evening of the 15th, a stubborn westerly wind returned, which forced me either to wait for a favourable wind or to change course. I ordered the engine to be switched off and we hoisted the sails.

9) The last phase of our protracted Odyssey began with our wait for an easterly wind. Lack of space prevents me from reporting on it more fully.

On the 16th, just before sunset, we were close to the African coast when a further storm, compelled us to spend the night anchored in the shelter of the Tres Forcas peninsula, about 2 miles north of Melilla. On two occasions during the night an MTB passed close to us at a distance of a few score metres, but luckily either failed to see us or was not suspicious.

Since Spanish Morocco seemed to be so closely guarded and patrolled, I weighed anchor at first light on the 17th and until the 18th meandered about in the region of Alboran Island, in the centre of the western basin of the Mediterranean.

On 18 January, we established our first contact with a Hudson aircraft sent out to look for us as a result of radio messages I had been sending to Gibraltar...until the British radio operator discovered that the batteries had not been completely charged at the time when we sailed from Gibraltar.

We spent the night of the 18th/19th anchored close to Alboran, so as not to move too far from the position the aircraft must have reported to base. We remained there the next day, under sail in the vicinity of the island, in the expectation that someone from Gibraltar would turn up.

Because of a further storm on the night of the 19th, we anchored again near Alboran Island and stayed there at anchor during the 20th and 21st. On the second day a lighthouseman with one of the soldiers from the little island (600 m. long) paid us a visit, begging us for some tobacco, since the inclement weather had prevented any ship from visiting since the end of December. Asked about our nationality, I said that we were Norwegians, not wanting them to report to Melilla by telephone the presence of a possibly suspicious English fisherman.

10) On 21 January we had what was to be our final adventure, which we expected would lead to our being interrogated in Melilla.

Just before sunset I sighted a patrol boat heading for the island from the direction of Melilla. From the faintness of its navigational lights, I guessed that it was some 6, 000m off and that it was Spanish—not the most desirable encounter in my position. I ordered the anchor raised but it was caught on some rock and this time we were not able to cut through the cable, which was chain not a grass warp, I therefore decided to re-enact the scene that had worked so well at Tarifa during the 4th mission.

In the meantime the patrol boat had reached the island, anchored and, having discovered us in its searchlight, let down a boat. Shortly the commander of the boat called to me that, as 'el capitán', I should come over 'con papel' [with the ship's papers] to his vessel.

I must add that, before he reached our side, I had ordered the men to throw overboard anything in the least compromising or that might indicate where we had been: grenades, revolvers, maps of the Oran region, notes and unfortunately French money, which, in the amounts we possessed (135,200 Francs), we would never have been able to explain away.

11) The captain of the patrol boat, a naval lieutenant aged around 35 years, received me on deck—to my astonishment, in quite friendly spirit. Having asked about my nationality ('British', I replied) he then asked to see my papers. He copied precisely my clearance paper, in which were recorded both my 'British' nationality and the direction and purpose of my voyage, namely east, to trawl for fish, Clearly convinced of my identity as a fisherman, the Spanish captain then very kindly invited me to have a glass of cognac with him. In the course of conversation he asked how we came to be anchored there, and I explained that it was because of a breakdown right at the beginning of our fishing run. I gave him many true details, leaving aside, of course, our sojourn on the French African coast. He himself confirmed that the weather was exceptionally bad there that year and said that he had come to bring supplies to the group on the island and a change of both lighthouseman and soldiers. He added, 'I should bring supplies to the island every ten days, but I have not been able to do so since 27 December because of the weather.'

Eventually, while the supplies and men were being put ashore and the existing garrison was embarking (25 soldiers guard the island's neutrality...), I had the honour (rather awkward, to tell the truth, because of the technical questions with which he punctuated the conversation) of eating supper on the ship's bridge with the captain. He evidently had a soft spot for the British, having at one time sailed in the waters around Ireland, fishing, and visited British ports. (For a foreigner he spoke English well.)

Asked if we needed anything, I told him that in recent days we had greatly felt the lack of sugar. He agreed to provide me with some in return for butter, since he apparently was very fond of English butter (he smiled as he said this). Eventually, we worked out an exchange whereby he received English tobacco, corned beef and biscuits, while we received two pounds of sugar and some oranges.

12) Early on the following day the wind at long last veered around (after three weeks...!) and by the 23rd we had made our way under sail or engine power to within 20 miles of Gibraltar, where again we were almost completely becalmed and

we had only enough fuel for port manoeuvring. But we were continually 'visited' by aircraft, which signalled to us that 'Everything is alright...help is coming'. That evening two Fairmile 'B'-Class MLs approached us, returning, as it turned out, from a second mission to locate us, which they had been unable to do as we had been forced in the meantime to change position.

Eventually, at 1900 hours on the 23rd, we entered harbour under our own steam using the remains of our fuel, and having thrown off the tow-line from the ML that had brought us to the port of Gibraltar. It was not before time, since for several days we had eaten only biscuits and dishes made from corned beef and for the whole 16 days of the voyage we had not managed to change our soaking clothing.

13) Analysing why the French shot at us, we may guess that the possible reasons were a) the usual suspicion of someone who attempts to run away; b) suspicion that we were smuggling, since we had no signs on the ship's side to indicate nationality; c) that the French in Africa were in possession of real information about us, through betrayal or idle talk, or perhaps the visit by that agent during the 9th mission. This last theory was supported by the most recent news received indirectly from Oran, recommending that I should not send a boat there at the beginning of February, as a trap was being prepared.

14) In addition, this journey proved indisputably that we can no longer use the *Dogfish* during the winter and spring transitional periods—in other words not until the beginning of April.

Luckily, the Seawolf, a much larger felucca with a new engine, will be ready in the meantime—although not until the end of this month (February).

15) In para. 4 I reported on Siembieda's contribution. In conclusion, I should like to report how Second Lt Gromnicki distinguished himself. In spite of the fact that he was at sea for the first time and has no previous knowledge of sailing, he set to the task with such enthusiasm and energy, in very difficult conditions, that he proved a great asset and in all senses a full member of the crew, which, given the reduced number of crew available (for sailing) was extremely valuable. I must emphasize that this officer, unlike the other members of the crew, volunteered for the voyage knowing that it would not bring him any material reward at all.

(signed) M.Krajewski.

Krajewski cannot have been best pleased to receive on 13 February, three weeks after his return from this ordeal, what amounted to a letter of reprimand from Mally.[14] The evacuation outpost in Africa had accused Krajewski of not having arrived at the rendezvous on the African coast where he had been expected about 11 January. From Krajewski's last report, Mally could not make out whether he had been on his way to North Africa or to France. Equally, Mally had asked, and now asked again, what was the situation about Roehr? Had Roehr yet made his way to French territory? As Mally had already pointed out several times, he was well aware of the great technical difficulties

Krajewski had to surmount as a result of having to depend on other people's repair workshops to keep his felucca in operational order. Mally nevertheless drew Krajewski's attention to the equally difficult conditions under which their people had to work in North Africa. They required him to overcome all technical difficulties and make every possible effort to arrive at the meeting-points at the agreed time. Krajewski should choose the day and hour for meeting, but thereafter would he please do everything possible to ensure the arrangements for the meeting were adhered to? A bit tough!

V
Krajewski's Further Plans for Operations to North Africa and Southern France: December 1941–March 1942

Slocum had cogent reasons for visiting Gibraltar early in December 1941.[1] Demands for clandestine transport were growing; German defences and controls were increasingly formidable, particularly on the north coast of France and in the Low Countries; attempts to carry out operations by sea from bases in the United Kingdom to these key areas had, in recent months, failed more often than they had succeeded.

The increased demand emanated mainly from SOE, whose Independent French Section had substantial numbers of agents under training, and from MI9, who were confronted with the task of rescuing from France growing numbers of shot-down aircrew.

By the end of April 1941, increased German vigilance had halted operations in and out of Brittany by fishing vessels, with the loss of two of the boats involved; and in the 13 months to September 1941 there had not been one successful cross-Channel operation to France by high-speed craft. Slocum expected shortly to be able to borrow a 'C'-Class MGB from Combined Operations and hoped that she would be allocated permanently to his Section in spring 1942. However, as the Germans tightened their hold on the occupied zone of France, it seemed all too likely that the increased vigilance and scale of their coastal, air and sea patrols, the building of their coastal defence system and the imposition of administrative controls on access to beaches and on the movements of fishing craft would make clandestine contacts with France by sea from the United Kingdom increasingly difficult. As the purveyor of physical communications to the SIS and the guardian of their priority over those of other agencies, Slocum urgently needed landing areas that offered access to France but were less heavily guarded than those directly accessible from the United Kingdom. The south coast of France, still not occupied by the Germans, seemed in every way suitable for his purpose, notwithstanding *Fidelity*'s limited success, and it was in pursuit of this line of inquiry that he went to Gibraltar.

Slocum found that the Poles, the Czechs and SOE were using what he termed 'their private means of transport' to mount forays into the western Mediterranean and down the Atlantic coast of Morocco. Although they had had a certain amount of success, he felt that this method of working left much to be desired. The craft employed were inadequate and the problem of maintaining them was insuperable. The dockyard would undertake no refits without the sanction of a recognised naval authority. This was almost unobtainable as the Navy, hard pressed for men and materials, viewed clandestine operations with suspicion and dislike, judging them a waste of ships and time. The Navy's indifference may perhaps be excused by the fact that requests for approval for such activities were inadequately explained although they came sandwiched between claims of importance.

In Slocum's view, there was, insufficient liaison with, and control by, the naval and air authorities in the operational sphere. The inadequate craft employed had, as a consequence, to counter the dangers of attack by Allied, as well as enemy, submarines, ships and aircraft. He recorded, though on what evidence is unclear, that in many instances they were hindered by the attentions of friendly patrols to such an extent that their operations had to be abandoned, or at least postponed to the next no-moon period. This in turn disorganised the plans of the shore parties, often in desperate straits, awaiting embarkation from enemy coasts. Finally, there was always the danger that two craft, each working for its own organisation, would arrive at the same pinpoint without previous knowledge of the other's existence and thus that either or both operations would be jeopardised. If a vessel became overdue, air reconnaissance and assistance could not be organised with the necessary speed. As 1941 drew to a close, Slocum claimed that there was mounting misunderstanding between the naval authorities at Gibraltar and what he termed 'the purely military ones', operating their own craft, as a result of which the latter had 'reached a peak of their unpopularity'. The Navy was irritated at the way in which 'private navy' ships were sailed without reference to the situation at sea and without warning to the local naval port commands. The secret organisations themselves were becoming conscious of the difficulty of laying plans for operations when they were compelled to use unreliable craft, which were constantly breaking down through faulty maintenance, and with the knowledge that, when at sea, they could expect scant assistance from a navy and air force whose sympathies had been 'so unfortunately alienated'.

In contrast to this untidy, unsatisfactory and even dangerous state of affairs in the Gibraltar Command, irregular operations in home waters had, as Slocum claimed, been a 'going concern' since 1940. The maritime interests of the clandestine departments were in the hands of a naval officer from the active list of the Royal Navy. This officer (Slocum himself) had built up a good liaison between the clandestine services, the Admiralty and local naval authorities. SOE would, of course, have regarded this description of the satisfactory state of affairs in home waters as quite unwarranted.

Krajewski's reports certainly bore out all Slocum's observations about inadequate craft and faulty maintenance, but Krajewski would hardly have been recommended for a DSO if his relations with the local naval authorities were as Slocum claimed. Perhaps Slocum's remark about the 'purely military ones' was meant to single Krajewski out from Quennell of SOE and the rest of the field. What is certain is that in December 1941 the Royal Navy at Gibraltar had its hands full: the Battle of the Atlantic was at its height and the difficulties of getting convoys through to beleaguered Malta were such that Gibraltar-based submarines of the Eighth Flotilla were being used to ferry aviation fuel through to keep the island's exiguous Spitfire fighter force flying. In such circumstances, it is hardly surprising that clandestine operations were merely tolerated rather than liked, and that Slocum's offer to take charge and reorganise them on a more satisfactory and coordinated basis should have been welcomed.

A series of consultations with Vice-Admiral Commanding North Atlantic (VACNA) and other interested parties culminated in a meeting at Government House, at which a universally acceptable course of action was agreed. Slocum, who presented himself as the delegate of the Admiralty, announced that a Special Flotilla would be formed and that, as a temporary measure, the existing feluccas would be placed under the administrative and operational control of the Captain Commanding the Eighth Submarine Flotilla (S/m 8). Arrangements would be made for maintenance to be provided by HMS *Maidstone,* the submarine depot ship, and the dockyard. As soon as possible, a suitable officer and staff would be sent out by NID (C) to direct, under VCNA, all clandestine operations from the Rock. Slocum undertook to provide extra vessels, including a 200-ton diesel trawler and a fast escort vessel.

As has been seen, Krajewski felt that Slocum's visit had at last got things moving: *Seawolf* would receive her new engine, which was to be an 88h.p. Kelvin, rather than the 50h.p. model for which he had originally asked, unless it were decided to install it in another felucca, the Vega (original name *Ville-de-Fedhala*), which had arrived in Gibraltar unexpectedly on 3 December from Casablanca, when stowaways forced her crew to proceed there.

Krajewski learned of this vessel's presence in the harbour only by chance.[2] She was an excellent open-sea type and very suitable for operations to the south coast of France. He hoped to be able to use her to begin his French evacuation scheme without needing to wait for the completion of *Seawolf*'s refit. The Contraband Control Office (CCO) had recommended to the Admiralty that the ship be released but, as de Bellaigue, the Free French liaison officer, independently needed a similar craft, he and Krajewski persuaded the CCO to rescind their advice and retain her for their clandestine operational purposes. They also wrote jointly to VCNA asking him to intervene in favour of their being allowed to have the boat.

Krajewski discussed his plans for using this vessel with Quennell, SOE's local representative, and it was agreed that she would be incorporated into the new Special

Flotilla, initiated by Slocum. But SOE had a special task to carry out, for which Quennell received priority to use the new ship: Krajewski was promised that he could have her afterwards for his first expedition to the south coast of France, projected for the end of December 1941. But, as so often before in connection with *Seawolf,* his hopes were frustrated.

Quennell needed a vessel for an expedition to Casablanca. He had recently received from England a complete Polish crew, consisting of a naval Lieutenant, Jan Buchowski, three Leading Seamen and three Ordinary Seamen, all of whom had been seconded to SOE by Admiral Swirski, the Polish naval Commander-in-Chief, at the request of Brigadier Colin Gubbins, SOE's Chief of Training and Operations. Buchowski, who had been awarded the Polish Cross of Gallantry for courage in Norwegian waters while serving in the destroyer *Blyskawica* and a Bar to this decoration for courage during the Dunkirk evacuation, had been acting gunnery officer of the ship prior to his secondment. He had been put through a course of intensive and specialised training by SOE before being sent out to Gibraltar.

This operation to Casablanca in the *Vega* was scuppered by bad weather, which made landing impossible. While they were off Tangiers, on the return passage to Gibraltar, they were summoned by a Spanish warship to heave to. When they failed to comply, the warship opened fire, and *Vega* was placed under arrest. As they were being escorted into Tangiers, they managed to throw their explosive materials and arms overboard. The crew were interned for three weeks, when they were released after the intervention of the British Consulate-General, but the boat remained impounded. Krajewski was therefore obliged to use the *Dogfish* for his very trying 16-day sortie to Algeria in January 1942; and also to postpone his first expedition to the south coast of France until the following April, when *Seawolf* had been fitted with her new engine and was at last ready for sea.

Early in 1942, Patrick Whinney, Slocum's Staff Officer for Mediterranean operations, now a Lt Cmdr, RNVR, arrived at Gibraltar to lay the foundations of the new organisation and prepare for the advent of Captain C.B.Osborne, RNR, who was to take up the post of senior officer. Osborne assumed control in the spring of 1942. The trawler *Tarana* and escort vessel *Minna* followed in quick succession. These two vessels and the operational felucca were, for purposes of cover, styled the Coast Watching Flotilla (CWF). Slocum felt, in retrospect, that the cover designation had proved a satisfactory choice.

Buchowski's unit, having been formed for SOE's needs, was initially distinct from Krajewski's evacuation mission and was known as the Diversionary Group, but the two were old shipmates from the *Blyskawica* and when Krajewski went to sea in *Dogfish* for a final sortie to Oran in March, Buchowski must have gone with him as second in command.

SOE held substantial stocks of arms, ammunition and explosives at Gibraltar in connection with contingency plans to destroy communications should the Germans move into Spain and invade North Africa. They no doubt wished to be able to transport these stores wherever they were needed, including southern France. But the fact that Buchowski had been given training by SOE suggests they may also have planned to use him to carry out raids or sabotage or to instruct others to do so. The exact nature of the operation he was sent to carry out at Casablanca in December, when *Vega* was lost, is not clear; nor is the nature of a second operation for which he was subsequently sent to Tangiers, probably in *Dogfish,* when they were shot at by coastal guards. It is, however, certain that SOE Gibraltar made up and smuggled into Tangiers a 341b. explosive charge, which was used on 11 January 1942 to destroy a cliff-top villa containing a German infra-red monitoring device. Used in conjunction with a similar installation on the Spanish side of the 16km-wide Straits, this would have enabled the Abwehr to detect the movement of Allied shipping in and out of the western Mediterranean under cover of darkness. The threat was discovered by none other than Kim Philby, who consulted R.V.Jones, scientific adviser to SIS. In Abwehr (German military intelligence) signals they noted references to an operation code-named BODDEN, which was also the name of an enclosed stretch of water near Peenemünde on the Baltic coast of Germany, a known centre of scientific research and development for operational purposes. From this and collateral intelligence, they correctly deduced what was being built by the Abwehr on the two sides of the Straits. The Abwehr scored a savage tit-for-tat by blowing up a British diplomatic bag and killing 29 people on the Tangiers–Gibraltar ferry some weeks later, but the Germans were never able to replace what they had lost, and thus the Allied invasion fleets destined for Oran and Algiers were able, in the first week of November 1942, to slip undetected through the Straits for the TORCH landings, an operation which, with El Alamein and Stalingrad, turned the tide of the Second World War.

On 8 March 1942, the new 88h.p. engine for *Seawolf* arrived. While it was being installed, Krajewski, cheered by the prospect that the vessel would at long last become available for operations, wrote formally to Captain Holland, Chief of Staff to the Governor and chairman of the local Joint Intelligence Committee, the body delegated to lay down priorities for clandestine operations from the Rock, outlining the tasks that the Polish mission wished *Seawolf* and her Polish crew to undertake.[3] Their object was to evacuate by sea the ex-Polish fighting forces immobilised in southern France, roughly estimated to number 3,000, though it was impossible to state how many could effectively be rescued. Krajewski noted that the plan to evacuate men went back to December 1940, when it had been discussed in outline between the Polish general staff and the Admiralty. In March 1941, he had been sent to Gibraltar, which he was to use as the base in carrying out the plan.

When the plan to organise a mass evacuation of the two main camps in the Marseilles area by means of the cargo steamer *Czardasz* was abandoned in April 1941 (see Chapter XXIV above), he was given the additional task of organising the rescue of Poles from Morocco and Algeria. At the same time he was to look for means to carry out the main scheme, evacuation from France.

The North African scheme had finally been put into effect from July 1941 onwards. In the course of ten expeditions, over 100 officers and men had been taken off, and he and his crew had gathered considerable experience in these rather unusual operations. On each journey at least 650km were covered in all weathers; there had been seven effective evacuations, five of which had been in heavy Atlantic surf; and three landings of officer-messengers.

The North African scheme, Krajewski continued, was based originally on the availability of the *Seawolf,* which he had taken over with the approval of VACNA and his Chief of Staff, Captain Duke, at the beginning of July 1941. Her engine having proved faulty, the boat was handed over to the dockyard about 20 July for an overhaul expected to last only two or three weeks. The African plan had been carried out mainly in the 10-ton *Dogfish,* which Quennell had kindly lent him. At the beginning of November, after a three-and-a-half-month refit, *Seawolf*'s engine had been declared unusable, so he had asked the Polish Government to buy a suitable replacement. This was done, but delivery from the United Kingdom had entailed considerable further delay in commissioning *Seawolf* and in the meantime other alterations were made, for instance to increase her radius of action.

At the beginning of December, when this refit was still in progress, Captain Slocum had informed a meeting of authorities and missions of the proposed new organisation of the Special Flotilla. From this point on, Krajewski had received effective and substantial help from the officer specialists of HMS *Maidstone*.

The Polish mission intended to land an officer in southern France to take charge of the landward side of the evacuation scheme. They would then carry out a succession of expeditions to take off the maximum number of men, whom the officer would assemble at the appointed place. The designated officer had already been very successful in organising the landward side of the North African scheme and was, moreover, well acquainted with the area in which he would be operating. Exact numbers to be embarked on each occasion and consequently the duration of the scheme could not yet be specified. Besides, the situation might change at any moment if the boat or the land-based organisation were compromised. A figure of about 80 at a time seemed likely. Security was of the utmost importance, since the plan was based on the premise that it would be possible to repeat the operations. More information would be available when the officer concerned had reached France and seen things at first hand. It might, for example, be possible to assemble men at several different points on the same night or to carry out embarkation on several consecutive nights: 'passengers' would then have to be transferred to another ship and the boat would have to wait during the day at a safe distance from the coast.

Extrapolating from the operation in August—September, when the much smaller *Dogfish* had embarked and brought back 48 'passengers' in addition to her crew of six, Krajewski estimated that *Seawolf* would be able to take off and bring to Gibraltar a group of 80 men or, if necessary, 100. He proposed to carry out a first and exploratory operation as soon as *Seawolf* had passed her speed trials and was ready for sea. A favourable date for the embarkation would be Saturday/Sunday, 18/19 April. This would mean sailing about the 14th.

A few days after the land-based officer was put ashore, when he had had time to make the arrangements, the boat would pick up the first batch of men and the captain of the *Seawolf* would confer on the beach with the officer to plan further moves.

Communications were the subject of separate planning but, in general terms, the W/T link between Polish military HQ in London and the south of France was supposed to be at their disposal. They would also use plain-language code, which had proved both simple and successful in the case of North Africa.

In submitting this plan, Krajewski thought it his duty to make clear that it would not be possible for the Polish mission to put their long-planned French scheme into operation unless they were assured beforehand of priority for the use of *Seawolf*. He added that they had taken charge of this vessel in July 1941 and that the Polish government had incurred expenses on her, including £1,000 on buying the new engine. This request for priority might appear superfluous, but the case of the *Vega* showed that no serious and far-reaching plan such as he outlined could be established unless the means to carry it out *in toto* were secured.

Krajewski then described how the *Vega* had arrived unexpectedly from Casablanca on 3 December, and said that she was a very suitable boat in which to start operations to the south coast of France while *Seawolf* was being got ready. He recounted how he had told SOE about her qualities and his plans for using her. As a result, the boat had been added to the Special Flotilla. SOE had then laid claim to her for an operation and Krajewski had been told he could have use of her only after their own priority operation.

Krajewski passed lightly over the unfortunate end of *Vega*, which caused a delay not of weeks but months in starting his French scheme. But he said that if he and his 'correspondents' in France had prepared an evacuation on a set date, the failure of *Vega* to arrive would have ruined the plan and exposed them to danger. He would in any case have had to postpone his arrival in France because of the delay caused by *Vega*'s use in the SOE operation. In point of fact, Krajewski had not been given even an approximate date for *Vega*'s availability and had therefore been unable to make any plans based upon her.

Krajewski said he would be very grateful if the Polish mission could have a written statement confirming that *Seawolf* would be available to them for the evacuation of Poles from southern France. He conceded that it was natural that *Seawolf* be used for other operations whenever she was not employed by the Polish mission for any length of time. He would be only too glad to help in any way by combining his operations off southern France with any similar operations planned by the authorities in Gibraltar. However, past experience told him that some sort of priority must be given to the use of the boat for one particular purpose if such a large scheme were to be put into effect. In support of his request for priority, Krajewski drew Captain Holland's attention to the potential contribution of the evacuated Polish personnel to the war effort, once they had been rescued from camps in southern France and incorporated in the Polish forces.

What reply Krajewski received to this cogently argued plea is not clear, but it must have been sufficiently emollient for him to continue with his proposed programme of operations to southern France. But by this time both SOE's Independent French Section and MI9 had emerged as potential users of any sea line of communications between Gibraltar and southern France and Captain Osborne's job as the staff officer responsible for allocating priorities fairly was clearly not going to be a sinecure.

SOE's interest in the unoccupied zone was growing. In September 1941, the month Dubourdin and Basin of their Independent French Section had been landed from *Fidelity,* Squadron Leader Ron Hockey of 138 Special Duties Squadron had parachuted to a reception party at Fonsorbes, near Toulouse, the first of many consignments of arms and explosives that were to be delivered to south-western France over the next three years.[4] Gibraltar became involved at the end of 1941, when SOE's Independent F Section urgently needed to infiltrate Captain Peter Morland Churchill into southern France with new instructions for Dubourdin and Basin. They also wanted him to find out more about an organisation named 'Carte' and its eponymous chief, who claimed to have good contacts with the Vichy general staff. Quennell had some difficulty in arranging for Churchill to be landed—or rather, to land himself by means of a Folboat canoe—from *P36,* one of the Gibraltar-based submarines, at Miramar-de-l'Esterel on 9 January 1942, when the submarine was on its way to Malta with supplies.[5] Churchill returned from the mission via Spain and set about arranging to carry out two further landings of agents for F Section from HM S/m P42 (later renamed *Unbroken*), as is described in Chapter XXVII below.

Krajewski seems himself to have undertaken yet another expedition to Oran on 22 March, presumably in *Dogfish.* It was evidently unsuccessful and, since afterwards he was preoccupied with mounting his first operation to France in the re-engined *Seawolf,* it was Buchowski who, on 25 April, carried out Operation ORKAN in *Dogfish,* embarking from the Oran area four Poles for the Polish missions and for Dunderdale. This mission, the first to North Africa recorded by Slocum's representatives on the Rock, shows that the new Coast Watching Flotilla dispensation had begun to work. Although Buchowski had been sent to Gibraltar to work for SOE, he was in this case operating for Krajewski's evacuation mission and either for the intelligence network that Slowikowski was very successfully running from Algiers, with an outpost at Oran, or for some other group linked with Dunderdale's Section of SIS. Slowikowski himself was still unaware that his 'Agence Afrique' was really working for SIS: Dunderdale had asked Colonel Gano, head of the *émigré* Polish Deuxième Bureau, to establish such an organisation for North Africa. This area was of little interest to the Poles as an intelligence target, but had considerable strategic importance for the British, though by no means easy for SIS to work in after Mers el-Kebir. French North Africa increasingly attracted the interest of Winston Churchill and of President Roosevelt: operations to it continued throughout the summer and autumn of 1942.

VI
Operations from Gibraltar to Southern France: April–June 1942

In the no-moon period of April 1942, operations from Gibraltar to the Côte d'Azur began with a bang. In the five nights between 18/19 April and 22/23 April, *Seawolf* landed Roehr at Port-Miou to organise a first evacuation, put three SOE agents ashore at La Napoule and embarked 41 Poles from Port-Vau;[1] HM S/m *P42* landed two SOE W/T operators at Antibes and embarked de Gaulle's future Commissaire a l'Interieur before proceeding to land two other SOE agents at Miramar-de-l'Esterel on the following night;[2] and Slocum's newly arrived 200-ton diesel trawler *Tarana* put Pat O'Leary and a W/T operator ashore in the Port-Vendres area.[3] So concentrated was this activity that the felucca and the submarine actually sighted each other when *P42* was underway on the surface without lights. *Seawolf* mistook her for a French naval patrol ship.

Of *Tarana*'s first operation, little is recorded. O'Leary, having escaped from Vichy police custody, had crossed the Pyrenees and made his way to Gibraltar for a meeting with Donald Darling, MI9's representative on the Rock, and Jimmy Langley, from their London headquarters. They discussed plans for mass evacuations of Allied evaders and escapers by sea from southern France. O'Leary and a W/T operator then took passage back to France in *Tarana,* which was commanded by Lt E.B.Clarke, RNR, whom Krajewski found 'a very pleasant and cheery fellow'.

Peter Churchill, having also returned from his first mission, embarked with four SOE agents on *P42,* under command of Lt Alastair Mars, RN.[4] He landed the two W/T operators, who were to work for 'Carte', by folboat at the Pointe-de-l'Ilet, just outside the ancient walls of the city of Antibes, and walked with them into the town to show them the way to their safe house, the home of a Dr Levy. Emmanuel d'Astier de la Vigerie, founder and head of 'Libération-Sud', was staying there and, when Churchill arrived, decided on the spur of the moment to take advantage of the opportunity to leave France and return with him to the waiting submarine.

On the following night, Churchill landed the other two agents at Miramar-de-l'Esterel, which had been his own disembarkation point in January. They were Vic Gerson, the organiser of Leslie Humphreys's remarkably efficient 'Vic' landline, who on an earlier mission to France had recruited as his deputy in the Paris area Jacques Mitterrand, a future general of the French air force and brother of François. His second passenger that night was Marcel Clech, the erstwhile Breton sailor and taxi-driver, who had survived 17 unsuccessful attempts to land him by sea in Brittany, 16 of them organised by Slocum. He had meanwhile trained as a W/T operator.[5]

The story of Operation JASMINE, Krajewski's first voyage to France in *Seawolf* is best told in his own words:

REPORT OF THE TWELFTH EVACUATION MISSION
(14–27 April 1942)[6]

1) *READINESS OF THE FELUCCA 'SEAWOLF'.* Once the new engine for the evacuation felucca had arrived and in particular been unloaded from the ship that brought it (but not until 1 April, in spite of many appeals from various quarters), the firm hurried to finish off the fitting and adjustment, although this did not prevent them from failing to keep their word over the deadline.

Eventually, however, the *Seawolf* was handed over to 'the company' on 10 April, despite a whole number of outstanding small jobs that I did not want the firm to do, since this would have involved further delay, or that needed by their nature to be carried out by specialists from HMS *Maidstone*.

We had very little time to get the felucca into seaworthy condition, since we were constrained both by the date agreed with Midshipman Chciuk at Cassis—18 April (we would have to raise anchor at least five days earlier)—and also by the approaching period of the new moon. Any slippage of the programme would mean postponing the long-awaited pioneering operation for almost a month.

As a result, the crew and I had barely three days to take charge of a completely bare felucca, equip it, test it and prepare it for a long voyage.

2) *PLAN OF OPERATION.* Lt Roehr[7] had arranged by letter with Midshipman Chciuk that he would meet him 'on a very important matter' in Cassis on 19 April. He was to brief him on current conditions in France and also smooth contacts with the local leaders.

My intention was to put Lt Roehr ashore at the same time so as to have someone permanently in France who is familiar with the techniques employed when evacuating by sea in our situation and with our resources, and to act as a personal link with the local leaders in France.

In order not to return empty-handed after a journey of 1,500 sea miles, Lt Roehr was to spend a few days collecting together a group of people for evacuation.

The authorities here asked me to put ashore three agents in the region of Antibes (near Cannes)—which readily fitted in with my operation, since I foresaw several days' wait in any case—so I agreed. I calculated that, as long as it did not clash with our evacuations, it would be to our advantage in that it would give me stronger grounds to put forward our requirements if the need for technical help arose.

3) THE RAISING OF THE ANCHOR took place on 14 April at 0500 hrs. Apart from the crew, the three above-mentioned 'passengers' were also taken on board. The composition of the crew apart from myself was: Mate Gorzelok, Leading Seaman Stanislawski (radio and deck-hand), Leading Seaman (Reserve) Chwastek (deck-hand), Petty Officer Siembieda (1st mechanic) and Seaman Kurzawa (greaser). Gorzelok had joined the crew on a permanent basis in place of Buchowski, which meant that none of my lads was familiar with the work of a deck-hand to anywhere near a satisfactory degree. I exchanged Seaman Schlauberg from my crew (cook) for Mate Gorzelok (deck-hand and also, of necessity, cook) in order to have someone who could help in case the engine broke down or if, at any other critical moment, it proved necessary to use the sails.

The journey began in a very strong wind (Force 4–5) but luckily it was a fair wind for us, which meant that I could exercise the crew in sail manoeuvres. In addition it meant a large saving in fuel and gave me experience in the art—totally new, and unknown to us—of lateen sailing. The results achieved were very interesting: under sails alone, our speed by the Walker log and in the prevailing wind conditions was 7. 1 knots. Our speed when powered by our 88h.p. diesel engine under the same conditions was not much greater—8.5 knots. Linking both forms of traction (engine +sails) produced little more than 8.9 knots, which is the maximum speed attainable on average by a hull of this length, and thus to be expected. By using the sails and half power, we could reduce our consumption of fuel while at the same time maintaining a speed of around 7–8 knots in the strong wind.

14 and 15 April were spent in making finishing touches and modifications to the vessel, since new needs arise with new experience. On 15 April we had one of those typical incidents that attests to the manner in which tasks at Gibraltar are carried out by Spanish workmen. We discovered a fire in the galley—luckily still at an early stage—the cause being an absence of asbestos between the coal stove and the wooden bulkhead. As a result, one of the spars had been charred and in none too favourable conditions we had to reinstall the stove provisionally with the means at our disposal.

From the very outset curious happenings began to occur with respect to the felucca's position. My instinct was to keep out of sight of land, since we had information that the Spaniards were observing every movement at sea by means of their coastguard network and reporting to the Germans. The only means I had of checking my dead reckoning (Walker log) were a sextant (which had come from a German ship) and a chronometer (brought from Oran, where a ship's officer, in gratitude for our having evacuated him to Gibraltar, had removed it from a requisitioned Yugoslav ship without the knowledge of the French). Our position according to the stars repeatedly showed large discrepancies from our dead reckoning, unexplained by any currents that we were aware of. After a few days, when I was sure that I had recovered my old skills and that the discrepancies were not attributable to my faulty calculations, I realised that the real deviation of the compass was very different from what I had been told by the flotilla navigator– by more than 10° (!). The difference on 15 April amounted to 35 miles, as was confirmed by the appearance of the African coast to starboard. The situation was very worrying since we were only at the beginning of our journey and it was going to be very difficult, without a reliable means of reckoning our position, to take on such delicate operations as approaching unfamiliar coastlines, keeping rendezvous, etc. I decided therefore to make a deviation table myself from the azimuth of the setting sun; however, for this I needed very good weather and a cloudless sunset.

At noon on the 16th I passed between the islands of Ibiza and Majorca. That evening a storm blew up, one of the heaviest of that season; worse to tell, this time it was against us. Because of the opposing swell, our speed was much reduced and a further reduction seemed inevitable to avoid damage to the hull (our average speed throughout the night was only 3.5 knots). A number of the crew were sick, which, together with the discovery of various defects in the new installations (e.g. a fault in the bilge pump, which sucked water into the boat rather than out of it), made it a rather unpleasant period for us.

On the 17th, the weather improved somewhat (speed 6.1 knots) and on the last day of our outward journey, arriving at the French coast, we encountered sunny weather. Behind us we had the best possible test of the excellent strength and endurance of our felucca, a successful sailing trial and a perfect idea of what still needed to be repaired on our vessel.

Astronomical observations continued to show a deviation of 18° (!) from our course. Fortunately I managed to catch sight of the sun or stars each day and in that way check the faults in our reckoning.

On 18 April we painted the French colours on our hull, as well as a registration number, and we carried out normal preparations for anchoring and putting someone ashore: lines, anchors, life-raft, etc. In the process the new crew had their first opportunity to familiarise themselves with the special techniques needed in these particular operations.

4) *PUTTING LT ROEHR ASHORE.* That same evening we saw the high coastline of the Marseilles region. Having waited until it grew dark, I moved in the direction of the Planier lighthouse, and then towards the little bay at Cassis. After midnight I entered the Port-Miou inlet, one of those known for their picturesque qualities as calanques, and dropped anchor. Lt Roehr was put ashore, having agreed to return in two hours' time with Chciuk. At 0200 hrs we did in fact make out the agreed signals, and then brought both of them off to the felucca, where we discussed the situation and our immediate plans.

The result was to fix a rendezvous for the night of 22/23 April—in four days' time —in En-Vau, the neighbouring *calanque*. Port-Miou had appeared busy of late; among other things, in a shack near the place where we had disembarked Lt Roehr a lamp was still burning, even at that late hour. In any case, while we were anchoring at a distance of around 300 m. from it, some man came to the door who appeared to have noticed the felucca. The number of people I asked for was 60.

At 0400 hrs I was already clear of the *calanque,* having landed both Lt Roehr and Midshipman Chciuk. I set a course for the east with the aim of putting the agents ashore. The distance to be covered was about 120 nautical miles.

5) *THE MEETING WITH THE 'MTB'.* The course I set for Antibes, where I was to drop the agents, was an average of 20 miles from the shore. On the evening of the 19th, being already to the south of the headland, I set a course for land, for the La-Garoupe lighthouse, a powerful light which we ought to have seen from a distance of 15 miles in spite of the poor visibility.

Here I made out a row of lights which seemed to me to be half-way between me and my objective, i.e. some five miles from the shore. Suspecting that it was a convoy, I began to manoeuvre in order to discover the direction in which they were travelling, when suddenly I saw, no more than about 1,500–2,000 metres in front of me, the outline of a small warship, the shape of the French *chasseurs de sousmarins* —but UNLIT. (French military vessels and merchant ships always carry lights.) I immediately turned about and took an opposite course, increasing speed to our maximum (8.7 knots in a calm sea), since he might equally have detected me under these conditions. I decided to give up for that night, assuming that the convoy would pass and that, since I had a few days in hand during which I had to wait for *my* operation to come to fruition, there was no hurry to put the agents ashore.

After waiting hove-to in a position some 50 miles south-east of Antibes from 0700 hrs until 1530 hrs (on 20 April), I once again set a course for Antibes.

At around 2100 hrs that day, I was some 20 miles S-E of Cap d'Antibes, or at the edge of territorial waters according to current French claims. *Once again* I had seen the line of lights and, mindful of this and of the previous night's encounter with the unlit patrol boat, I called the agents to a conference. In the end they thought that it would be better to take them back to Gibraltar rather than risk trying to penetrate the line of patrols, which—as I emphasized—was a wholly unusual phenomenon in French waters and was particularly dangerous because of the presence of unlit vessels, which might be noticed too late. I postponed a decision until the following day and withdrew to our former position offshore.

6) *PUTTING THE AGENTS ASHORE.* On the morning of the 21st I worked out a completely different plan for putting the agents ashore: namely, slipping along as close as possible to the shore, on the assumption that the line of patrols was stationed far out at sea (as our experience seemed to bear out), and that there was no way of saturating the coastal stretch with patrols too. Being still uncertain of my degree of deviation, I based the whole plan of our route on the known position of the Camarat lighthouse to the east of Toulon, at which I had to arrive as early as possible (there was little time to make my way from it to Antibes), but security considerations permitted this only at dusk.

On the way—making use of a calm and clear sunset—I determined the degree of error for all the basic courses we needed—and this completely confirmed my guesses as to the degree of deviation. Our deviation amounted to a maximum not of 5°, but of 10°. This was further confirmed by our landfall that evening, when the masts of the French naval radio station on Porquerolles in the Hyères Islands near Toulon appeared on our course, instead of the Camarat lighthouse.

The journey to the La-Napoule bay passed off without any incident: a solitary ship was all we saw. At 0115 hrs I entered the bay, where, because there was so little time left before dawn, the agents had agreed to disembark.

The rubber boat was put into the water and, after we had identified a suitable point on the generally very steep shoreline, the passengers were dropped off with their luggage. The landing-place turned out to be none too favourable, being not far from some huts in which, despite the lateness of the hour, we discerned some movement, no doubt because of the fierce barking of a dog. This sound, combined with the song of a nightingale in a nearby wood, created a strange and indescribable impression. What is more, our dinghy missed a passing fishing craft under oars by no more than a whisker. The craft must have been returning from a fishing trip and passed us at a distance of 50 metres, having, without doubt, seen the felucca.

At 0300 hrs I weighed anchor and set a course away from the shore. Then at a distance of some 20 miles from the coast, we set out for Marseilles, where a party of people was to be picked up the next night at a spot that was now familiar to me.

7) *EMBARKATION OF THE FIRST GROUP OF POLES FROM FRANCE.* On 22 April at 2330 hrs—as we had agreed with Lt Roehr—I was at the entrance to the Port-Vau calanque and gave the agreed signal. We immediately received a reply coming from the end of that rocky cleft in the shoreline, which was some 900m long and on average some 40m wide. The water, in these clefts is commonly deep in that region, which meant that I could go in almost to the very end. Accompanied by an oarsman (Gorzelok) I went ashore, where Lt Roehr was already waiting for me with three representatives of the Marseilles evacuation post and 41 other people. It was explained that the party numbered fewer that the 60 expected because of local difficulties. Given the short time available to organise collection, this did not surprise me at all. After discussing the local situation we went on to talk about plans for our next embarkation operation, which, as I emphasised, ought to involve a larger group of people—60, if the felucca *Seawolf* alone was at our disposal, and this figure could be increased by 100 if it proved possible to secure the 'special operations' vessel I was counting on from our flotilla. Marseilles was to send a signal when they were ready to dispatch the next party (I asked for a date around 9 May) and I had to confirm whether there would be the extra vessel or not. Lt Roehr was to remain in France.

The embarkation process continued during our conference. At 0100 I was already back on the felucca and, after turning about in that narrow *calanque* so that I had my bow facing seawards, I made my exit. Immediately after leaving, we encountered a ship which, to judge by its course, could only have been a patrol boat. Owing to the local conditions it was difficult to give him the slip, but eventually we managed to escape undetected.

8) The return journey passed without any noteworthy events. At noon on the first day, we sighted an aircraft flying from Marseilles. A second followed a few hours later. Also two seaplanes flew low over us on the 22nd when we were passing Toulon at a distance of 30 miles, but at no time did they seem to pay any particular attention to us: indeed this was the very reason I relied on a fishing vessel (felucca) for the evacuations.

The weather in general was not too good and, since most of the people had to remain on deck because of the lack of space below (others because of seasickness), conditions for them were very arduous. Nevertheless they were all in good spirits and after a few days it was evident they were also in good appetite, since, leaving aside other considerations, all of them had eaten very little meat or fat lately in France.

On 27 April at 0830 hrs, 13 days after we had originally weighed anchor at the start of our mission, we entered the port of Gibraltar.

9) *RADIO CONTACT* turned out to be very unsatisfactory. On the day before our departure I was given a radio set (pack set) which did not work because it was lacking a valve. This became evident during tests before we put to sea. I was promised that they would drop a valve to me by aircraft en route but the aircraft could not find us owing to the bad weather, and in any case the set was faulty in other respects. Because of this, I transmitted signals during the operation (after having completed particular tasks and after encountering the convoy) on a Polish-type set received from Commander Stoklas, but these, as it later transpired, were too weak and failed to be heard at all from that distance.

I was promised a set in better condition and better radio communications for future operations. Indeed, the receiver on my Polish set had broken down a long time before, but no-one here at Gibraltar was capable of repairing it, therefore we did not even attempt to receive signals.

10) *THE 'MTB' TURNED OUT TO BE…A SUBMARINE ON A SPECIAL OPERATION.* This was perhaps the most sensational aspect of this whole operation. When I gave the flotilla commander a report on the operation, the incident with the 'MTB' and the patrols, he informed me that at the time in question a submarine from our local flotilla was carrying out an operation, and they were due to return in a few days. When the submarine's commander did get back and we exchanged information, it turned out that, on the same day and more or less at the same time, he had sighted a mysterious fishing boat, and what had struck him was that it was NOT BEARING LIGHTS, and that suddenly, as if having sighted him, it had turned about and apparently taken flight…

'Perhaps I should have given chase and attempted to disable her, in order to prevent her betraying my presence', said the operational commander, 'but I was in a hurry myself, since I too had the task of putting agents ashore in that area.'

As it turned out, I had not been informed that one of our submarines was operating there, because it was supposed to have carried out its task *two days before* my operation, and the prospect of delay had not occurred to anyone. As it happened, the storm I encountered near Barcelona on the way to Marseilles had delayed the submarine by a whole 48 hours.

What was also interesting about this episode was that both our positions were imprecise: his was too close to the shore (3 miles) and, in addition, too far north, while mine was too far out (15 miles and, on the second day, 20 miles) because of the deviation error. I had thus assumed that the lights spotted 'not far off' belonged to ships, when in fact they were lights positioned on the high slopes of the shore, as is common in this region. I was all the more certain that they were not shore lights because the La-Garoupe lighthouse was not visible, and normally it would have been unmissable: on each occasion visibility was 25 miles. THE LIGHTS HOWEVER HAD APPARENTLY BEEN EXTINGUISHED NEAR THE ITALIAN FRONTIER and the last working lighthouse in this direction is the Camarat lighthouse near the Hyères Islands.

I requested my flotilla commander to inform me in future if any such operations were planned for the region in which I was engaged, and he agreed unreservedly, adding that he had not allowed for the possibility of such a delay on the part of the submarine.

(signed)
M.Krajewski (Captain)
Gibraltar, 25 May 1942

This episode—in which P42 and *Seawolf* sighted each other proceeding without navigation lights in suspicious circumstances near their respective operational objectives, and, thinking the other to be hostile, took evading action—delayed the landings Krajewski was due to carry out, but Mars, the submarine captain, made his way inshore, and Churchill landed his two passengers at Antibes in the early hours of 20 April, as described above. It is the only recorded case of its kind in four years of clandestine operations on French coasts during the Second World War. Ironically enough, this was the very danger that Slocum had invoked as part of his case for letting NID (C) take over the running of such operations in the western Mediterranean, yet it happened just after the new coordinating arrangements he had devised were in place, rather than under the previous free-for-all that he had deplored.

This was the beginning of one of the most intensive and successful phases of clandestine sea-transport operations to wartime France. Marian Krajewski and his colleague Jan Buchowski, backed by the resources of Slocum's 'private navy', were to be its star performers, but it must be remembered that the coast to which they worked was in Vichy France, rather than in German hands. Nevertheless, the distances covered, the overcrowding of the feluccas and the endurance demanded far exceeded anything experienced in operations from the United Kingdom base to the west and north coasts of France.

In the May no-moon period, Krajewski went back to the Côte d'Azur in *Seawolf,* this time accompanied by *Tarana*—an arrangement Krajewski had contemplated using during his operations to Morocco, but which had proved possible only once because of the unreliable physical condition of the back-up ship. His account of Operation MIMOSA was as follows:

> *REPORT FROM THE THIRTEENTH EVACUATION MISSION* (to France, from 5 to 21 May, 1942)[7]
>
> 1) *BACKGROUND AND PLAN OF THE OPERATION.* As I informed you in my report of the 12th mission, I came to an agreement with Lt Roehr, during our meeting at Calanque-en-Vau (near Cassis), that a second mission would take place at the beginning of May. They were to supply either 60 people if I was able to secure *Seawolf* alone or at least twice that number if I managed to obtain the use of one of the back-up ships. Our means of communication was to be radio via London, and Marseilles was to indicate if the situation permitted an operation; by way of reply, I was to let them know whether I had a back-up ship at my disposal.
>
> Meanwhile I had made clear during our conference that I anticipated spending a week in port on minor modifications, which our first expedition in the new *Seawolf* had shown to be necessary.
>
> France, however, did not keep to the letter of our Cassis agreement, since on the evening of 4 May I received an urgent telegram from London requiring my presence at the old meeting point to pick up 60 people during the night of 10/11 May. In other words I HAD LESS THAN A DAY IN WHICH TO GET READY AND SET OUT. Of course, I was presented with a *fait accompli* in terms of the number of people. I aimed, and still aim, to take as many people as possible during such missions, which are long—at least 2,000 miles—and exhausting because of the poor standard of accommodation. Indeed, I had been promised the additional ship and, if the Marseilles outpost had been true to their word and had had the courage to organise a larger group of people, we would have been able to take at least twice as many passengers.
>
> As luck would have it, the authorities here gave me the promised vessel anyway, because they asked me to put a further three agents ashore in southern France and they did not want them to be put at risk during the embarkation. Consequently they agreed to my plan to embark our people, take them to the Spanish-French frontier (one day's sailing) and there transfer them to the stand-by vessel (waiting 30 miles out at sea), collecting the agents at the same time. Indeed, I was going to suggest to

the local leaders in France that within a few days they provide me with an additional party of people, for whom I would wait at sea after putting the agents ashore: I would then return with them direct to Gibraltar. The plan was not particularly convenient since it prolonged an already lengthy voyage and exhausted a crew who, after the last two-week mission, had not had the rest in port they deserved, since there was so much work to be done in altering and modifying the boat. I was forced into it however by the action of the Marseilles leadership.

2) *CABLE FROM MAJOR A.CHOJNACKI.* Just as we were making our way back to port after the previous (12th) evacuation mission, I received a cable from the Marseilles post, which altered the background to the mission and made our decision more difficult. The last sentence of this cable stated that the 'French police know about the evacuations and may be hunting him [Krajewski]', in the light of which the author 'requested help'.

What kind of help Major Chojnacki envisaged I have no way of knowing: indeed, I was already in the open sea after taking people on board and was due any moment to leave the danger region. What is more, this is a distance that requires a few days' sailing even for a destroyer. Even if they had sent a warship it would only have met me somewhere near the Balearic Islands. The result was just what I had been trying my best to avoid—to cause the naval authorities here problems by continual requests for help in the form of MLs, aircraft, etc (which in any case had happened enough times in cases of real emergency, such as for example on the little *Dogfish* with its museum-piece engine). The illogicality or irrationality of the telegram was pointed out by the Admiral himself when he called me for a report of the operation ('We didn't really know in what way we could help you', our great friend declared).

The arrival of this telegram had a direct influence on the operation, because everybody here began to fear that the whole evacuation movement from France was, if not completely buried, at least rendered impossible for a period. We could not understand why a telegram suddenly requested us to come and pick up 60 people 'at the former place'. (Afterwards I understood the situation when one of the men evacuated during the previous mission, asked confidentially how he would explain the means by which the police could have discovered the operation, said, 'It is possible that Major Chojnacki sent that telegram just in case, because he is...very careful...')

3) We put to sea almost exactly 24 hrs after we received the telegram, which is never advisable because it imposes such haste on the last-minute preparations required for these special operations—things that one can do only when one knows the relevant conditions and the number of people (e.g. for supplies, since the space on a 20-ton felucca is limited and housekeeping must be very economical).

Crew: apart from myself—Petty Officer Siembieda (1st mechanic), Mate Tarnawski (2nd mechanic, newly sent), Seaman Kurzawa (greaser), Mate Zimny (helmsman, newly sent), Leading Seaman (of the Reserve) Chwastek (deck-hand, helmsman),

Leading Seaman Stanislawski (radio operator, helm) and Mate Gorzelok as cook and 'handyman'.

So we weighed anchor on 5 May at 2220 hrs—unfortunately in a strong storm, from the east. The first two days were a night mare, since the majority of the crew (not difficult to reach a majority among seven people!) fell sick. The worst affected however was the mate, Zimny, who, ironically, had been sent to me as chief and mainstay of the deck crew and my next in command. He became so terribly sick that he developed a temperature. Not only was he unable to steer—which others did despite being ill themselves—but I began to be concerned about him. He did not return to health and thus at the first opportunity I transferred him to the other ship, so that he did not continue to occupy a bunk (see below).

This weather lasted until 9 May when we were north of the Balearics. Unfortunately, the compass deviation had apparently again been wrongly plotted by the flotilla navigator, an error that had already convinced me of his incompetence. Luckily the conditions permitted astronomical observations almost every day, and usually I took three, sometimes more. We have an excellent chronometer and sextant too.

A new item on this voyage was the powerful radio receiver (of the British army officers' mess type), so that we had the opportunity not only to check our watches daily but also to hear the news bulletins and thus learn about current political events.

On 9 May, we painted the French colours and a registration number on the ship's side as usual (they had been painted over on our way back to Gibraltar after the previous mission). Then a Spanish aircraft flew over us, which, to judge by its course, was the communication flight between Valencia and Italy.

4) *EMBARKATION OF THE FIRST GROUP (31).* On the night of 10 May we were, in changeable weather conditions, at the entrance to Cassis Bay, where I began to look around for the familiar *calanque* (En-Vau). When we had found it and when the agreed light answered our signals, I entered and steered the felucca to the end of the calanque, before going ashore with the mate Gorzelok (0000 hrs on 11 May).

Once ashore we found Lt Roehr already waiting with 31 people. The embarkation began, while I had talks with Roehr and Cavalry Captain Iwaszkiewicz.

It turned out that 30 people had not turned up, as a result of local difficulties, I was told. Whatever the reason, this throws doubt on whether an operation to embark so few people is worthwhile, and not only from the strictly 'commercial' point of view: the risk to the 11 people involved in the operation and the enormous efforts of the crew must also be taken into account. Nor was the outlook in France much happier for clandestine evacuation by sea, according to a report by Lt Roehr. As a result, he anticipated being forced to leave with that same party. My plan, which depended on having someone in France who had experience of sea evacuations, lay in ruins.

All the more determined, in the light of the small party prepared for me, not to return to Gibraltar after putting the agents ashore, I asked Captain Iwaszkiewicz to have the next party ready for me in a few days' time. We decided to make it the night of 16/17 May and to choose a completely new location, namely by the Faraman lighthouse (at the mouth of the Rhône).

At 0115 we weighed anchor and set a course for the rendezvous with the ship.

5) TRANSFER OF THE PASSENGERS. The meeting with my colleague from the special flotilla had a particular significance. Since it was taking place at a considerable distance from the shore, it was a delicate operation not only from the point of view of the means of carrying out the transfer (which depended on the weather) but also in that it was to be something of a test of navigation. If we failed to meet, it would of course have been said that the *Seawolf* was in the wrong position. I had the feeling during our briefing that this test greatly intrigued everybody who was there; whether or not we succeeded in this mission might have a greater impact on our chances of obtaining this ship in future than at first appeared. So it was with the greatest care and effort that I took astronomical sights (luckily the sun, which that day had shown great reluctance to appear, came out from behind the clouds). The compass deviation, even after it had been defined, required repeated checking on a westerly course, because of the difficult conditions off Toulon under which I had swung the ship's compass.

It turned out that these astronomical observations rescued the situation for us, or at least saved us several hours' time and our reputation. After obtaining one position line and a noon latitude sight I discovered that I was 14 miles to the south-east of our meeting point (1255 hrs). I still had two hours before our rendezvous, so our honour was saved when, at 1425 precisely, we caught sight of the ship also steaming from the south. (In fact, rather more than saved, because in the Flotilla they talk about the *Seawolf* being accurate to the nearest mile, which makes pleasant hearing to Polish ears: our [British] hosts regard themselves as mariners without peer.)

The transfer took place without incident, other than an aircraft alert, during which the ship's captain asked me if I would hold away from his side while it lasted. It turned out—and the agents we took on board confirm this—that the ship's captain was a little edgy, after having apparently been tracked by aircraft earlier. Truth to tell, however, we could not make out the aircraft and after a further five minutes we came alongside again and completed the operation. Together with the 31 passengers I transferred the mate, Zimny, not only because he had requested it, but because I had come to the conclusion that he was no use at all to me at sea and was only taking up a bunk. We also transferred Lt Roehr but I kept behind Lt Biczysko in case the embarkation of the next party in a week's time became complicated and it was necessary to put someone ashore, which in fact proved to be the case.

All in all therefore the trans-shipment did not take more than ten minutes (the weather helped), after which the ship set course back to Gibraltar, where it arrived three days later; I however, turned to the east again, towards the Antibes region, where I had to put the agents ashore.

6) *PUTTING THE AGENTS ASHORE...AND OTHER ADVENTURES.* En route to the pinpoint there were no noteworthy events. We met only two steamers, which I always try to avoid in such a way as not to draw attention and not to let them get a close look at us. At present one does not see any fishermen along the French coast—mainly through lack of fuel—except for those in rowing boats and these are no more than a kilometre from the shore, and usually close to some centre of settlement; this sad inactivity holds sway as a symptom of the war in these doubtless once busy waters.

At sunset (2005 hrs) Camarat—the last lighthouse lit to the east of Toulon—was visible. From there I started to move along level with the shore, at a distance, to start with, of about 5km Visibility however grew worse. After a few hours I was not even sure of my own position since even the bearings I had taken from the lighthouse, some 20 miles distant from the disembarkation point, were out because of the degree of compass error, which again amounted to 10°. At 2320 hrs on 12 May I arrived, or thought I did, at the spot and ordered the log line to be hauled aboard, since we would shortly have to undertake manoeuvres in a small bay.

However, I soon began to have doubts about whether it was the right bay. I had never been in it myself before and there were certain indications that the next bay might be the one; we could see it, apparently not far off.

Unfortunately, after moving in that direction for an hour, I realised that I still had a long journey before me, and that I had probably passed the right spot. In order to recognise the place, however, I had to travel further on.

At 0130 hrs (on 13 May) we entered a bay, which I was already almost certain was not the right one. Before putting the agents ashore in the dinghy, I therefore told them frankly that the location was uncertain and asked whether it made any difference to them if it was e.g. Villefranche. Seeing their hesitation, I added that we had enough time to put the operation off until the following day, since we no longer had enough time to continue that night and dawn comes at about 0430 hrs. As a result, we exited the bay, becoming aware for the first time of the critical nature of our situation, since at the narrow entrance of the bay a number of fishermen were attempting to catch fish by dazzling them, which meant illuminating everything around them and creating almost an enclosure of spotlights.

At 0700 hrs we were again, as during the previous voyage, hove-to some 40 miles to the south-west of the Cannes region, half-way between Corsica and France.

Having thoroughly considered the events of the previous night, I had no doubts at all that the spot in which I had eventually ended up was the Anse-de-Canton Bay, in other words... MONACO, and I had anchored just alongside the marine observatory. The fact that I had been a significant distance from the frontier (around 6 miles, or an hour's sailing even for me) and 15 miles from the spot I was aiming for was evidence that the Italian armistice commission's request for the French authorities to switch off the lighthouses in the frontier region had not been a wasted gesture.

After fixing my position during the day and working out a course, I moved off again (1230 hrs) in the direction of the Camarat lighthouse.

At 2320 hrs we were already in the right bay (i.e. Antibes), where we again had to pass by the line of fishermen. Under normal conditions they must have seen me, but I assume that with this kind of fishing (using lights to dazzle the fish) they themselves must be dazzled to a certain degree.

At 2350 hrs the disembarkation was completed, we then hoisted the dinghy back on board and set a course that would distance us from the shore.

After waiting a further 24 hours, during which I established the degree of compass error (again very large and, on westerly courses, 12° not 0°, as the flotilla navigator had entered on the deviation table), I set a course to the west, towards the Marseilles region.

7) *THE CHASE.* The new embarkation point was some 30 miles west of Marseilles at the mouth of the River Rhône, near the Faraman lighthouse. My intention was to approach the shore in daylight and reconnoitre, since the shoreline in that area is flat and very monotonous.

At around 1530 hrs, when we were some 18 miles south of the mouth of the Rhône and 25 miles to the south-west of Marseilles, I made out a small steamer on the horizon, on our port side. I was following a course of 300°. In order not to approach too close and fearing that it might be a patrol boat, I changed course to starboard to 320° (I could not turn too far since I was in any case heading in the direction of land). The closer the boat approached, the more it resembled a patrol boat or a small boat of the trawler type converted into a small trading vessel, displacement around 200 tons.

He did not seem to be paying any attention to me for the moment but I watched him closely through my binoculars so as not to be caught out. When, however, he was level with me ('abeam') he suddenly altered *course towards me* and raised steam, as I concluded from the increased volume of smoke (coal-fired boiler) that he emitted, a characteristic effect of throwing more coal into the furnace. Just before this happened, a second patrol boat appeared, similar to the first, and began to behave in a similar manner. Having no longer any doubts as to their identity, I increased our speed to 'maximum', which produced (with the dinghy on the tow-line) 8.7 knots, as measured with my stopwatch. After a short while the patrol boats changed to a course that was parallel with mine (having reversed through 180° from their previous course), evidently realising that their route would be lengthened if they went *courbe de chien,* i.e. bow pointed towards me, instead of in front of me.

The situation was not at all pleasant, since it was only reasonable to expect that they had a speed advantage o ver me, and, furthermore, there were still more than five hours (!) to go until darkness, or rather until sunset. Worse, because of the proximity of the shore, the *Seawolf* would meanwhile have to change course *in their direction.* Accordingly I ordered that all our arms be prepared (pistols, machine-pistol, grenades) as well as radio codes, etc. and the detailed maps of the French coast—everything to be loaded into one bag to be sunk on my order. I checked too that the crew remembered my instructions on how to conduct themselves if we were taken prisoner.

In the midst of this predicament, yet another patrol boat appeared, this time off the starboard bow, and sailed as though intending to cut me off. Certain that they would get us this time ('He who is to hang will not drown,' one of the crew called out jokingly at this point), I gradually changed course to 250° (at 1635 hrs). I now had pursuers abeam on both sides, the first group having fallen back a little, and the race continued. The course this time was more favourable since it led to the open sea and almost to the French—Spanish border.

After an hour I realised to my considerable surprise, and indeed contentment, that they were evidently dropping behind us. In fact, at 1800 hrs, in order not to move too far away and make myself late for the rendezvous—since leaving people until daylight would have been a catastrophe—I stopped the engine. Half an hour later, I set a course of 340°, with the aim of closing in to the coast. When I saw a patrol boat again (1915 hrs), I again took a course of 250°: I already felt more certain of the situation, since from the point of view of speed I had now tested them, and the sun would set in a little more than an hour.

At 2000 hrs we set a course for the Beauduc lighthouse, not far from Faraman.

8) *THE ACCIDENTAL DISCOVERY OF PEOPLE FOR EMBARKATION.* The new pinpoint appeared unsuitable from the very moment we approached it; it was certainly a beach, but with a very shallow level of descent, so that even the *Seawolf* (draught 1.8m), had to be anchored some 600m away. Indeed, if it had not been for the very calm sea that night, there could have been no thought of bringing people on board by the dinghy, nor—because of the distance—by the technique used during the African evacuations in the 'Atlantic breakers', i.e. with the life-raft on a line.

What was worse, however, was that *no-one* replied to our pre-arranged signals (2330 hrs). Because of this I sent Lt Biczysko ashore in the rubber dinghy, since he knew this region well, and I even requested him, if need be, to make his way to the Polish 'work brigade' based some 7km away, from which our evacuation party was, at least partly, to be recruited. Also—most important—Capt Iwaszkiewicz, with whom I had arranged a meeting, came from this detail.

We received the agreed signal unexpectedly early: the dinghy was sent out and brought back (0115 hrs) ten people. Lt Biczysko explained the mystery: it seemed that the people had been waiting two kilometres away and on seeing our signal had thought it was a lighthouse… (This is why I made efforts to have someone in France who is familiar with our procedures.)

Happily everything ended well and at 0205 hrs we weighed anchor and set a course for the Balearic Islands.

Our return did not pass off without one more encounter with the patrol boats. At dawn, directly ahead of us, and at the exact edge of the 20-mile territorial waters, I saw the lights of a ship. I went past him by making a turn to starboard of 50° (0440 hrs) but he barely remained on the port beam and I had returned to our old course when a second boat appeared, again to starboard (0515 hrs). Since it was already light, I had no doubts whatsoever that this was a patrol boat similar to the one we had seen the day before, if not the very same one. On this occasion, however, they showed no inclination to intervene, possibly because at that time almost everybody on board was asleep (they were moving very slowly). Thus at 0655 hrs, having a clear horizon in every direction, we were able to return to our old course.

At 1030 hrs excellent visibility allowed us to sight the high cliffs of the Spanish-French frontier region. The weather was very good for almost the entire voyage, which was especially useful in view of our 36 passengers, most of whom had to spend the journey on deck in any case.

On 19 May a favourable wind even enabled us to use our sails in order to spare the engine, and of course to economise on fuel.

On 21 May at 0100 hrs we entered the port of Gibraltar, having covered our route in the record time of four days, instead of the usual five.

9) *RADIO COMMUNICATIONS* were not at all satisfactory on this occasion either. None of our signals was received when we transmitted from the French coast (the transmitter was of the British 'Pack-set' type, strength 40 watts).

Our signals were first picked up when we had reached Barcelona and then with a strength level of only '1' (one), in other words very faintly. We too heard them at the same strength, since, as it turns out, that organisation, has no transmitter on shore that is any stronger than ours (40 watts).

Indeed, proper communication was not established until we were south of the Balearic Islands. Near Barcelona we could hear only intermittently.

The reasons most probably lie both on the technical and the personnel side. My radio operator maintains that the people on land 'do not apply themselves' to getting hold of signals that are sent on the short wave by weak transmitters; if so, they will certainly miss ours, which are always in that category. This is an unacceptable state of affairs.

Indeed, the transmitter on land ought to be more powerful. I know that a stronger one is to be installed soon.

It is very likely too that the direction is very difficult because of geography, specifically because of the line of very high mountains on the track (through Spain). I know that from the Iberian peninsula there are greater difficulties in making contact on short wave with southern France than with London.

In the light of all this, it seems to me desirable in future operations of this type (southern France) to employ a stronger radio receiver of at least 50 watts, if not 100 watts. Even short-wave amateurs used this strength before the war...

10) *DISTINCTIONS.* Lt Biczysko distinguished himself during the operation, not only by volunteering to go ashore when the situation became complicated (which he settled most effectively) but also by acting almost as a member of the crew, as a result of which it was possible to use the crew for more specialised tasks.

Also worthy of note for his courageous and efficient execution of all landing tasks, associated as they are with the risk of arrest—Ernest Gorzelok.

Leading Seaman Chwastek demonstrated that he is currently the mainstay of my reduced deck crew.

M.Krajewski
(Naval) Captain
Gibraltar, 27 May 1942

On 17 May Lt Jankanty Roehr submitted a written report to Krajewski on his mission to France.[8] It throws interesting light on the prevailing conditions and the problems with which he had had to contend.

In preparation for his mission, he had written on 2 March to Commander Stoklas in London via British naval channels, forwarding samples of the identity documents that he would need. Stoklas replied by telegram, received on 25 March, that the matter was in hand but it would take between one and three weeks to produce them.

On 17 March, Roehr had written to Midshipman Chciuk in France indicating, in terms that only Chciuk would understand, the place and date of a meeting between them. The date proposed was 18 April or one of the immediately following days. Roehr was working on the assumption that his identity documents would arrive in Gibraltar by 14 April, the date on which the felucca would have to sail. Allowing time for sending messages and mail to and from London, this left four full weeks for preparing the documents. Chciuk confirmed by telegram on 4 April that he had received the letter designating their place and time of meeting.

On 11 April, a telegram arrived from London stating, 'Impossible to send documents for Roehr earlier. Would draw your attention to the fact that Roehr must be supplied with French ration cards and also coupons.' This telegram made clear neither when he could count on receipt of the documents (they had still not turned up by the time he wrote more than a month later) nor who was supposed to provide him with ration cards. Perhaps they expected Gibraltar to do this?

Roehr decided to give up counting on any concrete help from London and to land without any documents, so as not to postpone indefinitely the beginning of evacuation from France. He landed in France at 0100 hrs on 18 April at the agreed place, where he met Chciuk, with whom he made his way into Marseilles. Establishing contact with Major Chojnacki took the whole of the following day since the code name 'Hugo', given by London, was not known by anybody in the Marseilles area (Major Chojnacki seemed proud of this). Moreover, no one at the British Hospital, which was being used by the Poles, knew an address for Chojnacki (who seemed proud of this too).

The search through various intermediaries for Chojnacki alerted a considerable number of people to Roehr's arrival. Moreover, London had apparently given Marseilles his real name as early as January in anticipation of his arrival. This equally did not help to keep the whole operation secret. It would have been possible to avoid this situation by simply giving Roehr Chojnacki's private address.

Having finally located Chojnacki on 20 April, he made his way to Lt-Col. Ejsymont, to whom he explained that the first group of around 60 had to be embarked on the night of 22/23 April and of whom he requested that some people be allocated to help with the arrangements.

Roehr repeated the instructions from the Commander-in-Chief's headquarters that priority be given to the evacuation of NCOs and other ranks; that not more than 5 per cent should be officers; and that these officers should be of junior rank and not more than 30 years old. Priority was to be given to armoured-warfare specialists, R/T operators and airmen. Ejsymont and Chojnacki confirmed that they were familiar with this order, but that they were not observing it completely. In the light of this, Roehr made it clear that, since he had no say in the selection of evacuees, he would not assume any responsibility if any did not fit these criteria.

In a car rented from some friendly Frenchmen, Roehr took some helpers to show them the routes by which the evacuees were to be taken to the embarkation point and how they were to be moved. Along the journey into Marseilles and from Marseilles to the rendezvous, no one had his documents checked. All of them had legal safe conducts in any case. Subsequently, 41 people had been embarked efficiently at the pre-arranged place and time: this had not been observed from the landward side.

Roehr himself still had no documents at this point, but on the morning after the evacuation (23 April) he received from the French authorities, on the basis of a declaration by the Polish military office in Marseilles, a document directing him to be demobilised at Auch as a refugee from German captivity, which he had indeed been in September 1939.

At noon the same day, Major Chojnacki informed Roehr that he had sent London a telegram reporting that 41 people had been evacuated at Cassis (which was not in fact the pinpoint). The operation had come to the attention of the police, who might look for them. He demanded immediate help for the ship from the British. Roehr asked what proof he had for this and Chojnacki replied that the police had been at the English Hospital asking for Major Szydlowski (who had left) and at the Villa La Ravelle, where they had asked for Captain Szulc (who had also left). He further alleged that the whole of the Polish community in Marseilles, and especially those at the British Hospital, were abuzz and talking of leaving. There were French informers and the whole evacuation operation had been compromised. Roehr should disappear for a time because everybody knew he was organising sea evacuation operations.

Roehr replied that his information convinced him that he should keep out of sight for the next few days only, which fitted in with his plans to be demobilised at Auch. For his return from Auch in three to four days, he asked Chojnacki to prepare answers to two questions: (i) Could Chojnacki organise the escape of people from the work details in such a way as to concentrate at various points on the coast, which he would indicate, parties of around 60 people every 48 hours? (ii) Could Chojnacki prepare a first group of around 60 people for 10 May to be embarked at the previous place (Marseilles would serve as departure-point)? Decisions would be needed on these two points about 1 May. If plan (i) came off, Roehr would need to inform Krajewski at a reasonably early stage of the numbers and the dates of embarkation, so that he could organise the transfer of people at sea to a British vessel.

Roehr went to Auch, where, with the help of Captain Oscar Ejsymont, he was demobilised under a false name as an escaped prisoner of war of 1939 vintage. The documents he received enabled him to remain legally in the Marseilles area. Travel beyond the Marseilles area was still legally prohibited but if one were caught in a document check the consequences would not be too severe. He returned to Marseilles on 28 April but found Chojnacki was away. Eventually, on 2 May, he had a meeting with Chojnacki, at which Lt-Col. Ejsymont and Captain Ejsymont were present. Roehr was told that there had been no confirmation that the French authorities had discovered the evacuation plan and people had been needlessly alarmed that it may have been compromised. At present, it was not possible to bring parties of 60 to the coast every 48 hours, but a group of about that size could be made available for 10 May at Marseilles.

Roehr then asked for new helpers and for a telegram to be sent to Krajewski calling on him to come and take off these people on the night of 10/11 May. It was agreed that on this occasion nobody from the Marseilles area should be included in the evacuation, the better to maintain security; it was also agreed that Roehr and Iwaszkiewiez should go down to the Salins-de-Girod on 5 May to see whether it would be possible to carry out an evacuation from that area (the place was found suitable from the landward side and an embarkation took place from it on 16/17 May).

On the next day, 3 May, Major Chojnacki came to see Roehr at noon and told him that, after considering new elements, he had sent the telegram but had added his own suggestion that, because of a renewed risk of discovery of the whole operation (the French authorities were on their tracks and had already arrested the brother of Midshipman Chciuk), sea evacuation be suspended until further notice. On 4 May, Major Chojnacki nevertheless declared that everything was in order and demanded confirmation that Krajewski would arrive on the night of 10/11 May!

With Captain Ejsymont, who had been allocated to help him, Roehr checked out the new approach routes. Of the 60 people promised only 29 materialised, although there had been more than enough time to organise the operation. They argued that one of the work-detail companies had been broken up and they had decided to reduce the number and so lower the risk of discovery.

The journey from Marseilles and visit to the embarkation point took place without any difficulty. As on the previous occasion, there was no check of identity documents on the way over: the routes and the pinpoint were not 'blown'. Patrolling of the shore from the landward side and of coastal waters from seaward simply did not exist, as Roehr's observations showed and Captain Krajewski confirmed. Nevertheless, Lt Roehr acceded to Major Chojnacki's demand that he leave because his activities were too widely known, and embarked on 11 May himself. Before he left, he agreed with Chojnacki and Iwaszkiewicz details of how pinpoints should be chosen from both land and sea points of view, recognition signals, techniques of embarkation, telegraphic codes, etc. The embarkation on 16/17 May was to be carried out by Captain Iwaszkiewicz near the Salins-de-Girod: about 20 people were to be involved.

On 11 May, Krajewski transferred 29 evacuees, Roehr himself and Zimny (Mate) from the felucca to a British ship at sea. On arrival at Gibraltar, the following signal was sent to Stoklas: 'Roehr with 29 men arrived safely. K. should be back next week with approximately 20 men... Officers in France too talkative so Roehr suggests London orders France cease evacuation of officers only for two months. Evacuation should be carried out for other ranks only. K. sends back Zimny unfit for job...'.

On 28 May, Krajewski forwarded Roehr's report to Mally, with a copy to Stoklas, Naval Attaché at the Polish Embassy in London. At the same time he said that, in spite of the positive results achieved, for which they should thank Roehr, he would assess the effectiveness of the April to May operations at about 50 per cent: twice as many people should have been evacuated.[9] The organisation in France was weak and officers were talking too much. The French knew what was going on: the most up-to-date information on this subject was a report handed to them by Iwaszkiewicz at Faraman on 17 May. A French officer, in confidence, had shown the Polish officers of a work company at the Salins-de-Girod a warning from the authorities at Marseilles that in the Toulon district a group of Poles and their officers had made off to sea. The dates quoted coincided quite closely, if not exactly, with the first embarkation.

Indeed, Krajewski continued, evacuation by sea could not be continued with parties of 30–40 people as Marseilles seemed to contemplate, since it was highly uneconomic, not only from the viewpoint of expense but also taking into account the risks faced by the whole crew of the felucca in such difficult conditions. On each occasion, they had to undertake a voyage of not less than 2,000 miles, or almost the distance to America. Also, they might well have difficulties sooner or later from the British side, who periodically cast envious eyes on the Poles' successes and might argue, adducing the small numbers the Poles were bringing back, that their own operations were more important and that they needed the felucca.

Krajewski, indeed, had had enough. Having worked through the load of correspondence that faced him on return from his 13th evacuation mission, he wrote as follows on 25 May:[10]

> 8) *MY TRANSFER FROM GIBRALTAR.* Enclosed, amidst a whole pile of correspondence (it is a lot to send at once, but when do I have time to write except in port? and there are so many matters to be seen to), there is one that may come as a surprise to you: my request to the Chief of Staff to transfer me from Gibraltar and to appoint another naval officer to my post.
>
> The request I have submitted to the C-in-C's Chief of Staff is of course dry and formal, it cannot be anything else. You will be aware however of other, more understandable reasons—or rather, not only reasons, though the reasons are real—and…of my decision.
>
> I am already exhausted both mentally and even physically with this treadmill and this drudgery for well over a year. Not only do I have too few people to help me, on the one hand, but on the other there are many who are willing to put spokes in one's wheel. I have quite simply exhausted the fervour that allowed me to achieve things last year that I would perhaps not be capable of today. It is perhaps not completely irrelevant that I have not had a holiday for a very long time, although I must emphasise, Commander, that I am not here asking for a holiday, because after all at Gibraltar there can be no thought of a holiday. I HAVE ALREADY REACHED THE STAGE WHERE I NEED A CHANGE.
>
> I wanted very much to begin the evacuations from France, and I had placed a good deal of hope in them; they are progressing, perhaps even well, although not as I had wanted and I had the right to expect. The leaders over there were not up to the task of organisation and the operation had even been penetrated to a certain extent. This was what struck me, when—after a nightmare of a journey, during which I observed the efforts, dedication and COURAGE of the crew—I discovered that they had prepared 30 people for me. And then, when I had to return and expose myself to the comments of our various envious competitors at the base, I realised that…it was not worth it. Luckily, Capt Iwaszkiewicz agreed to have a second party ready in a week's time.
>
> Or that telegram of Major Chojnacki's 'just in case'.
>
> So—passing over my desire to return to the fleet, which I regard as a kind of self-indulgence at a time when I cannot withdraw without interrupting the evacuation programme—I most earnestly request you to intercede with the naval commander (Adm. Swirski) for him to pull me out, and to do it *now,* since I have delayed this decision for a long time (if I may recall my conversation with you last October). I understand that HQ may not agree, since they would always prefer to avoid the risks inherent in change. But in all honesty, *I can continue no longer.* The situation here is complicated even from angles that you would never imagine; certain British

institutions place obstacles in each other's way and...one of them becomes irritated when I associate with another in my complicated role as both head of the Polish mission and at the same time head of the evacuation post. I do not want to give any examples, because of the Censor, but there will be opportunities later. As it turns out, I have managed so far to remain on good terms with everyone, even though on occasion I have had to defend our interests in a forthright manner and intervene most forcefully—but it is all very tiring.

[The letter finishes with a recommendation that Sub Lt Gromnicki be promoted; also a written note thanking Stoklas for sorting out so many matters for him.]

(signed)
M.Krajewski

Krajewski also enclosed a formal request for a transfer:

Lt Comm Marian KADULSKI (Krajewski) Evacuation Outpost Gibraltar

To: The C-in-C's Chief of Staff
in London

28 May 1942

Request for release from present post[11]

1. Since it will soon be 18 months since I was transferred from shipboard duties to evacuation work–request that you release me from my post as head of the Polish Naval Mission at Gibraltar.

2. My hope is to return to service on Polish warships, with which I have completely lost contact since the time I was put at the disposal of the C-in-C's headquarters (that is, since December 1940).

3. I submit my request in the firm knowledge that today the situation of the mission here is on such a firm footing that changes in its command can take place without adversely affecting its work. Furthermore I submit this request in the knowledge that I have spent at this difficult outpost a period of such length that even British officers would in similar circumstances receive a transfer.

4. The main task of this outpost is currently the evacuation from southern France, the project which, while still experimental (sending a felucca a distance of 800 nautical miles), I proposed in my letter of 10 November 1941. This plan has now been successfully put into effect, as is proved by the first two missions in April and May this year, during which 106 people in total were evacuated and some 4,220 nautical miles were covered. The carrying capacity on this route could have been even greater, were it not for an excessive caution on the part of our evacuation leaders in France, who have observed already so many attempts at evacuation by sea, of which literally all in the course of the preceeding two years were unsuccessful.

5. This plan is now in a further stage of realisation, since a third mission to France is now being prepared (departure set for some time during the first ten days of June). I must however emphasise that in any case this is a plan intended to continue for at least one year; in other words, if I received orders to see it through to the end, this would mean that I would be cut off completely from the ranks of Polish navy officers and I would become a specialist in an area which does not have a great deal in common with the career of a naval officer.

6. The reasons that have led me to choose this moment to submit this request are, in addition, the gradual changes that have occurred at Gibraltar and the establishment of settled conditions, such that today any suitably chosen officer of the Polish navy could carry out the evacuation plan, since:

(a) we currently have a felucca whose thorough overhaul and fitting with a new engine lasted, thanks to local difficulties, more than nine months, but which has shown itself to be splendid for these duties and for which the expenses are now bearing fruit, since this felucca is capable of undertaking missions almost without a break;
(b) on technical-nautical grounds (repairs, supplies and equipment, etc), we are now dependent upon the local submarine base, and our felucca is released for an operation in almost the same way as their own regular warships. During the first phase, certainly, too many things depended upon the personal relationships established by the head of the mission, which would have meant, in the event of his replacement, that a newly dispatched officer would have to begin the evacuation work by...establishing good relationships and achieving a sound reputation among the (unfortunately numerous) authoritative agencies here;
(c) we have a crew from the navy which has been trained in the specific techniques of these difficult operations;
(d) we have an established operational practice for using feluccas; (equipping them; embarking passengers in difficult conditions, etc), which has been worked on and is effective to such an extent that on a number of occasions the authorities here seek to benefit from our experience.
(e) it is not without significance that we, as Poles at this base, enjoy considerable moral credit and an excellent reputation, which is expressed from time to time in confidences that are overheard: 'Only the Poles are doing something...' or 'The Poles are achieving things that we have not yet managed...'. Such prestige will strengthen the situation of the new head of the mission and will facilitate his adjustment at this base from the outset.

7. As my replacement in the position of head of the naval evacuation mission, I would suggest some young officer, a lieutenant commander or lieutenant.

8. I would also like to report that it is essential in the future (now even to a greater extent than heretofore) that the commander of the evacuation outpost here should be a post independent from that of head of the mission. I am concerned to ensure that the commander of the evacuation outpost here (who is also captain of the felucca, and as such has his hands full) should be relieved of such matters as contacts with military authorities with regard to the payment of our people, their quartering, disciplinary problems, etc. There is also to be considered the question of the welfare of what is sometimes a large number of Polish troops at Gibraltar, looking after them during their long stay here, discipline, etc. During the evacuation campaign, the number of our troops easily reaches 100 people.

(signed)
M.Krajewski
(copied to: Senior Commander of the Polish Navy)

Having fired these salvos Krajewski set about organising his 14th evacuation mission—the June no-moon-period voyage to the Côte d'Azur. It required a good deal of planning since, in addition to his own monthly evacuation, he had undertaken to do four further operations for SOE and MI9 and those for MI9 had to take place at a fixed date.

On the day before he was due to sail in *Seawolf,* a cable arrived from Stoklas announcing that he was arriving soon, presumably prompted by Krajewski's application for a transfer.[12] It was then far too late to change his plans, so he had to leave others to deal with the visitor from London.

Krajewski's report on this mission was as follows:

SECRET
REPORT OF THE FOURTEENTH EVACUATION MISSION
(to Southern France; from 4 to 19 June 1942)[13]

1) *BASIS OF THE MISSION.* This was to have been one of the normal, periodic missions to France. The situation in France, although not altogether satisfactory, did not give us any reason to suspect that the *details* of the evacuation action, such as embarkation point, dates, type of vessel, etc, had been discovered. Unfortunately general information about the evacuation was already in the hands of the French authorities...

We waited for a favourable period of the moon and also to complete certain small repairs and improvements on the felucca before setting out.

The first date suggested by the Marseilles outpost in a cable handed me by the Polish Naval Attaché in London was 8 June at 0000 hrs.

I could not accept this date however because of a previously arranged pick-up of agents and war materials for the local British authorities (for 15 June, 0000 hrs). This did not allow me to move earlier, since it would have meant that the felucca had to wait unnecessarily for several days longer (according to the plan worked out, it already had to wait five days between picking up the first group and the second).

So on this basis I had the following cable sent by the Admiralty here on the evening of 30 May:

URGENT. TOP SECRET. FROM VACNA to ADMIRALTY
From Polish Mission to Polish Naval Attaché
Your ref: 1712 B/38/5

1) For HUGO

a) intention is to take 80 (repeat 80) people from EN-VAU (repeat EN-VAU) during the night of 9/10 June.
b) please prepare discreetly the next party of 60 (repeat 60) people on the night of 14/15 June.
c) in the event of unforeseen difficulties on either side, all of these dates will be moved back automatically by 24 hours. (END HUGO)

2) Please emphasise to HUGO the necessity of making sure that the required numbers are available.
3) Regarding point a)—I propose that it be recommended to him that the party be split into two groups. The groups should arrive at the embarkation point each on a different night, with the proviso that they should be ready to be taken off on the night of 9/10June. I suggest that a similar plan be adopted for the evacuation party due to leave on 14/15June.
4) I intend to weigh anchor on the evening of 4 June.

2) It is true that the above cable shifted the pick-up date by two days, but on the other hand it gave ten days for a) the information to reach our authorities in London; b) to reach the Marseilles outpost; c) preparations in France to be set in motion.

Additional tasks that had to be carried out—during this mission—similar to those accomplished during both the previous missions for the British authorities—were:

a) to put ashore three agents in two separate places to the east of Toulon (the Cannes-Antibes region).
b) to pick up around three agents and bring them to Gibraltar or else to transfer them to a back-up ship together with some war material.

It was up to me to determine the pick-up point for the agents: since it had to be in the Marseilles region (luckily), I chose Port-Miou, which was familiar to me from the first mission to France. I did not wish to designate En-Vau on principle (so as not to deliver the Polish embarkation points into unknown hands). In fact, Port-Miou was not really suitable for taking aboard whole groups of people because of the number of buildings in the area, but for three people it seemed safe enough.

3) On the day before our departure (3 June) I received a cable from London announcing the imminent arrival of Commander Stoklas as Gibraltar. I realised that unfortunately I would be weighing anchor before he arrived, since there was no way of postponing our departure, owing to the meeting times already agreed.

4) *THE WEIGHING OF ANCHOR* took place on 4 June at 2230 hrs. To the last minute the coupler was being finished off, which isolated the dynamo while the radio was being used, since a sparking of the brushes, unavoidable in such a small dynamo, would have rendered even the most basic reception virtually impossible.

In fact, half an hour after weighing anchor the coupler began to burn and we were forced to return to our...earlier situation, that is...turning off the engine completely whenever we made attempts to contact Gibraltar. Of course I had to limit these to less than the necessary minimum since each attempt took at least half an hour.

Composition of the crew: Krajewski—captain; Siembieda—1st mechanic; Mate Tarnawski—2nd mechanic; Mate Gorzelok—cook and in charge of the dinghy in 'alarm manoeuvres'; Leading Seaman Stanislawski—radio operator and watch helmsman; Leading Seaman (Reserve) Chwastek—watch helmsman and deck-hand. Seaman Kurzawa remained behind at base. He had fallen ill with some stomach complaint the day before we left and had been taken to the infirmary (he has made a full recovery).

Unfortunately, as has recently become almost a tradition, the weather on the day of our departure was stormy and the wind coming from the east made the first few days of our voyage very difficult. Once again the majority of the crew suffered from seasickness to a greater or lesser degree; water was leaking in everywhere; cooking was impossible; nor did these conditions prove favourable to astronomical observations. Our speed was noticeably reduced (5 knots).

The weather did not improve until 7 June and this lasted through the next day; however, this short period of settled weather had to suffice until the end of the voyage. I must say that in this regard the voyage was exceptionally difficult, more so even than that in April, in spite of the better time of year.

After midday on 7 June we passed between Ibiza and Majorca (Balearics).

The only vessels we encountered—there were no aircraft sighted—were two small schooners near Majorca and, on the 8th at the level of Cape St Sebastian, a steamer of some 10,000 tons moving on a southerly course.

In spite of the bad weather, we arrived at the French coast very early, so that, on 9 June at 0730 hrs, I stopped the engine and waited hove-to at a distance of some 40km to the south of La Ciotat.

5) ARRESTS. At 1700 hrs I moved in the direction of Cassis, adjusting my speed so as not to be nearer than ten miles to those high shores at dusk. The short night at this time of year meant that we could not afford to wait until it had grown completely dark.

At 23.10 hrs I was situated at the entrance to the En-Vau *calanque*. In reply to our recognition signals—sent out as usual at the *entrance* to this narrow (around 40m) rocky gorge, with cliffs some 50m high and altogether about a kilometre in length—there came a reply—BUT NOT THE CORRECT ONE (a white light instead of blue). I decided nevertheless to enter, since circumstances indicated that the wrong signal may have been given because of technical difficulties rather than because the authorities had discovered the plan.

It took us a whole hour to turn around so that our bow was pointing towards the entrance and then to anchor, the conditions were so unfavourable (rocky bottom, and the anchor would not hold; strong wind and a swell *along* the *calanque,* which in that narrow space made the manoeuvres very risky indeed).

At 0045 hrs the raft we had sent out returned with Gorzelok and Stanislawski, bringing however only three people and the news of the arrests—or dispersal—of our group in the area of the embarkation point—that afternoon. In the light of this I immediately weighed anchor and left the *calanque,* leaving more exhaustive enquiries until later.

At 0100 hrs our course was for the agreed meeting spot with the back-up ship, which was to have taken off the expected party of 80 people.

The situation ashore was, in spite of everything, unclear, since it turned out that a group of 82 people had waited three days, having expected my arrival from the first day (in other words from 7/8 June). Not surprisingly, such a concentration of people eventually led to their being discovered by a forester, and they dispersed because: a) people were not aware that I had announced I would arrive on the night of 9/10; after being shot at, they lacked the determination and will to remain in the area until the evening, as had happened with three previous embarkations; b) the manner in which the people were concealed left, it seems, much to be desired, since they had no instructions as to what they should do in particular cases where complications might arise; c) discipline too was not at the level it should have been, since people went to Cassis (small village) for water, etc.

Knowing Major Chojnacki ('Hugo') from the accounts of others, I assumed that after these arrests he would immediately suspend all evacuation moves and certainly the embarkation arranged for 14/15 June.

6) *THE PLAN TO PUT ASHORE A COUIUER.* Knowing the french as I do, I did not assume that their level of watchfulness would be increased too greatly, and wanting at all costs to prevent such a long and tiring voyage from 'misfiring' completely because of some exaggerated danger, I decided to put ashore an officer-courier, who would clarify the situation on shore (i.e. at the Marseilles post) and whose arrival would give added motivation and prove that it was possible to slip through. I ordered him also to request Major Chojnacki most vigorously to send a party of people for the night of 14/15 June.

This is not to say that I prejudged the way the situation would develop; indeed, I ordered Lt Biczysko (courier) to have a good look around himself and form his own opinion about the situation and, if necessary to get someone else to prepare a party of people if the official leader was unduly fearful of the risks. I felt I could safely base such a plan on Lt Biczysko's assessment of the situation in the light of his character, as revealed to me by his exemplary conduct during the previous voyage.

The rendezvous with the ship taking off my passengers was to take place as previously—a point 30 miles east of Cap Creus (in other words the Spanish—French frontier). In spite of the fog which reduced visibility at the last moment to 4,000m, we managed to meet successfully, having fixed our position by observation during the morning. The meeting took place even earlier than had been anticipated in the programme, at 1240 rather than 1400 hrs. The transfer of passengers was effected successfully in spite of a swell, while at the same time we took on board the three agents who were to be put ashore, plus a number of packages, which were to be deposited together with the agents or at the time we took the people on board at Port-Miou.

We also picked up a series of signals, which unfortunately caused no small disturbance to the previous plan of my operation. I was warned that in the Antibes region, while putting ashore *two* of the agents, there MIGHT be an agent to pick up. I was not given the exact spot nor light signals or codes. I was further ordered to take on board at Port-Miou not three people but as many as ten, which made the whole Port-Miou operation very risky, since I had previously suggested it as a good embarkation point for three people but not for ten. It is too built-up.

All this showed up organisational shortcomings on the British side of my operation.

Not being able to influence or change any of the details, I decided to carry out the tasks insofar as possible.

7) *PUTTING ASHORE A COURIER AND THE AGENTS.* That evening (10 June) I was again in the Marseilles region, where, after avoiding a large steamer making its way from Marseilles to the south—and having avoided after sunset the lights of an extremely slow-moving ship not far from the coast in the Cassis-Toulon region (a patrol boat?)—we made the entrance to En-Vau. At 0135 hrs I dropped anchor. While manoeuvring in this very narrow *calanque* on such a dark night, however, I damaged the side of the ship's bow (bulwarks), having touched the almost vertical rock wall.

At 0210 hrs, after putting Lt Biczysko ashore, we were already heading south-east, in order to put the agents ashore.

In the morning, examination revealed that the collision had caused only a certain leakage of the deck and that the damage itself could be completely repaired, at least on a temporary basis. I had to wait for better weather, since the bow at that time was covered with water.

On 11 June at 2310 hrs we saw the coastal lights of the Cannes-Antibes region.

In the process of looking for the landing-point—though I had been there once already—there were some anxious moments as regards navigation. These give an idea of the particular difficulties of pilotage in wartime conditions, when one is putting people ashore at an agreed point on an enemy coast. As I have already pointed out in previous reports, lighthouses east of Toulon (in fact the Camarat light) have been extinguished.

For considerations of safety, I could not approach the shore before the sun went down, but I needed to fix my position by daylight—from the afternoon's observed position. Indeed, since the coastline in this area is extremely varied, with peninsulas and little islands, it is not easy to draw close to the shore and recognise a place even when one has been there before. At midnight I was certain that I had identified points that seemed to tally more or less with the log's indications (although the current of 1–2 knots demanded that it be treated with caution).

Having passed a familiar headland, I entered the familiar bay and went to an anchorage point about 200m from the shore.

In spite of the presence of many features that resembled those of the little bay of Antibes, however, something was different about the look of this place.

After we had consulted the chart and the contours of the shoreline, it turned out that we had not gone far enough and that this was not the Antibes bay but a small bay between Juan-les-Pins and the island of Saint-Marguerite, where I had all but put the agents ashore. Indeed, within ten minutes our course would have run us aground in two metres of water.

Eventually, at 0105, we were in the right place. The dinghy was launched and Gorzelok and Stanislawski took the two agents and their 'freight' ashore. There was no agent waiting to be brought on board ship. Consequently, at 0145 hrs we were already on our way to the second pick-up point (third agent)—Cap-d'Ail, near Monaco.

8) This agent was to be dropped—according to the instructions that the back-up vessel had brought me—in La-Napoule bay, where I had already put ashore three people during the first mission to France. As I discovered from talking with him, however, this disembarkation point was of no value at all to the agent, and had only been chosen because I was familiar with it. The agent, who was very shy and clearly did not want to cause me any trouble, did admit that if he were put down somewhere near Cap-d'Ail he would be far better off. The distance from Napoule to Cap-d'Ail was not insignificant (25 miles as the crow flies), which could have presented considerable difficulties to someone who was new to the area; to me, however, it did not make any difference to add this much to our journey, so I decided to put him ashore there—to the agent's undisguised satisfaction. The spot at La-Napoule was in any case not too favourable, but Capd'Ail I knew from having accidentally arrived there in the course of the 13th mission: it lies just below Monaco. The greatest potential difficulty—recognising the spot—did not arise, because the coastline there is very distinctive.

I aimed to carry out the landing on that same night, since the agent was reacting badly to his stay on the felucca, especially in view of the poor weather. The difficulty was that the night was going to be very short.

At 0430 hrs we had already reached Cap-d'Ail, a very steep, rocky slope. Having hove-to, I put the agent on to the dinghy under the command of Gorzelok and recommended that he put him ashore at any point he could find where it looked possible for him to climb up: it did not look too pleasant a pastime from the felucca.

After the dinghy had left us, there followed a period of waiting amid growing tension, since the dinghy had not returned and the dawn had begun to lighten the area; earlier we had already made out the lights of residential buildings on the rocky wall. I had already begun to fear that Gorzelok had mixed up the courses I had given him, when the dinghy reappeared. We hoisted it on board and then sailed away from the shore as fast as we could. Half an hour later a thick fog descended. At dawn, although we were still close to the shore, it was impossible for anyone to see us.

Gorzelok informed me that after searching around for a long time he had managed to find a sufficiently quiet spot between Cap-d'Ail and the small village of Eze, at the foot of some château.

9) *HOVE-TO.* We had a further three days' wait before the next party was due to be picked up, and we spent these lying hove-to almost exactly where we had been in previous missions to France, around 40 miles south-east of Antibes. We made use of one exceptional day's weather (12 June) to carry out temporary repairs to the ship's side. And we relaxed a little.

Unfortunately the very next day we experienced a storm, coming from the west. Anticipating that it might make me late, at 1420 hrs I had to move towards Marseilles.

The storm was one of the most violent experienced in those regions. I had to reduce our speed to 3½ knots in order to prevent our hull from being smashed. All the repairs we had carried out on the bow, although quite strong, were washed away. Our spare sail also was carried away during the night, in spite of the fact that it was securely fastened to the bow.

During the whole journey—that is until the evening of 14 June—we did not meet anyone except a three-masted schooner under French colours, running down full before the wind in the direction of Corsica.

A certain improvement in the weather (as it later turned out, only for a change of wind direction) occurred on the evening of the 14th, which we spent making good the damage to the sides with the remains of spare timber, which we always carry with us.

At 2315 hrs on the same day we were once again at the entrance to En-Vau. In response to my call signal we received the reply: 'DANGER'.

10) *WE TAKE ON BOARD A VERY MIXED PARTY.* Because of the recent penetration of our activities and arrests, as a result of which the police might have discovered our recognition signals, I had agreed with Lt Biczysko that the meaning of particular signal colours would be REVERSED: red would be 'All clear'; blue, 'Danger'. My call signal however would remain as it had been before (blue).

Having received the danger signal, therefore, I hesitated. As long as they were there, however, one had to assume that it could not be that dangerous, especially as from our position we could see nothing suspicious at all.

In addition, it occurred to me that Lt Biczysko might not have been able to remember that our call signal, i.e. that of the felucca, remained blue, and for some reason have assumed that the felucca was signalling danger.

In the light of the above I sent our call sign with a red light. The reply came back immediately: red. Everything was in order.

At 2345 hrs I was ashore where Captain Iwaszkiewicz was waiting with some people; others were still arriving in small groups led by guides. Also present was Lt Biczysko, who had acquitted himself extremely well, as the presence of so many people proved.

I was told that the signals had been understood perfectly but that Capt Iwaszkiewicz had quite simply used a different-coloured light by mistake.

As regards the situation on shore, it emerged that they had not received my cable—even by 14 June—although some 16 days had passed since I had sent it. What is more, as many as 82 people (among them two Free French) had been ready to leave earlier. However, 20 of them had been arrested in the end. The level of alertness of the authorities had been raised, although it was still possible to slip through, as we knew from the present embarkation.

According to Lt Biczysko's report, the leader of the Marseilles post was astonished when he arrived there, since, to his knowledge, the coast was—following the last penetration of the evacuation operations—cut off. He even declared that he would not allow him to return since 'it was only by a miracle that he had managed to get through'. On the first day he turned the idea down but on the second he agreed to provide a group of 20 people for 14 June. Luckily Capt Iwaszkiewicz persuaded Major Chojnacki to increase this figure to 40. (In the end I took 62 people on board that night.)

We agreed however that the boarding point we had used up until then (En-Vau) was now more or less compromised. I was not inclined to return to the Faraman site, though, owing to its openness to bad weather from almost every direction, and its very shallow waters, which rendered it impossible to sail close in. Furthermore, it was not a suitable site in that it was difficult to reach from the land side (small workers' settlements along the way, which foreigners seldom visited).

In the light of this, Capt Iwaszkiewicz proposed a completely new place very close to Marseilles, not far from La-Madrague tram stop. Its advantages: beaches frequented by crowds of people during the day, so that, the presence of large numbers of people would not arouse much attention; the tramline ran close by, so if the ship did not turn up it would be easy to disperse people again; there were apparently no inhabited buildings in the vicinity, although an anti-aircraft battery was situated near by on the headland, about two kilometres away.

Upon my return to Gibraltar I was to confirm the suitability of this place from the point of view of sea operations.

The next embarkation date we decided should be the 12 July at 0000 hrs.

In response to my proposal that we try to evacuate 100 people, Capt Iwaszkiewicz replied that it was not impossible. We agreed that I would, at a fairly early stage, indicate from Gibraltar whether I had the back-up ship at my disposal, since our ability to take off a large number of people depended on her availability.

I also gave him technical details of our operations, of our telegraphic communications and, above all, how many days our journeys lasted, since he seemed not to realise how slow communications were.

I also handed over a number of items I had been requested to get for him and for Major Chojnacki, and which it was impossible to obtain in France via normal trading channels.

Capt Iwaszkiewicz also passed on Major Chojnacki's wish that one of those who had been taken off (Dr Tomaszewski) should be sent back to them again(?!). 'What on earth for?' I asked. 'Intelligence duties?' 'I don't know myself what this is all about,' answered Capt Iwaszkiewicz.

I said that in general I did not believe that bringing people back served any useful purpose, and I was against it. The process was too arduous both for the passengers and for the crew (given that passengers occupy the sleeping berths) and too irregular for these matters to be decided so lightly. (A similar incident took place in the first party: Major Chojnacki wanted us to bring Mr Alvast back. According to Lt Roehr's information, however, this fellow had been under police observation for some time and was far too well known in Marseilles by the (unfortunately gossipy) Polish colony, for his disappearance by secret means and his equally mysterious reappearance to have been prudent.)

'If it is essential,' I replied, 'then I will always do it. But I would prefer Major Chojnacki to decide whether it is really necessary.'

11) At 0045 hrs the embarkation was complete, and we then moved to Port-Miou, which lies very close to En-Vau. At 0115 hrs I sent the raft commanded by Gorzelok into the *calanque* (we did not enter with the felucca itself since the *calanque* is inhabited, as we discovered during our first voyage to France). I gave him the password, so that he could collect people who would know the response.

To my amazement, after half an hour he brought back the first party, which included three women. He said that everything was in order, so I could not refuse to take them, in spite of the fact that our felucca can be used for almost anything except transporting women, especially since, for the whole of the journey lasting several days, it was to be crammed full of soldiers (there is, for example, no toilet on board).

At 0230 hrs we loaded the second group of people, after which I set course for home.

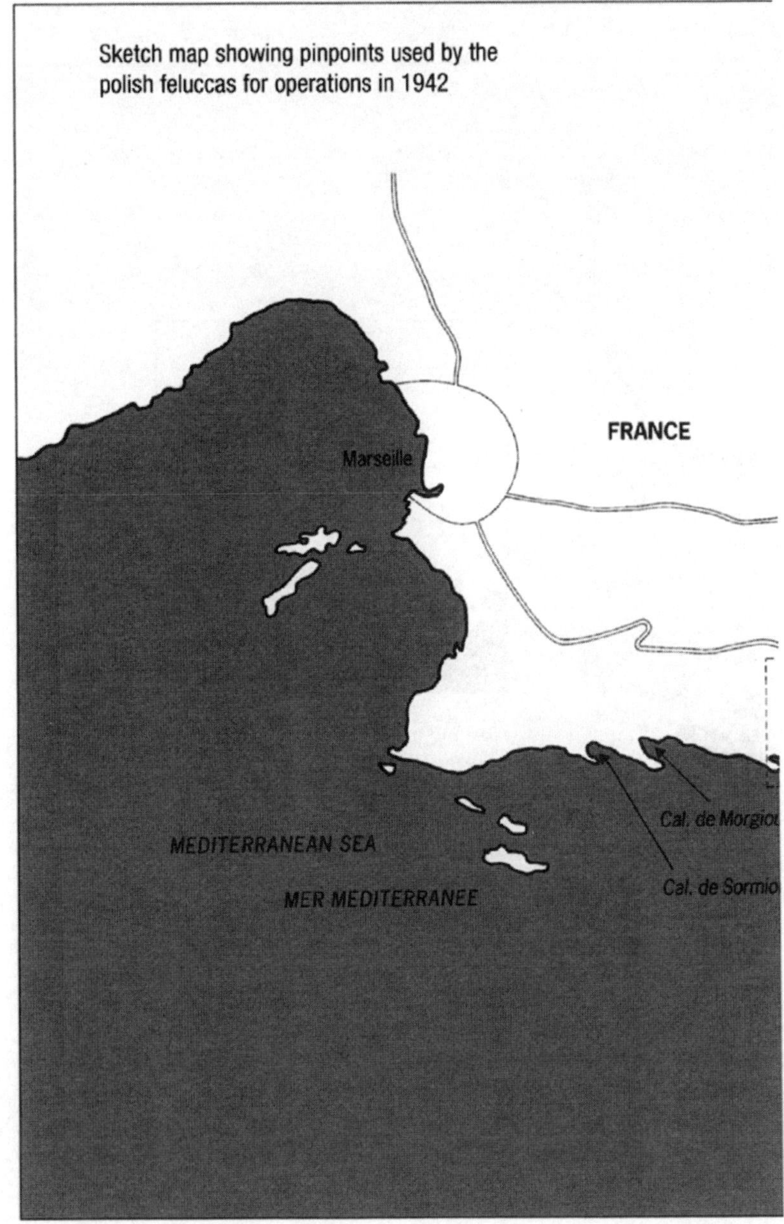

Sketch map showing pinpoints used by the polish feluccas for operations in 1942

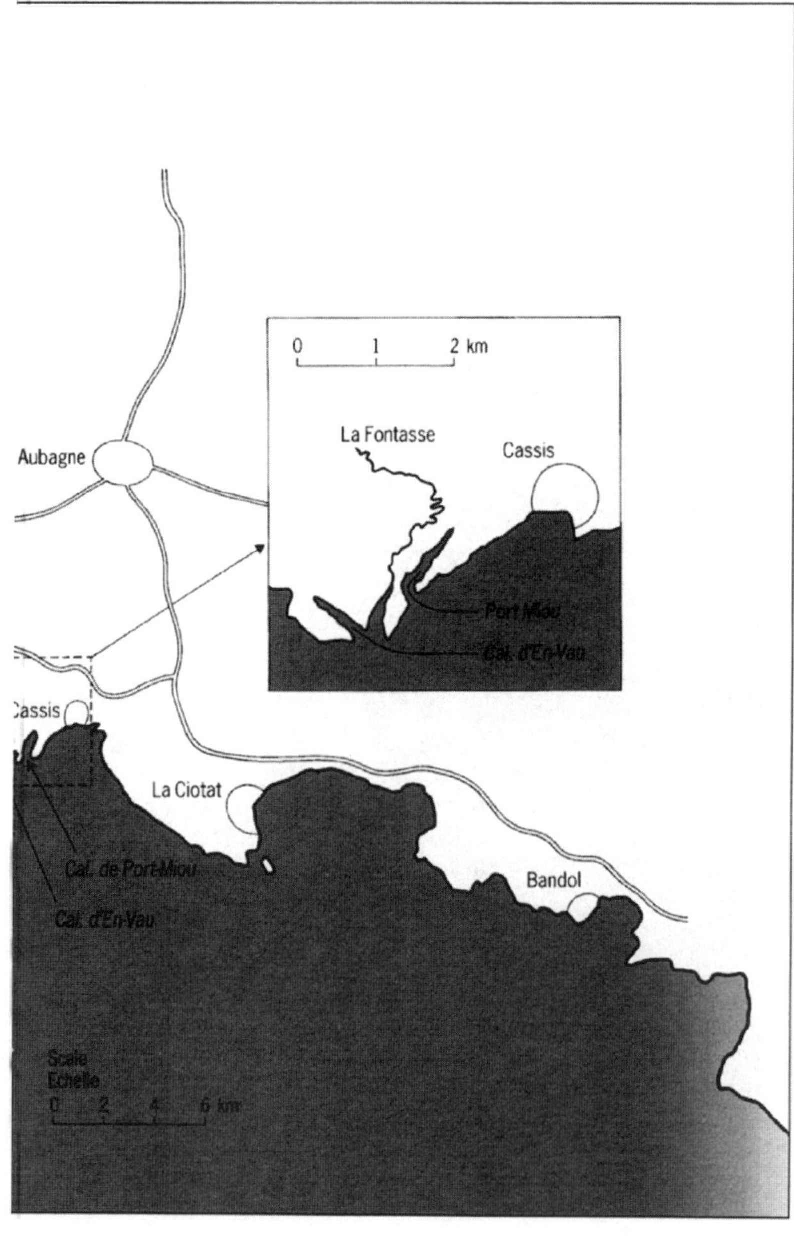
0 1 2 km
La Fontasse
Cassis
Port Miou
Cal. d'En-Vau
Aubagne
La Ciotat
Cal. de Port-Miou
Cal. d'En-Vau
Bandol
Scale
Echelle
0 2 4 6 km

An hour later we passed a large passenger ship of some 500 metres away. It was moving very slowly in the direction of Marseilles, apparently not wanting to arrive there by night.

12) *THE CURIOUS MYSTERY OF THE ST-CHRISTINE.* The first night was particularly difficult for the passengers, since we were taking a great deal of water on deck and almost all of them suffered from seasickness. Only after some time could we persuade our female passengers to go below to the cabin, which had been put at their disposal, since—as always in these cases—everyone was afraid that the suffering would be worse down below. The weather, which had been none too favourable for a considerable time, again turned into a heavy storm.

At 1105 hrs, being at the level of Cape Creus, in other words the Spanish frontier (at a distance of 65 kilometres), I made out on the starboard bow a steamer travelling most probably towards Marseilles. Anxious to pass her at a decent distance, which I habitually do during the day to prevent other seafarers getting too close a look at me, I changed course, doing my best to make the change imperceptible. However, when this ship saw us, it changed course...straight towards us. I made a further change of direction. Then, as though realising that it would pass too far away from us, the ship again changed its course towards us. There could no longer be any doubt: IT WAS HEADING FOR US ON PURPOSE. I therefore changed course gradually towards southeast. I ordered the passengers to hide themselves completely, an unimaginably difficult thing to do since there was no way that they could all be accommodated below. Some of them had to remain under the spare sails on deck.

The ship continued to approach, correcting its course regularly in order to intercept us. It was a ship of around 3,000 tons, with a single funnel, apparently quite modern and evidently with a speed of 12 knots, since my change of course put it on my starboard side, it still managed to catch up with us easily.

The name and colours were clearly visible: *St-Christine,* a French vessel.

And so it travelled behind us at a distance of around 500m for some 15 minutes. Anticipating trouble, I had prepared everything I could when our persecutor turned about and headed in a northerly direction. This mystery gave me no peace for the whole of the rest of the voyage. A merchant ship, however curious he might have been, however intrigued by a felucca seeking fish in the middle of the ocean where the water was 300 metres deep, would not have added so much distance to his journey simply to satisfy his private curiosity. The mystery was to be cleared up before long, however.

The storm continued to grow. Since it was coming from the north-west, it was hitting us abeam and causing our 20-ton felucca to pitch and roll, which was very unpleasant, especially with at least 50 people on deck. In addition we took a great deal of water on board.

Because of this I set a course for Cape Mahon (Minorca), with a view to leaving the Balearic Islands on my starboard side. All the time since we took our passengers on board I had been sending out a radio message in the hope of having them send me a transfer vessel, but we were unable to establish contact. I sent the message out 'into the ether' hoping that somewhere nearer I would be able to establish contact and would then find that the vessel was waiting for me along my course (I was giving out my position and course).

13) On the following day (16 June), from the morning on, we were sailing past the Balearic Islands. The weather improved for a time.

At midnight on the 17th we had a very odd meeting with a ship, which came towards us and then reduced its speed but did not approach us (the darkness was almost complete). Thinking that this might be the transfer vessel, I too reduced speed and gave out a call sign by switching off our navigation lights three times.

In response, an incomprehensible flashing came, after a time, from the other ship, whereupon I increased speed and moved off, leaving it still flashing.

14) *TRANSFER OF PASSENGERS.* At the level of Capo de Gata, in excellent weather, we encountered a squadron of the British fleet returning from convoy battles in the eastern Mediterranean, of which we had heard (on the radio). British patrol aircraft were in the air continually.

Taking advantage of the presence of a flying boat that dipped slightly and started to circle over us, I signalled by lamp, 'Please report my position. Here *Seawolf*', several times. He apparently had some difficulty reading it, but eventually answered, 'I will report your position.'

Because of my failure to make radio contact, I wanted to make sure that in Gibraltar they knew I was near, and would be prepared to receive this considerable number of passengers, something of a problem in that fortress. To prevent them from sending a ship out now, I signalled 'Need no help'.

The aircraft moved away. After a while we noticed a destroyer moving towards us at top speed. It ordered us to come alongside –and this was how in the end I transferred our passengers. I also took the astonished captain aside to give him some confldential information (1420hrs).

Unfortunately our already-damaged felucca was further battered in the course of our transfer operation. A deck beam in the engine-room was shattered and the bowsprit, which would normally have projected a metre and a half beyond the bow, was broken off; it was dangerous to lie side by side in a strong swell, which was all that remained of the many days of inelement weather.

The next day at 0830 hrs we reached Gibraltar. I discovered that the passengers had arrived there–at 2100 hrs on the day we had transferred them.

15) *THE SOLVING OF THE ST-CHRISTINE MYSTERY.* After our arrival in port I was told, while giving my report to Commander Osborne, that the following signal had been sent to Gibraltar from London on 13 June: 'Sources in Marseilles report that on 6 June, "All captains of merchant ships have received orders to be on the look-out for, and to report, a small, brown-coloured vessel of some 10 metres in length, 4 metres in width, with a *four-seater dinghy*. This ship carried out an *operation on 10 April*."'

Needless to add, I recognised my own *Seawolf* in the description of the ship and indeed the incident with the *St-Christine* also became clear.

But how did they get hold of so many details in Marseilles?

My theory is as follows: THE REAL SOURCE LIES IN GIBRALTAR. After all, absolutely nobody along the French coast saw me from close quarters. And only someone very close could have noticed that the dinghy is a four-seater. None of the Poles engaged in helping with the loading could see either; it was night and the ship was several hundred metres from the shore.

Equally, the date of 10 April—although one must not lay too much emphasis upon this detail—seems to confirm my thesis, because that was the day we received the *Seawolf* from the civilian shipyard. The Blanda shipyard lies alongside the Spanish border and is even easier to observe than the dockyard. And of course we had to tell the firm, which was always late finishing work, that they must complete the felucca on time because we needed it. On 10 April the felucca came round to the dockyard area; in other words, it disappeared from the view of whoever was watching it in the Blanda shipyard, which does work both for the army and the navy.

16) *VARIOUS.* Radio communication is, to date, ineffective. After raising anchor I am completely deprived of any contact with base. It is essential to get hold of a powerful transmitter/receiver (my previous report).

The following distinguished themselves in the course of this mission:

1) Lt Biczysko, Jozef—by taking on and executing the task of re-establishing contact with the Marseilles outpost; moreover, he faced the danger of landing in an area which, after all that had happened, must have been guarded and which we expected to be surrounded by the gendarmerie as soon as we landed.

In addition, during the whole voyage he distinguished himself by his willingness to help with deck work, at the same time learning such a lot that I used him as a helmsman and deck-hand, in spite of the fact that he had had no contact with the sea before.

2) Mate Gorzelok, Ernest—by courageously executing tasks associated with being in charge of the dinghy when we put agents ashore and when we brought people on board from difficult and sometimes dangerous spots. The fact that we carried agents considerably increased the risks if he were arrested, for then the charge would be not merely smuggling people (Poles) out but spying or indeed sabotage. The chances of being arrested were greater for him than for the rest of the crew on the felucca, which was at anchor a few hundred metres from the shore.

Gibraltar, 28 June 1942

The destroyer to which Krajewski transferred his passengers off Capo de la Gata was HMS *Middleton,* which belonged to the 'Hunt' class. As she steamed away from *Seawolf* at full speed to rejoin the anti-aircraft cruiser Cairo, Kinloch, her captain, told the ship's company that no-one should talk about the incident in case the Germans picked up a future 'run'. The refugees, who numbered over 60, included Pierre Fourcaud,[14] one of de Gaulle's first emissaries to return to France in the autumn of 1940, now returning from his third mission, and Henri Frenay, founder of the 'Combat' Resistance movement.[15] They were all placed in the tiller flat, under guard, and none of the crew was allowed to speak to them. It was a most uncomfortable compartment, right in the stern and above the propellers. Fortunately, they had to endure the discomfort for only seven hours before the ship berthed at Gibraltar. But Danny Jones, one of the ship's company remembered half a century later that they seemed so happy to have been picked up that they sang all the time.[16] The *Middleton*'s first lieutenant, Edward Ashmore, was a future First Sea Lord.

VII
The Coast Watching Flotilla and the Polish Special Operations Group

By the time Krajewski got back from his 14th evacuation mission on 19 June, Stoklas had returned to London and reported to Admiral Swirski, commander of the Polish navy, copying the report to General Klimecki, Sikorski's Chief of Staff.[1]

The object of his visit to Gibraltar, he said, had been to familiarise himself with the new Special Flotilla and to ensure that the principles on which it was organised conformed with Polish needs; to clarify the present situation of the groups commanded respectively by Krajewski and Buchowski in relation to the local British authorities; and to look into a variety of administrative problems such as manning, uniforms, leave and promotions.

Unfortunately, Stoklas continued, he arrived at Gibraltar just at the moment when the recently created organisation had been replaced with a new one. Although this was partly working, at this early stage it was impossible for him to sort out the problems that arose, since decisions were required from higher authorities in London and, above all, direct negotiation was needed with the British Admiralty.

After a series of meetings with the British authorities concerned, he put to Captain Osborne, senior officer of the so-called Coast Watching Flotilla (CWF), proposals regarding Krajewski's and Buchowski's groups, stipulating that these arrangements would still require the approval of his superiors in London. Osborne was in complete agreement with what Stoklas had in mind but said that once Stoklas had obtained the agreement of the Polish authorities, matters would have to be settled directly with Captain Slocum at the Admiralty, who was Osborne's immediate superior. Stoklas's proposals were as follows:

(1) Buchowski's unit, the so-called Diversionary Group, would cease to exist and that Buchowski together with his crew should be transferred to the Coast Watching Flotilla under the same conditions as were applied to Krajewski's group.

(2) Both groups would be transferred to the Polish navy and would form a Special Operations Group (SOG) seconded to the CWF at Gibraltar.
(3) The aim of the SOG would be to evacuate by sea from North Africa and southern France Polish citizens conducted to embarkation points by the relevant Polish evacuation missions.
(4) The SOG would comprise two complete crews under the command of officers of the Polish navy, who would take charge of feluccas provided by the British authorities in Gibraltar.
(5) For administrative and disciplinary purposes, the SOG would be subordinated to the head of the Polish mission in Gibraltar, who would be a staff officer appointed by the senior Polish naval commander (i.e. Admiral Swirski).
(6) Pay would be at the rates prevailing in the Polish navy and the necessary arrangements would be made to enable it to be issued by the Polish mission.
(7) The head of the Polish mission would cooperate with the senior officer of the CWF on all operational matters affecting the SOG.
(8) On all other matters such as accommodation, payments and the transfer of Polish personnel arriving at Gibraltar by sea or other routes, the head of the Polish mission would deal directly with the relevant British agencies in Gibraltar.
(9) Both crews of the SOG could be entrusted with any tasks resulting from their operational secondment to the CWF: that is, in addition to strictly Polish evacuation tasks, they might take on special tasks to benefit British intelligence. However, additional duties had to be subordinate to the basic aim of the group, which was to evacuate Polish citizens.
(10) Any proposals concerning duties not connected with the evacuation of Polish citizens would be received by the head of mission only from the Flotilla commander, with whom he would allocate priorities to tasks and operations. (A handwritten addition specified that the Head of the Polish mission would be directly subordinate to the [Polish] senior naval commander.)
(11) For the organisation of evacuations, the head of the Polish mission would follow the recommendation of the relevant department of Sikorski's headquarters. He would be a link between Sikorski's HQ and the relevant evacuation outposts. Operations concerning the evacuation of Polish citizens would be prepared by the head of the Polish mission, who would submit proposals to the Flotilla commander (i.e. Osborne), with proposed dates and places for embarking the evacuees.
(12) Operational orders would be issued by the Flotilla commander, whose responsibility it would be to ensure operational support from the British naval authorities at Gibraltar in the event that the operation undertaken by the SOG was threatened by enemy action.

As regards (1) above, the main problem connected with the creation of the CWF at Gibraltar had been the status of Buchowski's group.

Buchowski and his crew had been given four months' training in sabotage operations before they arrived in Gibraltar, where, Stoklas reported, Buchowski's group had been subordinated to a 'special organisation (non-military) headed, most probably, by the Ministry of Economic Warfare'. The head of this very conspiratorial organisation had representatives throughout the Empire and, under diplomatic cover, in neutral countries, they carried out sabotage and propaganda with the help of special agents and groups of specially trained people. The representative in Gibraltar of this organisation was Hugh Quennell, whose second in command was H. Morris. Initially, Quennell had had at his disposal a British sabotage group, whose operations had been unsuccessful. Then Buchowski's group had been sent to Gibraltar and placed under Quennell's orders.

Stoklas reported that Quennell's organisation (SOE) was not very popular at Gibraltar, especially in the military circles on the Rock. There seemed, moreover, to be a certain quiet rivalry between British military intelligence and Quennell's organisation. The head of intelligence on the Rock had made a whole series of attempts to have Buchowski's group removed from Quennell's authority. However, it seemed that the representative of British naval intelligence (affiliated to the Joint Intelligence Centre), Commander Clark, was fairly close to Quennell's organisation and had for a time played almost the role of naval Chief of Staff alongside Quennell.

Buchowski's group had been seven months at Gibraltar and, up to the time that Krajewski began to use individual members of it for his own evacuation operations, the activities of the group as a 'sabotage organ' for Quennell had been limited to a series of unsuccessful operations—or operations that were prepared on a grand scale and then called off. These culminated in an unsuccessful mission to Casablanca, at the end of which Buchowski and his whole crew were arrested at Tangier and his borrowed felucca was confiscated by the Spaniards.

General Klimecki agreed to Stoklas's proposals but suggested that, if Admiral Swirski approved Krajewski's request for a transfer, his replacement should be sent out to Gibraltar as soon as possible so that he might familiarise himself with the technical aspects of the job by making a few voyages with Krajewski.[2] Swirski must also have agreed, since by 17 July a draft directive had emerged from discussions with Slocum to give practical effect to the proposed reorganisation.[3] The Polish contingent would normally man the feluccas *Seawolf* and *Seadog,* but might be transferred to other feluccas of the CWF by agreement between CWF and the head of the Polish mission in Gibraltar.

The directive recognised that the main purpose of the Polish contingent of the CWF was the evacuation by sea from France and North Africa of Polish nationals, who would be delivered to the various points of embarkation by Polish evacuation missions established in those territories; but it went on to say that the primary task of the CWF was to provide sea lines of communication for intelligence organisations operating on behalf of the Allies. This latter objective, therefore, took precedence over all other operations of the CWF, including the evacuation of British, Polish and other Allied personnel. Thus the

Polish contingent might be called on to execute any operation on behalf of the Allied cause, provided that any approved Polish evacuation plan would not be jeopardised by diversion of the Polish contingent to other tasks, except in cases of critical emergency.

With this significant emendation, Stoklas's proposals were agreed and adopted. The directive stipulated that the W/T channel of communication on all operational matters between the head of the Polish mission in Gibraltar and his headquarters in London would be via the CWF's office.

Though Buchowski had not carried out any operation to the south coast of France before the end of June, on 25 April he had used *Dogfish* to pick up four agents from near Cap Falcon in Algeria.[4] Though he undertook the operation (ORKAN) for Krajewski, it is clear from the record that at least one of those embarked must either have belonged to Rygor-Slowikowski's 'Agence Afrique' intelligence network, which was working for Dunderdale of SIS, though Slowikowski was still ignorant of the fact, or was an agent of Dunderdale's on a separate mission.

Buchowski's next operation was also undertaken for Krajewski: he set off in *Dogfish* for Casablanca in May with Lt Roehr, but the operation failed because of bad weather and they were recalled to Gibraltar, having encountered French warships on two occasions.

Dogfish went back to Casablanca to complete what was probably the same evacuation mission (CASABLANCA) on 21 May, when she embarked 30 Allied evaders and escapers. It was the last large-scale venture of this kind to French North Africa by the Polish mission at Gibraltar. Who was in command is something of a mystery, as neither Krajewski nor Buchowski recorded it among his achievements.

At this point *Seadog,* a second 20-ton felucca, was ready for sea and Buchowski took her up to the Oran area in an attempt to put Gromnicki ashore. This operation (TANGERINE) failed on 9 June as they ran into a patrol on the Algerian coast and then encountered bad weather. After this there were no further felucca operations to North Africa: *Minna,* the fast escort vessel Slocum had sent out to join the CWF, took over this part of the Flotilla's work, leaving Buchowski and *Seadog* to join Krajewski and *Seawolf* on the run to the south coast of France.

Seadog's first appearance on the Côte d'Azur was at Cap-d'Antibes at the end of June.[5] Working without *Tarana,* which had just carried out a complex series of operations with *Seawolf,* she embarked one unidentified SOE agent and landed a consignment of SOE stores (Operation NETTLETREE). She returned a month later to the same area without *Tarana* to carry out Operation SASSAFRAS, in the course of which Buchowski landed Major Nicholas Bodington of SOE's F Section; Henri Frager, staff officer to Girard, head of the 'Carte' organisation, who had been in London discussing Girard's requests for propaganda broadcasts with the Political Warfare Executive (PWE); H.M.R Despaigne, an additional W/T operator for Peter Churchill; and Yvonne Rudellat, who was on her way to Tours to work as a courier for F.A.Suttill (PROSPER).[6]

VIII
Problems and Methods of Operating from Gibraltar to the South of France

Krajewski's three first voyages to France had lasted 13, 16 and 15 days respectively and had served to evacuate 171 Poles and three others. The distances involved—1,500–1,600 sea miles on passage, perhaps 2,000 miles in all, allowing for the extra distances steamed between operational pinpoints and waiting positions—greatly exceeded any previously tackled: it was by any standards a remarkable achievement.

Seawolf and the new *Seadog* were 47'6" long and, at 20 tons, twice the size of *Dogfish* (10 tons), but they were small, slow and extremely uncomfortable. There was no room below deck for the large numbers of passengers embarked, who had to be packed on deck like sardines, lying cheek by jowl along the felucca's gunwales. If it became necessary to conceal them from view or protect them from bad weather, they were covered by tarpaulins or sails.

All the feluccas employed were in a poor state of repair. Even *Seawolf*'s new Kelvin engine gave trouble, while *Seadog*'s Swedish semi-diesel was particularly temperamental and could be got going at all only with the aid of a blowlamp. Because of the shortcomings of her 30-year-old motor, which had required prodigies on the part of Siembieda, the mechanic who kept it going, *Dogfish* had been withdrawn from service after a year of voyages to the African coast. *Seawolf* was considered a better sea-boat than *Seadog:* she was of French Moroccan provenance, while *Seadog* was Spanish in origin. They used Spanish and French camouflage.

Things would have been a good deal worse if Krajewski had not found in Commander John Illingworth,[1] Maidstone's senior engineer officer, a firm friend and ally. Illingworth, a future Commodore of the Royal Ocean Racing Club, was already well known in that context and had on the bulkhead of his cabin a blown-up photograph of his very successful Laurent Giles-designed cutter *Maid of Malham*. Writing 50 years later from Oslo, Krajewski, who had of course long since resumed his true patronymic Kadulski, said he owed the success of his last operations in *Seawolf* and the markedly better conditions on board compared with *Dogfish* to Illingworth's keenness to help, his first-class technical engineering skills and his knowledge of the requirements of very small boats. Illingworth even arranged for electric light to be installed in the *Seawolf,* which helped Krajewski to do his navigation properly and read charts at night!

Tarana, which Slocum had sent out to operate in conjunction with the feluccas as well as on her own, was a Dutch-built, 200-ton deep-sea trawler. Under the command of Lt E.B.Clark, RNR, whom Krajewski describes as her 'jolly' captain, her mixed Anglo-Polish crew came to hold the record—six hours—for painting the ship overall during darkness, an operation that had to be undertaken at the beginning and end of each voyage. By transferring passengers to her from the feluccas at sea and thus saving a return trip of 750 miles to Gibraltar, it was possible for *Seawolf* and *Seadog* to embark twice—and, later, even three times—as many people in a fortnight as would otherwise have been possible. These rendezvous at sea also enabled the feluccas to embark agents for landing, without their having to make the whole uncomfortable trip from Gibraltar to the French coast in the smaller vessel; further, the agents avoided the risks inherent in being on board the felucca during preliminary operations that did not concern them—a distinct advantage from a security point of view. Of course, weather conditions had to allow the wooden felucca to come alongside the steel trawler without sustaining damage, since the difference in their respective sizes made the felucca very vulnerable.

In the summer of 1942 the Poles estimated that there were still roughly 3,000 of their officers and men immobilised in southern France. Krajewski and Mally were prepared to run considerable risks to get them out, even after it became clear that the French authorities knew quite a lot about the felucca traffic from Gibraltar—as a result, they thought, of indiscretions by other people's agents, but no doubt also of the propensity of the Poles in France to gossip.

The hazards of operating under fishing-boat cover were aggravated by the fact that the French fuel ration for fishing vessels was meagre and that the waters off the south coast of France were, even in normal times, not considered good fishing grounds. The triangle formed by Marseilles, Port-Vendres and Sète was something of an exception, since it was an area where the nature of the bottom and depths were suitable for trawling. There was very little sea traffic of any kind east of Marseilles and the few ships that did sail these waters kept close inshore. Practically no vessels were to be found near Corsica and there was no fishing east of Marseilles except that close inshore. Fishermen at such places as Antibes and the Anse-de-Canton in Monaco fished by night, employing acetylene arc lights. Not only were the long-lines and ring-nets of these boats a hazard on the feluccas' approach to the shore to land agents but their brilliant lights would produce a good silhouette of another boat at a distance of 300–400m. A felucca had therefore to be careful never to place herself between such lights and the shore.[2]

With a regular monthly service operating to the south coast of France, to a complex schedule involving combinations of three operating ships, and with *Minna* working to

North Africa, an enormous amount of preparatory work was needed to achieve maximum results for each sailing.[3] The requirements of each organisation calling on the CWF for transport had to be coordinated. Great distances were involved and the short no-moon period of each month restricted operating time. For these reasons, it was necessary to combine missions so that a felucca could carry them all out during her round voyage of about a fortnight.

The lion's share of this planning fell on Osborne himself. Apart from maintaining the flotilla, he was responsible for the conduct of operations while the ships were at sea. Before provisional plans could be drafted for VACNA's approval, the customer organisations had to say how many operations they would require during the period under review, while the field sections had to supply details of their proposed pinpoints. When the number of individual missions had been settled, the craft made their final preparations for sailing. The suggested pinpoints needed to be checked from the naval angle, adjusted where necessary to suit naval requirements and sent back to the field for final approval. Then the customer organisations were asked which of their missions could, with due regard for security, be combined and the final sailing orders were completed. These included full details of pinpoints, any alterations, times of rendezvous, ship-to-shore and shore-to-ship signals and passwords. The navigational notes consisted of times of moonrise and moonset, courses to and from the pinpoints and the most suitable areas for lying to during daytime. To these were attached silhouettes of the pinpoint areas. Although wireless silence was enforced, a list of crack signals was always carried in case of last-minute alterations in the sequence of landings and embarkations. VACNA's final permission to sail was then sought and relevant details were passed to Operations for onward routing to the RAF liaison officer (who informed any aircraft in the vicinity) and to Captain S/m 8, who warned submarines.

Routes to and from France had to be chosen bearing in mind that the Spaniards, though neutrals, maintained a strict coast-watching service with look-out posts located at vantage points all along the coast and in the Balearics. A report by the watch-post at Carnero opposite Gibraltar of the sailing of a 'special' felucca from Gibraltar might be followed, two days later, by a similar report by the watch-post at Dragonera light in the Balearics. These two reports would give the Spaniards a valuable insight into the movements of the vessel and there was no telling whether it would not be passed on to Axis agents or to the French.

Once the vessel disappeared out of sight of land, the enemy had no means of tracking her unless one of his or a neutral reconnaissance aircraft spotted her day by day, which was not likely. The conclusion that the felucca should therefore keep constantly out of sight of land on passage to or from France had one potentially serious disadvantage: a fishing vessel sighted many kilometres away from any fishing ground must immediately appear suspicious. Trawling is impossible beyond a depth limit of about 250 metres and where the bottom is rocky. Long-lining, on the other hand, is seldom carried out in depths of over 50 fathoms (90m) and never in depths of over 100 (180m). A felucca might pass muster if spotted in an unlikely area by air or sea reconnaissance, but not if seen by a genuine fisherman.

Ships at sea had to be avoided as far as possible, but without making an excessive change of course, which itself might attract attention. When Krajewski had passengers on board he used them to make up look-out watches during daylight hours, but at other times he had to do without, as he could not spare his few crew for this duty. The feluccas, being small, normally sighted ships before they were themselves sighted. Even when they sighted another vessel close to, it was sometimes possible to alter course gradually by as much as 40°, enabling *Seawolf* to pass the other ship at sufficient distance to avoid close inspection.

Plans had to be made in advance if it was thought likely that the felucca would meet patrol vessels. The external appearance of the boat had to be prepared, as did a cover story in case they were boarded or examined and arrangements on board were consistent with this. The feluccas on operations to the south of France were never in fact subjected to an examination such as *Dogfish* underwent at the hands of the Spanish authorities at Tarifa and in Alboran Island roads, though Krajewski had one narrow escape.

When it came to making a landfall, some moon was desirable, particularly where the pinpoint was inconspicuous or navigationally difficult to approach. The south coast of France offered a far better choice of places suitable for landing and embarkation in all states of weather than the Atlantic coast of Morocco. Port-Miou, near Cassis, was ideal in that it was sheltered against all winds. The *calanques* at Port-d'En-Vau and Sormiou were sheltered against all winds except from one direction.

IX
Operations by *Seawolf, Seadog* and *Tarana*: July–September 1942

At the beginning of July, Krajewski still had no news of the appointment of a relief to take over command of *Seawolf* from him or of the appointment of a staff officer to replace him as head of the Polish mission in Gibraltar. Exhausted as he was, he had no choice but to prepare his felucca for what was to prove the longest, most complex, most successful, but also one of the most trying of all his operations:

SECRET

REPORT OF THE FIFTEENTH EVACUATION VOYAGE
(to southern France, 7–26 July 1942)[1]

1) *TELEGRAMS PRIOR TO THE VOYAGE.* In the course of one of the embarkation operations during the 14th mission, Capt Iwaszkiewicz and I agreed that I was to let him know the *spot* where we would take on passengers, that is, I had to decide whether La-Madrague was suitable for that type of operation from the seagoing point of view. From the land side it had many advantages, such as its proximity to the tram stop, short journey time, etc. At the same time, its close proximity to Marseilles and to a fort was a disadvantage.

I was also to inform him by cable if I had a transfer vessel at my disposal; if so, Capt Iwaszkiewicz and I agreed, it would be better to aim to embark a larger group of around 100 people. He considered this to be quite feasible—and he was, after all, the one person (other than Major Chojnacki) entitled to give an opinion on what was clearly a local matter. I suggested this larger number to the local leaders of the evacuation, emphasising that we could mount only one voyage a month, encompassing at the most two pick-ups, because as a rule we spent a week at sea in the vicinity of the French coast. The period of bad weather due to start in October was another inducement to make the operation more productive by increasing the number of people taken off at each embarkation. The exact figures had to be decided by the people on the spot, i.e. in Marseilles, who had acknowledged that it would be possible to organise a *hundred* people at a time.

I emphasise the matter of numbers because of certain information received during the meeting with Major Chojnacki in France, about certain agencies in London intervening incomprehensibly with orders to reduce the number by *half* (!); I am submitting a separate report on this matter.

Against this background, I sent a cable on 22 June to Major Chojnacki...via London stating that from the seagoing point of view La-Madrague was a possibility and suggesting two embarkations; the first, of 100 people, the second, of 70 people. Further, I suggested a meeting with Major Chojnacki since there were many matters that required that I speak to him directly.

2) *MORGIOU AS A PROPOSED SITE.* Having sent my cable on 22 June I heard quite fortuitously, from one of the officers evacuated from Marseilles and from Major Chojnacki's immediate circle, that there was a spot for embarkation that was better, particularly from the seagoing point of view—at Morgiou. Accordingly, I sent a cable on 27 June suggesting this new site and—in case this caused the Marseilles outpost to change dates for technical reasons—an alternative date of 14 July. On 6 July I received a wire via London informing me that Major Chojnacki regarded Morgiou as inconvenient, and also that he could not change the dates. What struck me particularly about this wire was that the figures had been reduced by 50 per cent from those I had suggested (and had agreed with Marseilles). I thought however that conditions must have altered and that Major Chojnacki, and he alone, had set these new figures, which would have been natural in those circumstances.

In the light of this telegram, I brought forward our departure by 24 hours and before leaving sent a further cable (6 July) informing Major Chojnacki that I would arrive at La-Madrague on the required date.

3) We sailed at 2210 hrs on 7 July. The crew comprised: Capt Krajewski, Mate Tarnawski (1st mechanic), Leading Seaman Schlauberg (cook). Seaman Kurzawa (junior mechanic) remained behind in hospital in Gibraltar. For the first time Siembieda (mechanic from the merchant navy) did not take part, as he had been sent to England to have an essential operation on an advanced rupture and also he became increasingly demoralised with the conditions at Gibraltar, a problem on which I reported when the civilian crew were changed. He was kept on only because Bosun Buczek, sent out to Gibraltar as 1st mechanic, went to hospital before the first voyage and was judged unsuitable for service on seagoing units.

As the crew were considerably depleted, I received in addition merchant seaman Kreeman (Estonian) and Garcia (Spanish), both as mechanics. Futhermore, Sergeant Potter (British), who was familiar with the newer type of radio set which we were to use, travelled with us to establish proper radio communication.

As a passenger we took Mr Alvast—as requested by Major Chojnacki in his telegrams several times—with the aim of putting him ashore during one of our embarkation operations.

The first few days of the operation passed without incident. Our course led, as previously, far from land and was thus totally dependent on astronomical observations, except when it passed between the islands of Ibiza and Majorca (Balearics).

On 10 July, as we were having to regulate some valves, which during the short overhaul in port had been adjusted to completely wrong margins (too much tolerance), we took the opportunity to repaint the entire felucca, which I decided was advisable since our description had been passed out and was by now no doubt familiar to the captains of French merchant ships. The whole ship did not take longer than three hours.

On 12 July began the period of the severe mistral, which, I still imagined, should not have lasted longer than two to four days during this period.

Of our encounters with ships, the most interesting on the passage to Marseilles was our meeting with the *St-Christine,* known to us from the 14th mission (15 June), when she had changed course completely in order to examine our felucca from close quarters and then followed us for 15 minutes. This time, however, she did not undertake any suspicious manoeuvres whatsoever (this was 40 miles to the south of Marseilles) and, without changing course, disappeared in the direction of the above-mentioned port. In spite of everything, it did not seem to augur well, although it was possible that she had not recognised us because of the complete repaint.

4) *THE STORM RUINS OUR ORIGINAL PLANS.* Just after midnight on 13 July I was already close to the shore where Capt Iwaszkiewicz and I had fixed our rendezvous, not far from the La-Madrague tram station. It is a place lying some 5 km to the south of the port of Marseilles; the well-known little island of Château d'If lies even closer. The whole port can be seen from there like the palm of your hand. The shoreline is hardly less illuminated than it would presumably be in peacetime.

I received no reply to my signals at first and so, thinking that I had the wrong place moved closer to the port of Marseilles, where I again began the parade along the coast, sending out signals aimed as far as possible at the level of the water. Only at 0100 hrs, when I reached what I assumed was the meeting-place for the second time, did I receive a reply. Our people on the shore had probably been obscured from the sea in an oblique direction to the line of the shore and therefore had not seen our signals.

The storm however grew to an ever more threatening level. The anchor did not hold and a very strong wind was driving us on to rocks. Anchoring manoeuvres, or rather the attempt to locate a sufficiently shallow spot and suitable ground, lasted until 0300 hrs, after which, in the end, I decided to heave to offshore and send a boat only once in order to tell the reception committee to change the embarkation point to the familiar En-Vau. Mainly by luck, Leading Seaman Stanislawski managed to reach the narrow strip (some 20m) of beach and tell Capt Iwaszkiewicz of the postponement of the operation because of the weather, and of the new location.

5) *TAKING ON BOARD THREE 'AGENTS'.* The next day (13 July) I waited as the mistral intensified to the south of the Ciotat-Cassis region, having moved away to a distance of some 40 miles from the shore. Until shortly after sunset I did not want to be within 12 miles of the coast, the limit of visibility from the shore in these regions.

At midnight we were already entering Port-d'En-Vau. Our signals received the correct replies and so I sent the rubber boat ashore; out of the ten 'agents' expected it came back with two men and one woman (the wife of one of the men). The others 'had not made it'. After leaving Port-d'En-Vau we passed (0145 hrs) a patrol boat heading slowly in the direction of Toulon (under lights).

During our short stay in Port-d'En-Vau I put Mr Alvast ashore.

Meanwhile the storm, far from relenting, seemed to intensify further. The felucca showed more and more leaks, to the extent that the mechanics had to pump bilge-water for more than half a watch. The putty seals and caulking carried out by the Blanda shipyard in March were proving inadequate somewhere in the submerged portion of the hull. Heating up materials on such a small vessel in such bad weather was of course out of the question. The sea water was coming in everywhere, and we had no dry blankets in the cabin quarters (I underline this since, only yesterday, I had to resist Captain Osborne's requests that—in order to keep to some dates set in arbitrarity by the Admiralty for its operations—the *Seawolf* set out on its next operation as early as 5 August).

The original plan was to transfer the passengers in two batches: on 13 July, after the anticipated embarkation at La-Madrague, which of course had been cancelled because we had changed the pick-up of the Poles; and 14 July after taking on board the party of agents. Because of the storm I did not even move to the meeting-place but waited one more day riding out the storm beyond the extent of shoreline visibility, after which I moved once again towards d'En-Vau.

From the very beginning of the voyage I was in radio contact with Gibraltar, informing them of the changes in the situation. They sent on the information to the transfer vessel.

6) *RIDING THE STORM WITH 55 PASSENGERS.* At 2315 hrs I was again at the entrance to Port-d'En-Vau where I exchanged the normal signals with the shore. I made my way ashore on the dinghy, where it turned out that Major Chojnacki was waiting for me, as I had suggested in my previous cable, to confer with me on the current situation and plans for the future.

At 0030 hrs I returned to the felucca with the last group of evacuees, after which we weighed anchor and set a course to meet the transfer vessel. That night we took off 52 Poles.

Unfortunately, on that day too the weather was very stormy (waves 7–8 on the scale of sea conditions), so that when I eventually met the ship, transfers could not be contemplated. I did, though, let them know that I was forced to ride the storm with the swell (so as not to subject the passengers, most of whom were on the deck, to an irritating dousing from the waves, in testingly low temperatures); I also gave them a possible rendezvous in case we lost contact with the ship.

The ship moved against the swell to the north, but the *Seawolf* turned in a south-westerly direction, trying to travel at minimum speed—indispensable requirement for steering in such a heavy swell—and also not to distance ourselves too far from the area of operations (I still had to return to Cassis).

That day we sighted the first and only aircraft of that voyage—a two-engined plane travelling at altitude towards the south-east, not in any case showing any interest in our felucca. In the Marseilles region I normally encounter several merchant vessels daily; sometimes also in the Cannes-Antibes area, where, however, their course leads either to or from Italy; near Marseilles the course is to the south-west, or to Marseilles itself. To date I have never encountered any real warships (I do not count trawler-type patrol boats).

On the 15th conditions were very stormy.

When on 16 July the weather did not improve, the situation became ever more critical. Our whole strategic reserve was being used up; the dates of the operation were passing by; and the agreed date—which lay particularly near to my heart—was approaching ever closer—the night of 19/20 July, fixed for our second embarkation of Poles from Port-d'En-Vau. Apart from all this, we were drawing worryingly close to Sardinia (at 1710 hrs our observed position was lat. 40° 52' north, long. 6° 40' east, barely 75 miles from the north-west point of Sardinia), and along this coastline we could expect regular patrols by the Italian air force and later by patrol boats too. I therefore had to force a passage against the swell in order not to take too great a risk.

7) *THE TRANSFER OF OUR PASSENGERS.* Luckily, as evening approached, there were indications that the storm was weakening and the swell eased somewhat. At 1840 hrs I changed course, bringing her about and moving in the direction of Cassis, at the same time suggesting by W/T signal, after much consideration, the only means of saving the whole plan, namely: instead of the agreed rendezvous with the ship, we should meet as close as possible to my point of operation (Cassis region), I would approach the shore that night, after the anticipated transfer (17 July), and, having landed several agents on the shore, still have time to get to the Antibes region—and, above all, to make it in time to pick up the second group of Poles afterwards.

That day, in exceptionally beautiful weather (the last for a long time), there was an emotion-filled race to the changed meeting-points, since, what with the difficulties and limitations of radio communications, the explanations took up a great deal of precious time, and there was a point at which it seemed that the whole plan had already fallen apart.

Luckily, Gibraltar understood what I had in mind and eventually fixed a rendezvous so that the transfer could take place in the evening some 10 miles south of Cassis. The fact that I arrived at the meeting-point barely ten minutes before the ship itself shows how close the game was to being lost. To have arrived a couple of hours late would have meant the loss of a whole day, because of the huge distance

(140 miles) to the next point of our operation (Antibes). The agents we had agreed to pick up had in any case already been waiting for two days.

The transfer took place without any difficulties. Indeed I took a further six people to put ashore, and a certain amount of military stores. I also replenished our reserves of water and food and our fuel, just in case...(it turned out not to be necessary; as before, we had enough of everything for the place and the purpose).

At 2210 hrs, or 40 minutes later, I moved away from the side of the ship setting a course for the Bay of Cassis.

A few minutes after midnight four of the new passengers had already been put down at the spot discussed with them earlier in my cabin.

At 0500 hrs I set a course for the south in order to distance myself from the shore, after which we turned east.

8) *THE STORM RETURNS.* During the operation to put the agents ashore we again saw (at the same time of day as before) the lights of a patrol boat moving slowly along the coast, but he could not see us against a background of high cliffs.

The mistral in fact returned after a day's break and again reached the unusual strength of Force 7. It came at us from the west. It delayed my arrival at the embarkation and landing-spot until 0300 hrs, whereas the operational order had anticipated 0100 hrs. Indeed, as I received no answer to my signals, I could not be sure whether anyone was still waiting on the shore, or whether they had left after a couple of hours. Since the need to pick up the next group of Poles the following evening did not permit me to postpone the operation for a further 24 hours, I made my way to a place with which I was now familiar near Antibes (400 m. away) and I sent off the dinghy with the agents and material (0430 hrs).

Good fortune was not on our side at that point: the dinghy returned without having put anyone shore, since a few passers-by had taken an interest in her and one cyclist (it was already growing light) had even stopped to take a closer look.

I therefore left the bay at 0500 hrs, setting a course for Marseilles.

The storm however returned at its former strength.

With the direction of the swell and the wind against me, I realised by 1305 hrs on 19 July that I would not make it by the agreed time to pick up the Poles. Consequently I decided to turn about and make one more attempt to put the agents ashore and to take on board some of the people who would be waiting, or so we had been notified by signal. After midnight, that is, on 20 July at 0020 hrs, I received a reply to my signals from the shore, indicating that the reception committee was waiting, this time in the agreed place. The dinghy was sent out, taking the agents to the shore, at the risk of capsizing with its passengers and heavy load, and in a location that was less than ideal for this type of operation. The British authorities do not employ our system of choosing embarkation points: first, the land-side organisers suggest a location, having familiarised themselves with the hinterland, and only then do the seagoing people put forward their point of view. That spot had been chosen only from a nautical chart, which never gives a true picture of the coast.

The agents we were to have taken on board had not turned up and so at 0050 hrs I moved again in the direction of Marseilles, having successfully completed all the British tasks.

Our speed amounted to not much more than 4 knots because of the storm driving into us... In fact, it was obvious that we had been extremely unlucky in encountering this exceptional mistral, which lasted more than a fortnight.

9) *A FOREST FIRE NEAR CASSIS.* At 0130 hrs when I was approaching Cassis, but still a considerable distance away, I made out a phenomenon that we could not at first explain: the area projected for the pick-up seemed to be illuminated strangely for this area and this time of year. Drawing nearer, we discovered that it was a forest fire extending over a large area and fanned by the strong wind, which also made it extremely difficult to extinguish (as those we took on board confirmed later). I was afraid that no one would be waiting at d'En-Vau because the security agencies were bound to be present. However, the *calanque* itself was not affected by fire: in fact the couriers from the Marseilles outpost were waiting. They told us that the operation had been postponed for 24 hours precisely because of the presence of police, linked to the blaze. We took on board a woman and two children (the agent's family) who had not turned up for embarkation on 14 July and had now been brought along by a delegate of the British organisation in Marseilles, kept 'au courant' with my visits to Port-d'En-Vau by the British Admiralty.

10) *THE EMBARKATION OF 53 NEW PASSENGERS.* The next night at 0225 hrs (22 July), the second party of Poles were embarked at Port-d'En-Vau. While this was under way I had yet another onshore conversation with Capt Iwaszkiewicz about the situation in France with regard to evacuations.

The boarding had to be speeded up even further at the last moment because the lights of some ship became visible at the mouth of the *calanque*.

At 0350 hrs we left the Port-d'En-Vau *calanque,* cutting across the course of the above-mentioned ship (which was heading towards La-Ciotat) without incident.

I took a return course this time to Minorca so as to leave it on my starboard side, thus avoiding any encounters with merchant ships and any repetition of the incident with the *St-Christine* during the previous voyage.

This course was not too unpleasant, as the storm was coming at us from the north-west.

We had a further meeting as arranged with the transfer ship near the island of Formentera (Balearic Islands) on the morning of 24 July. After that, in changeable weather, I set a course onwards to Gibraltar, arriving there on 26 July at 1245 hrs, after a voyage of 19 days (the longest to date) some 2,520 nautical miles (the longest distance also).

It was a particularly arduous voyage because of the weather, which was tolerable for only a small proportion of the time.

In all, we evacuated 105 Poles and there would have been 50 more if it had not been for the interference of certain agencies in London (see below).

11) *INFORMATION FROM MAJOR CHOJNACKI AND CAPT IWASZKIEWICZ.* Something that came as a complete surprise to me, and astonished Major Chojnacki equally, was the fact that the reduction in the number of Poles—earlier agreed orally between the Gibraltar post and the Marseilles post—had come in orders from London and without any attempt to sound out the opinions of the two interested parties.

Another thing that struck both of us as very puzzling was the vehement tone of the telegram, which insisted that under no circumstances were the numbers given by London to be exceeded.

Major Chojnacki said that perhaps the Gibraltar post was not able to keep its word for some reason or could not guarantee to accommodate the promised number of evacuees on the felucca and on the transfer vessel. At the last moment (he emphasised the considerable delay in sending this telegram to him) he had been forced to change completely the instructions he and I had agreed, based on taking off 100 people.

We came to the conclusion that one of the newly arrived Polish officers in London had probably taken it upon himself to convince the evacuation department of the Commander-in-Chief's s headquarters that it was impossible to take off more than 50 people, and that he had prompted the staff there to issue a categorical order to THE ONLY PEOPLE COMPETENT TO TAKE SUCH A DECISION in this respect–the Marseilles outpost. It looked as though someone was bent on undermining the success of the evacuation operations being carried out by the Gibraltar and Marseilles missions.

Here I must reiterate that it would be quite uneconomical and irrational to organise such very arduous voyages on a small fishing boat—in conditions that are not comparable with any other and are unimaginable even to people who have seen action on a surface ship or a submarine—just to take off a few dozen people. What we should be aiming for is to increase the efficiency of such evacuations. Moreover only four more evacuation voyages can be mounted before the approaching winter season (the last of them in the first half of October), after which the weather conditions will be too bad for a small felucca to travel about 2,000 nautical miles and remain at sea for at least two weeks.

Major Chojnacki brought me up to date about the evacuation situation in France and told me that the French authorities are moving all Poles from the coastal region to the north (near the demarcation line). Amongst others, they are winding up the work detail at the Salins-de-Giraud (mouth of the Rhône) and the (Polish) section of the Red Cross at Marseilles. He expected further moves and thought that this was being done to hamper the Polish evacuations. He also considered it quite possible that they might move him and other Polish officers from Marseilles but added that he would continue to carry out the evacuation operations as before.

He requested me also to report to the central authorities in London that Capt Iwaszkiewicz deserves special distinction for his unstinting efforts in the organisational work of evacuation. Naturally I warmly support this assessment, having had the opportunity to observe the results of his work at first hand: it is Capt Iwaszkiewicz whom I always see on the shore leading the embarkation operation. There is a good deal of personal risk involved in this and the French prisons and treatment of prisoners have already achieved a sad notoriety. (I know of documented cases of arrested officers being beaten about the face, being manacled, being locked in cells together with common criminals, of appalling sanitary conditions, of being held in prison for several months despite orders from Vichy to free them, and so on.)

I passed on the news and agreed the dates of our next embarkation on the nights of 13/14 August and 16/17 August. The location: if we have suitable weather, La-Madrague; if not, then Sormiou.

Major Chojnacki and Captain Iwaskiewicz were equally surprised to have received the order from London to evacuate 50 per cent British personnel; they say that there are not that many of them in the unoccupied zone of France, adding that the British are also carrying out evacuation missions independently (by the sea route), begun after the successes of the Polish seagoing evacuations. The numbers involved though are considerably smaller.

In addition, I received a letter to be forwarded to the C-in-C's Chief of Staff. The envelope has been spoiled from being in Capt Iwaszkiewicz's pocket when he had to undertake a long walk in hilly countryside. I enclose the letter in the same state I received it.

(signed) M.Krajewski
Gibraltar, 31 July 1942

On his return to Gibraltar on 27 July from this very trying 19-day expedition to southern France, Krajewski was confronted with a crisis over his plans to resume evacuation from French North Africa.

After the unsuccessful operation to this area in June, he had managed, with the help of the Americans, to re-establish contact with Captain Szewalski in Oran with a view to fixing a date for a renewed attempt, using a felucca.[2] Since it must be assumed that the places used on previous occasions were guarded by the French, he proposed that they try a new stretch of coastline, one that had been recommended in April to Gromnicki in Oran by a trusted Spaniard who had been extremely helpful to the Poles. Not only was this man familiar with the topography of this part of the coast and with the Spanish fishermen who lived there but he also offered to lend a hand with arrangements for the landward side of an operation. Particulars of the new venue were forwarded in a letter to Szewalski by the Polish mission in Gibraltar on 16 June. In his interim reply on 22 June, Szewalski promised to send within a couple of days a suggested date and time for the felucca's arrival and detailed information about the stretch of coast proposed.

It was not until 19 July that Gromnicki in Gibraltar received this promised letter from Szewalski, who had by then visited the area with the Americans. He reported that, as in the previous year, guards were deployed lightly throughout the region but that there were none at the proposed landing point. A man referred to as 'Papa' would be waiting there on 30 July with a bicycle, identity card and a pass stamped by the police, which would enable Gromnicki to travel to Oran and to Algiers. A main purpose of the proposed operation was to land Gromnicki in Algeria, where, having established contact with Szewalski in Oran and Czapski in Algiers, he was to work out with them plans for an early resumption of evacuation of the Poles interned in French camps and specifically for a first operational project that took account of the new conditions. Gromnicki would also carry letters of introduction to very influential Frenchmen and to one in particular who actively supported the Polish cause. Both Gromnicki himself and Krajewski were counting on this mission to relaunch the evacuation programme.

On the very day on which Szewalski's letter reached Gibraltar, the mission had applied to Captain Osborne, commander of the Coast Watching Flotilla, for the operation to be carried out on 29/30 July: they asked CWF to make available either one of its new feluccas or some suitable British ship, since their own two feluccas with Polish crews were absent on operations to France.[3] Osborne assured them that the operation to land Gromnicki would be carried out and that the ship *(Minna)* would sail on 29 July in the morning. On 28 July, when all the preparations for Gromnicki's departure were complete, the British Admiralty (i.e. Slocum) cancelled the operation. Krajewski, now back in Gibraltar after his 15th evacuation mission, sent a signal on 29 July asking the reasons for this decision. The Polish Naval Attaché in London replied laconically that the cancellation of the operation was 'confirmed repeat confirmed'; the reason was that no details of the operation had been communicated to London, and the authorities there saw no possibility of carrying out evacuation operations from North Africa at that time.

Furious, Krajewski expostulated that decision-making had been taken out of his hands and that, without consultation with him, there had been a change of policy with regard to evacuation from North Africa. He wrote at length on 31 July to Klimecki, Chief of Staff to General Sikorski, quoting a directive he had received from him in April, after the failure of the attempt to carry out a mass evacuation of Polish internees from the Oran area. Klimecki had urged Krajewski to give priority to the task of evacuating even a few people each month from Algeria, as it was the only possible way of bolstering the morale of the other internees. Krajewski was at that point uncertain whether responsibility for the cancellation of Gromnicki's mission was Polish or British, but he feared that the intervention of officers who had been evacuated from North Africa might have been to blame. This suspicion was none the less galling for being unjustified.

The problem was, of course, that nobody had told the Poles anything about the decision taken by Roosevelt and Churchill to carry out a major landing of Allied forces in French North Africa, which made attempts to evacuate penny-packets of interned Polish troops clandestinely from the African coast quite pointless, since they would soon all be free.

Krajewski's frustration was compounded by uncertainty as to how long he would have to continue to bear, after more than a year of unceasing activity, the intolerable burden of being both head of the Polish mission at Gibraltar and captain, navigator, mate and factotum of exiguous and unreliable operational vessels. On his return to Gibraltar on 27 July he had heard that his successor as head of the mission would be Commander K.E. Durski-Trzasko, but on 1 August there was still no news that anyone had been appointed to take over his command of *Seawolf* and he wrote to Stoklas, the Naval Attaché in London, in a mood of considerable bitterness:

Dear Commander,[4]

This letter, by contrast with earlier ones, is of a private nature since it concerns exclusively my personal affairs, namely the matter of my transfer.

Since your departure I have received in all two telegrams (from you). I am drawing attention to these at the outset, because they are the only—fairly modest—evidence I have of our authorities' intentions with regard to me.

I must point out to begin with that I was cheered when I read the phrase in your telegram of 9 July that my 'early relief (was) under consideration'. At the same time I must admit to a certain sense of bitterness that, although both matters were set in motion at the same time, my successor as head of the mission, Commander Durski, is virtually on his way here, whereas my replacement as captain of the felucca is still only 'under consideration'. For more than a year now I have been roaming around in conditions with which no-one, literally *no-one,* in our navy can be even remotely familiar. Moreover, my plight is considerably worse than that of my crew (I have had two crews already), because they can at least partly relax in port—indeed, I try to ensure that they do, for the good of the evacuation. By contrast, almost the minute I return to port I have to set to work on correspondence, repairs to the feluccas, and many other matters—including those associated with being Polish mission representative here. After the last, long (20 days) and exhausting mission, I did go to the beach—only once, and then with a guilty conscience—and I would have liked to go there today in order to unwind a little (it is Saturday, 1800 hrs as I write), but I cannot as I want to send this important and urgent *courrier* tomorrow.

It has been like this continuously, after every mission, for more than a year.

As a result I am physically tired to the point of exhaustion. If I have come this far, it is only because I have been supported by strong reserves of health and, above all, by an eagerness to do a necessary job, supplemented lately by the hope that very soon my well-deserved 'change of guard' will come about… I was counting on handing over the August voyage to my successor but I see in fact that, when I complete my outstanding correspondence, I will have to begin preparations for my next voyage myself. And I really cannot keep going so long, and as a result the main thing that will suffer will be our very worthy cause.

So then […] I strongly and respectfully request you to make the necessary approaches to the competent authorities, so that before the end of August I may also be able to hand over completely my functions as captain of the felucca.

I can see that the evacuation department might, in the interests of blissful inertia, want to believe that this next evacuation, which will be important in terms of numbers, will go just like the previous ones, and to delay my departure by various means, of which they have many (e.g. 'There is no room on the plane', etc). But these gentlemen, apparently acting on information from people who do not always have disinterested aims, are precisely the ones who are beginning to put obstacles in my way (see my report by this same post on the limitations being placed on numbers to be evacuated). They who must know that, by putting off the change, they will bring the evacuation to a halt, by September at the latest. Because I now need a thorough rest before I will be fit for such demanding service at sea.

I declare today categorically that if my successor as captain of the felucca is not here before 5 September when we are due to weigh anchor, then there will be no evacuation mission that month. Indeed, I consider it my duty to myself and to the service to go to a doctor and request a check-up and a written certificate saying that I must have rest. I have no doubt at all that he will give me one.

A year of constant work and strain obviously takes its toll: I have been captain of the felucca, a junior officer (i.e. crew member, bosun *(sic)*, because I never had a good junior deck officer in the crew), a writer, a liaison officer and sometimes commander of the unit of evacuees, since in certain groups there were no good officers like Capt Ejsymont. On top of all this, I spent generally at least half my time at sea and the other half in port sorting out outstanding matters, which none of my helpers is competent to do.

Do I have to add that a warship officer's duties (and I speak from experience, having served on warships in 1940, during the height of battle) never involve a major effort such as has been exacted from me—an amalgam of ship/sea/land functions and administration?

I reiterate in the strongest terms that I will not be able to sail in September. Moreover, since Captain Osborne is giving *Seawolf* more and more tasks, and the Admiralty is basing more and more plans on her—setting dates, incidentally, completely arbitrarily — there could be no felucca available and the operation could well be called into question, in which case *there may be a great stir.*

I am writing to you frankly and in this detail because it is important to me that you, with your known positive attitude to our needs, understand the background to my request, which is all the more urgent and importunate for having been put off for so long.

While I am writing, a question: is it possible to find out who at HQ is queering the pitch? Why, inexplicably, from month to month HQ arbitrarily limits the number of people being evacuated without sounding out my opinion or that of the people in Marseilles? Or why Second Lt Gromnicki's operation was cancelled (the background to this he probably explained to you in detail) with the assertion that evacuation from North Africa is already impossible? Is it not Roehr, who is known to share this view (at some time I will be able to explain a great deal about his game to you)? I ask for my own information only, so as to have some insight into the Chief of Staff's decision.

Yours sincerely,
M.Krajewski

Having fired this salvo at Stoklas about his own affairs, Krajewski wrote to the head of the evacuation section at Sikorski's GHQ in London about the mysterious limitations that had been imposed on the numbers of Poles to be evacuated by his mission from the south coast of France.[5]

Krajewski explained how he had discovered from Chojnacki when they met at Cassis on 15 July that the latter had been instructed at the last minute by London to scale down by 50 per cent the numbers agreed with Iwaskiewicz in June. On that occasion, he had asked for 100 people to be available for the first July embarkation and 50 for the second. Chojnacki had been ordered to embark no more than 50 and 25. Though astonished by this peremptory change of plan, Chojnacki had concluded that Krajewski must have struck difficulty in obtaining a suitable back-up vessel and had therefore been compelled to make adjustments. He was as dumbfounded as Krajewski to discover that the restriction emanated from London.

Krajewski admitted that he knew nothing about the background to this decision but, if it were not the result of intervention by the British authorities or some other external factor, he wondered whether it was not based on false information brought back by an officer, whom he did not name but who was clearly Roehr. If so, it was an intolerable interference with responsibilities that belonged to the Marseilles and Gibraltar evacuation outposts and a stab in the backs of those who had to confront so many difficulties and dangers for the cause. He actually used the word 'crucified'.

On 8 August, a week after writing this letter, Krajewski was off to sea again, still without news of his relief. It proved to be another frustrating experience, for maintenance of the CWF feluccas had been handed back to the dockyard and was no longer carried out under the benevolent and rigorous scrutiny of Commander (E) John Illingworth of HMS *Maidstone*.

REPORT OF THE SIXTEENTH EVACUATION VOYAGE (aborted)
(8–13 August 1942)[6]

1) *OVERHAUL OF THE ENGINE AND FELUCCA BEFORE THE MISSION.* The felucca was last caulked during its major refit in March. The material employed in this work was putty which however quite quickly began to dry out and even fall out, which gave us some concern on the last few voyages, for in the bad weather the amount of water that collected in the bilge could certainly not be explained by a leak of the stern gland or anything of that kind.

During the very strong storm at the beginning of July (15th mission), with normal petty breakdowns of the (hand-operated) bilge-pump, the amount of water threatened the stability of the felucca and meant that the watch mechanic had to pump for 45 minutes every hour. I therefore sent a signal to tell Gibraltar that the felucca must at all costs be recaulked when it was hauled out on the slip.

On our return to port, the dockyard accordingly set to work giving her a thorough caulking and also took the opportunity to carry out other tasks such as repairing the freshwater tank, etc.

A second very important request we made was for the overhaul of the engine, which had run already for some 1,350 hours without being thoroughly serviced. The engine was taken to pieces (also by the dockyard) and reconditioned under a certain degree of 'supervision' by our senior mechanic Tarnawski.

2) *ENGINE TRIALS.* After the overhaul, with customary caution, I asked for a six-hour engine trial at sea in the presence of a representative from the mechanical workshop of the dockyard. Although this request was put forward by Commander Osborne, head of CWF, the dockyard commodore would not agree to put one of his mechanics at our disposal, arguing that they had an enormous amount of work in the workshop.

In the light of this I undertook tests with just my own crew; aboard as a guest I had Commander Osborne, who wished to take this opportunity to familiarise himself with sailing conditions on our felucca.

During the trial Tarnawski did not notice anything particularly worrying, although the temperature of the engine (crank-case, clutch) was certainly not normal. Since however this raised temperature had existed from the beginning, Tarnawski pronounced the engine in working order.

3) *THE RAISING OF THE ANCHOR* took place on 8 August just at sunset, in very good weather.

On board: Lt Cdr Krajewski—commanding officer; Chief Petty Officer Tarnawski—first mechanic; Leading Seaman Chwastek—helmsman; Leading Seaman Stanislawski—radio and helmsman; Seaman Schlauberg—cook and one turn at the helm daily; apart from this there were the foreigners, Garcia—second engine-room watch-keeper; Kreeman (Estonian)—third engine-room watch-keeper. Because of the shortage of crew, I myself had to take six-hour spells at the helm throughout the voyage, as well as my normal functions as captain. Not present: Seaman Kurzawa—in hospital once again.

4) *THE VOYAGE.* Only a few hours after weighing anchor (at 1020 hrs on 9 August) we again had cause to complain of the poor quality of work carried out by the Spanish workmen in the dockyard: there was a very serious leak, which was most strange in view of the very recent recaulking of the hull. After tearing away the ceiling in the commander's cabin aft we found that the leak had occurred through a seam puttied carelessly. In port, where the stern is not immersed so deeply as a result of the speed of the vessel, the unputtied spot was above the water-line and

was, of course, painted with great care. To stem this leak of water took us three hours and all our reserves of cement, which luckily we always carry in case the felucca is damaged while manoeuvring.

At 1700 hrs warships overtook us: they were two corvettes escorting two tankers heading in the direction of Malta.

At 2010 hrs when the convoy was passing us, one of the escorts (K140) became interested in us: it approached quite near on a couple of occasions, apparently to get a better look at us. When after a while we heard orders to man the boats, we knew what it meant.

Our papers were checked by a Naval Lieutenant (RNVR), without any special incident, although he seemed to realise that there was something curious about this felucca covered by British papers, which I did not want him to examine too precisely, since I feared they might discover a case of explosive material the British authorities had asked me to take to a certain point in France.

5) *THE ENGINE BREAKS DOWN.* During my watch at the helm and the Spaniard's watch over the engine, at 0730 hrs on 10 August, I noticed from the sound of the engine that something was wrong. I went down to the engine-room, which was filled with smoke; Garcia was evidently not unduly worried by this but I was familiar with the phenomenon from our first voyage with an engine of this type. We woke Tarnawski, who opened up the crank-case and then we discovered...that TWO BIG-END BEARINGS of the connecting-rods had melted, despite having been thoroughly oiled, at least in the part to which the watch technician had access. Further oiling did not help, neither did removing both forward pistons; the fuel pressure in this engine is too low for it to start under these conditions.

6) *UNDER SAIL.* Having a very favourable and fairly strong easterly wind, at least we did not worry about how to get home since our large area of sail gives us a sailing speed, in good conditions, of up to 7 knots. Here again, however, luck was not with us: at 1412 hrs, barely a few hours after we had started out under sail, the BOOM BROKE. Examination of a cross-section indicated that the wood had rotted. Our speed fell at once from 4 to 1? knots.

At 1755 hrs our observed position indicated a latitude of 36° 47'north, longitude 1° 18' west—still more than 150 miles from Gibraltar. (The breakdown had occurred a little less than 40 hours after starting up the engine after its overhaul in the dockyard; in other words, this engine, which had worked for 1,350 hours WITHOUT BEING SERVICED, had not been able to withstand being overhauled by the... Spanish mechanics.)

We did not manage to establish radio contact with Gibraltar until 2330 hrs on the same day (10 August), when I reported that we had a breakdown that could not be repaired, gave our position, speed and course and asked for Marseilles to be informed that the operation had been called off.

On the next day our observed position at 1415 hrs was latitude 36° 18' north, longitude 2° 29' west. Our speed increased to 3 knots as a result of using both parts of the broken boom to stretch out the sail and employing the lateen rig (completely different from ours)—which made the felucca look very strange.

On the same day (11 August) at 2330 hrs we received a signal from Gibraltar reading, 'Inform Gibraltar when you pass the Isle of Alboran. I will try to send destroyer to tow you back.' We were in any case already at the position requested.

On the morning of the 12th the wind dropped completely. Sending out hourly communiques of my position, I awaited the promised destroyer.

Around midday a heavily escorted British aircraft-carrier passed us, returning from the famous Malta convoy battle in which, among others, the aircraft-carrier *Eagle was* sunk.[7]

At 2015 hrs we sighted the destroyer. Half an hour later we were under tow.

We arrived at Gibraltar at 1100 hrs on 13 August.

7) *THE ENGINE REPAIR. CONCLUSIONS DRAWN FROM THE BREAKDOWN.* After my return I discovered at once from Commander Osborne that conclusions had been duly drawn from the breakdown. He had immediately requested the Admiralty to send an engineer officer to the Flotilla, saying that until then he had relied on the judgement of the dockyard regarding repairs, but that the dockyard was generally negatively disposed to such tasks, eager to see the back of them as quickly as possible and incapable of giving an assessment on which one could base the success of such important operations, not to mention the safety of the crew.

In addition, he reported that the mechanics tending the engine during the voyage—and making an excellent job of it—could not have had suitable training in regulating and adjusting an engine or in repairing the most serious breakdowns, since that demanded very good workshop specialists. We had such people on the *Maidstone* but they were no longer available to us, since the Flotilla had been made 'independent'.

Indeed, the first check of the engine by a 'borrowed' engineer officer showed that the filters were blocked up, the dockyard workers having cleaned the engine crank-case not with rags but with tow, leaving behind traces of fibre. Further, the senior mechanic recommended that the engine should most certainly have an oil-pressure manometer. But it was Tarnawski who pointed out that examination of the coupling showed a misalignment between the shaft and the clutch, which had caused the shaft to sag and the clutch consequently to run too hot, ever since it was installed.

As usual with this dockyard, the repair itself took longer than promised, here in spite of Commander Osborne's pleas.

Nevertheless it appeared that on 2 September everything would be ready. On that day, new white-metal bearings were installed, the alignment of the shaft was subjected to fresh examination and an already repaired universal coupling was fitted. We then set out on a six-hour test run. This time the dockyard did assign one of its mechanics to us as an observer. In addition there was an engineer officer on board, borrowed from one of the bigger ships in our Flotilla.

The test run already showed faults: the bearings were continuing to overheat. It was suggested that the oil could be cooled by installing piping to carry cooling water to the oil tank.

The issue of this cooling pipe (which requires very little work) is worth further mention as it is so characteristic of the technical difficulties we have to deal with.

The dockyard decided *not* to install it, their own engineer having concluded that it was not necessary.

I told Commander Osborne that it was indispensable: all engines designed for use on the open seas have an oil-cooling system, and our engine had always run too hot. The maker of the engine had probably not allowed for oil-cooling, since it was probably not designed for whole weeks in motion without a break but rather for intermittent work, perhaps in a port motor boat. We bought this engine because it was the only one of which we had full particulars and because there was a local mechanic representing the firm to carry out the installation. We also knew when that particular engine would be delivered to Gibraltar.

Commander Slocum, who is present here from the Admiralty, wrote a vigorous letter to the dockyard commodore, citing the above arguments and concluding that too much depended on this engine—from the viewpoint both of the operation and of the security of the crew and the felucca—for such simple tasks to be neglected, if there was just a chance that doing so might help the engine.

The results: none. The dockyard will not install an oil-cooling system and Commander Slocum's threats that the Admiralty will draw the appropriate conclusions if there is a further breakdown cut no ice.

As I write this report, we are preparing for a new sea trial of the engine (to take place on 9 September).

Gibraltar, 8 September 1942

While Krajewski was at sea on this abortive mission, Commander Durski-Trzasko arrived, to discover a poor state of morale among the Polish felucca crews, as he reported to Admiral Swirski:

Head of Polish Naval Mission,
Gibraltar[8]
Secret
25 August 1942

To: Commander of the Navy
(Adm. Swirski)

I wish to report that on the evening of 10 August I arrived at Gibraltar by flying boat, direct from Plymouth.

On the 11th I reported to Captain Osborne, head of the CWF (Coast Watching Flotilla). It took me a few days to pay all the necessary visits, first to the Governor and then to navy, army and intelligence organisations. I must point out that everywhere I went I heard the most sincere admiration expressed for the work of Captain Krajewski and Lt Buchowski.

At the time of my arrival, Captain Krajewski was engaged on a mission from which, however, he was forced to return, because of a major engine failure.

I chose 15 August to arrange a review of the crews of the feluccas and the army. It was on this occasion that I announced the creation of the Polish Naval Mission.

On the same day Lt Michalkiewicz [subsequently known as Lukasz or Lucas] and Bosun Zawistowski arrived by flying-boat from Plymouth.

On 19 August I carried out a detailed inspection of the crews of the feluccas and of the accommodation of the base ship, HMS *Araguana*. Earlier I had received information from Captain Krajewski and Lt Buchowski concerning the physical condition and state of morale of each member of the crews. I met each of them individually to discuss requests, complaints and regrets. Not surprisingly all of them wanted to return to England, adducing the most wide-ranging motives, and they all voiced various complaints about everyone and everything. Most of these grudges have been set out in detail by Captain Krajewski in his reports and are known to Commander Stoklas, but equally most of them have no foundation whatsoever, which suggests that they are the result of collusion. I can state with complete certainty that the men are nearly all exhausted and physically drained. Living on Gibraltar, with its very unpleasant climate, and in a completely isolated fortress, they spend their free time drinking, and their discontent manifests itself in a much more extreme form.

Lt Buchowski's crew in particular is suffering from low morale, one reason for which has been the failure to establish their relationship to the navy clearly and unequivocally. These people regarded themselves as civilians and were treated as such in most cases. The fact that on each occasion they were granted the best possible material conditions they demanded caused a loss of military identity and discipline.

My announcement that a new organisation was being created and my insistence that the crews of the feluccas are naval personnel and therefore soldiers in every respect caused dissatisfaction among Lt Buchowski's people, especially when I forbade them to walk about in civilian clothes and told them that they were subject to disciplinary regulations.

These symptoms of poor morale surfaced most clearly on 22 August, when Lt Buchowski reported to me that his crew members were asking for an immediate transfer and were refusing to put to sea.

I made my way to the warship *Araguana* and called Lt Buchowski's crew together. I explained to them that they are soldiers and work for the good of the homeland. I stressed that their refusal to carry out orders would inevitably harm their hitherto excellent reputation and might have far-reaching consequences, whereupon all of them announced their readiness to leave on the mission. Their commitment nevertheless was less than total, as evidence by the fact that they tried to negotiate an increase in their wages before setting out. I immediately cut short any discussion on that point. Lt Buchowski left on his mission today.

In spite of everything, these people work conscientiously and with a great sense of duty; they are undoubtedly very good and worthwhile material and will return to equilibrium when their conditions change.

I consider it impossible that Lt Buchowski's crew can be used for further work here; especially as some members of the crew are absolutely exhausted physically. After their return from the mission, I shall send the whole crew to England by the next transport, irrespective of when the replacement crew is due in Gibraltar.

Captain Krajewski's crew is also displaying the first symptoms of loss of morale. I have sent a signal asking for a further replacement crew be sent as soon as possible. A replacement is unquestionably needed, so I repeat the request here. The success of the missions depends in large part on the hard work of the individuals involved; even the most severe disciplinary measures will not have the desired effect on the recalcitrant element.

The new organisation, CWF, which was agreed between yourself and the British Admiralty, does not yet seem to be familiar to the local authorities here. I assume that Captain Slocum, who is due to arrive any day, will bring the appropriate orders and instructions with him.

I will be able to send Captain Krajewski to England after he has carried out a joint mission with Lt Lukasz. I assume this will be during the second half of September.

Head of Polish Naval Mission
Cmdr Durski-Trzasko

While this was going on at Gibraltar, *Tarana* (none of whose operation reports has come to light) went up to the Agde area, where Clark landed six agents for SOE on the night of 15 August (Operation BULL) before going on to pick up seven men and one woman near Narbonne later the same night. This operation was for Cohen's Section of SIS and was therefore ultimately either for the Free French BCRA or for the 'Alliance' network, which Cohen also handled. CWF reports describe the evacuees as 'POWs', though this designation can scarcely have applied to the woman passenger, who was presumably a member of MI9's 'Pat' escape organisation. Food, stores and W/T sets were landed on the same occasion. This was the first time Cohen's Section had made use of the CWF service, perhaps because their needs were so largely catered for by the fishing-boat operations that were being conducted concurrently on the west coast of Brittany.

With the immediate morale problems of *Seadog*'s crew reduced to operationally manageable proportions, Buchowski set off on 26 August for a further series of operations, on which he reported in due course as follows:

Lt Jan BUCHOWSKI
Report of voyage[9]

I beg to report, Commander, that, in line with the orders I received, on 26 August 1942 at 0630 hrs I left port. At 0800 hrs I rounded Europa Point and set a course that would take me past Cabo de Gata at a distance of 15 miles bearing north.

During the first two days the weather was awful, the wind easterly with a strength of 4–5 and sea conditions 4. The passengers did not feel too well and betrayed no inclination to partake of the meals. There were no unusual events to report at this time.

On 29 August at 0320 hrs we suffered a breakdown of the oil pump, which was repaired in 20 minutes. At 2300 hrs I passed Ibiza and Majorca, sailing between them, and headed in the direction of our first operation.

On 30 August I received a signal from the captain of the CWF: 'Begin Operation WATCHMAN as soon as possible on Monday.' I replied: 'Impossible for me before 2400 hrs stop Request instructions', to which I received the answer: 'Continue with the operation'.

Operation No. 1 (WATCHMAN)

On 31 August at 2300 hrs the shore became visible and I made out our location. On 1 September at 0300 hrs I entered the Rade-d'Agay and sent the first signal at the spot where the agents were supposed to have been waiting. Although I repeated the signal several times, I did not receive a reply. As a result I searched around the whole bay, giving signals at various points. I received a reply from beneath the railway bridge, but it was not given in the agreed colour, so I did not send out the dinghy. As I discovered later, it was most probably a police post. At 0145 hrs, I saw a signal correctly given from the right position. I sent the dinghy with one of the agents (female), whom I had to put ashore at this point. At 0205 hrs the dinghy returned in tow of a motorised fishing boat, and bringing with it seven passengers—five men and two women. I unloaded some 600 kilos of freight/cargo on to this motor boat. At 0220 hrs the loading and unloading was completed. After the fishing vessel had pulled away I moved to a position where I was to throw overboard (i.e. dispose of in the sea) the remainder of the freight. Unfortunately, one of the metal containers floated, but it was too late to do anything about it, since by this time a felucca was entering the bay, which is about 600 m. wide at this point. Owing to this, and not wanting to be noticed, I left the bay.

I discovered from the agents that they had been expecting me to arrive before 2400 hrs. It seems that they had sent a cable to London asking that the operation be completed by that time and, since I had not arrived by 2400 hrs, they went off to get some sleep, expecting me to turn up the next day. One of them happened to remain behind and, noticing my signal but not having a suitable lamp/torch, went to the nearest house and woke one of the others, who was able to give the signal. I feel, however, that we cannot blame the agents for the considerable delay in replying in this case, which is probably the result of a breakdown in communications between France, London and Gibraltar. Otherwise the organisation of the operation from the land side was excellent, proof of which this was that the embarkation of people and off-loading of a considerable amount of material was done simultaneously and took barely 15 minutes. On the same day at 1100 hrs I was hove-to some 50 nautical miles from the coast. At 1700 hrs I started up the engine and made my way to the point where the second operation was to be carried out.

Operation No. 2 (VAGRANT)

On 2 September at 0930 hrs I was at the place agreed and gave out the first signal. After five minutes I received a reply. I sent the boat to the shore. For the next hour the people on shore continued to signal to me but the boat did not return: I assumed that it had broken up on the rocks as the weather was none too good. At 0340 hrs I ordered the airman's rubber dinghy to be inflated and sent two people in it to render assistance.

Ten minutes after the dinghy had left, the boat returned bringing five passengers. I sent them back immediately for the rest of the passengers and ordered the dinghy to be hauled on board. After a further ten minutes both boats and the passengers were on the deck. I immediately weighed anchor. Asked the reason for the long delay on land, my crewman answered that when he reached the shore he could not find anybody. So he went off to search and after about half an hour he found one man at the top of a hillock intent on signalling out to sea. This fellow was startled by the appearance of my crewman and would have run off if it had not been for a well-aimed revolver under threat of which he led my crewman to the spot where the rest of the 'passengers' were hidden. Only here was he asked for the password. The passengers told me that they had been expecting a larger boat and had not come out of hiding when they saw the small boat, which they thought was only a fisherman. In my opinion, the land side of the operation failed in its duty here, since it is not desirable and is no part of our responsibility to force the passengers down at revolver point. Skilful use of the agreed signals should allow us to avoid that and the operation would take 30 minutes instead of two hours. Among the passengers was General Kleeberg.

Operation No. 3 (KUMMEL)

On 3 September at 0230 hrs I was situated at the predetermined location for operation No.3. Although I signalled several times I received no reply and consequently I sent out the boat with two people to search the rendezvous area, because it was possible that the passengers were again expecting something different. After an hour and a half the boat returned reporting that there was no-one there. On 4 September at the same time I returned to the rendezvous point, but the story repeated itself. When I returned to base I was told that there was indeed no-one there, as military manoeuvres were taking place in the area. It seems to me that one of the tasks of the organisers should be to find out about such occurrences at least a few days beforehand. Besides, the spot was one of the least secure on the whole of this coast (about 10 nautical miles from Toulon) and it would be desirable to avoid risking the two previous successful operations and the vessel by turning up there on two successive nights. Also, a signal that consists of two flashes on a white lamp for the party on shore seems rather ill-chosen, since I saw about 100 of these during my two-hour vigil there. If we were to put all these signals into service, we could, without much trouble, evacuate this entire stretch of shoreline, inhabitants, army units and all!

Operation No.4 (LEDA)

On 5 September at 0115 hrs I was at the spot appointed for the operation. At 0130 hrs I sent the first signal. I received an answer immediately. I sent the boat out together with one agent. Approximately 20–30 minutes after the boat had left I noticed a suspicious white light on the beach, as though someone were shining a torch. Ten minutes later the boat returned carrying five passengers and immediately departed for the rest. At 0250 hrs it returned bringing only one passenger, who told me that, after the first party had embarked and the boat had left the shore, the police materialised. So the rest of the party had scattered in all directions and he himself had struck a policeman. As he was running away, he was lucky enough to chance on one of my sailors, and thus come to board our vessel. He appealed to me to send a machine-gun and a few people to the beach to liquidate the police. Unfortunately, I had to turn down this enticing proposition of opening up the second front, not having the permission of either parliament or government and being under quite contrary orders from my superiors. I decided, however, to wait for 20 minutes, in case one of those who were left on shore managed to escape the clutches of the police, in which case he would give me the signal and I would be able to pick him up. Unfortunately nothing happened.

At 0320 hrs I left the operation area. That night, expecting to be pursued eventually, I painted Spanish colours on our bow and raised the Spanish flag, meanwhile setting a course that would enable us to reach the Spanish frontier as quickly as possible. At 1225 hrs (position: lat. 42°15′ N, 03°50′ E) I noticed a flying boat about 3 nautical miles away to the east. I sent all our passengers below deck. A few moments later the plane noticed me, flew lower and approached. For 15 minutes it circled us, flying very low. On his tail and wings he had Spanish colours, in the centre of which were Italian colours. He moved off in the direction of Cape San Sebastian. When the aircraft had disappeared from sight, expecting that a warship would eventually be sent to examine my Spanish identity, I changed course 90 degrees to ENE. I travelled this course for 30 nautical miles and then changed it again, heading for the western headland of Majorca. During the following few days there were no special events to report. On 9 September at 1310 hrs I moored near the pier at base.

Having in mind the safety of future operations, the vessel and the crew, I must submit that I regard the presence of high-ranking officers in uniform and a line of cars and limousines as highly undesirable, and the security risk heightened further by two tugboats just behind me, whose Spanish crew looked on with great interest at the ceremony of disembarking the passengers.

J.Buchowski (Lt)

Buchowski was not alone in his complaint about the public and indiscreet manner in which *Seadog* was received at Ragged Staff Steps. The Defence Security Officer wrote to Captain Osborne complaining that the entrance of a 'felucca'-type craft into the Admiralty Harbour was itself indicative of special operations.[10] A noteworthy number of important and well-known cars had arrived to pick up the passengers, who had disembarked in full view of many Spanish workmen, representatives of the Joint Intelligence Committee, the Assistant Chief of Staff and the Polish and French missions. The nature of the operation had been so evident that, as one report had pointed out, only the band, red carpet, press and news cameras had been lacking. The security officer recognised that there was perhaps no alternative to Admiralty Harbour, but suggested that a more discreet hour be chosen, rather than midday, that the incoming vessel be met by representatives of the Security Service only and that passengers be taken off immediately to a pre-arranged rendezvous, perhaps to a nearby building for the necessary particulars to be taken.

Osborne replied, pointing out 'facts which might not be quite obvious to those unconnected with the sea'.[11] Use of Admiralty Harbour was indeed inevitable, but the feluccas frequently entered and left it for non-operational purposes such as trials. The problem of the arrival and disembarkation of passengers was far from being satisfactorily solved, but other berths in it had been tried, including both the north and south moles and none had been found more secure than Ragged Staff Steps. The Spanish workmen never failed to notice what went on. The number of important cars could, and must, be eliminated and passengers should be taken away in a covered lorry, though this was not his responsibility, any more than was preventing mission representatives from meeting the vessel. Timing was difficult to control: the felucca travelled comparatively slowly and had no reserve of speed, so an earlier arrival was impracticable. In this instance, too, *Seadog* had covered a great distance and was at the limit of her endurance; moreover, it was not desirable to keep the crew and passengers on such a small craft any longer than could be helped. In his view, security was jeopardised more by the length of time the passengers were talking and hanging about after landing than by where they came ashore.

Commander Durski-Trzasko pointed out that he had been present in response to Osborne's 'express proposal'.[12] To avoid attracting attention, he had come in plain clothes and on foot. He had watched *Seadog*'s arrival from a distance and had approached only when General Kleeberg came ashore, to accompany him to the car.

By the time *Seawolf*'s engine repairs were completed, to Krajewski's relief, Lt Marian Michalkiewicz, who called himself 'Lukasz' or 'Lucas' while serving with the CWF, had arrived and it was decided that he and Lt Tom Maxted, RNR, who had been sent out by NID (C) to understudy the Polish felucca captains, would sail with Krajewski on his final expedition in September to learn how the job was done.

Slocum arrived at Gibraltar when this, Krajewski's 17th evacuation voyage, was being planned and considerable friction surfaced at a briefing meeting held by Osborne. Slocum complained that the Poles in France had been indiscreet in their preparations for the abortive August evacuation and Krajewski protested that the British side, to fit into their requirements, were obliging him to operate much too far into the moon period for safety. Krajewski's account of this acrimonious exchange is contained in the report he wrote nearly a month later on his return from his last mission. Durski-Trzasko, however, wrote straight away to Stoklas, the Polish Naval Attaché in London, on 11 September, the day on which Krajewski put to sea, saying that, after a month in Gibraltar, he noted a tendency to limit evacuation operations and to accord them lower priority;[13] and, moreover, to make Polish evacuation objectives subject to what he described as 'imperial' (i.e. British) aims.

REPORT FROM THE SEVENTEENTH EVACUATION VOYAGE (to France, from 11–26 September) [14]

1) *FREQUENT CHANGES OF DATES.* When we had grounds to assume that the dockyard would have the engine and the felucca ready for operations by the promised date, we established the following dates and locations for Polish embarkations:

The nights of 15/16 and 16/17 September; the number of people, 25 (in one night); pick-up point, Sormiou *calanque,* close to Marseilles, or La-Madrague, 5 km to the south of Marseilles—if the weather allows us to approach this coastline, which is open to winds from the west. Sormiou was suggested by Marseilles (Capt Iwaszkiewicz) during one of the earlier missions, but a personal inspection by Capt Iwaszkiewcz confirmed that En-Vau [or Calanque-d'En-Vau] was sufficiently safe too.

These first dates had already been imposed on me (indirectly) by the British side, which had settled the dates of *its* operations in advance, i.e. the tasks that *Seawolf* was to carry out under my command. As many as *six* of these operations had been anticipated initially.

When these first dates were being set, an incident occurred that was fairly trivial but nevertheless characteristic of a tendency by the British side (Capt. Slocum, of NID, Admiralty) to contend that it is the Polish side of our combined Anglo-Polish operations that has to adapt its plans to suit British desiderata.

Thus Capt. Slocum, who was present at my briefing with Capt Osborne, asked me to point out in my next cable to Marseilles (via London) proposing dates, that '...they should give an assurance that the preparations would be more discreet than during the preparations for the previous pick-up operation (which had failed because of our breakdown).' According to information received, apparently through the British authorities, Hugo's assistants were reportedly rounding up candidates and recommending that they make their getaway, giving the name both of the captain and of the felucca *(Seawolf)*. Capt Slocum apparently received this information before he left London and was intending also to send it on to our central authorities...

2) As regards the embarkation dates thus established, the Polish side already had reservations of a fairly fundamental nature; they were too close to the full moon, which was to be on 24 September. Beyond the limit of 'dark' nights, one can count on a period of more than eight days clear of the 'full', because then the moon is still not large and also it rises and sets fairly early. Since the felucca was ready to depart on 7 September and that 'limit' fell on 16 September—even allowing for the five days we needed to make our way to the French coast—we were still left with quite a lot of time, even for the British operations (12–16 Sept.), as long as we did not overwork *Seawolf* with too many of them.

3) These first operational dates were at the limit of the period of light nights—I should add that operation TITANIA was projected for the night after the Polish operation—this cannot be said of the dates established as the result of consequent changes. On 3 September, after the dates for the British operations had been altered on cabled orders from the Admiralty, the British side proposed new dates: 16/17 September and, for a second embarkation, 18/19 September…

4) However, yet another change soon followed: on 5 September, after still more adjustments to the British operations, we were offered new dates: the night of 18/19 Sept. for the first pick-up; 19/20 Sept. for second pick-up. Reporting this in our signal no. 455 of 5 Sept., we added in paragraphs C and D that these people could not gather at the agreed location before 0130 hrs Greenwich time, since Operation ORLANDO (putting agents ashore and taking materials on board) was also due to take place at Sormiou, and the British side wanted to ensure that this operation remained clandestine.

All the same it is worth pointing out that Sormiou was 'borrowed' by the British from the Polish side (just as En-Vau and Miou had been earlier) although Capt Osborne had, with commendable loyalty and on instructions from the Admiralty, approached the Polish mission to ask if we had anything against their use of that spot.

Unfortunately, we had no alternative but to accept these dates, although reservations were at once expressed about the almost reckless proximity of the dates to the full moon. The last operation (TITANIA) was scheduled for 20/21 September, three days before the full moon.

In the light of all this, I formally advised Capt Osborne before our departure that if we were arrested the situation would be clear and the conclusions…easy to draw. En-Vau, where I was to carry out Operation MULLET (taking on board two agents), also caused me misgivings because it had been visited too often.

We ruled out La-Madrague as a possible embarkation site, even in good weather, because of the unusually bright nights expected during our operations.

6) *COMPOSITION OF THE CREW.* Lt Cmdr Krajewski, in command; Lt Lukasz (Michalkiewicz), taking over command at some future point; Sub Lt Maxted, RNR, future commander of a British felucca, also along 'for practice'; Coxswain Maszczynski, helm; Leading Seaman Chwastek, helm; Leading Seaman Stanislawski, helm and radio; Chief Petty Officer Tarnawski, 1st mechanic; Leading Seaman Latka,

2nd engine watch; Seaman Kurzawa, 3rd engine watch; Mate Kuston, cook. Two of the officers and three of the crew were taking part in an evacuation mission for the first time.

7) *THE WEIGHING OF ANCHOR* took place on 11 September at 2045 hrs, i.e. when it was already dark, so as to preserve the secrecy of the operation.

The weather was unfavourable, with a fairly strong wind (the 'Levanto'—Force 4–5) blowing from the east.

On the following day, the 12th, we released in succession, at distances of 50, 60 and 100 miles, three pairs of mail pigeons, which we had received in order to train them. In our report to base we gave the time and estimated location (in code) of their release. As a rule, the pigeons circled over the spot where they had been released for about ten minutes, after which we lost sight of them.

It turned out after our return to port that only one of the six pigeons had not returned to base.

8) *BREAKDOWN.* At 0120 hours on 13 September a breakdown of the engine cooling pump occurred, when the shaft broke in two. The fault was a serious one. Luckily the mechanic on duty (Leading Seaman Latka) immediately realised what was happening and stopped the engine, thereby saving it from seizing up completely, which is what would have happened without any cooling. We were then about 5 miles away from Cabo de Gata.

Inspection of the cross-section of the shaft revealed that it had been split for a long time—most probably from the time it left the factory—and to such an extent that to the very last it could have been working only at 1/5 of its strength.

We managed to get around the fault by shortening the shaft, which had broken at one end, and by screw-threading it (we always have sets of screw stock and dies with us after so many accidents of this kind). Working by the light of a lamp, Tarnawski was able to get the engine started again at 0400 hrs. At 08.40 hrs we had to stop it again in order to carry out certain improvements to the pump– but afterwards, to the end of the mission, it worked faultlessly.

The breakdown was further proof that on this kind of small ship, with a small crew and only one engine, and where there are urgent and important tasks to perform, it is absolutely essential there be *at least one experienced mechanic* on board. Indeed in many cases the safety of the felucca and the crew depend on it. Neither Leading Seaman Latka nor Seaman Kurzawa would have been able to repair this breakdown, so without a mechanic all five operations would have been frustrated.

It is perhaps unnecessary to add that a mechanic with enough experience for this kind of task will never be less than 28–30 years old.

From the time the engine was overhauled by the dockyard, it in fact never ran properly during the voyage, so that for the most part we travelled at half speed, or rather half power.

9) On 14 September at 2125 hrs we were already level with the Tagomago lighthouse (Island of Ibiza) travelling between Majorca and Ibiza and moving away from the Balearic archipelago.

On 15 Sept. we had our first encounter with an Italian aircraft during the whole period of our voyages. We had in fact just finished painting the felucca, in order to change its appearance, and I was in the process of checking the ship's side, when I received the warning that an aircraft was approaching. It was then at a distance of some 800m and was making a turn (very low, at around 100m) in order to get a better look at us. When it began to circle, it was possible to make out its Italian markings without any difficulty.

We could not assume that nothing about us would arouse the suspicion of a critical observer; leaving aside the 'registration' letters, which we had only just painted on the bow, there was the very *position* of our felucca (very far from land and from waters usually frequented by fishermen) as well as its course. When the aircraft caught us unawares, we were heading straight for La-Ciotat, as we were already running out of time by then.

I ordered the helmsman to change course gradually to port by some 30°, which gave us a more 'natural' course, towards Cape St Sebastian. I also told the woman passenger and the second passenger (a man), who looked too refined to be a fisherman, to hide below deck. We carried out these manoeuvres while the aircraft was circling further away from the felucca. In addition I ordered all those on deck to wave 'in a friendly fashion' in the direction of the aircraft.

After almost a quarter of an hour of circling, the aircraft, a two-engined Caproni (bomber and long-range reconnaissance) moved off towards the north but, as I could see through my binoculars, still continued to circle for a time on the horizon on west-east courses…

I reported this encounter to the base at Gibraltar, as we were now already in contact

The fact that Lt Buchowski had had a similar encounter just a few weeks previously at the level of the Spanish-French border indicated a recently increased level of sea patrols to the north of the Balearic Islands. I had to take this into account in the next phase of my voyage.

10) On 15 September the weather turned very much worse and in the evening a storm, typical of the Golfe-de-Lyon, came from the WNW. We then observed an electrical storm lasting several hours, a phenomenon that I had never before witnessed on such a scale: the lightning extended for a distance of several kilometres.

On 16 September we approached the French coast so as not to reach the area of visibility from the coast-watching posts too early, but nevertheless to enable us to begin the operation as early as possible. Unfortunately the storm grew in strength, creating, as usual, almost unbearable conditions—everything got soaked through, the charts and cabins were showered with water, in a word there was not a dry spot on the vessel and it seemed that the felucca was dripping from all sides.

11) *PUTTING THE AGENTS ASHORE AT LA-CIOTAT.* Luckily our first operation was to take place in the Bay of La-Ciotat which is sheltered from winds from the WNW.

At 0002 hrs on 17 September we entered the Bay. Half an hour later I hove to at a distance of some 400m from the shore at what I thought was the agreed spot (in fact very difficult to recognise) and ordered the dinghy lowered; into it we loaded luggage and two agents (one of them the woman). The spot, it turned out, was not suitable after all, not least because it lay 2km from the brightly lit town of La-Ciotat, which, because of its shipyard, must inevitably be well guarded. The dinghy, under the command of Leading Seaman Stanislawski, nevertheless put ashore both passengers safely and without incident, and reported to me that the agents recognised the agreed spot without any difficulty near the point where they had landed.

At 0150 hrs the dinghy was back on deck, after which we made away from the shore.

At 0845 hrs we lay hove-to, awaiting the next operation in an observed position at mid-afternoon (1530 hrs) of lat. 42° north; long. 5°13′ east, around 40 miles to the south of the La-Ciotat area, a position to which I returned a few more times in breaks between operations. The weather had fortunately improved considerably.

This position, as my several earlier observations had indicated, was in something of a 'dead sector' as far as shipping movements were concerned.

12) *AN ERROR BY THE NEXT AGENT.* At 1605 hrs we set out once again. Since I found we were approaching the coast too early, at 2300 hrs (rendezvous was for 0100), and not wanting to spend that waiting period in the bay where we were due to meet (Sormiou) because it was populated, I hid behind the Isle of Riou, in whose shade (the moon, nearly full, was already shining very brightly) we passed the time by fishing. We repeated this manoeuvre several times, since it was the safest hiding-place, against the rocks, and not devoid of charm, because of the unusually picturesque scenery of that district. With each passing day (or rather, night) as we drew nearer to the full moon, it became increasingly lighter. In any case we had to spend our spare hours somewhere while waiting.

At 0030 hrs on 18 September I anchored in the *calanque* of Sormiou, to which, as with La-Ciotat, it was my first visit. My lamp signals, however, elicited no answer. When the situation did not change after 45 minutes, it became clear to me that the agent, who was to have met the other agent put ashore by me and collect some very heavy gear (radio station), was not there. Since my agent was not familiar with this region, I suggested putting him ashore in the Bay of Vau [*Calanque*-d'En-Vau], where I had to carry out the next operation that night, and where a reception committee was supposed to be waiting for us on shore.

At 0115 hrs I left the Bay of Sormiou, heading for En-Vau.

To our considerable surprise, as we passed the Morgiou *calanque,* which lies parallel with Sormiou, we perceived the AGREED SIGNALS. The agent had obviously made a mistake and taken up position in the adjoining bay. Finally, at 0230 hrs, our agent was put ashore and the delegate on land (the one who had made the mix-up) handed Leading Seaman Stanislawski, commander of the dinghy, around 50 kilos of material to take to Gibraltar (watches and stop-watches for the RAF).

13) *PICK-UP OF TWO AGENTS.* At 0310 hrs on the same night we were at the entrance of the En-Vau *calanque.* After an exchange of signals I entered it. Favourable weather conditions and our many past visits here saw to it that within minutes the dinghy had been put over the side, the two agents taken on board and we had left the *calanque* again, thereby establishing some sort of record for that kind of manoeuvre, which involves a certain amount of time taken to turn the felucca round in a *calanque only* 50m wide.

At 0815 hrs we were again lying hove-to at our former position.

Since the weather was exceptionally favourable, in the morning we had a bathing session with our passengers (Free French).

14) *TAKING ON BOARD THE FIRST 31 POLES.* At 0030 hrs on 19 September we were again at Sormiou (this time the Poles did not mistake the bay…). Signals were exchanged immediately: a moment later I was on the shore where, as usual, Capt Iwaszkiewicz was waiting for me.

While the group (31, of whom three were British) were being embarked, I held a conference with him. He said he thought Sormiou not completely convenient for our purposes, since passers-by were quite frequent. He therefore asked me if I would come to En-Vau the following night. Meanwhile he himself had to come aboard because his identity had been partially revealed.

At 0130 hrs we left the bay and moved to our usual position and hove to.

I now had enough people to organise, among other things, an anti-aircraft watch throughout the day, with changes of watch every two hours.

At 1400 hrs I ordered a general bathing session.

That day Tarnawski (1st mechanic) showed me a bearing newly made by the dockyard: white metal was falling off it, which threatened us with an unpleasant surprise at any moment. The engine too had been *heating up* more than usual ever since it left the dockyard.

At 1700 hrs we moved to the En-Vau *calanque.*

15) *TAKING A FURTHER 25 POLES ON BOARD.* That night at 2300 hrs we entered the En-Vau *calanque.* As we were still closer to the full moon the whole approach to the shore, which was fairly densely populated, was almost like a passage in full daylight. Almost every detail could be seen on the shore and also, we had to assume, on the felucca. I emphasise this because it gives an idea of the awkward situation in which the British Admiralty placed us by putting off the departure date, even though the felucca was ready; and how little in that institution

they allow for rational security considerations and the secrecy of operations for the longer run (indeed 'the long run' was supposed to have been the reason for limiting the number of people evacuated in any one operation to 25...).

Since Capt. Iwaszkiewicz himself had to go ashore in the dinghy, this time I remained on the felucca during the embarkation operation, leaving arrangements on shore to Lt Lukasz, while I continually manoeuvred the vessel as we lay hove-to among so many rocks.

Capt. Iwaszkiewicz came off again to the felucca to inform me that, despite everything, he would be *remaining* on land at the wish of Major Chojnacki, so we held our usual conference on the felucca (details below).

After taking 25 Polish evacuees on board, we left the *calanque* by 2350 hrs.

16) *THE INDISCREET BOARDING OF THE BRITISH PARTY.* The next operation (TITANIA), which involved picking up 15 POWs, was prepared by a British organisation [MI9] that apparently had an outpost at Gibraltar. The location: mouth of the River Tet below Perpignan. Having a considerable distance to cover, I set out to that point directly after leaving the En-Vau *calanque*.

Towards evening on that day we met a number of ships following the communication route from the Spanish border to Marseilles. Almost every night when we were in the vicinity of Marseilles we passed, at a decent distance, a few ships and perhaps even some patrol boats, but these were difficult to distinguish in the night, when we could see only their navigation lights.

The attempt to contact Gibraltar via the radio in order to arrange a new rendezvous with *Minna* (see para. 17) misfired. As the felucca was full to bursting—away above plan—I had suggested a meeting with the *Minna* to the *north* of the Balearic Islands, but received the answer 'Impossible'. *Minna* looks like a naval vessel and apparently they did not want to risk its being attacked by Italian aircraft.

Since all the lights are shining on that stretch of the French coast, I based our approach to the coast—which lacks any features by which to find one's bearings in the dark—on the red light of a fishing village and 'port' some 4km away to the north. At 0030 hrs, moving along the coast, which was lit up almost like daytime, we noticed the flashing of a light from a point that bore some resemblance to the agreed meeting point. THEY WERE HOWEVER IRREGULAR SIGNALS. After checking the position of a fort about ½km distant, I realised that it was one more case of unfortunate signalling from the land side. Our astonishment was all the greater when, after heaving to, WE HEARD CRIES AND SINGING AND SAW LAMPS BEING LIT among the party of people who were to be embarked. One even swam out towards us and in the water called out in our direction; in these conditions, as is well known, the sound carries a long way.

At 0130 hrs all of them had embarked. Again there were more in this party than anticipated: not 15 but 25 people, of whom the greater number were British from the RAF; there were also a few Frenchmen, one woman (Czech or, rather, 'Sudeten') and one Russian (the son of an emigrant).

1. *Seawolf,* with which Krajewski carried out his remarkable series of operations from Gibraltar to the South of France.

2. *Seawolf,* drawn by Lt Cdr Eric Honer RNVR when serving in the Adriatic.

31. MGB 179 (2 prints).

32. MGB191, Ancona, 1945.

All of them agreed that our vessel was visible 'as far as a mile out to sea', it was so clear.

17) *MEETING WITH THE MINNA.* Our journey back to base set a new record for our felucca in terms of numbers: in addition to the enlarged crew of ten for that voyage, we had *83 passengers* (54 Poles, 23 British, 4 French, 1 Russian, 1 Czech woman).

We therefore had 18 people altogether over the anticipated programme. Our drinking water being insufficient at the best of times, we had to ration this precious substance more than usual. Of course everybody had to be accommodated on deck, except the woman, a wounded Canadian (from the Dieppe raid), a wounded Pole and a wounded airman (who had been carrying out Special Operations flights and had had an accident on one of his missions).

The mood among the passengers was very good, irrespective of nationality, although I must state impartially that our people withstood the unspeakably awful conditions notably better than the others.

21 September was especially hard because of the return of the bad weather, and from a most impropitious direction (south, Force 4–5). Being virtually certain that we would meet Italian aircraft in this region (Lt Buchowski's report), we set up a specially rigorous anti-aircraft watch. In the end, we did not sight a single aircraft that day, possibly because of the poor weather…

We had to reduce our speed on a few occasions because of the heavy swell.

That day I had decided to change our usual return course (between Majorca and Ibiza) for a new one: between Majorca and Minorca, in spite of the narrowness of the straits. This enabled me to get to the south of the Balearic Islands during the night on the side that the Italian airmen 'did not like' to visit.

On 22 September, pouring rain, from which unfortunately not all our passengers were able to shelter, between 0600 and 0800 hrs we passed between the islands, luckily in poor visibility.

Because of the shallow seas in this area we passed many offshore nets set out by fishermen. We tried to pull some in, to improve the menu of the passengers and crew, but there was too little time, the weather was not in our favour and in the end we succeeded only in tearing away a few of the buoys.

On the next day we passed a large French passenger vessel, the *O.G.Grevy* going—judging by its course—to Oran; this was the second time we had met it in the same place.

On 23 September we were to have met the *Minna* at a position 30 miles east of the south-easterly headland of the island of Formentara (Balearics). The rendezvous had been arranged for 1000 hrs. At 0930 hrs, however, lying hove-to, we sighted the mast of the ship to the south. The transfer of passengers was completed by 0940 hrs. We passed over materials we had brought on board at the Morgiou *calanque* and were given fresh supplies of food and water.

18) *THE RETURN.* That day, with a favourable wind, we raised the sails; however it lasted no longer than half a day, after which we had a head wind again.

On 24 September we sailed the stretch between Cape Nao and Cabo de Gata, through—unusually—countless shoals of fish, so that it seemed as if the whole sea was alive with them…

On 26 September at 1030 hrs we were back in the port of Gibraltar, having this time covered 'only' 1,800 miles and spent 14 days at sea.

19) *MY CONVERSATION WITH MAJOR IWASZKIEWICZ.* He asked me to hand on a list for the C-in-C's Chief of Staff (delivered by me personally to the C-in-C's HQ, 9 October) and requested that:

a) we should not mention the names of the embarkation points, but use cryptonyms, namely: No. 1—La Madrague; No. 2—Sormiou; No. 3—Morgiou; No. 4—En-Vau;

b) we should add the figure 5 (five) to the date of the operation (which is to be understood as taking place at 0000 hrs), but at the same time give the real day of the week by way of confirmation;

c) the number of people being evacuated from France should be increased because of the great pressure of people;

d) we should support in London the suggestion of payment for the Marseilles evacuation 'outpost', because of the rising cost of living in France;

e) I should find out why orders had come from London reducing by ten the relatively modest number of 50 people to be evacuated, in order to take off ten Englishmen. The head of the British evacuation operation in Marseilles had shown him a signal from London notifying him that he 'might make use of the Polish organisation, but did not advise it';

The 'coding' of dates of evacuations (point b) above), even though the signals go by a Polish intelligence W/T link, was advisable as a safety measure, he said: the number of arrests lately in those regions has been worryingly high and caused some loss of confidence.

Gibraltar, 6 October 1942
Capt. M.Krajewski

Krajewski then returned to England, took three weeks' leave and, on 16 November 1942, rejoined *Blyskawica* as first lieutenant. He was awarded the Polish Cross of Gallantry and Bar 'for his courage, initiative and energy during special operations in the Mediterranean (1941–42) while evacuating Polish and Allied soldiers and citizens from occupied territories'. He served in the Battle of the Atlantic and in the North African invasion, but reckoned that his detachment to Gibraltar cost him his chances of a wartime command in the regular navy.

Buchowski sailed for France in *Seadog* again three days before Krajewski got back to Gibraltar from his epic 17th and last voyage. He took with him General Kleeberg[14] and Lt Cousens, RNR, who, like Maxted, had been sent out to Gibraltar by NID (C) to understudy the two Polish felucca captains and in due course relieve them in command. Buchowski's report on this expedition was as follows:

> BUCHOWSKI, Jan, Lt
>
> Report of voyage[15]
>
> I beg to report, Commander, that, following my operational orders I left port on 23.ix.42 at 2030 hrs. After circling Europa Point I set a course that would take us around Cabo de Gata at a distance of 15 nautical miles bearing north. On the 23rd and 24th the weather was fairly good, the wind easterly, Force 3–4, and the sea conditions level 3. On 25.ix at 0905 hrs a French passenger ship *(Marechal-Lyautey)* passed our stern at a distance of 3 miles, course N, speed 15 knots.
>
> The weather worsened, the wind westerly Force 3–4 and visibility poor. On 26.ix at 0900 hrs an Italian seaplane flew over the ship. Two-engined monoplane, two large floats, markings; a white cross on the rudder and wings. Position: lat.38°42' N, long. 01°58' E.Course changeable, presumably on anti-submarine patrol.
>
> On 27.ix from 0900 hrs to 1230 hrs we were passing through the straits between Majorca and Minorca. We noticed two French cargo vessels (coal-carrying), course S and N, speed around 7 knots. On 29.ix at 0800 hrs an Italian seaplane flew over the ship. The same type as that seen on the 26th. Changing course. The position at which we observed it: 42°57' N, 07°21' E. The plane remained visible to us until 1130 hrs. At 1330 hrs we were some 32 miles from the place of our first operation. I reduced our speed to 2½ knots. At 1500 hrs half speed. At 1600 full speed. At 1630 hrs the strong easterly wind suddenly dropped. At 1700 hrs there was an easterly wind Force 6–7, swell 4–5. We were in position at 2115. I began to give out the signals. By 2230 hrs I had received no reply, and as a result decided to move away. I could not travel to the second point, since it is impossible to land there in a strong easterly wind. On the 30th at 0420 hrs I was hove-to. We streamed the sea anchor. At 0630 hrs we had a breakdown of the engine, both bilge-pumps ceased operating. The ship started to take in a great deal of water. At 0900 hrs we had some 3 tons of water in the engine-room. We drew in the sea anchor in order to reduce the resistance and lifted the foresail, but within ten minutes the sail had been torn into shreds. The wind was blowing at Force 8–9, sea conditions 5–6. When we managed to repair the engine at 0930, we pumped out the water. On 1.x at 0930 hrs the weather was unchanged and we were unable to move to position. When the wind dropped at 1930 hrs to Force 4–5, the sea began to grow calmer. We set a course to the rendezvous spot. On 2.x at 1000 hrs the weather was fine. At 30 nautical miles from the meeting point we stopped the engine. We started the engine again at 1500 hrs, heading for the rendezvous. Entering La-Napoule Bay I passed at a distance of some 300 metres a French MTB making its way out into the open sea. In all probability, I was not observed. We were at the pinpoint by 2100 hrs and started to give out the requisite signals. There was no answer by 2100 hrs *(sic),* so I decided to put the two agents ashore, giving them the address and telling them how they could make contact

with the individual who was organising everything on the land side. I suggested that they should ask him to organise a reception for me the following night in the Rade-d'Agay at 2200 hrs and that they should bring all the passengers to that spot. I decided also to put ashore General Kleeberg since a delay in his arrival, even by so little as a day, would be dangerous for him and I was not sure whether his party of people would be waiting for him at position no. 2 (as it later turned out there was nobody there). I therefore landed General Kleeberg and two agents at the town of La-Napoule, 200m to the south of the railway station, half an hour before the departure of the train for Nice. At 2300 hrs I moved to the point fixed for our second operation. The place of the first operation was called Pointe-de-l'Aiguille, but two miles to the south there was a second point called Cap-de-l'Aguillon [? 1'Esquillon]: the similarity of the two names made me think that maybe they had made a mistake in London in giving out the position. I now had a lot of time in hand, since I did not need to be at the place of the second operation until 3.x at 0030 hrs, so I decided to move to 'Cap-de-l'Aguillon'. At 2330 hrs I sent out the first signal and received an answer immediately. I sent out the boat again with the two agents whom I had to put ashore. I could not offload the material since the promised motorboat had not materialised.

On 3.x at 0015 hrs I was at the position earmarked for the second operation. I remained there until 0130 hrs. I did not receive any reply to my signals. At 0136 hrs I moved out into the open sea. At 0900 hrs I stopped the engine some 35 miles from shore.

At 1500 hrs on 3.x I started up the engine and set a course for Rade-d'Agay. At 2200 hrs we were in position and I began to signal—but there was no answer. After about 20 minutes I saw a small boat moving in our direction. In the boat were two women—both French—who told me that I should make myself scarce since I had been observed by the gendarmes and police, and that I should go to the previous position. At 2230 hrs I left the Rade-d'Agay bay and had travelled half a mile from the shore when a flame about two metres long began to appear from the exhaust pipe. I covered the exhaust pipe in an old sail, but the sail caught fire, and so I organised three people with buckets to pour water on the sail.

On 4.x at 0000 hrs we were in position. I began to signal. By 0100 I had received no answer. The people pouring water on the sail were extremely tired, and so I decided to move out to sea. In the course of this short journey our engine stopped twice. At 1100 hrs I stopped the engine some 30 miles from the coast. The cause of our breakdown was coal-dust in the fuel. The filters were cleaned and the fuel tanks changed. At 1545 I started the engine and set a course for the site of the operation (Cap-de-I'Aguillon). At 2130 hrs we were in position—gave out the signal—received a reply. I sent out the boat which returned in ten minutes and the crew informed me that there was no motor boat. In the light of this I began to offload the material using our own small boat. The unloading was completed on 5.x at 0030 hrs. The people on the shore conveyed the news to me from General Kleeberg and the agents that everyone was safe and sound and that there were no more passengers to be taken off. At 0035 hrs I moved away from the coast–set a course for Gibraltar. Close to the Balearic Islands we had a breakdown of the radio, and thus were able neither to receive nor to send messages. I reached Gibraltar on 10.x at 0730 hrs, having covered 2,300 miles. In the tanks there were 5 gallons of fuel left.

(signed)
Lt Jan BUCHOWSKI

X
Last of the Polish Evacuation Missions

Patrick O'Leary, alias Albert Guérisse, having been landed near Port-Vendres on 18 April 1942 from *Tarana* in one of the first operations carried out under CWF auspices, set up one of the largest and most effective of MI9's wartime organisations for rescuing escaped prisoners of war and shot-down airmen who had evaded capture. The so-called 'PAT Line' had built on foundations laid by Ian Garrow at Marseilles and, by the autumn of 1942, its ramifications stretched up into the Pas-de-Calais and Belgium as well as into Brittany, which of course harboured many evaders.[1]

Most of these evaders and escapers were passed over the Pyrenees into Spain and, even if they fell into Spanish hands and were interned in the camp at Miranda, it was unlikely they would languish there for more than a few weeks, since the Spanish government was dependent on imported oil products and flour over, which the British contraband control system had a stranglehold. However, O'Leary did organise a small-scale first evacuation from Port-Miou in June, when, as recorded in Chapter XXX above, a mixed party of nine agents, refugees and airmen were embarked on *Seawolf* and subsequently transferred at sea to HMS *Middleton* (Operation LUCALITE I).[2] In July, *Tarana,* working alone, picked up 7 British escapers and evaders, mainly airmen, from the Saint-Pierre-Plage near Narbonne, among them Whitney Straight, a very distinguished American fighter pilot serving in the RAF, and did a smaller operation to the same point in August.

Those embarked by O'Leary on *Seawolf* on Krajewski's final expedition to France in September were mainly RAF aircrew who had escaped from internment by Vichy at Fort-de-la-Révère in the French hinterland behind Monaco. They included several well-known pilots and the complete aircrew of a Halifax bomber from 138 Special Duties Squadron, which flew missions for the clandestine services from Tempsford in Bedfordshire. Krajewski put the total number evacuated at 25, though other accounts speak of 38.[3]

The outward-bound passengers also included three French-Canadian commandos, who had been taken prisoner during the Dieppe raid a month previously but had escaped and fallen into Vichy hands. A fourth—a Sergeant Major Lucien Dumais—had already offered his services to O'Leary's escape line. He took part in the operation at Saint-Pierre-Plage that night, but stayed behind and was evacuated only a month later. He subsequently returned to France as head of MI9's SHELBURNE Mission, where, based in Brittany, he applied the formula of an escape line linked to largescale evacuation operations by sea, which O'Leary had copied from the Poles.[4]

As a result of the break-out from Fort-de-la-Révère, all the officers interned there were transferred to a camp in Italy. However, with the connivance of a Polish priest, the Abbé Mirda, and Caskie, the Missions to Seamen Scottish chaplain from Marseilles, who arranged for the internees to have access to a disused part of the fort once a week for recreation, 60 airmen and army other ranks made a second mass escape through the sewers in this area.

Thirty-four of these escapers were eventually collected by O'Leary at his safe house, a disused restaurant near Saint-Pierre-Plage. *Seawolf* should have picked them up on 5/6 October but made an error of some few hundred metres and thus failed to make contact with them. They had to cross and recross the River Tet four times, up to their necks in water, to get over to Saint-Pierre-Plage and back to the safe house before a new and more accurate rendezvous was arranged on the clandestine Gibraltar—Marseilles W/T link and they were all taken off by Lukasz on *Seawolf* on 11/12 October. Like those embarked by Krajewski at the same point on 20/21 September, the evacuees were so overwrought by fear, tension, boredom and frustration that their emotions erupted in a wave of reckless excitement when at last they saw the felucca's dinghy approaching the beach where they were assembled. Maxted, who was on board *Seawolf,* was appalled by the noise and feared that the French police or the dreaded *Milice* (Vichy auxiliary police units) would be alerted.[5]

Somehow, the whole party was ferried off safely and parked around the deck of the felucca. One man had escaped from hospital where he had been receiving treatment for a broken leg but had then broken an ankle jumping out the hospital window: he was propped against the wheel-house.

This was one of the few CWF missions from Gibraltar that consisted of a single operation, but it had proved a trying experience for the ship as well as for the passengers. Here is Lukasz's account of this first operation under his command:

> Lt M.Lukasz
> Report of voyage[6]
> (to) Head of Polish Naval Mission at GIBRALTAR
>
> I report below, Commander, on the progress of the voyage of the *Seawolf* carried out between 30.9.1941 and 16.10.1942. The crew was composed of the following members: Lt Lukasz (commanding), Lt Long (RNR), Sub Lt Maxted (RNR), Mate Tarnawski (1st mechanic), Leading Seaman Latka, Seaman Kurzawa (mechanic),

Mate Kuston (cook), Leading Seaman Stanislawski (radio operator), Leading Seamen Chwastek, Olesinski, Sieminski (deck-hands); PO Bates (British deck-hand).

AIM OF THE MISSION. Operation ROSALIND was intended to deliver a letter and two sacks of material to the British organisation in France as well as evacuate around 35 British POWs.

EXECUTION. In accordance with the orders of SOCWF I weighed anchor on 30 September at 2030 hrs and, at 2040, passed through the gate in the boom. After clearing Europa Point, I set a course that would take us along the Spanish coast so as to pass Cabo de Gata at a distance of 15 miles, continuing so as to stay 20 miles from the shore.

On 5 October at 1233 hrs, being some 42 miles from the embarkation point, I hove to, since we had around four hours to kill. At 1600 hrs I set out in the direction of the embarkation. I arrived at the location, i.e. on the southern bank of the River Tet estuary, at 0001 hrs on 6 October. A three-hour search of the coastline, continually signalling by lamp in the direction of the shore, produced no results (I covered a four-mile stretch of coast). At 0300 hrs I decided to withdraw and try my luck the following night. During the day I hove to at a distance of 36 miles from the coast.

On the next night I was at the agreed point at 0001 hrs (7 Oct.). On this occasion also, a two-hour search (covering some two miles of the coast) produced no results. At 0200 hrs I was forced to leave the area, as two vessels were heading in our direction, which I suspected were patrol boats. I decided to return to base, convinced that something must have happened ashore. I sent a radio report on the unsuccessful operation and of my decision to return to base. On 8 October at 1141 hrs I received a report giving the course followed by *Seadog* and requesting me to look out for her. Since my course was a little different from hers, I made a turn so as to arrive at her course as quickly as possible.

On 9 October at 1130 hrs I received a signal with the message: 'Return to embarkation point. The ROSALIND people have been waiting two nights and are still waiting…' I turned about immediately and went back. On 12 October at 0015 hrs I was at the embarkation point for the third time. This time when I signalled, I received the correct response immediately. At 0030 hrs I sent the dinghy to the beach and began to embark people. At 0200 hrs the operation was completed. I took on board 34 British former POWs, a Polish priest (a military chaplain called Mirda) and an officer of the French merchant navy. I left the letter and two sacks of material on shore. After hoisting the dinghy back on board, I set out on our return journey. On 16 October 1942 I passed through the gate in the boom at Gibraltar and at 0920 hrs handed over the passengers to the local authorities.

OBSERVATIONS. The journey passed off without any 'adventure'. I encountered over a dozen merchant ships and three transport aircraft, which did not pay us any attention. The weather, with the exception of the 2nd and 10th, was exceptionally fine. The wind did not go above Force 3. However on 11 October, the strong mistral (NW, Force 6–7) was in evidence. The swell did not ease until we were within three miles of the shore. At the embarkation point itself, conditions were calm and the use of the dinghy to embark the people did not present any problems.

RADIO COMMUNICATION. The radio operated effectively except on two days when we had no communication whatsoever with Gibraltar. It is difficult to find the reason for this. Probably on one day we were masked by high mountains, but on the second day the time assigned for communication with base was close to sunset (which on occasion causes problems).

The engine worked very satisfactorily. Small faults were caused by sloppy repair work in the workshops and perhaps too by ineffective servicing on the part of young, inexperienced mechanics.

GENERAL. I cannot explain how we were not seen on the nights of 5/6 and 6/7 October. I pulled along the shore at a distance of some 300 yards, certainly not more, and I touched the sandy bottom twice. Not only my light but the whole felucca must have been visible from the shore. According to eyewitnesses, during the first night even the fumes from the engine could be smelt… What is very curious is that, on my third approach to the embarkation point, I received a reply to my signal light immediately, although I was about a mile distant. There can be no question of our having made an error as to the embarkation point, since I checked our position several times with bearings taken from lighthouses.

(signed)
M.Lukasz, Lt

Even before Lukasz returned from this job for MI9's PAT escape line, Stoklas, the Polish Naval Attaché in London, had written to Slocum on 13 October, following up a conversation he had had with Lt Cmdr Madden of NID(C) on 24 September.[7]

Making it clear that he was acting on the instructions of the Chief of the Polish General Staff, Stoklas pointed out that the evacuation of Polish nationals from France and North Africa, for which purpose the Polish mission in Gibraltar had been organised, had lately been very considerably restricted by the Admiralty's giving precedence to special operations by feluccas attached to the CWF and manned by Polish crews.

The Polish General Staff regarded this as a particularly critical period. They wished to carry out as many evacuations from France as possible before the weather in the Golfe-de-Lyon broke and prevented any operations by these small boats. From experience of the previous year's campaign, they knew that September and October were the last favourable months.

On 1 September, they had been unexpectedly informed by the Admiralty that all sea operations both for the south coast of France and for the north coast of Africa, from Gibraltar as base, were suspended from 1 October for an indefinite period, probably until 15 November. According to this decision, which was communicated to Stoklas only on 13 September, the next evacuation from France, planned for the night of 4/5 and 5/6 October, had to be cancelled. This operation was considered especially important in view of the present serious deterioration of the situation of Poles in France.

Although the Poles were informed that all sea operations were to be stopped, both feluccas manned by Polish crews had been ordered to continue to carry out operations unconnected with the evacuation of Polish nationals from France. They were not informed whether any plans were being made for further such operations to be carried out during this period.

The Chief of the Polish General Staff instructed Stoklas to say that according to the *Proposals Concerning the Organisation of the Polish Mission in Gibraltar,* to which both sides had agreed, the Polish-manned feluccas might be used for such operations to a greater extent than originally anticipated, until special British crews were formed. As they had now heard that these crews had been put at the disposal of the senior officer CWF, Stoklas was further instructed to express the hope that from now on the Polish contingent would not be diverted from their main task—the evacuation of Polish nationals from southern France and north Africa; moreover that operations already proposed by the Polish mission in Gibraltar in cooperation with the Polish General Staff in London should, as far as possible, have first call on the Polish crews.

At any rate, the Chief asked for more detailed information, through the Polish Naval Attaché, about the way in which their crews were to be used in the immediate future, so that the Polish side might adapt their plans according to the circumstances in the countries from which evacuation was envisaged.

On the question of security and secrecy of the operations, which had already been raised, the Chief gave an assurance that he, for his part, had issued all the relevant instructions. He would be most grateful if the British authorities could note that very serious and dangerous indiscretions had allegedly been committed by non-Polish agents and possibly also by non-Polish civilians transported by their feluccas.

Such breaches of security, combined with the use of *Seawolf* and *Seadog* for British intelligence organisations had so increased the danger posed to operations purely for evacuation that the whole action to date might be compromised. Both sorts of operations had been carried out by the same boats, manned by Polish sailors, and their identity and the characteristics of the boats were now well known to the French authorities.

The Chief feared that all these factors might finally make the suspension of evacuation operations inevitable and consequently the existence of the Polish contingent in Gibraltar unnecessary. He had instructed Stoklas to say that he would be most grateful for an assurance that the task for which the Polish contingent had been attached to the CWF would not thenceforward be regarded as secondary, and that he would be informed, through the Polish Naval Attaché, of any important changes in the Admiralty's policy with respect to evacuation of Polish nationals from France to Gibraltar.

It was a good letter and it cannot, in the circumstances, have been an easy one to answer. Indeed, there is no evidence that it did receive an answer in written form.

That the Poles were compelled to cancel their own planned October evacuation from France and that *Seawolf* was then ordered by CWF to carry out an exactly similar operation on a smaller scale to rescue a group of British evaders and escapers was bound to engender resentment It entirely bore out Durski-Trzasko's warnings, at the end of his first month at Gibraltar, that Polish needs were being subordinated to British requirements. The Poles might have come round to accepting that, for reasons unknown to them, all forms of evacuation had temporarily to be relegated to lower priority than other forms of special operation; but that Slocum's organisation should then require a Polish crew to make a voyage to France to evacuate British nationals was a case of insult added to injury. Durski-Trzasko wrote to Admiral Swirski on 17 October, the day after Lukasz returned from his successful operation for MI9'S 'Pat' escape line, to say he saw no hope of further evacuation of Poles from France.[8] Since this was the main purpose for which the Polish crews were attached to the CWF, confirmed in the orders he had been given, he proposed that they wind up the Polish mission. From what he heard in Gibraltar, he concluded that, although the situation had completely changed, the British had no intention of dispensing with the services of the Polish feluccas, but wished to retain them for 'imperial' requirements. They made no secret of their view that, not only now but probably in the future too, the evacuation of large groups from the French coast must be entirely ruled out. The British understood perfectly well that they themselves were still not well enough prepared to take over the work carried out to date by Polish crews; nor did they have the experience and operational efficiency attained by the Poles through overcoming difficulties and set-backs. Durski-Trzasko imagined that the British would keep the Polish crews in place until they did have similar mastery of operational methods and means; but, equally, that the Poles would until then, be employed serving British, not Polish aims. If all this were so, however, the role of the Polish evacuation mission would have ended and, with it, the financing from Polish sources of seagoing evacuation operations. If the feluccas were to go on being manned by Polish crews under the command of Polish officers, it seemed essential to give them a proper official status. In other words, the feluccas should become regular men-of-war under command of a Polish naval officer, sailing under the Polish naval ensign. On board the feluccas, the crews should wear or at least carry uniforms in case they fell into enemy hands, when they might otherwise be treated as saboteurs, spies or even pirates.

By the time that Swirski replied to this letter, on 2 December,[9] the strategic situation in the western Mediterranean had changed radically.

XI
The Changing Strategic Context in the Western Mediterranean

Churchill claimed after the war that when the Japanese bombed the Pacific Fleet at its moorings in Pearl Harbour on 7 December 1941 and forced the United States into the Second World War, he knew that the war was won: Hitler and Mussolini would declare war on the United States and, in the prolonged coalition struggle that would follow, America's enormous resources, safeguarded by geography, would grind the Axis to defeat.[1] Great Britain, which had survived 17 months of lonely conflict under his leadership, would emerge, however mauled and mutilated, safe and victorious, as it had from eight earlier wars fought in the preceding two and a half centuries over the issue of hegemony in Europe. With the United States committed, all the rest was merely a question of what he called 'the proper application of overwhelming force'.

Churchill knew exactly where he most urgently needed the application of US force: in the Mediterranean, an area he feared the United States Joint Chiefs of Staff might 'too casually repudiate as not involving America's most vital interests'. Afraid that the whole fury of the United States would be turned on Japan, while Britain was left to fight Germany and Italy in Europe, Africa and the Middle East, the Prime Minister hastened to Washington. His object was to persuade Roosevelt and his service chiefs that the defeat of Japan would not spell the defeat of Hitler, but that, by contrast, if Hitler were defeated then finishing off Japan would be merely a matter of time and trouble.

Churchill, who was highly intuitive, suspected that Roosevelt might be sympathetic to some proposal for intervention in French North Africa.[2] The United States, unlike Great Britain, had maintained diplomatic relations with Vichy and the President had for some months had a personal representative in the Maghreb, Robert Murphy, entitled to report to the White House over the heads of the State Department. It was, in fact, an area of quite particular interest to the President. The policy pursued by Washington with regard to Vichy was very much Roosevelt's own and he had strong personal reasons for wishing to see it vindicated by positive benefits. North Africa was therefore the right card for Churchill to play and, as their first round of talks progressed in Washington over Christmas and the New Year of 1941–42, it was a subject to which the President returned with growing enthusiasm.

Before Churchill left in mid-January, the planners had been put to work on an Anglo-American project for landing in North Africa but the idea evoked little enthusiasm in the Washington military establishment: Admiral King wanted priority for the Pacific; General Marshall and General Eisenhower, his chief planner, thought the best way to beat Hitler was to build up large forces in Great Britain and launch them into Europe by the shortest sea route on a bee-line to Berlin. Despite the President's support for the North African plan, code-named SUPER-GYMNAST, Marshall and Eisenhower thought it a time-consuming diversion of resources, if not a devious Churchillian attempt to use American means to pluck British imperial chestnuts from the Middle Eastern fire. The case for the plan was further weakened by Auchinleck's resistance to Churchill's attempts to get him to mount an early offensive in the Western Desert. In the end it was laid aside by the US staff in favour of other projects.

However, the situation altered after Molotov's meetings in Washington in mid-May with the President, Hopkins, Marshall and King. He painted such a stark picture of what might happen on the Soviet front if no second front were opened in 1942 that Roosevelt, who faced mid-term elections in November, authorised him to tell Stalin that a second front could be expected before the end of the year. He did so without consulting Churchill and made the commitment public soon afterwards.[3]

During May, the British Chiefs of Staff had been conducting detailed surveys of available shipping resources, with particular attention to landing-craft availability, in order to assess their capacity for cross-Channel operations. They found that there were only enough landing craft to lift a force of 4,000 men to France: this finding demolished both General Marshall's SLEDGEHAMMER plan to seize a limited beach-head in the Cotentin, and Churchill's idea for a landing in Norway. On 2 May 1942 the British Chiefs directed SOE to facilitate a still-hypothetical landing in French North Africa.[4]

Churchill flew to Washington in June 1942. While he was with Roosevelt at Hyde Park, the combined British and US Chiefs of Staff decided, with rare unanimity, not to proceed with SUPERGYMNAST. Churchill held quite a different point of view, which he put to the President. If SLEDGEHAMMER was a non-starter, could they stand idle in the Atlantic theatre during the whole of 1942? Ought they not, while building up forces in the United Kingdom for a Continental invasion, to be preparing some other operation by which they might gain positions of advantage, and also directly or indirectly take some of the weight off Russia? That, the Prime Minister suggested, was the light in which the French North African operation should be studied.[5]

Churchill had made a careful study of the President's thinking and reactions and he was sure that Roosevelt was powerfully attracted by the North African plan. Stimson, the Secretary for War, who shared General Marshall's views on the matter, believed that

Churchill had taken up GYMNAST knowing full well that it was the President's 'great secret baby'.[6]

While Churchill was in Washington, news of the fall of Tobruk reached him and, as Rommel battered down the defences of Mersa Matruh and swept on to El Alamein, the Prime Minister faced a vote of censure in the House of Commons. He survived it by a massive majority, thanks partly to tactical errors by his critics. But from that point on, the needs of the 8th Army became a key factor in the ongoing strategic debate.

In July 1942, Roosevelt gave Marshall what was to prove a last chance to persuade the British Chiefs of the merits of SLEDGEHAMMER, but by then he had firmly overruled Marshall's arguments in favour of concentrating United States resources on the Pacific war rather than on SUPER-GYMNAST. He also told Marshall he wanted a decision within a week.

Marshall found the British Staffs adamantly opposed to SLEDGEHAMMER: it would have tied up 250,000 tons of shipping and precluded the sending of supplies to the 8th Army or to besieged Malta, a crucial factor in the attack on Rommel's communications. On 22 July he had to concede defeat. Eisenhower's immediate reaction was that it 'might well go down as the blackest day in history.'[7]

Since the President was both publicly committed to, and privately determined on, action in the 'European' theatre in 1942, GYMNAST in some form was now the only runner. Marshall wanted to postpone a final decision until 15 September, but Hopkins advised the President to reject this proposal, which would have entailed delaying the landings until the meteorologically unpropitious month of December: he urged that 30 October be fixed as the latest date for the beginning of TORCH, as the operation was now renamed. The President, in his capacity as Commander-in-Chief, decided that TORCH should take place at the earliest possible date, which turned out to be 8 November.[8]

In 1947, when General George Marshall had become Secretary of State, a young Brazilian diplomat, who had accompanied his minister on an official visit to Washington, asked Marshall whether he had read the first volume of Churchill's *Second World War*. 'Yes, I have read it: it's a great book', Marshall replied, 'but I am afraid of what he is going to say in the second volume.' Pressed to explain why, Marshall said that, in his wartime capacity as chairman of the Joint Chiefs of Staff, he had opposed Churchill's concept of attacking the soft underbelly of Europe as opposed to the cross-Channel alternative, because he feared the consequent losses of life and of time. As Secretary of State, he realised just what a mistake he had made.[9]

Eisenhower, too, later revised his opinion about SLEDGEHAMMER, when he came to realise how unseasoned the US troops were in 1942 and how inadequate the available air cover would have been.

From midsummer 1942, this high-level strategic debate began to influence the demands on the Allied clandestine services in the Western Mediterranean theatre and on the work of the CWF.

XII
Renewed Priority for Operations to French North Africa

The United States, having maintained diplomatic relations with the Vichy government, still possessed consular posts at Casablanca, Oran, Algiers and Tunis. When President Roosevelt decided that US strategic interests in French North and West Africa required him to appoint Robert Murphy as his quasi-diplomatic representative in the area, these served as a valuable infrastructure. The Americans were therefore far better placed to observe and influence events in the Maghreb during the run-up to TORCH than the British who, apart from their base at Gibraltar, had little more than their Consulate-General in Tangiers and were still suffering from the opprobrium of Mers el-Kebir. Murphy was, however, in no position to ask for the accreditation of attaches to represent the interests of the United States armed services, and the US was still groping its way towards the creation of a clandestine service with functions similar to those of SIS and SOE. The need for such capabilities in French North Africa was felt quite quickly after Murphy's arrival. Agreements concluded between Murphy and Weygand, Vichy's Delegate-General, for the supply of US economic assistance, served to justify the appointment of 12 additional Vice-Consuls or 'observers', whose agreed role was to ensure that US aid shipments did not find their way into Axis hands, but whose covert function was to collect military intelligence. These so-called 'Twelve Apostles' reported to a new Washington agency, the Office of the Coordinator of War Information, predecessor of the Office of Strategic Services (OSS). Its director was Colonel William J. Donovan, a highly decorated First World War veteran turned New York attorney and a personal friend of Roosevelt's, though he was a Republican and known to harbour political ambitions.[1]

'Big Bill' Donovan had visited London in the course of 1941 and had, by Churchill's decision, been very fully briefed on British arrangements in the clandestine sphere. This had materially strengthened his hand in pressing for the establishment of the OSS. During May and June 1942 Donovan was back in London for talks between OSS and SOE about combined working arrangements in the Western Mediterranean area in the event of Allied landings in North Africa.[2] It was agreed that an OSS headquarters should be set up in Tangiers under Colonel William Eddy to work with the SOE mission in Gibraltar. Hugh Quennell had been withdrawn from Gibraltar at the behest of Lord Gort, the Governor, after a disastrous explosion on board the Tangiers-Gibraltar ferry, and replaced by Colonel Brien Clarke, a New Zealander in the Coldstream Guards. It was decided that a network of clandestine W/T posts should be established with SOE's help, to cover at least the main centres– Tunis, Algiers, Oran and Casablanca. Since OSS was responsible for collecting intelligence as well as for subversion, they wished these stations to be linked to Tangiers, but both parties recognised that, if there were to be landings in North Africa, the operational headquarters would undoubtedly have to be Gibraltar.[3]

The still-hypothetical North African invasion plans lent enhanced importance to Rygor-Slowikowski's 'Agence Afrique', which he had built up into an extensive network concentrating on military targets and which provided SIS's main insight into this field. By great good fortune, the senior Vichy counter-espionage officer in Algeria, Achiary, was a secret sympathiser with the Allied cause. He became Rygor-Slowikowski's friend and protector, but he came under suspicion and was replaced by an inspector from Vichy who did not share his pro-Allied views and came close to unmasking the *réseau,* in which Rygor-Slowikowski used resident Poles as his sub-agents in Oran, Constantine, Casablanca and other centres.[4] Achiary himself was in touch with SIS, who arranged for a W/T receiver/transmitter to be delivered to him near Arzew in 1941 by a British submarine, which at the same time landed an agent of French nationality named Puech Sanson, who was on his way to Mostaganem, where his father had a factory producing Job cigarettes.[5]

Rygor-Slowikowski's published account of his mission[6] is detailed and impressive: the coverage he achieved, which was passed straight to Dunderdale by Colonel Gano in London, must have been particularly welcome to SIS, since Dunderdale's Section had by then (mid-1942) lost a high proportion of its sources in metropolitan France as a result of German countermeasures.[7] Rygor-Slowikowski also made contact with the Americans in Algiers, but found, to his extreme annoyance, that they were dilatory in passing on to Washington the copies of the reports he gave them.

The growth and success of the 'Agence Afrique' network and the enhanced strategic importance of French North Africa in the months leading up to TORCH meant that, just when the Polish evacuation missions to Casablanca and Oran came to a halt, new requirements, viewed by SIS and NID (C) as of even higher priority, took their place. The ensuing run of operations was carried out for CWF by *Minna,* Slocum's newly arrived fast escort vessel, which was by far the most suitable ship for the job.

Minna had been built in 1939 as a Scottish fishery protection vessel, but had never in fact served in that capacity, as she was sent straight from her builder's yard at Dumbarton to survey the west coast of Scotland for possible tanker anchorages, on behalf of the War

Department.[8] After four months, in August 1939, she was taken over by the Admiralty and allocated to the Firth of Forth as an examination vessel on blockade-enforcement duties. In June 1940 she captured an Italian merchant vessel off May Island but in December she was seriously damaged by one of the then new German acoustic mines. This put her into a repair yard for six months. Back in service, she was attacked and damaged by a Heinkel bomber in November 1941. When she had been repaired again, she was sent out to Gibraltar in April 1942 to join the CWF as the larger of the two ships Slocum had undertaken to provide as reinforcement for the Polish-manned feluccas.

Minna was 170 feet long, with a gross registered tonnage of 347. Designed to overhaul and arrest maritime poachers, she had been endowed with twin screws and the extra turn of speed necessary for that work. Ordinary deep-sea trawlers might well be capable of 9, or even 10, knots: *Minna*'s cruising speed of 14 meant that, if it came to a chase, poachers would not be able to show her a clean pair of heels. Her captain during this commission was Commander D.H.F. Armstrong, DSC, RNR, and her first lieutenant was another RNR officer, D.T.MacCallum. She carried a four-inch gun forward on her whale-back and sported the usual array of machine-guns on the wings of her bridge and aft for anti-aircraft protection.

Minna could even less afford to be seen close offshore on the Algerian or Moroccan coast than could *Tarana* on the south coast of France but, whereas *Tarana* under false Moroccan or Spanish colours might hope to pass muster as a genuine fisherman and thus avoid attack, *Minna* was unmistakably a minor warship and had to be prepared to fight her corner if sighted by a hostile patrolling aircraft. In mid-1942, there was always a chance of such an encounter in the western Mediterranean, but it was not a routine occurrence, so she was able to exploit the fact that the Germans had as yet no air-bases in southern France and that French coastal defences in Algeria were not sufficiently on the alert to include air-reconnaissance patrols. Nevertheless, her substantial silhouette and unsilenced engines meant that she needed to heave to at least a quarter of a mile offshore during a night operation; meanwhile, MacCallum would conduct any necessary boatwork, for which she carried one of the 25-foot SN6 surf-boats that Nigel Warington Smyth had developed and Camper and Nicholson had built for NID (C)'s clandestine needs.

Minna's first mission from Gibraltar for the CWF was a rendezvous in the Gibraltar Straits at the end of June 1942 with a felucca from Tangiers, to which she transferred a consignment of warlike stores for SOE—a method of shipment no doubt made necessary by the disaster in Tangiers harbour in March that had blighted Quennell's SOE career.

The fact that *Minna*'s next operation, GUYMAR, involved landing an agent near Oran for Kenneth Cohen's P1 Section of SIS is at first sight surprising. Cohen normally worked with de Gaulle's BCRA and the arrival of a Gaullist emissary in Algeria at that juncture would have been extremely unwelcome to President Roosevelt and Robert Murphy, his personal representative in the Maghreb. But, for historical rather than logical reasons,

Cohen was also SIS's point of contact with an important intelligence network, 'Alliance', whose chiefs, Commandant Loustaunau-Lacau and Jacques Bridou, alias 'Navarre', had refused to work with de Gaulle. The links between 'Alliance' and North Africa and Navarre's ambition to provoke a revolt of the French army there had led to the latter's arrest for the first time in May 1941. Commandant Léon Faye, chief of operations for 'Alliance', who was also arrested, had maintained close links with the small group of non-Gaullist conspirators in Algiers who were in touch with Murphy and planned to assist any Allied landings there.[9] The agent landed was a young officer of the Belgian merchant navy named Guy Verstraete, who had escaped from Dakar to Bathurst in a ship's lifeboat and on arrival in England had been recruited by SIS and trained as a W/T operator.[10] He was in touch with Ridgway Knight, one of Robert Murphy's OSS Vice-Consuls. His cover was that he was the son of a wealthy landowner. He and a considerably older local associate met the young and wealthy widow of a local colonist at an Oran hotel and were soon living with her in considerable style and comfort.

Minna's third operation, ORKAN II, successfully evacuated a subagent of Rygor-Slowikowski's from near Oran on 13 July, but the fourth, CASUAL, failed to land two, or possibly three, Polish agents in the same area on 19 July because the expected reception committee was not in place. This operation was successfully completed on 11 September, when it was combined with ZEBRA, an evacuation. The Oran sub-agent took the five men and one woman who were to be embarked on that night to the pick-up point as participants in an evening picnic party.[11] The agents landed on this occasion, Malinowski, Kowal and Piotrowski, had been on board *Minna* since May.

Another of *Minna*'s Algerian operations—ACCOST—an embarkation, failed at the beginning of October when a signal went astray leaving the agent too little time to arrive at the rendezvous. Last-minute intelligence was urgently required from Rygor-Slowikowski's 'Agence Afrique' in the run-up to TORCH, but the successful landing of an agent from *Minna* on 1 October, the embarkation of six on 3 October (GIRAFFE II) and of a further individual on the same night (ULTRAMARINE) were recorded as for the 'Poles', rather than SIS (P5), the description applied to other 'Agence Afrique' operations.

Minna was attacked by an enemy aircraft on the return voyage after the abortive operation on 19 July, but drove off her assailant. It is clear from the records that both she and *Tarana* were also used by CWF for a number of operations on the coast of Spain as well as in support of the Polish feluccas (see above).

XIII
SOE and OSS Prepare for TORCH

SOE's signals officer at Gibraltar, Squadron-Leader Mallory (real name Hugh Mallory-Falconer), and his staff had considerable difficulty in establishing the required W/T network to link all the US consular posts in French North Africa to Tangiers, let alone to Gibraltar. OSS brought various operators to Tangiers, where Mallory had made arrangements for them to be instructed in operating their sets, and sets were delivered to OSS in Tangiers for distribution. But by the beginning of September a major complication had arisen: the SOE signals station at the western end of the tunnels in the Rock was able to send and receive signals to and from Tangiers, Casablanca and Oran quite satisfactorily, but contact with Algiers was very temperamental and Tunis permanently out of communication.[1]

Mallory put in a prodigious amount of work trying to discover whether this difficulty was due to technical faults in the sets or to errors by the operators: the sets were changed and the Tunis operator brought back to Tangiers for further instruction. It eventually became clear that the trouble lay at the Gibraltar end: SOE needed a branch W/T station at the eastern end of the Rock directly connected with their main signals station.

Tunnelling in the Rock had been proceeding for a considerable time and plans existed for the garrison and civil administration to be dispersed in the tunnels in the event of siege, but the tunnelling operation had still not caught up with the final requirements and all the available space had been allocated with very high priorities. Colonel Brien Clarke of SOE decided that, in view of the vital importance of the SOE/OSS communications, he must approach Mason Macfarlane, who had succeeded Field Marshal Lord Gort as Governor in June 1942, to see whether the necessary further accommodation could be allocated to SOE.

Brien Clarke was unaware that his call on the Governor fell at an unfortunate juncture, because Mason Macfarlane had that very morning held an urgent conference to decide requirements and priorities for erecting further wireless installations on the Rock for the

Royal Navy and the RAF in connection with the planned landings. The Governor's first reaction to Clarke's request was distinctly hostile, but he relented when the problem was explained to him. Not only did he agree to provide the accommodation but he went so far as to allocate to SOE part of what would have been his own quarters, in case a crisis arose before tunnelling was complete.

Mallory and his staff worked day and night at the installation of this branch-signals equipment and, within a few days of the job's completion, Clarke was able to report that communications with Algiers had greatly improved and that a satisfactory link with Tunis had been established.

Clarke and Bill Eddy, his OSS opposite number, met quite frequently during this period, usually in Tangiers, as Eddy had no avowable reason for being seen frequently in Gibraltar. On these occasions they sent combined progress reports to London and Washington on the state of the clandestine W/T system and the assistance arrangements with the French groups with whom Murphy was working. In between these contacts, Major Wharton Tigar, SOE's man in Tangiers, who was working under cover as a clerk at the British Consulate-General, was in daily touch with his OSS counterparts.

Eddy, son of American missionary parents in the Middle East, was an Arabist and had taught at the American University in Beirut. After the war he became head of the US Mission in Saudi Arabia and in that capacity was reckoned by his British diplomatic colleagues as unfriendly to British interests. Clarke, on the other hand, considered that Eddy deserved the greatest credit for the cooperative spirit he showed and maintained throughout the planning and operational phases in the months leading up to TORCH.

The operational phase began for Brien Clarke at about tea-time on 19 October[2] when he was summoned to the drawing-room of Government House, where a conference of clearly distinguished visitors was in full swing. The Governor introduced him to Major-General Mark Clark, Colonel Lemnitzer, Colonel Hamblen and Colonel Julius Holmes, all of the US Army, though in civilian attire, and to Captain Gerald Wright, US Navy. It was evident to Brien Clarke that what he subsequently described as the long-expected, high-level staff talks with the French were about to begin.

At one point, VACNA, Sir Edward Collins, turned to Clarke and said, 'What do you know about all this? Do you realise that they are wanting to take one of my submarines to land on the North African coast? Isn't all this crazy?', or words to that effect. Clarke, who was evidently not fully informed about the state of negotiations between Murphy, General Mast and the self-appointed group of plotters under Lemaigre-Dubreuil, replied rather lamely that, in ancient days, before a tournament, the knights sometimes discussed whether lances, swords or clubs should be used, and how the tournament should be conducted; perhaps pending events should be viewed in the same light. Collins, widely known as 'the Giant Panda', seemed far from comforted.

The Governor suggested that perhaps General Mark Clark would like to question Captain Barney Fawkes, who commanded the 8th Submarine Flotilla from HMS

Maidstone, and Clarke himself about details of the impending submarine voyage and the W/T link between Gibraltar and Algiers. Mark Clark took the two officers concerned into a corner of the room to pursue these matters. One question he asked, among many others, was whether he and his party should land in North Africa in uniform or in plain clothes. Brien Clarke gave his opinion that they should to land in uniform, as even a US Major-General in plain clothes might have some difficulty in explaining to the Vichy authorities what he was doing there in civilian dress. Mark Clark said he received the same reply at Chequers from the Prime Minister a few evenings earlier.

Shortly afterwards the conference broke up and the American party adjourned to Captain Fawkes's quarters in *Maidstone*. Brien Clarke accompanied them. There the final details of the expedition were arranged. It was agreed that the party would leave Gibraltar in the submarine P219 (later named Seraph) under the command of Lt N.L.A.Jewell, RN, at about 2200 hours the same evening. For the first part of the voyage the submarine might maintain limited W/T communication with Gibraltar but when it reached the French North African coast W/T communication from the submarine would be prohibited. P219 would be equipped with the necessary Folboats for landing and taking off the party. Brien Clarke suggested that they should take a small radio set to act as a link between ship and shore. Captain Fawkes undertook to provide this.

The landing pinpoint and recognition signals had already been agreed with Murphy, who would be in charge of the reception party, which would be headed on the French side by General Mast. Brien Clarke undertook to send a signal to Algiers forthwith to tell them that the party was on its way. In the event of trouble at the Algerian end, General Mark Clark said his party would try to make for the large salt-flats south-east of Oran and hoped that a signal would be sent from Algiers to the Gibraltar SOE post, in case he wanted the Flying Fortresses in which the party had flown out from the United Kingdom sent to take them off.

Mark Clark also asked that, on the return journey when the submarine was in mid-Mediterranean and no longer needed to observe wireless silence, a Catalina flying-boat should be sent to take him and his party off the submarine, weather permitting, thus saving several hours on the return journey.

At Gibraltar there was a small detachment of the Special Boat Section (SBS), which was trained in the use of Folboat canoes for clandestine landings and which had therefore the equipment and experience to land and pick up General Clark's party.[3] Three of their officers, Captain G.B.Courtney (known to his friends as 'Gruff'), Captain R.P.Livingstone and Lt J.P.Foot, were embarked on P219 with their equipment before she sailed at 2100.

The departure from England of the two B17 Flying Fortresses had been delayed: instead of taking off on the evening of Sunday 18 October, they left only at dawn on the 19th, which meant that the party's sailing from Gibraltar was delayed. Before leaving, Clark sent Murphy a message to say he would meet Mast on the night of 21/22 October. Murphy had in the meantime sent a signal to say he and the French group would expect Clark on the night of 20/21 October and, if that rendezvous was missed, they would hope to meet him 48 hours later.

Jewell took the risk of running P219 on the surface in order to make the best possible speed, but further delay was caused by an indispensable exercise in the use of the Folboats in the dark and the submarine did not arrive at the agreed landing site of Messelmoun, some 12km west of Cherchell, until shortly before dawn on 21 October, by which time the reception party had left.

By then Murphy had received Clark's signal and the whole group was reassembled that evening, with some difficulty, at the villa on the unfrequented beach there. It had been chosen for the conference because it belonged to the father-in-law of an active member of the Cherchell Resistance. Shortly before midnight, the agreed light signal was shown to seaward and disembarkation began, using four Folboat canoes. This went very smoothly and Mark Clark and his colleagues were able to get some sleep while awaiting the arrival of General Mast and his team.

Historians have questioned whether General Clark's melo-dramatic mission accomplished anything useful. Tarbé de Saint Hardouin, one of the Group of Five with whom Murphy was negotiating the attempt to bring General Giraud into the affair, has argued that it actually did harm by creating an impression of too much confidence on the American side and too much distrust on the French.[4] The Allies were going to land in North Africa with or without French assistance, but A.L.Funk has pointed out that the planners of TORCH had grave reservations about the operation, at one time giving it no better than a 50–50 chance of success. They were very conscious of the lack of training, the shortage of equipment and, above all, the absolute novelty of an amphibious assault conducted from across the Atlantic. Any opportunity of securing an unopposed landing was therefore worth pursuing and far outweighed the risks of General Clark's capture. But those involved, both French and American, greatly overestimated Giraud's influence and relevance. Clark reported from Gibraltar that extremely valuable intelligence had been obtained and that the plan for the operation appeared sound.

The conference was brought to an abrupt and dramatic end at about 6p.m. on 22 October, when two coastguards, who had assisted the landing, telephoned to say that the local police commissaire was on his way to inspect the villa. One of the Arab servants, who had twice before been evicted at short notice for security reasons by Tessier, the owner of the property, had told the police that something abnormal was afoot—probably smuggling.

The whole landing party took refuge in the empty wine cellar, while the French participants flew in all directions: the trap-door to the cellar was closed on Mark Clark and his companions, barrels were rolled on top of it and, as a finishing touch, someone scattered dust on the boards. Some of this percolated into the cellar, causing Gruff Courtney to have a coughing fit. As he struggled in the darkness to control it, choking and spluttering, he whispered to Clark, 'General, I'm afraid I'll choke,' to which Clark replied

'I'm afraid you won 't.'[5] Clark slipped him a wad of chewing-gum, which he had already worked for a while, and this had the desired effect of silencing Courtney. They had to sit in pitch-darkness for two hours, getting more and more cramped, while Murphy, Ridgway Knight and Tessier explained that the American diplomats were his guests, that the occasion was a purely social one and included some imaginary ladies upstairs, and that the smuggling story was a ridiculous invention.

It was 8p.m. before the police went and General Clark and his fellow sufferers were allowed to emerge from the cellar. To Courtney's remark that 'your American chewing-gum' had so little taste, Clark replied that he had chewed all the taste out of that particular piece.

All the French, except Tessier and a young man named Karsenty, had driven back to Algiers. Those who remained carried the Folboats down to a wood near the beach, where a considerable sea was running. Clark, who could see he was going to get soaked, took off his trousers and rolled them up around his heavy money-belt, which contained several hundred dollars in gold. Not wishing to be weighed down by it in the surf and heavy undertow, he put the roll into the Folboat. He and Livingstone tried to launch one of the canoes, wading out waist-deep and making a dash for it at what seemed a favourable moment. Just when they thought they were clear, an exceptionally large wave hit them: the boat reared up almost vertically and was rolled over, leaving them struggling in a boiling turmoil of foam. It had been impressed on everybody that on no account must the paddles be lost: accordingly, all that could be seen of Clark at one time was one arm holding a paddle firmly aloft above the swirling water. But the trousers and the money had disappeared (they were subsequently recovered and given to Murphy).

The disconsolate group stayed on the beach, cold and wet, not daring to return to the villa. They discussed the possibility of buying, chartering or stealing a fishing boat at Cherchell, driving to Spanish Morocco or making their way to Algiers, but all these courses involved unacceptable risks. They decided therefore to wait. About four o'clock in the morning the sea seemed to have abated slightly and they decided to make another attempt. Courtney knew that on the West African coast natives launched their canoes through surf by carrying them out beyond the breakers before climbing aboard. The shore party, consisting of Tessier, Karsenty and the two coastguards, stripped off their clothes and waded out into the cold surf with the canoes held above their heads. This tactic worked, although two of the canoes capsized at the beach and had to be righted. The last Folboat to come alongside the submarine was swamped and had to be abandoned, taking with it Julius Holmes's musette bag and its contents, which included letters written by Murphy and more gold coins.

The sky was already announcing the advent of the dawn and Jewell decided they must submerge without delay. Soaked and exhausted, the landing party made their way below. Mark Clark asked Jewell whether they had a rum ration on submarines. 'Yes, sir', replied Jewell, 'but on submarines only in emergencies.' 'Well', said General Clark, 'I think this is an emergency. What about a double rum ration?' 'OK, sir', said the submarine's captain, 'if an officer of sufficient rank will sign the order.' Clark actually did put his signature to the order.

The submarine ran submerged during the day of 23 October except for a brief surfacing to send a message reporting that conditions were ideal for transfer to a flying-boat. On the morning of 24 October Mark Clark and his party were picked up from P219 by a Catalina and taken to Gibraltar, as planned. Before boarding the Flying Fortress for his return flight to London, General Clark dictated to Colonel Brien Clarke of SOE a signal reporting the main features of his talks with General Mast and outlining the more interesting episodes of his hazardous expedition. This was transmitted by SOE Gibraltar to SOE Baker Street with the prefix 'For Eisenhower's eyes only' and dated 24 October 1942.[6]

Mast had raised one matter with Clark that became SOE's direct concern: he said that if 2,000 Bren guns could be delivered to the young men under the orders of Henri d'Astier de la Vigerie and Colonel Van Hecke, the Belgian-born head of the local Chantiers de la Jeunesse youth training scheme, to replace the antique weapons on which they were relying, this group could become an underground force of political significance. Mark Clark foresaw no difficulty in meeting this request and agreed to make the arrangements.

During the previous few months, SOE had accumulated a stock of some 600 tons of arms, explosives and other warlike stores at Gibraltar for various contingency plans on which they had been working; these included distribution to the French resistance elements in North Africa who were collaborating with Murphy and the fledgling OSS. The stores included special flares for airborne landings, automatic pistols, Sten guns, anti-tank 'Gammon' grenades, demolition materials, miniature tyre-bursters camouflaged to look like mule droppings, samples of which had been collected in Tangiers and flown home. There were some Bren guns and rifles, together with large stocks of ammunition of the relevant calibres. Brien Clarke was thus easily capable of meeting Mast's request, but the quantities asked for were unrealistically high. Indeed, a certain amount of such equipment —particularly flares and recognition signals—had already been dispatched in small consignments to the Americans in Tangiers. Brien Clarke reported to Baker Street that Colonel Lemnitzer (a future NATO Supreme Commander) had turned over to him 16,500 Algerian Francs 'to cover expenses', though this sounds more like an attempt to dispose of the contents of his money-belt than even a notional transaction.

Brien Clarke and Eddy worked out a plan which they agreed with Murphy. It called for the landing of some 10 tons of small arms, ammunition, grenades and small mines somewhere in the vicinity of Algiers. Osborne chose *Minna* for the operation, which was not very different in kind from others she had carried out since the beginning of July on the Algerian coast, though it required her to venture considerably further east than on the previous six expeditions, all of which had been to the Oran area.

SOE Baker Street had formed a small mission to take part in the TORCH landings and in any subsequent military operations. This included a naval officer who had already distinguished himself during the final stages of the East African campaign by sinking, or forcing ashore, off Djibouti a German merchant vessel of 8,000 tons, which was attempting to escape from Massawa through Vichy-French territorial waters. This officer, Anglo-Irish by descent, had left the Royal Navy after the First World War as a Sub-Lieutenant and had spent the inter-war years as skipper of dhows in the Red Sea. His crews were Somali and he must have earned a living as a trader in pearls, arms and hashish. He had become a Muslim and, when recalled as a reserve officer at the outbreak of hostilities in 1939, was widely known as Lt Cdr Abdullah Bey, RN.[7]

His feat in sinking the *Elbe* and capturing her crew of nearly 40, with a force of two engineless dhows, whose armament consisted of a Bren gun and a three-pounder Hotchkiss quick-firing gun, such as was mounted on naval steam picket-boats at the turn of the nineteenth century, earned him a recommendation for the DSO. However, while in command of a schooner supplying beseiged Tobruk (petrol in the bottom of the hold, bully beef on top, because they were so regularly shot up from the air), Bey incurred the severe displeasure of Admiral A.B.Cunningham, his Commander-in-Chief at Alexandria. Quite what led to this fall from grace is difficult to establish: people said at the time that he had 'swung on too many chandeliers'. Whatever the reason, he was sent home and Cunningham advised that he be no further employed. The recommendation for a DSO was rescinded.

SOE, however, impressed by his operational record, were about to send Bey off to join the impending landings in French North Africa when they realised that Cunningham was not only Eisenhower's deputy for the TORCH operation but would thereafter again become Commander-in-Chief of the whole Mediterranean: the last person he would wish to see there was Abdullah Bey. The fact that the Bey was also reported to have been talking to a group of strangers in a bar off Trafalgar Square about the forthcoming invasion sealed his fate: he was sent off to 'the Cooler'—a particularly remote SOE establishment in the north of Scotland intended to keep such people out of harm's way. The present author was summoned from Helford and flown to Gibraltar to take his place as the naval member of SOE's BRANDON mission. He landed there on 29 October with orders to act as conducting officer on the gunrunning operation asked for by Mast. The matter was urgent: *Minna* would have to leave Algerian waters by dawn on 6 November at the latest, so as not to risk alerting the defences on the eve of the first major amphibious operation of the war.

XIV
The Last Phase of the CWF's Operation: October–November 1942

As winter approached, the weather broke and gale after gale made operations in the western Mediterranean hazardous. Gibraltar became a main forward base and concentration point for the impending North African invasion. Orders from London banned the passage of agents to and from the Rock, bringing the Poles' highly successful felucca service to a halt. Then, on 29 October, *Seadog* was sent to France again and, on the night of 3/4 November, only four days before TORCH, Buchowski used her to carry out four successful landing operations at Port-Miou near Cassis, an ideal pinpoint, sheltered from all winds. His report was laconic in comparison with those of Krajewski:

> On 29 October I left port at 2030 hrs and, in compliance with my operational orders, after rounding Europa Point, set an easterly course so as to pass by the south of Cabo de Gata at a distance of 15 nautical miles. During the voyage there were no events worth reporting.[1]
>
> Arriving at the position on 3 November at 2130 hrs, I transferred command to [Capt] Pohorecki and made my way via the dinghy together with two other people to the Port-Miou *calanque*. After an hour's searching along the shoreline, I found the agents, who had not been waiting at the position agreed, and we exchanged the correct signals and code-signs. At 2330 hrs I returned to the ship. Nine (9) agents were put ashore and six (6) embarked. On 4 November at 0200 hrs the operation was completed. We moved away from the shore and set our course for the next operation point.
>
> On 5 November at 2200 hrs we were at the agreed position and we exchanged signals. The dinghy could not make its way to shore because of rough weather. At 2400 hrs we made away from the shore. During the day we rode out the storm 30 nautical miles distant from the coast. The weather worsened.
>
> On 6 November at 1500 hrs I set a course for the operation point. The wind was Force 8, the sea conditions Force 6, and the wind was continuing to increase in

strength. At 2300 hrs, some five miles south of the point of the operation, the wind was Force 9–10 (from the NW). Working at full speed, the engine produced a speed of 1 knot. At 2330 hrs I changed course. We left the shore. The wind force of 10 increased to 11. On 7 November at 0200 hrs a wave destroyed and tore away the wheel-house and galley. At 0900 hrs I sent a signal to Gibraltar, reporting our situation. At 2000 hrs the engine broke down and the vessel drifted in the direction of Sardinia.

On 8th at 0100 hrs the fault was repaired. We were then some 60 nautical miles from the Sardinian coast. Set a course for Gibraltar. Weather unchanged.

On the 10th at 19.00 hrs we were about 20 nautical miles east of the north-eastern promontory of Minorca. The weather improved.

On 13 November at 1000 hrs we entered the port of Gibraltar.

J.Buchowski, Lt

The following were landed at Port-Miou in the course of Operations WATCHMAN III, OVERGROW and DUBONNET on 3/4 November for SOE:[2] George Starr, Marcus Bloom, Mary Herbert, Mme M.T.Le Chêne and Odette Sanson. Embarked were: J.A.R. Starr, I.Newman, a W/T operator with Peter Churchill, a person with the field name 'Richard', his son and 'Quintet' Jaboune, brother of Claude Dauphin, recruited by 'Carte' for Radio Patrie, the clandestine broadcasting station operated by the British Political Warfare Executive, whose existence and tenor exacerbated relations with 4 Carlton Gardens. George Starr, though initially destined for Lyons, was to end up in Gascony, where he became a Maquis organiser of such standing that the Germans believed him to be a British general: his homeward-bound brother John, whom he met briefly on the beach, was to return to France, where he was captured by the Sicherheitsdienst, taken to their Avenue Foch headquarters and manipulated in the hope of extracting information from other SOE prisoners. Odette Sanson, courier to Peter Churchill, was subsequently captured with him, survived Ravensbrück and was awarded the George Cross. One agent was also landed for MI9 at Port-Miou that night, along with 1,0001b of stores for SOE.

The pinpoint chosen by Algiers for *Minna*'s gun-running expedition (Operation LEOPARD for CWF, PICNIC for SOE) was 12km west of Cherchell and 120km west of Algiers. Though nobody mentioned it at the time, this was near the Tessier villa, where General Mark Clark and his colleagues had landed ten days before. Presumably, the complicity of the two local coastguards was thought to outweigh the risk of further trouble from the Arab servants and the police, though ten tons of cargo could hardly have been removed without at least one heavy truck.

Since *Minna* could not afford to be seen anywhere near French territorial waters and must therefore approach the landing from well offshore, a passage of some 400 nautical miles was involved. By the time the weapons had been degreased, repacked in waterproof packages of a suitable size to be manhandled and loaded on to the ship, it was clear that the earliest time she could reach the rendezvous was after nightfall on 2/3 November. Algiers was so advised by signal before *Minna* sailed.

Minna had no difficulty in maintaining the required timetable and she reached the area of the pinpoint on time. But she waited in vain for the agreed light signal and had to withdraw 20 miles offshore well before daybreak. On the night of 3/4 November, she crept back to the coast, confident that she was at the agreed place, but again there was no light signal and she withdrew, expecting to have to return for a third night's vigil, as called for by her operation orders. But on the afternoon of 4 November a signal was received from SOE Gibraltar saying that their friends would be prepared to receive the shipment that night but at an entirely different pinpoint, about 3km east of Alma Marine, which was 30km east of Algiers, and that they would, if necessary, repeat the reception arrangements on the following two nights.

The old and the new pinpoints were nearly 160km apart, as the seagull flies. *Minna* was lying 20 nautical miles offshore, and as she would have to skirt the coastal batteries on Cap Matifou just west of Alma Marine, she faced a passage of some 120 miles to reach the new venue. Obviously she could not arrive there in time to carry out the operation that night. *Minna* nevertheless steamed to the new operational area at top speed, determined to be in position on the second of the three appointed nights. The signal from the beach was to be a steady white light with a steady blue light beside it, starting at 2000hrs local time: the landing was to begin at 2130.

José Aboulker and Bernard Karsenty were in charge of the reception arrangements. Aboulker says they expected the delivery would be made by submarine and that on the night of 2/3 November they were on the beach at Messelmoun, where Karsenty had helped General Clark and his party ashore 12 days before.[3] They decided next morning, in consultation with Murphy, that this was too dangerous a landing-place and switched to the Alma Marine alternative, which they had previously reconnoitred. There must therefore have been a delay of 24 hours or more in transmitting the new arrangements to *Minna* via SOE Gibraltar.

Brien Clarke's report to SOE says that *Minna* was in the vicinity of the new landing point from the night of 3 November and that 'in spite of the most careful and audacious search by the ship's commander [Armstrong] on the night of 4/5 November', no recognition signals could be picked up and the project eventually had to be abandoned, as the Admiralty had insisted that *Minna* be clear of the African coast by dawn on the 6th, for fear that her presence would alert the defences and compromise the main landings.

Alma Marine beach was indeed used less than 48 hours later, for landings by troops that formed the easternmost flank of the invasion force. The present author confirms that *Minna* was operating within the time limit to which Clarke refers, but the 'careful and audacious' search took place not on the night of 4/5 November but on the night immediately before *Minna*'s withdrawal, that is to say, on 5/6 November. Moreover, *Minna* arrived in the vicinity not on 3 November but on the 4th.

Brien Clarke's errors are understandable. No sooner had *Minna* returned to Gibraltar than she was ordered to join one of the invasion force convoys sailing eastwards. There was no time for a post-mortem at Gibraltar on what had gone wrong, nor did the participants have occasion to discuss the matter in Algiers, where the unforeseen presence of Admiral Darlan raised matters of more immediate moment. But the reasons for the failure of Operation LEOPARD are of some interest in the light of Murphy's conviction, shared with Eddy, that the British let them down because they had 'no confidence in our judgement or our French underground'. John Knox, one of Murphy's Vice-Consuls sent to London to help with the planning of TORCH, told A.L.Funk in November 1972 that Brigadier Mockler-Ferryman, the relevant regional director of SOE in 1943, had admitted as much. But Mockler-Ferryman had not even joined SOE at the time of TORCH. Funk was also told by Karsenty and Aboulker that they learned after the war that the shipment had been sent, but to the wrong rendezvous. This may well be the reason why *Minna* failed to make contact at Messelmoun on 2/3 November: as in other cases, a navigational error of even a few hundred yards on an unfamiliar coast can wipe out the chance of picking up light signals. Aboulker told the present author in 1984 that he thought that the reception committee, which turned out at Alma Marine on 4/5 November and again on 6/7 November after *Minna*'s departure, might not have been there on the night in between, 5/6 November, which was the very night that *Minna* was cruising to and fro looking in vain for their lights, having been assured that the reception committee would be waiting on all three nights.

As for Murphy's suggestion that SOE had no confidence in 'our judgement and our underground', it should be recorded that, within a week of TORCH, most of the members of the Gaullist group who helped the Allies achieve an easy landing at Algiers had to be issued with British Army battledress and pay books by SOE's BRANDON mission, to save them from retribution at the hands of Darlan and his administration, whom Murphy and Mark Clark, Roosevelt's plenipotentiaries, had maintained in power.

XV
Final Preparations for TORCH

In the minds both of Murphy and of the anti-Gaullist French group with whom he was negotiating in Algiers, General Giraud had a key role to play in TORCH and its immediate aftermath because he was a figure behind whom the French forces in North and West Africa might rally. The problem was that he was not only in the wrong place—still in France—but that communication with him was difficult; besides, he had still not been won over to the idea of Allied landings in North Africa and was instead strongly arguing the case for southern France.

On 27 October, Brien Clarke received a signal from SOE Baker Street confirming and modifying a draft letter to Giraud from Murphy but no doubt emanating from Eisenhower, commander of the TORCH expeditionary force. It authorised Murphy to inform Giraud and Mast on 4 November of the date of the impending assault. The message also confirmed that, whether Giraud came to North Africa or not, Mast would be acceptable as his deputy.[1]

Another signal on 28 October indicated that Giraud's idea of a bridgehead in southern France to coincide with the launching of TORCH was out of the question. The final paragraph authorised Murphy to let Giraud know that the operation was now imminent and set for early November, so as to convince the General that his presence in North Africa was urgently needed. The message ended with the information that a British submarine under US command was moving in the direction of the Golfe-de-Lyon in order to expedite Giraud's removal from southern France.

At midnight on 31 October, by triple priority, a W/T message reached SOE Gibraltar. In it, Murphy stated that a messenger who had just returned from Giraud said that it was utterly impossible for him to leave France until about 20 November. Mast supported Giraud's plea for a delay, so Murphy suggested that TORCH be postponed until about that date.

Brien Clarke showed this remarkably silly signal to Admiral Sir Andrew Cunningham, Deputy Supreme Commander, who had just arrived in Gibraltar in HMS Scylla. The effect was dramatic. Cunningham pointed out that the assault forces were already well through the outer enemy submarine belt and that any change of plan would be quite disastrous. He told Brien Clarke that he would signal his view to the First Sea Lord through Admiralty channels and would be obliged if General Eisenhower could be notified that he had seen the telegram on its way through Gibraltar.

During the night of 1/2 November, a strongly worded reply from Eisenhower in London was received by SOE Gibraltar for onward transmission to Murphy. It was impossible to postpone the operation, he said: TORCH must proceed as planned.

On 4 November, SOE Gibraltar received a signal from Murphy asking them to inform Eisenhower that Giraud had decided to come over immediately and requesting that the submarine should be at the pre-arranged point at 2300 French time on 4 November, and again on 5 November if the first attempt to embark him failed.

The submarine despatched to fetch Giraud was P219 *(Seraph),* the same vessel as had been used for Mark Clark's mission. It was normally commanded by Lt Cdr Jewell, but on this occasion it was deemed politically necessary that it should be at least nominally under command of a US officer. Thus Captain Jerauld Wright, USN,—a future NATO Supreme Allied Commander Atlantic—to whom Gibraltar had wished Godspeed with Mark Clark's party on the night of 24 October, was back there on 28 October, ready for a second trip in the same submarine.[2]

A small ceremony took place in the captain's cabin of HMS *Maidstone* when Captain Barney Fawkes, Lt Cmdr Jewell, Captain Jerauld Wright and Colonel Brien Clarke were gathered together. Fawkes said that he had done considerable research into British naval history and believed the present to be a historic occasion, when for the first time a British submarine in war would be under command of an officer of another nation. He felt that great responsibility rested on Captain Wright and himself to make a success of the operation and he had therefore drafted certain rules, regulations and instructions, which he hoped Captain Wright could master before he took command of his ship in about an hour's time. Captain Wright, who had not had active duty in submarines for some years, was by this time somewhat pale and obviously weighed down by his impending responsibilities. However, with a somewhat shaky hand, he took the scroll from Captain Fawkes and, on undoing the binding tape, found it to be a picture of an extraordinarily attractive pin-up girl from La Vie Parisienne.

Wright's orders were to proceed to 42° N latitude and 6° E longitude and stand by for further instructions. By 1 November, P219 was on station, about 50 miles south of Toulon. At this time there were in fact two British submarines lying off the south coast of France. P217 *(Sibyl),* under Lt E.J.D.Turner, RN, having sailed from Gibraltar 24 hours after P219, was also standing by in response to a request, through SIS, from Commandant Faye, operations officer of the 'Alliance' intelligence network, for a submarine to be stationed off Nice. But Faye and Cdt Beaufre, who was planning to leave France with Giraud, signalled SIS on the afternoon of 3 November recommending an embarkation point nearer Marseilles. Faye later confirmed a rendezvous at Le-Lavandou, about 75 miles east of Marseilles, for the following night.

Difficulties of transmission again prevented P219 from receiving the order to proceed until 2100 on 4 November, when Giraud and his party were already waiting at Le-Lavandou. Giraud, his son Bernard and Cdt Beaufre were therefore picked up only on the next night, in rough sea conditions. P219 headed back to Gibraltar as fast as possible, running submerged by day and on the surface at night. She was at the time unable to transmit because of a radio breakdown. Some historians have stated that, because of the breakdown of W/T communications, Gibraltar and Eisenhower were not informed that Giraud had been picked up until the submarine docked in Gibraltar's Admiralty Harbour alongside *Maidstone* on the afternoon of 7 November. This is incorrect: P219 encountered a Catalina on pre-arranged patrol at 0850 on the morning of 7 November. After being contacted by signal, it landed and Giraud was paddled over by Lt Jimmy Foot of the SBS and transferred to the flying-boat. Sibyl picked up seven members of Giraud's entourage and Mme Beaufre from a small fishing boat that same night. The party had some problems with the French police just before embarking from Cros-de-Cagnes and three of the intended passengers were arrested.[3]

Though Cunningham had arrived in Gibraltar as scheduled on 30/31 October in *Scylla,* the weather had been extremely bad over a wide area during the previous ten days or so. Eisenhower and various members of his staff had been due to arrive there on 2 November and a second party the next night but impossible flying conditions—common enough during the Second World War in winter-time, since de-icing equipment was in its infancy —prevented any flights on Monday 2 November, Tuesday 3 November or Wednesday 4 November. In the meantime, Admiral Cunningham, who had taken up his temporary headquarters at the Tower, held the fort. During that time, the few people in Gibraltar who were aware of the date of D-Day began to wonder whether the operation would have to begin without the Supreme Commander and most of his staff in place at their forward headquarters. However, flying became possible on Thursday 5 November, on which date Eisenhower, Mark Clark and Al Grunther, acting Chief of Staff, arrived, to be followed next day by the remainder of the chief staff officers, including General Doolittle, the Air Force commander. The B17 Fortress in which Doolittle and his party were travelling was attacked by two German fighters and the co-pilot was wounded.

The garrison commander's mess had decided as a form of light entertainment for the new arrivals to take tickets for a film showing publicly that week in Gibraltar, *The First of the Few.* Doolittle watched himself (on the screen) being cheered and chaired some years earlier when he won the Schneider Trophy, but fortunately he was not recognised by the civilian audience.[4]

Eddy of OSS, after considerable urging on Brien Clarke's part, arrived in Gibraltar on 5 November, having previously sent over two of his officers from Tangiers, at the time of Mark Clark's secret mission to Cherchell, to acquaint the SOE signals staff with details of the OSS code and to assist generally with coding operations.

In the two or three weeks that followed, the US Army Signals Corps discovered that the Rock of Gibraltar was a lamentable place from which to transmit and receive radio communications without considerable previous experience and as a result the SOE/OSS network was to have heavy calls made upon it, particularly during the so-called 'Clark/ Darlan negotiations', for which it had not been intended. Owing to the excellent and tireless work of the operational signals staff in North Africa and Gibraltar, this additional traffic was successfully carried and, before Allied Force Headquarters (AFHQ) moved on to Algiers, Brien Clarke received a letter from the Chief of Staff conveying the Supreme Commander's thanks.[5] It was just as well that SOE had made itself useful: before the year was out, it was to need, in the upper echelons of AFHQ, whatever goodwill it had accumulated over TORCH.

The SOE signals arrangements during the assault phase of the invasion were in fact quite ramified, since SOE technical communications staff had been provided by their Baker Street headquarters for each of the three task forces. Thus, in addition to the SOE/OSS network previously set up by Squadron Leader Mallory to link Robert Murphy's 'observers' in Tunis, Algiers and Casablanca to the OSS base at Tangiers and the SOE base at Gibraltar, and to interlink the OSS and SOE base stations, on D-Day there were SOE signals links between Gibraltar and the forces landing at Algiers, Oran and Casablanca. These elements with the task force did sterling work and in the case of Casablanca—where the Allies experienced the most sustained opposition from the forces under General Noguès's command—they were used by Admiral Hall for some days for all his operational priority communications with Admiral Cunningham at Gibraltar. SOE received a special telegram of thanks for this cooperation. SOE's signals, weaned from those of SIS, had won their spurs.

XVI
Unsuccessful Attempts to Revive Felucca Operations

Attempts to restart the felucca operations from Gibraltar to the south of France after the Allied invasion of French North Africa were to prove fruitless. By the next moonless period at the end of November and beginning of December, the Germans were in control of the south coast of France and of airfields in its immediate vicinity. Ships as large as *Tarana* could no longer be used, because they would be bound to attract the attention of Luftwaffe reconnaissance flights and, having attracted it, would be unable to get away before enemy strike aircraft or surface vessels arrived to investigate and attack.

The feluccas, reinforced by another named *Welcome,* made voyages in December and January but, in the few cases where they were able to struggle through the prevailing bad weather and get to the pinpoint, the Germans were waiting for them with machine-guns and ambushes.

Buchowski's original unit of three Leading Seamen and three Able-bodied Seamen had been returned to the Polish navy during the autumn, though they were relieved by a new group to operate under the Coast Watching Flotilla. Buchowski himself was recalled to the United Kingdom at the end of October, but stayed on long enough to carry out the final series of operations with *Seadog* at the beginning of November, just before TORCH. He was accompanied on this expedition by his replacement, an officer named Pohorecki. Gubbins of SOE asked Admiral Swirski to be allowed to retain Buchowski's services for another 12 months.[1] Swirski replied that, in recalling him from Gibraltar, he acted as much on Buchowski's own request as for other reasons, which he set out in a letter dated 23 October. He said he did not consider it advisable to employ a very young officer for longer than 12 months outside the regular service of the navy and he had therefore agreed that Buchowski should return to normal service on board Polish ships. Buchowski was, moreover, a very capable gunnery officer and, as this branch was extremely short of Polish crew to man new ships, it seemed imperative to release him for an appointment on board one of their destroyers as soon as possible. The Admiral understood the arguments but preferred to postpone his final answer to Gubbins until Buchowski had reported to him in person and declared his preference.

Gubbins wrote again on 31 October and on 27 November to reiterate that Buchowski was urgently needed by SOE, particularly in view of developments in North Africa, but Swirski finally said that, on careful consideration, he was unable to spare him for work outside the Polish navy.

Buchowski's last contribution in the area of clandestine sea operations was the following report, apparently addressed to Colonel Mally:

Jan BUCHOWSKI, Lt
London, 18 December 1942
Top Secret

REPORT[2]

I wish to report to you, Colonel, my opinion that the occupation of France by the Germans has made evacuation by sea from the French coast impossible or in any event much more difficult. The French coastline is in all likelihood very strongly guarded by the Germans, so that the idea that a vessel might lie 30–40 miles offshore for the three days needed and remain unnoticed is unthinkable. The French patrolled a coastal strip of about five miles; it must be assumed that the current German patrols are covering more than 100 miles. The vessels used in clandestine work are fishing boats, which are very slow (7 knots). If there has been good observation from the air, a patrol ship can always be sent to check the identity of the vessel. Moreover, the Axis powers will be especially suspicious of a vessel travelling along a north-south route.

The only possible place for such operations at the moment on the southern French coast is the region of Perpignan, because it is close to the Spanish border (around 40 miles) and people can be taken on board and then...[typescript unclear] the vessel can be in Spanish territorial waters, with the Spanish flag raised, and can pretend to be a Spanish fisherman, heading for the Balearics.

There are two main obstacles:

1) As there are two German Panzer divisions stationed in the Perpignan district, that stretch of coast will presumably be strongly policed and it will be impossible either to gather groups of people together or to bring a vessel close in shore.

2) I know that this stretch of coast has been chosen by British intelligence (SOE) as the location of their operations. It is possible that they will not permit any other operations in this area. After all, they suspended the Polish evacuations from the Marseilles region three months ago when they began to increase their own activity in the area.

Thus it seems to me that evacuation by sea is feasible only if organised from the Spanish coast, north of Barcelona.

Organising an outpost in north-east Spain would spare the Poles who are continuing to trickle across into Spain the dangers of the overland journey towards Portugal. People currently in Spain would have to be chosen for the outpost, or suitable people sent there, who have an excellent knowledge of the country and could act on instructions from London. This outpost must have a hide-out, good communications with *centrala* [the 'centre'—presumably the Polish authorities in London] such that the ship would arrive within five days of the signal's being sent. The head of the outpost would have to be aware of the likely problems of the seaward side of the operation, as well as an expert in the land side.

The proposal to organise an outpost on Spanish territory would, in my opinion, meet with great opposition from the British, since the Foreign Office (especially Sir Samuel Hoare) are extremely scrupulous about observing Spanish neutrality (no British diversionary organisation has received Foreign Office permission to operate in Spain). I believe that the following is the only possible way of proceeding. First, Commander Durski, who has established very good relations with the British at Gibraltar, should try to gain the support of Mr Darling, head of the British evacuation operation, and of Col Codrington, head of SIS (Intelligence), in presenting this plan to the Governor of Gibraltar and the authorities in London, who will probably be won over by the fact that we will also be hiding and evacuating British airmen. Commander Durski should however immediately inform London (C-in-C's headquarters) of these overtures, so that the British authorities in London can be approached simultaneously with the notification of Gibraltar's consent.

If the plan receives official approval, it will be necessary to move the naval mission from Gibraltar to Algiers; since

1) it will shorten the voyage by some 600 miles;

2) it will allow the evacuation vessel to sail from Algiers to the Balearic Islands in 24 hours, to raise the Spanish flag there and to approach the coast as a fishing vessel. At present the only movement of neutral ships in the Mediterranean is between the Balearics and Spain, as Commander Durski is aware.

The transfer of our two vessels to Algiers should not present any problems since the CWF (Coast Watching Flotilla) is also going to transfer there shortly.

If the naval mission transfers to Algiers, I believe the consent of the American authorities should be sought, which I do not expect will present any difficulties, since they too are keen to see American airmen evacuated. Both Lt Cdr Kadulski and I have already been approached on this matter by Col. Holcomb, the American army liaison officer at Gibraltar, with whom Commander Durski is very friendly and who is extremely well disposed towards Poles.

It would further be desirable for the head of the mission to be accompanied by an officer who has excellent knowledge of North Africa and who enjoys good relations with both the American and the French authorities, since this would simplify administrative matters associated with the arrival and stay of Poles in Algiers and their speedy onward movement. It seems to me that Capt. Szewalski admirably meets the above conditions.

An officer should be left at Gibraltar to look after Poles escaping from Spain overland.

(J.BUCHOWSKI, Lt)

On 14 and 15 April 1943 the *Polish Daily* published announcements that Jan Buchowski, naval lieutenant, decorated twice with the Polish Cross of Gallantry, the Golden Service Cross with Swords (Polish) and the Distinguished Service Order, had met 'a sudden death' (described also on 15 April as 'a tragic death').

On 2 June 1943, *The Times* reported that at the Central Criminal Court on 1 June a Polish officer, Lt Lubomir Chieński, 43, was found not guilty of the murder of Lt Jan Buchowski, attached to the Polish naval headquarters in London, and was discharged. He had pleaded 'not guilty'. Lt Buchowski had been found shot dead at Lt Chieński's flat on 12 April. It was alleged that Lt Buchowski had 'formed an attachment for Lt Chieński's wife, to which the accused objected'.

XVII
Operations by Sea for SIS and SOE in Tunisia

Churchill now saw the task before the Allied armies in North Africa as twofold. They must conquer the African shore of the Mediterranean and set up the naval and air bases needed to open up an effective passage through it for military traffic. They should then use these facilities to strike at the 'underbelly of the Axis' in effective strength as rapidly as possible. Within ten days of the TORCH landings he was already directing the attention of the British Chiefs of Staff to the second of these objectives: North Africa, he said, was to be regarded as a springboard, not a sofa.

The United States Joint Chiefs of Staff, whom Roosevelt had had to overrule in ordering TORCH, continued to dislike very much the idea of committing US forces to operations east of the Straits of Gibraltar. For one thing, they viewed the whole North African enterprise and any ensuing operations in the western Mediterranean as a diversion of naval resources from the Pacific war and of land forces from the build-up in the United Kingdom for the planned assault on mainland Europe across the short sea route. For another, they felt that their armies might be cut off on the shores of an inland sea by the severing of communications through the Straits of Gibraltar by the Axis. Churchill had been forced to argue that American occupation of Casablanca and its hinterland would not be enough: the thrust of the invasion must extend to Oran, Algiers and further east. If the Americans could not supply forces for all these operations, British troops, accompanied by small US contingents, might undertake the more easterly of them and supply the naval cover required.

Accordingly, the Eastern Task Force that landed at Algiers consisted of the British First Army plus two US divisions. Eisenhower, having overcome his initial dismay at the decision to proceed with TORCH, now, as Supreme Allied Commander, shared the view that this task force should move as swiftly as possible up into Tunisia and that landings at Philippeville (now Skikda) and Bône (now 'Annaba) on D+3 should become an integral feature of the plan, though they could, of course, not be certain of reaching Tunis and Bizerta in time to forestall, or overcome, an enemy counter-landing.

Two SOE officers, Lt-Col. A.M.Anstruther and Major Hamish Watt Torrance, who, with Mr Knox of OSS, had been attached to the Eastern Task Force for the assault landings, were to accompany that Task Force up into Tunisia and, with the help of some of the other OSS Officers deployed in the area under consular cover before TORCH, were to organise any available resistance elements in support of whatever military campaign might develop.[1] This was a fairly tall order, since SOE had been forbidden to work in Algeria and Tunisia before TORCH and, apart from the group of under 200 young men–largely Jewish–who had been organised by OSS to help the Allies land in Algiers, there was little in the way of organised and effective pro-Allied resistance movements in either Algeria or Tunisia. Most of the French population were fence-sitters (referred to colloquially as *attentistes*) or worse: the Arabs were anti-French and, to a lesser extent, anti-European.

What became known as SOE's BRANDON mission, or the Special Detachments, came into existence only on D-Day. It consisted initially of two officers and a small signals detachment, all without previous knowledge of the country and the conditions in which they had to operate. There were no trained recruits and the mission arrived without transport of its own. They were quite pleased to be joined by the naval member of the mission, with HMS *Minna* at his disposal, together with the cargo of 10 tons of arms and explosives that would have been landed before TORCH if ship and reception committee had been able to make contact.

The first three days after the ceasefire, which became effective at Algiers on the evening of D-Day, were spent acquiring vehicles, discussing plans and policy with the local OSS representatives, negotiating with the Chantiers de la Jeunesse youth organisation—from which the Algiers resistance group had derived many of its volunteers—and recruiting candidates from among these volunteers to be trained for guerilla and other paramilitary activities. A headquarters, base and training camp were set up on a farm at Aïn Taya near Cap Matifou, and *Minna*'s cargo was offloaded in broad daylight into horse-drawn carts at a small jetty just behind a naval coastal battery that only 48 hours earlier had held up Allied troops advancing on Algiers from the east.

Although Colonel Van Hecke, head of the Chantiers de la Jeunesse, had failed at the last moment to take any active part in the coup on the night of the landings, his deputy, Henri d'Astier de la Vigerie, had been at the centre of it and it seems inherently likely that some of BRANDON's recruits remained in contact with him as long as they were in the Algiers area. D'Astier de la Vigerie was a Royalist and a former member of the extreme right-wing Cagoule, which was active in metropolitan France in the 1930s. Rygor-Slowikowski rated him a brilliant and enigmatic *condottiere* and, reporting to SIS on 15 November, said that he and Lemaigre-Dubreuil were the most adroit of those involved in the Algiers resistance; but at the same time he noted that his friend and erstwhile protector Achiary, ex-head of the Algiers counter-espionage police, considered d'Astier a 'man without scruples'. It was presumably from this source, via SIS, that Admiral Cunningham knew as early as 19 November that a royalist plot was afoot to replace Darlan by the Comte de Paris, pretender to the throne of France. He commented to the Admiralty in a signal of that date: 'such a step regarded as catastrophic'.[2] The Comte, whose adherents always referred to him as 'the Prince', was in Churchill's bad books not only for attempting to persuade Pétain to nominate him as his successor, but also because the Prime Minister knew he had been attempting to enlist the Italians in support of his cause.

The political backgrounds of BRANDON's recruits were heterogeneous, but they were all Gaullist in sympathy, so the US decision to negotiate the ceasefire with Admiral Darlan, who was Pétain's deputy and was fortuitously in Algiers provoked strong reactions among them. Seven of the group to which they belonged, under the command of Bernard Pauphilet, had actually placed the Admiral under house arrest on the night of the landings until Robert Murphy turned up at the villa where he was staying, as guest of his friend Admiral Fénard, and had Pauphilet's guard removed. The agreement with Darlan was no doubt justified in terms of military expediency, if only as a short-term measure, but it came as a bitter blow to a group united by their hatred of Vichy and all it stood for. In a barn at BRANDON's Cap Matifon camp, four officer-cadets of the Special Detachments, on a proposal by Philippe Ragueneau, one of their number, drew straws for the 'honour' of executing the new occupant of the Palais-d'Eté. Nothing was said at the time to any of BRANDON's officers, but Bonnier de la Chapelle, who drew the short straw, found reasons for staying in Algiers when most of the volunteers took passage in *Minna* on 16 November, under arrangements made by the author. They disembarked on the following day at Bône, where 1 and 6 Commandos had landed unopposed and were being followed ashore by the British 78th Division.

Another BRANDON recruit who stayed behind in Algiers was a man named Sabatier, who had presented himself as a captain and had been treated by BRANDON as its most senior recruit. He was in fact a sergeant, a Cagoulard and a henchman of d'Astier de la Vigerie. It was Sabatier who arranged with SOE's MASSINGHAM mission, which had begun to arrive in Algiers, for a Colt .38 Automatic pistol to be issued to Bonnier on the ground that he would be serving as an instructor at the Cap Matifon camp. It was Sabatier, too, who drove the car that fetched the Comte de Paris from the Moroccan border on 10 December. D'Astier had by then become deputy to Rigaud, Darlan's Commissaire à 1'Intérieur, and was in fact chief of the police. Rigaud, also a former Cagoulard, was not a convinced royalist and was seen by d'Astier as the main obstacle to his plan to restore the monarchy. In the end, d'Astier failed to remove this obstacle, though there is first-hand evidence that he had talked of doing so by force if necessary.[3]

BRANDON knew nothing of the viper's nest it had left behind it in Algiers. By arrangement with the commander of 78th Division, then still at Bône, Anstruther established BRANDON's main base at Guelma, well away from the probable front, and set up a training camp at La Mahouna, a nearby mountain resort consisting of chalets among the native cedar trees. Here the Special Detachments could continue to be trained in comparative seclusion. On 20 November, Ansthruther placed them at the disposal of 78th Division, the leading formation of General Anderson's 1st Army, which had crossed into Tunisia and had its headquarters at Souk el-Khemis (now El Khemis). When a formation called BLADE failed by a narrow margin to capture El Aouina, the airport of Tunis, one of BRANDON's first patrols led back to the Allied lines a parachute battalion that had been dropped south of Tunis and had lost all contact with the main Allied forces. There were other early patrols through the enemy lines, one of which attacked a German headquarters. Then the winter rains began, turning the RAF's improvised forward airstrips into quagmires, and 1st Army's thrust ground to a halt.

The 1 and 6 Commando had moved forward from Bône to Tabarka, a small port just over the Tunisian border, sending Captain Randolph Churchill ahead of them to requisition accommodation. The present author turned up there shortly afterwards to see what use might be made by BRANDON of the landing craft that had brought the Commandos forward and that were lying there under the command of the thoroughly cooperative naval officer, Captain N.V.Dickinson. It emerged that, without waiting for his unit to arrive or asking anyone's permission, Captain Churchill had disappeared in the general direction of Tunis on the pillion of a motor cycle driven by an OSS agent who had crossed the lines and come westward seeking contact with the Allied vanguard. This had presented his Colonel with something of a dilemma: if the escapade went wrong, the Prime Minister's son might well land in Colditz as a prisoner of war, or worse. Colonel Glendinning decided to accept responsibility and said that he had authorised the reconnaissance.

The coastal area running east from Tabarka to Bizerta was mountainous and difficult for large-scale movement of troops: it formed a broad stretch of 'no man's land', which lay open to infiltration by both sides. BRANDON was to try to disembark a two-man patrol by landing craft as near to Bizerta as possible: the patrol was to establish what positions were occupied by the enemy and then make its way back on foot. This involved a jump forward by night of nearly 60 miles. Captain Dickinson approved the plan and placed two small infantry assault craft at the author's disposal. But when the target area was reached, there was too much sea running to make landing possible. The expedition started on its way back to Tabarka but found itself not more than half-way there when day began to break, so they decided to lie up in the lee of Cap Serrat, hoping that, by covering the two landing craft with camouflage nets, it might escape the attention of any prowling enemy aircraft till darkness returned. The headland was crowned with a lighthouse and French naval signal station but these stood back from the top of the cliff and the landing craft were screened from their field of vision. After posting look-outs and eating a breakfast of compo rations, those who were not on watch retired to the shade of a nearby Muslim shrine standing on a rock at the end of a long sandy beach and turned in as the sun rose.

The area was sparsely populated, but the scrub vegetation of arbutus and tall Mediterranean heaths that covered it was grazed by flocks of sheep and goats, followed by Arab herdsmen from villages of brushwood huts standing back from the coast. The expedition's presence did not long remain undetected. In the middle of the morning their look-outs reported a man approaching across the beach; his shirt, trousers and large straw hat proclaimed him to be a European. As the man drew nearer, they saw that, for all the gaping holes in the toes of his boots, there was a distinctly military air about their elderly visitor, a dismounted and unarmed North African Don Quixote. He presented himself to the author in an educated French with old-world courtesy: 'Chef d'Escadrons Perrin, artilleryman in retirement' We were the first element of the Allied armies he had seen and he asked if there was anything he could do to help us. Well, as a matter of fact there was: if he could find us horses and guides, the reconnaissance begun by sea and defeated by weather might still be carried out by land. Had Monsieur le Commandant by any chance such resources? Yes, certainly he had.

The small BRANDON party—a Second Lt named Aynès, a Senegalese Sergeant named da Porto and the author, their conducting officer—walked back with the Commandant to his farm. He lived in a simple, single-storey building on the banks of a small river, the Oued Ziatine, spanned by a steel bridge. It was not like the substantial European colonists' farms of Algeria: the poorest peasants of the Cévennes or the Causses did not live more austerely than the Perrins, their son Jacques and their daughter-in-law, whose house stood nearby, though they belonged to a family whose factory at Grenoble produced the most famous gloves in France. But the Commandant had many hundreds of books in his living-room, in Arabic as well as French.

He had first come to the area in 1911 as a military surveyor and cartographer and he had liked the Ziatine valley well enough to retire from the army, obtain a concessionary grant of land and turn farmer. He was recalled to active service in 1914 and returned to Tunisia six years later to find that his house had been demolished, his cattle stolen and his fruit trees cut down by his Arab neighbours. He had started again from scratch and it was evident that he, the only European settler within 10km had come to enjoy some authority in the region, of which his knowledge was impressive. Arab villagers came from considerable distances to seek his advice, to ask him to write letters on their behalf or to seek first aid and medical advice from Mme Perrin.

Horses and guides were quickly forthcoming and soon the author made his way on horseback 5km up the hill to the lighthouse, which was manned by Tunisians, and the signal station, which had a crew of four French naval signals ratings, three of whom lived in married quarters with their families. What was termed the Semaphore was linked by telephone to the French naval headquarters in the Pêcherie at Bizerta; it seemed prudent to remove a substantial section of the telephone line before setting out on our mounted reconnaissance as dusk fell on the evening of 2 December. After we had been riding for five or six hours, the moon set and the guides lost their way, so we bivouacked until sunrise and, in due course, rode into a clearing where a German infantry platoon was drawn up for its morning inspection. We retreated over the brow of the hill before the bullets began to fly, but the object of the reconnaissance had been achieved: we knew how far west of Bizerta the Germans had deployed troops and that the Forestry Service track running west to Sedjenane and Cap Serrat was passable, even after rain, to light vehicles.

Our report, together with other reports indicating enemy penetration into the area, caused considerable anxiety to Fifth Corps, which had no Allied troops available to move into this sector. Further patrols by BRANDON personnel revealed that enemy penetration had not taken place on any large scale, but nevertheless the threat offered by this open flank continued to cause concern to the military authorities. It was therefore decided that BRANDON should establish two posts, one on the coast at Cap Serrat, the other further south at Sedjenane, from which observations could be made, unfriendly Arabs discouraged from cooperating with the enemy and sabotage and mining operations mounted against enemy communications, including the Bizerta-Tunis railway. These detachments were to operate under command of 36th Brigade. Torrance was given command of the post at Sedjenane and the present author, having valuable access to the knowledge and wholehearted cooperation of the Perrin family, was to return by sea to set up the post at Cap Serrat.

With the establishment of a front line half-way between the Algerian-Tunisian border and the main centres of population in the eastern half of the Protectorate, the Arab population constituted a definite threat to Allied military security. Though initially apathetic in a struggle between two groups of foreign powers, both of which were invaders of their country, the Axis could take heart from the fact that the Tunisian Arabs' balance of sympathies soon tipped in favour of the Axis cause against the Allies when the latter were joined by French forces. They were easily persuaded that an Axis victory would mean the removal of their former colonial masters. This attitude represented a considerable menace to the Allied forces during the period of military stalemate that prevailed until spring 1943. A substantial Arab population, engaged almost exclusively in agricultural and pastoral pursuits, lived in small villages scattered over the hills and mountains which formed the battlefield. The paucity of motor roads, the hilly nature of the country and the comparatively small size of the opposing forces meant that in large areas there was no continuous front line and that considerable tracts of territory were neither occupied nor disputed by either side. This, coupled with the apparent unawareness of the Arabs of the dangers of attempting to follow their normal patterns of life near the fighting zones and in no man's land meant that they could, and did, pass freely in and out of territory controlled by the opposing forces. This would have been a danger even if the Arab population had been sympathetic to the Allied cause, which they were not. The people were poor and favourably impressed by the high wages paid by General von Arnim's forces. The Germans had distributed large stocks of French textiles to them: they admired the Germans' apparent strength and had so far seen little to convince them that the Axis ultimately faced defeat. The enemy was quick to take advantage of this state of affairs and organised members of the Arab population to provide intelligence, to reconnoitre and carry out sabotage behind the Allied lines, as well as to give them assistance in patrols and labour.

BRANDON, whose recruits included speakers of North African Arabic as well as French, Italian and Spanish, the other relevant languages, became substantially involved in dealing with this problem on behalf of 1st Army, and detachments were sent to other parts of the line, expanding until the mission's strength was ultimately 700. It would stray too far from the subject of this work to attempt to deal with BRANDON's operations and activities along the whole of the front. However, as No.1 Special Detachment at Cap Serrat was landed by sea under cover of darkness, supplied initially in the same way and commanded by an officer of SOE's Naval Section, it may at least be worth summarising the relevant section of an official report on BRANDON written after the end of the campaign:

Cap-Serrat

No. 1 Special Detachment occupied the lighthouse at Cap-Serrat on December 16th and retained their position there until January 31st. Lieutenant Brooks Richards was in command with Sous-Lieutenant Ragueneau and 35–50 French troops, almost untrained and unfit owing to privations and, in some cases, imprisonment.

Provisioning was difficult owing to the weather, and communication by sea was possible on only two occasions. The landing place was 5 kilometres away with an unsatisfactory anchorage, and one assault landing craft was sunk there. Supply was finally brought by camel and horse 20 kilometres along the coast.

At first the local population was difficult partly because of enemy propaganda. The problem was dealt with in various ways, from taking hostages to supplying cloth and other stores to Arabs as a reward for assistance. This policy met with success and one of the villages formed an 'observer corps' to give notice of enemy activities and guard some of the French farms.

The detachment was attacked more than 50 times from the air; three enemy patrols penetrated to their defences and one attack by 200 Italians and armed Arabs was beaten off. A farm used by Italians was booby-trapped, agents were passed through the enemy's lines and reconnaissances made of Mateur, Ferryville, Tindja and Bizerta. There was a considerable amount of sickness and several men badly wounded. In the second half of January they were joined by Surgeon Lieutenant Chin, RNVR, who set up in addition a special clinic for the Arabs, which was much appreciated and useful in helping to extract information.

The detachment was faced by greatly superior numbers of enemy troops but, by tactical disposal of a very small number of men, the enemy was misled into

> believing that Cap Serrat was held by a much larger force than was the case, and the lines of communication were safeguarded on the whole northern flank of the front, this unit being the only one between Sedjenane and the coast.

Whatever No. 1 Special Detachment was able to achieve would have been inconceivable without the knowledge and wise counsel of Commandant Perrin. The Detachment was relieved by the RAF Regiment at the beginning of February.

The reason for the arrival of the RAF Regiment at Cap Serrat was that the RAF wanted to install there a ground-controlled interception (GCI) installation to monitor the take-off of German transport aircraft from airfields in Sardinia and in Sicily, so that when the Axis attempted to evacuate the 190,000 troops they had assembled in Tunisia, the twin-engined night fighters based at Souk el-Arba could shoot them down. One of the Atcherley brothers of Schneider Cup fame came to view the site and pronounced it perfect. But GCI had never been deployed in the front line and it took a decision by Roosevelt and Churchill at their Casablanca Conference to allow it to be done. They insisted that it be guarded by 4,000 troops. Ironically enough, only two weeks after No. 1 Special Detachment left the post, the unmetalled forest road leading eastwards to Mateur and Bizerta had dried out sufficiently to be used by motor vehicles and von Arnim launched an attack along it that dislodged the RAF Regiment from their Cap Serrat positions. The RAF were forced to run the GCI vehicles over the cliff and evacuate the vital radar tubes and the Perrin family by sea. The German thrust continued right through to Cap Negre, 25km further west. BRANDON's outpost had been very lucky.

Submarines based on Malta had been used in February and April 1942 both to pick up and land agents on the east coast of Tunisia for SIS (see Appendix E).

BRANDON organised a number of long-range operations during the Tunisian campaign but these were bedevilled by the same unpropitious environment as their tactical activities: the soil for an effective resistance movement was just not there. In five of these cases infiltration was arranged by sea and only one by parachute.

The first two of these operations also involved landings from submarines based on Malta. Operation FELICITY (also known as FELICE I) was an attempt to destroy a vital bridge south of Hammamet on the east coast of Tunisia. The personnel taking part consisted of Captain Eyre, Lieutenant Thomas, four British and six French other ranks. The party, which was in uniform, was to land during the night, attack the bridge and re-embark the same night. The operation took place on the night of 28/29 January 1943 and, although the party was put ashore safely from HM S/m P42, the firing of Very lights shortly afterwards from near the point of landing made it obvious to those watching from seaward that the alarm had been given. The submarine waited as long as it safely could but was forced to withdrew without regaining contact with the party ashore. It was hoped that its members would be able to disperse and make their way overland back to the Allied lines, but they were all captured. Little or no damage was done to the bridge.

The second landing carried out that night, also in the Hammamet area, but from HM MTB 307, involved Squadron-Leader Mallory, the SOE signals officer who had set up the North African signals system for OSS and SOE from Gibraltar before TORCH, and two French agents, Martinez and Bonjour. This party, code-named BLUE, was to organise resistance in the Tunis area.

After the end of the campaign, researches in Tunis showed that Mallory and his two associates must have been captured immediately upon landing, but the enemy made such skilful use of Mallory's W/T set that they were able to convince BRANDON right up until the capture of Tunis that it was Mallory himself who was working it. This deception seems to have stemmed largely from the inadequate signals arrangements made by Mallory before his departure, which contained no reliable security check. The BRANDON signals personnel receiving BLUE's messages claimed to be confident that they were being sent by Mallory himself and a later opportunity to detect what was going on was lost by an error on the part of MASSINGHAM's signals section.

As a result of this successful *Funkspiel,* BRANDON made preparations to reinforce Mallory, including sending in a party of agents to a reception arranged through the BLUE W/T link. This operation was known as BEAR (or the BEARS).

The party consisted of ten Corsican agents and saboteurs in civilian clothes with a W/T link. They had been briefed to disrupt communications and destroy dumps and aircraft in eastern Tunisia. The original plan had been to parachute the team into the field but it was finally decided to infiltrate them by sea to a reception provided by BLUE. The pinpoint chosen was at Kelibia near the southern end of the Cap Bon peninsula, where the wreck of HMS *Havoc,* a British destroyer that had to be beached following damage sustained during a Malta convoy, provided an unmistakable landmark. The operation was mounted from Malta, using two British motor torpedo-boats with the author as conducting officer. The landing took place on 6 April. Recognition signals and passwords were in order, and the author, who had gone ashore with the party, was allowed to re-embark safely and return to Malta under the illusion that all was well, unaware of the noose in which his head had reposed during the landing.

The BEARS were, of course, captured by the enemy as they left the beach. They tried unsuccessfully to escape and their leader Captain Brun was killed during the attempt. The enemy took possession of the W/T set and worked it back to BRANDON HQ as if things were perfectly normal, sending messages that reported considerable success by the BEARS and claiming the destruction of two ammunition dumps, an aircraft and three laden lorries, as well as the cutting of seven cables. At this point an opportunity arose to detect the deception that was being practised by the enemy. The first signal from CHAPTER, the new W/T set and signal plan that the BEARS had taken with them into the field, omitted the security check. MASSINGHAM signals, who were working this link, failed to notify the operations staff, but on their own authority pointed out the omission to CHAPTER and asked him to include the check in future. The facts of this incident were not brought to light until the campaign was finished.

As April progressed, it became obvious that the total defeat of the Axis forces in North Africa could not be long delayed. Allied Force Headquarters were extremely interested to know what plans were being made by the enemy for his evacuation from Tunisia. It seemed likely that von Arnim would use the sandy beaches of Cap Bon as an embarkation area and BLUE was accordingly asked to provide any available information. Meanwhile a representative of SIS had approached BRANDON on the same subject: they wished to land, blind, a W/T operator in Cap Bon who would observe and report back all movements.

SIS, however, had no operator available and therefore asked BRANDON's help in supplying one. BRANDON was not convinced of the soundness of the operation as proposed and agreed to supply an operator only after they had consulted with BLUE and he had agreed to provide a reception by him, which, not surprisingly, he did. He also asked that stores for himself should be sent in at the same time. An operation known as THIGH was consequently planned for the night of 6/7 May, to be mounted, in conjunction with SIS, from Sousse, which had just fallen to the advancing 8th Army. The present author travelled with two Jeeps from BRANDON's headquarters on the northern front all the way round the shrinking perimeter held by the Axis forces, to arrange this operation. It was to be carried out in two recently arrived and brand-new US Navy 72-foot Elco patrol torpedo (PT) boats. The party embarked according to plan but were forced back owing to engine trouble. Further delay was caused by bad weather on 8 May but the expedition sailed again before nightfall on 9 May and were half-way to the enemy-controlled reception in Cap Bon when they were recalled by a crack signal from the naval operating base at Sousse. Major Hamish Torrance had entered Tunis that day with the vanguard of the 1st Army, and had attempted to contact Mallory at an address given by him, but found he was unknown there. Further enquiries in the prisons of Tunis revealed that a British officer answering approximately to Mallory's description had arrived in one of them at Le Bardo in February, soon after the BLUE landing operation, but had since been removed. Conclusive proof that this was Mallory was provided by a graffito on the wall of the relevant room and prompt signalling by Torrance to BRANDON and by BRANDON to Sousse saved the THIGH expedition from falling into the trap that was no doubt awaiting them in Cap Bon peninsula. It seems unlikely that BRANDON's conducting officer (the author) would have been allowed to reembark unmolested as had happened on BEAR a month previously. After the defeat of Germany, both Mallory and eight of the ten members of the BEARS party were recovered from prisoner-of-war and concentration camps in Germany. One of the BEARS had been killed in an Allied air raid while in Germany. The only positive feature of this sorry tale is that in both cases (BLUE and CHAPTER) the W/T sets had been worked by the enemy without the knowledge and assistance of Mallory or the BEAR party.

On the night of March 4/5 BRANDON carried out one other landing of agents by sea. This was ZODIAC, which involved the infiltration of an organiser (David) and a W/T operator (Dupont) in civilian clothes near Bizerta. Their mission was to organise a resistance movement in enemy-held territory to carry out sabotage.

The operation, in which both Holdsworth from MASSINGHAM and the author from BRANDON were involved, was carried out in conjunction with the African Coastal Flotilla organisation set up by Slocum (see Chapter XVIII) from their forward base near Bône: it was the only BRANDON operation in which the ACF was involved. The landing was successfully completed from an air/sea rescue launch in ideal conditions, using two of the dories built in Cornwall to the author's design and brought out from Helford on *Mutin:* Holdsworth and the author did the boatwork. But the ZODIAC party were forced to cache their W/T equipment and supplies when it was found that Arabs had raised the alarm.

When the two agents returned to the spot a few days later, they found that their equipment had been stolen, presumably by the same Arabs. Although several attempts were made, ZODIAC was unable to contact BRANDON headquarters until 27 March, when a message was passed on an SIS link explaining their predicament and asking that a new set be sent. An attempt was made to deliver this set by means of Operation THIGH, but this was, of course, unsuccessful.

Meanwhile, David and Dupont proceeded to find safe houses for the W/T station and set about forming a band of 150 men who might be used for reception work, street fighting; etc. As no reply came to their messages, they decided to cross the lines in person and report to BRANDON. They were, however, captured by the enemy during the attempt and were imprisoned until the liberation of Tunis, when they were set free and reported back to base.

BRANDON's most successful long-range operation, KIPLING, involved the dropping by parachute on March 25/26 of a party of eight in uniform, headed by Captain Evans, to cut the Tunis-Sfax railway. It was carried out at the request of 18 Army Group, recently formed under General Alexander to control the 1st and the 8th Army, which had crossed from Libya into southern Tunisia. KIPLING was timed to interfere with the movement of enemy reinforcements to counter the 8th Army offensive which was to outflank and break the Mareth Line.

The dropping operation was successful and aerial observation carried out on 28 March showed that railway communications in the area had been interrupted. Although the party had elaborate plans for making their way back to the Allied lines after the attack, none of them in fact arrived and it was later learned that Evans had broken a leg on landing and they had all been taken prisoner.

Considerable interest in this operation was shown by the Allied military authorities, although fighter aircraft attacks on any-pile up of traffic that resulted from the break failed although fighter aircraft attacks on any-pile up of traffic that resulted from the break failed to materialise. Interrogation of a railway official from the area revealed later that the line had been interrupted for 24 hours.

XVIII
Clandestine Sea Transport Operations in the Western Mediterranean after TORCH

The advance guard of SOE's MASSINGHAM mission, which was to set up a base in Algeria to mount operations to Sardinia, Corsica, Italy and southern France, began to arrive at Algiers on 17 November 1942, as BRANDON and its recruits were moving up into Tunisia. Holdsworth and Laming, who were, with their crews, to provide MASSINGHAM with a naval component, sailed on 30 November from Helford for the Scillies in *Mutin* and *Serenini*. There they took on additional fuel and water before heading south under sail and power straight across the Bay of Biscay without escort. They reached Gibraltar in six and a half days—about the same time as was taken by convoys, which, of course, had to be routed far further out into the Atlantic because of the U-boat menace. After refuelling, they went straight on to Algiers, where they arrived, at the earliest, on 9 or 10 December. Neither of the ships was intended for operational use in the Mediterranean, but they provided accommodation for crews, transport for stores and personnel, as well as mobile base facilities from which operations could be organised, making use of such naval and local craft as might be available. SOE was concerned that SIS, in the shape of NID (C), should not be in a position to veto their use of clandestine sea transport in the new western Mediterranean theatre, which is what it had recently done with regard to the west coast of France.

Slocum, too, had received a directive to prepare for operations by sea to Corsica, Sardinia, Sicily and southern Italy, as well as to southern France. CWF had, of course, been operating from Gibraltar to southern France in the seven months before TORCH, mainly by means of the Polish-manned feluccas. This directive must have emanated from within SIS, as Slocum did not at that time hold any Admiralty appointment. He sent Lt Cmdr Patrick Whinney, his staff officer for Mediterranean operations, to requisition local craft and investigate the possibility of setting up new bases.

A first such forward base had already been established near Bône as a result of *Minna*'s visit to that port in mid-November, when she had landed BRANDON's recruits on their way forward to Tunisia. During the approach to Bône, Armstrong, *Minna*'s captain, had been impressed by the look of a secluded villa, tucked away under the lee of Cap de Garde. On closer examination, it seemed ideal as base for an advanced flotilla: the bay was sheltered from all directions except the south-east and was sufficiently far from the town to ensure security, yet near enough to allow full use of its maintenance facilities. The villa was requisitioned and, with the permission of the senior officer of the Inshore Squadron, Armstrong installed himself, one other officer and a number of ratings to form a nucleus for operating two craft. *Minna,* under the command of McCallum, his first lieutenant, then returned to Algiers. Slocum recorded that by the end of November two *balancelles,* the local form of felucca, were operating in support of the Allied armies in Tunisia, their duties being chiefly to run ammunition and supplies to isolated detachments marooned in the Cape Tabarka area. This rather overdramatises a useful but modest ration run to a ruined Genoese coral-fishing station at Sidi Mechrig, 20 kilometres to the rear of Cap Serrat, whence supplies were transported by camel or mule to BRANDON's No. 1 Special Detachment.

The base Armstrong had established was in fact of limited operational use, though it was employed in March 1943 for ZODIAC, BRANDON's one and only operation with a high-speed vessel on the north coast of Tunisia. The Villa la Vie, or 'Hatter's Castle', served mainly as an agreeable staging post. Slocum described it as 'a centre of cloak-and-dagger activity for the area and a veritable haven for those of SIS, SOE and MI9 who were travelling forward to advanced sectors and who wished to break their journey or communicate back to headquarters'. No. 30 Commando, a unit formed under the command of Dunstan Curtis, erstwhile captain of MGBs 314 and 501, now a Commander, RNVR, was based there during the whole of its time in Africa, to accompany the assault phase of an advance and to collect any material of value to naval intelligence.

While relations between the naval representatives of SIS and SOE were excellent in forward areas, Slocum's 1946 report records an acrimonious and wholly unnecessary dispute at Algiers between the two organisations over future control of clandestine sea transport in the theatre. Slocum's NID (C) reckoned that Allied Force Headquarters would require an officer on their staff to coordinate all irregular sea operations. Both locally and in London they considered that Osborne, senior officer of NID (C)'s Coast Watching Flotilla at Gibraltar, would be the most suitable choice for the appointment but 'another nominee was put forward and during the month of December the whole question was under heated discussion'.

Slocum says an operation had been planned involving the use of a French submarine without the prior concurrence of Commander-in-Chief, Mediterranean, and as a result the sailing had been peremptorily cancelled. What he describes as 'the inevitable repercussions' followed and, to avoid further recurrences of the kind, the 'only suitable officer' (i.e. Osborne) was applied for. Osborne arrived in Algiers at the beginning of 1943 and, from AFHQ, 'took control of clandestine operations under the title Senior Officer, African Coastal Flotilla (ACF)'.

The surviving SOE archives throw no direct light on this episode, but the 'other nominee' can only be a coded reference to Holdsworth, with whom Slocum's relations had reached a nadir over NID (C)'s last-minute ban on SOE operations to the west coast of France. Holdsworth himself can hardly have reached Algiers when the dispute began, since the French submarine in question, the *Casabianca,* far from having its sailing cancelled, merely had it postponed by 24 hours while the RAF and naval units were informed. She put to sea on 11 December. The operation in any case had nothing to do with SOE, but was a first Franco-American intelligence mission to Corsica: there were now two new players—OSS and what had been Vichy's Deuxième Bureau, operating out of Algiers under the somewhat uncertain and controversial auspices of Giraud and Darlan. Coordination would certainly be required, but the situation was radically different from that in home waters, where, except in relation to Norway, NID (C) had established a monopoly of the relevant operational means of transport, such as they were. But it quite quickly emerged that feluccas could not establish contact with Sardinia, Corsica or with southern France under German occupation, either from Gibraltar or from North Africa, and that *Minna* and *Tarana* could no longer be employed operationally, though useful for non-clandestine sea transport. Operations to Corsica, Sardinia, the west coast of Italy and south coast of France would in the next phase be carried out entirely by submarine.

By December 1942, the Royal Navy's submarine flotillas in the Mediterranean had long experience of carrying out special operations of the type required by the clandestine agencies: for nearly two years, they had been working from Alexandria with the Folboat canoe specialists of the Special Boat Section of the Commandos. This unit was created in July 1940, when Roger Courtney (elder brother of 'Gruff', who had landed General Mark Clark) demonstrated to the first Chief of Combined Operations, Admiral Sir Roger Keyes—of Zeebrugge fame-his ability to use Folboats to approach, and even to board, anchored ships at night undetected.[1] Courtney's unit, which became No. 1 Special Boat Section early in 1941, was attached to the 1st Submarine Flotilla, whose depot ship, HMS MEDWAY, lay at Alexandria. After a pioneering beach reconnaissance on Rhodes, Courtney had gone on to use Folboats from submarines for a variety of small-scale raids and other operations, including the evacuation from the south coast of Crete of British, Australian, New Zealand and Greek troops left behind when the island fell to German airborne forces in May 1941; and the landing and retrieval of agents for the clandestine services behind the enemy lines in Albania, Greece and Tunisia.

Courtney returned to the United Kingdom in December 1941 to form No. 2 Special Boat Section on similar lines and a first contingent of this new unit was sent out to Gibraltar in September 1942 and attached to *Maidstone* to operate, as we have seen, with submarines of the 8th Flotilla in preparation for TORCH. Some overcautious senior planner prevented No. 2 SBS from carrying out the requisite beach reconnaissance for fear of compromising the assault landings, with results that were operationally serious at Oran,[2] but the new unit did land General Mark Clark and his companions for talks with General Mast and Robert Murphy at Messelmoun; and they had also collected Giraud and his entourage from Le-Lavandou. CWF seems not to have been involved in these operations, since they kept no record of them. Submarine operations from Algiers were in practice arranged directly by the agencies concerned with HMS *Maidstone,* depot ship of the 8th Submarine Flotilla, where the operations officer, Lt Cmdr Cowell, and Captain Barney Fawkes showed great interest in their work.

The French submarine, whose sailing on the first operation to Corsica touched off the dispute about coordination and control, was the *Casabianca,* one of five that on the night of 26/27 November had disobeyed Admiral de Laborde's order to ships of the French fleet at Toulon to scuttle themselves and had escaped from the port. Two of the five slunk away to Spain and were interned at Cartagena, but *Casabianca, Marsouin* and *Glorieux* turned up off Algiers and joined the Allies. They had been attacked by German aircraft using bombs and laying magnetic mines as they left Toulon and *Casabianca* had had to make a hurried crash-dive, leaving her captain's naval cap floating where she submerged.

Casabianca's displacement of 1,500 tons was more than twice that of the British 'S'-class and larger than that of the 'T'-Class British submarines of the 8th Flotilla, so she offered great advantages in terms of carrying capacity for landing agents and supplies. This and the inspiring personality of her commanding officer, Capitaine de Frégate Jean L'Herminier, made her an obvious choice when a vessel was needed to carry a five-man mission, code-named PEARL HARBOR, to Corsica early in December.

L'Herminier came of a Breton family who had emigrated to the French West Indies at the time of the Revolution rather than live in France under a non-royalist regime, but they had never considered that sending their sons to serve in the French navy ('la Royale') was inconsistent with their monarchist allegiance. He was in his early forties, while British submarine captains were mostly in their mid-twenties. The fact that *Casabianca* was not equipped with Asdic and that her torpedoes proved erratic meant that her offensive potential was not rated highly by the Royal Navy and Captain (S)8 was the more ready for her to be used for 'cloak-and-dagger' missions.[3]

PEARL HARBOR was led by Commandant de Saule, a professional French intelligence officer of Belgian origin, whose experience in this field went back to the First World War.[4] He was accompanied by three Corsicans, all of whom had been on the fringes of the Algiers Resistance group. One, Pierre Griffi, was a W/T operator; a second, Regimental Sergeant-Major Toussaint Griffi, was his first cousin: the third, a socialist and trade-union activist named Laurent Preziosi, born in Algeria of Corsican parents, was a friend of Albert Camus, whom he had met when they were both working as journalists on the *Alger Républicain.*[5] They were to be escorted on the maritime stage of their expedition by an OSS agent of indeterminate east European origin, who called himself Frederick Brown. Brown, who had worked for a variety of intelligence services, owned a radio shop in Algiers and had been one of the W/T operators manning the link between the US Consulate-General in Algiers, the OSS base in Tangiers and the SOE signals station at Gibraltar. He was presumably responsible for PEARL HARBOR's signals arrangements, but the mission seems in other respects to have been briefed by General Ronin, who had been head of air intelligence at Vichy and had been put in charge of General Giraud's Deuxième Bureau; and by staff of Colonel Rivet's Service de Renseignements working under him. Their task was to set up a military intelligence network covering the whole of the island, which had recently been occupied by 80,000 Italian troops.

Casabianca had been in Algiers no more than a fortnight when she put to sea on the evening of 11 December, carried out the usual diving trial and was escorted by a Royal Navy vessel to a position ten miles north of Cap Caxine. Both the voyage and its landward aftermath have been recorded by participants.[6]

As the submarine headed north on the surface under cover of night using her two diesels, L'Herminier took the head of the table in the submarine's diminutive wardroom for a first meal at sea and said to de Saule and his four companions, 'Gentlemen, I am fully confident in setting about the mission that lies before us. If you agree, I should like now to consider how best to carry out what is for a submarine a rather unusual operation —that of landing five men on a beach.'

Toussaint Griffi and Laurent Preziosi found it rather odd that this question should be raised only when they were already at sea. Where, indeed, on the Corsican coast could the landing be undertaken with a minimum of risk to the submarine and the members of the mission? Their ignorance about the deployment of the Italian occupation forces on the island was total, so it was difficult to say what the best choice of beach would be. For navigational and technical reasons, the submarine, too, could not go just anywhere. The problem was not easy to resolve. Options on both east and west coasts were discussed at length but there was still no decision when the party broke up and the five agents climbed into the hammocks allocated to them in the submarine's after-torpedo-flat.

There was further lengthy discussion next morning; eventually, one of *Casabianca*'s officers pointed out that the choice must not only be suitable from the submarine's point of view but should put the mission ashore as near as possible to a point where they could make contact with known patriots. Toussaint Griffi and Laurent Preziosi, who had been in Corsica most recently, said Bastia and Corte were the two towns where such contacts could be established most rapidly and de Saule had potential contacts in Corte. L'Herminier said that, in that case, a west coast landing would be best: it was nearer to the mountain chain that divided the island into two and better for the submarine as the deeper water would allow her to come closer inshore.

De Saule agreed: he had noted from their earlier discussion that there were several beaches between Ajaccio and Saint-Florent that provided access to roads and mule tracks leading over the mountains to Corte, which offered the best prospect of reaching the centre of the island in safety. L'Herminier and Bellet, his first lieutenant, had a closer look at beaches lying on both sides of a line from Porto to Corte. Bellet said that the beach at Chioni seemed to have everything in its favour from both their points of view. His remark met with general approbation. L'Herminier, calm and resolute as usual, added, 'Well then, we will put you ashore on that beach, which does seem to provide the best conditions—300 metres length of sand and 40 metres depth of water within a mile of the coast—everything needed for a successful operation.'

The rest of 12 December gave the passengers leisure to see round the submarine and chat to the crew. Everyone seemed delighted to have escaped from the Germans and it was clear that their departure from Toulon had been carefully prepared. *Casabianca* had been due to be sent to a colonial station and, L'Herminier and his officers, with the agreement of the German armistice commission, had carried out engine trials, tested equipment and done a series of diving trials to a depth of 80m over a period of months. They had gone to considerable lengths to train the younger members of the ship's company. L'Herminier raised a laugh when he said that of course the Germans had refused him permission to put what he described as 'the finishing touches' to these preparations. But the essential thing was that they had managed to retain a considerable quantity of diesel fuel on board.

Casabianca surfaced soon after nightfall on 13 December and members of the PEARL HARBOR team were able to go for a walk on deck as the submarine's powerful diesels drove her northwards at a spanking pace. But while they were having dinner in the wardroom mess, an aircraft was sighted astern, so a quick dive to 40m was necessary. After a time, L'Herminier brought her up to 16 metres and took a look through the periscope. Nothing could be seen, so they resurfaced and started up the diesels. Three quarters of an hour later, enemy aircraft were again sighted circling round the point where they had crash-dived. They had to dive again, but soon they were back on the surface and on course.

After dinner, L'Herminier went up to smoke a cigarette and keep the officer of the watch company for a while. At about 2200hrs the starboard look-out reported land in sight. This was a great surprise, as their course should have taken them well clear of Sardinia and southern Corsica, but there was no doubt about it and they had to alter course sharply to port to take them out of the coastal zone, where they were likely to meet enemy patrols. The unexpected landfall gave rise to all sorts of conjectures, the most likely of which was that the gyro-compass was out of order, probably as a consequence of the shake-up it had received from the mine explosions as they were leaving Toulon. They decided that they must have sighted the island of Asinara off the north-west coast of Sardinia.

As they were unable to determine their position accurately, they set a course which they hoped would bring them to the point where L'Herminier planned to submerge—15 miles west of Cap Rosso. At 0100hrs on the morning of 14 December they judged they were in the right position and dived to about 40m, proceeding eastward at two knots, through the enemy's assumed patrol zone. L'Herminier meanwhile snatched some sleep.

At about 0730, he was wakened by the officer of the watch and they came up to periscope depth and took a look around. They were unquestionably off Corsica, but they were still too far from land to fix their position, though they spent an hour in fruitless attempts to do so.

They submerged to a depth at which enemy planes would be unable to spot them and made their way slowly inshore. L'Herminier retired to his cabin, having left instructions that he was to be informed as soon as soundings indicated a depth of 100 metres. The 100-metre contour line ran along the coast about two miles offshore, following the shore fairly regularly except near the headlands, where it was closer: that would be the time for another cautious look around with the periscope. Unfortunately, the supersonic Langevin-Florisson sounding machine, a delicate and rather capricious instrument, let them down and began to show soundings only when they were some way inside the 100-metre isobath.

L'Herminier ordered the submarine to periscope depth and made his way to the conning-tower in a hurry. The sounding machine was giving good readings now and showed that the sea-bed was rising rapidly. When the periscope broke surface, L'Herminier saw a reddish wall of rock straight ahead and quite close. He ordered 'hard aport'.

The rock face seemed so close that L'Herminier thought for a moment that he was using magnification 6 and turned the handle of the periscope to a different position. The texture of the cliff showed up in such detail that his head jerked back instinctively as though to avoid bumping against it. The periscope calibration had been set for magnification 1: they were very close inshore indeed! *Casabianca* answered her helm in time and they slid past an island almost close enough to touch it.

A look around with the periscope showed that they were in Focolara Bay, with Cap-Gargalo towering above them and the semaphore station on Cap-Cavalo visible away to the north. They were 12 miles to the north of their chosen landfall at Cap-Rosso and 14 miles from their destination in Chioni Bay. They set course accordingly but had to increase speed to arrive there before nightfall, even though it meant greater discharge of their precious batteries. This presented a problem as they could not hope to finish the job in one night. The moon did not set before midnight and the remaining hours of darkness would be too short to complete the agreed plan, so they would have to remain close inshore for the next 48 hours, with no chance to use their diesels to recharge the batteries.

Before nightfall, which comes early in December, they had sighted Cargèse and Omignia. They took a last periscope sighting and altered course towards the shore before setting *Casabianca* very carefully down on a sandy bottom at a depth of about 45m. Somebody made a joke about the lobsters they were probably crushing. Bellet, the first lieutenant, took in another five tons of water to anchor the submarine firmly to the bottom.

It had been a calm day and they hoped it would remain so, but they had wasted time in finding their destination and everyone except the watch gladly turned in to snatch a few hours' sleep.

Towards midnight, L'Herminier gave orders to prepare for the landing. One group of seamen under command of an officer was equipped with small arms and stood ready to take up covering positions on deck as soon as the submarine surfaced. A second group was detailed to launch a boat carried on top of the pressure hull. Then L'Herminier ordered the submarine to be brought to the surface, a manoeuvre carried out in impressive silence. Bellet, with his eyes glued to the periscope, reported all clear. A few seconds later, the hatch leading from the control-room to the conning-tower was thrown open and the two groups of seamen climbed up through it and set about allotted tasks. Then the PEARL HARBOR team were invited up on to the bridge, where L'Herminier and a junior officer named Chaillet had already stationed themselves. It was a moment of high emotion: *Casabianca* seemed very close to the shore and the mountains loomed above them with their summits outlined against a grey sky, though they were in fact about 800 metres from the shore. The sea was flat calm and a light offshore breeze carried the aromatic scents of arbutus, myrtle, lentisk and the giant Mediterranean heath, which flowers in winter.

L'Herminier and Chaillet accompanied the landing party aft, where the boat, manned by two seamen, was waiting for them. As the party embarked, L'Herminier said that the submarine would tow the boat as close to the beach as possible. Then, when the time came to cast off, *Casabianca* would be stationed at right angles to their approach course, so that she could cover their withdrawal should they come under small-arms fire. If there was not time for them to get on board before she had to dive, the submarine would be forced to abandon them.

Everything went as planned: *Casabianca* moved gently ahead, towing the dinghy: its wake left a striking phosphorescent track on the surface. For all the apparent nearness of the mountains, the submarine was still quite a long way from the shore when it cast off the tow-line and left PEARL HARBOR and Frederick Brown to be rowed into the darkness. Everyone on the dinghy shook hands, their excitement tinged with apprehension: they were closing in on enemy-occupied territory with no idea of what might await them.

Luck was on their side. After a quarter of an hour, in which the silence of the night was scarcely broken by rhythmic oar-strokes into unruffled water, they found themselves close to a small sandy beach on which the boat grounded. Delighted as the three Corsicans were to step ashore on to their native soil, they were certainly not on a 300-metre-long beach. It was not the moment for questions: they took leave of the boat's crew, who disappeared back to the submarine, and set about looking for somewhere to hide Pierre Griffi, his W/T set and Mr Brown, who was to help Griffi establish radio contact with the base station at Algiers. The plan was that the two-man signals team would remain close to the beach until the following night, while the other three went in search of contact with local patriots who might help them carry inland the food, arms and second W/T set that were due to be landed from the submarine during the second night.

Once Pierre Griffi and Brown had been suitably installed, de Saule, Toussaint Griffi and Preziosi set off inland with the aid of a compass and a pocket torch in search of the Ajaccio-Porto road. They had gone no further than the top of the first small hill when, only 200 metres on their right, they caught sight of an Italian sentry who had betrayed his position by using an electric torch. The three infiltrators thought their footsteps must have been heard and took cover under some bushes. The sentry shone his torch in their direction and came some way towards them, as though aware of their presence. It was a moment of extreme tension for the agents. They were unarmed and in a place to which they had to return only a few hours later. Toussaint Griffi and Preziosi suggested they should move before the Italian came upon them. De Saule, an old practitioner of clandestinity, said 'no', the last thing they must do was to move: the sentry would not come as far as their position. No doubt he would be more frightened than they were. Indeed, after coming 40–50 metres in their direction, the Italian stopped, turned and went back to his guard-post. Soon they were able to resume their march through the thick *maquis* scrub vegetation towards the mountain.

It was hard going and at the end of an hour, when they had reached the top of a ridge, they thought they had lost their way and halted. Crouched at the foot of an old tree, surrounded by thick scrub and using their overcoats to screen the light of their torch, they consulted both map and compass. They concluded they were moving in the right direction to strike the road somewhere between Piana and Cargèse.

Day was beginning to break. Then, only a few minutes after they had resumed their march, de Saule suddenly collapsed: he was in his fifties, walked with a stick and had been given none of the rigorous physical training to which agents were subjected in the United Kingdom before being allowed to go into the field. The two young Corsicans were seized by momentary panic. But Toussaint Griffi had been in action on the Ailette in 1940 and had seen something of the sort before. He decided to try to bring the prostrate Commandant round by slapping his cheeks. There was no immediate response and for some seconds the two younger men feared their leader was dead. But Griffi set to once more and this time de Saule regained consciousness. 'What happened to you, mon Commandant?' 'Don't worry, it's nothing. I have just had a slight turn, because I am beginning to feel very tired.'

Preziosi had a bottle of wine in his knapsack and he persuaded de Saule to take a drink from it. He also gave him some dates he was carrying. This brought some colour back into the Commandant's cheeks. He smiled, got up, said he felt better and suggested they should move on. They followed a mule track leading down into a valley, which they could just make out in the growing light. It was easier going now as the zigzag path was used by shepherds and their flocks of goats and sheep. It led down to a little stream, swollen by winter rains.

From time to time they stopped to take stock of the lie of the land and to listen for any unaccustomed sound. It was quite cold: a light breeze had got up but the aromatic scents of the *maquis* on it raised their spirits. After three nights of very little sleep, the long-awaited moment when they would make contact with one or more Corsican patriots was at hand. They had been walking for several hours now and wondered where, when and with whom that first encounter would occur.

They were still coming down the mountainside when they heard the sound of a motor-cycle. That meant they must be getting close to a road or some inhabited place. But under enemy occupation, a motor-cycle must be Italian. It was 6 o'clock and becoming light. They took another look at their map. Yes, it must have been on the road from Ajaccio to Calvi and, if they had not strayed too far from their chosen route, they were about two kilometres from a bridge over a river. They walked on for another quarter of an hour and came down to a stream along which eucalyptus trees were growing. They crossed it and saw, 500 metres down a bank, a shepherd's house, with wisps of smoke rising slowly to the sky from the chimney. As they watched, a woman in a long woollen skirt and with a kerchief round her head came out of the house to fetch logs from a pile at the foot of a big tree. De Saule asked Preziosi to go and make contact with her. Preziosi wondered what sort of reception he might expect at 7 o'clock in the morning, his face lined by lack of sleep, a felt hat on his head and wearing an extremely crumpled overcoat. As he approached the door, she was standing in front of the hearth trying to put life into the fire, which she had just refuelled, by fanning it vigorously with a piece of cardboard. He addressed her in Corsican, 'Good day, Madame, I am on my way to Revinda. Could you please tell me the way?' 'It is not far from here', she replied, 'but if you wait a short while my son, who has gone to the sheepfold, will be back to drink his coffee; he'll show you the way.' And she added, 'But come in, Monsieur. Come and sit down.' Preziosi did so, with profound relief and pleasure: he had made a first contact and the woman's touching hospitality lent strength to his faith in the Corsican Resistance. Though she showed no signs of mistrust, she went on to ask questions that proved that she found his presence at that early hour distinctly unusual. Where he had come from at such a time to go to Revinda? Preziosi said he had come from Piana; he had set out very early and he had taken a short cut across country to save time. Was he alone? No; he was with two friends, who had stopped 200 metres back to relieve themselves. 'Well, tell them to come', she replied. The lady's name was Santa di Notte and she wintered her sheep in the plain.

Preziosi fetched his companions and, by the time they reached the house, three cups had been set out on a small table by the fire. They had only just sat down when her son arrived; he was no doubt equally surprised to find visitors so early in the morning. As they sat sipping their coffee, the conversation turned to problems of everyday life under the Italian occupation. PEARL HARBOR learned that there were major Black Shirt units at Cargèse and some troops also at Piana: food supplies had become increasingly difficult as a result. However, troop movements on the nearby Route Nationale were infrequent.

This intelligence was most helpful, but they still had to decide where to go in search of the help that would be needed on the following night when the *Casabianca* would be landing further equipment and supplies. Revinda seemed as likely a place to look for such assistance as any, being well placed geographically in relation to their beach, so they decided to take advantage of their hostess's offer that her son guide them to that village. After breakfast he led them to the bridge they had noted on their map, where the Route Nationale crossed the nearby river. They followed the main road for some time in the direction of Piana and then took a track leading uphill to Revinda. The young shepherd told them they had only to follow this to reach their chosen destination. He then left them.

As they walked on alone, they discussed whom they should approach for help in Revinda. The mayor or the village priest seemed obvious choices, provided they were not Pétainists. De Saule thought the priest the better choice. Griffi and Preziosi were surprised: admittedly a priest was used to safeguarding the secrets of the confessional, but might he not be a collaborator, an Italian by origin or the product of an Italian seminary? De Saule dismissed the idea: the two Corsicans should have known better than to suggest such a thing. They had to concede that the priest in such a place would probably be a Corsican, but they wondered whether indeed there would be one at Revinda.

They had reached the top of the hill from which they could catch a glimpse of the sea, with the Baie-de-Chioni and some of the roofs of Cargèse. It was a point where the *maquis* grew particularly high and thick. Then, as though de Saule had spoken with foreknowledge, from a mule path, which joined their track on the right, appeared a priest riding a donkey: it was the Abbé Mattei, the incumbent from Cargèse, known locally as Prête Santu, who was on his way to Revinda to say mass on the feast of Sainte-Lucie. Yes, he said, he was Corsican but, above all, a Frenchman. He came to Revinda to say mass only three or four times a year!

The priest was obviously no friend of the Italian occupation, which he said weighed heavily on the population at Cargèse: the Corsicans had never accepted Genoese or other Italian tutelage. Clearly, PEARL HARBOR could have full confidence in him. He found them lodgings in Revinda and put them in contact with Dominique Antonini, a retired soldier, who had the mules they needed. Antonini was no fool and he subjected them to a searching cross-examination before he set out with them and his three mules at 5 o'clock that afternoon. Even then, he took care to bring up the rear of the procession and stay there.

It was completely dark when they got down to the beach. Their first calls to Pierre Griffi and Fred Brown produced no response. They tried several times more and were beginning to wonder what had gone wrong when the silhouettes of two men emerged from the night and came silently towards them. Dominique Antonini, still suspicious, had distanced himself from his companions and seemed ready to defend himself if need be. They called again and Pierre Griffi replied by switching on his torch. A few seconds later they were reunited. Antonini rejoined them, saying that he now knew that he was dealing with genuine members of the Resistance. He had been prepared for all eventualities: he showed them the automatic pistol that was stuffed into his belt.

The dinghy had got back to *Casabianca* at 0300 hrs on the previous night and, as it was hauled back on board, L'Herminier decided that it was really quite unsuitable for the work they were now engaged in: something far lighter was required and they must put in for it when they got back to Algiers. This had not been an ideal time for their operation, because the moon went down so late, but the urgency of establishing contact with the island had meant that they could not afford to wait for the next no-moon period.

On the night of 15/16 December, the sea, unlike on the previous night, was very rough. A cold north-west wind—the mistral, which in Corsica is called the *libeccio*—was blowing directly on to their beach. The sea was getting worse and the reception party wondered whether landing stores would be possible. The understanding with L'Herminier was that they would stand by from about 0130 hrs, which was when the moon set. At the appointed time, Pierre Griffi flashed the agreed signal to seaward with his torch; after he had done so three or four times, the submarine broke surface at the same point as on the previous night. She was visible to them on the beach and clearly seen and understood their signal: it remained only to wait for the boat to arrive. Some time went by and they could still not see any sign of its approach, so Toussaint Griffi and Preziosi climbed the hill that overlooked the beach. From this vantage point the boat could be made out at a distance of 300–400 metres. But, at that very moment, a big wave capsized the boat and it disappeared from sight. They rushed down the hill as fast as their legs would carry them. By the time they got to the beach, the boat's three occupants—Enseigne Lasserre, along with Lionnais and Vigot, the two seamen who had landed them the previous night—had swum ashore and were just emerging from the surf. Their sodden clothes were quickly replaced by three overcoats lent them by the reception party, so that everybody was left feeling frozen. But that was a small matter compared with the loss of the material the dinghy had been carrying.

For the three sailors to swim back to rejoin *Casabianca,* at her present position was out of the question but L'Herminier needed to be told that they were safe. The waves were by now large enough to make it difficult to see the submarine and Pierre Griffi was not confident of being able to send a message using his torch as a signalling lamp. The only possible course of action was to ask Mr Brown, who was said to be an excellent swimmer, to swim out to the submarine and ask Commandant L'Herminier to bring the *Casabianca* in as close as possible to the rocky point north of the Anse-de-Topiti. Then it might be possible for the three members of crew to swim the shorter distance to the submarine. After some initial hesitation, Brown agreed to undertake this mission. With exemplary courage, he plunged into the tumultuous breakers and, with a few powerful strokes, he was away from the beach, vanquishing wave after wave till he disappeared into the night. A state of acute anxiety reigned on the beach. The waiting time seemed interminable and their scantily clothed bodies got colder and colder under the impact of the chill north wind from the sea. An hour later they heard, quite distinctly, the sound of the submarine's diesels. They hoped this meant she would be standing closer inshore. In fact, however, the submarine's batteries were running dangerously low and, after Brown had reached her at 0345 hrs and been hauled aboard with the news that all was well with PEARL HARBOR, L'Herminier had decided they must be left to fend for themselves in Corsica for the time being. *Casabianca* was heading north to reconnoitre the coast as far as Calvi. At 1945 hours that evening, she turned and proceeded back to Algiers, the essential part of her mission successfully accomplished.

Though PEARL HARBOR had been sent into the field by professional French intelligence officers with OSS technical backing to collect military intelligence and de Saule had no wish to become involved in politics, political issues were inevitably raised: the Corsican Resistance being divided, which elements of it were to receive arms? Indeed, the politically unstable situation in Algiers in the aftermath of TORCH was itself a minefield, particularly for SOE's MASSINGHAM mission as it proceeded to set up its operational base.

As Admiral Cunningham reported to the Admiralty on 19 November, there was already a French royalist plot afoot to replace Admiral Darlan by the Comte de Paris, who was in Morocco. The pretender was in Churchill's bad books and Cunningham quite rightly considered that his advent would be a disaster. Roosevelt was equally determined not to become the restorer of ousted European monarchies, but Bob Murphy's right-wing French connections, both social and professional, led the plotters to hope for support from that quarter. There was also a small, but potentially important, Gaullist group in Algiers, centred on Capitant's and Coste-Floret's local offshoot of the 'Combat' Resistance movement in metropolitan France. Between these two hotbeds of anti-Darlan sentiment stood the enigmatic figure of Henri d'Astier de la Vigerie, who regarded himself as the main organiser of the Algiers Resistance group that had risen to support the Allied landings on 8 November. Henri was a royalist rather than a Gaullist,[7] but one of his brothers, Emmanuel, was head of the 'Libération-Sud' resistance organisation in metropolitan France and had visited London to meet de Gaulle earlier that year,[8] while a second brother, General François, had arrived in London by Lysander during the November moon and joined de Gaulle's staff.[9]

Since de Gaulle was in London and both SIS and SOE worked with his Bureau Central de Renseignements et d'Action as well as independently in the field, opponents of Darlan in Algiers looked to the British as their natural allies. In the absence of Foreign Office representation, other than Harold Mack, who was the British political adviser to Eisenhower and whose contacts with the French were thereby inhibited, Lt-Col. David Keswick, MASSINGHAM's intelligence officer, and his deputy, Major Jacques de Guélis of SOE's Independent French Section, became important sources of information about this complex and precarious political situation. Keswick reported to Baker Street on 27

November that he was most anxious about the position as the British had not gained the adherence of their previous enemies and had forfeited the trust of their friends. Giraud had been side-tracked, Béthouard had been dismissed and Darlan and the Vichyists were completely in power.[10]

Churchill came under increasing domestic political pressure as a result of the situation in Algiers and on 10 December, a month after the landings, he was led to seek refuge in a secret session of the House of Commons. The speech he made was one of the most brilliant of his career but such was the delicacy of Anglo-American relations at that juncture that its text was not shown to General Eisenhower until nearly two months later.[11]

Both SIS and SOE became involved in establishing links between the Algiers Gaullists and General de Gaulle in London. What Churchill called 'the patchwork arrangement', whereby Darlan was at the head of civil affairs and Giraud was in command of the French armed forces in North Africa, came under increasing strain. Matters came to a head when de Gaulle's first emissary, General François d'Astier de la Vigerie, arrived in Algiers on 19 December. He had been flown from Tempsford to Gibraltar on an aircraft belonging to one of the RAF's Special Duties Squadrons, and carried from Gibraltar to Algiers on a British submarine.[12] He brought funds for the Algiers Gaullists under Professor René Capitant. Darlan's fate was sealed at meetings François had with his brother Henri and with the Comte de Paris in Algiers on 19 December, though the respective roles of the Gaullist and the royalist brother, who was also chief of Darlan's police, have never been made clear.[13] On 20 December, General François formally offered the military cooperation of the Fighting French forces to both Giraud and to Eisenhower. He was then put on a plane and summarily removed from North Africa by the Americans.

MASSINGHAM had, apparently on 18 December, received a very strong warning that if they offered any assistance to anti-Darlan or Gaullist elements, General Eisenhower would order the removal of the mission. MASSINGHAM, in the words of a report in the SOE archives, therefore 'trod warily'. But it was with MASSINGHAM's full, if undeclared, support that a second Gaullist emissary, who had arrived in Algiers unostentatiously with General François d'Astier, remained there after the latter's expulsion. This second Gaullist envoy was travelling under the name Grimaldi. For most of 1942 he had called himself Severi but he was in fact Fred Scamaroni, the young Sous-Préfet who had been one of de Gaulle's emissaries on the ill-fated Dakar expedition in October 1940 and, after his release from Vichy prisons, helped to found the 'Copernic' intelligence network in the non-occupied zone (see Chapter XI above).[14] He had visited his native Corsica in 1941, where he found the Resistance divided and disorganised, and he longed to be sent back there to bring it into Gaullist allegiance. When he arrived back in England on New Year's Day 1942, he had adopted a new identity because he was well known to the Vichy authorities. Under the name Severi, he spent six months of 1942 working with Lagier on the Service Action side of the BCRA, which involved him in frequent liaison with SOE.[15] There seems to have been initial opposition in Baker Street to the idea of his returning to the field, on the grounds that he was compromised as an agent. However, Lt-Col. Jim Hutchison, head of SOE's RF Section, thought highly of the young man who in 1939 had torn up the paper that designated his post in the Préfecture at Caen a 'reserved occupation' in order to join the air force; who had joined de Gaulle in England on 27 June 1940; and who had made his way back from Dakar to rejoin de Gaulle in spite of immense difficulties. SOE eventually agreed to help him fulfil his ambition to return to Corsica as de Gaulle's representative.

Scamaroni's sister, who has had access to relevant BCRA archives, stated that he was on the same SOE-organised training course as Jean Moulin, and that Operation SAMPIERO, which was to land him in Corsica from a British submarine, was originally to have taken place in November 1942 but had to be postponed because of the Allied landings in North Africa. The operation had been renamed *Sea Urchin* by the time General de Gaulle signed his mission order on 9 December. In addition to Scamaroni, it included a French W/T operator named J.B.Hellier, provided by the BCRA, and a British arms instructor, James Anthony Jickell. It was the first time that BCRA agents and a member of SOE's Independent French Section, to whose existence de Gaulle objected strongly, had been sent into the field as members of a single team. Presumably, that was itself a measure of the Gaullists' urgent concern to strengthen their foothold in Corsica and not leave the island's Resistance movement to fall into the hands of the Darlan-Giraud Deuxième Bureau.

Four days after General François d'Astier de la Vigerie's expulsion and while the *Sea Urchin* team were waiting, under MASSINGHAM's care, to be sent to Corsica by submarine, Admiral Darlan was assassinated. SOE's in-house history of MASSINGHAM recorded that, 'prior to the general publication of the news, MASSINGHAM told London that the assassin was an officer from the 10th Corps Franc camp at Matifou'. What this rather bland statement omits is that this unit had been undergoing instruction by officers from BRANDON and OSS; that Bonnier de la Chapelle, the assassin, had at the request of Sabatier, Henri d'Astier de la Vigerie's henchman, been issued with a .38 Colt Automatic; and that Sabatier had been accorded asylum on Holdsworth's ship *Mutin.*[16] But the report of the autopsy on Darlan makes clear that the pistol used to kill him was not a Colt automatic but a weapon of French naval origin. It had been removed from a French naval gendarme in the Boulevard Baudin on the night of 8 November.[17]

Following the assassination, Darlan's immediate circle of friends persuaded General Bergeret that further violence was planned and he in turn persuaded General Giraud, who ordered Bonnier executed and a number of arrests to be made. These included everyone who had been in contact with General d'Astier during his visit and many who opposed the Darlan administration, notably the more prominent Gaullists, who were closely associated with many people recruited by BRANDON into the Special Detachments. The SOE report records that MASSINGHAM's intelligence officer Keswick attempted to find out who was the person responsible for the arrests. General Giraud began to regret his hasty action over the arrests and the execution of Bonnier and appointed General Ronin to sift the evidence.[18]

Allied Force Headquarters quickly discovered that Bonnier had been issued with a pistol by MASSINGHAM and ordered an inquiry of their own. Eisenhower would probably have carried out his threat to remove MASSINGHAM, lock, stock and barrel, if General Jock Whitely, his British deputy Chief of Staff, had not told him this would be politically serious and, further, that he knew Douglas Dodds-Parker, MASSINGHAM'S training officer, to be a reliable and efficient junior officer.[19] So the mission survived, minus Colonel Munn, its commanding officer, and 'Mouse' Glyn, his second in command. It acquired Dodds-Parker in Munn's place, and in mid-January 1943 moved to a new and better training camp and base at the Club des Pins, 20km to the west of Algiers.

How Scamaroni managed to avoid arrest in the aftermath of Darlan's assassination is not clear. No one had been in closer touch with General d'Astier de la Vigerie than he, and he already knew Professor René Capitant, the acknowledged head of the Gaullists in Algiers and a friend of General de Gaulle since the time when de Gaulle and he both served at the headquarters of the French 5th Corps in 1939. Indeed, Capitant confirmed to Scamaroni's sister and biographer before his death in 1971 that Fred had come to him as an accredited emissary of de Gaulle.[20] But he was also an SOE-sponsored agent on his way from London to the field: in that capacity he and his fellow members of the *Sea Urchin* team would have enjoyed MASSINGHAM's protection and support.

The BCRA archives consulted by Marie-Claire Scamaroni show that her brother wrote an eight-page report to the BCRA on 28 December, four days after Darlan's death. Its full contents were not disclosed to her but in the final paragraph he asked the BBC to broadcast the following message on 29, 30 and 31 December 1942: 'A nos amis de Corse, nous disons confiance: La Corse restera française, je répète, la Corse restera française. Gaston a mangé le saucisson, son ami ira manger la Coppa.'[21]

Gaston Taviani, alias 'Collin', was a BCRA agent who had been sent from London to south-eastern France and to Corsica in 1942 at Scamaroni's request. He had been in the island no more than a fortnight, but the object of the BBC message was to inform the people with whom he had already been in touch of *Sea Urchin*'s imminent arrival. Marie-Claire says that the mission should have been met by a reception committee on landing but apparently was not: indeed, in the absence of direct communications between Algiers and the island it is hard to see how the field could have been apprised of the intended time and place of landing.

The *Sea Urchin* mission left Algiers on 30 December 1942 in HM Submarine *Tribune,* which was under the command of Lt S.A.Porter, RN.[22] *Tribune* proceeded directly to Corsica to land Scamaroni and his companions (Operation SIDELINE), arriving there on New Year's Day 1943, exactly one year after Scamaroni had been picked up from Yves Le

Tac's Folboat canoe in the Aber-Benoît channel by MGB 314 and brought back to England. However, the weather was too bad for landing, so *Tribune* proceeded to the Cap-d'Antibes area to attack shipping until the weather looked more promising. On 3 January, while *Tribune* was patrolling on the surface at night off Cap-Ferrat, a searchlight was exposed in its direction several times, with a beam probably controlled by radar—a measure of the enhanced defences the Germans had established since their arrival on the coast in November.

By 4 January, the weather had moderated, so *Tribune* headed back to Corsica. Lava Bay, the pre-arranged landing-place, which lies north of Ajaccio, was reached soon after daylight on 5 January and the beach was reconnoitred from periscope depth at one mile. It appeared quite deserted but there was a heavy ground swell. Porter decided to land the agents at 0030 on 6 January in the north-east corner of the bay, the only part sheltered from the swell. However, at 2038 they observed a small searchlight sweeping the beach in Lava Bay and an area half a mile to seaward: it was shown from an elevation of about 30 metres in the very corner of the bay where Porter had planned to put *Sea Urchin* ashore. The submarine's presence had apparently not been detected, as the light did not sweep anywhere in her vicinity. This light could not have been brought hurriedly into position as there were no roads to Lava Bay, only a rough track; it must therefore have been part of the fixed beach defences. Indeed, Porter and Scamaroni concluded that the whole Ajaccio peninsula must be a defended area. Cupabia Bay on the north shore of the Gulf of Valinco, 20 miles south of Ajaccio, was selected as an alternative. *Tribune* proceeded to seaward, to arrive off the new pinpoint at dawn. She dived at 0623 on 6 January, closed Cupabia Bay and carried out close reconnaissance from half a mile. The beach was quite deserted and a rock landing point was selected at U-Scogliu-Biancu. Shore marks were noted for the run in. There was no current or tidal set and the landing-place was better than Lava Bay, being sheltered from the wind and swell. The only disadvantage was its distance from Ajaccio. *Tribune* withdrew, submerged, went southwards into the middle of the Gulf and then turned west. After dark, she surfaced and proceeded to seaward to charge batteries.

At 2140 Porter shaped course for the run in to the landing beach and proceeded on main motors. At 2345 the two rubber boats, baggage and a folding bicycle of SOE design were brought up on to the fore casing. The boats were inflated and the submarine trimmed down forward. At 0025, in position 41°44' N, 08° 15' E and 600 yards from the landing place, both rubber dinghies were launched and loaded: Porter noted in the log that the three agents embarked in high spirits. At 0035, the boats were slipped and proceeded shorewards on a steady course at a good speed. They were visible against the white rocks until they had nearly reached the shore. The night was bright with many stars and a haze to seawards. The boats' crews, presumably drawn from the men Holdsworth had brought with him from Helford, reported later that the submarine was invisible at a range of 140 metres, end on against the haze to seaward.

At 0125, the dinghymen reported on R/T that they had left the beach. *Tribune* was now beam-on to the shore at a distance of 550 metres, but they could not see her. R/T communication was maintained and the dinghymen eventually reported that they were 450 metres off the land. They flashed a torch to seaward at intervals but it was not sighted from the submarine. Porter was convinced that the rubber boats were now to seaward of him and had been blown to the westward by the offshore breeze. He instructed the boat to flash to the NE three times. The light was seen a mile south-west of the submarine's position and Porter closed in to the spot on the main electric motors. At 0230, he recovered the two boats and their crews. He then proceeded to seaward, still on the electric motors.

The dinghymen said the landing place was excellent: the agents reached shore with all their baggage without getting wet and were delighted with the pinpoint At 0315, *Tribune* was clear enough of the land to change over to main diesel engines, and at 0632 she dived and shaped course to the NW with the intention of making a situation report later in the day. She resurfaced at 1848 hours and headed NW on main engines. At 1924, she received Captain (S) 8's signal ordering a situation report to be made 'as convenient before daylight on 9 January'. At 2047, *Tribune* reported completion of operation SIDELINE and shaped course for the Cassingdene Reef light, to arrive at dawn to intercept traffic between Marseilles and Toulon.

Scamaroni set off alone through the *maquis* for Ajaccio, 30km away, with the bicycle on his back. He left Hellier and Jickell near the beach to hide the W/T set, the team's baggage and a sealed suitcase, of whose contents only Scamaroni was aware: it carried the greater part of his total funds, which amounted to a million Francs, intended to finance the mission's operations.

Scamaroni made his way across country until he reached the River Taravo, where he fell into a ditch and slept till dawn. He then proceeded by road on his bicycle to Ajaccio, arriving at nightfall, cold and hungry. Under cover as a commercial traveller, he knocked at the door of a man named Raimondi, a public-works contractor and cinema-owner, who had been chosen by Achille Peretti, future President of the French Assemblée Nationale, to be Scamaroni's deputy head of mission. Scamaroni did not know Raimondi, but he identified himself by saying, *'Je viens de la part de Monsieur Tainturier.'* This was the name of a close family friend who had worked for many years with Fred's father in the Prefectural Corps and been sacked by the Vichy administration after many years of service at Toulouse. To Scamaroni's great relief, the man who had opened the door replied: *'Ah oui, Monsieur Tainturier de Toulouse.'* Peretti must have laid on these pre-arranged passwords before Fred left London. Raimondi was equally relieved, as he had received the BBC message but did not know what had become of his designated chief and had no means of making contact with him.

He gave Fred a meal and rapidly assembled some members of his Resistance team, which belonged to the 'Combat' movement: Colonel Ferrucci, who was to become deputy head of the military side of the organisation; Antoine Serafini, the departmental architect, a future mayor and parliamentary deputy for Ajaccio; Fernand Poli, a journalist; whom he introduced to Scamaroni, their new chief and representative of the mythical General de Gaulle, who was known to them only as a voice on the BBC's French broadcasts. Fred immediately impressed them with his appraising gaze.

Jickell and Hellier, after hiding their baggage, seem also to have set off for Ajaccio. Poli and a man named Vignocchi went by car from Ajaccio to look for them and found them, ravenously hungry and having frequently lost their way. They were taken into Ajaccio and installed in a safe house.

Next day, 9 January, Hellier, with the help of Bianchi and three other members of the Ajaccio Resistance, set out in a taxi to collect the hidden baggage. They were disguised as fishermen and even greeted a passing Italian patrol. They pressed an errant donkey into service and readily found the spot where the material had been hidden, but unfortunately one of the suitcases was missing. By four in the morning, the rest of the luggage was by the roadside ready for departure when the group was challenged by an Italian patrol. They explained that they were taking the early-morning postal bus to Ajaccio and were allowed to continue. The bus was searched by a gendarme who tapped the cases without opening them.

When they arrived in Ajaccio it was discovered that the missing suitcase belonged to Scamaroni and contained the greater part of the mission's war chest, 600,000 Francs and $500, as well as clothes, weapons and spare crystals for Hellier's W/T sets. Scamaroni dismissed speculation that the Italian OVRA must have discovered the cache: if they had, he said, they would have taken everything or nothing, and then lain in wait for whoever came to collect the kit.

Bianchi installed the W/T set in a safe house. Hellier's first signals were heard by MASSINGHAM in Algiers on 25 January but were unintelligible. This seems to have remained the case throughout the time the mission were in the field. SOE London received a first message from *Sea Urchin* on 2 February 1943. It read, Team safely housed stop. Equipment Ajaccio stop. Congratulate submarine crew. POT A [Jickell] leaves tomorrow in search of landing grounds stop. Fishing days authorised and limited to certain gulfs.'[23]

Meanwhile, discreet enquiries were being made in the Gulf of Valinco area about the missing suitcase. A 17-year-old shepherd was spending wildly in the local bar with freshly minted bank notes. After a few traditional Corsican death threats and a vow of silence, the shepherd's parents finally handed over the suitcase and its contents, including three-quarters of the money. The new notes the mission had brought contrasted with the ragged, soiled ones in circulation on the island, and Raimondi therefore arranged for all their cash to be exchanged for less conspicuous notes.

On 5 February, MASSINGHAM were informed by SOE London that a reinforcement party, code-named MECHANIC/GURNET, had left London for Algiers and that

MASSINGHAM were to arrange details of their infiltration direct with *Sea Urchin*. MASSINGHAM explained that they had still not been able to establish radio contact with *Sea Urchin*. They asked London to get *Sea Urchin* to suggest a landing point on the west coast; but GURNET was never landed.[24]

Whether Scamaroni had deliberately arranged to communicate exclusively with London is not clear: he may have found MASSINGHAM's links with the Giraudist Service de Renseignements disturbing. He was finding that various Resistance groups in Corsica, particularly 'Franc Tireur', under General Mollard, who had been the military commander in the island in 1939 and 1940, and the 'Front National' under Benielli in Bastia and Giovoni in Ajaccio, both Communists, were reluctant to amalgamate behind de Gaulle. He discovered, too, that one of Benielli's men, Tavera, who had been offered to Scamaroni as liaison, was cultivating Hellier and plying him with drink to get information about the Free French. Scamaroni protested to Benielli about this, but the latter denied responsibility.

XIX
Missions to Sardinia and Corsica: January–March 1943

On the night of 8/9 January 1943, when *Tribune* had just resumed her offensive patrolling on the south-east coast of France, HM S/m P228, subsequently renamed Splendid, under command of Lt Ian McGeoch, RN, carried out a first infiltration of agents for the Italian Section of SOE's MASSINGHAM mission in Algiers.[1] The operation, code-named CONVERSE, involved landing two men, Adler and Pisani (alias 'Serra'), on the east coast of Sardinia and it was destined to have a direct effect on events in Corsica.[2] It had been planned in conjunction with Emilio Lussu, a brave and brilliant anti-Fascist leader from the days of Mussolini's 1922 march on Rome. Lussu, who combined left-wing politics with the cause of Sardinian separatism, had made a spectacular escape from the prison camp on the Lipari Islands in 1939. SOE had told Jack Beevor, their man in Lisbon, to arrange for Lussu to be brought out of France, where he was living under a false name, but Lussu and his wife turned up in Lisbon in 1941 without any action on Beevor's part. Beevor sent them on to London, but they were returned to France in June 1942 by felucca.[3]

The night of 8/9 January, which had been provisionally selected for CONVERSE, was perfectly suitable in terms of weather under the lee of Sardinia. The sea was calm; there was a light offshore breeze and an overcast sky, which made the night exceptionally dark. McGeoch closed the beach to within half a mile by 0230 on the 9th and then quickly sent the eight-man rubber dinghy away, manned by two men from Holdsworth's *Mutin,* Leading Seaman Taylor and Able Seaman Webb.[4]

Adler, who inspired great confidence in McGeoch and was certainly very intelligent, asked that the submarine return the next night, if she could do so without undue risk, to take him and Serra off, in case they thought their presence had been compromised and that they would soon be discovered. McGeoch felt that giving the agents some hope of retreat if events turned out against them would boost their morale and justified P228's allotting another 24 hours of her patrol time to providing it. He therefore arranged a comprehensive set of light signals for use by Taylor and Webb. If Taylor were unable to find the submarine when coming away from the shore, McGeoch told him to proceed to seaward on a compass bearing due east from Mount Ferru, as far as possible, since it was not unlikely that P228 would be forced by patrol or other craft to dive or withdraw. Taylor had instructions from SOE to land with the agents and help them to carry their W/T gear a mile or so inland, where it would be buried. He was ordered to leave shore not later than 0430.

The rubber boat left P228 at 0250 and was seen heading slowly but surely for the shore. At this time, some rather heavy gusts of wind were coming offshore, which must have slowed the boat down.

At 0445, one green flash was sighted to northward. McGeoch moved the submarine one cable in that direction but they did not see the light again. The flash was reported to be on the beach, some little way above the water; Taylor was intending to leave the shore shortly but, knowing it was after 0430, had flashed the signal before actually leaving. P228 therefore returned to the exact waiting position.

At 0540, the boat had not returned and dawn was imminent P228 moved offshore, dived and then proceeded further to seaward on the line due east from Mount Ferru. During the forenoon one aircraft flying up the coast and one auxiliary schooner under sail and power, steering south, were seen.

Just after noon, they were proceeding very slowly towards the shore along the agreed line when Sub Lt Robert Balkwill, with his eyes glued to the search periscope, said, There they are, Sir!' The rubber boat was bearing 300,° 2,000 yards distant. They were four miles from land and it was sunny day with a calm sea: McGeoch decided it would be better to surface and risk being seen than to leave Taylor and Webb drifting about in the Tyrrhenian Sea. As he subsequently reported: '1223 Surfaced. Embarked boat and its occupants who were understandably relieved that we were not a U-boat, the periscope having looked at them, they said, in a hostile way.' They dived again quickly, Balkwill having first leapt over the side to rescue the dinghy paddles, which were floating away and could have aroused suspicion. The dinghy was slashed with a knife so that it would deflate more quickly. A tot of rum restored Taylor and Webb's morale and they seemed thereafter entirely unmoved by their adventure. No enemy response followed P228's brief stay on the surface. But it was not until a couple of nights later, when the submarine was well away from the scene of the operation, that McGeoch felt able to signal to Captain (S)8 that CONVERSE had been completed.

Taylor reported that the landing had been successfully carried out and that no alarm had been raised. He and Webb had helped the agents carry the W/T gear some distance inland and bury it. On the way inshore, one of the agents (Pisani, alias Serra) had been absolutely useless and, as he would not paddle, the efforts of Adler, the other agent, were largely wasted because the boat turned round. The offshore breeze came in stronger gusts inshore and impeded the boat, so that the shoreward passage took an hour. He also reported that the agents had asked him not to flash any signals until 15 minutes after the boat had left the beach. In agreeing to this, Taylor had not realised how much faster he would move downward away from the shore. In fact, Webb saw the submarine and alerted Taylor, who thought they still had much further to go. They therefore paddled on and, not finding the submarine, continued to seaward as instructed.

McGeoch reported that both ratings had behaved admirably and cheerfully in trying circumstances, though not more so than was expected in view of their magnificent record in earlier operations.

In normal times, Algiers was not a French submarine base, though Oran had the requisite facilities. From a maintenance point of view, it would have made good sense for *Casabianca,* which at the beginning of 1943 was the only French submarine in the Mediterranean in seagoing condition, to be transferred to Oran, but L'Herminier was determined to remain based on Algiers. The Allied intelligence services operated from Algiers and L'Herminier felt that his submarine, though less well equipped for offensive patrol duties than her smaller, but more modern, sisters of the Royal Navy's 8th Flotilla, was particularly qualified to serve their needs for clandestine sea transport. He persuaded the Deuxième Bureau without too much difficulty that *Casabianca* was big enough to carry out an operation to Provence as well as to Corsica in the course of a single patrol, but he stipulated that their next sortie should be delayed until the new moon, so that they could take advantage of the long, dark nights for what promised to be protracted and heavy work when they began landing arms and explosives in Corsica.[5]

Casabianca's second mission was in fact threefold: she had, first of all, to land two secret agents in Corsica—Regimental Sergeant Major Bozzi and a W/T operator named Chopitel, together with two British B7-type suitcase sets, several accumulators and a transformer. ACF listed this operation, code-named AUBURN, as being for Cohen's Section of SIS and the mission was, therefore, supposed to work independently, but it was decided that the security advantages of doing so were outweighed by access to the experience gained by PEARL HARBOUR, and that they should therefore put themselves under the orders of Commandant de Saule.

The second part of the programme involved landing a cargo of Sten guns and ammunition for PEARL HARBOUR at the Anse d'Arone. At the same time it was hoped that *Casabianca* would be able to re-embark the three members of her crew who had been left behind in December.

The third, and most important, part of the *Casabianca*'s mission in the February no-moon period was to land a three-man team on the coast of Provence, consisting of Captain Caillot, a cavalry officer who was to serve as W/T operator; Lieutenant Guillaume of the French counter-espionage service and Fred Brown of OSS.[6] Caillot was to operate an OSS signals plan code-named YANKEE. Brown had six SOE B-type suitcase sets with him: he thought in big terms, but his notions of security were, in the view of most wise men, quite unacceptable.[7]

A secondary task for *Casabianca* while on the coast of Provence was to embark a group of French officers who wanted to join the French Forces in North Africa.

The arms were supplied by SOE's MASSINGHAM packing station in watertight packages, none of which weighed more than 70lb, but the boxes of ammunition were heavier and awkward to handle through the hatches and into their stowage places in the submarine. SOE could not immediately supply the secure R/T link that L'Herminier had requested or a lightweight replacement for *Casabianca*'s own heavy dinghy. Col. Eddy of OSS, however, was able to produce a number of large, American, eight-man, inflatable aircraft dinghies, which MASSINGHAM modified by removing the inflatable centre thwarts and fitting removable, but rigid, bottom boards to distribute the weight of the cargo evenly over the bottoms of the boats, which consisted otherwise of no more than a reinforced rubber skin.[8]

Casabianca sailed on the evening of 31 January, after a last-minute change of plan when the 'field' in Provence signalled that they would be standing by on the night of 4/5 February. This was potentially awkward, as PEARL HARBOUR was expecting them at the Anse-d'Arone on the night of 6 February.[9]

The rendezvous in Provence was supposed to be at Cros-de-Cagnes and *Casabianca* crossed the Mediterranean without incident. Her navigator checked the position whenever possible with star sights, as they had rather lost confidence in their gyro-compass, which, having let them down on their first mission, could not be replaced or repaired at Algiers. They made a good landfall and, on the night of 3/4 February, observed searchlights in the vicinity of Toulon, on the Iles-d'Hyères and near La-Garoupe, the unlit lighthouse on the Cap-d'Antibes. The coast was obviously now well watched by the Germans and the British submarine *Tribune* had reported that the searchlights were apparently linked to a well-organised radar system. At 0150, *Casabianca* was just about to submerge: everybody was below and L'Herminier was ready to press the klaxon for the dive when the control-room reported on the voicepipe that a W/T signal addressed to them was being received. L'Herminier instructed his British liaison crew to take the message and acknowledge receipt: it could be decoded at leisure after they had dived to 40 metres.

The signal was from the commander of the British 8th Submarine Flotilla. Referring by code name to the French agent who was due to meet them, it reported that reconnaissance of 'No. 1' was unfavourable. No. 1 was their chosen pinpoint at Cros-de-Cagnes. The warning had arrived just in the nick of time to save them from falling into a potential trap.

The message gave no clue as to what they were supposed to do about an alternative landing place but L'Herminier decided to take the initiative. He went into conference with his three passengers. They decided against the Esterel, because the road and the railway followed the coast too closely and because there were a number of strategic key-points in that vicinity that were likely to be well guarded. The area south and west of Saint-Tropez was more promising: the coast there was broken and the main communications ran well inland. There was good cover for concealment of passengers and material. Cap-Camarat had a lighthouse and a semaphore station and Cap-Lardier was an obvious choice for an enemy observation post, but between the two lay Taillat Point, which might be less well guarded. They decided to feel their way along the coast either east or west of this feature, making themselves as inconspicuous as possible, and penetrate into one or other of the two bays, where, L'Herminier assumed, they would be completely safe both from the prowling searchlights on the Ile-du-Levant and from the enemy's radar network. Taillat itself, joined to the mainland by a narrow isthmus, would be silhouetted against sea and sky at night like an island and should be easy to identify.

They set course westwards, knowing they could not arrive before nightfall and that, when they got there, the submarine's batteries would be practically exhausted. During that day, the sea became rough and it was difficult to keep *Casabianca* at periscope depth, so that it was impossible to keep track of their exact position. Then, at nightfall, it became calmer and they had to dive deeper to avoid being spotted from the air. At 1800 hours they were proceeding at 2 knots when they touched bottom. That at least resolved doubts about their position, as there was only one shoal in the area: they knew that they must be 410 metres off the Tourelle-de-l'Esquillade. The current, reinforced by the east wind, had carried them further to the west than they had reckoned and they were now close to the Pointe-du-Titan, on which a searchlight was mounted. By 2000 hours, they were far enough from it to risk surfacing and switching over to diesels, but remaining in deep trim so that as little as possible of their superstructure was clear of the surface.

They passed Lardier and could see Camarat on the horizon, but Taillat was lost against the background. Fortunately, the sounding machine was working well enough to enable them to avoid shallow points in the sea-bed, many of which had never been properly charted.

At 2100 hours, they headed into Bon-Porté Bay, which was quite shallow. The dinghymen and the three agents stood ready to leave and the submarine hove to about 275 metres short of the beach. The dinghy was launched and loaded and the shore party took their places on board. The indicator of the storage batteries read so low that the submarine would have been unable to submerge had anything gone wrong. At 2125 hours, the dinghy left for the shore.

As their eyes became accustomed to the darkness, they became aware of the presence of what looked exactly like a blacked-out ship, less than 200 metres away to starboard. The gun crew, who were closed up and standing by, trained their weapon on to the target and were ready to fire: it was a moment of intense emotion for all on deck and for the shore party, who were still near enough to see what was happening. But the target did not move and gradually confidence returned. In reply to L'Herminier's whispered question down the voice-pipe from the bridge to the control-room, one of the officers confirmed that there was a large, detached rock jutting out of the water in the middle of the bay. It was called Escudelier rock and it became a well-known landmark to everyone who undertook subsequent operations to this pinpoint. There was in fact a German block-house only a short distance beyond it.

Within the record time of 17 minutes, the dinghy was back alongside, having successfully completed the first landing from Algiers on the German-occupied south coast of metropolitan France. It was a good pinpoint, but suitable for use in only calm weather, as they were to learn on subsequent visits. Apart from the block-house, which lay 300 metres to one side of where the agents had landed, it subsequently transpired that there was a machine-gun nest only 200 metres in the other direction. A German-occupied farmhouse lay only a short distance above, north-east of the beach: it was badly blacked out and they had wrongly assumed that the light escaping from it was a star, although L'Herminier did think it strangely motionless among the myriad stars that twinkled through the pine trees.

Their success was cheering but this was countered by the ordeal they then had in engineering the submarine's withdrawal. The batteries, which had never been so low, had to provide power not only for the electric motors, to make a silent retreat, but thereafter to start the heavy diesels, which could not be brought into action by any other means. L'Herminier ran the motors dead slow so as to use a minimum of current.

At 2230, when they were still uncomfortably close to the coast, they saw a small white light behind them and to port. It went out, but they eventually made out the unmistakable silhouette of a small German patrol vessel, not very far away. L'Herminier decided that he had no alternative but to start up his diesels and rely on the submarine's surface speed of 17 knots to make their escape. While in Algiers there had been no time to arrange fitting of the exhaust-guards designed by Kerneur, their chief engineer, and, when the diesels started, there was a display of fireworks at water-level that must, L'Herminier thought, have greatly surprised the watch on the enemy patrol boat. They still had two more operations to do in Corsica before they could head for home.

By this time, Pierre Griffi's PEARL HARBOR W/T link had passed several dozen signals to base reporting progress in establishing the network and transmitting detailed intelligence of Italian military dispositions.[10] When Algiers told de Saule to stand by for a first consignment of arms to be landed from *Casabianca* on 6 February at the Anse-d'Arone, south of the Gulf of Porto—a region difficult of access because of its precipitous topography—Toussaint Griffi, Preziosi and four members of the Front National group from Ajaccio had piled into a large taxi and gone north along the coast through Sagone. They were particularly apprehensive about a permanently manned check-post at Cargèse, where there was a concentration of Italian troops, and were prepared to shoot if stopped, but, to their immense relief, they sailed past the road-block of sandbags without raising a movement from the Italian sentries behind it. As the taxi climbed from Cargèse to Piana and away from the sea, Preziosi and Griffi caught sight of the bay at Chioni and the spot where they had landed two months previously. It was a small creek close to the main beach and the beach was guarded by an Italian military unit; so they had had a very narrow escape. They drove past the little house with the eucalyptus trees where they had made their first contacts on their way to Revinda and shortly came to the point where they were to meet the two Nesa brothers, who had a sheep-fold not far from the road at U Solognu. This was beginning to be a place of refuge for the local Resistance. The family were taking care of four of these patriots in addition to the three castaway members of *Casabianca*'s crew. Commandant de Saule joined them during the morning. It was the first meeting in the Maquis of a party of combatants from outside the island with a group of local patriots and everyone felt pleased to be involved in such an important step forward. *Casabianca*'s crew members were particularly happy at the prospect of being able to rejoin their submarine.

Soon they had to go down to the Baie-d'Arone, which lies just north of the Baie-de-Chioni on the way to the Gulf of Porto. Access to the beach was difficult as all the paths leading to it ran through the thick scrub that covered very steep hillsides. For reasons of prudence they went down in small groups and met at a small hut not far from the beach. A surprise awaited them when they reached the foreshore at about 1 o'clock in the morning and found four men there: the two agents, Sergeant Major Bozzi, Chopitel, the W/T operator, and two sailors named Asso and Cardot had been there since the previous night. *Casabianca* had arrived 24 hours earlier than expected and L'Herminier had decided to send them ashore without waiting for the reception party. But the submarine's heavy boat had run so hard aground that it had defied their efforts to refloat it, and once again, two sailors had been unable to return to their submarine. They told de Saule that the arms and ammunition would not be landed until the following night—7 February—so the whole party went back to the hut. This information was misleading: *Casabianca* surfaced again on the night of 6 February and sent a flat-bottomed boat ashore, towing four of the rubber boats, which were loaded with a cargo of 450 Sten sub-machine-guns and 60, 000 rounds of 9mm ammunition. The landing party, who, on the previous night, had gone to check why the dinghy had not returned and had found it half-buried in the sand, unloaded their cargo and hid it under branches before returning to the submarine. The reception committee were unaware that they had come and gone, but fortunately they decided to return to the beach shortly before dawn to remove the stranded boat from sight, whereon they discovered the arms dump. They set to work and in less than an hour the arms and boxes of ammunition had been hidden provisionally in a more secure place half-way between the beach and the hut. They had finished before day broke. Toussaint Griffi and Preziosi noticed that quite a lot of the stranded boat remained visible, although it was supposed to have been broken up while the arms were being hidden, so they made a renewed attack on the wreckage with pick-axes and hid the pieces in the thick scrub that ran right down to the beach.

While this was being done, other members of the reception party had moved the material again. Some of it was stored in the shepherd's hut, some was loaded on to donkeys for early distribution to reliable local hands, starting with the Maquisards already gathered at the Nesa family's sheep-fold, who thus became the first armed Maquis group in the island; here PEARL HARBOR was soon to establish its base. It took a couple of hours for the first donkey convoys to scale the steep ascent from the shore and deliver their loads, but when they returned to the beach they brought back bread and good Corsican *charcuterie* for the 15 or so exhausted people at the hut with the remainder of the cargo.

The Sten guns and ammunition that had been landed represented less than half the total cargo *Casabianca* had on board, but the weather had deteriorated during the landing and L'Herminier had to use the electric motors all the time to prevent the submarine from drifting ashore.[11] He anchored to save his batteries and decided to wait another day in the hope of being able to land the rest of the arms cargo the following night. But the shore party, on leaving the beach, had to row off in the teeth of what had become a strong onshore wind. Seeing how difficult they found it to make headway towing the four rubber boats, L'Herminier weighed anchor and stood inshore to pick them up. As he did so, the rudder-guard bumped heavily on the bottom and the flat-bottomed boat was so damaged in coming alongside that it sank. They had now lost both their rigid boats and could only hope that the weather would improve substantially before the following night, as the rubber boats would be able to be used alone only in calm conditions. They waited on the bottom off the Anse-d'Arone all day but when they surfaced after dark that evening it was still blowing hard and they had to renounce the idea of further landings. They had seen lights on the beach before they submerged that morning and surmised that the reception party had at least turned up to collect what they had managed to put ashore.

Casabianca was back in Algiers on 10 February. On the same night, the British submarine Saracen, under the command of Lt M.G.R.Lumby, RN, entered the Bay of Cupabia and landed three further agents there for SIS. The party's leader and W/T operator was Guy Verstraete, the Belgian merchant marine officer landed by *Minna* near Oran in July 1942, who had been in contact with Ridgway Knight. The mission, whose other two members were Corsicans named Antoine Colonna d'Istra and Simon Charles Andrei, recruited by SIS in Algiers, was known locally as FREDERICK.[12]

They used the same landing-place as Porter had used a month earlier to infiltrate Scamaroni and his *Sea Urchin* team. Lumby was not warned by S (8) that he would be using a 'hot bed' and subsequently complained of this omission.[13]

The Italians had indeed heard that a landing by submarine had been made in the Golfe-de-Valinco area. At 0210 on 11 February, when *Saracen* was less than 750 metres from the shore and on the surface preparing for the boatwork, a small searchlight on the beach one mile to the eastward started searching the sea. The submarine was illuminated six times but, though beam-on to the light, was apparently not detected. Lumby thought great credit was due to the three agents and two boat's crew, who carried on loading their boats as if they had not noticed the light. Verstraete and his companions were dispatched five minutes later in two rubber dinghies of the American type. The landing was successfully accomplished and the boats were re-embarked only 40 minutes after they had left the submarine.

Lumby reported on his return to Algiers that the American-type rubber dinghy appeared to have every advantage for landing agents. It carried a very heavy load, as well as being seaworthy and robust. The latter point was very important. When the two dinghies were going inshore on 11 February they ran aground on a sharp reef and remained there until the swell managed to lift them right over. A Folboat would have sunk instantly and an ordinary rigid boat would have been holed; and as they were still over 25 metres from the beach, all the gear would have been lost. The only damage to the dinghies was a number of severe gashes in the canvas. The boats' crews had been supplied with binoculars and an R/T set, which were not used in this case as the dinghies had no trouble finding the submarine. However, they must be considered essential equipment for operations of this nature, where the burning of searchlights could compel the submarine to shift position violently.

Saracen's remarks on the American-type rubber dinghies confirmed Captain (S)8's views based on his flotilla's previous experience. Their only disadvantage seemed to be that they could not navigate accurately over any great distance. (S)8 thought therefore that the Folboat should be retained and, for certain operations where an unknown distance had to be traversed to and from shore, that the submarine should carry both types of boat.[14]

There was no reception committee on 11 February at Cupabia Bay and the FREDERICK team hid their luggage among the rocks. It consisted of a mountain rucksack, two suitcases of clothes, a suitcase W/T transmitter/receiver, another containing spare parts and a tin box containing an accumulator. They then made their way east to the small mountain village of Olmeto, some 18km away, where they arrived exhausted in the evening. Andrei had an old friend named Joseph Tramoni living there, who gave them food and a bed for the night. Andrei and Verstraete went back to the beach to collect their luggage on 15 February in company of a 16-year-old boy, Benoît Mondolni, and his donkey.[15]

All four submarine operations to Corsica so far had been to the west coast. At about this time, however, the Front National, under the leadership of Arthur Giovoni, the Communist chief at Ajaccio, conceived a plan to capture and abduct one of the four Italian divisional generals in the island, whose headquarters was at Petreto-Bicchisano, an operation whose effect would be all the more spectacular if he could be shipped out to Algiers as a prisoner of war. For this, an embarkation point on the east coast would be more suitable, as they wanted to take their prospective captive in that general direction via Aullène and Solenzara. Though far from convinced of the merits of the scheme, de Saule agreed to put it to his chiefs in Algiers and asked them to study the possibility of sending *Casabianca* to the east coast in the course of her next patrol. His feeling that the planned abduction involved disproportionately great risks was shared by the Palais d'Eté, so the plan was abandoned.[16]

De Saule worried that Toussaint Griffi and Preziosi were getting altogether too mixed up in the Front National, of which they had both become members, so he sent them off to join the Maquis group at U-Solognu, where the original castaways from *Casabianca,* Lasserre, Lionnais and Vigot, had now been joined by Cardot and Asso, left ashore after the second operation. The idea of a submarine operation on the east coast in March went ahead meanwhile and de Saule decided to send Toussaint Griffi and Preziosi back to Algiers by means of it. He felt that their close links with the Front National would make it difficult for them, in the coming paramilitary phase, to achieve effective coordination with all the other Resistance movements in the island.

The point for the operation, the Anse-de-Canelle, some way north of Porto-Vecchio, had originally been selected because a member of the Resistance had a farm near by capable of providing shelter for a substantial party, which made it particularly suitable in connection with the plan to kidnap the Italian general.

Casabianca sailed from Algiers on 2 March and on the night of 5/6 March made an unsuccessful attempt to land agents and pick up Captain Caillot and Lieutenant Guillaume (whom L'Herminier had landed a month before) and three other officers, including a general, from the Taillat pinpoint.[17] She then sailed to the Canelle rendezvous, where de Saule had assembled the whole PEARL HARBOR party and the five sailors. The coast in that area is featureless, with a sandy beach stretching away north and south for some 30km The party were in position on the night of 8/9 March, but Pierre Griffi flashed the recognition signal to seaward for two hours in vain and they got caught in a rainstorm as they were making their way back to their hotel at Solenzara, where they arrived drenched.[18] Preziosi and Toussaint Griffi had to go to bed naked, leaving their clothes to dry by the embers of the fire in their bedroom. They slept late and that night again made their way towards the Anse-de-Canelle, which lies 4–5km from the town. The area was malarial and the Italians had not deployed troops in it but, as they walked towards Favone, they saw the headlights of a car stopped on the road about 400–500 metres away. The lights were tinted blue, which suggested the vehicle was Italian, and, as they were shining in the direction of their rendezvous, which was only a kilometre away, they feared that an ambush was being prepared. Some of the party thought they should return to the hotel but in the end they agreed to split up into three groups and try to ensure that the submarine came to no harm. It fell to Preziosi and two of the local Resistance to act as the reconnaissance group. One of them, a man named Nicoli, went on alone to prospect. An hour later they saw a figure approaching, wearing hat with its brim pulled down. They thought at first he must be an enemy and prepared to shoot. Preziosi called his name twice without response but the third time, just as they were on the point of firing, Nicoli identified himself. The vehicle did indeed belong to the enemy but it had broken down and was abandoned. Anyway, it seemed better to call off the operation for that night.

On 10 March they had better luck. During the day, they made contact with a local fisherman who had a big boat moored in the creek at Favone and who was prepared to take everyone who was due to leave off to the submarine. They set off for the third time at about 1930 hours. It was less dark than on the two preceding nights and there was enough moonlight to enable them to find their way without difficulty. At 2000, one of the sailors, who was an engine-room rating, said he could hear the submarine's diesels. Everybody stopped and listened: other members of the submarine's crew thought they could perhaps also hear the sound. They had scarcely resumed their march when Lasserre said there was no doubt at all: the submarine was in the offing, expecting them, of course, at Canelle, whereas they were planning to embark at Favone. Unfortunately, an east wind had arisen within the previous quarter of an hour which, as Lasserre observed, would not help the embarkation process. He set to work straight away with the signal torch to try to attract the submarine's attention and get L'Herminier to come closer to Favone. At 2300 hours, they were on the little quay at Favone. Pierre Griffi was to board the fishing boat with the seven men who were due to leave, as he had messages from de Saule to deliver to L'Herminier. The motor started and less than quarter of an hour later they were in contact with the submarine, which was lying about two miles offshore. The fishing boat came alongside the submarine's bow and, although the fresh breeze complicated the manoeuvre, the sailors climbed on board, followed by Toussaint Griffi and Preziosi. L'Herminier was standing on the forward casing waiting for them. Pierre Griffi also came on board, had a few words with L'Herminier and then returned to the fishing boat, followed by two Corsicans from the Corps Franc French commando unit, who had been sent with six million Francs, arms and ammunition to prepare the insurrectional phase of the Resistance. The fishing boat was loaded and moved off slowly towards Favone, where de Saule and three members of the Resistance were awaiting them.

On board *Casabianca* L'Herminier still had the three intelligence agents he had been unable to land at Taillat. He was due to go back for a second attempt to do so and to pick up Captain Caillot and Lt Guillaume;[19] the revised rendezvous had been fixed for the night of 13/14 March. He decided to use the intervening time to fit in an offensive patrol off Bastia on his way north. He cross-examined Lasserre, who had spent part of his time ashore in Corsica at Bastia, where he and his companions had been taken care of by the local Resistance, about the timing of the shipping service organised by the Italians between Livorno, Elba and Bastia, which was the only port of any consequence in that part of the island. Lasserre told him that the small passenger ferry-boat *Francesco Crispi* and the cargo steamer *Tagliamento* maintained a weekly service, which would normally arrive on that very day. *Casabianca* therefore took up station off Bastia. At the beginning of the afternoon, the expected convoy appeared. L'Herminier fired four torpedoes but they missed their targets and hit the breakwaters of the Old Port. The submarine was then subjected to a prolonged depth-charge attack by the convoy's escorting destroyers. She dived to 80m and was pursued northwards almost to the Gulf of Genoa, or so it seemed to Preziosi. However, no sooner had the alert passed than L'Herminier, vexed by his failure, decided to return to Bastia next day with a view to shelling a large Italian military petrol dump close to the cemetery. Unfortunately, the torpedo attack had alerted the whole of the enemy defence system in the area and, even before they surfaced, the submarine was detected and subjected to a renewed and intensive depth-charge attack. By an adroit manoeuvre, L'Herminier managed to escape from his pursuers again, but he was deeply disappointed by this second failure and made no attempt to hide it. Though they performed yeoman service in opening up and maintaining clandestine sea lines of communication with Corsica and south-eastern France, they all longed to strike at the enemy- a role for which their lack of Asdic and their unreliable torpedoes fitted them less well. On this occasion, bad luck followed them back to the French coast: when they arrived in Bon-Porté Bay on 13 March, a combination of bad weather and the multiplicity of the German coastal batteries made it impossible to land the three-man team of intelligence agents they were carrying or to pick up the waiting party.

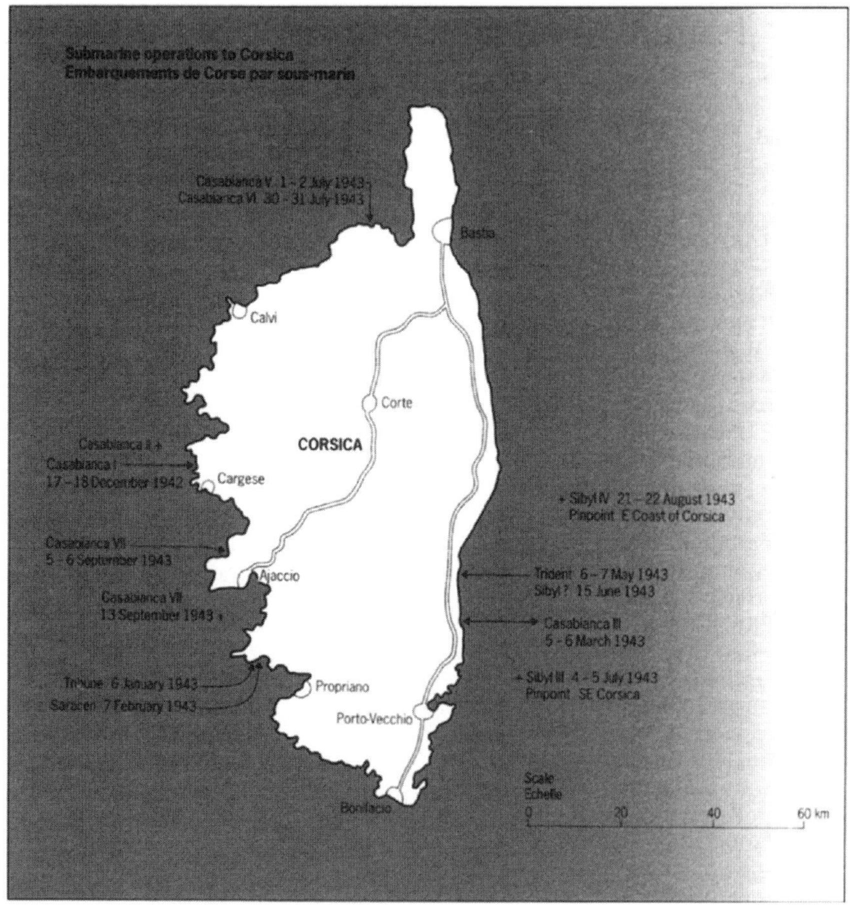
Submarine operations to Corsica
Embarquements de Corse par sous-marin
Casablanca V 1 – 2 July 1943
Casablanca VI 30 – 31 July 1943
Bastia
Calvi
Corte
CORSICA
Casablanca II +
Casablanca I
17 – 18 December 1942
Cargese
+ Sibyl IV 21 – 22 August 1943
Pinpoint E Coast of Corsica
Casablanca VII
5 – 6 September 1943
Ajaccio
Trident 6 – 7 May 1943
Sibyl ? 15 June 1943
Casablanca VII
13 September 1943 +
Casablanca III
5 – 6 March 1943
Tribune 6 January 1943
Saracen 7 February 1943
Propriano
+ Sibyl III 4 – 5 July 1943
Pinpoint SE Corsica
Porto-Vecchio
Bonifacio
Scale
Echelle
0
20
40
60 km

XX
Last Missions to Corsica before the Italian Armistice and its Liberation

SOE's W/T contact with SEA URCHIN ceased abruptly on 15 March and reports trickled in from Deuxième Bureau sources that Scamaroni and Hellier were under arrest, which turned out to be true. Their undoing patently stemmed from the very prompt arrest of Adler and Serra, the SOE Italian Section agents landed in Sardinia in February, and their willingness to cooperate with the OVRA, Italian counterpart of the Gestapo. Serra had known Hellier in Algiers when they were waiting to be sent into the field by MASSINGHAM. The OVRA brought him over to Corsica, where he identified Hellier, doubtless without difficulty as he had taken to drinking heavily in the bars of Ajaccio. Hellier in turn betrayed his chief.[1]

Scamaroni, who had found it hard to unite the Corsican resistance behind de Gaulle because the Front National's Communist leadership were suspicious of de Gaulle and thought they could get the arms they needed from PEARL HARBOR, took his own life, having disclosed nothing under torture. Hellier told his captors enough to compromise not only his chief but a number of his local contacts as well. A fresh start was necessary. Verstraete and Andrei of FREDERICK had, incidentally, also been arrested by the Italians when they returned to Cupabia Bay, hoping for another submarine landing operation.[2]

It so happened that MASSINGHAM had already found and trained the man who stepped into the breach and became the leader of the Corsican Resistance. His name was Paul Colonna d'Istria, a cousin of Antoine Colonna d'Istria who had been landed in Corsica in February as a member of SIS's FREDERICK mission. He came of a family long established in the Sartenais and was a Commandant in the gendarmerie, serving on the staff of the General commanding that force at Algiers.[3]

MASSSINGHAM discovered Colonna as a volunteer for a mission to Corsica in rather unusual circumstances.[4] Like many people from southern Corsica, where Arab cultural influence has left its mark, he was in the habit of having his horoscope cast each year. When this had last been done, some months before the Allied landings in North Africa, his astrologer had forecast that he would return to Corsica in dangerous circumstances within the year. At the time, this prediction had not made much sense, as he could then travel to Ajaccio on the ferry from Algiers with no particular difficulty or danger. But after TORCH and the Italian occupation of the island, he realised that he was destined to return to his native island clandestinely, just as Sampiero Corso had in 1564, when he attempted, with the support of Catherine de Medici, to deliver it from Genoese domination. This historical precedent had appealed also to Fred Scamaroni, whose family background was not dissimilar: SAMPIERO was the name he chose for the original operation that was to have returned him to Corsica as an emissary of de Gaulle.[5]

Paul Colonna was prepared to work for SOE, as was his cousin for SIS. Although SOE had been willing to support Scamaroni as a BCRA agent, it had no doctrinal difficulty about sending a successor into the field who would be working directly for MASSINGHAM. Although de Gaulle much disliked the practice, Baker Street's Independent French Section under Maurice Buckmaster sent Frenchmen as well as British officers into France as agents all the time and Jacques de Guélis, head of MASSINGHAM's French Country Section, belonged by background to that side of SOE's French activities. On 17 January, he had sent back to London via Gibraltar six young Frenchmen (Sihol, Kahn, F. Vallée, Gaillot, Maloubier and Reynaud) whom he had found in Algiers as volunteers for training and service with F Section. Bob Maloubier and Pierre Reynaud were both destined to win DSOs in France working for F Section. Paul Colonna was to earn one in Corsica.

Colonna, whom MASSINGHAM called 'Whiskers' or, more familiarly, 'Cesari', was not politically minded. MASSINGHAM hoped that his status as a British agent would allow him to hold himself aloof from the power struggle between de Gaulle and Giraud that was to be the principal preoccupation of the French in Algiers in the summer of 1943. They believed subsequently that his political independence had enabled him to weld together the disparate elements of the Corsican Resistance.[7] In retrospect, this was perhaps a somewhat naive view, but at the time it fitted in well enough with the need to work with the Americans, both in OSS and at AFHQ, who were still strongly anti-Gaullist. Indeed, Arthur Roseborough, head of OSS's Secret Intelligence (SI) operations at Algiers, lost his job because of his strong pro-de Gaulle views.[8]

By the end of March 1943 Scamaroni was dead and de Saule of PEARL HARBOR was on the run. It was decided to bring him out of Corsica during the operation (LEG) that would land Colonna d'Istria and his British W/T operator. The rendezvous fixed was on the east coast above the 42° parallel at the mouth of a river and the submarine chosen for the job was *Trident* (Lt P.E. Newstead, RN), which also carried an SOE prize crew to take over, it they could, an Italian schooner and bring it back to Algiers.[9]

Holdsworth had gone forward with *Mutin* to Bône for ZODIAC, but John Newton, skipper of Serenini, was embarked as captain of the prize crew and as conducting officer for SOE. The boatwork was to be carried out in conjunction with a Special Boat Section team consisting of Courtney and Lt E.J.A.Lunn.[10]

While *Trident* was 'dived' during the day before the operation, Newstead received a message altering the rendezvous to a point about 20 miles further south, at the mouth of the River Travo.

The operation itself, which took place on the night of 6 April at quarter moon, was comparatively straightforward: the SOE party paddled towards the shore in an inflatable rubber dinghy guided by Courtney and Lunn in a Folboat canoe, whose task was to keep the party on the right compass bearing for the river mouth. They approached the shore in silence, smelling the aromatic *maquis* stronger and heavier on the wind. Courtney noted that the whiteness of the sand at the river mouth first appeared as a long, grey, horizontal smudge, broken by the dark shapes of bushes.[11]

Once on shore, the men landing from the rubber boat threw restraint to the winds and clustered on the sand talking to the reception committee at the tops of their voices. De Saule told Colonna to get in touch with Pierre Griffi, who would brief him about the situation. Courtney and Lunn tried in vain to quieten them and the hubbub only grew when other members of the reception committee arrived and told them that a beautiful Maquisarde had been waiting to embrace the brave British Commandos. She had, however, gone home about an hour before.

Courtney and Lunn were impatient to get away: de Saule and Jickell, who had avoided arrest when Hellier and Scamaroni were rounded up by the OVRA, were escorted into the rubber dinghy, which was taken in tow by their Folboat. Courtney recalled it making its unwieldy way, swaying across the crests of the rollers, until they reached the safety of the submarine.

Although de Saule had been picked up, other people connected with his PEARL HARBOR mission who were due to be evacuated had gone to the original rendezvous on the coast 20 miles further north, in case the message changing the venue had not got through to the submarine. Newstead therefore turned north, hoping the next night to collect these people, who must have included Pierre Griffi, de Saule's W/T operator.[12]

During the day he made an unsuccessful attack on a merchant vessel. This upset de Saule, who feared that it might prejudice the attempt to rescue the remaining members of his party.[13]

The attempt to make contact with them failed in any case, and Newstead, knowing that the unsuccessful attack would have stirred up the defences off Bastia, proceeded to the northernmost limit of his patrol area, on the coast west of Genoa. There, *Trident* sighted what appeared to be a small coastal tanker of a few hundred tons close inshore. She was too small to justify using a torpedo, so they surfaced and prepared to engage her with their guns. But appearances proved deceptive: she was in fact an Italian Q-ship, which proceeded to mount an intensive and accurate counter-attack on the submarine. *Trident* only just survived this. On 18 April she returned to Algiers.[14]

Trident sailed again from Algiers on 1 May, apparently under orders to attempt again to evacuate the remaining members of de Saule's party, as well as to land two Soviet agents on the Italian coast (Operation ETNA).[15] The Corsican operation on 10 May was again unsuccessful. Pierre Griffi, whose relationship with Colonna proved difficult, was arrested by the Italians on 16 June and executed in August.[16] By the time *Trident* was free to attempt ETNA, moon conditions were no longer suitable and the operation was not carried out. She returned to Algiers on 18 May.

Colonna found that, despite Scamaroni's valiant efforts, the Resistance, though strongly anti-Fascist, was far from united. After carefully taking stock, he concluded that the Communist-led Front National provided the only nucleus around which a unified Resistance effort could be built.[17] De Gaulle, who was still in London at the time, was furious not to have been able to replace Scamaroni with one of his own men and chalked up yet another grievance against SOE's Independent French Section. Though Colonna had gone into Corsica under British auspices, the mission quite rapidly came under Giraud's aegis: Eisenhower involved Giraud, as Commander-in-Chief of French forces in North Africa, in the contingency planning for Corsica, which, if American strategy had prevailed in the Mediterranean theatre, would have had a more central role than the Quebec Conference decision to land in Sicily eventually awarded it.[18] When de Gaulle arrived in Algiers in June 1943, Colonna's mission was an accomplished fact.

Within two months, Colonna had achieved some sort of coordination of the Resistance movement under his leadership, but it was an arrangement that conceded pride of place to the Front National. He claimed to have some good men at his command. He had also organised 12 dropping grounds for supplies. It was difficult for MASSINGHAM to keep pace with the demand for supplies created by this swift expansion. Colonna rightly insisted that arms must be sent without delay as a token of confidence, otherwise his men would lose heart and melt away.[19]

By June MASSINGHAM had four RAF Halifaxes from Tempsford temporarily based in Algeria for supply operations to Corsica, but the island proved difficult to supply by air.[20] Much of the eastern coastal plain was so heavily garrisoned by the Italians as to make clandestine reception impossible. The rest of the island was so mountainous that it was difficult to find dropping zones that were large enough and even approximately level: aircraft had to fly between mountain peaks and supplies that dropped wide of the mark fell down precipices. Supply by submarine therefore continued. In June, HM S/m *Sibyl* (Lt E.J.D.Turner) was sent to south-eastern Corsica with a consignment of arms. It carried, too, Lt R.J.Laming, RNVR, and PO Sam Smalley of SOE's Naval Section as a conducting party. Laming was to meet Colonna by arrangement and discuss the situation with him. Colonna was at the pinpoint and came aboard the submarine for this discussion while the stores were being landed. As the boats pulled away from the beach after landing the last boatload, the Italians raised the alarm and began firing out to sea. The patriots on the beach fought their way out with the stores, but Colonna was marooned on the submarine.

After failing next night to regain contact with his men on shore, he had to submit to returning on the submarine to Algiers.[21] This apparent mischance proved fortunate. The Allied Command, having decided on a major landing in Sicily (Operation HUSKY), ruled on 21 June that the liberation of Corsica should be a French military responsibility. SOE's —and hence Colonna's—activities in the island thus came under the operational control of the French general staff. In Algiers, Colonna was able to meet the French officers responsible and try to impress them with the potential represented by his organisation, of which they were, and remained, somewhat sceptical.[22]

The formation of the Bataillon de Choc under Commandant Fernand Gambiez was the limit of 'irregularity' the French officers concerned were capable of comprehending. For the training of this unit they gladly accepted the assistance of SOE instructors from MASSINGHAM, and conceded that its function should be to stiffen Colonna's patriot units rather than to fight independently.

While he was in Algiers, Colonna was awarded the DSO. King George VI, who was on a visit to the British forces in North Africa and on more than one occasion came to MASSINGHAM's base at the Club des Pins for a swim and lunch, broke with precedent and bestowed it on Colonna personally, a rare honour for a non-British subject.[23] Colonna also took advantage of his stay in Algiers to have a new horoscope cast. He was told that he would be surrounded by his enemies but that he would escape from them against all the odds.[24]

On the night of 1/2 July he was landed back in Corsica from the *Casabianca*. He had the satisfaction of knowing that his persistent demands for supplies were now being energetically met by MASSINGHAM, for on his return he brought with him an unprecedentedly large consignment of 11½ tons of arms. Many of these weapons had been salvaged by SOE after the surrender of the Axis forces in Tunisia, under an arrangement made by Dodds-Parker with AFHQ. They had been cleaned, greased and packed by SOE into manhandleable loads, using a variety of coverings, including Axis shell containers, to protect them from spray and damp while in transit.[25]

MASSINGHAM's Naval Staff and Training Section had been closely involved with *Casabianca*'s crew in devising and practising methods for landing these supplies, which were used operationally for the first time on this occasion. SOE had now been able to make available two of the lightweight plywood dories that the author designed and had built while at Helford in 1942. These had been adapted for submarine use by fitting to their bottoms large, brass screw plugs or bungs—'Kingstons' in submarine parlance—which, when removed, allowed the dories to flood and drain as the submarine dived or surfaced. With their thwarts removed, two of these dories could be nested one inside the other, like the heavier prototypes carried on the Grand Banks cod-fishermen which worked out of ports such as Saint-Malo under sail until the inter-war years. Two of these Helford dories were carried upside-down in a compartment on top of *Casabianca*'s pressure hull, under the forward deck casing. They had the directional stability that the aircraft rubber dinghies lacked, and the latter could, when loaded, be formed into a train of four or five boats, which would follow docilely in the dory's wake as a tow when the dory was rowed ashore. Lightweight and secure radio-telephones had also been made available and were used for the first time to link the dories and the shore party back to the submarine.

Eight of *Casabianca*'s Seamen and Petty Officers had been put through a Commando-type assault course by MASSINGHAM at the Club des Pins and were sent ashore first to reconnoitre, to 'stake out' the landing point and find the best place to cache the landed material. While this was being done, the rubber dinghies provided by OSS were brought up on deck, fitted with their rigid wooden bottom boards and inflated by a lead from the ship's compressed-air system. They were then put into the water and aligned along one side of the surfaced submarine's deck casing; the submarine was in deep trim, with her bow resting on the sandy bottom, so that the boats could be more easily reached and loaded and there was no risk of her changing position while the landings were being carried out.

The beach chosen for the operation was the Plage-de-Saleccia, near Curza Point in the Désert-des-Agriates on the north coast—a region then so malarial that the Italians kept no permanent guard-posts there. It lies between the Genoese tower on Mortella Point—the prototype of British Martello towers—and the cove where Nelson landed cannon from his squadron for the siege of Calvi.

It was a flat calm night and the scent of the *maquis* was pungent. As soon as the rubber boats were afloat and the dories had been lowered quietly into the water, *Casabianca*'s crew of 85 men were all put to work. A human chain was formed to convey the packages from the stowage-places that Bellet, the first lieutenant, had found for them in every part of the pressure hull—under the floor of the mess decks, in the shaft tunnels, in places where spare torpedoes would normally have been carried and even alongside the main diesel engines. The chain of despatchers manhandled the packages, which weighed anything up to 70lb, along slippery gangways and up through the hatches to a further chain of willing hands, which carried them forward and passed them down into the rubber boats. The men worked rapidly and noiselessly, stripped to the waist and sweating like galley-slaves. They knew that a single slip, resulting in a metallic clang, might be picked up by enemy hydrophones and could lead to the loss of the submarine and all her crew.[26]

Each rubber boat could carry up to half a ton of material and, as soon as a 'train' of boats had been loaded, one of the dories would tow it ashore. The beach-reconnaissance party, reinforced by men who had come ashore with the stores, then proceeded to unload the boats, passing the heavy packages from hand to hand to the place where they were to be concealed, pending collection by the Resistance. Though the whole ship's company toiled at the task all night, the job was not finished when imminent dawn brought proceedings to a halt not long after 0300 hours. All traces of the night's work were carefully effaced and everybody was brought back on board, except Colonna, who decided to mount a discreet guard over the site until the following night and retained a radio-telephone for use when *Casabianca* surfaced after dark. The rubber boats were hauled on deck and deflated, the dories stowed away on top of the pressure hull, hatches closed and water was expelled from the ballast tanks so that *Casabianca*'s keel floated clear of the bottom. Then she slid silently astern into deep water to submerge and spend the daylight hours on the sea-bed a mile-and-a-half offshore.

The present author was on board as conducting officer for SOE, with Skipper Lt John Newton, Ldg Seaman Frank Taylor and Able Seaman Don Miles, and went ashore at the outset. He had been involved for nearly two years in the problems of clandestine landings of material on enemy coasts, and found *Casabianca*'s achievement uniquely impressive. In one short summer's night L'Herminier and his crew had succeeded in landing and hiding eight tons of arms and explosives in hostile territory without any outside help. No British submarine captain would have been allowed to take his submarine inshore to the point where she grounded, as a preliminary to sending the boats away. The way in which his large crew had worked together to make an operation of this size possible was in itself a remarkable tribute to L'Herminier's and Bellet's powers of leadership and to the efficiency and high morale of their crew.

It was much darker on the following night and one of the dories returning from the beach with a train of empty rubber boats missed *Casabianca*. Its departure from the beach had been reported by radio-telephone and, when it failed to appear alongside, L'Herminier decided to risk showing a few short flashes of light to seaward. It was not until 0230 hours that it came alongside, after an unnerving interlude in which it had pulled all round the bay looking for the submarine. But it was the only mishap in an otherwise flawless operation and by 0315 everyone was back on board except Colonna and his new W/T operator, Luc Le Fustec, who remained ashore, which was where their mission lay. Colonna was able to arrange for the entire cargo to be collected by the Resistance.

The present author went down with malaria before the end of *Casabianca*'s 12-day patrol and, while he was away convalescing, L'Herminier was called upon to deliver a further large cargo of arms and ammunition to Corsica (Operation SCALP II). Colonna had told us that the next delivery would have to be made further south, because the material already landed would cater for the needs of the Resistance in the northern part of the island and it would be difficult for him to distribute to other areas because of Italian checks on movements by road. He asked MASSINGHAM by W/T to arrange that the next consignment be landed in the Gulf of Porto on the western coast of the island.[27]

Bellet again took careful stock of the available stowage space and this time all the rest of the ship's company joined in the hunt. With what L'Herminier later described as care and grim determination, they managed, by utilising every nook and cranny from one end of the submarine to the other, to stow away 20 tons of warlike stores, again carefully packaged by MASSINGHAM.

The Gulf of Porto is six miles deep and the dangers involved in mounting a large-scale landing of material in it on two successive nights were obvious, but L'Herminier felt that, if that was what Colonna needed, they must do their level best to respond. Four potential pinpoints were identified and Holdsworth arranged for high-level photographic reconnaissance to be carried out. L'Herminier's choice fell on the Anse-de-Gradella, though there were indications that there might be Italian coastal batteries not far from it.

MASSINGHAM's conducting party this time was led by Newton and included Captain Michael Gubbins, son of SOE's chief executive, as well as PO Frank Taylor and Able Seaman Duff.

On the night of 29/30 July, L'Herminier could not sleep and went up on to the bridge at 0100 hours. The smell of *maquis* was so strong that he could not help thinking they must be very much nearer land than they had reckoned, and he ordered the engines to be stopped. It was a warm, humid and very beautiful night, but he could see absolutely nothing through his night binoculars. He expected at that time to be 15 miles to the west of Cap Gargalo, where he planned to make his landfall at 0400 hours. The place had unpleasant memories for him, dating from their first mission to Corsica. He decided to stand north and south until the time came to submerge before dawn, when a quick periscope sighting would enable them to fix their position.

They proved to have been much closer to Gargalo than expected: indeed, they might have run straight on to it if L'Herminier's intuition had not told him to stop. They proceeded into the middle of the gulf at a depth of 50 metres, travelling at 2 knots on the electric motors, and at 1430 hours settled down on the sea-bed within a short distance of their objective. They surfaced at 2250 hours that night. Owing to the illusion that makes distances seem shorter at night, the southern shore of the gulf looked as if it was almost on top of them.

The coastal road passed above the Anse-de-Gradella but they hoped that they would be so close to the shore that they would be hidden from it by the dead angle of the cliffs. There was no signal from the reception committee they were expecting this time. L'Herminier set aside his misgivings and nosed in between the rocks until *Casabianca*'s stern touched bottom about 100 metres from the beach.

The rubber boats were brought up on deck. The dories entered the water soundlessly and the reconnaissance group took their places on board them, but they had gone no more than a few metres when heavy firing broke out from both sides and machine-gun bullets began to whistle around them. The dory crews clambered back on board and L'Herminier ordered full astern, instructing Bellet to put the submarine into deep trim by the stern as they disengaged themselves from the rocks and headed towards the open sea, six miles to the westward. L'Herminier did not dive because he was anxious to save the boats spread out on the foredeck, but the dories broke free and were lost in the darkness. Gradually, the firing died away and it was possible to send men out on to the foredeck to collect the rubber boats. It had been a close shave.

But L'Herminier was *vir tenax propositi*. When he got to the open sea, he headed north at 17 knots under the diesels towards the Curza pinpoint they had used successfully four weeks earlier. Though bereft of their dories, they managed, with the help of their rubber dinghies and an ungainly steel boat they had had made in the dockyard at Oran, to land and conceal what must surely have been a world record of 20 tons of arms on the nights of 30/31 July and 31 July/1 August, again without the help of a reception committee.[28]

After this second success, *Casabianca*'s stock stood high with MASSINGHAM and Holdsworth attempted to get her permanently allocated to SOE for operations of this type. There had, however, been some friction between *Casabianca*'s crew and the SOE conducting party in the course of SCALP II and, consequently, Holdsworth's proposal was turned down.

Casabianca did one further, though smaller, supply run to the Golfe-de-Lava on 5/6 September, when she landed Lt Giannesini, a Gaullist agent, together with a radio operator and five tons of stores, this time without any SOE conducting party. The reception party was organised by Henri Maillot, de Gaulle's cousin, who was prominent in the local Front National. This brought the total landed by this submarine to 61 tons. She also picked up Arthur Giovoni, the Communist leader of the Front National at Ajaccio. He was carrying a copy of the Italian defence plan for the island, which had been made available to the Resistance by a Lt-Col. Gagnoni, whose father had been a Republican senator and who had served three years in prison for his anti-Fascist views.

Weather had been bad for aircraft supply in July but in August and September the number of air drops was substantially increased to bring the total of supplies delivered by air to well in excess of 160 tons. A final delivery of 28 tons by *Serenini,* under temporary command of Lt C.Long, RNR, of the African Coastal Flotilla, and another by one of the ACF feluccas on 16 September, after the Italian armistice, brought the total of stores landed by sea and by air from MASSINGHAM to approximately 250 tons.[29]

After his return to Corsica at the beginning of July, Colonna had had a very narrow escape in circumstances that strikingly bore out the prediction of his astrologer. Circulating from one Maquis cell to another, frequently on bicycle and in the uniform of a gendarme, he was caught up one day in a major drive by Italian troops designed to flush Maquisards out of their protective scrub cover. He sought refuge by lying down on the ground in the middle of a flock of sheep and goats. If the flock had moved on, as they do when grazing, he would have been exposed and captured but they did not, perhaps because they were resting in shade from the heat of the day. He continued to arm his organisation, and faced the problems of D-Day in Corsica with 12,000 armed men at his back.[30]

The nucleus of this force was the Communist-led Front National. Colonna believed he had persuaded this organisation temporarily to lay politics aside and to accept in alliance any group that was genuinely patriotic and sought affiliation. Colonna saw to it that the supplies of arms, which he controlled, went only to those groups that were prepared to do so.

In the last days of August, the probability of an Italian capitulation—well known to MASSINGHAM, which was handling the signals traffic between the Badoglio government and General Eisenhower, though not to General Giraud—began to have its effect on the Italian troops in Corsica. Colonna was in touch with Colonel Cagnoni at Bastia who controlled the defences of the port and the airfield. Shrewdly suspecting what was about to happen, Cagnoni promised to bring the troops under his command into action against the Germans and to persuade some of his colleagues to do the same. In the event, this was indeed the only area in which Italian troops played an active part in hampering the German withdrawal.[31]

The Germans already had 5,000 troops in southern Corsica and it was known in Algiers that they planned to withdraw their much larger force in Sardinia under command of General Ritter von Senger und Etterlin to Corsica. In view of this, proposals for a paramilitary insurrection of patriot forces in the island were rejected as too hazardous. Eisenhower knew from ULTRA that, though the Germans had originally intended to hold Corsica, they changed their minds on 13 September and proceeded to withdraw, via the ports and airfields of the island's eastern coastal plain, to the Italian mainland.[32]

When the armistice was made public on 8 September and the Corsicans saw the Germans executing an orderly and unhampered withdrawal, there was no holding them. It was their last chance to strike a blow at the enemy who had aroused their resentment in a way the easygoing Italians had never succeeded in doing. They brought their weapons out from their hiding-places and started an insurrection. Led by Colonna, who narrowly escaped being betrayed to the Germans (there was a price on his head), the Corsicans joined with the Italians and seized Bastia. But the German-held area was limited to a narrow strip along the east coast, which was the only site of enemy movement. Elsewhere, the Resistance had no enemy to attack, for the bulk of the 80,000 Italian troops followed their General into passive and ignominious neutrality. The bands were prepared to conduct guerilla warfare against second-rate troops in their own locality, but not to undertake a long march across country to fight far from their homes. Of two thoroughly practical prerequisites—boots and food—there was a lack that could not be made good. Consequently, the brunt of the fighting was borne by the bands in the eastern coastal strip; the bulk of what SOE called at the time 'the patriot forces' were never engaged.[33]

Help was now on its way, and on 11 September General Giraud sent Colonna an order to dispose his patriots in defence of Ajaccio in order to ensure a bridgehead for the landings of French troops.

Two days later, the *Casabianca* arrived at Ajaccio, having made the passage from Algiers on the surface, carrying 109 men, almost all members of the Bataillon de Choc: L'Herminier had achieved his ambition to have *Casabianca* become the first French ship to enter a liberated port in metropolitan France. The French submarine *La-Perle* (under Lt Paumier) followed on 16 September in support. Paumier persuaded the captain of the Toulon-Ajaccio ferry to sail to Algiers and he also landed three tons of much-needed flour. The French submarine *Aréthuse* (Lt Goutier) arrived on 18 September carrying five tons of munitions, before going on to Cap-Camarat to land five officers and embark seven, together with the colours of the 2ième Dragon Regiment.[34]

Casabianca had also landed a joint SOE-Deuxième Bureau mission consisting of Major Jacques de Guélis, head of MASSINGHAM's French Country Section, and Commandant Clipet from General Ronin's office, for liaison with the patriot forces.[35] The task of the Bataillon de Choc was to consolidate and extend the bridgehead, which was held throughout the brief campaign. Colonna was by now a sick man, so Clipet assumed command of all patriot forces. He was handicapped in his task by the French professional soldier's characteristic dislike of the 'irregular'. Instead of using the patriot bands for sabotage and ambushes, to which they were suited, and supporting them with more highly trained and disciplined troops, Clipet wanted to incorporate them as an integral part of the Bataillon de Choc and make them fight 'in the line'. One company of picked men, to whom he was able to give boots, rations and transport, fought with spirit and success; but other units, obliged reluctantly to leave their home areas and march on foot to the front, arrived there so hungry and exhausted as to be valueless as combatants.

On 13 September, the day the Bataillon de Choc landed at Ajaccio, the Germans, recovering from their surprise, drove the Italians out of Bastia and cleared their line of withdrawal up the coast road from Bonifacio and Porto-Vecchio. For a few days, their retreat was hampered by demolitions and skirmishes with the local patriots and the Italians who had joined forces with them. But ammunition and explosives soon ran short and the penury of available transport in the island apart from Italian military vehicles meant that no reinforcements could be brought up. Thus, although many of the patriots had ammunition but no occasion to use it, others operating in vital areas were soon reduced, by lack of it, to guides and intelligence scouts. Certainly, they did good service, but these were not the capacities for which they had been recruited and equipped by SOE.[36]

Meanwhile, the Germans executed a leisurely withdrawal with the precision of a textbook manoeuvre. The French 'offensive', launched with African troops on 20 September, never caught up with them; indeed, it interfered with their movements far less than the Italians and the patriots had done in the first few critical days at Bastia, when the German commander on three occasions sent emissaries to Colonna endeavouring to persuade him, by a mixture of threats and promises, to call the patriots off. Two SOE parties established with their W/T sets in the forward areas could only report the day-to-day dispositions of the German units: they could not make good the French troops' lack of transport or clear the minefields that slowed their methodical advance. When the motorised 4th Spahis at last swept round Cap-Corse into Bastia on the morning of 4 October, they found that the last Germans had left the previous night.

SOE found it difficult to assess MASSINGHAM's contribution to the campaign: it was not clear whether the existence of a formidable patriot force in Corsica, of which the Germans were certainly aware, influenced the Germans' decision to withdraw their forces from Corsica as well as Sardinia. If it did, SOE's work in the island might be judged to have paid a handsome dividend in saving many French lives, which would certainly have been lost if a landing had encountered determined German opposition. If it did not, SOE itself conceded that the fruits of MASSINGHAM's labours were less easy to determine. Elaborate plans to isolate and hamper bodies of Italian troops scattered throughout the island could not abruptly be switched to provide a concentration of force against a narrow, though extended, area on one side of the island held by the Germans. The Corsican population had not been persecuted under Italian occupation to anything like the extent that the population of metropolitan France had been by the time the Allies landed there in 1944. Patriotic young Corsicans had not been driven into the mountains by the threat of forced labour in Germany, as befell their contemporaries in southern mainland France during 1943 and much of 1944. Nor had they experienced the savagery of reprisals against their relations and homes. When, in September 1943, the Corsican patriot thought, in the peaceful security of his village, about the duty he had undertaken to perform, it was to wish he had a long-range rifle rather than a short-range Sten-gun. If he failed to answer a blunt call to leave his home and undertake the unforeseen hazards of a campaign of movement, it was an understandable human failure.[37]

Colonna's insistence that SOE provide weapons for long-range fighting in mountainous country—rifles, anti-tank rifles and light machine-guns—was an important lesson, which certainly had an effect on SOE's future thinking.

In a memoir published 20 years after the end of the war, Senger und Etterlin described the reasons that led to the decision to evacuate Corsica rather than to defend it. The mission to evacuate Sardinia and defend Corsica, with which he was charged by Kesselring at the beginning of September, was political as well as military: he had to convince General Magli, the Italian corps commander in Corsica, to cooperate with him even in the event of a separate Italian armistice and, in the event of a refusal, to disarm the Italian troops.[38]

From the outset, on 9 September, the Germans were sufficiently mistrustful to take charge of strategic points on the east coast of Corsica. Magli had received Etterlin on the evening of 8 September and, Etterlin claims, had offered 'to support him in so far as was possible, to facilitate the transfer of German troops from Sardinia, to checkmate the rebellion of armed French bands and to have his coastal artillery reply to any bombardment from the sea'. Etterlin was pleased to have made these arrangements 'by the diplomatic channel' and considered them indispensable to allow him to act on his own initiative.

The agreement, if indeed it existed, fell to pieces immediately: the German garrison at Bastia, on an order given by the German naval authorities without Etterlin's knowledge, attempted to seize the port and the Italian vessels lying in it. The *coup de main* failed: Etterlin described it as foolish and contrary to Germany's own interests.

Magli, who asked for nothing better than to stay neutral, was informed by Colonna d'Istria on 9 September that an Allied expeditionary force was on its way. Called on to state immediately his position, 'With us, against us or neutral', Magli replied, 'With you.'

On 12 September, the first elements of Senger und Etterlin's 90th Panzer-Grenadier Division landed at Bonifacio and on the mainland the Wehrmacht began to disarm the Italians. Magli realised that his two-faced posture was untenable: he was not going to be able to 'continue to collaborate with the Germans even as a neutral'. That evening, there was a meeting between him and Etterlin, which the latter described as 'dramatic'. From that point on, the German commander realised that he, with one division and one brigade, 35,000 men in all, would be in no position to disarm four divisions of Italians. Still less would he be able to disarm the Corsican Resistance, whose numbers he did not know but who had given 'unmistakable proof of their fanaticism'. He decided to hold the eastern side only of the island's dorsal mountain chain. He was relieved next day, 13 September, to receive fresh orders not to defend Corsica but to transfer the German forces to the mainland. As he proceeded to put this plan into effect, he was disturbed by an astonishing order, brought to him on 16 September by General Westphal, Kesselring's Chief of Staff, to seize control of the road from Ajaccio to Bastia—an order he subsequently described as requiring him to reconquer the island before evacuating it. He managed to persuade his superior to renounce this stupid idea. MASSINGHAM's achievement in arming virtually every mobilisable male member of the Corsican population had not been in vain.

On the political plane, the spectacle of the Front National taking over every Mairie in the island added fuel to the crisis in the relations between de Gaulle and Giraud. Giraud was forced out of his co-presidency of the Committee of National Liberation by de Gaulle even while the island was in the throes of liberation. De Gaulle put paid to Giraud's plans to install military government in the island and sent Charles Luizet there as Préfet. De Gaulle held SOE partly responsible for a situation he was determined to avoid in mainland France and de Guélis had to be replaced as head of MASSINGHAM's French Country Section. The present author, instead of going to Corsica to conduct clandestine sea-transport operations for SOE to north-western Italy and south-eastern France, was asked to take over the Section.

Submarine operations had paid a unique part in the liberation of Corsica and it is no accident that when *Casabianca* came to be scrapped after the war, her bridge, conning-tower and gun-platform were preserved as a monument in the citadel at Bastia.

It is sad to have to record that Jean L'Herminier—far too old by the Royal Navy's standards for service in submarines—paid a terrible price for his determination to remain at his post until he had completed the job: a clot developed in one of his legs, and by the time his doctor had decided they must amputate, it had moved to the other leg, which had also to be sacrificed. His courage in affliction was as great as in war, but he died in 1947.

XXI
Operations from Bastia

In April 1943, as a result of negotiations between SIS and the Admiralty and a suggestion that NID (C) should be merged into the Admiralty's Operations Division, Captain Slocum again visited North Africa. Admiral Cunningham, Commander-in-Chief Mediterranean, agreed to this proposal. He made it clear to Slocum that irregular operations did not interest him in the least but that he would suffer them, provided that a clear-cut policy was laid down and they came under one central control. Slocum became Deputy Director Operations Division (Irregular)—DDOD(I)—in June and his African Coastal Flotilla (ACF) was accepted by Allied Force Headquarters as the controlling authority for clandestine sea transport in the western Mediterranean theatre of operations. In due course, this arrangement was extended as far east as the Adriatic, but it was effectively rejected by Middle East Command, with the result that SIS, SOE and the Special Boat Squadron continued to operate separate flotillas of caiques and schooners in the Aegean, while sea transport to Yugoslavia, Albania and western Greece involved a complex interface of command responsibilities.[1]

In the meantime, Captain Osborne had handed over command of the ACF to Captain R.E.T.Tunbridge, DSC, RNR. On the advice of the clandestine authorities in London, a Special Operations Committee was set up under the chairmanship of Brigadier Sugden of Allied Force Headquarters to decide transport priorities. Captain Tunbridge and Holdsworth, as naval representative of SOE, both attended as nautical advisers until Holdsworth was appointed head of SOE's MARYLAND mission to Italy, following the Italian armistice.[2]

Submarine transport, which played such a substantial part in operations to Corsica before the Liberation, in practice escaped the jurisdiction of ACF and DDOD(I). The feluccas, *balancennes* and a small, local motor trawler named *Cyrus-Joseph,* which were the only potentially operational craft under the direct control of ACF, made a peripheral contribution only to the liberation of Corsica. *Seawolf* was sent in April to attempt to land two agents in the north-west of the island, but failed owing to bad weather and active enemy shore patrols; the experiment was not repeated, as submarines were available and more effective. Indeed, with the eviction of the German and Italian forces from North Africa, enemy shipping targets had become scarce and the 8th Submarine Flotilla were glad to carry out cloak-and-dagger operations; these, when successful, were added to the submarine's battle honours, in the form of a small dagger symbol on the piratical black flag with skull and cross-bones that British submarines had adopted and flew in celebration on their return from patrol.

United States PT boats—the equivalent of the Royal Navy's MTBs—were used in June and July to land agents for SIS in north-western and south-western Sicily before the Allied invasion of the island (HUSKY), but attempts by the ACF's feluccas *Welcome, Seawolf, Seadog* and the trawler *Cyrus-Joseph* to carry out operations to Sardinia and the Naples area failed in five cases out of seven; on three occasions the vessels were attacked by friendly aircraft.

As the invasion of Sicily progressed, the demand for intelligence from Italy increased. Local fishing activities in Italian waters were so scarce that operations by vessels of fishing types were unlikely to provide a solution of the needs of the clandestine agencies. However, once Sicily was in Allied hands, operations by fast craft out of Palermo seemed to be a good way of meeting their requirements. After preliminary arrangements with the US naval commander, DDOD(I)'s local organisation was given permission to use United States PT craft out of that port, which was under complete American control. In July, Slocum visited the area to obtain the approval of the British naval authorities for this arrangement. In spite of American willingness to co-operate, Admiral Cunningham categorically refused to release any craft possessing offensive potentialities for clandestine operations. Slocum returned to London and subsequent suggestions and request from the Admiralty achieved nothing. Again all irregular operations had been brought to a standstill, as by now it was quite impossible to operate fishing vessels in the areas from which intelligence was so desperately required.[3]

However, Slocum sent Whinney out to the Mediterranean to carry out a reconnaissance of Bastia to assess the damage to the port. Geographically it offered important advantages for operations to the Italian mainland, as compared with Maddalena in Sardinia: whereas Maddalena and Anzio, which lie in the same latitude, are 320km apart, Bastia is a mere 40km from Elba.[4]

Maddalena had been in Allied hands since the German withdrawal in September 1943 and a British naval base had been established there under the redoubtable Captain N.V.Dickinson, who had been so helpful to SOE's BRANDON mission in the early days of the Tunisian campaign. Plans were already afoot to move the British, Canadian and US fast craft assembled at Maddalena forward to Bastia as soon as practicable and Whinney took passage northwards on a 'B'-Class ML to prospect.

SOE had already formed and sent forward from Algiers to Corsica a mission code-named BALACLAVA, which was the first unit to arrive in the island with the intention of carrying out operations from there to the adjacent coasts of Italy and south-eastern France. Through an emanation of MASSINGHAM's Naval Section, it was under the command of Major N.A.C.Croft, well known before the war as an Arctic explorer, with Lt Fisher Howe, US Naval Reserve, an OSS officer, as his deputy. An advance party left Algiers on 28 September in *Serenini,* loaded down with 15 tons of boats, stores and equipment, which Croft had assembled with the care born of his experience in Greenland, North East Land and Spitzbergen. Skipper Lt John Newton, *Serenini*'s commanding officer, was in the United Kingdom on sick leave, so his place was taken by Lt Long of Slocum's African Coastal Flotilla. ACF volunteered the use of all their feluccas but only one of them proved able to carry a worthwhile amount of cargo. The expedition put in first to Ajaccio, where Croft made contact with de Guélis's mission, with Brigadier-General Peake, AFHQ's representative, and with General Martin, who commanded the French troops in the island. *Serenini* then proceeded to Calvi, where a base was established. A few days later, when the Germans had completed their leisurely evacuation of Corsica by air and sea, Croft moved to the port of Bastia, where he set up BALACLAVA's main headquarters.[5]

BALACLAVA's arrival at Bastia had preceded Whinney's and, on the morning after Whinney landed from Maddalena, he made contact with Croft with a view to sending a signal back to Maddalena. He found SOE's unit installed in a modern villa, with a tidy garden and a pleasant patio overlooking the sea, though the furniture consisted for the most part of ration boxes and army trestle tables. Over a bottle of gin, Croft offered Whinney all the help he might need. Cooperation between SIS and SOE seemed to have got off to a good start, but it was still quite unclear what vessels would be available to exploit the geographical advantages of Bastia as an operational base for the needs of the clandestine agencies.[6]

When Whinney reported back to Dickinson at Maddalena, a wonderful surprise awaited him. Maddalena had been an important base for the Italian navy's MAS boats—the equivalent of the Royal Navy's Coastal Forces craft or PT boats—and, as a result of the armistice and the Badoglio government's co-belligerency, these flotillas had passed under Allied command. The problem that faced Dickinson, however, was what operational use could be made of them. As he had pointed out when he took them over, it would be foolish in the extreme to expect the crews of these vessels to go out and engage their ex-Allies or, even worse, their own compatriots, at sea.[7]

While Whinney was making his report about the state of Bastia, Dickinson cut him short. After enquiring casually about Whinney's plans, which centred, perforce, on the ACF's unusable array of fishing vessels, he went on to explain his predicament over the MAS boats. He suggested that Whinney should consider using them as a better alternative to his fishing craft. It was a solution that would relieve him of the embarrassment of

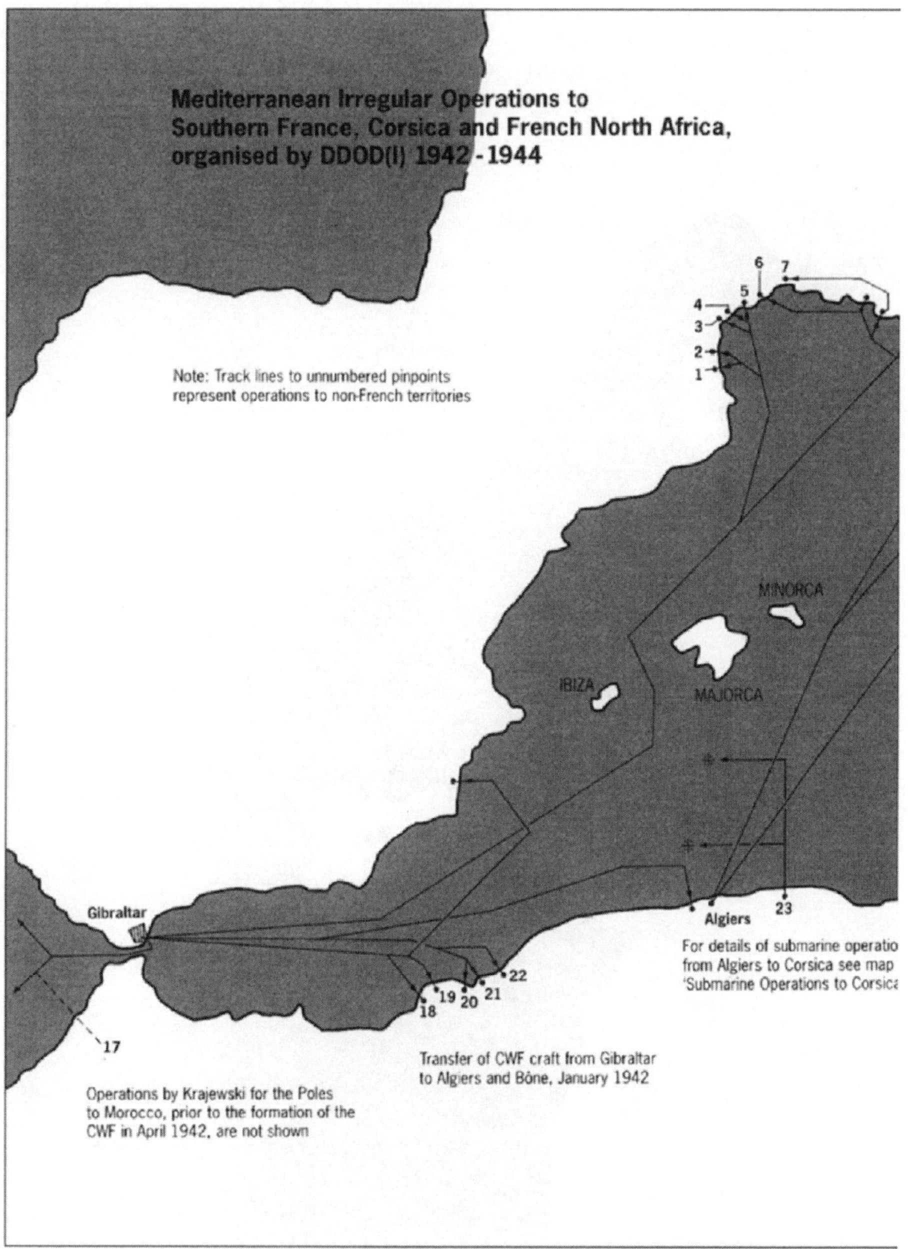
Mediterranean Irregular Operations to Southern France, Corsica and French North Africa, organised by DDOD(I) 1942 - 1944
Note: Track lines to unnumbered pinpoints represent operations to non-French territories
1
2
3
4
5
6
7
MINORCA
MAJORCA
IBIZA
Gibraltar
Algiers
23
For details of submarine operatio from Algiers to Corsica see map 'Submarine Operations to Corsica
22
21
20
19
18
17
Transfer of CWF craft from Gibraltar to Algiers and Bône, January 1942
Operations by Krajewski for the Poles to Morocco, prior to the formation of the CWF in April 1942, are not shown

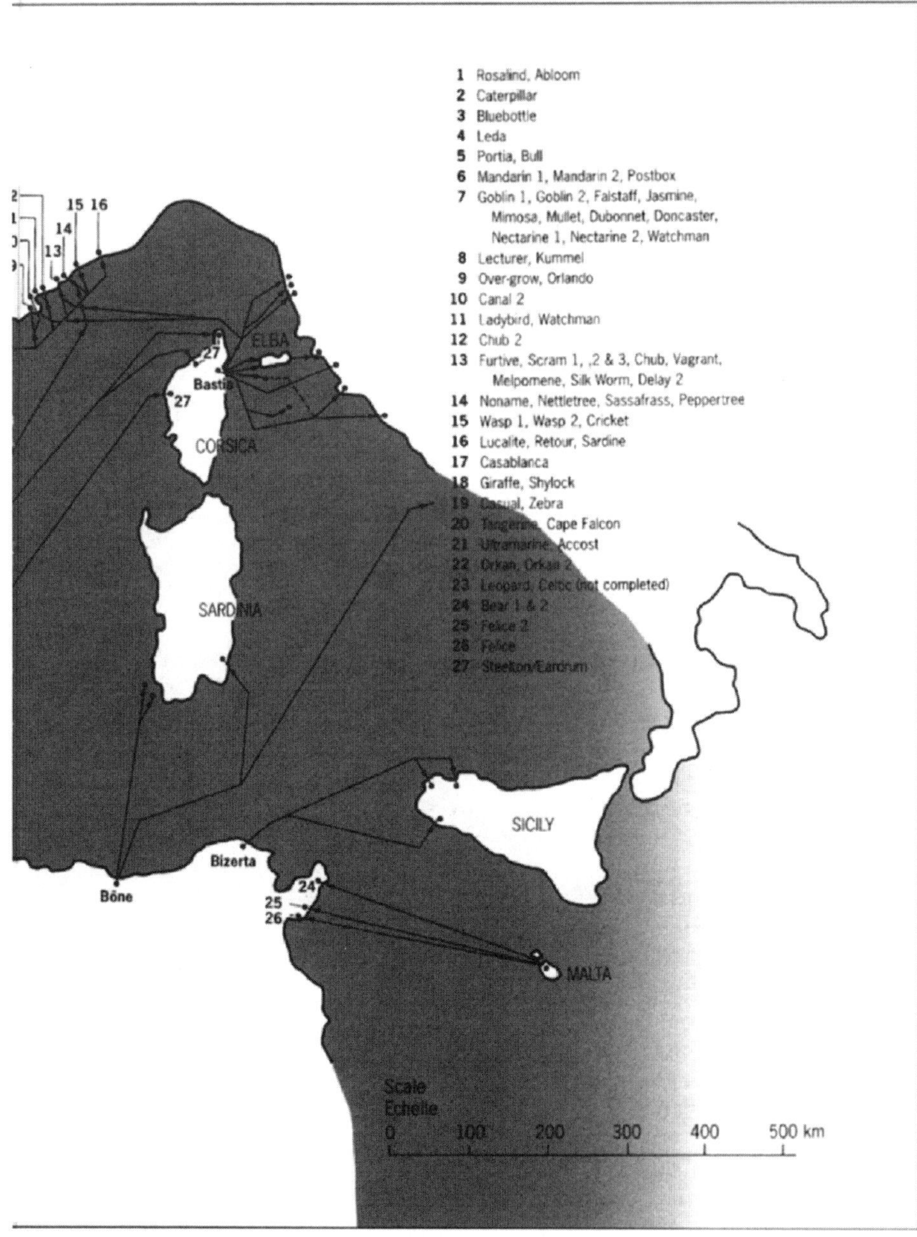

1 Rosalind, Abloom
2 Caterpillar
3 Bluebottle
4 Leda
5 Portia, Bull
6 Mandarin 1, Mandarin 2, Postbox
7 Goblin 1, Goblin 2, Falstaff, Jasmine, Mimosa, Mullet, Dubonnet, Doncaster, Nectarine 1, Nectarine 2, Watchman
8 Lecturer, Kummel
9 Over-grow, Orlando
10 Canal 2
11 Ladybird, Watchman
12 Chub 2
13 Furtive, Scram 1, ,2 & 3, Chub, Vagrant, Melpomene, Silk Worm, Delay 2
14 Noname, Nettletree, Sassafrass, Peppertree
15 Wasp 1, Wasp 2, Cricket
16 Lucalite, Retour, Sardine
17 Casablanca
18 Giraffe, Shylock
19 Casual, Zebra
20 Tangerine, Cape Falcon
21 Ultramarine, Accost
22 Orkan, Orkan 2
23 Leopard, Celtic (not completed)
24 Bear 1 & 2
25 Felice 2
26 Felice
27 Steelton/Eardrum
15 16
14
13
ELBA
27
Bastia
27
CORSICA
SARDINIA
SICILY
Bizerta
Bône
24
25
26
MALTA
Scale
Echelle
0 100 200 300 400 500 km

finding something for them to do and provide Whinney with fast craft suitable for clandestine sea-transport needs.

Whinney could hardly believe his luck, though he was by no means certain that DDOD (I) would approve the idea. He knew that for Slocum the safety of his passengers was always paramount and there were undeniable risks in employing those who had so recently been enemy crews in a conflict in which Italian Fascists loyal to the ousted and discredited dictator were still fighting alongside the Germans.

There were three types of MAS boat: the largest, 120 feet long, was a copy of the German E-boats and fitted with diesel engines; there was a 60-foot variety with twin 500 h.p Isotta-Fraschinis and a 47-foot version of rather similar Italian design. Whinney signalled all the relevant particulars to his master and, after a certain amount of humming and hawing arising out of his natural caution, Slocum accepted that there was really no alternative and sent his approval and good wishes.

Whinney concluded that the 60-foot boats were the most suitable for his purposes. By removing their torpedo tubes, which increased the deck space available for carrying dinghies, their top speed could be enhanced from 37 to 47 knots, speeds vastly superior to those of which even Slocum's 15th Motor Gunboat Flotilla working in the English Channel were capable. The MAS boats' auxiliaries gave them a cruising speed of 6 knots and they were supposed to be silent, though Whinney found that, with an onshore light air, they could be heard as a rather high-pitched whine when the boat was a mile or more from the beach.

Dickinson told the senior officer of the Italian naval base to arrange for his MAS boats to be sent to Bastia as 3 as he had finished what could be only a fairly perfunctory vetting of the crews. By this time, several of the feluccas and other fishing vessels of the African Coastal Flotilla had joined *Seadog* at Maddalena and Whinney proceeded to select from their crews eight dinghymen to form four operational teams to accompany his conducting officers when work with the Italian MAS boats began. When he was ready to return to Bastia, Dickinson instructed him to find accommodation there for both himself and his staff, as he wished to move forward as soon as possible and begin the new operational phase in which he was to become Senior Officer Inshore Squadron.

Tom Maxted, one of the ACF's conducting officers, who arrived at this point in Corsica, had already experienced Dickinson's helpfulness at Tabarca, a small port near the frontier between Algeria and Tunisia, as had the author at the beginning of the Tunisian Campaign. Sixty years later his memory of that first contact is worth quoting:

> From Bône to Tabarca. *Annonciada* was a small 45 ft. coastal sand carrier. She had a lateen rig, diesel engine, hold, a tiller and that's about all. A few bunks were rigged up and additional diesel tank. A few days before we left for Tabarca we were lying in Bône harbour and it was attacked by Stuka dive bombers. One bomb hit the jetty a

> few yards from *Annonciada*. It broke open and spilled white explosives all over us. I will always remember the picture of that bomb lying by us, all broken open.
>
> We sailed one evening for Tabarca. The hold was full of explosives and ammunition for the naval commandos who had recently occupied the small town. I dropped our anchor in what appeared to be a harbour, a commando landing boat came out and on board was Captain Dickinson, senior officer of the commandos. He ordered the cargo to be transferred then looked round *Annonciada*. The first thing he said was that he would send a chippie over to fix up a galley for us. I did not know that this was the first of many times he would help me in the future when he became SOIS. As he went ashore he said "Oh by the way Maxted, if you hear the church bells ring, look out for German aircraft". Half an hour later, the church bells rang and immediately two Messerschmitts flew over us and sprayed us with gunfire. Fortunately only a small amount of damage was done and nobody was injured. We sailed that evening for Bastia.

Croft found it a great advantage during the critical settling-in period at Bastia to have an American, in the person of Fisher Howe, as his first lieutenant.[8] Before leaving Algiers, both officers had privately told the author, who was still handling SOE's Naval Section business while taking over MASSINGHAM's French Country Section, that they had doubts as to whether they could work well together, but their fears proved groundless: they rapidly came to appreciate each other's qualities and became firm friends. It was a very effective partnership. Liaison with the United States 63rd Fighter Wing and the OSS mission at Bastia under Lt Col Russell Livermore was excellent. Livermore had under his command two of the 15-man Operational Groups (OG)s, created by 'Big Bill' Donovan as an integral part of OSS, on the lines of the British SAS. These particular OGs were composed of Italian-speaking officers and enlisted men. Donovan, who was up to his eyebrows in Washington politics and anxious for OSS to be seen to be where action lay, had rushed them to Corsica as soon as opportunity offered, and was in a hurry to see them operationally involved. Dickinson personified inter-Allied cooperation. The uniquely friendly atmosphere that emerged at Bastia in the closing months of 1943 was enhanced by the fact that the headquarters of Fighter Wing, Coastal Forces, ISLD (as SIS called itself for cover purposes), OSS and SOE's BALACLAVA mission were all situated within 150 metres of one another. Attached to BALACLAVA was an 'A' Force unit, which dealt with Allied escapers and evaders and operated usually under SIS auspices. In this case, for convenience, it joined up with Croft's mission. Also attached briefly to BALACLAVA was Commander Dunstan Curtis's intelligence procurement force, which also normally operated under the wing of SIS. This section was soon withdrawn to the United Kingdom for use in OVERLORD, but Croft retained the services of its highly qualified intelligence officer, Lieutenant 'Paddy' Davies. At BALACLAVA's headquarters, Davies helped Croft organise what proved to be a first-class intelligence 'pool' which was shared by members of the various special services and certain officers of Coastal Forces, the French general staff, Deuxième Bureau and Lt-Col. Fernand Gambiez's *Bataillon de Choc.* It was against this background of goodwill and efficiently coordinated planning that the local operational difficulties of the Allied Special Forces were tackled and resolved. The wise and firm guidance of Captain N.V. Dickinson was all important. The author was present when Croft invited Dickinson to dinner at Bastia early in the New Year for a council of war. Something had to be done, Croft said, to keep SIS in general—and Lt Cdr Pat Whinney in particular—from swallowing up SOE's BALACLAVA mission whole and removing all his freedom of action. Dickinson was firm: BALACLAVA could certainly help SIS when asked; they could also land agents for the Americans and the French, of course, since they had the expertise; but they were an independent group and must remain so.[9]

To Croft's regret, Howe, whose role in sorting out relations with the local American authorities had been so valuable, was ordered back to OSS headquarters in London two months after BALACLAVA's arrival in the island and before operations out of Bastia had begun. He was not replaced.

The crew of the Italian MAS boats, the first six of which were now at Whinney's disposal, remained an unknown quality. Whinney, in his book *Corsican Command,* recalled how, on the day after their arrival from Maddalena, the crews were drawn up for his inspection, fallen in along the jetty with their backs to the water. Each crew was separated from its neighbour by a gap of two or three metres. Whinney felt that a formal inspection of this type was not really his form at all: he would have preferred to go round each boat while the hands were working but, as he discovered then and on a number of subsequent occasions, the Italians could be sticklers for formality. After a very grand salute from the Italian commanding officer, a formal handshake and a second, even grander, salute, the commanding officer led off to introduce the first of the MAS boat captains, who were all somewhere between 25 and 30 years of age. The salute, which Whinney described as a sort of abrupt shading of the eyes, as if from a sudden blinding light, and the handshake were repeated and off they went to inspect the next crew, which was rigidly at attention, looking smart and clean.

They were half-way along this second crew when one of the ratings took a brisk pace forward, raised his arm palm downward in the Nazi salute and said quite loudly, 'Heil Hitler!' There followed a moment of acute embarrassment for everybody, not least for the man himself, who looked round sheepishly to see what his shipmates thought. They afforded him no comfort. Something had to be done. Whinney resisted an impulse to push the man into the water, which was only about two metres behind him. Turning to the commanding officer, whose face was locked in horror, he asked him to tell the man that he was now supposed to be fighting on the other side. The commanding officer favoured Whinney with an understanding shading of the eyes and then addressed himself to the offender. Under the ensuing avalanche of reprimand, the man dissolved into what Whinney described as a "grease-spot". The effect was not lost on his shipmates, although further down the long line there were one or two other 'Heil Hitler's. Each got the same impressive treatment, which Whinney felt would have done credit to a Whale Island instructor. It did provide some sort of rough yardstick of unreliability, but the changes made at that time did not, alas, eradicate all the culprits.

Over a glass of wine after the inspection, Whinney said that the episode should perhaps be regarded as a blessing in disguise—a means of separating goats from sheep. As he outlined what the MAS boats might be expected to so, the formality of the proceedings gradually relaxed. There would be no offensive activity against their compatriots fighting on the other side or against their erstwhile allies, the Germans. Of course, if the other side attacked, they would have to reply in kind. But, as proof of their new peaceable vocation, the Allies would be asking them to remove their torpedo tubes, leaving them a couple of light machine-guns and a 20mm cannon mounted on the stern to discourage pursuers. It was impossible at that stage for him to go further, but the Italians seemed relieved by what they had heard.

The weather during the no-moon period of November was so bad that the offensively tasked US PT boats and their British Coastal Forces counterparts based at Bastia could manage no more than half a dozen sorties. But the Germans proved highly sensitive even to this limited scale of attack on their maritime supply lines. Bastia was bombed on 24 November. The fire of the Italian AA (anti-aircraft) gunners who were supposed to defend the port was so ineffective that the Allied naval craft lying there were forced to put to sea. Later, when Allied attacks on convoys along Ligurian coast were stepped up, the Kriegsmarine was forced, as their War Diaries disclose, to ask the Wehrmacht and Luftwaffe to 'eliminate' what they described as this 'nest of pirates' which they could not do alone. Fortunately, the other services were too busy to take the job on but there were hit-and-run raids from both air and sea. In mid-December, there was an invasion scare at Bastia after enemy destroyers had appeared off the port and attempted to shell the tactical signals interception station. At the time heavy rains had virtually isolated the port, breaking down bridges, flooding roads and putting airfields out of action. Mines, too, were a constant menace and on 31 December a minesweeper was blown up and an Italian landing-craft approaching the harbour was sunk with heavy RN and RAF casualties.

Whinney had acquired a British 'B'-class Fairmile Motor Launch 576 and had used it to land two agents for OSS on 8 November in the Livorno area and, three nights later, to put ashore three OSS officers and eight enlisted men with stores on the island of Capraia. He also tried to use the same vessel to carry out a first operation for SOE's MARYLAND mission, of which Holdsworth was chief, but bad weather compelled cancellation of the first attempt. Croft recorded either this or a second similar operation but after two hours the short, choppy seas were too much for the ML and they had to return to harbour. The 576 presumably was deemed not to fall within the C-in-C's ban of use of vessels with an offensive capability, but she was also not fast enough for clandestine operations and Whinney had to turn to the MAS boats. The Italian commanding officer had chosen a young red-headed lieutenant, who was captain of one of the boats, to be Whinney's guide. He proved to a member of the well-known Triestine ship-owning family of Cosulich. Because of his wiry red hair, he quickly became known to his new British colleagues as 'Ginger'. Whinney found MAS 541, under 'Ginger''s command, all that he could have wished: a minimum of spit and polish, but with everything neat, tidy and well maintained. Good morale prevailed on board and Whinney was favourably impressed by the personality and high professional competence of 541's engine-room chief, Capo Pulchri. When invited into the diminutive ward-room for a first glass of wine, Whinney discovered 541's battle honours, inscribed on a bulkhead, included HMS *Fiji,* the British cruiser sunk during the German airborne invasion of Crete in April 1941.

By the end of November, Whinney's ACF unit was ready to operate with the Italian MAS boats. Careful observation had convinced him that 'Ginger' Cosulich was the most experienced and reliable of the young Italian MAS boat captains; he was also the one with whom he had worked first and got to know best. Fortunately the Italian commander concurred in Whinney's choice of Cosulich for this all-important first operation. In his book Whinney described the operation that he and Andrew Croft undertook in MAS 541 on the night of 2/3 December, in which two SOE agents were landed at Deiva, between Sestri Levante and Moneglia on the east side of the Gulf of Genoa. He called it the first such expedition, but Slocum's records show a successful operation for SOE to the Porto Potenza area on 27 November using an Italian MAS boat to land an 'unspecified force'.[11]

Shortly after Christmas, two operations to France became necessary—one for OSS, the other for SIS. This posed a new problem because the pinpoints involved lay 150 miles from Bastia—a round trip of 300 miles, which was far longer than previous operations to the Italian mainland. This meant shipping extra fuel tanks in the form of mattress-like plastic bags and lightening the MAS boats by cutting down on crew numbers, though the sorties were certain to be protracted. Cosulich had often had to do this when fighting on the side of the Axis, but it was something no captain of a high-speed fighting vessel liked doing as it made the ship more vulnerable.

The first expedition involved landing two French agents for OSS, and was undertaken by Croft.[12] Tom Maxted of ACF was in overall charge of the expedition. In his report (to the author) dated 9 January 1943, Croft says that, owing to a misunderstanding, they sailed on 28 December later than had been planned but, after three and a half hours at 30 and 35 knots, they switched over to the auxiliaries and, at about midnight, the loom of the Ile-du-Levant appeared ahead. Course was altered to the northward but, with a speed of only 6 knots, they did not reach the target area until 0425 hours. Five minutes later, some 800 metres ESE of the Cap-du-Pinet, the rubber dinghy, manned by himself and Able Seaman Don Miles, left with the two passengers.

The coast between Cap-du-Pinet and the Pointe-du-Capon had been marked in a beach interpretation report as precipitous and studded with offshore rocks and shoals. The shallowness of the offshore water and the fact that the highest peak near the coast was only just over 120 metres had, however, been taken into account; and these factors, combined with a promising-looking stream valley, indicated that a suitable place for a 'blind' landing could be found, even though the hinterland appeared from intelligence to be well defended.

As it turned out, the landing place was almost ideal, as the inshore rocks provided a natural camouflage for the rubber dinghy. Miles made a reconnaissance and discovered a track leading up through thick woods from the coast to the interior. The agents, who throughout had shown complete unconcern, now disembarked and went their way. Croft and Miles were back on board within 50 minutes of leaving the boat. The operation had proved surprisingly easy, the only difficulty being to find the MAS boat, since she had shifted her position nearly a mile. In this one respect it was fortunate that the night was brightly starlit.

When dawn broke, 541 was only 30 miles from the French coast. Croft wrote that great credit was due to Maxted and Cosulich for their determination in proceeding with the operation, in spite of their late arrival in the target area, and in carrying it out with decision and judgement.

The second operation, which was for SIS, involved handing over a parcel containing money to a member of Marie-Madeleine Fourcade's 'Alliance' network and collecting in return a parcel containing intelligence.[13]

On the morning of 29 December, Whinney received a signal from London giving a pinpoint near Cavalaire, which, when plotted on to the chart, differed by about 900 metres from that previously indicated. He sent an urgent signal pointing out this discrepancy and asking for clarification, but the matter had not been resolved by the time they put to sea. It was a familiar problem, since agents in the field used map coordinates on Michelin maps, while sailors worked in latitude and longitude. Then there was a hold-up owing to late delivery of petrol, which was in very short supply in the island. They sailed an hour late but, by the time they reached Cap-Corse and turned west, they had used up enough fuel to increase speed from 30 to 35 knots. There was just enough swell to cause the plastic deck tanks to wallow awkwardly and make the boat lurch from time to time, but the problem resolved itself as the fuel was used and finally the extra tanks were empty and could be rolled up and stowed amidships. Whinney found three and a half hours at 35 knots, with minimal protection on the bridge against wind and weather in mid-winter, a chilling experience, and was glad when they reduced speed and switched over to the auxiliaries for the final approach, which lasted two full hours.

It was glassy calm as they closed in with the Iles-d'Hyeres to port and Cap-Camarat to starboard. The noise of the auxiliaries was worryingly loud to Whinney, but they had made up for their late start and arrived punctually at the pinpoint. Whinney thought he had ordered the ship to stop 680 metres from the shore, but it turned out to be nearly double that distance. He and Petty Officer Bates reached the shore in their rubber dinghy at 0210 hours, ten minutes after schedule; but was it the right pinpoint? When nobody had turned up after 20 minutes, they decided to try the alternative position, about 900 metres to the east. There was nobody there either and, after another 20 minutes they paddled round into the next bay before returning to their original position. While they were waiting beside the jetty that was supposed to be the meeting-place, a searchlight was switched on three times from somewhere just above their heads: it shone in the direction where the MAS boat had been when they left her but did not pick her up.

At 0400, half an hour before the agreed time-limit would be up, they realised they must leave if they were to rejoin MAS 543 before she left for Bastia. Indeed, they had cut the time rather too fine, but, fortunately, Ranald Boyle, one of Whinney's officers, who was in charge of the MAS boat in Whinney's absence, realised that they were further from the shore than they had reckoned and stood inshore to collect them. Just when they were beginning to despair of finding 543 before the deadline ran out, there she was, bearing down on them. Five minutes later, they were on the way back to base.

On two successive nights, Cosulich and the Marchese Centurioni and their crews had done 300-mile expeditions, a feat achieved by none of the MGBs of Slocum's Dartmouth Flotilla. The operation was successfully completed at a third attempt on 28 January. Slocum's Sea Operations Analysis perhaps for reasons of security, recorded the pinpoint of the three FURTIVE operations as the Pointe-des-Issambres, which is between Sainte-Maxime and Saint-Aygulf, whereas Whinney's own report on the last such operation makes it clear that the landings took place near Cavalaire on the other side of Saint-Tropez.

Between 6 December 1943 and 24 July 1944, there were 18 clandestine sea-transport operations to the coast of Provence by highspeed craft operating from Corsica. Five of these were undertaken by Italian MAS boats, the rest by the United States PT craft. Details of these are listed in Appendix D. There were also ten operations to the Barcelona area on behalf of the French Deuxième Bureau, all by French submarines; this provided an alternative route to and from France after the Bon-Porté Bay pinpoint had to be abandoned.[14]

Since there were no Lysander or Dakota pick-up operations into southern France until June 1944, these contacts by sea were more important than their number might suggest and provided Rivet's Service de Renseignements and Paillole's Direction de Securité Militaire with a large volume of intelligence. SOE's MASSINGHAM would have made greater use of operations by sea from Corsica if an agent named François Pelletier, whom they had trained and sent in to carry out the landward end, had not been betrayed, arrested and executed.[15] The main importance of the Bastia base was, however, in relation to the campaign in Italy: Allied high-speed craft mounted more than 90 operations to the Ligurian coast and the off-lying islands between November 1943 and the end of July 1944 for the Allied clandestine services.

Whinney had been to Algiers in the dark period of December to work out with Captain Tunbridge and AFHQ's Special Operations Committee a schedule of the jobs to be done for the various agencies (the 'Sked') during the next dark phase of the moon and by mid-January a first such full programme was under way.

On 10 December, MAS boat 541 had landed five OSS personnel and a W/T set on Gorgona Island, 20 miles off Livorno, and had removed from it eight Fascist guards, thereby establishing a useful forward observation post for the Allies: on 15 January 541 went back to Gorgona to land stores and establish better W/T communications. On the 17th PT 215 escorted by PT 203 was to land four OSS agents and supplies south of the Argentario promontory on which Porto Ercole stands, 70 miles north of Rome. On the outward passage 203 broke down and returned to port: 215, with the very useful radar that the US PT boats alone carried, detected two enemy vessels between her and the pinpoint, but she avoided them and completed the job (operation RICHMOND). On 18 January, MAS 541 landed two US officers on Elba and a MAS boat landed and picked up a 15-man OSS Operational Group raiding Pianosa. On 19 January, MAS 541 made an unsuccessful attempt to land four SOE agents (two Italian women, an Italian man and a Canadian W/T operator) at Moneglia north of Spezia. Once again compass error (there was no compass adjuster at Bastia) had led to an unsatisfactory landfall and too late an arrival at the pinpoint.

This group had been flown from SOE's operational headquarters (MARYLAND) at Monopoli at the end of December with Captain Dick Cooper—a former regimental Sergeant-Major of the Foreign Legion—after failing to get through the British 8th Army Lines. ACF had already made unsuccessful attempts to land them on 2 and 3 January. On the first of these expeditions they were accompanied by a small SIS party making for the same area. Unfortunately, the noise of the PT boat's engines alerted the shore defences and the approach of two E-boats obliged Maxted to abandon the operation. On the following night, Whinney, with Croft and Coltman as surf-boat's crew, made a further attempt, using another PT boat. They arrived late on schedule and, when the dinghy was launched the radar misleadingly indicated 300 yards from the shore, but this was a gross underestimate. The dinghy was heavily overloaded with six people on board. At the end of a very hard row, Croft searched the precipitous coastline in vain for a point which would have provided a practicable landing for the lady passengers and their gear. It was another very hard row back to the PT boat and three oars were broken in the process. As this was the end of the no-moon phase, Cooper took them off to Calvi for a rest. They proved a difficult quartet to manage: both men were in love with the same woman, Fiametta; and the radio operator looked ill. On 21 January, a further attempt was made to land them. Maxted was in charge of MAS 543, with Newton and Robinson as the shore party and Croft and Cooper accompanying the agents. After five hours at sea, MAS 543 suffered a broken fuel pipe, leaving no alternative to a return to harbour.

By this time Anna, the second of the two ladies, complained of sickness and low morale: they were flown back to Monopoli. Though it seemed a disaster at the time, the outcome was probably no bad thing as Ranieri, one of the two male agents, was subsequently found to be a Fascist.

On 20 January, MAS 541, with 543 in support, landed six agents at Porto Ercole for OSS and embarked seven Italians and one escaped British prisoner of war (POW) (Operation RICHMOND II). More escapers had been expected but failed to show up because they feared they were walking into a trap set by the Fascists.

There had been 73,000 Allied POWs in camps in Italy at the time of the Armistice and at least 12,000 escaped, mainly into the Appenines, where they received much help from the contadini, but attempts to organise their rescue from the west coast were disappointing. Fergus Dempster, one of the ACF's officers, proved particularly unlucky. As Slocum later recorded, 'His patience and morale were severely tested as a number of the operations on which he served as Senior Officer were for MI9. Although the expeditions were invariably faultless from a naval point of view, on frequent occasions the escaped POWs failed to arrive at the pinpoint, with the result that Dempster, after a troublesome passage, had a gruelling voyage back empty-handed.

In Operation POSSUM on 21 January, MAS 507 landed stores for Allied forward positions on Capraia. Slocum's Sea Operation Analysis records similar routine supply operations by an ML on 6 January and by 'A' Force's Air Rescue Launch P. 403 on 19 March.

On 22 January, MAS 543 landed two agents for SIS south of Livorno. On that same night, MAS 541 had tried to land agents south of Sestri-Levante, was fired on but managed to evade (no reference to this in Slocum's Sea Operations Analysis). On that same night there was an unsuccessful attempt by MAS 541 to land two agents for SOE at Cap-Camarat, near Saint-Tropez—in France. Maxted was Senior Officer in charge of the operation, with Croft, Bourne-Newton and Seaman Ashton to handle the boat-work. Boyle was understudying Maxted. It was considered particularly important to infiltrate these agents, who had spent several weeks in Corsica being instructed in the tricky business of dinghy-handling, landing techniques, the selection of potential landing areas and so on, in order to be able to instruct others of their own choosing, and studying aerial photography of the French coast between Marseilles and Menton. The senior agent in question was François Pelletier; his field name was Ruben and the operation was called LADBROKE.

MAS 541 left Bastia at 1715 hours on 17 January, but once again her compass proved faulty and she had to heave-to three times on this outward passage for a positional check. The French coast was sighted at 2100 hours but, as this was earlier than expected, she had to cruise round killing time. Then began the search for the small village near which was the pinpoint. But visibility was poor and, after creeping along for several hours on auxiliary motors, the area could not be identified. At 0900 hours, with daylight not far off, the operation had to be abandoned.

Maxted, incidentally, found the MAS boats, though fast and with a usefully low silhouette, very noisy on main engines, unreliable and poor sea boats. Their only navigational equipment was a compass.

Next night, Operation LIVINGSTONE was mounted for MARYLAND. This involved landing two agents near Voltri, west of Genoa harbour. The pinpoint was risky owing to the proximity of the Ansaldo shipyards. MAS 509 was chosen for the job and Maxted was to be in charge. The conducting and shore party provided by BALACLAVA consisted of Croft himself, Coltman and Seaman Miles, plus Captain Ken Carson, Croft's newly arrived second-in-command in place of Fisher Howe. The MAS boat sailed from Bastia at 1800 hours in ideal conditions—calm sea and no wind. They reached the target area half an hour after midnight and the shore party were preparing to disembark when flares burst overhead, illuminating the scene, and the MAS boat was challenged by signal-lamp. The challenges came from more than one vessel: it was no time to dither. The 509 turned on her heel and fled, pursued by enemy gunfire, which fortunately did no damage.

That same night (28 January) Patrick Whinney was completing Operation FURTIVE near Cavalaire for SIS. It was his third attempt, and involved landing money, collecting mail and what proved to be two, rather than one, agent from Marie-Madeline Fourcade's intelligence network, who had used a rope to climb down the cliff. Whinney's report can be found in the Appendix, but does not explain the references in the Sea Operation Analysis to the Pointe-des-Issambres, which is on the other side of St-Tropez.

Maxted was already becoming very familiar with that part of the French coast and with Cap-Camarat in particular. It was a pinpoint which the African Coastal Flotilla was to visit at least once a month to land or pick up a courier. This was one of two adjacent headlands—the other being Cap-Lardier—which French submarines had been visiting monthly for similar purposes until the preceding November 26, when their shore party ran into a German patrol, an agent named Alfasser being killed and General Giraud's daughter having a narrow escape. The French then transferred their submarine operations to Barcelona.

The following night, January 29, Slocum's Sea Operations Analysis logged three successful operations—NEUTER to Monte-Christo Island to land two agents for the Italians, CONTENTION to land three on Elba for OSS and GENERAL STRIKE to embark ten and mail from the Italian mainland opposite the south end of Elba, also for the Italians. Hampshire recorded a fourth (POSSUM VIII) that night, when John Newton's FPV 2017 *(Serenini)*—not normally regarded as an operational craft—was apparently pressed into service to carry out the regular ration-run to Capraia. That same night Croft and Maxted were involved in a fifth, though unsuccessful, operation (BROKERAGE), probably an attempt to repair the failure of LADBROKE, using an alternative pinpoint. The pinpoint for the latter was recorded by Slocum as the 'Pointe-de-l'Aiguillon'. There is in fact no headland of that name, but there are at the eastern end of the Massif-de-l'Esterel a 'Pointe-de-l'Aiguille' and a 'Pointe-de-1'Esquillon', and it is pointless to speculate which was intended. PT 200, supported by PT 217, ran into a patrol of two E-boats off the pinpoint, whichever it was. Croft proposed that they should wait offshore until the patrol had passed, that PT boat 217 be used as a decoy and that his two dinghies should then be launched and attempt to carry out the landing before the E-boats returned. But the Captain of the PT boat rejected Andrew's advice, and suggested that the two agents be put into a dinghy and left to make their own way ashore. This proposal was indignantly rejected by Croft. Deadlock ensued and BROKERAGE had to be called off. It was not the only occasion when an US PT boat captain, inexperienced in this kind of work, demurred at approaching pinpoints when enemy patrols had been detected by radar in the vicinity. But usually the tact and determination of their British colleagues prevailed on them to complete the operation.

On the night of 31 January, PT 217 was sent back to the Genoa area to land three agents for SOE and OSS (Operation VALENTINE), which was successfully done by Croft. That night an operation code-named X-2, to put ashore two SIS agents on the mainland of Italy failed for lack of a reception committee.

The pace was hotting up. During the nine moonless nights of February, 15 operations were undertaken by the ACF and another 19 on the 11 dark nights of March. At least half of these failed for one reason or another.

Croft was a perfectionist: he devoted the moonlit periods to training his boats' crews at Calvi and other points on the west coast of Corsica in boat handling, field-craft and use of small arms. He experimented with camouflage and discovered that the first sight of an approaching boat at night-time was its loom or shadow and that this could be eliminated by painting the boat with aluminium paint: they measured down to a few feet the distance at which a boat's approach could be seen by the enemy and this knowledge gave his crews great confidence in subsequent operations.

Croft had for some time been in touch with a Capitaine Hagé of the French Deuxième Bureau, whose office was in Bastia but whose chief, a Colonel Cappart, was on the staff of General Martin, the French military commander at Ajaccio. SOIS having ruled, as we have seen, that BALACLAVA was free to conduct operations for the French and the Americans, Andrew and Hagé got down to detailed discussions about landing agents on Elba, which was the French Command's planned objective. Hagé contributed actively to the coverage of 'Paddy' Davies' intelligence pool and Croft found both him and Cappart extremely cooperative colleagues. Operations for the French to Elba began on 18 February with the landing of two agents and a W/T operator. There was great rejoicing at the French headquarters when the latter came up on the air a couple of days later. BALACLAVA's signals station was reinforced to allow the Elba station to be worked from there.

On 21 January, an Allied landing took place at Anzio but the break-out towards Rome was slow to develop; high priority attached to all forms of attack against German communications by sea and by land. Because of the mountainous character of much of the Italian peninsula, railway lines frequently follow the coast and they and their many tunnels are vulnerable to attack by amphibious forces. Long before the tide of war begun to turn in the Allies' favour, British submarines based in Malta had been used frequently to carry special forces to attack rail targets and SOE's MARYLAND quickly found itself in the same line of business, particularly in the Adriatic.

MARYLAND's Naval Section was making use of *Motosilurante* 24, one of the largest type of motor torpedo-boat serving in the Italian navy—a 63-ton vessel powered by three Isotta-Fraschini engines and capable of a top speed of 34 knots. This vessel, commanded by Sottoten. vasc. Salvatore Scire, arrived at Bastia early in February to land eight Italian commandos in the Moneglia area near Spezia. She belonged to II Flottiglia MAS at Capri and had been the first ship serving in the Allied Fleet to enter Naples. She brought with her her own SOE dinghy party, but Croft, whose knowledge and experience were essential to a successful outcome of the venture, quickly involved himself and took charge when the operation was carried out on 21 February (not recorded by MacCallum, who had succeeded Whinney as DDOD(I)'s local representative). MS 24 was also used for Croft's most spectacular operation to the pier at Voltri near Genoa on 17 March when he landed eight agents for SOE plus two for SIS. Andrew said he would not have taken so many had he not been there before and reconnoitred the beach and the German positions. The fact that the enemy's guards smoked while on duty had been most helpful.

But this run of success was punctuated with setbacks, such as the Capraia episode of 21 February 1944, as Maxted recalls:

> I was told to join air-sea rescue boat P 403 and sail with a party to investigate an enemy raid the night before. I was told also to take Lt Charles Buist, SOO (Staff Officer, Operations) to SOIS. He did not appear and I was told to sail without him. I was also warned of mines in the small harbour. As we entered the harbour at dead slow, we lay on the bows looking down on the bottom, the water was very clear and I saw no mines. We landed the party, then headed back to Bastia. Very soon, we saw MAS 546 heading for Capraia. She was taking Charles Buist who had missed us. MAS 546 went alongside in the small harbour where we had been, and exploded a mine. All were killed except four, who were badly wounded. I lost a good friend in Charles Buist. There is a plaque in the Convent in Bastia in his memory. The next day I was sent in ML 576 to bring back the bodies. We had an American Colonel on board. As we approached Capraia we were attacked by three American Mitchell bombers who nearly sank us, but we managed to limp back to Bastia. They dropped a stick of bombs, machine-gunned and finally opened fire with 75mm cannon, leaving the motor launch with two big holes in her side, her engines out of action, her telegraphist wounded and the ship drifting down on a lee shore.

It was a fine feat of seamanship to have staunched the leaks with an improvised collision mat, re-started one engine and limped back home.

Thirty-two operations were scheduled for March. Fifteen were unsuccessful and four were defeated by bad weather. But there was an outstanding performance by MARYLAND's MS 24, which on 17 March not only did the operation to Voltri, but landed two further agents in what was rather curiously logged as 'the Turin area'. Then, six nights later, 'Ginger' Cosulich's MAS 541 was lost with all hands in the course of an operation to land two men in the Savona area for the French *Bataillon de Choc.* An explosion was heard from the shore, which strongly suggested she was victim of a mine. This was confirmed after the war, when the wreck was located. With her went Lt Dow, one of the ACF's operational officers, two French officers and Cosulich, who was, with the Marchese Centurioni, one of the most experienced, outstanding and generally liked of the original Italian MAS boat captains.

On 17 March, the night of MS 24's three successful operations, MAS 541 had done her last successful operation (AMLOCH), landing five agents for SOE in the Castiglioncello area. On the same night, MAS 543 landed two for SIS at a pinpoint dangerously close to Spezia but, while the boatwork was proceeding, three E-boats closed in. Just as the boat's crew under Boyle was scrambling aboard, the moon rose and she was challenged three times by the E-boats. She started her main engines and had reached 40 knots before the enemy found the range. She got back to Bastia with only superficial damage and no casualties.

During the March dark period, five operations were successfully completed for OSS to Gorgona but the last brought back two wounded and three dead SOE agents, victims of an enemy raid on the previous night. After a reconnaissance of Pianosa carried out by the *Bataillon de Choc* on the 16th, an armed raid by 120 of the latter, carried out on 18 March from two French *chasseurs,* took 120 prisoners.

On 19 March, PT boats 206 and 210 had been scheduled to carry out Operation CROMER to land an SOE woman agent in Morgiou Bay near Marseilles. Because of the distance involved the expedition was due to sail from Calvi instead of Bastia with Maxted in overall command and with Croft and a BALACLAVA dinghy crew accompanying him. The weather that night was so bad that the operation was postponed. On 21 March, the expedition did sail, but PT 206 broke a propeller shaft and both boats had to return. A third attempt on 24 or 25 March was defeated by weather and the operation was then stood down until the ensuing dark period.

On 22 March, Operation GINNY II was mounted for OSS. It involved landing one of 1677th Headquarters Company's two 15-man Operational Groups (OGs) near Sestri Levante to blow up a tunnel on the main Genoa-Spezia railway line. The Group was put ashore from PTs 210 and 214 with Brian Smith as Senior Officer and an ACF dinghy crew. But, while waiting to re-embark the raiders, the PT boats were confronted by an enemy patrol and came under fire. They were compelled to withdraw, leaving the raiding party ashore. On his return to Bastia Croft was asked to help with an operation to rescue them and this was attempted on the following night. Croft brought with him two of his seamen and the largest type of boat available to him—an 11′-6″ Goatley, with solid bottom and collapsible canvas sides. They embarked on PTs 204 and 207, but unfortunately encountered hostile vessels four miles off the pinpoint. A further expedition was mounted 24 hours later and was able to land: they found nobody waiting. Though the OG had all been in uniform and had no civilian clothing with them, they had been taken prisoner soon after landing and had been shot without trial in accordance with Hitler's infamous 'extermination' order issued after the Dieppe raid of August 1942. After the war, General Anton Dostler, one of Kesselring's Corps Commanders, was tried by a US War Crimes Tribunal at Rome and condemned to death for the summary execution of the GINNY II Operational Group.

Senior Officer Inshore Squadron's report for March stressed that shortage of craft was becoming a serious problem. He was making increasing use of PT boats: they were efficient and very cooperative, but had no time to train for the clandestine role. Early in April this problem was exacerbated by the defection of MAS 505, which, while on passage from Maddalena, which was still the MAS boats' maintenance base, to Bastia, was taken over by mutineers. They shot their Captain, Sub-Lieutenant Carlo Sorcinelli, and two other Italian officers who were taking passage. They threw the bodies overboard and took the boat over to Porto-San-Stefano on the mainland, where they surrendered to the Germans. The boat had never been used on special operations, but they brought much useful information to the enemy. When rumours of the mutiny reached Bastia, all the other Italian-manned boats were withdrawn from special operations lest they might prove untrustworthy. The Commander-in-Chief decreed, moreover, that no Italian ship was to sail without Allied escort, a requirement very difficult to meet. Once again, SOIS proved most helpful.

Twenty-nine operations had been proposed for April: 12 were successfully completed, four failed and 13 were postponed or not attempted. PT boats were solely employed and on several occasions the enemy was lying in wait at the pinpoint. An operation (ABRAHAM) for the newly organised *Direction General des Services Spéciaux* at Algiers failed on 18 April, when PTs 202 and 216 encountered an enemy destroyer at Cap-Camarat, which opened fire without challenging. Operation YOUNGSTOWN III for OSS failed on that same night, when PT 303 encountered two enemy patrols off Portofino and ran into a severe storm, which delayed the landing of two agents until it would have been too late. Operation ABRAHAM was successfully completed at Cap-Camarat on 21 April. There were no hostile craft waiting this time but, as the dinghy was approaching the shore, an enemy patrol appeared and opened fire with rifles: one of the bullets went through a tool-box on which Maxted was standing to supervise the operation. The landing took place and the dinghy returned while PT 209 laid down a smokescreen, behind which the expedition withdrew without loss. Operation CROMER was, at a fourth attempt, completed for SOE at Morgiou, near Marseilles just over a week later, two agents being landed and the mail embarked.

The German garrison on Elba was by now very much on the alert and Boyle's landing of two agents there on 23 April from PTs 205 and 202 (Operation ARCTIC IV), with Skipper Newton and Seaman McDuff as surf-boat's crew, was a distinct success. So smoothly did it go that the whole expedition was back in Bastia before dawn next day. Four days later the same agents were exfiltrated. On the morning of 27 April, the weather outlook seemed very unpromising and the sea at Bastia was so rough that it seemed doubtful whether the prearranged pick-up would be possible. But a signal received on BALACLAVA's W/T link with the French agents on Elba read 'Ici mer calme—mission terminée'. This led to a decision that NOSTRUM II must be attempted. PTs 218 and 214 sailed therefore with Maxted in charge and Newton and McDuff as dinghy crew.

But when 218 was due to enter the bay in which the pinpoint lay, her radar showed that either an E-boat or an R-boat was lying there. The 218 continued cautiously and worked her way into a position between the enemy vessel and the shore pinpoint. When a shaded torch spelled out the agreed signal from the waiting agents, Maxted and the Americans wondered whether the enemy vessel had seen it too. But the enemy made no move and seemed to be unaware either of the PT boat or of the waiting French agents. John Newton, fully aware of the precarious situation, insisted on taking the dinghy inshore and, after a long and nail-biting wait, his boat reappeared with the three agents aboard and transferred them and their gear up and into the PT boat, which slipped out of the bay still unobserved by the enemy patrol. SOIS described NOSTRUM II as the most outstanding operation of the month.

In May 1944, 31 operations were scheduled and 21 were successfully completed in spite of unseasonable weather. Four were failures and six were either cancelled or failed to materalise. The most remarkable feature was the absence of enemy interference. For the first time British Coastal Forces MTB's were used to relieve pressure on the PT boats. They were slower than their American counterparts and the Italian MAS boats, but proved in other respects very suitable. There was at the time considerable enemy traffic along the Italian coast and French lighthouses were lit, though reduced in power.

On 15 May, MTB 375 was tasked to carry out Operation ASHWATER, which involved landing three MARYLAND (i.e. SOE) agents in the San Remo area near the Franco-Italian frontier. Unfortunately, the MTB and her escort must have been picked up by enemy radar as they approached the coast. Maxted hove the MTBs to off the pinpoint. Croft and Miles embarked the agents in the dinghy but, when they were no more than 50 yards from the beach, a lorry full of German troop drew up on the road opposite and deployed to positions along it. Andrew was unwilling to give up and withdrew, looking for another landing point. But, on closing the beach again, he could hear footsteps approaching and it became clear that the whole area was thoroughly alerted: coastal batteries opened up with starshell and the lights of nearby Alassio were switched on. There was no alternative but to withdraw as quickly as possible.

A further attempt two days later using PT boats, with Brian Smith as Senior Officer, was defeated by weather at Cap-Corse. Two days later still Cooper told Croft that the agents had got cold feet and were to be flown back to Monopoli. At the last minute, they changed their minds and wanted to carry out their mission, but MARYLAND had had enough and cancelled the operation. In June 1944, considerable opposition was encountered on all sorties. Some 31 operations had been proposed, but 17 of these did not materalise. Ten were successful and four failed.

Allied military commanders and planners had for some months been conscious of the importance of Elba as a safeguard for the enemy's coastal shipping, on which it depended increasingly as Allied air supremacy systematically destroyed the traffic routes on land. But Allied plans for the capture of Elba had to wait until Allied forces broke out of the bridgehead at Anzio, captured Rome and moved north of it. The assault on the island was to be a French operation, using troops drawn from a Colonial Infantry division training in Corsica, reinforced by the *Bataillon de Choc,* Moroccan *Goumiers*—and two British Commandos. Before the assault, which began on 17 June, General de Lattre de Tassigny went out of his way to say that French forces had never been sent into action with better intelligence, but the frontal assault on the south-facing beaches cost him heavy casualties before he succeeded in outflanking the garrison of 4,000, half of whom were Germans and half troops loyal to Mussolini. Croft recorded in his private diary, 'We have played a major part in the landing of Elba, as the CHARLES Mission was put in four times and exfiltrated three times, once with enemy close on heels. In addition we have maintained wireless contact and supplied and maintained equipment.'

Andrew much admired Hagé, but Hagé came to him in great distress only a few weeks later and disappeared from the island without trace. Croft heard that he was in prison in Marseilles and inferred that, notwithstanding de Lattre's praise, he must have been made scapegoat for the heavy looses suffered by the 9th Colonial Infantry Division and the British Commandos. Neither Andrew nor four of his men who had been recommended by Hagé and Cappart the for the Croix de Guerre actually received such an honour.

On the night of 19/20 June, MI9's 'A' Force needed to infiltrate three agents into the Spezia area on the mainland and P 403, the US Air-Sea Rescue craft, was chosen for the job: Croft considered it a suitable choice, as it had a low profile like an Italian MAS boat but much quieter engines. Sergeant Bernard Jones, First Mate of John Newton's *Serenini,* and Corporal Bourne-Newton made up the shore party for FERRET and had no major difficulty in landing the three agents, though the sea was rough and the dinghy men had initial problems in finding a suitable beach. A search failed to find any of the prisoners of war they had expected. They rowed half way to where they expected to find the Air-Sea Rescue Boat when a light began to blink from the point they had just left. Jones reported this to Captain Fowler by walkie-talkie, who told them to go back and investigate. They did so but found nobody, though they heard movements in the undergrowth. Deciding that the light could not have been for them, the dinghymen pushed off again and headed for the Air Rescue Boat. They heard engines and saw what they thought to be 403, but it was an enemy patrol vessel and they paddled away: the walkie-talkie seemed no longer to be working and neither of them was wearing a watch. The prospect of returning to the shore was uninviting as the area seemed to be swarming with Germans and news of the fate that had befallen the GINNY II OG had filtered back to Bastia. They courageously and rapidly rowed their rubber boat out to sea. To cut a long story short, they were extremely fit and they had with them the provisions Croft always insisted his boats' crews carried. By sunrise, they had made good five miles to the south-west and could see Moneglia clearly.

ARB 403 had had to withdraw to seaward, having run into a hostile vessel; when it was safe to do so, she returned to the pin-point, but there was no sign of the dinghy and no answer when they tried to contact them on the walkie-talkie. After one and a quarter hours, they could delay no longer and returned to Bastia to report.

By late afternoon, rowing two-hour stretches in turn and making extremely swift change-over so as not to lose momentum, the dinghymen could see Corsica in the distance and set a compass course. They took half an hour's rest and were off again all through the night. Late on the 22nd, they could see the unoccupied island of Gorgona away to port. On the 22nd, two whales surfaced and cruised slowly past at a distance of 30 yards. By late afternoon, the northern tip of Corsica was only three or four miles to southward of them, but, however hard they rowed for the next three-and-a-quarter hours, they could make no progress against tide and wind. They changed course for Capraia, which they knew to be in the hands of one of Colonel Russell Livermore's OGs. By midnight, they gave up and slept till dawn. It was now 23 June and they battled against a strong current to make the last mile and a half to the island's shore.

By this time, hope was stirring at Bastia: Peter Fowler had received a signal from the FERRET agents ashore on the mainland: they had found no trace of the two sergeants or of their rubber dinghy. The two dinghymen had meanwhile managed to make a cup of cocoa with water collected from the rocks in the cove where they had landed. They stored everything away tidily and continued rowing to the local port, where they fired their sten-gun to attract attention and were towed into harbour by two fishermen. They had covered more than 90 miles in 86 hours—and sent BALACLAVA a signal addressed personally to Major Croft, 'Beg to report safe arrival Capraia 1830 GMT June 23.' As Ken Carson wrote in BALACLAVA's log, 'Beg to Report!' This happy breed…!' It was a feat of presence of mind, initiative, skill, courage and endurance which Croft, a highly qualified judge in such matters, considered of the highest order. They would not have succeeded but for the meticulous attention with which Croft equipped all his boats' crews for emergencies. But the enemy presence on the decreasing Italian coastline in his hands was making clandestine operations from Bastia increasingly difficult. When Croft went to see McCallum about the still-missing FERRET dinghymen, he found the latter depressed, because members of another shore party had been left behind in an ACF operation named

LOCUST. The object of this had been to land four OSS agents in the Spezia area, but when this was first attempted on 16 June, PT boat 310, escorted by 309, with Brian Smith in charge, had been driven off by gunfire from enemy destroyers and coastal craft without recovering the US surf-boat party. On 21st, the operation had been tried again with PT boat 309, escorted by PT 308, but they were prevented from reaching the pinpoint by heavy enemy coastal traffic, the vanguard, as it subsequently transpired, of a convoy which anchored in the bay where the pinpoint was situated. On 23rd of the month, Smith, with a strong escort of four British Coastal Force MTBs which remained offshore, dashed in with PT boat 305 and reembarked his men, who had rescued the stranded Americans, before the enemy opened fire with inaccurate starshell.

One of the last clandestine infiltration operations from Bastia (KINGSTON) was a failure. MAS boat 543 was attacked on 24 July by three enemy E-boats and the dinghy with the two OSS agents and Leading Seaman Luff (ACF) had to be abandoned. Luff was later known to be a prisoner of war, but the fate of the agents is unrecorded.

Successful operations for OSS continued to Cap-Lardier until 20 and 24 July, and BALACLAVA's last sea operation was successfully completed on 29 July. They had infiltrated nearly 100 agents into enemy-occupied territories—all of them delivered safely—and brought out nearly half that number.

On 5 August, the best all-rounders of BALACLAVA flew back to MASSINGHAM and a week later parachuted into the Hérault Department under the command of that most versatile of SOE's officers, Andrew Croft. Half a century later Croft wrote,

> If I could relive any chapter of my life during the war, it would undoubtedly be Corsica. From September 1943 to August 1944 I had the fun of running my own show to a large extent unsupervised. Furthermore it was a Naval/Military enterprise which was very much to my liking and for which my experiences as an Arctic explorer stood me in good stead. After all, the loss of a torch or a pair of gloves on the Greenland ice-cap would have been a major disaster, consequently I left nothing to chance when preparing for the fifty-two sorties which we undertook to the enemy-held coasts of Italy and France. We had to land agents and their equipment of arms and radio sets. Sometimes we went in again to take off those same men, or possibly escaping prisoners of war, with the Germans hard on their heels. Only during the fortnight's dark period of the moon would such operations be practicable; of course if the Germans had caught any of us we would have been shot on the orders of some local Hitlerite, hence a very high standard of training was essential.'

Tom Maxted wrote, even more recently,

> As you know, we only operated in the non-moon period. The other two weeks were spent doing the odd trips to the islands, practising boat work and enjoying ourselves, and this we did! There were a number of attractive girls in Bastia, most of

them lived in Paris but they were sent to their family summer-houses in Corsica to get away from the Germans. We had an Italian Fiat pick-up each and we would muster these and have great bathing parties. There were some lovely bathing places near where we were. Then in the evening there were the Soirées. I visited Bastia five years ago in a friend's yacht. A few of the 'girls' were still there and they told me how much they had enjoyed those days and how much they looked forward to the time of the month when there was a moon and we thought our security was complete. I found Bastia unrecognisable with dual carriageways and underpasses etc. but the mountains were still as beautiful as ever. That year in Corsica was the most memorable of the war and—I can almost say—my life.

XXII
Early Operations in the Adriatic and Southern Italy

BALACLAVA had been sent forward to Corsica by SOE's MASSINGHAM mission in Algiers even before the island was completely free, so as to be able to exploit its geographical advantages for clandestine sea operations both to south-eastern France and north-western Italy. In practice, as we have seen, the greater part of the 52 missions in which it was involved from Bastia were to Italian destinations or to the islands. SOE's MARYLAND mission was at the outset also seen by SOE as an operational outstation to take advantage of southern Italy as a jumping-off base for irregular naval operations to Greece, Albania and Yugoslavia as well as the Adriatic coast of Italy, though the three Balkan countries were the concern of Force 133, SOE's headquarters in Cairo, rather than MASSINGHAM.

SOE, building on experience with BRANDON, had also sent forward from Algiers a third mission, codenamed BROW, under Major Malcolm Munthe, son of Dr Axel Munthe author of *The Story of San Michele,* to take part in the HUSKY landings in Sicily, though British First Army needed to be persuaded by Lt-Col. Rosebery, head of SOE's Italian Section at its Baker Street headquarters, that this would be worthwhile. Rosebery himself landed at Taranto, as soon as Mussolini was ousted, and established direct contact with the Badoglio government and with the King. SOE'S overall prestige had been powerfully reinforced when it served, as much by luck as by good management, as the communications link between the Badoglio Government and General Eisenhower's Algiers headquarters during the armistice negotiations (MONKEY).

Indeed, when the Italian royal government set themselves up in Brindisi on 10 September they had brought with them from Rome Dick Mallaby, the SOE agent who had operated MONKEY and he had established radio contact with MASSINGHAM while AFHQ were making arrangements to send over an Allied Military Mission under General Mason Macfarlane, summoned by Eisenhower from Gibraltar. MASSINGHAM at once despatched Captain Teddy de Haan, who had acted as interpreter for the Italian surrender talks in Sicily, to pick up and build on the relationship with SIM, the Italian Military Security Service, already initiated through MONKEY. With him had gone Captain Freddy White and two signallers from MASSINGHAM to supplement Mallaby's efforts in developing radio communications on a broader basis.

Gerry Holdsworth had in two respects prepared the ground for a rapid development of SOE's involvement in southern Italy. He had, at a meeting called in Algiers in early July by Captain Bowlby RN of SIS, established that ACF was not adequately equipped with suitable craft and personnel to meet the needs of the organisations entitled to its services, though they were taking steps to improve the situation. In forward areas where, owing to shortages of staff, ACF had no local representative and where, in order to be successful, immediate action was essential, individual organisations would be permitted to make their own arrangements informing Commander ACF as quickly as possible—in some cases after the event—of what was about to, or had, taken place. Secondly, he had visited Cairo and discussed with SOE's Force 133 the possibility of contacting a local craft engaged in the Dalmatian coastal trade and the possibility of using trans-Adriatic craft for this same purpose and also the infiltration of stores.

On 23 September, Admiral Cunninghan and Admiral de Courten, his Italian opposite number, signed an agreement at Taranto about the deployment and use of the Italian fleet. Under this agreement, the First MAS Flotilla, consisting of six MS and seven MAS boats at Brindisi and Taranto under Commander (Cap. Freg.) Giorgio Manuti became available to the Allies as well as six submarines based at Brindisi.

There was at this time strong pressure from General Montgomery to avoid his 8th Army battlefront becoming encumbered with liberated Allied prisoners of war. This led to Brigadier Crockett, head of MI9, sending misconceived orders instructing prisoners in Italian camps to remain where they were in the event of an Italian armistice. This order was widely disregarded and, though in at least two camps the majority stayed put until the Germans collected them and shipped 50,000 of them off to Austria and Germany, something between 12,000 and 20,000 escapers were free, largely in the Appenines. Lt-Col. Anthony Simonds, of MI9's 'A'-Force in the central Mediterranean Theatre, a regular officer with plenty of experience in the clandestine sphere, was on 23 September called upon to mount and run an extensive operation (SIMCOL) to rescue Allied POWs behind the 8th Army front between Pescara and Ancona. This operation was mounted in haste and without adequate means or sufficient preparation.

For planning purposes the area was divided into four sectors:

1. Ancona to Civitanova (Ancona Sector).
2. Civitanova to San Benedetto (Fermo Sector).
3. San Benedetto to Pescara (Ascoli Piceno Sector).
4. Pescara South (Chieti Sector).

In essence, the plan was to drop by parachute in each of these four sectors uniformed parties to contact escaped Allied POWs and convoy or direct them to four pre-selected rendezvous points on the coast. At these points, other uniformed parties were to be landed from the sea to help round up the POWs, give them protection and supervise their embarkation.

The troops to form these operational parties were hastily assembled from 1st Airborne Division, two SAS and an OSS Italian Operational Group (composed of Italo-Americans) which had just arrived in North Africa.

To deliver the airborne parties, since there were no suitable aircraft on hand in southern Italy, it was decided at the last minute to summon some Albermarles from Sicily. There was no sea transport immediately available, apart from eight Italian fishing vessels which had been hurriedly commandeered.

SOE's main advance party for Italy under Gerry Holdsworth arrived at Brindisi from North Africa via Malta on *Mutin* (FPV 2013) on 28 September: she was commanded by Lt Dick Laming, RNVR, a pre-war Dutch merchant navy officer, with Tom Long as coxswain. On board were also Lt Hilary Scott RNVR, Capt. Edward Renton and Telegraphist Prince as passengers. She was followed some 48 hours later by *Gilfredo* (MFV 2019), commanded by Sub Lt R.O. Richards, the present author's brother, with Major Hewitt, Captains Lee, Michael Gubbins and Donaldson (a Field Security Section NCO, commissioned on arrival in Italy, the only Italian-speaker in the Maryland combined advance party). There to meet them were Douglas Dodds-Parker and Major Bruce (Training Officer). Holdsworth went ashore and *Mutin* celebrated the arrival of his Commander's 'brass hat'. It should be noted that at this stage MARYLAND was conceived of not just as a unit for operations in Italy, but as a forward base and advance HQ for MASSINGHAM, which it was anticipated would in the near future move forward (apart from its French Section) along with AFHQ itself.

Laming had been told by Holdsworth to make contact with the Italian navy and he was in due course escorted into the august presence of Admiral de Foscary, Chief of Staff—Intelligence, whose family had provided Doges of Venice. He gave Laming, who found him a 'charming gentleman', the address of his Palazzo and said with a grin that Laming would no doubt arrive there long before he himself got home.

MARYLAND'S Naval Section personnel hoped to be able to use the Italian MS boats, which were Italian versions of German E-boats, for the operations they envisaged behind the fighting front. Laming found Manuti, who commanded the flotilla, 'a lovely rogue' and discovered that he had 18 months earlier, when commanding MS 63 off Cap Bon in Tunisia, sunk the British cruiser *Manchester*. *Manchester*'s silhouette was painted on the bridge of MS 63, one of the boats which SOE was most to use, together with MS 73. Their captains were, respectively, Lieutenant Tedesci and Lieutenant Manusardi.

As Laming was now in command of *Mutin*, it crossed his mind that she, a sailing vessel belonging ultimately to the French navy, was to be treated with the greatest respect and he decided, in accord with Holdsworth, that she was to be kept well away from the 'shooting war'. He stuck to his view right up to the moment she sailed for her return to the United Kingdom in November 1944. Thanks to his care, she is now the oldest ship serving in the French Marine Nationale.

MARYLAND, known more widely as No. 1 Special Force, set up shop at Monopoli, a small port half way between Brindisi and Bari. Lt Hilary Scott, a future President of the Law Society, Lt Laming, Lt Michael Gubbins, and six of MARYLAND's naval ratings took part in SIMCOL, but the naval side of that operation was under the command of the Senior Naval Officer Landing Adriatic (SNOLA). Dodds-Parker reported that many such requests for help were outside Holdsworth's formal SOE charter but he considered it important for Gerry to undertake them where possible in the hope of getting as a quid pro quo the support he needed from other parties for his primary tasks. London agreed, provided SOE needs did not suffer. Scott and Laming left Monopoli and took the Italian trawler *San Vito* and another ship up the coast around the Gargano peninsula. They were anchored off Lake Varano on the north shore of the peninsula when the 8th Army steamed by in their landing craft bound for Termoli. Fishing boats with troops hidden below decks followed the initial landings. The troops landed on the quay and advanced quickly along it, taking the town. For several days at the beginning of October the Luftwaffe bombed the area at regular intervals: a German was discovered in the church tower giving them directions. Shortly after the occupation of the town, Dick Laming had the *San Vito* moored at the end of the harbour mole. At mid-day, Luftwaffe planes came over on their regular daily visit. Two small bombs dropped on either side of her, while Laming stood at the end of the gangway. They opened up all her underwater seams and she settled on the bottom quietly. One SAS was killed and four SAS and OSS injured. Bert Ramsdale, a pre-war Yorkshire professional footballer who was a member of the crew, was badly shaken. Termoli became the starting point for operations up the coast, but *Mutin* moved forward only as far as Manfredonia.

Tom Long had some time before this been sent from Brindisi to Taranto for an operation off Sardinia, which surrendered on 18 September. He went alone on an MS acting as a covering force to another MS carrying out a special operation. His instructions were that if anything went wrong regarding the first boat, he was to make sure that the boat he was on did not clear off without attempting a rescue. He was aboard for several days and remembered it as a particularly miserable time—nobody to talk to, food reeking of garlic and no tea or coffee to drink—only *vino,* which tasted to Tom like a ¼ pint of port with ¾ of a pint of vinegar added. When he returned to *Mutin,* John Macdonald was dishing up dinner. It was corned beef and mash; he has always regarded that as the most enjoyable meal of his entire life.

Another naval problem in which Holdsworth was immediately involved was that of supplies for the partisans in Yugoslavia—a matter of personal concern to the Prime Minister, whose chosen personal representative to Tito, Fitzroy Maclean, had just been sent in and who had lost no time in calling urgently for deliveries by sea. This was primarily SOE Cairo's problem but, as subsequently commented by General Gubbins, they had shown 'fantastic incompetence and dilatoriness' and it was not until 15 October that a small party arrived from Cairo to set up an Advance HQ MO4 in Bari. Meanwhile, an OSS officer named Huot had stolen a march on them, thereby seemingly relieving Holdsworth of the responsibility for arranging the unloading in Brindisi of 400 tons of stores despatched from Protville (RINGLET) in the *Brittany* on 8 October and their onward despatch to the Dalmatian coast or islands by whatever craft might be found.

Adrian Gallegos, whose father had been a Spanish artist established in Rome, but who had worked at Lloyds before the war and was completely tri-lingual, had joined the RNVR before the war and had served in armed merchant cruisers before being sent by SOE to Gibraltar as one of a linguistically qualified group of officers posted there to be ready to conduct guerrilla warfare in Spain should Hitler invade that country. He had been sent forward by MASSINGHAM to Malta and thence to Syracuse on the south coast of Sicily to help Malcolm Munthe's BROW mission requisition *Gilfredo,* a rat-infested schooner, which would enable the author's brother Robin to ship arms salvaged by SOE from the Sicilian battlefield to Tunis, where SOE had set up a station at Protville for cleaning, servicing and packing enemy weapons destined for supplying the needs of partisans in the Balkans. Thereafter, Gallegos was formally attached to Munthe's expanded party, codenamed VIGILANT, which was assembling at Palermo and was attached to the US 5th Army for the AVALANCHE landings on the Italian mainland. This party included two of the leading Italian political exiles, Alberto Tarachiani and Alberto Cianca, whom Max Salvadori (also a member of the party) had recruited in the USA and Mexico and who had been brought by SOE via the UK to North Africa. The idea was to infiltrate some of them into enemy-occupied Italy by land or sea. This may have been a specific reason for sending in Gallegos with his fluent Italian with the advance party for VIGILANT, not just general anticipation of opportunities for possible para-naval operations on the west coast as and when the 5th US Army advanced.

The VIGILANT party landed at Paestum on 10 September. Munthe decided to make a dash up the coast to Salerno (in the British sector) to establish a base as far forward as possible, taking Tarachiani and Cianca with him and leaving Gallegos in charge of the rest of the party at Paestum. A few days later, after learning of the liberation of Capri (which surrendered to the Allies on the 12th), Munthe drove back to Paestum to collect Gallegos and take him across to Capri in one of Lt Quentin Riley's craft from 30 Commando. Tarachiani and Cianca were also withdrawn from Salerno to Capri if only for greater safety, though doubtless also with a view to possible infiltration by sea, which was preferable to a passage through the lines while the battle raged on the mainland.

More immediately, Munthe seized on the idea of rescuing Benedetto Croce, the Liberal philosopher and historian, from his villa near Sorrento, before the Germans laid hands on him. For such purposes, Munthe and Gallegos were pleased to find Italian naval craft of the II *Flottiglia* MAS lying at Capri. With the agreement of Rear Admiral Morse (FOWIT-designate for Naples) and Captain Andrews USN (i.e. Allied Forces north of Salerno), the CO of the Italian flotilla, Cap. Freg. Alessandro Michelagnoli, was persuaded to allot a suitable motor launch (AS13) with his best crew for the rescue of Croce. So after dark on 15 September Gallegos set off in AS 13 with Avvocato Brindisi, an old friend of Croce and Mayor-designate of Capri, to guide and introduce him, to persuade Croce to leave his villa before the Germans arrived and seek safety on Capri. They succeeded in overcoming the old man's initial reluctance to leave and came back with him and three of his daughters, leaving behind Croce's wife and eldest daughter to pack up a few more things in daylight and shut up the house, with a promise to return for them next night. But it was Munthe who went back on the 16th to fetch them, as an opportunity occurred for Gallegos to go over to Ischia, where Munthe was keen for him to find and requisition a suitable property for eventual SOE use.

By 19 September, the plan to land Tarachiani and Cianca, using an Italian MS boat somewhere near Rome had had to be abandoned because of news of the end of Italian military resistance there and German occupation of the city. Instead an operation was mounted for Gallegos to land an Italian agent at a point on the coast between Gaeta and Terracina, with a mission apparently to reconnoitre the Terracina area and carry out certain specific acts of sabotage, after which he would be picked up from the same point four nights later. For this operation, which had been authorised by Admiral Morse, it had been intended originally to use a British MTB or US PT boat but, when they claimed shortage of fuel, recourse was had to one of the Italian fast craft, whose crews, having been based on Gaeta, were familiar with the area. As Italy was not yet formally at war with Germany, the Italian flotilla commander, Michelagnoli, impressed on Gallegos, the importance, in the event of capture, for the protection of the crew, who would risk being shot, of not revealing that the operation was being carried out for the Allies. The craft used for the operation was MS21 (Sottoten. vasc. Luciano Marengo) and the agent was landed safely, but on its way back MS21 struck a mine, and sank, with the loss of one member of the crew. The rest, with Gallegos, were picked up 36 hours later and taken to Rome for interrogation, under which Gallegos succeeded throughout in passing himself off as one of the Italian crew and was shipped off with them as an Italian prisoner to Germany.

MASSINGHAM reported Gallegos missing on 28 September. This happened to coincide with the despatch to MASSINGHAM of Lt P.T. Simpson-Jones (ex-RN and SOE since 1941, with operational service in Madagascar), who had been in training (with others) at Helford for North Africa since the Summer, in response to a request by MASSINGHAM for para-naval reinforcements. Chosen no doubt as the senior and most experienced of the then available naval officers at MASSINGHAM to replace Gallegos with two ratings (ABs Wood and Lawson), they were sent to hitch their way to Naples, where they arrived on 14 October.

In the meantime, Munthe had acquired for VIGILANT the use of at least one small craft (VAS 222) of the II flottiglia MAS with a volunteer crew. Simpson-Jones found the VAS, however, unsuitable for operational purposes as too slow and noisy, but, having learnt of the availability of MS boats in Capri he approved of them on sight and by the end of the month had arranged for MS24 and 52 to be brought over to Naples, towing a third (MS72) for eventual cannibalisation to keep the other two going.

These formed the nucleus of the Naples Special Service Flotilla, formally instituted on the authority of FOWIT in a memorandum issued on 2 November 1943. The flotilla was to operate under the orders of FOWIT and to be based on Ischia with 'the British Special Force attached G2 5th Army' (i.e. VIGILANT) responsible for maintenance and victualling of crews. It was specified that two MS (24 and 52) and 2 MAS (206 and 222) were to be available for special service operations approved by FOWIT and to operate on the instructions of officers of 'the British Special Force organisation'. Craft of the flotilla were also to be similarly available for operations of OSS approved by FOWIT. Of the craft specifically allocated to VIGILANT only the two MS were used operationally. The two VAS plus a third (VAS 211) proved useful initially for ferrying bodies and supplies between Naples and Ischia.

In reporting this satisfactory arrangement to MARYLAND Simpson-Jones explained that the MS and MAS were on loan from the RN 'on the understanding that we will do any jobs they need', for exmple, air/sea rescue or beach reconnaissance (for which a COPP party would shortly be provided), and that an agreement had been reached with OSS to carry out operations for them. His report also mentioned the requisitioning through the Navy of an Italian 10-ton vessel *(San Angelo)* also to be used for bringing supplies to Ischia from Naples. His report ended with a plea for MARYLAND to send him as his first lieutenant either R.A.Clark or Carnachan, with both of whom he had done training at Helford and who were at MASSINGHAM when he left. He asked also for dories and folboats. It was now well into an operational no-moon period and one operation had already been planned by VIGILANT for Simpson-Jones, who after no more than two days in Naples had crossed over to Ischia and established himself in the port there alongside the Italian naval craft and their crews. The operation was WORDSWORTH and its object was to land two Italians behind enemy lines. But on 26 October it was 'reluctantly abandoned' by VIGILANT, owing to the 'present state of mind' of the agents, who were to be infiltrated instead by land, and then prepare to receive a W/T operator later by sea. The records show that three agents were sent through the lines on 28 October with a mission to operate about 100km behind the front, organising resistance. However, there is no further record of this operation and no evidence of any W/T operator having been sent in by sea.

Simpson-Jones was luckier next time and achieved his first successful operation just before the end of the no-moon period: TIDEWAY, on 5/6 November. Using MS24, he landed a single Italian 'blind' near Sabandia on the coastal area of the drained Pontine Marshes with two cases of explosives. This was one of VIGILANT's recruits, a communist who had come through the lines from Rome and was being sent back there after a course of training at VIGILANT's school on Ischia (the property requisitioned by Gallegos), with instructions and guidance for the military committee of the Italian Communist Party in Rome. The landing was successful and the Italian subsequently praised the courage of the British sailor (presumably Wood or Lawson) who helped carry the explosives inland in potentially threatening circumstances. During the ensuing moonlit period, Simpson-Jones, now convinced that the MAS boats were of no use to him even as support craft, came to an arrangement with FOWIT to swap them for an Italian vessel on which he had cast his eye and which he judged ideal for his purposes—as parent ship to the MS craft and base ship for himself in all future eventualities. This was the *Eduardo,* of 130 tons gross, built in 1941 for the Atlantic fishing trade but immediately requisitioned by the Italian navy and converted into a minesweeper. He took it over with an Italian crew and began to have it modified and fitted out to SOE's requirements.

Early in the next dark period, Simpson-Jones received a directive from FOWIT (23 November) to carry out beach reconnaissances in the Anzio/Nettuno area (for Operation SHINGLE) with the aid of a COPP party and the SBS. Two reconnaissances were carried out using MS craft in this dark period: the first on X-RAY (American) and the second on PETER (British) beach. Simpson-Jones reported the first as a complete success but the second as only partially so, in obtaining the required soundings and having lost one canoe. He recorded no details of this first reconnaissance, but Christopher Woods, the official historian of SOE in Italy, has a copy of the proposals (operational plan 'PWQ') which he submitted to FOWIT on 30 November (approved 1 December) for the second: they refer to it being carried out by '1 unit of a COPP party and 2 units of the SBS' in three canoes under the command of Sub-Lt K.G.Patterson RANVR, to be transported in MS52, with Simpson-Jones in MS24 as support ship. G.B.Courtney gives some details of both these reconnaissances in his book *SBS in World War Two* (pp. 117–18), including dates (28/29 November and 2/3 December) and the fate of the lost canoe party (Patterson and AB Lockhead), who, late in returning and having missed the rendezvous, paddled ashore and avoided capture until 3 February, thus avoiding compromising SHINGLE.

Also scheduled for this dark period was a second operation for VIGILANT (GERARD III), being a third attempt (the preceeding two by land having failed) to infiltrate a party of four Italian saboteurs to operate behind the lines in the British X Corps coastal sector of the US 5th Army front. On 29 November, Simpson-Jones submitted a proposal to land the men (plus their stores in three Helford containers) using MS24 in the same area in which he had carried out TIDEWAY earlier in the month. The operation was carried out successfully, but the exact date is uncertain (2/3 December is quoted but this date clashes with that given for a beach reconnaissance and both cannot be right). The eventual landing point according to one of the participants was 'in a small cove south of M.Circeo'. At this time, the Royal Navy appointed an NOIC in Ischia, Lt Cdr John Gibbons RNVR, with whom Simpson-Jones now shared a villa. This led to the issue on 4 December of a memo from FOWIT establishing a modified procedure for the clearance of SOE operations and the use of craft allocated to SOE. There followed on 5 December a meeting convened by FOWIT and attended by representatives of SOE ('British Special Force') and OSS to coordinate operations by the two organisations. But the dark period, beginning on 21 December, when eight operations were scheduled for SOE and OSS, was a grave disappointment owing to bad weather: the only thing that was satisfactorily carried out was a further reconnaissance of PETER beach, the navy lending a US PT boat specially for the job. Thanks to this boat's radar, the place was found accurately, but again a canoe was lost with an American officer and enlisted man. Captain W.G. Davis of SBS, who had taken part in the earlier reconnaissance, was in command of the US beach survey party in two canoes and it appears that in fact all three American ensigns involved were killed, although Davis survived. Two agent-landing operations were attempted, but both were unsuccessful due to adverse weather. Both Simpson-Jones and Carnachan have commented adversely on the behaviour of the MS boats in heavy seas: Simpson-Jones said that they lost speed and became unmanageable in anything over force 5–6 ahead of the beam.

The end of the December dark period coincided with the end of VIGILANT; after two visits by General Colin Gubbins in the course of a long Mediterranean tour, it was decided to amalgamate the various elements of SOE in Italy working in support of the Italian military campaign into a single unit with its headquarters under Holdsworth in Monopoli. It was this which led to the idea of sending Simpson-Jones and his Ischia para-naval party and MS24 to reinforce BALACLAVA's efforts from Bastia. But before this could happen, the SHINGLE operation which had earlier been shelved, was revived and Simpson-Jones was summoned to Caserta on 15 January to be requested, as the only available British officer who had actually visited PETER beach, to carry out one further, final reconnaissance of it, taking with him a new COPP party which had been hastily summoned from India, to familiarise them with the beach area. In order to test the alertness of the defences and the degree to which the beach might have been compromised, particularly by the fate of the Americans on the previous reconnaissance of 29/30 December, he was asked to take his MS as close to the shore as possible. The reconnaissance was carried out successfully on 18/19 January and no sign of activity was detected on the beach.

For the landing itself, Simpson-Jones was again to go with the COPP party. He was on this occasion not allowed to use either of the MS boats because of the difficulty of informing all concerned that an Italian boat would be taking part. He took with him for the actual SHINGLE operation AB Wood and they were embarked in US Submarine Chaser 508. Simpson-Jones and his party received congratulations from Admiral Troubridge and General Alexander, whom they had taken ashore to inspect the beachhead. On his next visit to Naples he arranged for a signal of congratulations to be sent by FOWIT to the II MS flotilla for their part in the preliminary reconnaissances.

MS24's subsequent part in operations from Bastia during February and March have been dealt with in the preceding chapter. It would seem that Croft did not get on well with Simpson-Jones, who is scarcely mentioned in BALACLAVA's log. In the southern Adriatic, owing to the SIMCOL operation, matters developed somewhat differently: German air attacks on Termoli resulting in the loss of fishing vessels and shelling caused the crews of the remaining vessels of this type to run from the port to shelter at Bari, though that port was to be devastated later by a massive German air-raid. There was, moreover, a complete lack of cover offshore from fishing vessels by the end of the first week of October as the Germans had destroyed the fleet. German resistance frustrated the 8th Army's plan to reach Pescara on 10 October, so the plan had to be revised and faster craft requested. Laming took part in a SIMCOL pick up on the 5/6 October, using a Landing Craft Infantry (LCI): the three escapers they picked up at D-beach south of Pescara said there were thousands more further inland, who had been afraid to come to the beach because they did not trust the available information and feared falling into a trap. Tom Long accompanied Laming on the LCI to go ashore (at San Vito near Ortona), hoping to contact agents with escaped prisoners and took an operational scow and equipment with him, but the long-retired Admiral Cowan, who had been in command of the Baltic squadron blockading St Petersburg in 1920, talked himself on to the operation and took charge of the landing party consisting of himself and two elderly Brigadiers (one British, the other Polish) who needed three walking sticks between them. Tom was furious at having the operation 'messed up by decrepit geriatrics'.

All in all, SIMCOL was not a great success. Laming took part in one further SIMCOL pick-up on 9/10 October, after which the beginning of the moon period precluded further sea operations for a fortnight, by which time a new series had been organised, using the Italian MS craft as well as LCIs. Dick Laming recalls that on his first operation for MARYLAND, as opposed to SIMCOL, MS 61, escorted by MS 73, sailed from Viesti (Gargano). He was standing on the bridge near the Quartermaster when Tedesci, the captain, came up to him and said in English, 'Lt Laming, I want you to know that if you were not standing there now, my men would not go to sea with me." Dick was very touched and just shook his hand, without reply. Tedesci and his boat both 'turned up trumps', as Laming put it. And so did the Italian navy more generally: DDOD(I)'s Sea operations analysis for the Adriatic shows no fewer than 190 operations carried out by Italian vessels and Italian crews out of the remarkable total of 250 'irregular' operations. Laming found the Italians 'marvellous to work with'. Tom Long, notwithstanding his initial unhappiness when sent to take part on an Italian *Motosilurante*'s first operation to Sardinia, writes today 'We had found these Italians to be tip-top in every way.'

Laming's first operation with MS 61 must have been GEARBOX, which on or about 27/28 November successfully landed six agents for SOE at the mouth of the River Chienti near Porto Potenza Picena and nearer still to Porto Civitanova. These were a mission code-named OPAL to work in the Marche, a team coednamed ZIRCON destined for the Romagna and an agent belonging to A-Force (MI9), who had all been embarked originally on FPV 2013 *(Mutin)* and transferred, probably either at Manfredonia or Vieste, to MS 61. An unsuccessful attempt was made to put them ashore near Ancona before their successful landing on the south bank of the Chienti. Dick was supported by my brother, Sub-Lt R.O.Richards, and Tom Long. It was not literally MARYLAND's first operation by sea, as will be seen from the Appendix, but their first use of a *Motosilurante* (MS) for their own needs.

Laming had done three operations for A-Force using other types of vessels. The first three MS boats arrived at Termoli only on 18 October and did their first operation for A-Force (MI. 9) three nights later.

The navy at Termoli was run by a Captain Black, whom Dick described as 'a hard thing if ever you met one'. Black must have taken to Laming for all that as he invited him up to Termoli for Christmas (1943). Dick hitch-hiked up, as that was by far the quickest way to move along the coast. He found Captain Black in bed with flu and with the local Marchesa nursing him. Christmas Eve was, in Dick's own words 'a real boozy party' and he spent a lot of time in Black's bedroom longingly eyeing the Marchesa. He even attended the local midnight Mass, but with little recollection and, in his own words, it must have been 'near cracker-dawn' when he got to bed. At 8 o'clock breakfast, where they sat blearily, contemplating the snowstorm and howling wind outside, the local Commander invited him to the Operations Room and told him that there was a US Air Force raft drifting down the coast, assisted by the tramontana. The last position was eight miles off Pescara. Captain Black was not about when Dick stepped on board one of the LCIs, with which they started making an extremely wet passage north in the general direction of Ortona. And there was the yellow raft with five airmen in it, one-and-a-half miles off the Ortona breakwater. The front line was the Sangro River, away to the south, so the Germans must have seen what they were doing, but not a shot was fired at them. 'Frohliche Weinachten!' (The battle for Ortona extended over 20 December to 28 December.) When they got back to Termoli, it was still snowing.

After the Germans fell back to Pescara, Dick for a time used Ortona as a starting point for his operations (AVONMOUTH/ AINTREE and AMPTHILL in March); according to the MI9 history, Termoli was closed by the navy for use by the clandestine services between the end of January and early April.

As the front line moved north, the Italian navy said they would not be able to assist SOE further as they were constrained to have their MS boats based at Brindisi and Taranto and would not, Tom Long says, have the necessary range. Tom left *Mutin* to become skipper of an Italian trawler, which had a good capacity for carrying 40-gallon drums of fast-craft diesel and between operating periods his job was to go to Brindisi, load up with drums and take them up to Ortona. Everyone was very satisfied with this arrangement and MS operations went on as before. When up at Ortona Tom was frequently asked by the Naval Officer-in-Charge to put to sea as airmen were reported drifting in dinghies and the Air-Sea Rescue flotilla was still based back at Manfredonia. They had sent one vessel up to Ortona and the American skipper moored her alongside the quay. Tom told him it was a dangerous position as it was open to the German guns. The skipper said it was handy for going ashore and the crew backed him up, until the next day, when one of them had his private parts shot away and was killed. So back the vessel went to Manfredonia.

The Tremiti Islands were also used at this stage as an advanced refuelling base for the MS boats; one of which (MS 31) achieved the remarkable feat of leaving Termoli under command of Manuti with about 20 officers, commandos and civilian agents on board, doing a landing of men and materials at the mouth of the River Po that same night and returning to base 22 hours after she set out, having done 530 miles at an average of 25 knots. Early in January 1944, the Commanding Officer of Advanced Landing Forces at Termoli reported, 'During the period concerned I have had at my disposal an average of 4 Italian MTBs (scl. MS boats). They have given proof of real ability and efficiency in all the tasks they have been called on to perform. The personnel of this flotilla has always collaborated with enthusiasm and high morale, and their cordial co-operation in all fields is most satisfying.' The flotilla's main base was transferred from Brindisi to Manfredonia at the end of January.

By that time Dick's Italian was becoming quite passable, and he used to spend quite a lot of time in their company, especially when they operated from way-out places like Ortona 'To me', he said, 'the Adriatic was a great picnic, and on the main landings we made I only played the role of figurehead.' I interpret this as meaning that he left the boat-work to Bob Clark, my brother and Tom Long, who were also used to carry out demolitions, mainly of railway targets. The records show that my brother and Lt Clark each also took a much-needed cargo of petrol to Vis, and that Tom used *Mutin* to ship over camouflage nets, under which they then spent the night moored at the foot of a cliff.

XXIII
African Coastal Flotilla (Adriatic)

When the final plans for the invasion of Italy were maturing, Slocum, in his capacity as Deputy Director Operations Division (Irregular) (DDOD(I)), had asked the secret organisations regarding their future transport requirements. A large number of operations in the Adriatic were envisaged, to both the Italian and the Yugoslav coasts. Later on, too, they had hopes of reopening operations to the south coast of France (closed since the German invasion of the formerly Non-Occupied Zone in November 1942, following the Allied landings in French North Africa) as well.

The ACF were not, as we have seen, initially well-equipped to undertake operations either on the west coast of Italy or in the Adriatic: their African vessels were of little use in the new context and Admiral Cunningham's refusal to let the US PT boats at Syracuse or, indeed, any other vessels with an offensive capacity, be used for clandestine transport, produced a temporary deadlock but the 8th Army, keeping up the momentum of their final North African pursuit, swept into and up south-eastern Italy. ACF, slower than SOE's Naval section, sent their first craft (*Seahawk,* an especially built large felucca just out from home) into the Adriatic. Sailing from Bône with Commander K. Michell, DSO, MVO, DSC, RN and Sub-Lt B.W.Levy RNVR on board as DDOD (I) representatives she arrived during the first week of October, by way of Syracuse, Taranto and Brindisi. Commander Michell left the vessel at Taranto to present his credentials to Flag Officer Taranto and liaison with the Italians (FOTALI) and rejoined the advance sea borne party by road. Their object was to establish a base on the east coast and take over such local craft as necessary. The only suitable port, apart from Bari—whose harbour was already overcrowded and much bombed—seemed to be Molfetta, 20 miles north. It had not only a usable harbour but excellent repair facilities which were as yet untapped. Living and office accommodation were obtained in the town and harbour precincts respectively. Arrangements were made without delay and on 18 October Molfetta base was commissioned as ACF(A).

The first of the Bône MFVs had arrived but after a bad voyage was considered not worth an extensive refit. She was replaced by the brand new Italian motor trawler *Seastar.* Two others, *Seamaid* and *Seaflower,* were taken over at the same time and converted, while a third, *Dentice,* on the stocks, but expected to complete within a few weeks, was added as a spare. *Sea-giant* was taken over shortly after, when it was seen that *Dentice* would not complete according to schedule. The Polish vessel *Seawolf arrived* before Christmas and her crew transferred on to *Seaflower.*

Bône base had closed down on 20 October, after *St Vincent* sailed for Italy. She was destined never to arrive, but after many breakdowns managed to make Syracuse, where she was handed over to the SAS for training purposes. She was last seen steaming out into the blue at her modest 4 knots, commanded by an intrepid soldier, who, it is believed, eventually managed to make his home port in Africa after 'thumbing' tows from passing naval ships. But before she left Syracuse, *St Vincent* achieved the distinction of holding up all the traffic across the narrow bridge there by the simple expedient of ramming her 20-foot bowsprit through its railings. Ship and bridge were 'two blocks' for quite 20 minutes until someone was found who really knew how to reverse her engine, whereupon she disengaged and backed sedately away to her proper berth. The remaining two Bône craft, *Annonciade* and *St Anne,* were handed back to their owners. They had never been much of a success.

In November, as ACF(A) was getting into its swing, 'three organisations', as ACF(A) saw it, 'took it upon themselves to start forming their private flotillas'. Permission had been obtained (contrary to Admiralty policy as laid down) from C-in-C for SOE, MI9 and OSS to run their own craft. The old trouble seemed to be recurring, for, in addition, an officer in Bari was running arms to Albania—an SOE Mid-East commitment—and the Adriatic would soon therefore be the happy hunting ground for four independent 'navies'. To forestall certain trouble in this connection, DDOD(I) requested, and received, permission to appoint an officer to Taranto to coordinate irregular operations. The operating of the re-born 'private navies thus came under Admiralty control', as did all other clandestine traffic, through SOSO(A) on FOTALI's staff: round one to Slocum.

A few days before Christmas 1944, Commander Clark relieved Commander Michell at Molfetta and Lt Levy took over the duties of SOSO(A) at Taranto.

The ACF(A) Flotilla was now working at full pressure. A large number of operations had been undertaken and, in spite of the bad weather for which the Adriatic is notorious, a great many had been successful. This gratifying state of affairs continued until June. Originally, on account of enemy air activity in the northern and central waters, it was customary to sail all ACF(A) craft on operations first to Vis Island. From there, they would make their way north under the lee of the Yugoslav islands to the latitude of San Sego, where they would cut across to the Italian mainland. Astronomical navigation was an impossibility during the winter months and this policy also allowed a fairly short DR run to the pinpoint. Later, as the Germans became wise to the activities of the so-called 'innocent' vessels (Marshal Tito's partisan navy relied exclusively on this form of transport as well), they also used similar craft, only armed to the teeth. As a result, both air forces were ordered to shoot anything moving in that area during daytime. ACF(A) policy had to be altered, and craft made only night passages, lying up amongst the islands during daylight. By February this, too, was ineffective as Coastal Forces were operating from Vis and with their periodical beatings-up of enemy shipping were stirring the whole eastern Adriatic into activity. Flotillas of E-boats and F-lighters eventually arrived on the scene and so made further use of the islands out of the question.

The question of MFVs' (Motor Fishing Vessels') armament had always been a controversial subject, and flotilla opinion was equally divided. No one had had any experience of surface action in a fishing vessel, and air interference had been confined to the mere shooting-up and bombing of the Bône ships by 'friendly' aircraft. In both cases the aircraft had not been over thorough, and those in favour of plenty of guns and the shooting down of any enemy attackers had, perhaps, the stronger opinions until the *Seastar* was efficiently beaten up by a couple of enemy fighters. After that it was generally accepted that with 8 knots, a small crew and an unstable gun-platform, it was best for everyone to put discretion before valour, and six inches of hard oak between themselves and the bullets, by getting below decks quickly. To retaliate cheekily with a Bren and a few Sten guns would only provoke further attention. So it was, that when mid-sea courses were forced on the ships as the only alternative, the policy of 'take it quietly' was adopted as the best means of achieving the object of the operation—namely, the safe landing of passengers on board.

By August, the capture of Ancona had shortened the distances necessary to operate to the northern Italian areas and Istrian Peninsula. Better still, additional harbours were available for starting off points, and this brought all areas within range of night operations in fast craft. Also, with the prevailing weather it was possible to sail an MTB during the short calms (too short for MFV voyages) between gales to complete the operation when a fishing vessel would become weather-bound by the following storm before even reaching the pinpoint. The reputation of irregular operations had been steadily improved in the Adriatic and the Commander-in-Chief had sent his congratulations on results achieved. FOTALI was also keenly interested and had visited Molfetta several times to meet the ACF staff, so when suggestions were put forward that fast craft would be more useful they were quickly forthcoming. A flotilla of Higgins MGBs was allocated to ACF(A) and manned by its officers and crews. Of the now out-of-favour MFVs, two had seen considerable service at Vis, where they had landed partisan and Allied reconnaissance parties, and units for howitzer support of partisan attacks, and, on occasion, had even broadcast to enemy garrisons. Of these two, *Seahawk* and *Seastar,* the latter became permanently attached to SNOV until paid off in October. The remainder of the requisitioned craft were paid off to NOIC Bari in September and their crews manned the newly acquired MTBs. Shortly after, Malta became *Seahawk*'s final resting place and her Commanding Officer and crew also joined an MTB.

A certain amount of experience in operating fast craft in the Adriatic had been gained as an American Air-Sea Rescue boat, P42, formerly operating from Corsica, had been working for ACF(A) since April. She was commanded by a US Air Corps officer, Lt G.Moritz, and had rendered useful service, chiefly for MI9, in operations to northern Italy and Yugoslavia. Bastia base having been closed down, its officers and crews transferred to the Adriatic sector.

After a period of working up at Malta, Higgins Craft 179, 180 and 191 under the command of Lieutenants Cosens, Maxted and Hamilton, respectively, steamed round to the Adriatic and were finally based at Ancona. The Ancona base of ACF(A) had been preparing for their arrival for some time, and soon, under the direction of Lieut. Commander B.D.Youatt, R.N., they were sallying forth on operations to the limited coastlines still in the enemy's hands from just north of the River Po to the Istrian Peninsula.

The remaining craft, MGB 177, of ACF(A)'s 45th Flotilla, was allocated to Leghorn for operations on the west coast. She was commanded by Lt B.H.T.J.Smith, DSC, RNR, and came under the control of Lt Commander D.T.MacCallum, RNR.

Meanwhile, the Ferry Service, described in Chapter XLIV, which had been the mainstay of the Molfetta base, had by this time dwindled to a trickle and *Laurana* had been handed over to General Service use. *Prodigal,* which had been employed in the Aegean, was ready to return to the United Kingdom to be converted for tropical waters. Accordingly, during the latter part of November and the early part of December, all essential stores were shipped north to Ancona, and three days after Christmas, just 15 months ten days after commissioning, ACF(A) Molfetta was declared closed.

XLIV
The Ferry Service

Towards the middle of May 1943 the trawler *Prodigal* arrived in the Mediterranean, but the swiftly changing conditions in this theatre of operations had made it impossible to use her on clandestine activities after the manner of *Tarana* in the Gibraltar days. She did, however, carry out a few irregular operations from Algiers and, in the following month, she became the pioneer of the Mediterranean Ferry Service. This service was run by ACF for the benefit of the numerous secret organisations then operating, who, owing to the shipping scarcity, were finding it difficult to obtain transport for priority stores and personnel.

After the Sicilian landing, *Prodigal* undertook the trans-shipment of the greater part of the SIS Algiers base to Sicily, afterwards, as the advance continued up Italy, carrying personnel and equipment from the Syracuse base and Algiers to Bari. In addition, during this period she made voyages to Malta and Alexandria.

In January 1944, *Prodigal* became the chief means of supply to the Yugoslav Island of Vis, and during the ensuing eight months carried many hundreds of Allied and partisan troops and many tons of stores between Italy and Komiza. Another of her duties was to escort the small Island convoys, and on many occasions she was called upon to tow the supply LCTs to and from Komiza. She saw action, too, when she was included in the partisan attack on Brac Island and towed a broken down LCT out of range of the defence guns.

In February, another ACF vessel was helping this all important business of supplying the last Allied stronghold in the eastern Adriatic. *Laurana,* an ex-Fiume/Pola ferry boat, had been taken over by SOE the previous month, and found unsuitable. ACF had taken her over, and after a few alterations she was running for SNO Vis. Later she was converted into a hospital ship and ran a regular schedule between Bari and Komiza.

By August the situation in the islands had turned in the Allies' favour. Most of the strategically important islands such as Korcula, Sulta and Mljet, had been captured by joint Allied and partisan efforts and the threat to Vis had been removed. Shipping was available, so *Prodigal* was sent for refit preparatory to playing her part in the Greek campaign.

Laurana was sent to Taranto to be regunned and properly converted, and the responsibility of supplying the Yugoslav islands fell on SOSO(A), in conjunction with the SNO Vis and the local LCI Flotilla. Control of this service eventually devolved on to SOSO (Bari), who was exclusively interested in all things Albanian and Yugoslav.

In June, the available ships for the ferry service were supplemented by the addition of *Tarana*. After a brief stay at Molfetta she was returned to the west coast, and plied between North Africa, Naples, Corsica and Maddalena. She also, after the southern France landing (DRAGOON), transported the personnel and equipment of the interested organisations to France on the second day of the attack.

XXV
SOSO(A) Taranto

The appointment of one of Slocum's DDOD(I) officers as Staff Officer, Special Operations (Adriatic), to the staff of FOTALI was the direct result of the forming of 'private navies' by SOE's MARYLAND and VIGILANT Missions, MI9's 'A' Force and the existence of an SOE Cairo arms supply service to Albania. It was felt by ACF(A) as DDOD(I)'s representatives that, 'to avoid a recurrence of the early troubles both of Gibraltar and North Africa', all clandestine traffic in the Adriatic should once more come under a central control. All ACF (A) operations were submitted to the Admiral at Taranto through SOSO(A) as well, and this officer was suitably placed to forward the views of Captain Tunbridge (whose duty it was to lay down the general policy) to this particular regional control. The 'higher levels' controlling the Adriatic sector at this time were unaware of the many ramifications of clandestine operations and believed them to be merely 'gun-running'. After the full importance of these operations had been explained, first sympathy and then interest arose, and the path was smoothed for future users.

Lt Levy assumed this duty at the end of 1943, and apart from coordinating the Adriatic traffic started a supply and passenger service to the western Greek islands. In most cases Italian vessels were used, sometimes TBDs, often LCIs and LCTs and on occasion Allied destroyers.

Until the middle of June, 'pure' clandestine operations were undertaken by the ACF(A) fishing craft, but, as the nights became shorter and more and more of the agents reported that long voyages in rough weather made them so ill as to be practically useless when finally landed, passages by this means lost favour. MS and MAS Boats had been used by SOE for short voyages up the coast, and occasionally MI9 had been loaned an LCI for one of their mass evacuations. As the Allied front line progressed northwards and gave the navy more advanced ports, the use of fast craft became general, although even then, some of the longer voyages had to be undertaken by the MFVs. Most of these craft were outside the DDOD(I) control, and were loaned merely for operations so their running came under

SOSO(A). A satisfactory liaison had been built up with the Italian navy and their officers were extremely keen and willing to do these operations. As a result, Italian craft were always available for clandestine duties, and, ironically enough, were employed for the whole of the Greek traffic.

During the transitional period, when ACF(A) were changing over from MFVs to fast craft, all Adriatic irregular traffic came under the control of Taranto. Previous to this, steps had been taken by higher levels to abolish the private navies then in existence. A number of MI9 craft were lying idle, and, with this type of shipping at a premium, attention had once again been drawn to the undesirability of private enterprise. The highly irregular sailing of an SOE vessel which took place on the west coast finally brought matters to a head, and instructions were issued by the Commander-in-Chief that all private craft employed on clandestine operations were to be placed under the control of the Senior Officer, ACF. Thus the abolition of this particular branch reduced some of Taranto's worries at the peak of a busy period, but SOSO(A)'s duties were still numerous and can best be explained in detail by the inclusion of his letter replying to DDOD(I)'s request for full particulars of his activities.

From: SOSO (A)

Date: 2nd May 1944

To: DDOD(I), Admiralty.

The following information is submitted as requested. The individuals with whom I have the most contact are:

SOE.......... Lieut Comdr Scott.

'A' Force....... Wing Comdr Dennis.

Major Fillingham.

Major Lefroy.

OSS(Brindisi).. Captain Corvo.

Captain Clementi.

Lieut Dadario.

OSS (Naples}.... Captain Paccata.

Lieut Hollinshead.

ISLD.......... Squadron Ldr. Armitage-Smith.

Major Bruce-Lockhart

SBS...... Lieut Taylor.

Lieut Young

SAS (now rtd.

U.K.)......... Major Power

Force 155......... Greek Section

Major Higgins

Captain Hewer

Albanian Section

Captain Wattrous
Captain Squires
Task Group
80.4........... Lieut Comdr Douglas Fairbanks, USN
Captain Andrews, USN

2. My own procedure, of which you asked for an account, is best described by a hypothetical example:

(a) Major Klandestein of Force 666 arrives in my office and asks if I can arrange for operation INCREDIBLE, by which he would like to land a half ton of stores and 5 agents in Istria, and evacuate three Italians, two White Russians, four Resurgent Abyssinians, and, if there is room, two British General officers with a corresponding number of American nurses. His proposed pinpoint is three miles south of Pola and the date 29th February, and could he have an MS?

(b) I point out that an MS has insufficient range and that he has chosen a pinpoint which, intelligence reports have disclosed, is protected by two minefields, a Radar, 5 M/G posts, a coastal defence battery and a small garrison, so that possibly some other spot might be nicer. I investigate the nearest alternative and propose 5 miles north of Umago. He says this would be all right except that the Generals are not very good at walking; so we eventually compromise on a point 5 miles south of Umago.

(c) The question of craft. Would he be prepared to share an MFV that is already scheduled to land a party in the vicinity? Yes, he would be quite satisfied provided I am not referring to a certain ISLD party. In that case he thinks it inadvisable to mix his White Russians with a couple of Gladstonian Liberals he has heard ISLD are proposing to infiltrate into Montenegro. His objection is accepted and I decide to combine his operation with one for OSS, who are looking forward to inserting a pair of Cypriots into the Chioggia area.

(d) Date. There is too much moon on February 29th. Also OSS could not wait so long. Also I have another submarine operation towards the end of the dark period and would prefer to sail this one towards the beginning, for the Adriatic is a small sea. The Generals, it appears, have a top secret reason for not wishing to be hurried back to the war before St. Valentine's day; but he will communicate with the Field and let me know.

(e) A visit to OSS in Brindisi to secure their concurrence for the proposed operation. They are reluctant to have anything to do with Major Klandestein, with whom they have not been on bowing terms ever since the unfortunate incident of the hatpin and the rubber boat. This rankling reminiscence is assuaged by my admiration for the Californian climate, a disparaging allusion to King George III and a packet of Senior Service cigarettes. The combination is agreed to.

(f) I wait in Brindisi to discuss matters with the Italian Captain (S) whose lunch hour terminates at 1650. We route the submarine together arranging that the Chioggia landing shall be carried out, on the 11th at 2300 and the Istrian operation at midnight the following night, with the intervening hours lying on the bottom in the

Gulf of Venice. Various other matters are brought up. Could the submarines be supplied with 'waste' and an Aldis lamp? And their crews with boots? Italian stocks are at zero. I promise to do what is possible. What about recognition signals? They consider Minor War Vessels are insufficient. I satisfy them with the assurance that that it is all our own submarines carry. And so on.

(g) Back in Taranto, it is now necessary to telephone ISLD in Bari and revise the date allocated for the sailing of the MFV on their Istrian operation which, since no reception committee is involved, is a movable feast. I communicate the new date to Commander Clark.

(h) A further visit from Major Klandestein. He has been in touch with the Field who are satisfied with the ante-dating of the operation as the Generals have decided not to come out this month in any case. Also we are to take off three American nurses instead of five.

(i) Signals between ship and shore are arranged. It is confirmed also that Major K. will supply rubber boats and an accompanying officer.

(j) Details of operation are signalled to Algiers and London and now appear on my Daily State.

(k) A visit from the Italian Captain (S). We arrange a suitable time and place for (a) loading stores and dinghies and (b) embarkation of personnel. I advise Klandestein accordingly. Captain (S) is informed that I have been successful over his 'waste' but have drawn a blank in the matter of boots. He is also told the ship-to-shore signal arrangements.

(l) Having laid out the course and fixed the points, times and dates of submersion, I issue a Warning Signal communicating these details to the relevant Air Force Groups and NOICs, CFW, C-in-C Mediterranean, and such destroyers and other craft as Operations may designate. I make out the Sailing Orders for the Admiral's signature, to be passed on to the Italian Minister of Marine and O.C. submarine.

(m) A few hours before sailing, an enemy submarine is reported to have been seen 30 miles west of Dubrovnik. A hunt is hurriedly planned which, of course, involves postponement for the Special Operation. I telephone Brindisi Operations and the Italian Ministry, confirm by signal and instruct Klandestein to advise the Field. This postponement perhaps has to be repeated daily for three or four days. The whole jigsaw of the Special Operations programme has therefore inevitably to be overhauled, dates revised, organisations consulted afresh in Bari, Brindisi, Monopoli, Mola and Molfetta, and the NOICs from whose ports sailings had been planned, duly advised of the new arrangements. These in turn will probably need to be modified again later owing to a bad spell of weather. (Actually a submarine postponement usually involves a little less general dislocation than in the case of other craft.)

(n) The hunt is eventually called off. The submarine can sail and, if I can arrange other business at the same time to make the trip worth while, I go across to Brindisi to see her off.

(o) I advise FBSO that on February 15th at 0800 an Allied submarine is expected back with a miscellany of passengers some of whom he will have to arrange to have met by Field Security Police for purposes of interrogation. This course does not apply to vouched-for agents or British escapees.

(p) A signal from the submarine a few days later asks approval to exceed the 24 hours' grace allowed her in sailing orders as weather has been too bad to effect, the second landing. It is approved and three days later she returns successful.

(q) The result of the operation is signalled to London and Algiers and telephoned to Major Klandestein who is duly promoted to Lieut. Colonel.

(r) A copy of the Commanding Officer's report is received, translated and included as an appendix in my monthly summary of Special Operations for C in C Mediterranean.

3. On re-reading this account, it appears, even to me, to err on the side of extravagance but, in fact, it contains no incident that has not actually happened and, of course, omits many that have. It is a fairly routine example of the history of an operation from my end of it, but, apart from routine, naturally a great number of tributary questions continually arise to be dealt with, which are really too miscellaneous to summarise. This, however, will probably give you the picture you want in, I hope, not too irregular a manner.

The Taranto activities continued until, coincident with the expulsion of the enemy from Greece, the coasts of Albania and Yugoslavia, operations became more and more offensive in nature, until, by the end of October, SOSO(A) was interested, chiefly, in offensive patrols. In fact, by November, the situation in the southern Adriatic was that enemy activity consisted of sporadic E-boat sorties designed to harry our shipping supplying the Allied liberation armies operating in the Balkans. It was against one of these sorties that Lt Levy, acting as Conducting Officer for a division of MAS boats, was severely wounded during a sharp engagement.

When fit to travel, Lt Levy was returned to UK, his place being taken by Lt P.C.Sylvester-Bradley, RNVR. By December 1944, no DDOD(I) representative was required on FOTALI's staff, all clandestine operations in the Adriatic being mounted from Ancona. The post of SOSO(A) was therefore redundant, and another chapter in the history of clandestine operations in this theatre was concluded.

XXVI
A Pyrrhic Victory

The 'highly irregular sailing' which led to the abolition of the 'private navies' was a piece of ill-judged private enterprise by John Newton, the erstwhile small-time smuggler from Guernsey. Readers of the beginning of this story will have encountered him as the man whose help Lord Portsea and the Channel Islands Emergency Committee sought when faced with imminent German occupation in June 1940. Ian Fleming, personal assistant to Admiral Godfrey, Director of Naval Intelligence, introduced him to Holdsworth and he was the first recruit for SOE's Helford Flotilla. His intimate knowledge of the Casquets Lighthouse enabled Gus March-Phillips to capture the German lighthouse crew without firing a shot: Newton had been promoted Skipper-Lt and decorated. He had been a star performer in BALACLAVA's shore parties, though Croft quite rightly saw him as someone who needed firm control. That control lapsed when Croft was parachuted into France and MASSINGHAM failed to provide the required supervision when Newton was sent to take over a schooner in western Sicily that they wanted for their move forward after the DRAGOON landings in Provence. The schooner, the *Marietta Madre,* was carrying a cargo of Marsala wine and Newton sailed for Algiers with at least part of that cargo aboard. He compounded this picaresque misdemeanour by trying to sell arms to the Communists when he reached France: he was sent home and discharged from the Service. But Christopher Woods, the official historian of SOE in Italy, points out that ACF(A)'s triumph was of little practical consequence, as MARYLAND's sea operations in the Adriatic, like those on the west coast of Italy, had died a natural death during the summer of 1944. As far as concerned the proper main purposes of SOE sea operations, the last actual 'body' operation was AINTREE in mid-March and stores operations by sea to Italy, though planned and actually attempted, were never successful: the idea was abandoned altogether in favour of air supply by the end of April 1944.

On 10 April, Holdsworth told Admiral Taylor, SOE's most senior Naval Officer in their Baker Street headquarters, that, 'Just for the present MAKYLAND's Naval Section has very few commitments owing to the fact that the coasts to which we have been working are now very heavily guarded. It will be necessary for things to quieten down a little before the good work can proceed.' Holdsworth no doubt still hoped at that stage there would still be 'good work' for his Naval Section to do in the Adriatic, but two attempts later in the month to deliver stores by sea to the MARCASITE mission in the Marche (Operation ABERGELE), which had been planned since February, failed mainly because of enemy activity on and off-shore. No further attempts to carry out this or any other 'body'-, or store-landing operations seem to have been made after this date. The only subsequent MARYLAND sea operations in the Adriatic (ANON in May and LEYTON in July) were carried out at the request of the army or the navy.

It was much the same on the west coast: the last successful BALACLAVA operations to Italy for MARYLAND were carried out in March. Thereafter, only one other infiltration operation for MARYLAND (ASHWATER in May) was mounted from Corsica and, that proving unsuccessful, the party concerned was parachuted in instead.

The fact is that RAF facilities were now available and, after the early operations on both coasts to the areas readily accessible from the sea, SOE found it generally more convenient to infiltrate both bodies and stores direct to their destinations by air to British Liaison Officers in the mountains further north. Moreover, as the Allied armies advanced in the summer, the amount of coastline available for landings by sea diminished and consequently became more intensively defended by the enemy. In this respect, MARYLAND's needs differed from those of 'A' Force, for whom evacuation of evaders and escapers continued to be a prime necessity.

From early 1944, MARYLAND also began to come under increasing pressure to release bodies and craft for service in the Far East. Thus the return in the summer of 1944 of *Mutin,* and the withdrawal of *Eduardo,* plus their crews. Hilary Scott, too, went home at the beginning of August 1944. The remaining naval officers in MARYLAND were incorporated in SOE's plans for what was termed 'RANKIN conditions', i.e. parachuting in British officers to key centres in the event of German surrender or withdrawal. Sub-Lt Robert Clark, for example, was parachuted into snow-covered mountainous terrain and taken prisoner of war. My brother was fortunate enough to be ill when this took place or he would probably have suffered a similar fate. It was just as well that the RANKIN plan never had to be implemented on any wider scale.

XXVII
LEGHORN 1944: The ACF's Last Phase

In November 1944, MI9, anticipating requirements for the seaborne evacuation of escaped prisoners of war from the south coast of France between Nice and Genoa, discussed with SOACF the possibility of setting up a small ACF base at Leghorn, Italy, to implement this requirement. The naval authorities agreed to this proposal and in December 1944 Lt Comdr D.T.MacCallum, DSC, RNR, established himself as the ACF representative at Leghorn on the staff of SOIS (Senior Officer Inshore Squadron), assisted by Lt P.C.Sylvester-Bradley, RNVR.

The flotilla based on Leghorn consisted of the Coastal Force craft MGB 177 (one of the Higgins PT craft) and the American-manned ex-Air-Sea Rescue P 568 and P 584.

During the base's brief existence, operations were carried out mainly for SOE, the anticipated evacuation operations for MI9 having failed to materialise. The only noteworthy operation was Operation TOAST for SOE, the object of which was to sink the aircraft carrier AQUILA, a prospective blockship lying in Genoa harbour. SOE intended to employ San Marco swimmers as limpeteers. The operation was successfully carried out by MGB 177, acting as pilot, and the Italian MS 74, each towing one MTS/M (Mobile Transport Submarine) to a position five miles off Genoa harbour. The MTS/Ms then towed SOE Chariots to within one mile of the harbour, which was entered without opposition. The limpets were attached to the aircraft carrier and the Chariots left to rejoin the main force outside the harbour, still without encountering any enemy opposition.

No further operations were envisaged before the end of April 1945 and the Leghorn base was consequently closed. In May 1945, the ACF came to an end, the main Naples office closing down on 24th May. The Coastal Forces craft were sailed to Malta to be incorporated in the Mediterranean Coastal Force organisation; HM Trawler *Tarana* returned to the UK, to be paid off and returned to her original French owners. ACF personnel also returned to the UK, it being anticipated at that time that they would all be required for further Special Service with DDOD(I) in the Far East.

XXVIII
Clandestine Sea Operations to and from Nice

Though the requirement for seaborne evacuation of escaped Allied prisoners of war did not materialise between Nice and Genoa on the scale anticipated by MI9, and it proved a dangerous part of the front for ACF(A) operations, there was considerable clandestine activity by sea around Nice in the final phase of the war: with help and encouragement from SOE, OSS and the French clandestine services, Italian local fishermen rowed round the end of the lines. I owe the following account of this successful local enterprise to Christopher Woods, who served No. 1 Special Force in the field, became the official custodian of the SOE archives and, finally, the official historian of SOE in Italy. Though his history is still not in print, he has been unstintingly generous in making the results of his researches available to me in working on the Italian section of this book.

At the end of September 1944, Capt. Michael Lees, an SOE officer with a British Mission in south-west Piedmont, left to cross the border into southern France, in order to return to base in southern Italy, leading a party which included (as well as two Italian delegates, four escaped British POWs and three evading US aircrew), a Canadian war correspondent (Capt. Paul Morton) and a South African war artist (Capt. Geoffrey Long) who had been parachuted in by SOE with Lees to observe and record scenes of partisan life in nothern Italy.

Having arrived at Pigna in Liguria, then occupied by partisans under the local command of LEO (Stefano Carabalona) the party split up, Lees deciding to press straight on with four others to cross into Allied lines over the border with France on foot. This they accomplished, arriving on 2 October and reporting to a US Brigade HQ in Menton, after which they were driven to Nice, where Major Havard Gunn, an SOE liaison officer from the French Section in North Africa (SPOC) arranged for their onward passage by air the next day to southern Italy.

Of those left behind at Pigna, some decided to emulate Lees and follow a route through the mountains, but Morton and Long (with two others, including one of the US airmen) elected to try an alternative route suggested by LEO—to cross into France by sea from Ventimiglia. LEO made the necessary arrangements and so the four duly landed at Monte Carlo a week later in the early hours of 9 October, having been rowed out from Ventimiglia by two Italian fishermen, Giulio Pedretti and Pasquale Corradi, in a 14 foot rowing boat owned by the latter's father.

From Monte Carlo, after checking by the FFI garrison, they were driven to Nice next morning (10 October) and reported to Major Gunn. Morton and Long submitted to G-2 HQ ABTF, in addition to their observations of German dispositions on the Italian side of the lines, details and impressions of Italian partisan formations in the rear area and their capacity to harry the enemy. They mentioned in their report the desire of LEO to have contact with the Allied military command and to receive supplies of arms, and included a suggestion that the two fishermen from Ventimiglia who had rowed them out might be used to take back an Allied Liaison Officer with radio operator to work with LEO at Pigna. The two fishermen, who themselves provided valuable information to the Photographic Interpretation Section of the US HQ, were then handed over by Gunn to Capt. Jones of OSS with testimonials to their willingness and skill.

It was no doubt largely on the strength of the reports which Lees, and Morton and Long brought back that SOE HQ in Monopoli (No. 1 Special Force) decided towards the end of October to re-route a British Liaison Mission for western Liguria—which had been standing by for a month to go in by air via another established Mission in Piedmont but had been held up by a combination of bad weather and non-availability of aircraft—and to infiltrate it instead direct from southern France, where they were simultaneously in the process of establishing a unit (20 Detachment) in Nice (under Sqn Ldr Betts). Around the same time, a similar advanced base was set up in Grenoble (Detachment 25) to support operations in the more northerly area.

1SF's primary purpose in setting up these two Detachments was to find alternative ways of infiltrating bodies and supplies into north-western Italy to help alleviate the increasing problem of reaching these areas from the only currently available air bases in southern Italy (or North Africa). This was due partly to adverse weather conditions but also to severe restrictions on the availability of aircraft for this purpose, owing partly to heavy losses of planes and trained crews in operations over Poland in August and September and partly to imposed rationing in favour of other military requirements when 15 Army Group dictated a policy of maximum concentration on north-eastern Italy in support of its military drive on that axis to the exclusion of north-western Italy.

The problem of north-western Italy had become particularly acute for 1SF on account of its RANKIN commitment in that area. This was, paradoxically, a byproduct of the same military imperative of maximum support in north-eastern Italy for OLIVE, the offensive launched towards the end of August, in view of the expectation that this would force a German withdrawal from north-western Italy, creating a military/administrative vacuum in that area which the British Army would not have troops immediately available to fill.

Hence the requirement for 1SF to have a sufficient spread of Missions already there on the ground in liaison with the local partisan formations and Committees of National Liberation, so as to ease any difficulties in the transition to Allied military government.

For 20 Detachment this spelt primarily help towards the establishment of a Mission in the westernmost province of Liguria with its provincial capital at Imperia. In September 1944, 1SF assembled a Mission (CLARION) for this purpose. It was headed by Major Duncan Campbell with Capt. Robert Bentley (a fluent Italian-speaker, born and educated in Cairo and recently posted to 1SF from Civil Affairs in Tripolitania) as his second-in-command. It also contained a para-naval component in the shape of Sub-Lt Robert Clark, Petty Officer Cauvain and Telegraphist Banks. These three were all volunteers from the lately disbanded Para-naval Section of 1SF and had no doubt been allotted to this Mission, because its southern boundary would lie along the Ligurian coast with possibilities for sea supply operations.

The Mission was originally scheduled to be dropped to the nearest 1SF British Mission already in the field (FLAP) headed by Major Temple (Neville Darewski), who was operating in the southern part of Piedmont. But a month later, CLARION was still, for reasons cited above, awaiting infiltration. It was then decided, with the establishment of Detachment 20 in Nice, to withdraw Capt. Bentley from the main body of Mission CLARION and send him (with his own radio operator) to Nice to try his luck at speedier infiltration from there to Liguria to act as advance party for the main body of CLARION, which it was still intended to drop in southern Piedmont to FLAP. A revised Operation Instruction issued on 30 October to Bentley specifically directed him on arrival in Nice 'to contact Capt. Jones of OSS or Col Blythe of the ABTF and ask to be put in touch with the two fishermen who had come out with Capt. Long; and to discuss with them and Allied naval authorities the possibility of a sea landing at Ventimiglia or elsewhere on the Ligurian coast'.

Whether Capt. Bentley carried out this particular recommendation is unknown but, for whatever reason, he seems to have preferred, after his arrival in Nice, and presumably in conjunction with Betts, to attempt infiltration of his mission by land rather than sea. It was not until mid-December, after he had made at least one unsuccessful attempt to cross the mountains in adverse weather conditions, that he turned to planning entry by sea.

This coincided with the arrival from Italy by sea of the very LEO who had arranged the exfiltration of Morton and Long. Having apparently somehow got wind of Capt. Bentley's Mission, he had decided to go himself to France to help with the arrangements for its infiltration. His arrival with a large group, including four women, was followed a few days later by that, also by sea, of another partisan emissary, Dott Kahnemann (alias NUCCIA). Bentley saw both of them (the LEO courtesy of OSS) and with their advice and aid finally organised the infiltration of his Mission (CHIMPANZEE or SAKI) by sea on the night of 7/8 January 1945. This operation was carried out in a Chris-craft by Lt Robin Richards and a crew of two British seamen, who constituted the para-naval section of 20 Detachment, and apparently with the participation of Giulio Pedretti, presumably on loan from OSS for the occasion (Operation DAYLIGHT/CORINTH).

On 18 January, 20 Detachment recorded the arrival of a 'PT boat' (presumably MGB 179, the ex-PT boat decommissioned by the US Navy, transferred to the Royal Navy and operated by the ACF base at Livorno) to carry out a combined landing and pick-up operation for OSS and IS9. Bentley was informed and told that it would be landing 1800lb of stores as well as one agent. No doubt it was the arrival of this craft with a longer range than anything hitherto available locally that prompted 20 Detachment to raise with Bentley the possibility of sending in a three-man Italian Mission (HERRIN) to operate under his control in the Alassio area. This proposal coincided with a move by Bentley, who had attached his Mission to CURTO's HQ (now redesignated I Ligurian Zone, covering the partisan forces in Imperia province recently reorganised into two divisions: the 2nd Div. F. Cascione in the West and the 6th Div. S.Bonfante in the East). This move took him and Zone HQ further east to a position from which he was able to organise a new landing point (pinpoint DESPERADO) in the vicinity of Arma di Taggia.

A first operation using the 'PT boat' to pinpoint DESPERADO to land 1,8001b of stores plus (if MARYLAND's authority was received in time) the HERRIN party was planned for the night of 5 February but then postponed to the 6th (by which time Bentley had reported that he would also have two British officers and two American pilots standing by for evacuation). The operation, however, was unsuccessful, the naval party reporting that they had seen no signals from the reception party and that the boat had been illuminated by searchlights and fired on from the East. Asked for his account, Bentley replied that reception had been there flashing their signals, and that 'fireworks' had been observed but coming from west of the pinpoint. Bentley then shifted the landing point slightly to pinpoint PIPPO and called for a repeat operation on the night of the 8th. This, however, was cancelled due to engine trouble, and a mistral prevented another attempt the following night. But on the night of the 11th a second sortie to pinpoint PIPPO (to land stores only) was made but without success when a heavy swell caused the 'PT boat' to turn back. The operation was laid on again for the night of the 12th (this time including the HERRIN party) but once more the naval party reported having been lit by searchlight and shelled (as before, from the east). Bentley reported that the reception had waited till 0210 and had once more heard firing but (as before) from the west, an assertion which, when queried, he repeated the following day.

On 14 February, 20 Detachment discussed with Lt Cdr McCullum, visiting CO of the ACF Base at Livorno, how the two sea operations could have failed in the same manner. McCullum accepted that it was impossible that the reception party could have been wrong about their position and improbable that they would have been wrong about the direction from which the firing came. On the other hand, it seemed equally unlikely that the boat could have made such a considerable mistake as to its position despite its radar equipment. McCullum felt that in any case this sector of the coast must now be considered sufficiently alerted to rule out any further attempt for the rest of the non-moon period.

On the same day the wider question as to whether in the light of this experience further sea operations of any sort would be possible in the present dark period or whether indeed the whole idea of sea operations must be ruled out for the future was referred to Lt-Col. Hanson, the senior SOE coordinating officer for the two 1SF Detachments in France: 20 Detachment was concerned because they had offered Bentley on the 13th the alternative of short-range small boat operations, to pinpoints BANDITO or BRIGANTE. After consulting Lt Cdr McCullum Hanson ruled: (a) that no more operations should be planned for the present non-moon period due to the state of alert; but (b) that the wider aspect of the future of sea operations in general should be referred to Capt. Tunbridge, the senior officer of ACF.

No early reply seems to have been received on this wider question, for on 26 February 20 Detachment was telling Bentley that they were still hopeful of ‘PT operations’ from 6 March (presumably, the start of the next no-moon period) and they were particularly anxious to infiltrate Bartali, the leader of HERRIN. But two days later, the order came from Livorno for MGB to return there forthwith. To Lt Richards’s enquiry about whether this meant that no further PT boat operations could be considered on the coast of western Liguria, the reply came on 1 March that Capt. Tunbridge would not operate on this alerted part of the coast. 20 Detachment, however, concluded that this did not rule out sea operations altogether, only long-range operations requiring the use of craft from ACF. In any case, at this time Bentley was coming under heavy enemy pressure which compelled him to withdraw with Zone HQ to positions further from the coast and to turn his thoughts more towards the possibility of supply by air.

This, however, did not prevent him on 5 March from putting up a plan for a sea rendezvous off Bordighera between a local fishing vessel and a boat from 20 Detachment to take off his Allied escapers and evaders (now numbering five) and to transload a small quantity of stores including some much-needed wireless equipment. The 20 Detachment’s immediate response was to dismiss this plan as impracticable and to urge Bentley to stay clear of the coast and forget about sea operations but to get his escapers and evaders rowed out by fishermen, whom IS9 would recompense. This, however, was not the end of the matter, for during the night of the 7th a certain RENZO and FRANCESCO arrived from Bordighera (in a rowing boat bringing out two badly blown OSS agents), claiming instructions from Bentley to arrange a sea reception for the 10th. Their story was that this had now become practicable once more, since the landing area was now guarded by an Italian Bersaglieri post, who had been persuaded by bribery to collaborate with the partisans. With Bentley having confirmed the reliability of RENZO and the feasibility of the project, 20 Detachment decided to attempt the operation planned for the 10th but had to cancel it due to a heavy sea. It was not rescheduled for a following night as RENZO maintained that his arrangement had been limited to the one night only and he could not guarantee reception signals on subsequent nights. However, only a few nights later (the 15th), the five Allied escapers arrived, duly rowed out from RENZO's beach and with the news that reception had been laid on after the 10th for the following two nights.

RENZO now proposed a new arrangement whereby reception could be alerted to stand by. It involved the firing from Cap Martin of two rockets so as to be visible from the Bordighera area, and this was duly laid on with the French commander at Menton. On the 17th a boat sailed from Villefranche with RENZO and two others, taking three packages of arms and ammunition for the partisans, but no rockets went up, so there was no reception and the boat returned. The operation was repeated two nights later (the 19th). This time the French company was presented with two white mortar parachute flares and instructed to fire them at 10p.m. Still there was no sign of reception but the landing was made just the same and one hour later an OK signal was received from the shore. Bentley's radio was off the air at the time but, when it came up again on the 23rd, he confirmed the arrival of RENZO and thanked them for the stores.

Meanwhile, on 21 March, as arranged with RENZO before he left, the boat had gone out again, this time to attempt the sea rendezvous off Villacrosia. No contact was made, though a light was seen, but it receded too fast for the motor boat, which was being rowed at the time for silence, to catch up with it. The next night (22nd) RENZO came out again with three others, rowing a rubber dinghy which he had kept for the purpose. He brought news of Bentley, from whom little had been heard for the past fortnight, and reported that the stores taken in had reached Divisional HQ. As already noted, radio contact with Bentley was resumed on the 23rd.

Before radio contact with Bentley had lapsed, he had been asked on the 5th whether a Liaison Officer and WTO could be sent in to him to work with the 6th Bonfante Div. He replied that Bartali (of HERRIN) would do, and on the 8th 20 Detachment sought HQ 1SF's permission to infiltrate him and his WTO for this purpose 'by local enterprise', by which no doubt they meant the means already used with RENZO. HQ 1SF signalled approval on the 12th but the matter was not proceeded with while Bentley was off the air.

On the 26th, radio contact having been restored, Bentley was asked whether he still needed HERRIN with WT for intercom with 6 Div. On 2 April he suggested that HERRIN be sent in overland but 20 Detachment believed the route proposed now blocked and impracticable. On the 5th Bentley passed a warning from the CLN San Remo that the Villacrosia beach was watched by the SS, so HERRIN should not be landed there. This warning was, however, discounted by 20 Detachment in the light of their successful experiences with RENZO. Indeed, only the previous night (the 4th) they had successfully landed on this beach two trained Italian sabotage instructors with two others (specially briefed members apparently of RENZO's reception team). For this operation 20 Detachment recorded the use of a French Sea Rescue boat.

In view of this success, 20 Detachment determined to proceed with plans to land the HERRIN party, now reduced from three to two (Bartali and his WTO) and re-designated SIAMANG II, on this beach, provided the correct beach signals were received. A first immediate attempt was aborted when the boat encountered en route two enemy MAS craft seemingly attempting a similar operation on Cap Martin. The boat returned at once and the information was phoned straight through to the 2ème Bureau of the French Division in the coastal area. Further attempts were frustrated by weather conditions until the night of the 11th when Bartali and his WTO (plus a two-man French Mission and one more member of RENZO's reception team) were all successfully landed on the beach at Villacrosia.

The following night (12th) 20 Detachment despatched its penultimate sea operation: to land RENZO once again with two more sabotage instructors. But the boat returned having found no reception. This operation was not repeated but on the 13th 20 Detachment asked Bentley on RENZO's behalf if the CLN San Remo would object to his reception team's receiving a French DGER Mission with a tactical intelligence brief. Bentley asked in return that the French boat should pick up a report which he was sending down to the Bordighera reception committee, and suggested that this could start a regular mail service which might even be extended to the delivery of stores. But none of this could be carried through as various circumstances prevented the operation being successfully mounted before the end of the no-moon period: on the 15th the French boat was fired on from the shore at the pinpoint: two nights later its radar screen picked up a MAS craft lurking in the Bordighera area; and on the last night of the dark period heavy seas precluded any sortie.

This still was not quite the end of sea operations, as a DGER party (led by a French officer already known to Bentley and who would contact him on arrival) was landed at San Remo on the night of 25/26 April, the eve of liberation.'

So much from the SOE side of the fence. What follows is drawn from Italian sources, notably a contribution by Francesco Biga to the records of a conference held in Genoa in 1989 and published under the general title *Resistance in Liguria and the Allies*. Biga's piece is entitled 'Ligurian Resistance and its contacts with Resistance and the Allies in Provence (1943–1945)', and includes sections on 'Mission CORSARO of OSS' and on 'Mission CHIMPANZEE of SOE'. The main sources quoted are a longer work by the same author (which Woods had not seen) and an unpublished personal record by Giulio Pedretti (CORSARO).

Giulio Pedretti (CORSARO) and Pasquale Corradi (PASCALIN), having reached (on 9 October) the port of Monte Carlo with their four passengers, were taken to the Hotel Excelsior, where, after interrogation by a Scottish Major (Gunn), they were fed and reclothed with uniforms from a military store. They were accommodated for a while in Rue Victor Hugo in Nice and were debriefed by the 'Operations Office of the American HQ' on their personal backgrounds and activities and on the partisan situation in the province of Imperia. They were then recruited into the US OSS organisation in Nice comprising some 25 Italians. From them OSS formed Mission CORSARO (later known as LEO after the partisan leader who came to play a leading role in it), whose tasks were to maintain liaison between the Allied HQ and partisan HQs in the area Ventimiglia-Limone-Nava-Oneglia-Albenga, to collect and transmit military intelligence and to help Allied missions in transit. The two fishermen went sent back to Ventimiglia with two radios and began their work there enlisting various collaborators (including Alpini Major Raimondo and his son) to contact partisan formations and procure military intelligence.

Following the German occupation of Pigna on 8 October and the subsequent withdrawal further north of partisan brigades I and V on 17–18 October, LEO (Stefano Carabalona), having learnt of the designation by the Allies of British Capt. Robert Bentley (Bob) to establish a liaison mission with the HQ of Garibaldi Division 'F Cascione' (the formation on which he depended), arranged to go personally to France to make the necessary arrangements for the arrival of this mission. On the night of 10 December he (along with at least seven others, among them Luciano Mannini (ROSINA), and members of their families including four women) were brought out by Pedretti in a large rowboat (the availability of which at Ventimiglia had been noted earlier by Capt. Long) from Vallecrosia to Villefranche. There on arrival they were housed in the Villa Petit Rocher at St Jean Cap Ferrat. Their arrival was followed only a few nights later by that of another partisan Dott Kahneman (NUCCIA), bringing with him a plan of German coastal defences.

On 15 December, LEO joined OSS and contacted Capt. Bentley, while Pedretti (under the new name of CARONTE replacing CORSARO) was given command of four motor boats in the bay of Villefranche by the Villa Rochet, which became an Allied sabotage and commando training school.

In mid-January 1945, Stefano Carabalona was sent back to Italy on an OSS Mission with Luciano Mannini. After making contact with the CLN at Bordighera he established himself in the Vallecrosia area to collect information on German forces in the frontier zone, which, using a young courier named Irene, he sent for transmission to a radio operator working in San Remo. Then Irene and the radio operator became blown and the Germans discovered where Carabalona and Mannini were living. Two agents came to arrest them there and a firefight ensued in which all four seem to have been wounded, Carabalona seriously, but he and Mannini succeeded in escaping to Bordighera. Eventually, on 6 March, Carabalona and Mannini were evacuated from Vallecrosia by Pedretti together with Renzo Rossi, who had sheltered Carabalona for three weeks in Bordighera, and a certain Gianni. On their arrival, Carabalona was transferred to hospital and Renzo Rossi took over his position with OSS.

Renzo Rossi made four trips to France by sea, finally returning to Italy on the night of 27 April with two French lieutenants, landed at San Remo by Pedretti.

Pedretti worked in practice for three Allied Missions (American, British and French), which operated independently, and altogether made 27 crossings between Italy and France. These included a number of deliveries of arms and supplies for the partisans, for instance on 10, 11 (which included the infiltration for 20 Detachment to Bentley of a two-man Italian sub-mission) and 12 April, followed by seven more trips later in the month. There was also an occasion in mid-March, when he brought out five Allied officers.

Embarcations from Vallecrosia were arranged by an especially trained group numbering up to twenty under the command of Renzo Rossi of Bordighera. RENZO also figures in SOE documents of 20 Detachment relating to the activities of Mission CHIMPANZEE. The earliest mention is that of his arrival by boat from Bordighera during the night of 7/8 March with LEO and ROSINA (described as 'two OSS agents who had to return to France because completely blown in Ventimiglia-Bordighera district'). RENZO claimed to have come with instructions from Bentley to organise a supply of arms to be delivered by sea three nights later for reception under special arrangements he had laid on at a landing point at Vallecrosia which 20 Detachment and Bentley had been warned in mid-February (evidently by OSS) to discontinue because 'Irene (the OSS courier) had turned traitor'. Later they had been told that 'a local OSS agent named Gino had been killed while in possession of a notebook with names of agents and safe houses in the Bordighera area' and this was taken to explain the 'treachery' of Irene. After Bentley had vouched for RENZO as 'a good chap', 20 Detachment decided to go ahead with the proposed stores delivery on the 10th but it had to be cancelled due to rough seas. It was, however, carried out later.

Thereafter, RENZO is mentioned as playing a part in most, if not all, further deliveries by sea to CHIMPANZEE, some of which are recorded as having been carried out using craft provided by a French service.

Epilogue

Immediately after the fall of France, the Admiralty's reluctance to appoint a serving officer to take charge of clandestine sea transport for the undercover agencies forced SIS and SOE to improvise in difficult circumstances. This worked well enough in the cases of Norway and Greece, where the sea lines required by both organisations could be started up with minimal demands on scarce British naval resources, but operations to the north coast of France and the Low Countries could not. Friction developed between SIS and SOE—the junior service, whose urgent needs could not be met.

The trouble was compounded by the Admiralty's initial refusal to allocate high-speed craft to the job on a permanent basis. This meant that operations had to be carried out by vessels borrowed from Coastal Forces, which could not be fitted with such specialist navigational equipment as was available and whose crews could not be trained to land boats on open beaches. The success rate was therefore low: there was, in fact, no successful operation by highspeed craft to the north coast of France between 2 August 1940 and September 1941. This was particularly serious for SOE, which was under political pressure to 'set Europe ablaze' and had fewer alternative means of transport than SIS.

The RAF, by creating the Special Duties Squadrons, avoided such a direct conflict of interest between SIS and SOE, but when Slocum, while remaining head of SIS's Operations Section, became the Admiralty's controller of all irregular operations to the north and west coast of France he was placed in a difficult position: he admitted at the end of the war that he never wholly gained SOE's confidence.

Though SOE maintained autonomous contact by sea with Norway, and on a larger scale than SIS, Slocum came by stages to control all clandestine operations by surface craft to the rest of German-held western Europe as far east as the Adriatic. As we have seen, SIS's attempt to bring the flotillas of local craft serving Greece under his authority as DDOD(I) foundered because of opposition by GHQ Middle East. At the end of the war, he was preparing to send operational high-speed craft and a small depot ship to the Far East. He reckoned in 1946 that his Section under its various guises had landed 1,000 agents in enemy-occupied territory and extracted 3,500 agents and Allied evaders and escapers in the course of 1,150 operations involving 1,500 voyages, 75 per cent of which were successful. It was an impressive achievement, and attained in the face of enormous obstacles.

For all that, clandestine sea transport to France and French North Africa was never in practice controlled by any single authority. The present record has thus had to be compiled from a variety of sources.

In the period between the armistice of June 1940 and the spring of 1941, two Sections of SIS and also de Gaulle's Deuxième Bureau all operated more or less independently on the north and west coasts of France and SOE prepared to do likewise. Then, by the time Slocum's Section had emerged from the scrum as the controlling agency for all operations in the Narrow Seas, the Poles had begun to conduct felucca operations independently from Gibraltar to Morocco and western Algeria.

The creation of the Coast Watching Flotilla in spring 1942 extended Slocum's authority to clandestine operations by surface craft in the western Mediterranean and opened up a remarkable run of operations to the south coast of France, mainly by the Polish feluccas; but operations by submarines from Gibraltar, such as those that landed General Mark Clark in Algeria and picked up General Giraud from France, were not under the operational control of the CWF.

After the TORCH landings in North Africa the situation became more complex: both the US Office of Strategic Services and Giraud's Service de Renseignements began to operate from Algiers to Corsica and to France and a phase began in which submarine operations predominated. Slocum's African Coastal Flotilla had little, if any, involvement in missions for the Allied clandestine services by British or French submarines based on Algiers.

Between June 1940 and the liberation of 1944 there were in all 77 successful or partly successful contacts with France by sea from bases in the United Kingdom. Details of these are set out in Appendix A. Though figures are in some cases approximate, it seems that 88 individuals were landed and 218 embarked.

The number of relevant operations in the western Mediterranean was higher, though the tactical character of some of the sea transport during the Tunisian and Corsican campaigns makes precise reckoning difficult. There were certainly over 100 successful operations to French territory in this theatre, in the course of which 211 persons were landed and 665 evacuated.

Except in the case of Corsica, the quantities of warlike stores carried were insignificant by comparison with the 10,485 tons delivered to France by air. Though SOE exacerbated its relations with SIS by its insistence in 1941 and 1942 on planning for deliveries of arms and explosives by sea, it was driven to do so because Dalton had oversold the immediately available potential of the French Resistance and because it was still not known whether aircraft would be available. By 1944, SOE's Country Sections had come to think exclusively in terms of parachute deliveries for the supply of stores and the ships at Helford that had been fitted out for the job were never used.

Notwithstanding the large number of Lysander pick-up operations, particularly in 1943, sea transport remained important throughout as a means of collecting qualitatively important intelligence, too bulky to be transmitted by W/T. Even in 1943, runs of bad weather over northern France frequently made pick-up operations impossible for weeks at a time. Rémy's 'Confrérie Notre Dame', the most productive and long-lasting of all the intelligence networks in France, remained more dependent on its monthly collection of mail by sea than on the Lysander pick-up operations that were supposed to alternate with it. The nine GLOVER operations carried out in 1944 by the 15th MGB Flotilla continued to deliver vitally important intelligence from all over the northern half of France to SIS right up to the liberation of Brittany.

For SOE, submarine operations to Corsica were of great importance and Buckmaster's F Section became dependent on clandestine sea transport to Brittany at a critical period before D-Day OVERLORD: they had been obliged to close down Gilbert Déricourt's far too extensive Lysander operations because of well-founded suspicions that he was a double agent.

For the evacuation of groups of substantial size, sea transport had no competitor. Though by August 1944, Dakota aircraft were being landed clandestinely in southern France, this was exceptional: the Special Duties Squadrons would never have been able to tackle the Polish evacuation problem or the large numbers of evaders and escapers collected by MI9's PAT and SHELBURNE escape lines.

Just when Slocum seemed to have made good his case for permanently allocating suitable high-speed craft for operations to the north coast of Brittany, bad luck intervened. MGB 314, the first vessel to achieve a run of successful expeditions in this area, was lost at Saint-Nazaire; then MGB 501, first of the ex-Turkish gunboats allocated to NID(C), was sunk by misadventure only weeks after delivery. Finally, four of the ex-Turkish gunboat hulls that Slocum had expected to take over were reallocated to the Ministry of Economic Warfare and an inexplicable 12 months elapsed in bringing MGB 503, the first diesel-engined gunboat of this class, into operational service. In November 1943, while German diesel-engined E-boats capable of 35 knots ranged as far west as the Scillies, DDOD(I) was still largely dependent on that old and tired workhorse MGB 318, capable of only half that speed.

In the western Mediterranean Captain Fawkes was outstandingly helpful in making submarines available to the clandestine services in 1943. The chance availability of French submarines after the TORCH landings in North Africa allowed what Slocum considered the best of all forms of clandestine sea transport to be extensively used. However, after September 1943 the progress of the Italian campaign and the availability of Corsica as a base called for the use of highspeed craft. Admiral Cunningham's initial refusal to release a single British or American vessel of this type caused a deadlock, which was broken only when Italian MAS boats fortuitously became available after the Italian armistice. The cooperation of Captain Dickinson was invaluable in this and Cunningham's ban had by the end of January 1944 been relaxed.

Losses in the course of operations to France were surprisingly small: two fishing boats and their Breton crews early in 1941; two ratings killed by gunfire.[1] Boats' crews left ashore on five occasions were all safely rescued. But a number of ambushes were narrowly avoided. MGB 502 was lost by mine with only two survivors, but this happened after VE day and in Scandinavian waters. MAS 541 was also lost by mine with all hands, including one of ACF's officers, though on an Italian operation. Because of Hitler's infamous secret instructions, no one knew quite what fate might await them if they were captured in the course of special operations: two British captains of local craft taken prisoner in Greek waters were executed: one survivor of Gus March-Phillipps's raid on Saint-Vaast who escaped into Spain was extradited back into German hands and executed in France.

Though casualties were thus far smaller than in the RAF's Special Duties Squadrons, clandestine sea-transport operations involved very considerable feats of seamanship, navigation and endurance.

Krajewski's felucca operations from Gibraltar were outstanding: those to the south of France, which greatly benefited SOE and MI9, inexplicably received no official British recognition, his DSO having been awarded before the expeditions to France began. By the time this small Polish unit was disbanded in the Adriatic it had carried a total of over 600 people into or out of Vichy controlled or enemy-held territory and landed around 120 tons of war material. Their feluccas had spent 350 days at sea and travelled 35,000 nautical miles. Yet one has to search hard to find even an incidental reference in print to these feats.

The motor gunboat operations in the English Channel were equally impressive. The 'C'-class MGB 318, too slow to operate safely in the short summer nights, was often at sea in weather that kept the regular Coastal Forces flotillas tied up in port. She and her larger sisters 502 and 503 worked, moreover, to a coast with notoriously strong tides and a daunting array of offshore dangers on moonless nights, without the normal navigational facilities, finding their way time and again to pinpoints inshore of these hazards.

The first edition of this book dealt only with the clandestine sea lines to France. Since Corsica was and still is an integral part of metropolitan France, the operations from Algiers to it belonged naturally to the account. But Bastia is geographically nearer to the west coast of Italy and the offshore Italian islands than to south eastern France and from the time of the island's liberation the flotillas based there worked predominantly to Italian pinpoints. Andrew Croft was disappointed to discover that *Secret Flotillas* made only passing reference to BALACLAVA'S operations in support of the Italian campaign, though they were nearly five times as numerous as those to France. It was this among other factors that has led me to extend the book's scope and it would have been wrong to have included only the operations which took place on the west coast of Italy, to the exclusion of those in the Adriatic.

There were 84 'irregular' operations on the west coast to Italian objectives and 17 to French pinpoints. The situation in the Adriatic was more complicated, with 117 successful operations in support of the Italian campaign, with another 33 unsuccessful ones, which is not bad, considering the poor reputation which the weather there enjoys. Only 14 operations to Yugoslavia are recorded as carried out by DDOD(I)'s vessels, but the total to Vis carried out by sea for SOE's Cairo Headquarters must have been very much higher, since Yugoslavia received a greater tonnage of SOE military supplies than any other country.

There were 57 operations logged by Slocum's ACF(A) to Albania and 35 to western Greece. Italian naval vessels and crews operating under command of British officers from ACF(A) and SOE carried out half the operations recorded by DDOD(I). One Italian MAS boat defected to the Germans, killing her Italian officers; but she had never been used by the Allies for ACF(A) operations. Under the de Courten-Cunningham agreement of September 1943, both Italian submarines and destroyers were made available to the Allies, as well as MS and MAS boats, the counterparts of our Coastal Forces. Though the cooperation between what had so recently been enemy forces must have been initially nerve-wracking for both parties, it worked extraordinarily well and there are warm tributes from various British participants and authorities to the efficiency and helpfulness of their new partners.

This book will have succeeded in its *raison d'être* if it rescues from impending oblivion or from the realms of misleading myth the epic achievements of those, including the Poles, who opened up and maintained these clandestine sea lines of communication; and if it does justice to filling in colourful and significant chapters of Anglo French and Anglo Italian relations in the Second World War.

Notes

Chapter I

1 The account in this and the following seven paragraphs of the Polish government-in-exile's attempts to reconstitute their armed forces, of the fate of those forces in the Battle of France and of the immediately ensuing evacuation to the United Kingdom is based on Garliński's *Poland in the Second World War.*
2 M.Z.Rygor-Slowikowski, *In the Secret Service: The Lighting of the Torch,* Chapter II.
3 Tadeuz Wyrwa, The Polish Embassy in Madrid, 1940–44', *Zeszyty Historyczne* (Paris), No. 95 (1991).
4 Ibid.
5 The author's name is differently spelt at top and bottom of this document (A.XII.4/140), viz. Kpt CIECHONSKI Czeslaw, former staff officer of 2nd Infantry Division, and Czeslaw CICHONSKI Kapitan.
6 Rygor-Slowikowski, *The Lighting of the Torch,* pp. 15–18.
7 Ibid.
8 R.Pichavant: *Clandestins de l'Iroise,* Vol. I: *1940–42,* p. 151.
9 Rygor-Slowikowski, *The Lighting of the Torch,* pp. 15–18.
10 Personal communication to the author by Air Chief Marshal Sir Lewis Hodges.
11 A.XII. 4/140 (Sikorski Institute Archives).
12 Rygor-Slowikowski, *The Lighting of the Torch,* pp. 23–6.

Chapter II

1 Documents from Sikorski Institute Archives.
2 Ibid., MAR A V 12/82.
3 M.Jullian, HMS *FIDELITY,* and information from British official archives.
4 Ibid. and P.Kingswell, *FIDELITY Will Haunt Me till I Die.*

Chapter III

1 Sikorski Institute Archives MAR A V 10/1 (HQ of the Commander-in-Chief); 1 st Bureau; 1084 tjn/41/O.1/Ewak London, 8 April 1941, signed General Klimecki, Chief of Staff to the Commander-in-Chief.
2 Note de Renseignments No. 30 issued by Deuxième Bureau, EM Marine au Maroc on 20 Sept. 1940 and report dated 1 Oct. 1940, ref. 707 EM2. Affaire PECHERAL, Jacques: communicated to the author by Capitaine de Vaisseau Claude Huan, together with the document in note 4 below.
3 On 13 Nov. 1941, headed 'A/S de Manuel PEREIRA RAMAHEIRA'. Note de Renseignments dated 13 Nov. 1941 and issued from Casablanca.
4 Annex to a letter dated 23 October 1941 from Capitaine de Frégate Tariel to Amiral de la Flotte, Secrétaire d'Etat a la Marine (Darlan). The author is grateful to Capitaine de Vaisseau Claude Huan for bringing him this document, which is in the French Naval Archives, to his attention.
5 Sikorski Institute Archives MAR A V 10/1.
6 Ibid.
7 Ibid.
8 Ibid., L 614.
9–26 Sikorski Institute Archives MAR A V 10/1.

Chapter IV

1 Letter from Captain M. Kadulski (Krajewski) to author dated 12 Oct. 1992.
2 Letter from Amiral de la Flotte, Secrétaire d'Etat a la Marine, FM3—SECA dated 22 October, in French Naval Archives, tracked down and communicated to the author by C.de V.Claude Huan.
3 Reply to the above letter dated 23 October 1941 signed by Capitaine de Frégate Tariel.
4–9 Sikorski Institute Archives MAR V A 10/1.

Chapter V

1 The following two-and-a-half pages are based on British official records made available to the author by Gervase Cowell.
2 Sikorski Institute Archives MAR A V 10/2.
3 Ibid.
4 Information received from Group Captain H.B.Verity.
5 P.M.Churchill, *Duel of Wits*.

Chapter VI

1 Sikorski Institute Archives MAR A V 10/2.
2 Churchill, *Duel of Wits;* M.R.D.Foot, *SOE in France;* and the relevant British official records.
3 Relevant British operational records made available to the author by Gervase Cowell.
4 Churchill, *Duel of Wits*, pp. 20–33.
5 Foot, *SOE in France*.
6 Sikorski Institute Archives MAR A V 10/2.
7 Ibid.
8 Ibid.
9 Ibid.
10 Sikorski Institute Archives MAR A V 10/5.
11 Sikorski Institute Archives MAR A V 10/2.
12 Ibid.

13 Ibid.
14 Letters from Admiral Sir Edward Ashmore and from Danny Jones, the historian of HMS *Middleton,* to the author.
15 Personal communication to the author by Colonel Pierre Fourcaud, DSO.
16 As note 14.

Chapter VII

1 Sikorski Institute Archives MAR A V 10/5; records of Polish Naval Attaché in London.
2 Ibid.
3 Sikorski Institute Archives MAR A V 10/2.
4 Report by Buchowski, listing his operational achievements from Gibraltar, in MAR A V 10/5.
5 Relevant British official records.
6 Foot, *SOE in France:* personal communication to the author by C.M.Woods, CMG, then SOE Adviser to the Foreign and Commonwealth Office and custodian of the SOE Archives.

Chapter VIII

1 Letter to the author from Captain M.Kadulski.
2 Memorandum in English to NID(C) by Krajewski/Kadulski (copy in Sikorski Institute Archives MAR A V 10/2).
3 Relevant British official records made available by Gervase Cowell; and Krajewski's memorandum referred to above.

Chapter IX

1 Sikorski Institute Archives MAR A V 10/2.
2 Ibid.
3 Ibid.
4 Ibid.
5 Ibid.
6 Ibid.
7 Operation PEDESTAL.
8 Sikorski Institute Archives MAR A V 10/2.
9 Sikorski Institute Archives MAR A V 10/1.
10 Sikorski Institute Archives MAR A V 10/2.
11 Ibid.
12 Ibid.
13 Ibid.
14 Ibid.
15 Ibid.
16 General Kleeberg had been in London to report to General Sikorski.

Chapter X

1 See pages xxx–xxx.
2 See pages xxx–xxx.
3 Huguen, *Par les Nuits les Plus Longues,* page 221.

4 See Chapter XVIII p. xxx.
5 C.Hampshire: *Undercover Sailors,* p. 155.
6 Sikorski Institute Archives MAR A V 10/5.
7 Ibid.
8 Ibid.
9 Ibid.

Chapter XI

1 W.S.Churchill, *The Second World War,* Vol. III, p. 539, quoted in A.L.Funk, *The Politics of TORCH: The Allied Landings and the Algiers Putsch 1942,* p. 27.
2 Ibid.
3 Funk, *The Politics of TORCH,* p. 30.
4 SOE Archives.
5 *The Politics of TORCH, Chapter 4.*
6 Ibid.
7 Ibid.
8 Ibid.
9 Personal communication to the author by the Brazilian diplomat in question, Mario Gibson Barboso.

Chapter XII

1 Funk, *The Politics of TORCH,* pp. 32–3.
2 Report by Col. Brien Clarke to SOE Headquarters, communicated to the author by Sir Douglas Dodds-Parker.
3 Ibid.
4 Rygor-Slowikowski, *The Lighting of the Torch,* pp. 91, 95, 144–5, 166–70.
5 Information communicated by L'Hostis, W/T operator to Henri d'Astier de la Vigérie, to C. de V.Claude Huan.
6 Rygor-Slowikowski, *The Lighting of the Torch.*
7 Of 95 reports circulated by Dunderdale in June 1942, all but five came from his Polish liaison.
8 P.N.Thomas, 'Ships that Served: The Scottish Fishing Protection Vessel *Minna*', *Model Shipwright, 2, 3* (Spring 1973).
9 Funk, *The Politics of TORCH.*
10 The wartime career of Guy Verstraete was pieced together by Mr Terry Hodgkinson.
11 Rygor-Slowikowski, *The Lighting of the Torch.*

Chapter XIII

1 Report by Col. Brien Clarke to SOE Headquarters previously mentioned.
2 Col. Clarke misdated his summons to Government House but it is clear from other sources that General Mark Clark and his party arrived at Gibraltar on 19 October and that the conference in question took place immediately thereafter.
3 R.Courtney, *The Special Boat Section.*
4 *The Politics of TORCH,* p. 164.
5 Courtney, *The Special Boat Section.*
6 Report by Col. Clarke referred to above, note 1.

7 This officer's unusual background was common knowledge among his colleagues in SOE's Naval Section.

Chapter XIV

1 Sikorski Institute Archives MAR A V 10/5.
2 Foot, *SOE in France*; and a private communication to the author by C.M.Woods, when SOE Adviser to the Foreign and Commonwealth Office and custodian of the SOE archives.
3 Letter to the author by Professor José Aboulker.

Chapter XV

1 Report by Col. Brien Clarke referred to above (see Chapter XIII, note 1).
2 Ibid.
3 Letter from Captain N.L.A.Jewell to the author.
4 Report by Col. Brien Clarke.
5 Ibid.

Chapter XVI

1 This correspondence is in the Sikorski Institute Archives MAR A V 10/5.
2 Ibid.

Chapter XVII

1 These officers, the 'Twelve Apostles', had been deployed in North Africa before the creation of the Office of Strategic Services but Donovan's organisation had become OSS by the time of the TORCH landings. This chapter draws on a report on the BRANDON mission in the SOE archives as well as on the author's knowledge.
2 Admiral Cunningham's signal is in Churchill's files in the Public Record Office, ref. PREM. 3/442.
3 Private communication to the author by Capitaine de Vaisseau Claude Huan.

Chapter XVIII

1 G.B.Courtney, *SBS in World War Two.*
2 The five 'marking' submarines from the 8th Submarine Flotilla sent to lead in the landing forces at Algiers and Oran received a last-minute instruction from Gibraltar based on considerations of secrecy that periscope reconnaissance only was to be made. The Combined Operations Pilotage Parties (COPP) carried on these submarines were, however, allowed to show the 'marking officers' the inner pilotage approaches to the landing beaches by means of canoe trips. This was carried out successfully in all cases but one. HM S/m *Shakespeare's* (P221) party was caught by a sudden storm on 4 November and the canoe was driven out to sea. The next day, waterlogged and suffering from cramp and exhaustion, the party was picked up by a trawler and taken into Algiers. Their cover story had been well rehearsed and was so well played that they were in danger of being shot as spies, but it was at least successful and nothing was given away to the French. (See Admiralty printed report BR 1736 (B1), Battle Summary No. 38 and *Role of Submarines in TORCH,* both in the Public Record Office.)

3 Author's personal knowledge.
4 De Saule's real name was Robert de Schrevel. He was a Belgian magistrate who had joined the French Foreign Legion at the outbreak of war. Also known as Dudule and René Tournier.
5 T.Griffi and L.Preziosi, *Première Mission en Corse Occupée, avec le Sousmarin Casabianca* (Dècembre 1942-Mai 1943).
6 Ibid. and Captain J.L'Herminier: *Casabianca: The Secret Missions of a French Submarine.* This chapter relies on L'Herminier's account of the maritime aspects of this operation and on Griffi's and Preziosi's record of PEARL HARBOUR once ashore.
7 This emerges from published and unpublished material communicated to the author by Capitaine de Vaisseau Claude Huan.
8 See Chapter VI above.
9 H.B.Verity, *We Landed by Moonlight.*
10 Letter in SOE Archives.
11 Copy in PREM. 3/442/14.
12 Author's personal knowledge.
13 Published and unpublished material communicated to the author by Capitaine de Vaisseau Claude Huan.
14 M.-C.Scamaroni, *Fred Scamaroni: 1914–1943.*
15 Ibid.
16 Author's personal knowledge.
17 A copy of the report on the autopsy was made available to the author by Capitaine de Vaisseau Claude Huan. The circumstances of Darlan's brief arrest on the night of the TORCH landings are recorded in Funk, *The Politics of TORCH.* That this was the origin of the naval pistol seems virtually certain.
18 SOE report on MASSINGHAM mission.
19 Private communications to the author by Sir Douglas Dodds-Parker.
20 Scamaroni, *Fred Scamaroni.*
21 Capitaine de Vaisseau Claude Huan has searched the BCRA archives for this document in vain. The archives are in some disorder and it may have migrated into a file where one would not expect to find it. But it may equally have been withdrawn because of its sensitivity.
22 Extracts from the operational report of HM S/m *Tribune* in the Public Record Office, made available to the author by Terry Hodgkinson.
23 SOE Archives. Extracts from the relevant files were made available to Terry Hodgkinson by Gervase Cowell in a letter, of which a copy was made available to the author by the latter.
24 Ibid.

Chapter XIX

1 I. McGeoch, *An Affair of Chances: A Submariner's Odyssey 1939–42.*
2 It was Terry Hodgkinson who drew the author's attention to the connection between the Adler/Serra case and the fate of Scamaroni, which had emerged from his correspondence with Gervase Cowell.
3 J.G.Beevor, *SOE: Recollections and Reflections, 1940–1945.*
4 McGeoch, *An Affair of Chances.*
5 L'Herminies, *Casabianca.*
6 Ibid. The author is indebted to C. de V.Claude Huan for a list of many of those who travelled to or from France on the French Submarines based on Algiers. He derived his information on the subject from Capitaine P.Paillole. The results of his researches have been incorporated in Appendix D.

7 Lt-Col. F.C.A.Cammaerts, DSO, ('Roger'), SOE's most successful agent in south-eastern France, formed a particularly adverse impression of Brown's blatant disregard for security when in occupied France. The author has a letter from him on the subject.
8 Author's personal knowledge.
9 L'Herminies, *Casabianca.*
10 Griffith and Preziosi, *Première Mission en Corse Occupée.*
11 L'Herminies, *Casabianca.*
12 The author is indebted to Terry Hodgkinson for information about FREDERICK, a subject he researched most thoroughly with a view to a possible television programme.
13 Private communication to the author by Captain M.G.R.Lumby.
14 Operational report by Lumby, made available to the author by Terry Hodgkinson.
15 See note 12.
16 Griffith and Preziosi, *Première Mission en Corse Occupée.*
17 L'Herminies, *Casabianca.*
18 Griffith and Preziosi, *Première Mission en Corse Occupée.*
19 L'Herminies, *Casabianca*; and Huan, see note 6.

Chapter XX

1 See Chapter XIX, note 2.
2 Unpublished memorandum by Terry Hodgkinson on FREDERICK referred to above.
3 Author's personal knowledge.
4 Ibid.
5 Scamaroni, *Fred Scamaroni.*
6 G.Fleury and R.Maloubier, *Nageurs de Combat.*
7 Unpublished SOE report on operations in Corsica by MASSINGHAM.
8 Personal communication by A.L.Funk.
9 Courtney, *SBS in World War Two*; and letters from Captain P.E.Newstead, RN.
10 Courtney, *SBS in World War Two.*
11 Ibid.
12 Information from the Submarine Museum, Gosport, kindly made available by Gus Britton.
13 Griffith and Preziosi, *Première Mission en Corse Occupée.*
14 Official Admiralty report on submarines operating in the western Mediterranean; also see note 12.
15 Records of Slocum's Section; report by Captain (S) 8 dated 17 July 1943 states that 'one of the agents had refused to land from *Trident*'.
16 P.Silvani,...*et la Corse fut libérée.*
17 As footnote 7; and author's personal knowledge.
18 Personal communication by A.L.Funk to the author.
19 As note 7.
20 Author's personal knowledge.
21 Ibid.
22 As note 7.
23 Author's personal knowledge.
24 Ibid.
25 Ibid.
26 L'Herminier, *Casabianca.*
27 Ibid.
28 Ibid.
29 As note 7.

30 Ibid.
31 Silvani, *...et la Corse fut libérée;* and author's personal knowledge.
32 Personal communication by A.L.Funk to the author.
33 As note 7.
34 L'Herminier, *Casabianca.*
35 As note 7; also personal communication by A.L. Funk to the author.
36& 37 As note 7.
38 General von Senger und Etterlin wrote in *Neither Fear nor Hope,* p. 175: 'I believe that the inhabitants have become entirely apolitical due to their foreign rulers. This accounts for the fact that the numerous partisans, who were supplied with arms by air-drops, were not as active as might have been expected from their numerical strength and the contacts they had with the Allies along the open west coast. The ambush that I ran into after the Italian capitulation was laid by French gendarmes. The French were far more anti-German than the native Italians *[sic].*'

Chapter XXI

1 Author's personal knowledge.
2 MARYLAND, SOE's first mission established in ex-enemy territory, came, under the cover title No.1 Special Force, to be the main source of supply and strategic direction to the Italian partisans, with around 70–80,000 guerillas operating under its orders.
3 Report by F.A.Slocum; and P.Whinney: *Corsican Command.*
4 *Corsican Command.*
5 Report by N.A.C.Croft to the author in Algiers.
6 Whinney, *Corsican Command;* and as note 5.
7 Whinney, *Corsican Command.*
8 As note 5.
9 N.A.C.Croft, *A Talent for Adventure.*
10 As footnote 5.
11 *Corsican Command.*
12 As note 5.
13 Whinney, *Corsican Command.*
14 Ibid.
15 A.Pelletier, 'Autrement qu'ansi', unpublished manuscript in the SOE archives.
16 P.Whinney, *Corsican Command',* confirmatory evidence of the fate of MAS 541 and the position where she sank was communicated to the author by Capitaine de Vaisseau Claude Huan, from the French Naval archives.
17 A.Croft, *A Talent for Adventure.*
18 As note 5.
19 Ibid.

Epilogue

1 Losses in Holland were more severe: six French 'fuseliers marins', forming part of 8 Commando, were killed or drowned conducting a reconnaissance at Wassenaar-Slag on 28 February 1944 to see whether it would be possible to resume sea landings of agents, notwithstanding the German coastal defences.

Appendix A: Clandestine Sea Transport Operations from Gibraltar to French North Africa and the South Coasts of France and Spain

Operation Code name	*Department*	*Pinpoint*	*Ship*	*Object*	*Results and remarks*
			Period: September 1940–May 1941		
	Free French 2e Bureau	Agadir Bay	HM destroyer? (from Gibraltar)	To land 3 agents: Guérin & Ter-Sarkissof – both officers – and Second Maître Jacques Pècheral.	21 Sept. 1940 – Agents successfully landed but arrested by French authorities in following month. They had taken passage to Gibraltar on 26 July from Scapa Flow in HMS *Barham*.
	Free French 2e Bureau	Near Mostaganem	Small ship *Johan*, flying the Belgian flag, operating from Gibraltar	To land 3 agents: Lieutenants Puech-Samson and Bazaucourt, with W/T operator Papin.	26 Sept. 1940 – Agents successfully landed and remained in Algiers until mid-November. Taken prisoner in mid-November 1940, 30 miles west of Oran when they failed to embark for Gibraltar.
	SOE DF (Humphries) Section and EU/P (Polish Liaison) Section	Etang-du-Cannet	HMS *Fidelity*	To land 2 agents: E.H. Rizzo (DF) and Bitner (Polish).	25 April 1941 – Successful.
	Polish Evacuation Section	Cerbère	HMS *Fidelity*	To embark a party of Polish servicemen.	26 April 1941 – Unsuccessful. Attempt was made in broad daylight from within port of Cerbère. French gendarmerie intervened and Lt Cmdr P. O'Leary (Albert Guérisse) attempted to put to sea in the boat they were using but they were pursued by a French motor launch and arrested, except for one sailor who swam into Spanish waters.
	SIS/MI9	Gulf of Lyons	HMS *Fidelity*	To embark British POWs.	6 May 1941 – Attempt frustrated by appearance of French seaplane.

Operation Code name	*Department*	*Pinpoint*	*Ship*	*Object*	*Results and remarks*
			Period: July–September 1941		
KRAJEWSKI	Polish mission	Between Casablanca and Fedhala	*Seawolf* (felucca)	To evacuate Polish troops interned by Vichy authorities.	19–25 July 1941 – Krajewski's first attempt. Unsuccessful owing to poor communications with the organiser at Casablanca. Crew consisted of 3 Norwegians.
KRAJEWSKI I; 'First Evacuation Mission	Polish Mission	As above	*Seagull* (lent by Quennell of SOE)	As above, and to land Major Brzozowski.	4–8 August – Successful, 6 August: 27 people evacuated, including 3 Czechs. 13 others arrested by Vichy police. Lt Killick (British, SOE) on board as observer.
KRAJEWSKI III	Polish Mission	Between Sali and Mehedia (Port-Lyautey)	*Dogfish* (felucca)	To evacuate Polish escapers and to land Staggart (Czech volunteer).	17–25 August – Unsuccessful. Staggart lost his nerve and was unable to land. Krajewski called this his third evacuation mission, though he described its immediate predecessor as his first such operation. It was his third expedition to Morocco.
KRAJEWSKI IV	Polish Mission	near Casablanca	*Dogfish*	To evacuate Polish evaders and escapers.	30 August–3 September -Successful. Embarked 48, including 4 Belgians, on night 1/2 September. Cadet Officer Kleybor and 2 Norwegians as crew. Lt Killick (British) on board.
IVz/SLO1	SIS/MI9	Gulf of Lyons	HMS *Fidelity*	To embark party of escaped British POWs.	14 September – Unsuccessful. *Fidelity* arrived 24 hours late, having sailed from UK with brief call at Gibraltar during the night. Subsequent attempts on 20 and 21 September also failed.

Operation Code name	*Department*	*Pinpoint*	*Ship*	*Object*	*Results and remarks*
			Period: July–September 1941 continued		
ABRICOT	SIS/MI9	Algeria (Cap Ténès)	*Fidelity*	To embark a party of escaped British POWs.	16 September – Unsuccessful. No-one at pinpoint.
KASBAH	BCRA	Algeria (nr Cherchell-Tipaza)	*Fidelity*	To land 2 agents: Second Lt Jacquelin and Sgt Radio Carton; and 2 W/T sets.	17 September – Unsuccessful owing to presence of Italian submarine.
AUTOGYRO/ URCHIN	SOE	Barcarès, NE of Perpignan	*Fidelity*	To land 4 agents: F. Basin ('Olive'), R. Leroy ('Louis'), R.B. Roche, and A.J.R. Dubourdin ('Alain').	19/20 September – Successful.
			Period: October–November 1941		
KRAJEWSKI V	Polish Mission	Fedhala	*Dogfish*	To pick up Polish evaders and escapers.	7–10 October – Successful. Embarked 13 Poles and two Belgians, and Mr Wysocki, owner of the safe house the Poles had been using.
KRAJEWSKI VI	Polish Mission	Mostaganem (DORULA)	*Dogfish*	To embark 2 agents: Major Wysoczanski and Lt Roehr.	23-29 October – Successful.
KRAJEWSKI VII	Polish Mission	Mostaganem Bay	*Seagull*	To land supplies for 150 people for four days.	1–6 November – Unsuccessful. Saw people on shore at pinpoint, but they showed incorrect recognition signal (3/4 November). Trawler *Quarto*, which was to have been used as back-up, not available owing to boiler trouble.

Operation Code name	*Department*	*Pinpoint*	*Ship*	*Object*	*Results and remarks*
			Period: October–November 1941 continued		
KRAJEWSKI VIII	Polish Mission	(1) Mostaganem Bay (BRZOZA) (2) Cap-Falcon nr Oran (Zorra)	*Dogfish*	(1) To pick up Polish escapers from R/V nr Mostaganem. (2) To land 1 agent nr Cap Falcon	18–25 November – Planned evacuation of about 40 Polish soldiers, who had escaped from two interment camps, failed, as French authorities got wind of plan and frustrated it.
BUCHOWSKI I	SOE	Casablanca	*Vega*, ex-*Ville-de-Fedhala* (Buchowski)	To land SOE stores.	December 1941 – Unsuccessful. Ship intercepted by Spaniards on return voyage and taken into Tangiers, where the crew were detained for several weeks and the ship was confiscated.
KRAJEWSKI IX	Polish Mission	ZORRA nr Cap Falcon (Andalousses Bay)	*Dogfish*	1) To land Lt Gromnicki carrying funds (600,000 Fr. Francs) for 'Szewalski' intelligence organisation. 2) To re-embark him.	13–18 December – Landing successful. Re-embarked Gromnicki two days later with 5 Polish officers. *Dogfish* not really fit for operations in winter: motor old and unreliable.
			Period: January – April 1942		
? DELAY	SOE	Miramar-de-l'Esterel	HM S/m P36 (Lt H.N. Edwards, RN)	To land Capt. P.M. Churchill, using his own Folboat	9 January 1942 – *Successful.* P36 left Gibraltar on 1 January and arrived back there on 15 January. The Naval Staff History omits this patrol completely but it was clearly offensive and took place in the Gulf of Lyons area as Naval Historical Branch have record of two Gibraltar signals telling her where merchant ships were to be.

Operation Code name	*Department*	*Pinpoint*	*Ship*	*Object*	*Results and remarks*
			Period: January–April 1942 continued		
KRAJEWSKI X	Polish Mission	Cap Falcon, nr Oran, Algeria	*Dogfish*	To land 1 agent (Lt Gromnicki) and to evacuate a party of Polish evaders and escapers.	8–23 January 1942 – Unsuccessful. Storm conditions made landing impossible at Cap Falcon. Motor broke down. Entered Oran Bay hoping to reach Arzew for shelter but could not. Blown 100 miles to the east. Continuous gales. Fired on in Oran Bay. Investigated by Spanish patrol boat at Alboran Island.
KRAJEWSKIXI	Polish Mission	Oran area	*Dogfish*	? To evacuate Polish evaders and escapers.	22 March – Unsuccessful. There is no report on this operation in the Sikorski Institute archives. Buchowski accompanied Krajewski on it.
ABLOOM	SIS/MI9	Port-Vendres area	*Tarana* (Lt E.B. Clarke, RNR)	To land Pat O'Leary and W/T Operator.	18 April – Successful. This was the first operation to France under CWF auspices. *Tarana*, a Dutch-built trawler with secret armament, had a British and Polish crew. Operated sometimes under Moroccan, sometimes Portuguese flags.
			Period: April–June 1942		
JASMINE (KRAJEWSKI XII)	Polish mission, SOE and PWE	Cassis area, Antibes	*Seawolf* (Krajewski)	(1) To land Lt Roehr at Port-Miou. (2) To land 3 agents at Antibes. (3) To evacuate Polish evaders and escapers from En-Vau.	18 April – Roehr successfully landed. 21/22 April – SOE & PWE agents successfully landed at Antibes. 22/23 April – 41 Poles evacuated. The SOE agents were Menesson ('Prunus') and Pertschuk ('Birch'). Le Chêne ('Plane') was for PWE.

Operation Code name	*Department*	*Pinpoint*	*Ship*	*Object*	*Results and remarks*
				Period: April–June 1942	
DELAY II	SOE	Antibes and Miramar-de-l'Esterel	HM S/m P42 (UNBROKEN) (Lt A.G.C. Mars, RN)	(1) To land 2 agents (Zeff and Newman) at Antibes. (2) To land 2 agents (Gerson and Clech) at Miramar, near Cannes.	(1) 19/20 April – Successful. P. Churchill landed them using Folboat canoes & brought out Emmanuel d'Astier de la Vigerie ('Bernard'). (2) 20/21 April – Successful. Peter Churchill places this second landing in the Baie d'Agay.
ORKAN	Polish Mission and SIS (P5)	Oran	*Dogfish* (Buchowski)	To evacuate 4 Poles.	25 April – Successful. Buchowski in command.
MIMOSA (KRAJEWSKI XIII)	Polish mission and SOE	Cassis area, Antibes and Rhône delta	*Seawolf* *Tarana*	To evacuate Polish evaders and escapers and land SOE agents (Denis Rake and Charles Hayes).	10/11 May – 31 Poles evacuated from En-Vau and transferred to *Tarana* at R/V on 11 May, when *Seawolf* embarked the agents from *Tarana*. 13/14 May – Agents successfully landed at Antibes. 15/16 May – 30 Poles embarked from nr Beauduc lighthouse in Rhône delta.
CASABIANCA	Polish mission	Casablanca area	*Dogfish* (Buchowski)	To evacuate 30 Polish evaders and escapers.	23 May – Successful.
* GOBLIN Ia (KRAJEWSKI XIV)	Polish mission	Cassis area (En-Vau)	*Seawolf* *Tarana*	To evacuate Polish evaders and escapers.	9 June – Picked up 3 Poles. Police had arrested others and group had dispersed. * Operation combined with GOBLIN II, SARDINE, LUCALITE I and LUCALITE II below; all one voyage.

Operation Code name	*Department*	*Pinpoint*	*Ship*	*Object*	*Results and remarks*
				Period: April–June 1942 continued	
	Polish mission	En-Vau	*Seawolf*	To land Polish courier (Lt Biczysko).	10/11 June – Courier landed.
* GOBLIN II	SOE	Antibes area	*Seawolf* *Tarana*	To land 2 SOE agents: Jickell & Boiteux; and stores.	11/12 June – Agents successfully landed. 1 embarked, according to Slocum.
* SARDINE	SOE	Cap-d'Ail, Monaco area	*Seawolf* *Tarana*	To land 1 SOE agent.	11/12 June – Agent (?Coppin) successfully landed.
* LUCALITE I	SIS (MI9), Polish mission	Port-Miou	*Seawolf* 1)	To embark a non-Polish party. 2) To embark Polish evaders and escapers.	14/15 June – 9 mixed agents and refugees, including 3 women, successfully embarked.' 62 Poles successfully evacuated.
* LUCALITE II	SIS (VIb)	Port-Miou	*Seawolf*	To land 70lb. of war material.	14/15 June – Successful.
TANGERINE	Polish mission	Oran area	*Seadog*	To land 1 Polish courier (Gromnicki).	9 June – Failed. Bad weather.
NETTLETREE	SOE	Cap-d'Antibes	*Seadog* *Tarana*	To embark 1 and land SOE stores.	30 June – Successful. Possibly Frager.
				Period: June–July 1942	
No name	SOE	Gibraltar Strait	*Minna*	To R/V at sea with felucca from Tangier and transfer stores.	26–30 June – Successful.
GUYMAR	SIS P1 Section (Cohen) (Cohen)	Oran area (Cohen) (Cohen)	*Minna*	To land 1 agent (J. Verstraete).	7 July – Successful.

Operation Code name	*Department*	*Pinpoint*	*Ship*	*Object*	*Results and remarks*
				Period: July 1942	
* LUCILE	SIS (P1) (BCRA réseau 'Ronsard')	Port-d'En-Vau	*Seawolf*	To embark up to 10.	13/14 July – Successful. Embarked 2 men & 1 woman (wife of one of the men). * Operation combined with MANDARIN I & II, 'KRAJEWSKI XV' and PEPPERTREE below; all one voyage.
* MANDARIN I & II; (KRAJEWSKI XV)	Polish	Port-d'En-Vau	*Seawolf* *Tarana*	To embark Polish evaders and escapers.	14/15 July – Successful. 52 embarked and transferred. 22 July – Successful: 53 embarked.
* PEPPER-TREE	SOE	(1) Cassis Bay, Cap-Gros (2) Antibes	*Seawolf* *Tarana.*	(1) 15 July – to land 4 agents transferred from *Tarana* (2) To land remaining 2 agents.	(1) 15/16 July -Successful. 4 agents landed. (2) 19/20 July – Successful, after failed attempt on 19 July, because of too much traffic on the road. Passengers landed included R.H. Heslop ('Mahogany'), R. Leroy ('Buckthorn'), ?Lt Krumhorn ('Mangrove'), Capt Barnard.
**POST BOX	SOE Italian Section	'Marseilles area' (Port-Miou)	*Seawolf* *Tarana*	To land 2 (Emilio and Joyce Lussu)	18 July ? – Successful. ** Operation combined with BLUEBOTTLE below; all one voyage. Krajewski's report does not in fact distinguish this operation from PEPPERTREE and LUCILE above.

Operation Code name	Department	Pinpoint	Ship	Object	Results and remarks
			Period: July 1942 continued		
**BLUE-BOTTLE	P15 (MI9)	'Gulf of Lyons area' (Saint-Pierre-Plage, near Narbonne)	*Tarana*	To embark British escapers and evaders.	14/15 July[2] – Successful. Coast Watching Flotilla's first evacuation for the 'Pat' line. Carried out directly by *Tarana*. 7 identified British evaders and escapers evacuated, including Sqn Ldr Whitney Straight, a very distinguished fighter pilot and André Simon of SOE.
ORKAN II	SIS (P5) (Dunderdale)	Oran area	*Minna*	To evacuate 1 agent.	13 July – Successful. Group concerned was Rygor-Slowikowski's 'Agence Afrique'.
			Period: July–September 1942		
CASUAL	SIS (P5) (Dunderdale)	Oran area	*Minna*	To land 2 Polish agents to Rygor-Slowikowski's 'Agence Afrique'.	19 July – Failed: No reception committee present. *Minna* attacked by enemy aircraft on return voyage. Aircraft driven off.
SASSAFRAS	SOE	Cap-d'Antibes	*Seadog*	To land 4 agents: N. Bodington ('Professor'), Frager ('Architect'), Despaigne ('Magnolia') and Rudellat ('Soaptree').	30 July – Successful. Auguste Floiras left either on this operation or PEPPERTREE.
BULL	SOE	nr Agde	*Tarana*	To land 6 agents, including 1 woman, and stores.	15 August – Successful. Included Sevenet, Déricourt, Cdt Charles Clasen (Belgian) and 'Mercure' (BCRA).[3]

Operation Code name	*Department*	*Pinpoint*	*Ship*	*Object*	*Results and remarks*
			Period: July–September 1942 continued		
BLUE-BOTTLE (LEDA I for BCRA)	SIS (P1) (Cohen) (BCRA *réseau* 'Phalanx')	Saint-Pierre-Plage, near Narbonne	*Tarana*	To pick up evaders and escapers and to land stores.	15 August – Successful. 7 men and 1 woman embarked. Food, stores and W/T sets landed.
WATCHMAN	SOE	Agay	*Seadog*	To land agent and stores.	1 September – Successful. Landed 1 agent (Blanche Charlet) and 2,000lb stores. Brought off 5 men and 2 women: Bodington, André Gillois and wife and daughter; two Belgians.
VAGRANT	SIS (P5) (Dunderdale)	Agay area	*Seadog*	To evacuate mixed party.	2 September – Successful. Ten people evacuated, including General Kleeberg.
KUMMEL	SOE	nr Toulon	*Seadog*	To evacuate 5.	3 September – Failed. No one at R/V. Military manoeuvres in area.
			Period: September 1942		
LEDA (LEDA II for BCRA)	SIS (P1) (Cohen for BCRA *réseau* 'Phalanx')	Narbonne	*Seadog*	To land 1 agent and evacuate others.	4 Sept. – Successful. 'Porthos' (W/T op.) landed. Brossolette, Charles Vallin, Denis Cochin, Dutrex, Sq Ldr Guy Lockhart (Lysander pilot), organiser 'Ronsard' (Quartier Maître Richard) evacuated. Christian Pineau, Jean Cavaillès and Saint Génies left behind owing to shore interference by customs patrol and arrested.

Operation Code name	*Department*	*Pinpoint*	*Ship*	*Object*	*Results and remarks*
				Period: September 1942 continued	
ZEBRA	SIS (P5) (Dunderdale)	Oran area	*Minna*	To land 3 agents to Slowikowski's 'Agence Afrique': Malinowski, Kowal, Piotrowski.	11 September – Successful. Agents had been on board since May. Also picked up Polish agents from Paris, refugees from treachery of 'La Chatte'. (see CASUAL below).
CASUAL	SIS (P5) (Dunderdale)	Oran area	*Minna*	To evacuate agents from 'Agence Afrique'.	1 September – Successful. 5 men and 1 woman embarked.
FALSTAFF (TRITON)	SIS (P1) (Cohen)	La-Ciotat	*Seawolf*	To land 2 agents (1 a woman).	17 September – Successful. (CND *réseau*). Passy says Henri Frenay and Emmanuel D'astier were embarked.
ORLANDO	SIS (P5) (Dunderdale)	Sormiou, but Morgiou was point used	*Seawolf*	To land 1 agent and heavy W/T station.	18 September – Successful, but reception committee was at wrong pinpoint. Picked up 50 kilos of watches and stop-watches for the RAF.
MULLET	SOE	Port-d'En-Vau	*Seawolf*	To embark 2.	18 September – Successful.
NECTARINE I (KRAJEWSKI XVI)	Polish mission	Sormiou	*Seawolf*	To embark Polish evaders and escapers.	19 September–31 embarked, including 3 British.
NECTARINE II	Polish mission	Port-d'En-Vau	*Seawolf*	As above.	20 September – Successful. 25 Poles embarked.

Operation Code name	*Department*	*Pinpoint*	*Ship*	*Object*	*Results and remarks*
			Period: September–October 1942		
TITANIA	P15 (MI9)	Canet-Plage, west of Perpignon, at mouth of Tet River	*Seawolf*	To evacuate British evaders and escapers from the 'Pat' line.	21 September – Successful. Krajewski puts number of those embarked at 25. Another account put it at 38. The party included a few Frenchmen, 1 Sudeten woman and a Russian, according to Krajewski.
SILKWORM	Poles & SIS (P5) (Dunderdale)	La-Napoule	*Seadog*	To land 1 and embark 6.	2 October – Buchowski landed 2 agents and General Kleeberg at La-Napoule. His record does not distinguish between the operations as listed in British records.
WATCHMAN II	SOE	Cap-de-l'Esquillon	*Seadog*	To land stores, etc.	2/3 October – Promised motor boat did not appear. Material landed 4/5 October using own boat.
CHUB I	SOE (? and PWE)	La-Napoule, Cap-de-l'Esquillon	*Seadog*	To land two parties of 2 agents at different pinpoints.	2/3 October – Buchowski landed all 4 agents including S.G. Jones, J. Goldsmith and Chalmers-Wright. He also decided to land General Kleeberg at the first pinpoint.
CHUB II	SOE	Rade-d'Agay	*Seadog*	To embark 6.	4 October – Failed. French police interfered.
ACCOST	SIS (P5)	Oran area	*Minna*	To embark 1.	Beginning October – Failed. A signal went astray and agent thus had too little time to arrive at R/V.

Operation Code name	Department	Pinpoint	Ship	Object	Results and remarks
			Period: September–October 1942 continued		
GIRAFFE I	'Poles'	Oran area	*Minna*	To land 1.	1 October – Successful.
GIRAFFE II	'Poles'	Oran area	*Minna*	To embark 6.	3 October – Successful.
ULTRAMARINE	'Poles'	Oran area	*Minna*	To embark 1.	3 October – Successful.
ROSALIND	P15 (SIS for MI9)	Canet-Plage, west of Perpignon, at mouth of Tet River	*Seawolf* (Lukasz)	To embark British evaders and escapers from the PAT line.	11/12 October – Successful. 34 embarked at a second attempt. No contact on 5/6 October.
SERAPH I	General Eisenhower	Messelmoun, near Cherchell, Algria	HM S/m P219 (later named *Seraph*) (Lt N.L.A. Jewell, RN)	To land Lt-Gen. Mark Clark and four staff officers for talks with General Mast, Col Jousse and Mr Robert Murphy.	21/22 October – Party successfully landed and re-embarked by No. 2 SBS.
* WATCHMAN III * OVERGROW * DUBONNET	SOE (F Section and Italian Section)	Port-Miou	*Seadog* (Buchowski)	To land stores and personnel (Buchowski says 9 landed and 6 embarked).	3/4 November – Successful. 3 women, 5 men and 1,000lb stores landed; 4 men and 1 boy embarked. SOE records identify following landed: George Starr ('Wheelwright'); Marius Bloom ('Bishop'; W/T operator); Mary Herbert ('Jeweller'); Mme M.-T. Le Chêne ('Wisteria'); Odette Sanson ('Clothier'); plus Giacomino Galea for Italian Section. Embarked: J.A.R. Starr ('Walnut'); I. Newman ('Dividend'); 'Quintet' (Radio Patrie); 'Richard' and his son.
* PORTIA	P15 (SIS for MI9)	Port-Miou	*Seadog*	To land 1.	3/4 November – Successful. * Part of WATCHMAN III.

Operation Code name	Department	Pinpoint	Ship	Object	Results and remarks
				Period: November–December 1942	
LADYBIRD	SIS (P5) (Dunderdale)	Fréjus	*Seadog*	To land 1 and embark stores.	5 November – Failed owing to rough weather. 6 November – Further attempt failed for same reason.
SERAPH II		Le-Lavandou, 20 miles E of Toulon	HM S/m P219 (Lt N.L.A. Jewell, RN)	To embark General Giraud and 4 others, including his son and Viret, his bodyguard.	5 November – Successful. Party had been waiting since previous night. Party picked up by Catalina amphibious aircraft at 0900 7 November.
LEOPARD (PICNIC for SOE)	SOE	(1) Messelmoun (2)Alma-Marine (Algeria)	*Minna*	To land 10 tons of stores in preparation for TORCH landings at Algiers.	2/3 and 3/4 November – No reception found at Messelmoun. Ordered to new 5/6 November – No reception found at alternative R/V.
SIBYL		Cros-de-Cagnes	HM S/m *Sibyl* (Lt E.J.D. Turner, RN)	To embark 10 French staff officers and 1 woman.	8 November – 7 successfully embarked: Mme. Beaufre, Cdt V. Boutron, 3 French Officers and 2 men. Party had problems with French police just before embarking and 3 men were arrested.
WASP	SIS (P1) (Cohen)	Cros-de-Cagnes	*Seawolf*	To embark 2.	30 November & 4 December – Failed.
MELPOMENE	SIS (P1) (*réseau* 'Denis')	La-Napoule	*Seawolf*	To embark 7. (André Manuel, René Massigli, Louis Guiringand, Col Eric Sawyer and 2 English friends see Passy 'Memoires'	1 & 5 December – Failed.

On first attempts of above three operations, no contact with agents on shore. On second attempt at WASP and MELPOMENE, weather prevented mbarkation.

Operation Code name	Department	Pinpoint	Ship	Object	Results and remarks
			Period: December 1942–February 1943 continued		
LADYBIRD	SIS (P1)	nr Fréjus	*Seawolf*	To embark stores for Ministry of Economic Warfare.	2 December – Failed.
CRICKET	SIS (P5) (Dunderdale)	Nr Agay (Cros-de-Cagnes)	*Seawolf*	To embark party of agents.	3 December – Cancelled by field after ship had sailed. Further attempts to be made.
LADYBIRD II	SIS (P1)	Fréjus	*Welcome*	To embark MEW stores.	2 January 1943 – Failed. Atmospheric conditions prevented ship receiving W/T signal changing date after ship had sailed.
* WASP II	SIS (P1) (Cohen)	Cros-de-Cagnes	*Seawolf*	To embark 7.	January – Failed. Opposition from machine-guns at WASP/CRICKET pinpoint.
* MELPOMENE II	SIS (P1)	La-Napoule	*Seawolf*	To embark 7.	January – Failed. Weather very bad.
* CRICKET II	SIS (P5) (Dunderdale)	Cros-de-Cagnes	*Seawolf*	To embark party.	January – Failed.
* LADYBIRD III	SIS (P1)	nr St-Aigulf	*Seawolf*	To embark MEW stores.	29 January – Failed. Ambush laid on beach. Felucca returned owing to illness of commanding officer. * Operation combined on same voyage with MELPOMENE III below.

Operation Code name	Department	Pinpoint	Ship	Object	Results and remarks
			Period: December 1942–February 1943 continued		
* MELPOMENE III	SIS (P1)	Cap-de-l' Aiguillon	*Seawolf*	To embark 7.	29 January – Failed.
MELPOMENE IV & ROMEO	SIS (P1)	Cap-de-l'Aiguillon & Cavalaire	*Welcome*	To embark 7 at one pinpoint and up to 10 at another.	February – Failed. Agents cancelled arrangements after *Welcome* sailed. *Welcome* kept R/V but saw nothing and returned to Gibraltar 15 February.

Notes:

1 Alya Aglan's *Mémoires Resistantes: Historie du Réseau JADE-FITZROY 1940–44* identifies these passengers as Claude and Denise Lamirault, Emile Champion ('Parrain') with wife and son. Henri Frenay and Pierre Fourcaud were also evacuated on this occasion. All were transferred to HMS *Middleton*, met by chance at sea.

2 Some accounts quote 13 July as the date of this pick-up operation.

3. The BCRA archives show an agent Code named 'Mercure' as passenger on an operation near Narbonne on 10 August.

Appendix B:
Clandestine Sea Operations from Various Bases to Tunisia

Operation Code name	*Department*	*Pinpoint*	*Ship*	*Object*	*Results and remarks*
			Period: December 1942–April 1943		
?	SIS (Malta)	Cap Kamart (E Coast of Tunisia)	HM S/m *Urge*	To land agents.	16/17 February 1942 – Only 1 agent landed owing to foul weather.
?	SIS (Malta)	Off Sousse	HM s/m UTMOST (Lt Cdr Cayley RN)	To pick up Cdt. Breuillac and mail from Tunis at R/V with yacht belonging to Mounier.	15 April 1942 -Successful. Breuillac returned to Tunisia on 19 April by same means.(See Fleury and Maloubier: *Nageurs de Combat*, pp. 499–56.)
FELICE I (called FELICITY by BRANDON)	SOE (BRANDON Mission)	South of Hammamet	HM S/m P42 (*Unbroken*) (Lt A.G.V. Mars, RN), from Malta	To land party of 12 to demolish bridge.	28/29 January 1943 – Party successfully landed in uniform but captured during attack on bridge. Party consisted of Capt Eyre, Lt Thomas, 4 British and 6 French ORs.
FELICE II (BLUE)	SOE (BRANDON Mission)	Gulf of Hammamet	HM MTB 307, from Malta	To land 3 agents: Sqn Ldr Mallory, Martinez and Bonjour (leader was W/T operator).	28/29 January 1943 – Agents successfully landed but captured almost immediately afterwards.
ZODIAC	SOE (BRANDON Mission)	Bizerta	Air/sea rescue launch from Bône	To land 1 agent and 1 W/T operator: David and Dupont.	4/5 March 1943 – Agents safely landed.
BEAR	SOE (BRANDON Mission)	Kelibia (east Coast of Tunisia)	MTBs, from Malta (? MTB 307)	To land 10 agents to carry out sabotage in conjunction with BLUE.	6 April – Agents successfully landed, but to a reception party organised by the enemy. Conducting officer (Lt F.B. Richards) and boats' crews allowed by enemy to re-embark none the wiser.

Operation Code name	*Department*	*Pinpoint*	*Ship*	*Object*	*Results and remarks*
			Period: May 1943		
BEAR II	SIS	Cap Bon area	2 US P/T boats from Sousse	To land W/T operator to reception committee provided by BLUE/BEAR organisation.	Early May 1943 – First attempt failed owing to mechanical breakdown. Expedition recalled from second attempt because the BLUE/BEAR organisation had been discovered to be under enemy control.

Appendix C:
Operations from Algiers to Corsica, South Coast of France and Spain

Operation Code name	*Department*	*Pinpoint*	*Ship*	*Object*	*Results and remarks*
			Period: December 1942–February 1943		
CASABIANCA I/ PEARL HARBOUR	OSS & Deuxième Bureau	Anse-de-Topiti (nr Chiuni, west coast of Corsica)	French S/m *Casabianca* (Captaine de Frégate L'Herminier) 1)	To land 4-man intelligence mission and OSS W/T officer (F. Brown). (2) To land stores and arms; and re-embark OSS representative.	14/15 December – Successful landing of Cdt de Saule, Adjutant-Chief Toussaint Griffi, Sergeant Pierre Griffi, L. Preziosi and Fred Brown. 15/16 December – Attempt to land stores and arms failed. Dinghy lost and Lasserre, Lionnais and Vigot left ashore with PEARL HARBOUR mission. Brown swam off.
SEA URCHIN	SOE and BCRA	Cupabia Bay, Gulf of Valinco, Corsica	HM S/m *Tribune* (Lt S.A. Porter, RN)	To land BCRA/SOE team of 3 agents: Scamaroni, Jickell and W/T operator.	6/7 January 1943 – Successful. Original choice of pinpoint in Lava Bay proved unsuitable.
CASABIANCA II/ AUBURN	OSS/Deuxième Bureau/SIS (P1)	(1) Bon-Porté Bay nr Cap Lardier (2) Baie-d'Arone (Corsica)	French S/m *Casabianca*	(1) To land 3 Deuxième Bureau and OSS agents. (2) To land 2 SIS agents on west coast of Corsica: Adj Bozzi and Sgt Chopitel ('Auburn'). (3) To land arms and ammunition to PEARL HARBOUR.	4/5 February – Operation (1) successfully completed without reception committee. Landed Capt Caillot, Lt Guillaume and Fred Brown (OSS) 5/6 February – Operation (2) successfully completed without reception committee. 2 crew stranded (Asso,Cardot). 6/7 February – Operation (3): 450 Sten guns and 60,000 rounds of ammunition successfully landed without reception committee.

Operation Code name	*Department*	*Pinpoint*	*Ship*	*Object*	*Results and remarks*
			Period: December 1942–February 1943 continued		
FREDERICK	SIS (P1)	Cupabia Bay	HM S/m *Saracen* (Lt M.G.R. Lumby, RN)	To land 3 agents: Guy Verstraete, Antoine Colonna d'Istria, Andrei.	10/11 February – Successful.
			Period: March–May 1943		
CASABIANCA III/ PEARL HARBOUR	Deuxième Bureau	(1) Pointe-de-Taillat, Bon-Porté Bay (2) Anse-de-Canelle (east coast of Corsica)	French S/m *Casabianca*	(1) To land 3 agents: Capt de Peich, 'M Jean' and another. To pick up 2 of agents landed in Provence in February and Lt Col Bonneteau, General Arlebousse and Capt Raymond Bernard. (2) To pick up 2 members of PEARL HARBOUR Mission and 5 members of S/m's crew stranded in Corsica during two previous missions. Land 2 members of Corps Fanc d'Afrique.	5/6 March – Operation (1) unsuccessful. 10/11 March – Operation (2) successfully completed after two unsuccessful attempts. Motor fishing boat from Favone used to make contact with s/m. 13/14 March – Second unsuccessful attempt to carry out (1). A further attempt to take these people off on the following night also failed.
LEG	SOE	S.E. Corsica (mouth of Travo River)	HM S/m *Trident* (Lt P.E. Newstead, RN)	(1) To land Paul Colonna d'Istria and Lionel Lee (W/T operator), plus stores. (2) To evacuate Cdt de Saule and others. (3) To attempt to capture an Italian schooner and sail her back to Algiers.	6 April – Successful landing operation. De Saule and Jickell evacuated. (3) not attempted.
			Period: March–May 1943 continued		
CATERPILLAR I	SIS (P5) (Dunderdale)	NW Corsica	*Seawolf*	To land 2 agents.	10 April – Failed owing to bad weather and shore patrols.

Operation Code name	*Department*	*Pinpoint*	*Ship*	*Object*	*Results and remarks*
			Period: March–May 1943 continued		
ETNA	SOE	(1) NW coast Italy (2) East coast of Corsica	HM S/m *Trident*	(1) To land 2 Soviet agents in Italy. (2) To make a further attempt to evacuate remainder of de Saule's mission from Corsica (? Pierre Griffi).	(1) Not carried out (2) 10 May – Unsuccessful.
MARSOUIN	Deuxième Bureau (Giraud); OSS/SIS	Bon-Porté Bay	French S/m *Marsouin*	To land 5 agents: Jean Avallard, Christian Durrmeyer, E. Bolot (W/T operator) for OSS/SIS; Louis Gay for OSS, Gabriel Francart for SIS. To land 500kg of arms for OSS. To pick up Ingénieur Huet, Fred Brown (OSS).	8 May – Successful. Fabrizio Calvi lists Capitaine Jean Marie and Christophe Dunoyer (Service de Renseignements) among passengers. Submarine ran aground.
			Period: May–August 1943		
CASABIANCA IV	Deuxième Bureau	Barcelona	French S/m *Casabianca*	To land 4 agents (unidentified).	23 May 1943 – Successful. Patrol 20–24 May from Algiers.
LEG II/SKIN	SOE SE	Corsica (? mouth of River Travo)	HM S/m *Sibyl* (Lt E.J.D. Turner, RN)	(1) To contact agent (Paul Colonna d'Istria) for consultations and then and him again. (2) To land stores (conducting party: I Lt R.J. Laming, RNVR, and PO Sam Smalley).	Approx. 15 June – Only partly successful. Agent taken aboard s/m and stores successfully landed, but shooting broke out before agent could be disembarked. A further attempt was made on following night but there was no contact with shore party and it was decided it would be unwise for him to land 'blind'. He therefore returned to Algiers.

Operation Code name	*Department*	*Pinpoint*	*Ship*	*Object*	*Results and remarks*
			Period: May–August 1943 continued		
SCALP/ CASABIANCA V	SOE	Curza Point, Désert-des-Agriates, N Corsica	French S/m *Casabianca*	(1) To land Paul Colonna d'Istria and W/T operator (Luc Le Fustec). (2) To land 13 tons stores (conducting party: Lt F.B. Richards, Skipper Lt J.L. Newton, PO F. Taylor, Seaman D. Miles).	1/2 and 2/3 July – Successful.
LA PERLE I	Deuxième Bureau	Cap-Camarat area	French S/m *La-Perle*	(1) To land 2 agents: Lt de Gasquet and Capitaine Vellaud alias Desforges. (2) To pick up a party	2/3 July – Failed. Those due to be embarked were Estienne, Lt Col Bégue, Col. Agostini, Col. Serre and his son, Paul Schlochoff, Dautry.
SIBYL I	?	SE Corsica	HM S/m *Sibyl*	To land 1 agent.	4/5 July – Successful, according to Naval Staff History of submarine operations.
SCALP II/ CASABIANCA VI	SOE	Curza Point, N Corsica	French S/m *Casabianca*	To land 20 tons of stores (conducting party: Skipper Lt Newton, Capt. M. Gubbins, PO F. Taylor, Seaman).	30/31 July and 31 July/1 August – Successful, after abortive attempt on W coast.
			Period: August–September 1943		
SIBYL II	?	E coast of Corsica	HM S/m *Sibyl*	?	21/22 August – According to Naval Staff History (p. 172), carried out a special operation in Corsica and then patrolled east of the island.

Operation Code name	*Department*	*Pinpoint*	*Ship*	*Object*	*Results and remarks*
			Period: August–September 1943		
ARÉTHUSE	Deuxième Bureau	Cap-Camarat	French S/m *Aréthuse* (Lieutenant de Vaisseau Goutier)	To land 6: Lt Chevée, Jean-Marie Sévère alias Bertino (W/T), E.V. Flichy, Claude Château, Jean-Paul Klotz ('Faure'), and an 'inspecteur de police'. To evacuate mail and personnel.	29 August – Successful. Also embarked: Ingénieur-Général Ziegler, 2 'inspecteurs de police' (Grino and another), Jacques Rivet, son of the General.
SCALP III/ CASABIANCA VII	SOE	Golfe-de-Lava, due S of Piombata rock	French S/m *Casabianca*	(1) To bring off 1 of leaders of Corsican Resistance (Giovoni). (2) To land 2: Lt Giannesini and W/T operator. (3) To land 5 tons of arms, ammunition and explosives.	5/6 September – Successful. Reception committee organised by Henri Maillot, de Gaulle's cousin.
CASABIANCA VIII	French general staff	Ajaccio, Corsica	French S/m *Casabianca*	To land 109 (members of Bataillon de Choc and SOE/Deuxième Bureau mission).	13 September – Successful. Passage carried out on the surface. Mission covered period 11–15 September.
			Period: September–October 1943		
LA PERLE II	French general staff	Ajaccio	French S/m *La-Perle* (L de V Paumier)	To land 3 tons of flour.	16 September – Successful. Mission undertaken in support of *Casabianca*. Paumier persuaded captain of the Toulon–Ajaccio ferry to sail to Algiers.
STEELTON/ EARDRUM	SOE	Gulf of Porto, Corsica.	*Serenini* *Seawolf* *Seadog* *Welcome*	To land 1 agent and material.	16 September – Successful.

Operation Code name	*Department*	*Pinpoint*	*Ship*	*Object*	*Results and remarks*
			Period: September–October 1943 continued		
ARÉTHUSE II	French general staff	Ajaccio	French S/m *Aréthuse* (L de V Gouttier)	To land 5 tons of munitions.	18 September – Successful. Mission in support of *Casabianca* and Bataillon de Choc.
ARÉTHUSE III	Deuxième Bureau	Cap-Camarat	French S/m *Aréthuse*	To land 5: Capitaine Pauly (alias Pierson), 1 Lt, 3 *aspirants* (incl. Alfasser). To pick up mail and a party of French officers.	28 September – Successful. Picked up: Col Zeller, Col Chouteau, Col Granier, Cdt Etienne Rivet, Capitaine Vellaud, Capt de Neuchèze, Capitaine de Corvette Barthélemy and standard of 2e Dragons.
LA PERLE III	Deuxième Bureau	Barcelona	French S/m *La-Perle*	To land 1 agent (Capt d'Hoffelize) and stores.	16–17 October – Successful.
LA PERLE IV	Deuxième Bureau	Cap-Camarat	French S/m *La-Perle*	To land agents: Capt de Saint-Hilaire, Henri Bron (W/T), Paul-Marie Dubuc (W/T), Serge Deyres. Also to land stores.	26/27 October – Successful.
			Period: November 1943–January 1944		
CREVASSE/ ORPHÉE I	Deuxième Bureau	Barcelona	French S/m *Orphée* (L V Dupont)	To land 5 agents, including Capitaine E. Bertrand and Lt d'Hénin and a W/T set.	20 November – Successful.
CASABIANCA IX	Deuxième Bureau	Cap-Camarat	French S/m *Casabianca* (L de V Bellet)	Embarkation?	26 November – Operation interrupted by Germans. Alfasser shot and killed. Monique Giraud, daughter of General Giraud, managed to escape.

Operation Code name	*Department*	*Pinpoint*	*Ship*	*Object*	*Results and remarks*
			Period: November 1943–January 1944 continued		
PROTÉE	Deuxième Bureau	Barcelona	French S/m *Protée* (L de V Millé)	To land 4 (?) agents: Capitaine Elie Rous ('Sera'), Capitaine Demettre ('Van der Brouck'), Georges Alain de Beauregard ('Gérard'), Georges Maignon ('Rivière').	6 December – Successful.
ORPHÉE II	Deuxième Bureau (DGSS)	Barcelona	French S/m *Orphée* (L de V Dupont)	To land 4 (?) agents: Marie-Andrée Bécu, wife of Capitaine de Corvette Mourman, C.C. Sanguinetti, Georges Espardeillat ('Christian'), Caubet ('Serge Patte'). To embark Auguste Larovier.	28 December – Successful.
ORPHÉE III	Deuxième Bureau (DGSS)	Barcelona	French S/m *Orphée* (L de V Dupont)	To land and embark agents and mail.	25 January 1944 – Successful. 9 agents picked up or landed (unidentified).
			Period: February–June 1944		
ORPHÉE IV	Deuxième Bureau (DGSS)	Barcelona	French S/m *Orphée*	To land & embark agents & mail.	22 February – Successful. Landed 7 agents. Picked up Lt Boffy, Lt Georges Ribollet ('Jojo').
DEPLETION ORPHÉE V	Deuxième Bureau	Barcelona	French S/m *Orphée* (L de V Dupont)	As above.	1/2 March – Landed 12, including Paul Leduc ('Ledoux'; W/T operator), Lt Jeunot ('Tam'), André Marcel Pierrat ('Poiret'), Régis Witrand (W/T operator).

Operation Code name	*Department*	*Pinpoint*	*Ship*	*Object*	*Results and remarks*
			Period: February–June 1944 continued		
SULTANE	Deuxième Bureau (DGSS)	Barcelona	French S/m *Sultane* (L de V Javouhey)	As above.	28 March – Landed 6 agents: Capitaines Vellaud, 'Sapin', Meiglen and Mireille Molbert (W/T operator) plus 2 unidentified men. Picked up Capitaine Demettre.
ARCHIMÈDE I	Deuxième Bureau (DGSS)	Barcelona	French S/m *Archimède* (Capitaine de Corvette Bailleux)	As above.	20 April – Landed 5 or 6 agents, including a woman. Picked up Jean Diraison.
CASABIANCA X	Deuxième Bureau (DGSS)	Barcelona	French S/m *Casabianca* (L de V Bellet)	As above.	22 May – Landed Chartier, Perrier, Duchemin, Latour, Lt Ribollet, Abadie, Claire Dreyer ('Lenoir'). Picked up Marcel Picot, Jean-Marie Bresand.
ARCHIMÈDE II	Deuxième Bureau (DGSS)	Barcelona	French S/m *Archimède*	As above.	2 June – Landed Lt Lucien Bardet, (W/T operator), Charles Farelle (W/T operator), Isidore Fillion. Picked up a Lieutenant and Mireille Molbert.
SULTANE II	DGSS	Barcelona	French S/m *Sultane* (L de V Javouhey)	As above.	26 June – Picked up 3 or 4 agents, including a Colonel.

Appendix D:
Clandestine Operations from Corsica to South Coast of France

Operation Code name	*Department*	*Pinpoint*	*Ship*	*Object*	*Results and remarks*
			Period: November 1943–January 1944		
BOLIDE	Deuxième Bureau	Off Cap-de-l'Aiguillon	*Jeaninou* (French motor launch)	R/V at sea with Spanish ss REBECCA.	1 November 1943 – Failed owing to engine breakdown.
CLINTON (known to OSS as CANAL II)	OSS	Cap-du-Pinet (Cap-Camarat)	MAS 541 (Tenente di Vascello Cosulich) (ACF)	To land 2 agents.	28/29 December 1943 – Successful. Lt Maxted in command. Conducting party; Major Croft and OS Miles.
FURTIVE	SIS (P1/1.0)	Pointe-des-Issambres	MAS 541 (Tenente di Vascello Cosulich) (ACF)	To land 1 parcel and embark mail for 'Alliance'. 3 voyages.	29–30 December – Failed to find agents at pinpoint. Lt Cmdr Whinney in charge of expedition. 3 January 1944 – Failed. Again no agents at pinpoint. 28 January – Successful. 2 agents also embarked.
BROKERAGE	SOE	Cap-de-l'Aiguillon	PT200 PT217	To land 2.	29 January – Failed. Enemy patrol encountered off pinpoint.
			Period: January–April 1944		
LADBROKE	SOE	Cap-Camarat	(1)MAS 541 (Cosulich) (2) 2 PT boats	To land 2.	(1) 27/28 January – Failed owing to poor navigation. Lt Cmdr Whinney in command. Party included Major Croft, Bourne-Newton, Ashton. (2) 30 January – Failed owing to hostile craft. Lt Maxted i/c. Party included Croft, Sgt Bourne-Newton, PO Smalley and OS Chalmers.

Operation Code name	*Department*	*Pinpoint*	*Ship*	*Object*	*Results and remarks*
			Period: January–April 1944 continued		
CROMER	SOE	Morgiou Bay	2 PT Boats	To land 2 and embark mail.	19 March – Failed owing to bad weather. Maxted in command. 24 March – Failed (bad weather). 25 March – Failed (bad weather).
ABRAHAM	DGSS/BCRA	Cap-Camarat	PT 202 PT 216	To land 2.	18 April – Failed. Enemy destroyer encountered at pinpoint. Opened fire without challenging. No damage or casualties.
			Period: April–May 1944		
ABRAHAM (repeat)	DGSS/BCRA	Cap-Camarat	PT 209 PT 216	To land 2.	21 April – Successful.
CONISTON	SOE	Morgiou Bay PT 203	PT 207	To land 2 and embark mail to Pelletier ('Reuben'). Meteorological mission: Marcel Chaumien, operations officer and Jean Soupiron (W/T). Passed on to the Luberon.	28 April – Successful. Maxted in command. Conducting party: Capt Carson, PO Smalley, Sgt Bourne-Newton.
GORGE	SOE	Morgiou Bay (KARIKAL)	PT 556 + another	To land 4 and embark 5 including H. Rosencher ('Raoul').	19 May – Failed owing to fog and faulty navigation. Maxted in command. Conducting party: Major Croft, PO Smalley.
GORGE (repeat)	SOE	Morgiou Bay	PT559	To land and embark agents.	20 May – Successful. Landed Henri Rosencher. Embarked Camille Rayon ('Archiduc'), Sobra ('Hercule') and W/T operator.

Operation Code name	*Department*	*Pinpoint*	*Ship*	*Object*	*Results and remarks*
				Period: May–July 1944	
CHATHAM	OSS (AZUR mission)	Cap-Lardier	PT 217	To embark evaders and escapers.	24 May – Successful.
GRAPEFRUIT	OSS (AZUR mission)	Cap-Lardier	PT 218	(1) To embark 2: Marius Chavant ('Clement') and Lt Jean Veyrat. (2) To land agents named 'Damprun and Riant'.	24 May – Embarkation successful but it took place under enemy control: those landed were immediately arrested.
CORTE	DGSS/BCRA	Cap-Lardier	PT 558	To land 2.	26 May – Successful.
GORGE II	SOE	Morgiou Bay	PT 557 + another	To land 4 and embark 5.	23/24 June – Failed twice owing to bad navigation. Boyle in command. Conducting party: Croft and Smalley. 25 May – 3rd attempt called off as SPOC had learned of arrest of 'Octave' (W/T Operator) and Rayband family at La-Motte-d'Aigues on 21 May.
SWEET PEA	OSS	Cap-Lardier	PT 557	To land 2.	20 July – Successful.
SWEET PEA II	OSS	Cap-Lardier	PT 555	To embark 3.	24 July – Successful.

Appendix E:
Sea Operations Analysis—West Coast Italy and Islands except Corsica

Operation Code name	*Department*	*Pinpoint*	*Ship*	*Object*	*Results and remarks*
			WEST COAST ITALY AND ISLANDS (EXCEPT CORSICA)		
			Period: May–September 1943		
ETNA	SOE for Russians	Near Bordighera	S/m TRIDENT	Land 2 Soviet agents. Early May.	Failed: owing to delay on LEG operation could not be executed as by that time moon conditions were unsuitable.
ZOUAVE I	SIS	N.W. Sicily	US MTB	Land 2	Successful 7th June.
ALPHA	SIS	S.W. Sicily	US MTB	Land 2 to establish shelters for further agents	Successful 8th June.
ZOUAVE II	SIS	N.W. Sicily	US MTB	Embark ZOUAVE I agents	Failed on 27th June (bad weather) and 28th June (agents not at pinpoint). Successful 5th July.
ETNA II	SOE for Russians	Gulf of Genoa	S/m SPORTSMAN	Land 2	Successful 27th June. One agent landed. Attempt to blow up railway line abandoned.
LEGIONNAIRE	SIS	N.W. Sicily	US MTB	Land 2 and W/T	Successful 30th June.
MOLECATCHER III	Deuxieme Bureau	N.W. Sicily	US Fast craft PT.203	Embark 1	Successful 6th July
OKAPI	SIS	San Pietra, S.W. Sardinia	SEADOG	Land 1 and Ascension R/T link	Successful 30th July

Operation Code name	*Department*	*Pinpoint*	*Ship*	*Object*	*Results and remarks*
			Period: May–September 1943 continued		
SUNSHINE	SIS/OSS	South Italy	American P.T. craft	Land 1 Ascension equipped agent and 1 O.S.S. agent	Successful 12th August.
CONFINE	SIS	Sicily	PRODIGAL	Transport SIS party and stores from Malta	Successful 25th August
GAMMA III	BMT	Capo Ferrato, S.E. Sardinia	WELCOME	Land 2 and W/T	Failed 26th August. Craft shot up by friendly aircraft. Operation abandoned.
GAMMA II	BMT	Capo Ferrato, S.E. Sardinia	WELCOME	Land 2 and W/T	Failed 28th August. Abandoned owing to attack by friendly aircraft.
GREENGAGE	SIS	Sassari area, N.W. Sardinia	SEAWOLF	Land 1 and W/T	Failed 28th August owing to very heavy weather.
THUNDER	SIS	Naples area	CYRUS JOSEPH	Land 1 and Ascension	Successful 31st August. Craft attacked by aircraft on return voyage.
BURROW	SOE	Portofino area	S/m SERAPH	Land and bury stores	Successful 1st September. Andrew Croft
GREENGAGE (2nd attempt)	SIS	San Antioco Is. Sardinia	SEAWOLF	Land 1 and W/T	Failed 5th September owing to heavy weather.
LEVIS	MI9	Naples area	WELCOME	Land 1	Failed 6th September owing to heavy weather.
RUSHWORTH	MI9	Gulf of Genoa	S/m from 8th S/m Flotilla	Land 2 and W/T	Successful September.

Operation Code name	Department	Pinpoint	Ship	Object	Results and remarks
			Period: September 1943–January 1944		
GALLEGOS 1	SOE	Sorrento	AS 13 from Capri	To persuade Benedetto Croce to leave home and be evacuated to Capri	15 Sept. Croce and 3 daughters successfully evacuated by Gallegos.
MUNTHE 1	SOE	Sorrento	AS 13	To rescue Signora Croce and her eldest daughter. 16 Sept.	Successfully carried out.
GALLEGOS II	SOE	Gaeta/Terrac from Ischia	MS 21	To land 1 agent (Farina)	24 Sept. Landing successfully accomplished but MS sunk by mine and crew captured.
TIDEWAY	SOE	Sabandia	MS 24	To land 1 agent (Magnacracchi)	5 Nov. Successfully accomplished by Simpson-Jones.
ABNEGATE	OSS	Leghorn area	ML.576	Land 2	Successful 8th November.
BOORISH	OSS	Capraia Is.	ML.576	Land 3 officers and 8 men and stores	Successful 11th November.
PWQ	RN(FOWIT)	Anzio/Nettano (from Ischia)	MS 24 and 52	Beach Reconnaissance X-RAY US Beach	28/29 Nov. Simpson Jones SBS and COPP party report complete success
PWQ	RN(FOWIT)	Anzio/Nettuno (from Ischia) area	MS 52 and 24	Beach Reconnaissance PETER British Beach	2/3 December. Simpson-Jones SBS and COPP party report only partial success. One canoe lost.
EMPLACEMENT	SOE	Gulf of Genoa	Italian MAS boat 541	Land 2	Successful 2nd December.
GERRARD III	SOE	Sabandia area	MS 24	To land 4 saboteurs	? 2 Dec

Operation Code name	*Department*	*Pinpoint*	*Ship*	*Object*	*Results and remarks*
		Period: September 1943–January 1944 continued			
BIG GAME	OSS	Gorgona Is.	Italian MAS Boat	Land OSS Personnel	Successful 10th December. 6 OSS personnel and W/T/ landed and 8 Fascist guards embarked.
NOISY	RN (FOWIT)	Anzio/Nettuno area		MS 24 Radar search mission	12 December
CROFT/MEADOW	SIS	Leghorn area	ACF craft	Land 2 and W/T	Successful 27th December.
PWQ	RN(FOWIT)	Anzio/Mettuno area	US PT boat	Beach Reconnaissance PETER British Beach	29 December. One canoe lost.
HILLSIDE II/ KELVIN SOE	SOE	Genoa area	PT boats	Land 2 men and 2 women	2/3 and 3/4 January unsuccessful
POSSUM	OSS	Is. of Capraia	M.L.	Land stores	Successful 6th January.
BIG GAME III	OSS	Is. of Gorgona	MAS boat	Establish W/T Communications	Successful 15th January
RICHMOND	OSS	S. of Argentario Promontory	P.T.215	Land 6 (?)	Successful 17th January. Other accounts show 4 agents landed. PT203 sent as escort.
CHICAGO	OSS	Is. of Pianosa	MAS boat	Armed raid	Successful 18th January. Armed raid involving 15 men.
ARCTIC	OSS	Is. of Elba	MAS boat 541	Land 21	Successful 18th January

Operation Code name	*Department*	*Pinpoint*	*Ship*	*Object*	*Results and remarks*
			Period: January–March 1944		
PWQ	RN(FOWIT)	Anzio/Nettuno area	MS 24 and 52	Beach Reconnaissance PETER British beach	18/19 Jan 1944. Successful.
SHINGLE	RN(FOWIT)	Anzio/Nettuno area	US Submarine-Chaser 508	Assault landing	19–23 Jan 1944. Simpson-Jones lands Admiral Troubridge and General Alexander
RICHMOND II	OSS	Italian coast – opposite Giannutri Island	MAS.541 and MAS.543	Land 6 and embark 8	Successful 20th January
BARLEY	SIS	Leghorn area	MAS.500	Land 2	Successful 22nd January
CONTENTION	OSS	Is. of Elba	ACF craft	Land 3	Successful 29th January.
GENERAL STRIKE	OSS	Italian mainland	ACF craft opposite S.Elba	Embark 10 and mail	Successful 29th January.
NEUTER	Italians	Monte Cristo Is.	ACF craft	Land 2	Successful 29th January.
TAIL-LAMP	SOE	Cap Arenzano area N.W. Italy/Voltri	PT.217	Land 4, embark 8	Successful 31st January.
VALENTINE	SOE/OSS	Genoa area	ACF craft	Land 3	Successful 31st January.
ARCTIC III	OSS	Is. of Elba	MAS.509	Embark 3	Successful 1st February.
? HILLSIDE III	SOE			To land 1 woman agent	? Feb. Carnachan

Operation Code name	*Department*	*Pinpoint*	*Ship*	*Object*	*Results and remarks*
			Period: January–March 1944 continued		
ALNMOUTH	SOE	2km N.E. of Ostia	MS 24	Land 8 Italian Commandos to blow up railway bridge	Successfully landed 21/22 February
JOLLY	SIS	South of Turin N.W. coast	MAS.543	Land 2	Successful 21st February.
GINNY	OSS	Gryassola, N.W. Italy	P.T.	Land raiding party	Successful 27th February.
GINNY II	OSS	Pointa de Marmi	PT.s 210 and 214	Land raiding party and re-embark	Successfully landed but enemy patrol off pinpoint forced craft to withdraw leaving raiding party ashore, 27th February.
DOUGHBOY II	Deuxieme Bureau	Is. of Elba	MAS.541	Embark 4	Successful 2nd March.
BIG GAME V	OSS	Gorgona Is.	P.402	Land stores	Successful 10th March.
AMLOCH	SOE	Castiglioncello area	MS.24	Land 5 (2 organisers for Florence: 2 for Grasseto)	Failed 14th March – enemy patrol encountered. Successful 17th March in MAS.541.
POSSUM (repeat)	OSS	Capraia Is.	P.403	Land stores	Successful 15th March.
PRE-BALKIS	Battn.de Choc	Pianosa Is.	MAS.543	Land and re-embark recce. party	Successful 16th March.
ANSTEY	SOE	Voltri area	MS.24	Land 8 and embark party	Successful 17th March.
MARIOT	SOE	Castiglioncello area	MAS.543	Land 2	Successful. Craft shot up on return, 17th March

Operation Code name	*Department*	*Pinpoint*	*Ship*	*Object*	*Results and remarks*
			Period: March–May 1944		
ZEAL	SIS	Urin area	MS.24	Land 2	Successful 17th March.
FLOCK	SIS	Voltri area	MS.24	Land 2	Successful 17th March.
SAND	SIS	South of Levero	MAS.543	Land 2	Successful 17th March.
BALKIS	Battn.de Choc	Pianosa Is.	C.F. craft	Armed raid involving 120 men	Successful 18th March.
STEADFAST	SIS	Punta Invrea area	MAS.541	Land 1	Successful 18th March.
CADIX	Battn. de Choc	Savona area	MAS.541	Land 2	Failed. Explosion heard from shore thought to be MAS.541 hitting mine – presumed lost. 21st March.
BIG GAME VI	OSS	Gorgona Is.	P.403	Land stores and equipment	Successful 22nd March
GINNY III	OSS	Pt. de Marmi	PT.s 214 and 208	Embark raiding party	Failed 25th March – no one at pinpoint.
BIG GAME VII	OSS	Gorgona Is.	P.403	Land stores	Successful 26th March.
POSSUM Second Repeat	OSS	Capraia Is.	P.403	Embark 3 escapees from Elba	Successful 27th March.
BASSAM	Battn. de Choc	Montalto area	P.210 and 204	Demolition raid involving 1 officer and 6 men.	Successful 27th March.
BIG GAME VIII	OSS	Gorgona Is.	P.403 and MGB.s 657 and 663	Bring back dead and wounded from enemy raid on Gorgona	Successful 28th March.
BIG GAME IX	OSS	Gorgona Is.	P.403	Exchange personel	Successful 31st March.

Operation Code name	*Department*	*Pinpoint*	*Ship*	*Object*	*Results and remarks*
			Period: March–May 1944 continued		
BIG GAME X	OSS	Gorgona Is.	MAS.543 and P.403	Remove O.P.	Successful 9th April.
POSSUM	OSS	Capraia Is.	P.403	Remove O.P.	Successful 12th April.
GOOSEBERRY I	Force 'A'	Fosse delle Cazzanelle	PT.212 and 215	Embark P.O.W.s.	Failed. Nobody at pinpoint. 17th April.
YOUNGSTOWN 3	OSS	Portofino area	PT.209 and 211	Land 2	Failed. Enemy patrol at pinpoint. 18th April.
JULOT	S.R. (French)	Is. of Elba	PT. craft	Land 2	Successful 20th April.
ARCTIC IV	OSS	Is. of Elba	PT.s205 and 202	Land party	Successful 23rd April.
HIPPO	OSS	Capraia Is.	PT.s 216 and 209	Land 2, exfiltrate 1	Successful 25th April.
GOOSEBERRY II	Force 'A'	S. of Montalto	PT.214 and MGB.659	Embark P.O.W.s.	Failed. Nobody at pinpoint. 25th April.
HIPPO II	OSS	Capraia Is.	FPV.2017	Contact HIPPO party	Successful 26th April.
NOSTRUM II	SOE	Is. of Elba	PT.218 and PT.214	Embark 3	uccessful 27th April. Enemy patrol at pinpoint failed to sight craft.
SENECA II	OSS	Gorgona Is.	PT.s 215 and 213	Land 6	Successful 28th April.
SENECA III	OSS	Gorgona Is.	PT.303	Exchange personnel	Successful 14th May.

Operation Code name	*Department*	*Pinpoint*	*Ship*	*Object*	*Results and remarks*
			Period: May–June 1944		
ASHWATER	SOE		San Remo area	MTB.375	Land 3 and stores Failed – enemy shore patrol at pinpoint 15th May.
IOTA	SR	Genoa area	PT.216	Land 2	Successful 15th May.
POOL I	Deuxieme Bureau	Is. of Elba	PT.214	Land 7	Successful 15th May.
SENECA IV	OSS	Gorgona Is.	PT craft	Exchange personnel	Successful 18th May.
POOL II	Deuxieme Bureau	Is. of Elba	PT.218	Embark 6	Successful 20th May
YAKIMA	OSS	Giglio Is.	PT craft	Small raid	Failed.
YOUNGSTOWN III	OSS	Portofino area	PT.303	Land 2	Failed. Craft encountered 2 enemy patrols and ran into Severe storm, delaying landing until too late.
BUTE	OSS	Montalto area	PT craft	Embark party	Failed – craft forced back by heavy weather, 21st May.
GORGEOUS	RN	Gorgona Is.	PT.553	Survey island for berthing landing craft	Successful 23rd May.
OMAHA II	OSS	Capraia Is.	PT.553	Land stores	Successful 23rd May.
READING	OSS	Portofino area	PT.217	Land 1	Successful 24th May.
SENECA V	OSS	Gorgona Is.	P.403	Exchange personel	Successful 28th May.

Operation Code name	*Department*	*Pinpoint*	*Ship*	*Object*	*Results and remarks*
			Period: May–June 1944 continued		
OMAHA III	OSS	Capraia Is.	P.403	Land stores	Successful 28th May.
OMAHA IV	OSS	Capraia Is.	P.403	Land stores and exchange personnel	Successful 3rd June.
OMAHA V	OSS	Capraia Is.	P.403	Exchange personnel	Successful 10th June.
SENECA VI	OSS	Gorgona Is.	P.403	Land stores and exchange personnel	Successful 10th June.
LOCUST	OSS	Spezia area	P.403 and PT.218	Land 4	Successful 16th June, but craft attacked by enemy force and had to withdraw Leaving US personnel on shore. Successfully re-embarked 23rd June.
SCRAM I	'A' Force	Near Bonassola	P.403	Embark P.O.W.s	Failed – craft forced back by heavy weather, 17th June.
FERRET	'A' Force	North of Bonnassola	P.403	Land 3	Successful 19th June but 2 dinghymen left behind – convoy encountered off pinpoint, forcing craft to withdraw. The 2 dinghymen rowed more than 90 miles to Capraia.
OMAHA VI	OSS	Is. of Capraia	P.403	Land stores	Successful 24th June.
SENECA VII	OSS	Is. of Gorgona	P.403	Land stores and personnel	Successful 24th June.

Operation Code name	*Department*	*Pinpoint*	*Ship*	*Object*	*Results and remarks*
			Period: June–July 1944		
CYCLAMEN	BCRA	Spezia area	PT.306 MAS boat	Land 2	Failed 25th June – heavy coastal traffic prevented craft reaching p.point. Failed 26th June – craft attacked by aircraft and surface craft.
SCRAM I	'A' Force	Near Bonassola	PT.306	Embark POWs	Failed – craft attacked by enemy aircraft, 26th June.
OMAHA VII	OSS	Is. of Capraia	P.403	Evacuate OSS personnel	Successful 17th July.
SENECA VIII	OSS	Is. of Gorgona	P.403	Exchange personnel	Successful 21st July.
SCRAM III	'A' Force	Near Bonassola	MTB.378 Escorted by 3 PT boats.	Land 4 and embark POWs.	Landing successful but no POWs at pinpoint. Slight damage and casualties Caused by attack by enemy surface craft. 23rd July. 25th July – POWs embarked.
KINGSTON	OSS	Spezia area	MAS.543	Land 2	Failed 24th July. Craft attacked by 3 enemy E-boats; dinghy with the 2 Agents and Ldg. Seaman Luff (A.C.F.) had to be abandoned. (Luff later known to be POW)
POST-KINGSTON	OSS	Spezia area	PT.308 (escorted by PTs 311 and 313)	Evacuate KINGSTON Party	Failed to find party either at pinpoint or R/V at sea.Spitfire sweep also failed to find any trace. 25th July.
SENECA IX	OSS	s. of Gorgona	P.403	Evacuate malaria patient and land relief	Successful 30th July.

Operation Code name	*Department*	*Pinpoint*	*Ship*	*Object*	*Results and remarks*
			Period: February–April 1945		
CORINTH	SOE	Nr. River Canevai (San Remo area)	MGB.177 (escorted by PT.s 303 and 304)	Land 500 lbs. stores to reception committee and embark 2 POWs	Failed 6th February. No reception committee. Craft waited 50 minutes off pinpoint then shore defences opened fire forcing craft to withdraw. Abandoned.
TOAST	SOE	Genoa harbour	MGB.177 with MS.74 owing MTS/M's to 5 miles off Genoa	Sink aircraft carrier AQUILA (prospective blockship)	Successful. SOE used San Marco swimmers as limpeteers. MGB.177 used for towing purposes. Chariots entered and left harbour without opposition. All personnel recovered. 18th April.

Appendix F:
Sea Operations Analysis—Adriatic (including Eastern Italy, Yugoslavia, Albania and Greece)

Operation Code name	*Department*	*Pinpoint*	*Ship*	*Object*	*Results and remarks*
		ADRIATIC (INCLUDING EASTERN ITALY, YUGOSLAVIA, ALBANIA AND GREECE).			
			Period: October–December 1943		
ACOMB	SOE		MAS 514	Land 2	4 Oct 1943
SIMCOL	MI9		MS31, 33 and74 Joined end Nov and early Dec 1943 by MS61, 56, 55, 53, 73, 65 and 54 in that order.	To land commandos and pick up POWs	18 Oct. onwards: after 21 Oct from Termoli. MS33 sunk off Pescara on 2 Nov. having carried out 4 other missions in previous 10 days.
QUINTET	SOE and MI9		MS and LCI	To land 5 agents for SOE and pick up POWs 25/26 Oct.	Laming landed 5 (RUBY/MARCASITE) picked up 22 POWs
MANARA I	SOE and SIS with SIM supports	Giulianova and 2 other pinpoints.	Italian s/m MANARA (Ten vasc. Gaspare Cavallina).	To land 3 gps. of agents at 3 points on Italian coast of upper Adriatic.	27 Oct.–3 Nov. from Brindisi. One of those landed was a naval W/T operator (RUDDER), sent as reserve W/T op. For a network in Rome established by SOE/ISF and SIM jointly. Difficult landing: had to swim ashore but reached Rome 8 Nov. and survived the war. Other agents landed were for SIS and 3 of these were captured and executed in Pesaro.

Operation Code name	*Department*	*Pinpoint*	*Ship*	*Object*	*Results and remarks*
			Period: October–December 1943 continued		
GOOSEBERRY IV	MI9	Cervia area, N.E. Italy	SEAHAWK	Embark P.O.W.s	Failed 29th October – bad weather.
MAREA I	SOE and SIS	Pesaro/Cattolica	Italian S/M MAREA (Sotten.vasc. Attilio Russo).	To land 5 agents in 2 parties on Italian Coast of upper Adriatic	3–9 Nov. from Brindini Cap.corv. Raul Galletti, head of naval intelligence at Brindisi on board. GARNET(2) for SOE; FURROW(3) for SIS. Both parties got away from Pesaro. GARNET never made radio contact, but FURROW eventually did and operated over a long period to good effect.
SPLENDID	SIS	Istrian coast	SEASTAR	Land 2	Failed 23rd November – bad weather, but craft evacuated Partizans from Dugi.
CRAB I and II	MI9	Cervia area	SEAHAWK	I – embark 10 British officers. II – R/V naval craft and transfer party	Failed owing to weather – 24th November.
GEARBOX	SOE	Civita Nova/Porto Polenza area	MS 63	To land 5 (ZIRCON/OPAL)	Successful 27th November
HEADLAMP I	SIS	Pesaro area	S/m NICHELIO	Land party	? Successful 28th November.
HEADLAMP II	SIS	Gulf of Venice	S/m NICHELIO	Land party	? Successful 29th November. 7 ISLD agents land S. of Chioggia.
AMAZING	SIS	Numana area	Italian vessel	Land party	Successful 30th November.

Operation Code name	*Department*	*Pinpoint*	*Ship*	*Object*	*Results and remarks*
			Period: December 1943–January 1944		
LAMP	SIS	Hvar and Brac Is. Yugoslavia	SEAHAWK	Land 5 and W/T	Successful 4th December.
BIGAMY I	OSS	Valona Bay Albania	SEASTAR	Land arms etc.	Failed 4th December owing to weather. Successful 7th December by M.L.
			Period: October–December 1943		
Q.W.Q.	15th AG	Pelagosa Is.	SNO craft	Recce. by 40th Commando	Successful 6th December.
Q.W.R.	15th AG	Civitanova	SNO craft	Land 1	Successful 10th December.
Q.W.V.	15th AG	Civitanova	SNO craft	Land 8	Successful 14th December.
			Period: December 1943–January 1944		
BIGAMY II	OSS	Valona Bay Albania	SEAMAID	Land arms etc.	Successful 21st December.
			Period: October–December 1943		
SPLENDID II	SIS	Istria	SEASTAR	Land 2	Successful 21st December.
			Period: December 1943–January 1944		
QWU	15th AG	North of R.Po	MS	Embark POWs	Failed 21st December owing to weather.
LAYSHAFT	SOE	Pesaro area	MS31	Land party	Failed 23rd December – bad weather.
QWW/X	MI9	Civitanova	MS	Embark POWs	Successful 23rd December.

Operation Code name	*Department*	*Pinpoint*	*Ship*	*Object*	*Results and remarks*
			Period: October–December 1943 continued		
QWY	MI9	S. of Ancona	MS	Embark POWs	Failed 24th December owing to weather.
			Period: October–December 1943		
CHERRY/MAYFLY	SIS	Cesanatico	SEAFLOWER	Land 3	Successful 28th December.
			Period: December 1943–January 1944		
QWS/QWT	15th AG	Rimini/Ravenna	MS	Beach recce.	Failed 28th December owing to weather.
DANGLE/ DECENCY	OSS	Pesaro area	S/m AXUM	Land 10 and W.T	Successful 30th December.
RODNEY RENOWN	SOE	Nr. Chioggia Istrian coast	Italian S/m MAREA	Land 3 Land 2	Failed 30th December Successful 30th December
QWO.2	SAS	Civitanova	MS	Embark POWs	Failed 31st December. No one at pinpoint.
MAPLE	SAS	Fano area	SEAHAWK	Land 8 and stores	Successful 31st December.
			Period: December 1943–January 1944		
ENDEAVOUR	SIS	San Giorgio	SEAHAWK	Land 2	Successful 2nd January 1944.
MERMAID	SIS	Dugi	SEASTAR	Land 1 and stores	Failed. Craft shot up – 2 killed and 3 wounded. 7th January.

Operation Code name	*Department*	*Pinpoint*	*Ship*	*Object*	*Results and remarks*
			Period: January–February 1944		
SPAM	SIS	N.Yugoslavia	SEAMAID	Land stores and party	Failed 19th January. Enemy in occupation of pinpoint.
			Period: January 1944		
(ABBERLEY) COMEBACK I	SOE	Pesaro	S/m NICHELIO	Land 3	Successful 19/20th January. Italian team BEAUMONT
			Period: December 1943–January 1944		
ABBERTON	SOE	Mouth of R.Tenna near Civitanova	MS65	Land 4 (including Italian General)	Two ops combined 20th January from Termdi. Both successful.
QWQ II	MI9	Mouth of R.Tenna near Civitanova		Land 1 and evacuate Captain Fowler and POWs	23 POW evacuated. Sub-Lt.RA Clark, Sub Lt Macpherson (borrowed from SEAHAWK) Sub-Lt Bruce
			Period: January–February 1944		
LAYSHAFT	SOE	San Benedetto	MS73	Land 2 Italian saboteurs	Successful 20th January Laming Conducting Officer
ENDEAVOUR II	SIS	San Giorgio	MS73	Land 2 Italian agents	Successful 20th January.
SPEEDOMETER	SOE	San Giorgio	MS73	Land party to blow train (R. O. Richards)	Successful 20th January. Combined with LAYSHAFT and ENDEAVOUR II
TOURING	Italians	St. Tesdona	Italian MS	Recover troops	Successful 21st January. 180 recovered.
WINDY	SIS	Commachio	SEAFLOWER	Land party	Successful 21st January.

Operation Code name	*Department*	*Pinpoint*	*Ship*	*Object*	*Results and remarks*
			Period: January–February 1944		
BRILLIANT II	SIS	Fano	SEAFLOWER	Land party	Successful 22nd January
			Period: January 1944		
FAIR II	SIS	Cortelazzo	SEASTAR	Land 2	Successful 22nd January.
PAPERCHASE	OSS	Ravenna	MAS boat	Land 1	Successful 22nd January.
BIGAMY Series III to XX	SOE	Valona Bay Albania	–	20 operations by various MS craft and fishing-vessels in support of the Allied Mission in Albania – evacuation of personnel, landing of stores, equipment and agents.	
COMEBACK II	SIS	Cortelazzo	S/m NICHELIO	Land 2	Successful 23rd January. (OAT) GRAIN LANE
ENGRAVE I	SIS	Istria	S/m NICHELIO	Land 2	Successful 27th January.
ENGRAVE II	SIS	Pesaro	S/m NICHELIO	Land 2	Successful 28th January.
STRAW	SIS	Ravenna	SEAMAID	Land 2	Successful 28th January.
FORMULATE	SAS	Fano	SEAGIANT	Land W/T and 1 officer	Successful 29th January.
VOUCHSAFE III	F.133	Morea Is.	Italian MS	Embark party	Successful 29th January.
			Period: January–February 1944		
PRUNE	OSS/SI	Cattolica, Italy	S/m PLATINO	Land 8	Successful 29th January.
LEMON	OSS	Istria	S/m PLATINO	Land 6	Successful 30th January.

Operation Code name	*Department*	*Pinpoint*	*Ship*	*Object*	*Results and remarks*
			Period: January 1944		
DEATHRAY	SAS	Fano	Italian MS	Land party to blow up bridge	Successful 30th January.
Q.W.R.II	MI9	Grottomare	MS73	Land 3	Successful 30th January.
			Period: January–February 1944.		
MICAWBER	Italians	Albanian coast	Italian destroyer	Evacuate 300 troops	Successful 2nd February.
MALVOLIO	F.133	Dedeil Cove (Albania)	Italian destroyer	Land stores and evacuate troops	Successful 3rd February. 50 troops evacuated.
			Period: February–March 1944		
COCKROACH	SIS	Pesaro	SEAMAID	Land 9	Successful 16th February. Craft ran aground and was lost on return from operation.
IAGO	SOE	Cortalazzo	S/m PLATINO	Land 3	Successful 18th February.
FALSTAFF and CORDELIA	OSS/SI	Commachio	S/m PLATINO	Land 9	Successful 19th February.
JUG	MI9	River Aso, S. of Ancona	MS	Land 2	Successful 20th February.
PETER	MI9	Civitanova	MS	Land 2	Successful 27th February.
ADVENT	SOE	Pesaro	S/m NICHELIO	Land 10	Successful 27th February.
RAT I and II	MI9	Ancona area	MS	Land 6	Successful 27th February.

Operation Code name	Department	Pinpoint	Ship	Object	Results and remarks
			Period: February–March 1944 continued		
ALMER AVONMOUTH AUSTWICK ACCRINGTON AINTREE AMPTHILL CAGE EQUALITY	SOE SOE SOE SOE SOE SOE MI9 SIS	SIS San Giorgio San Benedetto San Benedetto Civitanova Fano San Giorgio Cattolica San Giorgio	MS MS MS MS MS MS MS SEAHAWK	Land party Land 4 Land srores Land stores Land 6 Land party Land 2 Land party	Failed owing to weather During the period ending March 2nd.
BANNER	SBS	Merlera Is.	SEAHAWK	Land 1	Successful 9th March.
EQUALITY	SIS	S. of Fano	SEAHAWK	Land 1	Successful 16th March.
			Period: March 1944		
CAGE II AINTREE	MI9 SOE	Cattolica R. Chienti	MS MS 56	Land 2 Land 6 saboteurs	Successful 18th March. Successful 19th March. Mounted from Ortona. Lt. R. Laming assisted by Sub-Lt R. Clark
AVONMOUTH	SOE	R. Chienti	MS 56	Land 2 sabotage instructors and stores	Successful 19th March. Combined with above. To join with MARCASITE.
BEDLAM	OSS	Dedeil Cove	S/m	Land 3 tons stores and party of 15	Successful 19th March.
VOUCHSAFE V	F.133	Gulf of Arcadia	Torp. boat destroyer	Evacuate British and US airmen and land stores	Successful 19th March.
ALPHA	SAS	Merlera Is.	MFV	Recover agent and land stores	Successful 21st March.

Operation Code name	*Department*	*Pinpoint*	*Ship*	*Object*	*Results and remarks*
			Period: March 1944 continued		
ROSSINI	F.133	Dedeil Cove	MS 54 and 74	Land 3 tons stores and evacuate personnel	Successful 21st March. (22nd March in Italian Naval records).
AMPTHILL	SOE	Ancona area	MS 56	Land party from 1 SF MFV under Sub-Lt RO Richards	Successful 21st March. Lt Laming in charge. Sub Lt Clarks and Lt Taylor as covering party. Bridge blown.
ATHOS	OSS/SI	Commachio	S/m PLATINO	Land 4	Successful 21st March.
PORTHOS	OSS/SI	Cortellazo	S/m PLATINO	Land 4	Successful 22nd March.
D'ARTAGNAN	OSS/SI	River Adige	S/m. PLATINO	Land 4	Successful 23rd March.
JOCK I	MI9	R. Chienti	MS	Land 4	Successful 23rd March.
HARVEST	SIS	Umago, Istria	S/m NICHELIO	Land 2	Successful 28th March.
TURF	SIS	Umago	S/m NICHELIO	Land 2	Successful 28th March.
			Period: March–April 1944		
TRIBUTE	SIS	Rovigno, Istria	S/m NICHELIO	Land 3	Successful 29th March.
ALPHA II	SBS	Fano Is.	SEAHAWK	Land stores	Successful 31st March.
PICNIC I	SBS	Gulf of Drin	MAS	Land 1	Successful 31st March.
VOUCHSAFE VI	F.133	G. of Arcadia	TBD	Evacuation and land 2 tons stores	Successful 31st March. 40 Allied personnel evacuated.

Operation Code name	*Department*	*Pinpoint*	*Ship*	*Object*	*Results and remarks*
				Period: March–April 1944	
ILLEGAL	F.133	Grava Bay, Albania	M.A.S.	Land 3 and evacuate Italian Gen. Staff	Failed 3rd April.
TARDY	F.133	Dedeil Cove Albania	MAS	Land 2 and stores	Successful 3rd April.
PICNIC II	F.133	Gulf of Drin	MS 54	Evacuate 1, land 3 tons	Failed. Craft fired on by shore battery. 3rd April.
				Period: April–June 1944.	
SHOOT I	SBS	Mljet Is.	SEAGIANT	Land recce. party of 2. R.M. Commandos, 3 US signals, W/T and Partizan guide	Successful 13th April.
SHOOT II	SBS	Mljet Is.	SEAGIANT	Land Partizan Capt. and 8 other ranks with W/T and evacuate SHOOT I Party	Successful 15th April.
				Period: March–April 1944	
ABERGELE	SOE	S. of Tenna	MS	Land 3 tons	Failed 19th April. No signals from shore.
ANYHO	MI9	S. of Tenna	MS	Recover 6	Failed 19th April. No signals from shore.
BETA	OSS	Merlera Is.	MS	Land 2	Successful 20th April.
SHEFFIELD	MI9	N. of Tenna	SEAHAWK	Recover 6	Failed 21st April. Flares on pinpoint.

Operation Code name	*Department*	*Pinpoint*	*Ship*	*Object*	*Results and remarks*
			Period: April–May 1944		
PINEAPPLE	MI9	Chioggia	SEAFLOWER	R/V and recover 3 from schooner	Failed, 21st April. No contact established with schooner.
			Period: April–June 1944		
SHOOT III	SBS	Korcula Is.	SEAGIANT	Tow 2 LCA.s to place howitzer support on Korcula for Partizan attack	Successful 21st April.
			Period: March–April 1944		
WISHFUL	MI9	Chioggia	SEAFLOWER	R/V F/V in G. of Venice	Failed 22nd April. No one at R/V. Craft waited 3 hours.
			Period: April–May 1944.		
GLASSHOUSE	F.133	Parga	LCI and MTB	Land 37 tons and embark party	Successful 22nd April.
DASTARD	F.133	Zante	S/m. PLATINO	Land 3 and stores	Successful 22nd April.
BUTTERDROP	F.133	Western Greece	TBD	Land 3 tons and evacuate Allied personnel	Successful 24th April.
ACORN	OSS	Cortelazzo	S/m. PLATINO	Land 3	Successful 24th April, but firing ashore.
			Period: March–April 1944		
WISDOM	SIS	Ancona area	DENTICE	Land 2	Failed 25th April – firing ashore.

Operation Code name	*Department*	*Pinpoint*	*Ship*	*Object*	*Results and remarks*
			Period: April–May 1944.		
VIRGINIAN	AFHQ	Kunje Bay, S.Yugoslavia	Destroyer GRECALE	Land beach recce. party	Successful 29th April.
			Period: April–June 1944		
SHOOT IV	SBS	Ulto Is.	SEASTAR	Place howitzer support and medical aid on Sulto for Partizan attack on garrison	Successful 9th May.
			Period: April–May 1944		
MOONSHINE	F.266	Dedeil Cove	MS	Recover 5, land 2	Successful 11th May.
BETA II	SBS	Merlera Is.	MAS.	Contact and land 2	Successful 13th May.
ANON	SOE	Western Greece	MS 56 and 64	Land British recce. party	Successful 14th May.
INDEPENDENCE	F.266	Is. of Corfu	MS	Land recce. party	Successful 16th May.
			Period: April–June 1944		
SHOOT V	SBS	Mljet Is.	SEASTAR	Land 1 officer and 1 Rank with W/T	Successful 16th May.
			Period: April–May 1944		
INDEPENDENCE I	F.266	Is. of Corfu	MS	Recover recce. party	Successful 19th May.
			Period: April–June 1944		
SHOOT VI	SBS	Korcula Is.	SEASTAR	Land 1 officer and 1 rating with W/T and stores	Successful 19th May.

Operation Code name	*Department*	*Pinpoint*	*Ship*	*Object*	*Results and remarks*
			Period: April–May 1944		
DARLINGTON	MI9 R.	Tenna	MS 74 and 64	Recce. and land 2	Successful 19th May.
HUMBER	MI9	R. Tordino	MS	Embark 20 POW.s	Successful 20th May.
			Period: May–June 1944		
GLASSHOUSE III	F.133	N.W. Greece	LCI	Land 60 tons and 70 personnel	Successful 21st May.
EPIGRAM I	F.266	Grava Bay	TBD	Land 30 tons	Successful 22nd May.
BUTTERDROP II	F.133	Morea Greece	TBD	Evacuation	Successful 22nd May.
KAPPA	SBS	Merlera Is.	MS	Land 3 tons	Successful 22nd May.
HULL	MI9	R. Tordino	P.402	Recover POWs	Successful 22nd May – 20 evacuated.
			Period: April–June 1944		
FOOTHOUND	SBS	Mljet Is.	SEAHAWK	Reproduce speeches in German during attack on garrison	Successful 23rd May.
			Period: May–June 1944		
SPURN	MI9	R. Tordino	MFV	Recover POWs	Failed 23rd May – no shore signals.
INDEPENDENCE III	F.266	Merlera Is.	MS	Land 2 for recce.	Successful 23rd May.
PINTAIL	SOE	Dedeil, Albania	MAS	Land 2	Successful 24th May.

Operation Code name	*Department*	*Pinpoint*	*Ship*	*Object*	*Results and remarks*
			Period: May–June 1944 continued		
ANON II SOE	Western Greece	MS 64 and 74	Beach recce.	Successful 24th May.	
DARLINGTON II	MI9	R. Tenna	LCI and MS	Recover POWs	Successful 24th May. 130 POWs evacuated.
EPIGRAM II	F.266	Grava Bay	TBD	Land 30 tons	Successful 24th May.
TRENT	MI9	R. Tordino	MS	Recover POWs	Failed 25th May. No signals from shore
DASTARD II	F.133	Zante, Greece Cephalonia	S/M.	Land 1 ton Land 2 tons	Successful 25th May.
			Period: April–June 1944		
SHOOT VII	SBS	Brac Is.	SEAHAWK	Pick up 3 American airmen and party of Partizans	Successful 27th May.
SHOOT VIII	SBS	Brac Is.	SEASTAR and SEAHAWK	Land large force to divert enemy from the mainland where they were harrassing Tito's forces	Successful 2nd June.
			Period: May–June 1944		
LANDLUBBER	LRDG	Grava Bay	MS	Recover 4	Successful 4th June.
			Period: April–June 1944		
SHOOT IX	SBS	Brac Is.	SEAHAWK	Land 100 Commandos to re-capture Brig. Churchill (taken Prisoner on SHOOT VIII	Successful 5th June.

Operation Code name	*Department*	*Pinpoint*	*Ship*	*Object*	*Results and remarks*
				Period: May–June 1944	
BELINDA	F.266	Grava Bay	TBD	Land 60 tons	Successful 10th June.
CELIA	F.266	Grava Bay	TBD	Land 60 tons	Successful 12th June.
				Period: June 1944	
ASTROLABE I	PPA	R. Tenna	P.402	Land Popski's Private Army	Successful 12th June.
ASTROLABE II	PPA	R. Tenna	LCT and ML	Land Major Popski	Successful 16th June, but decided to abandon operation with PPA after patrol.
EQUALITY II	SIS	S. of Fano	SEAHAWK	Recover 2	Failed 17th June owing to weather.
BRACING I	F.133	N. Greece	LCI	Land 60 tons	Successful 18th June.
OSSENING I	OSS	Fano area	MS	Land demolition party	Successful 19th June.
LANDLUBBER II	LRDG	Grava Bay	MS	Land 6	Successful 20th June.
BUTTERDROP III	F.133	Morea, Greece	TBD	Land 4 tons	Successful 20th June.
BRACING II	F.133	N. Greece	LCI	Land 60 tons	Successful 20th June.
BETA III	SAS	Merlera Is.	MS	Land stores	Successful 21st June.
LANDLUBBER III	LRDG	Dedeil Cove	MS	Land stores	Successful 23rd June.
DRUPE	OSS/SI	Commachio	S/m. PLATINO	Land 9 tons	Successful 24th June.
HARROGATE	MI9	Fano area	MS	Land 2	Successful 26th June.

Operation Code name	*Department*	*Pinpoint*	*Ship*	*Object*	*Results and remarks*
			Period: June 1944 continued		
LAVENDER	F.399	Grava Bay	MS	Recover 3	Successful 27th June.
LANDLUBBER IV	LRDG	Albania	MS	Land 25	Successful 28th June.
LANDLUBBER VA	LRDG	Orso Cove	MS	Recover 25	Successful 29th June.
			Period: July 1944		
DAKOTA	F.399	Grava Bay	MS	Recover 4	Failed 2nd July. No one at pinpoint.
LANDLUBBER V	LRDG	Orso Cove	MTB	Land 4 and 500 lbs	Successful 5th July.
BARBARY	F.399	Grava Bay	MTB	Recover 4	Successful 5th July.
BETA IV	SBS	Merlera Is.	SEAHAWK	Land 3	Successful 7th July.
LANDLUBBER Vb	LRDG	Orso Cove	MS	Land 2 and recover stores	Successful 14th July.
LANDLUBBER VIa	LRDG	Grava Bay	MS	Land 4	Successful 14th July.
BETA V	SBS	Merlera Is.	MS	Recover 2	Successful 16th July.
BRACING III	F.133	Parga	LCI	Land 30 tons	Successful 16th July.
LEYTON	ISF (SOE)	Montignano	2 MS	Land 12 for demolition on road into Ancona	Successful 18th July. Laming and R.O. Richards
DRUPE II	OSS	Commachio	MS	Transfer 3 and 1? tons	Successful 18th July.

Operation Code name	*Department*	*Pinpoint*	*Ship*	*Object*	*Results and remarks*
				Period: July 1944 continued	
BUTTERDROP IV	F.133	Morea, Greece	TBD	Land 6 tons	Successful 19th July.
BRACING IV	F.133	Parga, Greece.	LCI	Land 30 tons	Successful 19th July.
LANDLUBBER VIb	LRDG	Grava Bay	MS	Recover 4	Successful 20th July.
OSSENING II	OSS	Fano area	MS	Land demolition party	Successful 20th July.
DASTARD III	F.133	Cephalonia, Grecce	S/m.	Land stores	Successful 22nd July.
				Period: July–August 1944.	
DASTARD IV	F.133	Zante Is.	S/m.	Land stores	Failed 23rd July. No one at pinpoint.
OSSENING III	OSS	Fano Is.	MS	Land demolition party	Failed 25th July. Firing from shore.
BEAR I	SBS	Dedeil Cove	MS	Land 4 and 500 lbs.	Successful 25th July.
HEALING I	F.399	Spilea, Albania	MS	Land 12 and 900 lbs.	Successful 26th July.
HEALING II	F.399	Orso Cove	MS	Recover 2	Failed 30th July. No one at pinpoint.
HEALING III	LRDG	Spilea	TBD	Land 4 and stores	Successful 14th August.
GENEVA I	F.399	Spilea	TBD	Land 10 tons and recover 100 personnel	Successful 14th August.

Operation Code name	Department	Pinpoint	Ship	Object	Results and remarks
				Period: July–August 1944 continued	
BOAR III	S.B.S.	Spilea	TBD	Land 4 and stores	Successful 14th August.
BIRDLET III	SBS	S. of Orso	MS	Land 3	Successful 14th August.
BETA VI	.SBS	Merlera Is.	MAS	Land 3	Successful 14th August.
DIGAMMA	SBS	Merlera Is.	MAS	Land 2	Successful 14th August.
OSSENING III	OSS	N. of Fano	MS	Land demolition party	Successful 16th August.
BRACING V	F.133	Parga	LCI	Land 90 tons	Successful 17th August.
DASTARD V	F.133	Zante Is.	S/m.	Land stores	Successful 18th August.
				Period: August–September 1944.	
BIRDLET IV	SAS	S. of Orso	MS	Land 3 and stores	Successful 22nd August.
OSSENING IV	OSS	Cattolica	MS	Land demolition party Fired on by shore battery.	Failed 22nd August.
PACKARD	OSS	N. of Pesaro	MS	Land 1	Successful 23rd August.
GLADIATOR	F.399	Spilea	MS	Land 3 tons	Successful 24th August.
BRACING VI	F.133	Parga	LCI	Land 90 tons	Successful 25th August.
BUTTERDROP V	F.133	Morea Greece	TBD	Land 4 tons	Successful 25th August.

Operation Code name	*Department*	*Pinpoint*	*Ship*	*Object*	*Results and remarks*
			Period: August–September 1944 continued		
PACKARD II	OSS	Pesaro	TBD	Land 4 tons	Successful 26th August.
BETA VII	SBS	Merlera Is.	MAS	Land 1	Successful 27th August.
NUTSHELL	F.399	Spilea	TBD	Land 20 tons and recover wounded	Successful 28th August.
GENEVA II	F.399	Spilea	MS	Land 2 and stores	Successful 29th August.
BRACELET	F.133	Paxos Is. Greece	PRODIGAL	Trans-ship 25 tons to caiques	Successful 5th September.
GYROSCOPE	LRDG	Orso Cove	MS	Land 10 and 1? tons stores	Successful 10th September.
BIRDLET V	SBS	Orso Cove	MS	Collect intelligence	Successful 10th September.
PROGRESS	F.399	Spilea	TBD	Evacuate wounded	Successful 14th September.
GYROSCOPE II	LRDG	Orso Cove	MS	Recover 10	Successful 15th September.
			Period: November 1944–March 1945.		
SEXTANT	PPA	Ravenna area	MS	Land recce. party	Failed after 3 attempts. 1st – no contact with shore; 2nd – adverse weather; 3rd – adverse weather 20th October.
BOND VI (R)	OSS	Ravenna area	P.402	Land 4 and stores	Successful 24th November.
BEE	OSS	Ravenna area	P.402 and MGB. 180	Land 3	Successful 16th December.
ANT	OSS	Gulf of Venice	MGB.180	Land 3	Successful 21st January 1945.

Operation Code name	*Department*	*Pinpoint*	*Ship*	*Object*	*Results and remarks*
			Period: November 1944–March 1945		
ANISEED	LRDG	Lussin Is.	MGBs 180 and 181	Land recce.party	Successful 12th February.
DRAGONFLY	OSS	S. of Chioggia	MS	Land 6 and stores	Failed 15th February – fog Failed 16th February – arrived late at pinpoint due to engine trouble. Agents landed but no reception so re-embarked and returned.
HORNET	OSS	N. of Venice	MTB. 700	Land 10 and stores	Failed 20th February – weather. Failed 21st February – enemy craft encountered at pinpoint.
HORNET II	OSS	N. of Venice	MGB.191	Land 6	Successful 9th March.
BEE II	OSS	R. Po area	P.402	Land stores	Successful 11th March.
HORNET III	OSS	N. of Venice	MGB.191	Land 10 and embark P.O.W.s	Successful 16th March. 13 P.O.W.s evacuated.
			Period: September–November 1944.		
CROOKSON	F.399	Spilea, Greece	TBD	Land 90 tons	Successful 4th October.
BIRDLET VI	SBS	Orso M.S.	Collect intelligence	Successful 4th October.	
LOLLIPOP II	LRDG	Spilea and Orso	MS	Land and evacuate party	Failed 14th October.
BOND V	OSS	Ravenna area	MS	Land stores and exchange personnel	Successful 16th October.

Operation Code name	*Department*	*Pinpoint*	*Ship*	*Object*	*Results and remarks*
			Period: September–November 1944 continued		
HALTER II	LRDG	Istria	MTB	Pick up 10 and W/T	Successful 16th October.
CHISHOLM	Force 399	Spilea	LCT	Land 50 tons	Successful 17th October.
TOMTOM	LRDG	S. of Durazzo	MS	Recover 2	Successful 24th October.
BOND VI	OSS	Ravenna area	MS	Land 4 and small quantity stores	Failed 18th November. No contact at pinpoint. 6 O.S.S. Italians landed for recce. failed to return.
SEAKITE I	OSS	Gulf of Venice	MS	R/V F/V	Failed 10th November. No contact.
CONCORD II	LRDG	Gulf of Drin	MS	Land 20 and recover 3	Successful 27th October.
			Period: September 1944.		
BETA VIII	SBS	Merlera Is.	MS	Land 1 and 2 tons stores	Successful 15th September.
CHAFFEE	F.399	Spilea	TBD	Land 30 tons	Successful 16th September.
BRACING VII	F.133	Parga, Greece	LCI	Land 30 tons	Successful 16th September.
LOLLIPOP	LRDG	Orso Cove	MS	Land 6 and recce. party	Successful 16th September.
DIGAMMA II	SBS	S. of Corfu	MS	Land 1 ton stores	Shore party failed to appear. Failed 16th September.
BOND	OSS	Ravenna area	MS	Collect intelligence	Successful 17th September.

Operation Code name	*Department*	*Pinpoint*	*Ship*	*Object*	*Results and remarks*
			Period: September 1944. continued		
MERCERISED	40th Commando	Cape Kiephal, Greece	LCT	M.S. Land party for reconnaissance	Successful 19th September.
BRACING VIII	F.133	Parga	LCI and TBD	Land 160 tons	Successful 20th September.
BUTTERDROP VI	F.133	Morea, Greece	MS	Land 10 tons	Successful 20th September.
CROSBY	F.399	Spilea	TBD	Land 70 tons	Successful 20th September.
STRANGE	SIS	Istria	P.402	Land 3	Successful 22nd September.
CLAWSON	F.399 Spilea	TBD	Land 90 tons	Successful 23rd September.	
			Period: September–November 1944.		
Un-named " " "	8th Army	(a) Rimini area (b) Nr. Vignole (c) Ravenna area	MS MTB MS	Evacuation Land stores Pick up	(a) Successful 22nd September. (b) Failed 27th September. E-boats encountered at pinpoint. (c) Successful 27th September.
BRACING IX	F.133	Paxos Is.	PRODIGAL	Transport 10 tons and 50 personnel and transfer to caiques	Successful 28th September.
MERCERISED II	40th Commando	Cape Kiephal	MS	Recover wounded and recce. work in the area.	Successful 29th September.
BRACING X	Force 133	Paxos Is.	PRODIGAL	Trans-ship 10 tons and 50 personnel to ship	Successful 30th September.

Operation Code name	*Department*	*Pinpoint*	*Ship*	*Object*	*Results and remarks*
			Period: September–November 1944 continued		
ADDICT I	LRDG	Vignole Bay, Istria	MGBs 180 and 191	Land 10 and 1½ tons stores	Successful 21st February.
ADDICT II	LRDG	Istria	MGB.179	Embark 8	Successful 6th March
ADDICT III	LRDG	Istria	MGB.179	Embark 8	Successful 7th March.
ADDICT IV	LRDG	Istria	MGB.179	Land look-out post	Failed 8th March – severe weather
ADDICT V	LRDG	Istria	MGB.179	Land stores	Successful 10th March.
ADDICT VI	LRDG	Istria	MGB.179	Land W/T	Successful 12th March.
ADDICT VII	LRDG	Istria	MGB.179	Land W/T	Successful 15th March. Struck mine on return voyage, no casualties.
ADDICT VIII	LRDG	Is. of Cherso	ML.576 and ML.238	Pick up 2 agents	Successful 21st March.
ADDICT IX	LRDG	Olib Is.	MGB.180	Land 2	Successful 27th March.
ADDICT X	LRDG	S. of Trieste	MGB.180	Land stores, embark 7	Successful 30th March.
ADDICT XI	LRDG	E. of Pola	MGB.180	Embark 10	Successful 30th March.
			Period: April 1945.		
ADDICT XII	LRDG	Bucina Cove, E. of Pola	MGB.180	Land raiding party	Failed 2nd April – enemy opposition.
ADDICT XIII	LRDG	E. of Pola	MGB.180	Land 3	Successful 3rd April.

Operation Code name	*Department*	*Pinpoint*	*Ship*	*Object*	*Results and remarks*
			Period: April 1945.		
ADDICT XIV	LRDG	Istrian coast	MGB.180	Land 15	Successful 5th April.
ADDICT XV	LRDG	Istrian coast	ML.576	Land and embark raiding party	Successful 6th April. Seven prisoners also taken.
ADDICT XVI	LRDG	Istrian coast	ML.576	Land raiding party and re-embark	Successful 6th April.
ADDICT XVII	L.RDG	Istrian coast	MGB.180	Land 27 and stores	Failed 9th April due to enemy opposition.
ADDICT XVIII	LRDG	Istrian coast	MGB.191	Evacuate 8	Successful 16th April.
ADDICT IXX	LRDG	Istrian coast	MGB.191 and MGB 180	Evacuate 8	Successful 25th April. Coastal guns fired on MGB.s – minor damage and no casualties.
BEE III	OSS	River Po area	Italian MS	Land stores from Corsini spoilt by weather.	Sundry attempts since 6th April – in MS O.S.S. made 4 attempts in Chris-Craft which failed due to weather.
HORNET IV	OSS	Chioggia area	MGB.191 and P.402	Land stores and evacuate P.O.W.s; also land I.S.9 recce. party	Successful 8th April. 12 POWs evacuated. Enemy convoy off p.p. evaded.
HORNET V	OSS	Venice area	MGB.191 and P.402	Embark P.O.W.s	Successful 13th April.
JOHN IV	IS9	N. Gulf of Venice	MGB.191 and P.402	Land 4	Successful 13th April, but dinghy's crew failed to return.

Bibliography

Unless otherwise stated, books in English were published in London, those in French in Paris.

AGLAN, Alya: *Mémoires Resistantes: Historie du Réseau JADE-FITZROY 1940–44* (Editions du Cerf, 1994).

ANDREW, Christopher: *Secret Service* (Heinemann, 1985).

BARBER, Noël: *The Week that France Fell: June 1940* (Macmillan. 1976).

BEESLY, Patrick: *Very Spetial Admiral: The Life of Admiral J.H.Godfrey, CB,* with a Foreword by Stephen Roskill. (Hamish Hamilton, 1980).

BEEVOR, J.G.: *SOE: Recollections and Reflections 1940–1945* (The Bodley Head, 1981).

BIRKIN, David: The Aber-Wrac'h Saga', unpublished typescript communicated by the author and by Judy Birkin.

BOTT, Lloyd: *Some Wartime Memoires of Lloyd Bott,* privately circulated in typescript by the author (Melbourne, 1991).

CALVI, Fabrizio, in collaboration with Olivier Schmidt: *OSS: La Guerre secrète en France, 1942–45: Les Services Spéciaux Americans, la Resistance et la Gestapo* (Hachette, 1990).

CAMPOS, Christophe, ed.: *Franco-British Studies* (Journal of the British Institute in Paris)

——No. 2 (Autumn 1986), 'British Aid to Armed French Resistance': I Maurice Hutt: The 1790s and the Myth of "Perfidious Albion'"; II M.R.D.Foot: 4940–44 and the Secret Services';

——No. 7 (Spring 1989), 'Operation TORCH and its Political Aftermath: A Franco-Anglo-American Gordian Knot': papers by J.B. Duroselle, Anthony Verrier, Arthur Funk, Philippe Masson, Philip Bell, Jean-Pierre Azéma, Jean-Louis Crémieux-Brilhac, Charles-Robert Ageron. [Discussions of the roles of OSS and SOE in North Africa, Anglo-American policy towards Darlan and the Vichy administration, the death of Darlan.]

CHALOU, George C., ed.: *The Secrets War: The Office of Strategic Services in World War II* (National Archives and Records Administration, Washington, DC, 1992).

CHURCHILL, P.M.: *Of their Own Choice* (Hodder & Stoughton, 1952).

CHURCHILL, P.M.: *Duel of Wits* (Hodder & Stoughton, 1955).

CHURCHILL, Winston: *The Second World War, Vols I-V* (Cassell, 1948–52).

COLLIER, Richard: *D-Day: June 6, 1944: The Normandy Landings* (Cassell, 1992).

COON, Carleton S.: *A North African Story: The Anthropologist as OSS Agent 1941–43. With Historical Settings from the Editors of Gambit* (Gambit, Ipswich, MA, 1980).

COURTNEY, G.B.: *SBS in World War Two* (Robert Hale, 1985).

COUTAU-BEGARIE, Hervé and HUAN, Claude: *Darlan* (Fayard, 1989).

CRAWLEY, Aidan: *De Gaulle: A Biography* (Collins, 1969).

CROFT, Andrew: *A Talent for Adventure* (SPA Ltd, Hanley Swan, in conjunction with Andrew Croft, 1991).

DEACON, Richard: *A History of the British Secret Service* (Frederick Muller, 1969).

D'ESTIENNES D'ORVES, Family, eds: *La Vie Exemplaire du Commandant d'Estiennes d'Orves: Papiers, Carnets, Lettres* (Plon, 1950).

DILKS, David: *The Diaries of Sir Alexander Cadogan, 1938–45* (Cassell, 1971).

DODDS-PARKER, Douglas: *Setting Europe Ablaze: Some Account of Ungentlemanly Warfare* (Springwood Books, Windlesham, 1984).

DUMAIS, Lucien A.: *The Man Who Went Back* (Leo Cooper, 1975).

FLEURY, Georges and MALOUBIER, Robert: *Nageurs de Combat* (La Table Ronde, 1989).

FOOT, M.R.D.: *SOE in France: An Account of the Work of the British Special Operations Executive in France 1940–1944* (HMSO, 1966).

FUNK, Arthur Layton: *The Politics of TORCH. The Allied Landings and the Algiers Putsch 1942* (University Press of Kansas, Lawrence/ Manhattan/Wichita, KS, 1974).

FUNK, Arthur Layton: *Hidden Ally: The French Resistance, Special Operations, and the Landings in Southern France, 1944,* Contributions in Military Studies, No. 122 (Greenwood Press, New York, Westpoint, CT, and London, 1992).

GAULLE, Charles de: War Memoirs, Vol. I: *The Call to Honour 1940–42* (Collins, 1955).

GILBERT, Martin: *Second World War* (Weidenfeld & Nicolson, 1989).

GILLOIS, André: *Histoire Secrète des Francais à Londres de 1940 à 1944* (Hachette-Littérature, 1973).

GRIFFI, Toussaint and PREZIOSI, Laurent: *Première Mission en Corse Occupée, avec le Sousmarin CASBIANCA (Dècembre 1942-Mai 1943),* Preface by Henri Noguès (Editions L'Harmattan, 1988).

HAMPSHIRE, A. Cecil: *The Secret Navies* (William Kimber, 1978).

HAMPSHIRE, A Cecil: *Undercover Sailors: Secret Operations in World WarII* (William Kimber, 1981).

HINSLEY, F.H., with E.E.Thomas, C.F.G.Ransom and R.C.Knight: *British Intelligence in the Second World War: Its Influence on Strategy and Operations,* Vol. I (HMSO, 1979).

HUAN, Claude. See COUTAU-BEGARIE.

HUGUEN, Roger: *Par les Nuits les Plus Longues: Réseaux d'Evasion d'Aviateurs en Bretagne 1940–1944* (Editions Breiz, La Baule, 4th edn, 1978).

JULLIAN, Marcel: *HMS FIDELITY* (Souvenir Press, 1957).

KINGSWELL, Peter: *FIDELITY Will Haunt Me till I Die* (privately published by the Royal Marines Historical Society, 1991).

LACOUTURE, Jean: *De Gaulle: The Rebel, 1890–1944,* trans. Patrick O'Brian (Collins Harvill, 1990).

LANGLEY, Mike: *Anders Lassen: VC, MC, of the SAS: The Story of Anders Lassen and the Men who Fought with Him* (New English Library, 1988).

LE GRAND, Alain and THOMAS, Georges-Michel: *39–45 Finistère* (Editions de la Cité, Brest-Paris, 1987).

LE TAC, Joel *et al*: *Les Réseaux Action de la France Combattante, 1940–1944* (Amicale des Réseaux de la France Combattante, 1986).

LE TRIVIDIC, Dominique-Martin: *Une Femme du Réseau Shelburn: L'Histoire de Marie-Thérèse Le Calvez de Plouha, en Bretagne recueillie par Dominique-Martin le Trividic,* Preface by Jacques Chaban-Delmas ('Témoignages', Editions le Cercle d'or, Les Sables d'Olonne, 1979).

L'HERMINIER, Captain J.: *CASABIANCA: The Secret Missions of a French Submarine;* trans. Edward Fitzgerald (Frederick Muller, 1953).

McGEOCH, Ian: *An Affair of Chances. A Submariner's Odyssey 1939–42* (Imperial War Museum, 1991).

MACLACHLAN, Donald: *Room 40* (Weidenfeld & Nicolson, 1968).

MACMILLAN, Harold. *War Diaries: The Mediterranean, 1943–45* (Macmillan, 1985).

MERRICK, K.A.: *Flights of the Forgotten: Special Duties Operations in World War Two* (Arms and Armour Press, 1989).

MINSHULL, Merlin: *G(u)ilt Edged* (Bachman and Turner, 1975).

MOREAU, Hubert:'Premières Missions', *Revue de la France Libre,* Nos 80, 81 and 82 (1955) (three articles).

MOREAU, Hubert *et al.*: 'Lieutenant de Vaisseau Hubert Moreau', typescript booklet. (Communicated to the author by Capitaine de Vaisseau Claude Huan. Includes a separate and, in some respects, fuller account of Moreau's escape from France in june 1940 and his first two missions, a press release dated 25 August 1941 by the Free French information service entitled 'Le Leopard', and a biographical note headed MOREAU (Hubert Arnold Pierre), Lieutenant de Vaisseau, *Résistant-Premier Agent do Renseignment Français en Frnace Occupée—1920–1959,* compiled 13 October 1980 by le Maître Principal Dominique Lemaire from the Archives Centrales de la Marine, CC7 4ème Moderne 1331/4 and 3040/11.)

PASSY (A.Dewavrin): *Souvenirs, Vol. I: 2e Bureau, Londres* (Raoul Solar Editions, Monte Carlo, 1947).

PELLETIER, Antoine: 'Autrement qu'ansi', unpublished manuscript.

PICHAVANT, René: *Clandestins de l'Iroise,* Vol. I: *1940–42—Récits d'Histoire;* Vol. II: *1942–3;* Vol. III: *1943–4;* Vol. IV: *1940–44* (Editions Morgane, Douarnenez, 1982, 1984, 1986, 1988).

RÉMY (Gilbert Renault alias 'Roulier'): *Mémoires d'un Agent Secret de la France Libre* (Editions Robert Laffont, 1945).

RÉMY: *Le Livre du Courage et de la Peur: Juin 1942-Novembre 1943,* 2 vols (Aux Trois Couleurs et Raoul Solar Editions, 1945).

RÉMY: *La Maison d'Alphonse* (Librairie Académique Perrin, 1968).

RYGOR-SLOWIKOWSKI, Major-General M.Z.: *In the Secret Service: The Lighting of the Torch,* trans. George Slowikowski; ed., Introduction and Afterword John Herman (Windrush Press, 1988).

SCAMARONI, Marie-Claire: *Fred Scamaroni: 1914–43* (Editions France-Empire, 1986).

SENGER und ETTERLIN, Ritter von: *Neither Fear nor Hope* (Presidio, Novato, CA, 1988).

SILVANI, Paul:...*et la Corse fut libérée* (La-Marge, Ajaccio, 1993). SPEARS, Sir Edward: *Assignment to Catastrophe,* 2 vols (Heinemann, 1947).

THOMAS, Georges-Michel. See GRAND, Alain.

VERITY, Hugh: *We Landed by Moonlight* (Ian Allan, 1973).

WHINNEY, Patrick: *Corsican Command* (Patrick Stephens, 1989).

WILKINSON, Peter and ASTLEY, Joan Bright: *Gubbins and SOE* (Leo Cooper, 1993).

Index

Note. maps are designated by italicised references to the pages on which they appear; illustration references are to Illustration number, not page. Code names appear in capital letters in the main text but in upper/lower case and within quote marks in the index, with the agent's real name in parentheses.